UNIX® SYSTEM V RELEASE 4

Integrated Software Development Guide

for Intel Processors

UNIX
SYSTEM LABORATORIES

Published by Prentice Hall, Inc.
A Simon & Schuster Company
Englewood Cliffs, New Jersey 07632

IMPORTANT NOTE TO USERS

While every effort has been made to ensure the accuracy and completeness of all information in this document, USL assumes no liability to any party for any loss or damage caused by errors or omissions or by statements of any kind in this document, its updates, supplements, or special editions, whether such errors, omissions, or statements result from negligence, accident, or any other cause. USL further assumes no liability arising out of the application or use of any product or system described herein; nor any liability for incidental or consequential damages arising from the use of this document. **USL disclaims all warranties regarding the information contained herein, whether expressed, implied or statutory, including implied warranties of merchantability or fitness for a particular purpose.** USL makes no representation that the interconnection of products in the manner described herein will not infringe on existing or future patent rights, nor do the descriptions contained herein imply the granting of any license to make, use or sell equipment constructed in accordance with this description.

USL reserves the right to make changes to any products herein without further notice.

TRADEMARK

Intel386 is a registered trademark of Intel Corporation.
OPEN LOOK is a registered trademark of UNIX System Laboratories, Inc. in the USA and other countries.
UNIX is a registered trademark of UNIX System Laboratories, Inc. in the USA and other countries.
X Window System is a trademark of the Massachusetts Institute of Technology.

10 9 8 7 6 5 4 3 2 1

ISBN 0-13-879479-0

UNIX
PRESS
A Prentice Hall Title

P R E N T I C E   H A L L

ORDERING INFORMATION

UNIX® SYSTEM V, RELEASE 4 DOCUMENTATION

To order single copies of UNIX® SYSTEM V, Release 4 documentation, please call (201) 767-5937.

ATTENTION DOCUMENTATION MANAGERS AND TRAINING DIRECTORS:
For bulk purchases in excess of 30 copies please write to:
Corporate Sales
Prentice Hall
Englewood Cliffs, N.J. 07632
Or call: (201) 461–8441

ATTENTION GOVERNMENT CUSTOMERS: For GSA and other pricing information please call (201) 767-5994.

Prentice-Hall International (UK) Limited, *London*
Prentice-Hall of Australia Pty. Limited, *Sydney*
Prentice-Hall Canada Inc., *Toronto*
Prentice-Hall Hispanoamericana, S.A., *Mexico*
Prentice-Hall of India Private Limited, *New Delhi*
Prentice-Hall of Japan, Inc., *Tokyo*
Simon & Schuster Asia Pte. Ltd., *Singapore*
Editora Prentice-Hall do Brasil, Ltda., *Rio de Janeiro*

Contents

8 Application Software Packaging

9 Modifying the sysadm Interface

10 Driver Software Packaging

A Manual Pages

I Index

Figures and Tables

Preface to this Volume

PREFACE

PREFACE

Introduction

This book, the *Integrated Software Development Guide* (ISDG), concentrates on an application programmer's view of how to develop and package application software under UNIX System V, using the system services provided by the UNIX operating system kernel. The ISDG is designed to give you information about application programming in a UNIX system environment. It does not attempt to teach you how to write programs. Rather, it is intended to supplement texts on programming by concentrating on the other elements that are part of getting application programs into operation. The ISDG supplies information on how to write application software and installable drivers for new hardware additions to UNIX System V Release 4.0 for the Intel386 microprocessor.

Throughout this chapter and the rest of the ISDG, you will find pointers and references to other guides and manuals where information is described in detail. In particular, you will find numerous references to the *Programmer's Guide: ANSI C and Programming Support Tools*.

The *Programmer's Guide: ANSI C and Programming Support Tools* describes the C programming environment, libraries, compiler, link editor, and file formats. It also describes the tools provided in the UNIX System/C environment for building, analyzing, debugging, and maintaining programs. The *Programmer's Guide: ANSI C and Programming Support Tools* and the *Integrated Software Development Guide* are closely connected. Much of the information from both used to be in the Release 3.2 version of the *Programmer's Guide*. For Release 4.0 of UNIX System V, the information has been made into a series of guides.

If you are unsure of which book to reference, check the *Product Overview and Master Index*. It explains how the document set is organized and where to find specific information.

Audience and Prerequisite Knowledge

The *Integrated Software Development Guide* (ISDG) is intended for the Independent Software Vendor (ISV) who develops UNIX System software applications to run on Intel386 microprocessor-based computer systems.

As the title suggests, we are addressing software developers. No special level of programming involvement is assumed. We hope the book will be useful to people who work on or manage large application development projects.

Programmers in the expert class, or those engaged in developing system software, may find the ISDG lacks the depth of information they need. For them we recommend the *Programmer's Reference Manual*.

Knowledge of terminal use, of a UNIX system editor, and of the UNIX system directory/file structure is assumed. If you feel shaky about your mastery of these basic tools, you might want to look over the *User's Guide* before tackling this one.

Related Documentation

A variety of documents support the UNIX System V/386. Refer to the *Product Overview and Master Index* to help you get acquainted with the documents you can use with UNIX System V/386 Release 4.0 for the Intel386 microprocessor.

The *Master Index* helps you to understand general relationships among the documents and to identify which documents you want to order.

Throughout the ISDG, references are made to certain specific documents listed in the *Product Overview and Master Index*. Rather than list the complete title each time the document is referenced, the following convention is used:

- The *UNIX System V/386 Release 4 Programmer's Guide* is referred to as the *Programmer's Guide*.

- The *UNIX System V/386 Release 4 User's Reference Manual* is referred to as the *User's Reference Manual*.

- The *UNIX System V/386 Release 4 System Administrator's Reference Manual* is referred to as the *System Administrator's Reference Manual*.

- The *UNIX System V/386 Release 4 Programmer's Reference Manual* is referred to as the *Programmer's Reference Manual*.

- The *UNIX System V/386 Release 4 System Files and Devices Reference Manual* is referred to as the *System Files and Devices Reference Manual*.

- The *UNIX System V/386 Release 4 Device Driver Interface/Driver-Kernel Interface (DDI/DKI) Reference Manual*, is referred to as the *Device Driver Reference Manual* or as the *DDI/DKI Reference Manual*.

Organization

The material in the ISDG is organized into the following sections and chapters:

- Preface — Application Programming in the UNIX System Environment

  Briefly describes what application programming is, introduces programming tools and languages supported in the UNIX system environment and other UNIX system services you can use to develop and package application programs, and indicates where to read about them.

- Chapters 1 through 7 — Application and Driver Software Development

  This section begins by introducing the UNIX system calls and libraries you can use to develop application programs, then goes on to provide detailed information about the use of many of the UNIX system services. It includes with a sample application that pulls together a lot of the techniques from the preceding chapters. The section concludes with a chapter on device driver software development which includes two samples of device driver implementations.

- Chapters 8 through 10 — Application and Driver Software Packaging

  This section includes detailed descriptions and case studies about the use of tools for building application and driver software packages. It outlines the procedure you use to install the UNIX System software and provides the details necessary to create a software installation floppy disk set for your computer. Some broad guidelines are also presented for installing and removing UNIX programs, as well as examples of installing and removing scripts. The final chapter, "Driver Software Packaging", contains the rules and procedures you need to follow for packaging device driver software to work on UNIX System V Release 4.0 for the Intel386 microprocessor.

Following all the chapters in the ISDG is an appendix of manual pages unique to *Application and Driver Software Packaging*.

An index is included at the end of the ISDG.

The C Connection

The UNIX system supports many programming languages, and C compilers are available on many different operating systems. Nevertheless, the relationship between the UNIX operating system and C has always been and remains very close. Most of the code in the UNIX operating system is written in the C language, and over the years many organizations using the UNIX system have come to use C for an increasing portion of their application code. Thus, while the ISDG is intended to be useful to you no matter what language(s) you are using, you will find that, unless there is a specific language-dependent point to be made, the examples assume you are programming in C. The *Programmer's Guide: ANSI C and Programming Support Tools* gives you detailed information about C language programming in the UNIX environment.

Hardware/Software Dependencies

Nearly all the text in this book is accurate for any computer running UNIX System V Release 4.0, with the exception of hardware-specific information such as addresses.

If you find commands that work a little differently in your UNIX system environment, it may be because you are running under a different release of the software. If some commands just don't seem to exist at all, they may be members of packages not installed on your system. If you do find yourself trying to execute a non-existent command, talk to the administrators of your system to find out what you have available.

Information in the Examples

While every effort has been made to present displays of information just as they appear on your terminal, it is possible that your system may produce slightly different output. Some displays depend on a particular machine configuration that may differ from yours. Changes between releases of the UNIX system software may cause small differences in what appears on your terminal.

Where complete code samples are shown, we have tried to make sure they compile and work as represented. Where code fragments are shown, while we can't say that they have been compiled, we have attempted to maintain the same standards of coding accuracy for them.

Notation Conventions

Whenever the text includes examples of output from the computer and/or commands entered by you, we follow the standard notation scheme that is common throughout UNIX System V documentation:

- All computer input and output is shown in a `constant-width` font. Commands that you type in from your terminal are shown in constant-width type. Text that is printed on your terminal by the computer is shown in constant-width type.

- Comments added to a display to show that part of the display has been omitted are shown in *italic* type and are indented to separate them from the text that represents computer output or input. Comments that explain the input or output are shown in the same type font as the rest of the display. An italic font is used to show substitutable text elements, such as the word "*filename*" for example.

- Because you are expected to press the (**RETURN**) key after entering a command or menu choice, the (**RETURN**) key is not explicitly shown in these cases. If, however, during an interactive session, you are expected to press (**RETURN**) without having typed any text, the notation is shown.

- Control characters are shown by the string "CTRL-" followed by the appropriate character, such as "D" (this is known as "CTRL-D"). To enter a control character, hold down the key marked " (**CTRL**) " (or " (**CONTROL**) ") and press the (**D**) key.

- The standard default prompt signs for an ordinary user and `root` are the dollar sign ($) and the pound sign (#).

- When the # prompt is used in an example, the command illustrated may be executed only by `root`.

Manual Page References

When software components are mentioned in a section of the text for the first time, a reference to the manual section where the software component is formally described is included in parentheses: component_name(section_number). The numbered sections are located in the following manuals:

Sections (1), (1C), (1G)   *User's Reference Manual*

Sections (1), (1M)   *System Administrator's Reference Manual*

Sections (2), (3)   *Programmer's Reference Manual*

Sections (4), (5), (7), (8) *System Files and Devices Reference Manual*

Note that Section 1 is listed for both the *User's Reference Manual* and the *System Administrator's Reference Manual*. These manuals describe commands appropriate for general users and system administrators as well as for programmers.

Application Programming in the UNIX System Environment

This section introduces application programming in a UNIX system environment. It briefly describes what application programming is and then moves on to a discussion on UNIX system tools and where you can read about them, and to languages supported in the UNIX system environment and where you can read about them.

Programmers working on application programs develop software for the benefit of other, nonprogramming users. Most large commercial computer applications involve a team of applications development programmers. They may be employees of the end-user organization or they may work for a software development firm. Some of the people working in this environment may be more in the project management area than working programmers.

Application programming has some of the following characteristics:

- Applications are often large and are developed by a team of people who write requirements, designs, tests, and end-user documents. This implies use of a project management methodology, including version control (described in the *Programmer's Guide: ANSI C and Programming Support Tools*), change requests, tracking, and so on.

- Applications must be developed more robustly.

    - They must be easy to use, implying character or graphical user interfaces.

    - They must check all incoming data for validity (for example, using the Data Validation Tools described in Chapter 9).

    - They should be able to handle large amounts of data.

- Applications must be easy to install and administer

    (see Chapter 8, "Application Software Packaging" and Chapter 9, "Modifying the `sysadm` Interface").

UNIX System Tools and Languages

Let's clarify the term "UNIX system tools." In simple terms, it means an existing piece of software used as a component in a new task. In a broader context, the term is used often to refer to elements of the UNIX system that might also be called features, utilities, programs, filters, commands, languages, functions, and so on. It gets confusing because any of the things that might be called by one or more of these names can be, and often are, used simply as components of the solution to a programming problem. The chapter's aim is to give you some sense of the situations in which you use these tools, and how the tools fit together. It refers you to other chapters in this book or to other documents for more details.

Tools Covered and Not Covered in This Guide

The *Integrated Software Development Guide* (ISDG) is about tools used in the process of creating programs in a UNIX system environment, so let's take a minute to talk about which tools we mean, which ones are not going to be covered in this book, and where you might find information about those not covered here. Actually, the subject of things not covered in the ISDG might be even more important to you than the things that are. We couldn't possibly cover everything you ever need to know about UNIX system tools in this one volume.

Tools not covered in this text:

- the login procedure

- UNIX system editors and how to use them

- how the file system is organized and how you move around in it

- shell programming

Information about these subjects can be found in the *User's Guide* and a number of commercially available texts.

Tools that are covered in this text apply to application software development. This text also covers tools for packaging application and device driver software and for customizing the administrative interface.

Programming Tools and Languages in the UNIX System Environment

In this section we describe a variety of programming tools supported in the UNIX system environment. By "programming tools" we mean those offered for use on a computer running a current release of UNIX System V. Since these are separately purchasable items, not all of them will necessarily be installed on your machine. On the other hand, you may have programming tools and languages available on your machine that came from another source and are not mentioned in this discussion.

The C Language

C is intimately associated with the UNIX system since it was originally developed for use in recoding the UNIX system kernel. If you need to use a lot of UNIX system function calls for low-level I/O, memory or device management, or interprocess communication, C is a logical first choice. Most programs, however, don't require such direct interfaces with the operating system, so the decision to choose C might better be based on one or more of the following characteristics:

- a variety of data types: characters, integers of various sizes, and floating point numbers

- low-level constructs (most of the UNIX system kernel is written in C)

- derived data types such as arrays, functions, pointers, structures, and unions

- multidimensional arrays

- scaled pointers and the ability to do pointer arithmetic

- bitwise operators

- a variety of flow-of-control statements: `if`, `if-else`, `switch`, `while`, `do-while`, and `for`

- a high degree of portability

Refer to the *Programmer's Guide: ANSI C and Programming Support Tools* for complete details on C.

It takes fairly concentrated use of the C language over a period of several months to reach your full potential as a C programmer. If you are a casual programmer, you might make it easier for yourself if you choose a less demanding programming facility such as those described below.

Shell

You can use the shell to create programs (new commands). Such programs are also called shell procedures. Refer to the *User's Guide* for information on how to create and execute shell programs using commands, variables, positional parameters, return codes, and basic programming control structures.

awk

The awk program (its name is an acronym constructed from the initials of its developers) scans an input file for lines that match pattern(s) described in a specification file. Upon finding a line that matches a pattern, awk performs actions also described in the specification. It is not uncommon that an awk program can be written in a couple of lines to do functions that would take a couple of pages to describe in a programming language like FORTRAN or C. For example, consider a case where you have a set of records that consist of a key field and a second field that represents a quantity, and the task is to output the sum of the quantities for each key. The pseudocode for such a program might look like this:

```
SORT RECORDS
Read the first record into a hold area;
Read additional records until EOF;
{
If the key matches the key of the record in the hold area,
  add the quantity to the quantity field of the held record;
If the key does not match the key of the held record,
  write the held record,
  move the new record to the hold area;
}
At EOF, write out the last record from the hold area.
```

An `awk` program to accomplish this task would look like this:

```
        { qty[$1]  += $2  }
END     { for (key in qty) print key, qty[key]  }
```

This illustrates only one characteristic of `awk`; its ability to work with associative arrays. With `awk`, the input file does not have to be sorted, which is a requirement of the pseudoprogram.

For detailed information on `awk`, see the "awk" chapter in the *User's Guide* and awk(1) in the *User's Reference Manual*.

lex

`lex` is a lexical analyzer that can be added to C or FORTRAN programs. A lexical analyzer is interested in the vocabulary of a language rather than its grammar, which is a system of rules defining the structure of a language. `lex` can produce C language subroutines that recognize regular expressions specified by the user, take some action when a regular expression is recognized, and pass the output stream on to the next program.

For detailed information on `lex`, see the "lex'' chapter in the *Programmer's Guide: ANSI C and Programming Support Tools* and lex(1) in the *Programmer's Reference Manual*.

yacc

`yacc` (Yet Another Compiler Compiler) is a tool for describing an input language to a computer program. `yacc` produces a C language subroutine that parses an input stream according to rules laid down in a specification file. The `yacc` specification file establishes a set of grammatical rules together with actions to be taken when tokens in the input match the rules. `lex` may be used with `yacc` to control the input process and pass tokens to the parser that applies the grammatical rules.

For detailed information on `yacc`, see the "yacc'' chapter in the *Programmer's Guide: ANSI C and Programming Support Tools* and yacc(1) in the *Programmer's Reference Manual*.

m4

m4 is a macro processor that can be used as a preprocessor for assembly language and C programs. For details, see the m4 chapter of the *Programmer's Guide: ANSI C and Programming Support Tools* and m4(1) in the *Programmer's Reference Manual*.

bc and dc

bc enables you to use a computer terminal as you would a programmable calculator. You can edit a file of mathematical computations and call bc to execute them. The bc program uses dc. You can use dc directly, if you want, but it takes a little getting used to since it works with reverse Polish notation. bc and dc are described in Section 1 of the *User's Reference Manual*.

Character User Interfaces

curses

Actually a library of C functions, curses is included in this list because the set of functions comprise a sublanguage for dealing with terminal screens. If you are writing programs that include interactive user screens, you will want to become familiar with this group of functions.

For detailed information on curses, see the *Programmer's Guide: Character User Interface (FMLI and ETI)*

FMLI

The Form and Menu Language Interpreter (FMLI) is a high-level programming tool having two main parts:

- The Form and Menu Language, a programming language for writing scripts that define how an application will be presented to users. The syntax of the Form and Menu Language is very similar to that of the UNIX system shell programming language, including variable setting and evaluation, built-in commands and functions, use of and escape from special characters, redirection of input and output, conditional statements, interrupt signal handling, and the ability to set various terminal attributes. The Form and Menu Language also includes sets of "descriptors," which are used to define or customize attributes of frames and other objects in your application.

- The Form and Menu Language Interpreter, fmli, which is a command interpreter that sets up and controls the video display screen on a terminal, using instructions from your scripts to supplement FMLI's predefined screen control mechanisms. FMLI scripts can also invoke UNIX system commands and C executables, either in the background or in full screen mode. The Form and Menu Language Interpreter operates similarly to the UNIX command interpreter sh. At run time it parses the scripts you have written, thus giving you the advantages of quick prototyping and easy maintenance.

FMLI provides a framework for developers to write applications and application interfaces that use menus and forms. It controls many aspects of screen management for you. This means that you do not have to be concerned with the low-level details of creating or placing frames, providing users with a means of navigating between or within frames, or processing the use of forms and menus. Nor do you need to worry about on which kind of terminal your application will be run. FMLI takes care of all that for you.

For details see the FMLI chapter in the *Programmer's Guide: Character User Interface (FMLI and ETI)*

ETI

The Extended Terminal Interface (ETI) is a set of C library routines that promote the development of application programs displaying and manipulating windows, panels, menus, and forms and that run under the UNIX system. ETI consists of

- the low-level (curses) library
- the panel library
- the menu library
- the form library
- the TAM Transition library

The routines are C functions and macros; many of them resemble routines in the standard C library. For example, there's a routine printw that behaves much like printf and another routine getch that behaves like getc. The automatic teller program at your bank might use printw to print its menus and getch to accept your requests for withdrawals (or, better yet, deposits). A visual screen editor like the UNIX system screen editor vi might also use these and other ETI routines.

A major feature of ETI is cursor optimization. Cursor optimization minimizes the amount a cursor has to move around a screen to update it. For example, if you designed a screen editor program with ETI routines and edited the sentence

        ETI is a great package for creating forms and menus.

to read

        ETI is the best package for creating forms and menus.

the program would change only "the best" in place of "a great." The other characters would be preserved. Because the amount of data transmitted—the output—is minimized, cursor optimization is also referred to as output optimization.

Cursor optimization takes care of updating the screen in a manner appropriate for the terminal on which an ETI program is run. This means that ETI can do whatever is required to update many different terminal types. It searches the terminfo database to find the correct description for a terminal.

How does cursor optimization help you and those who use your programs? First, it saves you time in describing in a program how you want to update screens. Second, it saves a user's time when the screen is updated. Third, it reduces the load on your UNIX system's communication lines when the updating takes place. Fourth, you don't have to worry about the myriad of terminals on which your program might be run.

Here's a simple ETI program. It uses some of the basic ETI routines to move a cursor to the middle of a terminal screen and print the character string BullsEye. For now, just look at their names and you will get an idea of what each of them does:

Figure 1: A Simple ETI Program

```
#include <curses.h>

main()
{
    initscr();

    move( LINES/2 - 1, COLS/2 - 4 );
    addstr("Bulls");
    refresh();
    addstr("Eye");
    refresh();
    endwin();
}
```

For complete information on ETI, refer to the ETI chapter in the *Programmer's Guide: Character User Interface (FMLI and ETI)*.

Graphical User Interfaces

XWIN Graphical Windowing System

The XWIN Graphical Windowing System is a network-transparent window system. X display servers run on computers with either monochrome or color bitmap display hardware. The server distributes user input to and accepts output requests from various application programs (referred to as "clients"). Each client is located on either the same machine or on another machine in the network.

The clients use Xlib, a C library routine, to interface with the window system by means of a stream connection.

"Widgets" are a set of code and data that provide the look and feel of a user interface. The C library routines used for creating and managing widgets are called the X Intrinsics. They are built on top of the X Window System, monitor events related to user interactions, and dispatch the correct widget code to handle the display. Widgets can then call application-registered routines (called callbacks) to handle the specific application semantics of an interaction. The X Intrinsics also monitor application-registered, nongraphical events and dispatch application routines to handle them. These features allow programmers to use this implementation of an OPEN LOOK toolkit in data base management, network management, process control, and other applications requiring response to external events.

Clients sometimes use a higher level library of the X Intrinsics and a set of widgets in addition to xlib. Refer to the *XWIN Graphical Windowing System* for general information about the design of X. The *Xlib–C Language Interface* is a reference guide to the low-level C language interface to the XWIN System protocol.

OPEN LOOK Graphical User Interface

The OPEN LOOK Graphical User Interface is a software application that creates a user-friendly graphical environment for the UNIX system. It replaces the traditional UNIX system commands with with graphics that include windows, menus, icons, and other symbols. Using a hand-held pointing device (a "mouse"), you manipulate windows by moving them, changing their size and running them in the background. You can have multiple applications running at the same time by creating more than one window on your screen.

For more information, refer to the *OPEN LOOK Graphical User Interface User's Guide* and the *OPEN LOOK Graphical User Interface Programmer's Guide/Reference Manual*.

UNIX System Calls and Libraries

This section describes the UNIX system services supplied by UNIX system calls and libraries for the C programming language. It introduces such topics as the process scheduler, virtual memory, interprocess communication, file and record locking, and symbolic links. The system calls and libraries that programs use to access these UNIX system services are described in detail later in this book.

File and Device Input/Output

UNIX system applications can do all I/O by reading or writing files, because all I/O devices, even a user's terminal, are files in the file-system. Each peripheral device has an entry in the file-system hierarchy, so that device-names have the same structure as file-names, and the same protection mechanisms apply to devices as to files. Using the same I/O calls on a terminal as on any file makes it easy to redirect the input and output of commands from the terminal to another file. Besides the traditionally available devices, names exist for disk devices regarded as physical units outside the file-system, and for absolutely addressed memory.

File and Record Locking

The provision for locking files, or portions of files, is primarily used to prevent the sort of error that can occur when two or more users of a file try to update information at the same time. The classic example is the airlines reservation system where two ticket agents each assign a passenger to Seat A, Row 5 on the 5 o'clock flight to Detroit. A locking mechanism is designed to prevent such mishaps by blocking Agent B from even seeing the seat assignment file until Agent A's transaction is complete.

File locking and record locking are really the same thing, except that file locking implies the whole file is affected; record locking means that only a specified portion of the file is locked. (Remember, in the UNIX system, file structure is undefined; a record is a concept of the programs that use the file.)

Two types of locks are available: read locks and write locks. If a process places a read lock on a file, other processes can also read the file but all are prevented from writing to it, that is, changing any of the data. If a process places a write lock on a file, no other processes can read or write in the file until the lock is removed. Write locks are also known as exclusive locks. The term shared lock is sometimes applied to read locks.

Another distinction needs to be made between mandatory and advisory locking. Mandatory locking means that the discipline is enforced automatically for the system calls that read, write, or create files. This is done through a permission flag established by the file's owner (or the superuser). Advisory locking means that the processes that use the file take the responsibility for setting and removing locks as needed. Thus, mandatory may sound like a simpler and better deal, but it isn't so. The mandatory locking capability is included in the system to comply with an agreement with /usr/group, an organization that represents the interests of UNIX system users. The principal weakness in the mandatory method is that the lock is in place only while the single system call is being made. It is extremely common for a single transaction to require a series of reads and writes before it can be considered complete. In cases like this, the term atomic is used to describe a transaction that must be viewed as an indivisible unit. The preferred way to manage locking in such a circumstance is to make certain the lock is in place before any I/O starts, and that it is not removed until the transaction is done. That calls for locking of the advisory variety.

Where to Find More Information

Chapter 2 in this book discusses file and device I/O including file and record locking in detail with a number of examples. There is an example of file and record locking in the sample application in chapter 4. The manual pages that specifically address file and record locking are fcntl(2), lockf(3), and chmod(2) in the *Programmer's Reference Manual* and fcntl(5) in the *System Files and Devices Reference Manual*. fcntl(2) is the system call for file and record locking (although it isn't limited to that only) fcntl(5) tells you the file control options. The subroutine lockf(3) can also be used to lock sections of a file or an entire file. Setting chmod so that all portions of a file are locked will ensure that parts of files are not corrupted.

Memory Management

The UNIX system includes a complete set of memory-mapping mechanisms. Process address spaces are composed of a vector of memory pages, each of which can be independently mapped and manipulated. The memory-management facilities

- unify the system's operations on memory

- provide a set of kernel mechanisms powerful and general enough to support the implementation of fundamental system services without special-purpose kernel support

- maintain consistency with the existing environment, in particular using the UNIX file system as the name space for named virtual-memory objects

The system's virtual memory consists of all available physical memory resources including local and remote file systems, processor primary memory, swap space, and other random-access devices. Named objects in the virtual memory are referenced though the UNIX file system. However, not all file system objects are in the virtual memory; devices that the UNIX system cannot treat as storage, such as terminal and network device files, are not in the virtual memory. Some virtual memory objects, such as private process memory and shared memory segments, do not have names.

The Memory Mapping Interface

The applications programmer gains access to the facilities of the virtual memory system through several sets of system calls.

- mmap establishes a mapping between a process's address space and a virtual memory object.

- mprotect assigns access protection to a block of virtual memory

- munmap removes a memory mapping

- getpagesize returns the system-dependent size of a memory page.

- mincore tells whether mapped memory pages are in primary memory

Where to Find More Information

Chapter 2 in this book gives a detailed description of the virtual memory system. Refer to mmap(2), mprotect(2), munmap(2), getpagesize(2), and min-core(2) in the *Programmer's Reference Manual* for these manual pages.

Process Management and Scheduling

The UNIX system scheduler determines when processes run. It maintains process priorities based on configuration parameters, process behavior, and user requests; it uses these priorities to assign processes to the CPU.

Scheduler functions give users absolute control over the order in which certain processes run and the amount of time each process may use the CPU before another process gets a chance.

By default, the scheduler uses a time-sharing policy. A time-sharing policy adjusts process priorities dynamically in an attempt to give good response time to interactive processes and good throughput to CPU-intensive processes.

The scheduler offers a real-time scheduling policy as well as a time-sharing policy. Real-time scheduling allows users to set fixed priorities— priorities that the system does not change. The highest priority real-time user process always gets the CPU as soon as it is runnable, even if system processes are runnable. An application can therefore specify the exact order in which processes run. An application may also be written so that its real-time processes have a guaranteed response time from the system.

For most UNIX system environments, the default scheduler configuration works well and no real-time processes are needed: administrators need not change configuration parameters and users need not change scheduler properties of their processes. However, for some applications with strict timing constraints, real-time processes are the only way to guarantee that the application's requirements are met.

Where to Find More Information

Chapter 3 in this book gives detailed information on the process scheduler, along with relevant code examples. See also priocntl(1) in the *User's Reference Manual*, priocntl(2) in the *Programmer's Reference Manual*, and dispadmin(1M) in the *System Administrator's Reference Manual*.

Interprocess Communications

Pipes, named pipes, and signals are all forms of interprocess communication. Business applications running on a UNIX system computer, however, often need more sophisticated methods of communication. In applications, for example, where fast response is critical, a number of processes may be brought up at the start of a business day to be constantly available to handle transactions on demand. This cuts out initialization time that can add seconds to the time required to deal with the transaction. To go back to the ticket reservation example again for a moment, if a customer calls to reserve a seat on the 5 o'clock flight to Detroit, you don't want to have to say, "Yes, sir; just hang on a minute while I start up the reservations program." In transaction-driven systems, the normal mode of processing is to have all the components of the application standing by waiting for some sort of an indication that there is work to do.

To meet requirements of this type, the UNIX system offers a set of nine system calls and their accompanying header files, all under the umbrella name of inter-process communications (IPC).

The IPC system calls come in sets of three; one set each for messages, sema-phores, and shared memory. These three terms define three different styles of communication between processes:

messages	Communication is in the form of data stored in a buffer. The buffer can be either sent or received.
semaphores	Communication is in the form of positive integers with a value between 0 and 32,767. Semaphores may be con-tained in an array the size of which is determined by the system administrator. The default maximum size for the array is 25.
shared memory	Communication takes place through a common area of main memory. One or more processes can attach a seg-ment of memory and as a consequence can share what-ever data is placed there.

The sets of IPC system calls are:

```
msgget    semget    shmget
msgctl    semctl    shmctl
msgop     semop     shmop
```

The "get" calls each return to the calling program an identifier for the type of IPC facility that is being requested.

The "ctl" calls provide a variety of control operations that include obtaining (IPC_STAT), setting (IPC_SET) and removing (IPC_RMID), the values in data structures associated with the identifiers picked up by the "get" calls.

The "op" manual pages describe calls that are used to perform the particular operations characteristic of the type of IPC facility being used. msgop has calls that send or receive messages. semop (the only one of the three that is actually the name of a system call) is used to increment or decrement the value of a semaphore, among other functions. shmop has calls that attach or detach shared memory segments.

Where to Find More Information

Chapter 4 in this book gives a detailed description of IPC, with many code examples that use the IPC system calls. An example of the use of some IPC features is included in the liber application in chapter 4. The system calls are described in Section 2 of the *Programmer's Reference Manual*.

Symbolic Links

A symbolic link is a special type of file that represents another file. The data in a symbolic link consists of the path name of a file or directory to which the symbolic link file refers. The link that is formed is called symbolic to distinguish it from a regular (also called a hard) link. A symbolic link differs functionally from a regular link in three major ways.

- Files from different file systems may be linked.

- Directories, as well as regular files, may be symbolically linked by any user.

- A symbolic link can be created even if the file it represents does not exist.

When a user creates a regular link to a file, a new directory entry is created containing a new file name and the inode number of an existing file. The link count of the file is incremented.

In contrast, when a user creates a symbolic link, (using the ln(1) command with the -s option) both a new directory entry and a new inode are created. A data block is allocated to contain the path name of the file to which the symbolic link refers. The link count of the referenced file is not incremented.

Symbolic links can be used to solve a variety of common problems. For example, it frequently happens that a disk partition (such as root) runs out of disk space. With symbolic links, an administrator can create a link from a directory on that file system to a directory on another file system. Such a link provides extra disk space and is, in most cases, transparent to both users and programs.

Symbolic links can also help deal with the built-in path names that appear in the code of many commands. Changing the path names would require changing the programs and recompiling them. With symbolic links, the path names can effectively be changed by making the original files symbolic links that point to new files.

In a shared resource environment like RFS, symbolic links can be very useful. For example, if it is important to have a single copy of certain administrative files, symbolic links can be used to help share them. Symbolic links can also be used to share resources selectively. Suppose a system administrator wants to do a remote mount of a directory that contains sharable devices. These devices must be in /dev on the client system, but this system has devices of its own so the administrator does not want to mount the directory onto /dev. Rather than do this, the administrator can mount the directory at a location other than /dev and then use symbolic links in the /dev directory to refer to these remote devices. (This is similar to the problem of built-in path names since it is normally assumed that devices reside in the /dev directory.)

Finally, symbolic links can be valuable within the context of the virtual file system (VFS) architecture. With VFS, new services, such as higher performance files, network IPC, and FACE servers, may be provided on a file system basis. Symbolic links can be used to link these services to home directories or to places that make more sense to the application or user. Thus, you might create a data base index file in a RAM-based file system type and symbolically link it to the place where the data base server expects it and manages it.

Where to Find More Information

Chapter 5 in this book discusses symbolic links in detail. Refer to symlink(2) in the *Programmer's Reference Manual* for information on creating symbolic links. See also stat(2), rename(2), link(2), readlink(2), and unlink(2) in the same manual, and ln(1) in the *User's Reference Manual*.

Application and Driver Software Packaging

This section gives the software package developer information on the interfaces provided by SVR4, specifically package software for SVR4 and how to modify the administrator's interface.

The interface modification tools allow you to generate files to deliver as part of your package. When these files are installed, your package administration tasks are added to the interface.

Packaging Application Software

Packaging software that will be installed on a computer running UNIX SVR4 differs from packaging in a pre-SVR4 environment. Pre-SVR4 packages deliver information to the system through script actions, but an SVR4 package does this through package information files.

A software package is made up of a group of components that together create the software. These components naturally include the executables that comprise the software, but they also include at least two information files and can optionally include other information files and scripts.

The contents of a package fall into three categories:

- required components
- optional package information files
- optional package scripts

A packaging tool, the pkgmk command, is provided to help automate package creation. It gathers the components of a package on the development machine and copies and formats them onto the installation medium.

The installation tool, the pkgadd command, copies the package from the installation medium onto a system and performs system housekeeping routines that concern the package.

Where to Find More Information

Chapter 8 in this book gives complete details on packaging application software, including package installation case studies. For details on a specific tool, refer to admin(4), compver(4), copyright(4), depend(4), installf(1M), pkgadd(1M), pkgask(1M), pkgchk(1M), pkginfo(1), pkginfo(4), pkgmap(4), pkgmk(1), pkgparam(1), pkgproto(1), pkgrm(1M), pkgtrans(1), proto-type(4), removef(1M), and space(4) manual pages at the end of this volume.

Modifying the sysadm Interface

The UNIX system provides a menu interface to the most common administrative procedures. It is invoked by executing sysadm and is referred to as the "sysadm interface."

You can deliver additions or changes to this interface as part of your application software package. Creating the necessary information for an interface modification can be done using the tools UNIX provides.

Two commands can be used to modify the interface. edsysadm allows you to make changes or additions to the interface. It is interactive (much like the sysadm command itself) and presents a series of prompts for information. Which prompts appear depend on your response to them. The delsysadm command deletes menus or tasks from the interface. In addition to these commands, a group of data validation tools are provided to simplify and standardize the programming of administrative interaction.

When you execute edsysadm to define menus and tasks and save those definitions to be included in your application software package, it creates the package description file, the menu information file, and a prototype file.

- The package description file contains information used by edsysadm to change interface modifications already saved for packaging.

- The menu information file contains the menu or task name, where it is located in the interface structure and, for tasks, what executable to use when the task is invoked.

- The prototype file created by edsysadm contains entries for all of the interface modification components that must be packaged with your software (for example, the menu information file and, for tasks, the executables).

You must take a number of steps if you intend to modify the sysadm interface by adding the administration to your package. You have to

- plan your package administration
- write your administration actions
- write your help messages
- package your interface modifications

Where to Find More Information

Chapter 9 in this book gives complete details on modifying the sysadm interface. For details on a specific tool, refer to the manual pages at the end of this volume, which includes the manual pages for delsysadm(1M) and edsysadm(1M). The *System Administrator's Guide* gives a complete description of the interface and how to use it. See also the *Programmer's Guide: Character User Interface (FMLI and ETI)* for complete information on FMLI.

Data Validation Tools

Data validation tools are written to help you write any administrative programs and routines that are part of your software package (this is known as package administration). They help standardize the appearance of administration interaction in the UNIX system environment and also simplify development of scripts and programs requiring administrator input.

There are two types of data validation tools:

- shell commands (to be used in shell scripts)
- visual tools (to be used in FMLI form definitions)

The shell commands perform a series of tasks; the visual tools perform a subsection of the full series. These tasks are:

- prompting a user for input
- validating the answer

- formatting and printing a help message when requested
- formatting and presenting an error message when validation fails
- returning the input if it passes validation
- allowing a user to quit the process

Where to Find More Information

Chapter 9 in this book describes the characteristics of these tools and introduces you to the available tools for all two types. For details on a specific tool, refer to the manual pages at the end of this volume, which includes ckdate(1), ckgid(1), ckint(1), ckkeywd(1), ckpath(1), ckrange(1), ckstr(1), cktime(1), ckuid(1), ckyorn(1), dispgid(1), and dispuid(1). The visual tools are also documented in the Section 1 manual pages.

Driver Software Packaging

The final chapter in this section, "Driver Software Packaging", contains the rules and procedures you need to follow for packaging device driver software to work on UNIX System V Release 4.0 for the Intel386 microprocessor. As you may know, writing a device driver carries a lot of responsibility because, as part of the UNIX operating system kernel, it is assumed to always take the correct action. "The Trace Driver", presents a pseudo-device, called the "trace driver," that allows the UNIX operating system kernel or other device drivers to report debugging information without the use of console printf's. "A Prototype Floppy Disk Driver", contains some selected portions of the UNIX System V/386 Release 4.0 floppy disk device driver source files. "A Sample Driver Software Package", shows the ID modules needed to install a device driver and describes the Install and Remove scripts.

Where to Find More Information

Chapter 10 in this book describes the characteristics of the Installable Driver (ID) facility and introduces you to the available tools for the ID facility on UNIX System V/386. For details on a specific tool, refer to the manual pages at the end of this volume, which includes idbuild(1M), idcheck(1M), idconfig(1M), idinstall(1M), idmkinit(1M), idmknod(1M), idmkunix(1M), idspace(1M), idtune(1M), mdevice(4), mfsys(4), mtune(4), sdevice(4), sfsys(4), stune(4).

1 UNIX System Calls and Libraries

1. UNIX SYSTEM CALLS AND LIBRARIES

Introduction

The chapter introduces the system calls and other system services you can use to develop application programs. Each application performs a different function, but goes through the same basic steps: input, processing, and output. For the input and output steps, most applications interact with an end user at a terminal. During the processing step, sometimes an application needs access to special services provided by the operating system (for example, to interact with the file system, control processes, manage memory, and more). Some of these services are provided through system calls and some through libraries of functions.

Libraries and Header Files

The standard libraries supplied by the C compilation system contain functions that you can use in your program to perform input/output, string handling, and other high-level operations that are not explicitly provided by the C language. Header files contain definitions and declarations that your program will need if it calls a library function. They also contain function-like macros that you can use in your program as you would a function.

In this part, we'll talk a bit more about header files and show you how to use library functions in your program. We'll also describe the contents of some of the more important standard libraries, and tell you where to find them in the *Programmer's Reference Manual*. We'll close with a brief discussion of standard I/O.

Header Files

Header files serve as the interface between your program and the libraries supplied by the C compilation system. Because the functions that perform standard I/O, for example, very often use the same definitions and declarations, the system supplies a common interface to the functions in the header file stdio.h. By the same token, if you have definitions or declarations that you want to make available to several source files, you can create a header file with any editor, store it in a convenient directory, and include it in your program as described in the first part of this chapter.

Header files traditionally are designated by the suffix .h, and are brought into a program at compile time. The preprocessor component of the compiler does this because it interprets the #include statement in your program as a directive. The two most commonly used directives are #include and #define. As we have seen, the #include directive is used to call in and process the contents of the named file. The #define directive is used to define the replacement token string for an identifier. For example,

```
#define NULL    0
```

defines the macro NULL to have the replacement token sequence 0. See the section on "C Language", in the *Programmer's Guide: ANSI C and Programming Support Tools*, for the complete list of preprocessing directives.

Many different .h files are named in the *Programmer's Reference Manual*. Here we are going to list a number of them, to illustrate the range of tasks you can perform with header files and library functions. When you use a library function in your program, the manual page will tell you which header file, if any, needs to be included. If a header file is mentioned, it should be included before you use any of the associated functions or declarations in your program. It's generally best to put the #include right at the top of a source file.

assert.h	assertion checking
ctype.h	character handling
errno.h	error conditions
float.h	floating point limits
limits.h	other data type limits
locale.h	program's locale
math.h	mathematics
setjmp.h	nonlocal jumps
signal.h	signal handling
stdarg.h	variable arguments
stddef.h	common definitions
stdio.h	standard input/output
stdlib.h	general utilities
string.h	string handling
time.h	date and time
unistd.h	system calls

How to Use Library Functions

The manual page for each function describes how you should use the function in your program. Manual pages follow a common format; although, some manual pages may omit some sections:

- The **NAME** section names the component(s) and briefly states its purpose.

- The **SYNOPSIS** section specifies the C language programming interface(s).

- The **DESCRIPTION** section details the behavior of the component(s).

- The **EXAMPLE** section gives examples, caveats and guidance on usage.

- The **FILES** section gives the file names that are built into the program.

- The **SEE ALSO** section lists related component interface descriptions.

- The **DIAGNOSTICS** section outlines return values and error conditions.

The **NAME** section lists the names of components described in that manual page with a brief, one-line statement of the nature and purpose of those components.

The **SYNOPSIS** section summarizes the component interface by compactly representing the order of any arguments for the component, the type of each argument (if any) and the type of value the component returns.

The **DESCRIPTION** section specifies the functionality of components without stipulating the implementation; it excludes the details of how UNIX System V implements these components and concentrates on defining the external features of a standard computing environment instead of the internals of the operating system, such as the scheduler or memory manager. Portable software should avoid using any features or side-effects not explicitly defined.

The **SEE ALSO** section refers the reader to other related manual pages in *The UNIX System V Reference Manual Set* as well as other documents. The **SEE ALSO** section identifies manual pages by the title which appears in the upper corners of each page of a manual page.

Some manual pages cover several commands, functions or other UNIX System V components; thus, components defined along with other related components share the same manual page title. For example, any references to the function calloc cite malloc(3) because the function calloc is described with the function malloc in the manual page entitled malloc(3).

As an example manual page, we'll look at the strcmp function, which compares character strings. The routine is described on the string manual page in Section 3, Subsection 3C, of the *Programmer's Reference Manual*. Related functions are described there as well, but only the sections relevant to strcmp are shown in the following figure.

Figure 1-1: Excerpt from string(3C) Manual Page

NAME

> string: strcat, strdup, strncat, strcmp, strncmp, strcpy, strncpy, strlen,
> strchr, strrchr, strpbrk, strspn, strcspn, strok - string operations.

SYNOPSIS

> #include <string.h>
>
> ...
>
> int strcmp(const char *sptr1, const char *sptr2);
>
> ...

DESCRIPTION

> ...
>
> strcmp compares its arguments and returns an integer less than, equal to, or greater than 0, according as the first argument is lexicographically less than, equal to, or greater than the second.
>
> ...

As shown, the DESCRIPTION section tells you what the function or macro does. It's the SYNOPSIS section, though, that contains the critical information about how you use the function or macro in your program. Note that the first line in the SYNOPSIS is

```
#include <string.h>
```

That means that you should include the header file string.h in your program because it contains useful definitions or declarations relating to strcmp.

In fact, `string.h` contains the `strcmp` "function prototype" as follows:

```
extern int strcmp(const char *, const char *);
```

A function prototype describes the kinds of arguments expected and returned by a C language function. Function prototypes afford a greater degree of argument type checking than old-style function declarations, and reduce the chance of using the function incorrectly. Including `string.h`, assures that the C compiler checks calls to `strcmp` against the official interface. You can, of course, examine `string.h` in the standard place for header files on your system, usually the `/usr/include` directory.

The **SYNOPSIS** for a C library function closely resembles the C language declaration of the function and its arguments. The **SYNOPSIS** tells the reader:

- the type of value returned by the function;

- the arguments the function expects to receive when called, if any;

- the argument types.

For example, the **SYNOPSIS** for the macro `feof` is:

```
#include <stdio.h>

int feof( FILE *sfp )
```

The **SYNOPSIS** section for `feof` shows that:

- The macro `feof` requires the header file `stdio.h`

- The macro `feof` returns a value of type `int`

- The argument *sfp* is a pointer to an object of type `FILE`

To use `feof` in a program, you need only write the macro call, preceded at some point by the `#include` control line, as in the following:

```
#include <stdio.h>   /* include definitions */
main() {
   FILE *infile;      /* define a file pointer */
   while (!feof(infile)) {   /* until end-of-file */
      /* operations on the file */
   }
}
```

By way of further illustration, let's look at how you might use strcmp in your own code. The following figure shows a program fragment that will find the bird of your choice in an array of birds.

Figure 1-2: How strcmp Is Used in a Program

```
#include <string.h>

/* birds must be in alphabetical order */
char *birds[] = { "albatross", "canary", "cardinal", "ostrich", "penguin" };

/* Return the index of the bird in the array. */
/* If the bird is not in the array, return -1 */

int is_bird(const char *string)
{
     int low, high, midpoint;
     int cmp_value;

     /* use a binary search to find the bird */
     low = 0;
     high = sizeof(birds)/sizeof(char *) - 1;
     while(low <= high)
     {
          midpoint = (low + high)/2;
          cmp_value = strcmp(string, birds[midpoint]);
          if (cmp_value < 0)
               high = midpoint - 1;
          else if (cmp_value > 0)
               low = midpoint + 1;
          else /* found a match */
               return midpoint;
     }
     return -1;
}
```

The format of a **SYNOPSIS** section only resembles, but does *not* duplicate, the format of C language declarations. To show that some components take varying numbers of arguments, the **SYNOPSIS** section uses additional conventions not found in actual C function declarations:

- Text in `courier` represents source-code typed just as it appears.

- Text in *italic* usually represents substitutable argument prototypes.

- Square brackets [ ] around arguments indicate optional arguments.

- Ellipses ... indicate that the previous arguments may repeat.

- If the type of an argument may vary, the **SYNOPSIS** omits the type.

For example, the **SYNOPSIS** for the function `printf` is:

```
#include <stdio.h>

int printf( char *fmt [ , arg ... ] )
```

The **SYNOPSIS** section for `printf` shows that the argument `arg` is optional, may be repeated and is not always of the same data type. The **DESCRIPTION** section of the manual page provides any remaining information about the function `printf` and the arguments to it.

The **DIAGNOSTICS** section specifies return values and possible error conditions. The text in the **DIAGNOSTICS** takes a conventional form which describes the return value in case of successful completion followed by the consequences of an unsuccessful completion, as in the following example:

> On success, `lseek` returns the value of the resulting file-offset, as measured in bytes from the beginning of the file.
>
> On failure, `lseek` returns −1, it does *not* change the file-offset, and `errno` equals:
>
> > EBADF if `fildes` is not a valid open file-descriptor.
> >
> > EINVAL if `whence` is not SEEK_SET, SEEK_CUR or SEEK_END.
> >
> > ESPIPE if `fildes` denotes a pipe or FIFO.

The `<errno.h>` header file defines symbolic names for error conditions which are described in `intro(2)` of the *Programmer's Reference Manual*. For more information on error conditions, see the section entitled "UNIX System Call Error Handling" in this chapter.

C Library (libc)

In this section, we describe some of the more important routines in the standard C library. As we indicated in the first part of this chapter, libc contains the system calls described in Section 2 of the *Programmer's Reference Manual*, and the C language functions described in Section 3, Subsections 3C and 3S. We'll explain what each of these subsections contains below. We'll look at system calls at the end of the section.

Subsection 3C Routines

Subsection 3C of the *Programmer's Reference Manual* contains functions and macros that perform a variety of tasks:

- string manipulation
- character classification
- character conversion

Figure 1-3 lists string-handling functions that appear on the string page in Subsection 3C of the *Programmer's Reference Manual*. Programs that use these functions should include the header file string.h.

Figure 1-3: String Operations

strcat	Append a copy of one string to the end of another.
strncat	Append no more than a given number of characters from one string to the end of another.
strcmp	Compare two strings. Returns an integer less than, greater than, or equal to 0 to show that one is lexicographically less than, greater than, or equal to the other.
strncmp	Compare no more than a given number of characters from the two strings. Results are otherwise identical to strcmp.

Figure 1-3: String Operations (continued)

strcpy	Copy a string.
strncpy	Copy a given number of characters from one string to another. The destination string will be truncated if it is longer than the given number of characters, or padded with null characters if it is shorter.
strdup	Return a pointer to a newly allocated string that is a duplicate of a string pointed to.
strchr	Return a pointer to the first occurrence of a character in a string, or a null pointer if the character is not in the string.
strrchr	Return a pointer to the last occurrence of a character in a string, or a null pointer if the character is not in the string.
strlen	Return the number of characters in a string.
strpbrk	Return a pointer to the first occurrence in one string of any character from the second, or a null pointer if no character from the second occurs in the first.
strspn	Return the length of the initial segment of one string that consists entirely of characters from the second string.
strcspn	Return the length of the initial segment of one string that consists entirely of characters not from the second string.
strstr	Return a pointer to the first occurrence of the second string in the first string, or a null pointer if the second string is not found.
strtok	Break up the first string into a sequence of tokens, each of which is delimited by one or more characters from the second string. Return a pointer to the token, or a null pointer if no token is found.

Figure 1-4 lists functions and macros that classify 8-bit character-coded integer values. These routines appear on the conv(3) and ctype(3) pages in Subsection 3C of the *Programmer's Reference Manual*. Programs that use these routines should include the header file ctype.h.

Figure 1-4: Classifying 8-Bit Character-Coded Integer Values

isalpha	Is *c* a letter?
isupper	Is *c* an uppercase letter?
islower	Is *c* a lowercase letter?
isdigit	Is *c* a digit [0-9]?
isxdigit	Is *c* a hexadecimal digit [0-9], [A-F], or [a-f]?
isalnum	Is *c* alphanumeric (a letter or digit)?
isspace	Is *c* a space, horizontal tab, vertical tab, new-line, form-feed, or carriage return?
ispunct	Is *c* a punctuation character (neither control nor alphanumeric)?
isprint	Is *c* a printing character?
isgraph	Same as isprint except false for a space.
iscntrl	Is *c* a control character or a delete character?
isascii	Is *c* an ASCII character?
toupper	Change lower case to upper case.
_toupper	Macro version of toupper.
tolower	Change upper case to lower case.
_tolower	Macro version of tolower.
toascii	Turn off all bits that are not part of a standard ASCII character; intended for compatibility with other systems.

Figure 1-5 lists functions and macros in Subsection 3C of the *Programmer's Reference Manual* that are used to convert characters, integers, or strings from one representation to another. The left-hand column contains the name that appears at the top of the manual page; the other names in the same row are related functions or macros described on the same manual page. Programs that use these routines should include the header file `stdlib.h`.

Figure 1-5: Converting Characters, Integers, or Strings

a64l	l64a		Convert between long integer and base-64 ASCII string.
ecvt	fcvt	gcvt	Convert floating point number to string.
l3tol	ltol3		Convert between 3-byte packed integer and long integer.
strtod	atof		Convert string to double-precision number.
strtol	atol	atoi	Convert string to integer.
strtoul			Convert string to unsigned long.

Subsection 3S Routines

Subsection 3S of the *Programmer's Reference Manual* contains the so-called standard I/O library for C programs. Frequently, one manual page describes several related functions or macros. In Figure 1-6, the left-hand column contains the name that appears at the top of the manual page; the other names in the same row are related functions or macros described on the same manual page. Programs that use these routines should include the header file `stdio.h`. We'll talk a bit more about standard I/O in the last subsection of this chapter.

Integrated Software Development Guide

Figure 1-6: Standard I/O Functions and Macros

fclose	fflush			Close or flush a stream.
ferror	feof	clearerr	fileno	Stream status inquiries.
fopen	freopen	fdopen		Open a stream.
fread	fwrite			Input/output.
fseek	rewind	ftell		Reposition a file pointer in a stream.
getc	getchar	fgetc	getw	Get a character or word from a stream.
gets	fgets			Get a string from a stream.
popen	pclose			Begin or end a pipe to/from a process.
printf	fprintf	sprintf		Print formatted output.
putc	putchar	fputc	putw	Put a character or word on a stream.
puts	fputs			Put a string on a stream.
scanf	fscanf	sscanf		Convert formatted input.
setbuf	setvbuf			Assign buffering to a stream.
system				Issue a command through the shell.
tmpfile				Create a temporary file.
tmpnam	tempnam			Create a name for a temporary file.
ungetc				Push character back into input stream.
vprintf	vfprintf	vsprintf		Print formatted output of a varargs argument list.

Math Library (libm)

The math library, libm, contains the mathematics functions supplied by the C compilation system. These appear in Subsection 3M of the *Programmer's Reference Manual*. Here we describe some of the major functions, organized by the manual page on which they appear. Note that functions whose names end with the letter f are single-precision versions, which means that their argument and return types are float. Programs that use math functions should include the header file math.h.

Figure 1-7: Math Functions

erf(3M)		
erf		Compute the error function of x, defined as $$\frac{2}{\sqrt{\pi}} \int_0^x e^{-t^2} dt.$$
erfc		Compute 1.0 - erf(x), which is used because of the extreme loss of relative accuracy if erf is called for large x and the result subtracted from 1.0 (e.g., for $x = 5$, 12 places are lost).
exp(3M)		
exp	expf	Compute e^x.
cbrt		Compute the cube root of x.
log	logf	Compute the natural logarithm of x. The value of x must be positive.
log10	log10f	Compute the base-ten logarithm of x. The value of x must be positive.
pow	powf	Compute x^y. If x is zero, y must be positive. If x is negative, y must be an integer.
sqrt	sqrtf	Compute the non-negative square root of x. The value of x must be non-negative.

Figure 1-7: Math Functions (continued)

floor(3M)		
floor	floorf	Compute the largest integer not greater than x.
ceil	ceilf	Compute the smallest integer not less than x.
copysign		Compute x but with the sign of y.
fmod	fmodf	Compute the floating point remainder of the division of x by y: x if y is zero, otherwise the number f with same sign as x, such that $x = iy + f$ for some integer i, and $|f| < |y|$.
fabs	fabsf	Compute $|x|$, the absolute value of x.
rint		Compute as a double-precision floating point number the integer value nearest the double-precision floating point argument x, and rounds the return value according to the currently set machine rounding mode.
remainder		Compute the floating point remainder of the division of x by y: NaN if y is zero, otherwise the value $r = x - yn$, where n is the integer value nearest the exact value of x/y, and n is even whenever $|n - x/y| = 1/2$.
gamma(3M)		
gamma	lgamma	Compute $\ln(|\Gamma(x)|)$, where $\Gamma(x)$ is defined as $\int_0^x e^{-t} t^{x-1} dt.$
hypot(3M)		
hypot		Compute $\mathrm{sqrt}(x * x + y * y)$, taking precautions against overflows.
matherr(3M)		
matherr		Error handling.

Figure 1-7: Math Functions (continued)

trig(3M)		
sin	sinf	Compute the sine of x, measured in radians.
cos	cosf	Compute the cosine of x, measured in radians.
tan	tanf	Compute the tangent of x, measured in radians.
asin	asinf	Compute the arcsine of x, in the range $[-\pi/2, +\pi/2]$.
acos	acosf	Compute the arccosine of x, in the range $[0,+\pi]$.
atan	atanf	Compute the arctangent of x, in the range $(-\pi/2, +\pi/2)$.
atan2	atan2f	Compute the arctangent of y/x, in the range $(-\pi, +\pi]$, using the signs of both arguments to determine the quadrant of the return value.
sinh(3M)		
sinh	sinhf	Compute the hyperbolic sine of x.
cosh	coshf	Compute the hyperbolic cosine of x.
tanh	tanhf	Compute the hyperbolic tangent of x.
asinh		Compute the inverse hyperbolic sine of x.
acosh		Compute the inverse hyperbolic cosine of x.
atanh		Compute the inverse hyperbolic tangent of x.

General Purpose Library (libgen)

libgen contains general purpose functions, and functions designed to facilitate internationalization. These appear in Subsection 3G of the *Programmer's Reference Manual*. Figure 1-8 describes functions in libgen. The header files libgen.h and, occasionally, regexp.h should be included in programs that use these functions.

Figure 1-8: libgen Functions

advance step	Execute a regular expression on a string.
basename	Return a pointer to the last element of a path name.
bgets	Read a specified number of characters into a buffer from a stream until a specified character is reached.
bufsplit	Split the buffer into fields delimited by tabs and new-lines.
compile	Return a pointer to a compiled regular expression that uses the same syntax as ed.
copylist	Copy a file into a block of memory, replacing new-lines with null characters. It returns a pointer to the copy.
dirname	Return a pointer to the parent directory name of the file path name.
eaccess	Determine if the effective user ID has the appropriate permissions on a file.
gmatch	Check if name matches shell file name pattern.
isencrypt	Use heuristics to determine if contents of a character buffer are encrypted.

Figure 1-8: `libgen` **Functions** (continued)

`mkdirp`		Create a directory and its parents.
`p2open`	`p2close`	p2open is similar to popen(3S). It establishes a two-way connection between the parent and the child. p2close closes the pipe.
`pathfind`		Search the directories in a given path for a named file with given mode characteristics. If the file is found, a pointer is returned to a string that corresponds to the path name of the file. A null pointer is returned if no file is found.
`regcmp`		Compile a regular expression and return a pointer to the compiled form.
`regex`		Compare a compiled regular expression against a subject string.
`rmdirp`		Remove the directories in the specified path.
`strccpy`	`strcadd`	strccpy copies the input string to the output string, compressing any C-like escape sequences to the real character. strcadd is a similar function that returns the address of the null byte at the end of the output string.
`strecpy`		Copy the input string to the output string, expanding any non-graphic characters with the C escape sequence. Characters in a third argument are not expanded.
`strfind`		Return the offset of the first occurrence of the second string in the first string. −1 is returned if the second string does not occur in the first.
`strrspn`		Trim trailing characters from a string. It returns a pointer to the last character in the string not in a list of trailing characters.

Integrated Software Development Guide

Figure 1-8: libgen Functions (continued)

strtrns	Return a pointer to the string that results from replacing any character found in two strings with a character from a third string. This function is similar to the tr command.

Standard I/O Library

The functions in Subsection 3S of the *Programmer's Reference Manual* constitute the standard I/O library for C programs. In this section, we want to discuss standard I/O in a bit more detail. First, let's briefly define what I/O involves. It has to do with

- reading information from a file or device to your program;

- writing information from your program to a file or device;

- opening and closing files that your program reads from or writes to.

Three Files You Always Have

Programs automatically start off with three open files: standard input, standard output, and standard error. These files with their associated buffering are called streams, and are designated stdin, stdout, and stderr, respectively. The shell associates all three files with your terminal by default.

This means that you can use functions and macros that deal with stdin, stdout, or stderr without having to open or close files. gets, for example, reads a string from stdin; puts writes a string to stdout. Other functions and macros read from or write to files in different ways: character at a time, getc and putc; formatted, scanf and printf; and so on. You can specify that output be directed to stderr by using a function such as fprintf. fprintf works the same way as printf except that it delivers its formatted output to a named stream, such as stderr.

Named Files

Any file other than standard input, standard output, and standard error must be explicitly opened by you before your program can read from or write to the file. You open a file with the standard library function `fopen`. `fopen` takes a path name, asks the system to keep track of the connection between your program and the file, and returns a pointer that you can then use in functions that perform other I/O operations.

The pointer is to a structure called `FILE`, defined in `stdio.h`, that contains information about the file: the location of its buffer, the current character position in the buffer, and so on. In your program, then, you need to have a declaration such as

```
FILE *fin;
```

which says that `fin` is a pointer to a `FILE`. The statement

```
fin = fopen("filename", "r");
```

associates a `FILE` structure with `filename`, the path name of the file to open, and returns a pointer to it. The `"r"` means that the file is to be opened for reading. This argument is known as the mode. There are modes for reading, writing, and both reading and writing.

In practice, the file open function is often included in an `if` statement:

```
if ((fin = fopen("filename", "r")) == NULL)
    (void)fprintf(stderr,"Cannot open input file %s\n",
        "filename");
```

which takes advantage of the fact that `fopen` returns a `NULL` pointer if it cannot open the file. To avoid falling into the immediately following code on failure, you can call `exit`, which causes your program to quit:

```
if ((fin = fopen("filename", "r")) == NULL) {
    (void)fprintf(stderr,"Cannot open input file %s\n",
        "filename");
    exit(1);
}
```

Once you have opened the file, you use the pointer `fin` in functions or macros to refer to the stream associated with the opened file:

```
int c;
c = getc(fin);
```

brings in one character from the stream into an integer variable called `c`. The variable `c` is declared as an integer even though we are reading characters because `getc` returns an integer. Getting a character is often incorporated in some flow-of-control mechanism such as

```
while ((c = getc(fin)) != EOF)
    .
    .
    .
```

that reads through the file until `EOF` is returned. `EOF`, `NULL`, and the macro `getc` are all defined in `stdio.h`. `getc` and other macros in the standard I/O package keep advancing a pointer through the buffer associated with the stream; the UNIX system and the standard I/O functions are responsible for seeing that the buffer is refilled if you are reading the file, or written to the output file if you are producing output, when the pointer reaches the end of the buffer.

Your program may have multiple files open simultaneously, 20 or more depending on system configuration. If, subsequently, your program needs to open more files than it is permitted to have open simultaneously, you can use the standard library function `fclose` to break the connection between the `FILE` structure in `stdio.h` and the path names of the files your program has opened. Pointers to `FILE` may then be associated with other files by subsequent calls to `fopen`. For output files, an `fclose` call makes sure that all output has been sent from the output buffer before disconnecting the file. `exit` closes all open files for you, but it also gets you completely out of your process, so you should use it only when you are sure you are finished.

How C Programs Communicate with the Shell

Information or control data can be passed to a C program as an argument on the command line, which is to say, by the shell. When you execute a C program, command line arguments are made available to the function `main` in two parameters, an argument count, conventionally called `argc`, and an argument vector, conventionally called `argv`. (Every C program is required to have an entry point named `main`.) `argc` is the number of arguments with which the program was invoked. `argv` is an array of pointers to character strings that contain the arguments, one per string. Since the command name itself is considered to be the first argument, or `argv[0]`, the count is always at least one. Here is the declaration for `main`:

```
int
main(int argc, char *argv[])
```

For two examples of how you might use run-time parameters in your program, see the last subsection of this chapter.

The shell, which makes arguments available to your program, considers an argument to be any sequence of non-blank characters. Characters enclosed in single quotes (`'abc def'`) or double quotes (`"abc def"`) are passed to the program as one argument even if blanks or tabs are among the characters. You are responsible for error checking and otherwise making sure that the argument received is what your program expects it to be.

In addition to `argc` and `argv`, you can use a third argument: `envp` is an array of pointers to environment variables. You can find more information on `envp` in the *Programmer's Reference Manual* under `exec` in Section 2 and in the *System Files and Devices Reference Manual* under `environ` in Section 5.

C programs exit voluntarily, returning control to the operating system, by returning from `main` or by calling the `exit` function. That is, a `return(n)` from `main` is equivalent to the call `exit(n)`. (Remember that `main` has type "function returning int.") Your program should return a value to say whether it completed successfully or not. The value gets passed to the shell, where it becomes the value of the `$?` shell variable if you executed your program in the foreground. By convention, a return value of zero denotes success, a non-zero return value means some sort of error occurred. You can use the macros `EXIT_SUCCESS` and `EXIT_FAILURE`, defined in the header file `stdlib.h`, as return values from `main` or argument values for `exit`.

Passing Command Line Arguments

As described above, information or control data can be passed to a C program as an argument on the command line. When you execute the program, command line arguments are made available to the function `main` in two parameters, an argument count, conventionally called `argc`, and an argument vector, conventionally called `argv`. `argc` is the number of arguments with which the program was invoked. `argv` is an array of pointers to characters strings that contain the arguments, one per string. Since the command name itself is considered to be the first argument, or `argv[0]`, the count is always at least one.

If you plan to accept run-time parameters in your program, you need to include code to deal with the information. Figures 1-9 and 1-10 show program fragments that illustrate two common uses of run-time parameters:

- Figure 1-9 shows how you provide a variable file name to a program, such that a command of the form

    ```
    $ prog filename
    ```

    will cause `prog` to attempt to open the specified file.

- Figure 1-10 shows how you set internal flags that control the operation of a program, such that a command of the form

    ```
    $ prog -opr
    ```

    will cause `prog` to set the corresponding variables for each of the options specified. The `getopt` function used in the example is the most common way to process arguments in UNIX system programs. `getopt` is described in Subsection 3C of the *Programmer's Reference Manual*.

Figure 1-9: Using `argv[1]` to Pass a File Name

```
#include <stdio.h>

int
main(int argc, char *argv[])
{
        FILE *fin;
        int ch;

        switch (argc)
        {
        case 2:
                if ((fin = fopen(argv[1], "r")) == NULL)
                {
                        /* First string (%s) is program name (argv[0]). */
                        /* Second string (%s) is name of file that could */
                        /* not be opened (argv[1]). */

                        (void)fprintf(stderr, "%s: Cannot open input file %s\n",
                                argv[0], argv[1]);
                        return(2);
                }
                break;
        case 1:
                fin = stdin;
                break;

        default:
                (void)fprintf(stderr, "Usage: %s [file]\n", argv[0]);
                return(2);
        }

        while ((ch = getc(fin)) != EOF)
                (void)putchar(ch);

        return (0);

}
```

Figure 1-10: Using Command Line Arguments to Set Flags

```
#include <stdio.h>
#include <stdlib.h>

int
main(int argc, char *argv[])
{
      int oflag = 0;
      int pflag = 0;          /* Function flags */
      int rflag = 0;
      int ch;

      while ((ch = getopt(argc, argv, "opr")) != -1)
      {
            /* For options present, set flag to 1.         */
            /* If unknown options present, print error message. */

            switch (ch)
            {
            case 'o':
                  oflag = 1;
                  break;
            case 'p':
                  pflag = 1;
                  break;
            case 'r':
                  rflag = 1;
                  break;
            default:
                  (void)fprintf(stderr, "Usage: %s [-opr]\n", argv[0]);
                  return(2);
            }
      }
      /* Do other processing controlled by oflag, pflag, rflag. */
      return(0);
}
```

System Calls

UNIX system calls are the interface between the kernel and the user programs that run on top of it. The UNIX system kernel is the software on which everything else in the UNIX operating system depends. The kernel manages system resources, maintains file-systems and supports system-calls. `read`, `write` and the other system calls in Section 2 of the *Programmer's Reference Manual* define what the UNIX system is. Everything else is built on their foundation. Strictly speaking, they are the only way to access such facilities as the file system, inter-process communication primitives, and multitasking mechanisms.

Of course, most programs do not need to invoke system calls directly to gain access to these facilities. If you are writing a C program, for example, you can use the library functions described in Section 3 of the *Programmer's Reference Manual*. When you use these functions, the details of their implementation on the UNIX system are transparent to the program, for example, that the system call `read` underlies the `fread` implementation in the standard C library. In other words, the program will generally be portable to any system, UNIX or not, with a conforming C implementation. (See Chapter 2 of the *Programmer's Guide: ANSI C and Programming Support Tools* for a discussion of the standard C library.)

In contrast, programs that invoke system calls directly are portable only to other UNIX or UNIX-like systems; for that reason, you would not use `read` in a program that performed a simple input/output operation. Other operations, however, including most multitasking mechanisms, do require direct interaction with the UNIX system kernel. These operations are the subject of the first part of this book. This chapter lists the system calls in functional groups, and includes brief discussions of error handling. For details on individual system calls, see Section 2 of the *Programmer's Reference Manual*.

A C program is automatically linked with the system calls you have invoked when you compile the program. The procedure may be different for programs written in other languages. Check the *Programmer's Guide: ANSI C and Programming Support Tools* for details on the language you are using.

Input/Output and File System Calls

File and Device I/O

These system calls perform basic input/output operations on UNIX system files.

Figure 1-11: File and Device I/O Functions

open		open a file for reading or writing
creat		create a new file or rewrite an existing one
close		close a file descriptor
read	write	transfer data from/onto a file or device
getmsg	putmsg	get/put message from/onto a stream
lseek		move file I/O pointer
fcntl		file I/O control
ioctl		device I/O control

Terminal Device Control

These system calls deal with a general terminal interface for the control of asynchronous communications ports.

Figure 1-12: Terminal Device Control Functions

tcgetattr	tcsetattr	get and set terminal attributes
tcdrain	tcflush	line control functions
tcflow	tcsendbreak	line control functions
cfgetispeed	cfgetospeed	get baud rate functions
cfsetispeed	cfsetospeed	set baud rate functions
tcgetsid		get terminal session ID
tcgetpgrp		get terminal foreground process group ID
tcsetpgrp		set terminal foreground process group ID

Directories and File Systems

These system calls allow creation of new directories (and other types of files), linking to existing files, obtaining or modifying file status information, and allow you to control various aspects of the file system.

Figure 1-13: Directory and File System Functions

link			link to a file
access			determine accessibility of a file
mknod			make a directory, special, or regular file
chmod	fchmod		change mode of file
chown	fchown	lchown	change owner and group of a file
utime			set file access and modification times
stat	fstat	lstat	get file status
pathconf	fpathconf		get configurable path name variables
getdents			read directory entries and put in file system-independent format
mkdir			make a directory
readlink			read the value of a symbolic link
rename			change the name of a file
rmdir			remove a directory
symlink			make a symbolic link to a file
unlink			remove directory entry
ustat			get file system statistics
sync			update super block
mount	umount		mount/unmount a file system
statfs	fstatfs		get file system information
sysfs			get file system type information

Process and Memory System Calls

Processes

These system calls control user processes.

Figure 1-14: Process Management Functions

fork			create a new process
execl	execle	execlp	execute a file with a list of arguments
execv	execve	execvp	execute a file with a variable list
exit	_exit		terminate process
wait	waitpid	waitid	wait for child process to change state
setuid	setgid		set user and group IDs
getpgrp	setpgrp		get and set process group ID
chdir	fchdir		change working directory
chroot			change root directory
nice			change priority of a process
getcontext	setcontext		get and set current user context
getgroups	setgroups		get or set supplementary group IDs
getpid	getppid	getpgid	get process and parent process IDs
getuid	geteuid		get real user and effective user
getgid	getegid		get real group and effective group
pause			suspend process until signal
priocntl			process scheduler control
setpgid			set process group ID
setsid			set session ID
kill			send a signal to a process or group of processes

Signals

Signals are messages passed by the UNIX system to running processes.

Figure 1-15: Signal Functions

`sigaction`		detailed signal management
`sigaltstack`		set/get signal alternate stack context
`sigignore`	`sigpause`	simplified signal management
`sighold`	`sigrelse`	simplified signal management
`sigset`	`signal`	simplified signal management
`sigpending`		examine blocked and pending signals
`sigprocmask`		change or examine signal mask
`sigsuspend`		install a signal mask and suspend process
`sigsend`	`sigsendset`	send a signal to a process or group of processes

Basic Interprocess Communication

These system calls connect processes so they can communicate. `pipe` is the system call for creating an interprocess channel. `dup` is the call for duplicating an open file descriptor. (These IPC mechanisms are not applicable for processes on separate hosts.)

Figure 1-16: Basic Interprocess Communication Functions

`pipe`	open file-descriptors for a pipe
`dup`	duplicate an open file-descriptor

Advanced Interprocess Communication

These system calls support interprocess messages, semaphores, and shared
memory and are effective in data base management. (These IPC mechanisms
are also not applicable for processes on separate hosts.)

Figure 1-17: Advanced Interprocess Communication Functions

msgget	get message queue
msgctl	message control operations
msgop	message operations
semget	get set of semaphores
semctl	semaphore control operations
semop	semaphore operations
shmget	get shared memory segment identifier
shmctl	shared memory control operations
shmop	shared memory operations

Memory Management

These system calls give you access to virtual memory facilities.

Figure 1-18: Memory Management Functions

getpagesize		get system page size
memcntl		memory management control
mmap		map pages of memory
mprotect		set protection of memory mapping
munmap		unmap pages of memory
plock		lock process, text, or data in memory
brk	sbrk	dynamically allocate memory space

Miscellaneous System Calls

These are system calls for such things as administration, timing, and other miscellaneous purposes.

Figure 1-19: Miscellaneous System Functions

`ulimit`		get and set user limits
`alarm`		set a process alarm clock
`getrlimit`	`setrlimit`	control maximum system resource consumption
`uname`		get/set name of current UNIX system
`profil`		execution time profile
`sysconf`		method for application's determination of value for system configuration
`uadmin`		administrative control
`time`	`stime`	get/set time
`acct`		enable or disable process accounting
`sysi86`		machine-specific functions

UNIX System Call Error Handling

UNIX system calls that fail to complete successfully almost always return a value of −1 to your program. (If you look through the system calls in Section 2, you will see that there are a few calls for which no return value is defined, but they are the exceptions.) In addition to the −1 returned to the program, the unsuccessful system call places an integer in an externally declared variable, errno. In a C program, you can determine the value in errno if your program contains the statement

```
#include <errno.h>
```

The C language function perror(3C) can be used to print an error message (on stderr) based on the value of errno. The value in errno is not cleared on successful calls, so your program should check it only if the system call returned a −1 indicating an error. The following list identifies the error numbers and symbolic names defined in the <errno.h> header file, and described in intro(2) of the *Programmer's Reference Manual*.

Error Number	Symbolic Name	Description
1	EPERM	**Not super-user** Typically this error indicates an attempt to modify a file in some way forbidden except to its owner or the super-user. It is also returned for attempts by ordinary users to do things allowed only to the super-user.
2	ENOENT	**No such file or directory** A file name is specified and the file should exist but fails to, or one of the directories in a path name fails to exist.
3	ESRCH	**No such process** No process can be found corresponding to the that specified by PID in the kill or ptrace routine.
4	EINTR	**Interrupted system call** An asynchronous signal (such as interrupt or quit), which the user has elected to catch, occurred during a system service routine. If execution is resumed after processing the signal, it will appear as if the interrupted routine call returned this error condition.
5	EIO	**I/O error** Some physical I/O error has occurred. This error may in some cases occur on a call following the one to which it actually applies.
6	ENXIO	**No such device or address** I/O on a special file refers to a subdevice which does not exist, or exists beyond the limit of the device. It may also occur when, for example, a tape drive is not on-line or no disk pack is loaded on a drive.
7	E2BIG	**Arg list too long** An argument list longer than ARG_MAX bytes is presented to a member of the exec family of routines. The argument list limit is sum of the size of the argument list plus the size of the environment's exported shell variables.
8	ENOEXEC	**Exec format error** A request is made to execute a file which, although it has the appropriate permissions, does not start with a valid format (see a.out(4)).

Error Number	Symbolic Name	Description
9	EBADF	**Bad file number** Either a file descriptor refers to no open file, or a read [respectively, write] request is made to a file that is open only for writing (respectively, reading).
10	ECHILD	**No child processes** A wait routine was executed by a process that had no existing or unwaited-for child processes.
11	EAGAIN	**No more processes** For example, the fork routine failed because the system's process table is full or the user is not allowed to create any more processes. Or a system call failed because of insufficient memory or swap space.
12	ENOMEM	**Not enough space** During execution of an exec, brk, or sbrk routine, a program asks for more space than the system is able to supply. This is not a temporary condition; the maximum size is a system parameter. The error may also occur if the arrangement of text, data, and stack segments requires too many segmentation registers, or if there is not enough swap space during the fork routine. If this error occurs on a resource associated with Remote File Sharing (RFS), it indicates a memory depletion which may be temporary, dependent on system activity at the time the call was invoked.
13	EACCES	**Permission denied** An attempt was made to access a file in a way forbidden by the protection system.
14	EFAULT	**Bad address** The system encountered a hardware fault in attempting to use an argument of a routine. For example, errno potentially may be set to EFAULT any time a routine that takes a pointer argument is passed an invalid address, if the system can detect the condition. Because systems will differ in their ability to reliably detect a bad address, on some implementations passing a bad address to a routine will result in undefined behavior.

Error Number	Symbolic Name	Description
15	ENOTBLK	**Block device required** A non-block file was mentioned where a block device was required (e.g., in a call to the `mount` routine).
16	EBUSY	**Device busy** An attempt was made to mount a device that was already mounted or an attempt was made to dismount a device on which there is an active file (open file, current directory, mounted-on file, active text segment). It will also occur if an attempt is made to enable accounting when it is already enabled. The device or resource is currently unavailable.
17	EEXIST	**File exists** An existing file was mentioned in an inappropriate context (e.g., call to the `link` routine).
18	EXDEV	**Cross-device link** A link to a file on another device was attempted.
19	ENODEV	**No such device** An attempt was made to apply an inappropriate operation to a device (e.g., read a write-only device).
20	ENOTDIR	**Not a directory** A non-directory was specified where a directory is required (e.g., in a path prefix or as an argument to the `chdir` routine).
21	EISDIR	**Is a directory** An attempt was made to write on a directory.
22	EINVAL	**Invalid argument** An invalid argument was specified (e.g., unmounting a non-mounted device, mentioning an undefined signal in a call to the `signal` or `kill` routine. Also set by the functions described in the math package (3M).
23	ENFILE	**File table overflow** The system file table is full (i.e., SYS_OPEN files are open, and temporarily no more files can be opened).

Error Number	Symbolic Name	Description
24	EMFILE	**Too many open files** No process may have more than OPEN_MAX file descriptors open at a time.
25	ENOTTY	**Not a typewriter** A call was made to the ioctl routine specifying a file that is not a special character device.
26	ETXTBSY	**Text file busy** An attempt was made to execute a pure-procedure program that is currently open for writing. Also an attempt to open for writing or to remove a pure-procedure program that is being executed.
27	EFBIG	**File too large** The size of a file exceeded the maximum file size, FCHR_MAX (see getrlimit).
28	ENOSPC	**No space left on device** While writing an ordinary file or creating a directory entry, there is no free space left on the device. In the fcntl routine, the setting or removing of record locks on a file cannot be accomplished because there are no more record entries left on the system.
29	ESPIPE	**Illegal seek** A call to the lseek routine was issued to a pipe.
30	EROFS	**Read-only file system** An attempt to modify a file or directory was made on a device mounted read-only.
31	EMLINK	**Too many links** An attempt to make more than the maximum number of links, LINK_MAX, to a file.
32	EPIPE	**Broken pipe** A write on a pipe for which there is no process to read the data. This condition normally generates a signal; the error is returned if the signal is ignored.

Error Number	Symbolic Name	Description
33	EDOM	**Math argument out of domain of func** The argument of a function in the math package (3M) is out of the domain of the function.
34	ERANGE	**Math result not representable** The value of a function in the math package (3M) is not representable within machine precision.
35	ENOMSG	**No message of desired type** An attempt was made to receive a message of a type not existing on the specified message queue (see msgop(2)).
36	EIDRM	**Identifier removed** This error is returned to processes that resume execution due to the removal of an identifier from the file system's name space (see msgctl(2), semctl(2), and shmctl(2)).
37	ECHRNG	**Channel number out of range**
38	EL2NSYNC	**Level 2 not synchronized**
39	EL3HLT	**Level 3 halted**
40	EL3RST	**Level 3 reset**
41	ELNRNG	**Link number out of range**
42	EUNATCH	**Protocol driver not attached**
43	ENOCSI	**No CSI structure available**
44	EL2HLT	**Level 2 halted**
45	EDEADLK	**Deadlock condition** A deadlock situation was detected and avoided. This error pertains to file and record locking.
46	ENOLCK	**No record locks available** There are no more locks available. The system lock table is full (see fcntl(2)).

Error Number	Symbolic Name	Description
60	ENOSTR	**Device not a stream** A putmsg or getmsg system call was attempted on a file descriptor that is not a STREAMS device.
61	ENODATA	**No data available**
62	ETIME	**Timer expired** The timer set for a STREAMS ioctl call has expired. The cause of this error is device specific and could indicate either a hardware or software failure, or perhaps a timeout value that is too short for the specific operation. The status of the ioctl operation is indeterminate.
63	ENOSR	**Out of stream resources** During a STREAMS open, either no STREAMS queues or no STREAMS head data structures were available. This is a temporary condition; one may recover from it if other processes release resources.
64	ENONET	**Machine is not on the network** This error is Remote File Sharing (RFS) specific. It occurs when users try to advertise, unadvertise, mount, or unmount remote resources while the machine has not done the proper startup to connect to the network.
65	ENOPKG	**Package not installed** This error occurs when users attempt to use a system call from a package which has not been installed.
66	EREMOTE	**Object is remote** This error is RFS specific. It occurs when users try to advertise a resource which is not on the local machine, or try to mount/unmount a device (or pathname) that is on a remote machine.
67	ENOLINK	**Link has been severed** This error is RFS specific. It occurs when the link (virtual circuit) connecting to a remote machine is gone.

Error Number	Symbolic Name	Description
68	EADV	**Advertise error** This error is RFS specific. It occurs when users try to advertise a resource which has been advertised already, or try to stop the RFS while there are resources still advertised, or try to force unmount a resource when it is still advertised.
69	ESRMNT	**Srmount error** This error is RFS specific. It occurs when an attempt is made to stop RFS while resources are still mounted by remote machines, or when a resource is readvertised with a client list that does not include a remote machine that currently has the resource mounted.
70	ECOMM	**Communication error on send** This error is RFS specific. It occurs when the current process is waiting for a message from a remote machine, and the virtual circuit fails.
71	EPROTO	**Protocol error** Some protocol error occurred. This error is device specific, but is generally not related to a hardware failure.
74	EMULTIHOP	**Multihop attempted** This error is RFS specific. It occurs when users try to access remote resources which are not directly accessible.
76	EDOTDOT	**Error 76** This error is RFS specific. A way for the server to tell the client that a process has transferred back from mount point.
77	EBADMSG	**Not a data message** During a read, getmsg, or ioctl I_RECVFD system call to a STREAMS device, something has come to the head of the queue that can't be processed. That something depends on the system call: read: control information or a passed file descriptor. getmsg: passed file descriptor. ioctl: control or data information.

Error Number	Symbolic Name	Description
78	ENAMETOOLONG	**File name too long** The length of the path argument exceeds PATH_MAX, or the length of a path component exceeds NAME_MAX while _POSIX_NO_TRUNC is in effect; see limits(4).
79	EOVERFLOW	**Error 79** Value too large to be stored in data type.
80	ENOTUNIQ	**Name not unique on network** Given log name not unique.
81	EBADFD	**File descriptor in bad state** Either a file descriptor refers to no open file or a read request was made to a file that is open only for writing.
82	EREMCHG	**Remote address changed**
83	ELIBACC	**Cannot access a needed shared library** Trying to exec an a.out that requires a shared library and the shared library doesn't exist or the user doesn't have permission to use it.
84	ELIBBAD	**Accessing a corrupted shared library** Trying to exec an a.out that requires a shared library (to be linked in) and exec could not load the shared library. The shared library is probably corrupted.
85	ELIBSCN	**.lib section in f4a.out** corrupted Trying to exec an a.out that requires a shared library (to be linked in) and there was erroneous data in the .lib section of the a.out. The .lib section tells exec what shared libraries are needed. The a.out is probably corrupted.
86	ELIBMAX	**Attempting to link in more shared libraries than system limit** Trying to exec an a.out that requires more static shared libraries than is allowed on the current configuration of the system. See the *System Administrator's Guide*.

Integrated Software Development Guide

Error Number	Symbolic Name	Description
87	ELIBEXEC	**Cannot** exec **a shared library directly** Attempting to exec a shared library directly.
88	EILSEQ	**Error 88** Illegal byte sequence. Handle multiple characters as a single character.
89	ENOSYS	**Operation not applicable**
90	ELOOP	**Number of symbolic links encountered during path name traversal exceeds** MAXSYMLINKS
91	ERESTART	**Error 91** Interrupted system call should be restarted.
92	ESTRPIPE	**Error 92** Streams pipe error (not externally visible).
93	ENOTEMPTY	**Directory not empty**
94	EUSERS	**Too many users** Too many users.
95	ENOTSOCK	**Socket operation on non-socket** Self-explanatory.
96	EDESTADDRREQ	**Destination address required** A required address was omitted from an operation on a transport endpoint. Destination address required.
97	EMSGSIZE	**Message too long** A message sent on a transport provider was larger than the internal message buffer or some other network limit.
98	EPROTOTYPE	**Protocol wrong type for socket** A protocol was specified that does not support the semantics of the socket type requested.
99	ENOPROTOOPT	**Protocol not available** A bad option or level was specified when getting or setting options for a protocol.

Error Number	Symbolic Name	Description
120	EPROTONOSUPPORT	**Protocol not supported** The protocol has not been configured into the system or no implementation for it exists.
121	ESOCKTNOSUPPORT	**Socket type not supported** The support for the socket type has not been configured into the system or no implementation for it exists.
122	EOPNOTSUPP	**Operation not supported on transport endpoint** For example, trying to accept a connection on a datagram transport endpoint.
123	EPFNOSUPPORT	**Protocol family not supported** The protocol family has not been configured into the system or no implementation for it exists. Used for the Internet protocols.
124	EAFNOSUPPORT	**Address family not supported by protocol family** An address incompatible with the requested protocol was used.
125	EADDRINUSE	**Address already in use** User attempted to use an address already in use, and the protocol does not allow this.
126	EADDRNOTAVAIL	**Cannot assign requested address** Results from an attempt to create a transport endpoint with an address not on the current machine.
127	ENETDOWN	**Network is down** Operation encountered a dead network.
128	ENETUNREACH	**Network is unreachable** Operation was attempted to an unreachable network.
129	ENETRESET	**Network dropped connection because of reset** The host you were connected to crashed and rebooted.
130	ECONNABORTED	**Software caused connection abort** A connection abort was caused internal to your host machine.

Integrated Software Development Guide

Error Number	Symbolic Name	Description
131	ECONNRESET	**Connection reset by peer** A connection was forcibly closed by a peer. This normally results from a loss of the connection on the remote host due to a timeout or a reboot.
132	ENOBUFS	**No buffer space available** An operation on a transport endpoint or pipe was not performed because the system lacked sufficient buffer space or because a queue was full.
133	EISCONN	**Transport endpoint is already connected** A connect request was made on an already connected transport endpoint; or, a *sendto* or *sendmsg* request on a connected transport endpoint specified a destination when already connected.
134	ENOTCONN	**Transport endpoint is not connected** A request to send or receive data was disallowed because the transport endpoint is not connected and (when sending a datagram) no address was supplied.
143	ESHUTDOWN	**Cannot send after transport endpoint shutdown** A request to send data was disallowed because the transport endpoint had already been shut down.
144	ETOOMANYREFS	**Too many references: cannot splice**
145	ETIMEDOUT	**Connection timed out** A connect or send request failed because the connected party did not properly respond after a period of time. (The timeout period is dependent on the communication protocol.)
146	ECONNREFUSED	**Connection refused** No connection could be made because the target machine actively refused it. This usually results from trying to connect to a service that is inactive on the remote host.
147	EHOSTDOWN	**Host is down** A transport provider operation failed because the destination host was down.

Error Number	Symbolic Name	Description
148	EHOSTUNREACH	**No route to host** A transport provider operation was attempted to an unreachable host.
149	EALREADY	**Operation already in progress** An operation was attempted on a non-blocking object that already had an operation in progress.
150	EINPROGRESS	**Operation now in progress** An operation that takes a long time to complete (such as a connect) was attempted on a non-blocking object.
151	ESTALE	**Stale NFS file handle**

2 File and Device Input/Output

2. FILE AND DEVICE INPUT/OUTPUT

Input/Output System Calls

The lowest level of I/O in UNIX System V provides no buffering or other such services, but it offers the most control over what happens. System-calls that represent direct entries into the UNIX System V kernel control all user I/O. UNIX System V keeps the system-calls that do I/O simple, uniform and regular to eliminate differences between files, devices and styles of access. The same read and write system-calls apply to ordinary disk-files and I/O devices such as terminals, tape-drives and line-printers. They do not distinguish between "random" and "sequential" I/O, nor do they impose any logical record size on files. Thus, a single, uniform interface handles all communication between programs and peripheral devices, and programmers can defer specifying devices from program-development until program-execution time.

All I/O is done by reading or writing files, because all peripheral I/O devices, even a user's terminal, are files in the file-system. Each supported device has an entry in the file-system hierarchy, so that device-names have the same structure as file-names, and the same protection mechanisms work on both devices and files.

A file is an ordered set of bytes of data on a I/O-device. The size of the file on input is determined by an end-of-file condition dependent on device-specific characteristics. The size of a regular-file is determined by the position and number of bytes written on it, no predetermination of the size of a file is necessary or possible.

Besides the traditionally available devices, names exist for disk devices regarded as physical units outside the file-system, and for absolutely addressed memory. The most important device in practice is the user's terminal. Treating a communication-device in the same way as any file by using the same I/O calls make it easy to redirect the input and output of commands from the terminal to another file; although, some differences are inevitable. For example, UNIX System V ordinarily treats terminal input in units of lines because character-erase and line-delete processing cannot be completed until a full line is typed. Programs trying to read some large number of bytes from a terminal must wait until a full line is typed, and then may be notified that some smaller number of bytes were actually read. All programs must prepare for this eventuality in any case, because a read from any disk-file returns fewer bytes than requested when it reaches the end of the file. Ordinarily, reads from a terminal are fully compatible with reads from a disk-file.

File Descriptors

UNIX System V File and Device I/O functions denote a file by a small positive integer called a *file-descriptor* and declared as follows:

```
int fildes
```

where `fildes` represents the file-descriptor, and the file-descriptor denotes an open file from which data are read or onto which data are written. UNIX System V maintains all information about an open file; the user program refers to the file only by the file-descriptor. Any I/O on the file uses the file-descriptor instead of the file-name to denote the file.

Multiple file-descriptors may denote the same file, and each file-descriptor has associated with it information used to do I/O on the file:

- a file-offset that shows which byte in the file to read or write next;
- file-status and access-modes (e.g., *read, write, read/write*) [see open(2)];
- the 'close-on-exec' flag [see fcntl(2)].

Doing I/O on the user's terminal occurs commonly enough that special arrangements make this convenient. When the command interpreter (the "shell") runs a program, it opens three files, called the *standard input*, the *standard output* and the *standard error output*, with file-descriptors 0, 1 and 2. All of these are normally connected to the terminal; thus, a program reading file-descriptor 0 and writing file-descriptors 1 and 2, can do terminal I/O without opening the files. If I/O is redirected to and from files with < and >, as in:

```
prog <infile >outfile
```

the shell changes the default assignments for file-descriptors 0 and 1 from the terminal to the named files. Similar conventions hold for I/O on a pipe. Normally file-descriptor 2 remains attached to the terminal, so error messages can go there. In all cases, the shell changes the file assignments, the program does not. The program can ignore where its output goes, as long as it uses file-descriptor 0 for input and 1 and 2 for output.

Reading and Writing Files

The functions read and write do I/O on files. For both, the first argument is a file-descriptor, the second argument is a buffer in the user program where the data comes from or goes to and the third argument is the number of bytes of data to transfer. Each call returns a count of the number of bytes actually transferred. These calls look like:

```
n = read(fildes, buffer, count);
n = write(fildes, buffer, count);
```

Up to count bytes are transferred between the file denoted by fildes and the byte array pointed to by buffer. The returned value n is the number of bytes actually transferred.

For writing, the returned value is the number of bytes actually written; it is generally an error if this fails to equal the number of bytes requested. In the write case, n is the same as count except under exceptional conditions, such as I/O errors or end of physical medium on special files; in a read, however, n may without error be less than count.

For reading, the number of bytes returned may be less than the number requested, because fewer than count bytes remained to be read. If the file-offset is so near the end of the file that reading count characters would cause reading beyond the end, only sufficient bytes are transferred to reach the end of the file; also, typewriter-like terminals never return more than one line of input. (When the file is a terminal, read normally reads only up to the next new-line, which is generally less than what was requested.)

When a read call returns with n equal to zero, the end of the file has been reached. For disk-files this occurs when the file-offset equals the current size of the file. It is possible to generate an end-of-file from a terminal by use of an escape sequence that depends on the device used. The function read returns 0 to signify end-of-file, and returns -1 to signify an error.

The number of bytes to be read or written is quite arbitrary. The two most common values are 1, which means one character at a time ("unbuffered"), and 512, which corresponds to a physical block size on many peripheral devices. This latter size is most efficient, but even character at a time I/O is not overly expensive. Bytes written affect only those parts of a file implied by the position of the file-offset and the count; no other part of the file is changed. If the last byte lies beyond the end of the file, the file grows as needed.

A simple program using the read and write functions to copy its input to its output can copy anything, since the input and output can be redirected to any file or device.

```
#define  BUFSIZE  512
main()    /* copy input to output */
{
    char buf[BUFSIZE];
    int  n;
    while ((n = read(0, buf, BUFSIZE)) > 0)
       write( 1, buf, n);
    exit(0);
}
```

If the file size is not a multiple of BUFSIZE, some read will return a smaller number of bytes to be written by write: the next call to read after that will return zero indicating end-of-file.

To see how read and write can be used to construct higher level functions like getchar and putchar, here is an example of getchar which does unbuffered input:

```
#define  CMASK    0377  /* for making char's > 0 */
getchar() /* unbuffered single character input */
{
    char c;
    return((read(0, &c, 1) > 0) ? c & CMASK : EOF);
}
```

The variable c *must* be declared char, because read accepts a character pointer. The character returned must be masked with 0377 to ensure that it is positive; otherwise, sign extension may make it negative.

The second version of getchar does input in big chunks, and hands out the characters one at a time.

```
#define  CMASK    0377  /* for making char's > 0 */
#define  BUFSIZE  512

getchar()  /* buffered version */
{
    static char   buf[BUFSIZE];
    static char   *bufp = buf;
    static int    n = 0;

    if (n == 0)  {   /* buffer is empty */
        n = read(0, buf, BUFSIZE);
        bufp = buf;
    }
    return((--n >= 0) ? *bufp++ & CMASK : EOF);
}
```

Opening, Creating and Closing Files

Other than the default standard input, output and error files, you must explicitly open files in order to read or write them. The two functions that do this are: open and creat [see open(2) and creat(2) in the *Programmer's Reference Manual*]. To read or write a file assumed to exist already, it must be opened by the following call:

```
fildes = open(name, oflag);
```

The argument name is a character string that represents a UNIX System V filesystem path-name. The oflag argument indicates whether the file is to be read, written, or "updated", that is, read and written simultaneously. The returned value fildes is a file-descriptor used to denote the file in subsequent calls that read, write or otherwise manipulate the file.

The function open resembles the function fopen in the Standard I/O Library, except that instead of returning a pointer to FILE, open returns a file-descriptor which is just an int [see fopen(3S) and stdio(3S) in the *Programmer's Reference Manual*]. Moreover, the values for the access mode argument oflag are different (the flags are found in /usr/include/fcntl.h):

> O_RDONLY for read access.

> O_WRONLY for write access.

> O_RDWR for read and write access.

The function open returns −1 if any error occurs; otherwise it returns a valid open file-descriptor.

Trying to open a file that does not exist causes an error; hence, creat is used to create new files, or to re-write old ones. The creat system-call creates the given file if it does not exist, or truncates it to zero length if it does exist; creat also opens the new file for writing and, like open, returns a file-descriptor. Calling creat as follows:

```
fildes = creat(name, pmode);
```

returns a file-descriptor if it created the file called name, and −1 if it did not. Trying to creat a file that already exists does not cause an error, but if the file already exists, creat truncates it to zero length.

If the file is brand new, creat creates it with the *protection mode* specified by the pmode argument. The UNIX System V file-system associates nine bits of protection information with a file, controlling *read, write* and *execute* permission for the *owner* of the file, for the owner's *group*, and for any *other* users. Thus, a three-digit octal number specifies the permissions most conveniently. For example, 0755 specifies *read, write* and *execute* permission for the *owner*, and *read* and *execute* permission for the *group* and all *other* users.

A simplified version of the UNIX System V utility cp (a program which copies one file to another) illustrates this:

Figure 2-1: simplified version of cp

```
#define   NULL 0
#define   BUFSIZE 512
#define   PMODE 0644 /* RW owner, R group & others */

main(argc, argv)      /* cp: copy f1 to f2 */
   int argc;
   char *argv[ ];
{
   int  f1, f2, n;
   char buf[BUFSIZE];

   if (argc != 3)
      error("Usage: cp from to", NULL);
   if ((f1 = open(argv[1], 0)) == -1)
      error("cp: can't open %s", argv[1]);
   if ((f2 = creat(argv[2], PMODE)) == -1)
      error("cp: can't create %s", argv[2]);

   while ((n = read(f1, buf, BUFSIZE)) > 0)
      if (write(f2, buf, n) != n)
         error("cp: write error", NULL);

   exit(0);
}

error(s1, s2)  /* print error message and die */
   char *s1, *s2;
{
   printf(s1, s2);
   printf("\n");

   exit(1);
}
```

The main simplification is that this version copies only one file, and does not permit the second argument to be a directory.

As stated earlier, there is a limit, OPEN_MAX, on the number of files which a process may have open simultaneously. Accordingly, any program which intends to process many files must be prepared to re-use file-descriptors. The function close breaks the connection between a file-descriptor and an open file, and frees the file-descriptor for use with some other file. Termination of a program via exit or return from the main program closes all open files.

Random Access — lseek

Normally, file I/O is sequential: each read or write proceeds from the point in the file right after the previous one. This means that if a particular byte in the file was the last byte written (or read), the next I/O call implicitly refers to the immediately following byte. For each open file, UNIX System V maintains a file-offset that indicates the next byte to be read or written. If *n* bytes are read or written, the file-offset advances by *n* bytes. When necessary, however, a file can be read or written in any arbitrary order using lseek to move around in a file without actually reading or writing.

To do random (direct-access) I/O it is only necessary to move the file-offset to the appropriate location in the file with a call to lseek. Calling lseek as follows:

```
lseek(fildes, offset, whence);
```

or as follows:

```
location = lseek(fildes, offset, whence);
```

forces the current position in the file denoted by file-descriptor fildes to move to position offset as specified by whence. Subsequent reading or writing begins at the new position. The file-offset associated with fildes is moved to a position offset bytes from the beginning of the file, from the current position of the file-offset or from the end of the file, depending on whence; offset may be negative. For some devices (e.g., paper tape and terminals) lseek calls are ignored. The value of location equals the actual offset from the beginning of the file to which the file-offset was moved. The argument offset is of type off_t defined by the header file <types.h> as a long; fildes and whence are int's.

The argument whence can be SEEK_SET, SEEK_CUR or SEEK_END to specify that offset is to be measured from the beginning, from the current position, or from the end of the file respectively. For example, to append a file, seek to the end before writing:

```
lseek(fildes, 0L, SEEK_END);
```

To get back to the beginning ("rewind"),

```
lseek(fildes, 0L, SEEK_SET);
```

Notice the 0L argument; it could also be written as (long) 0.

With lseek, you can treat files more or less like large arrays, at the price of slower access. For example, the following simple function reads any number of bytes from any arbitrary point in a file:

```
get(fd, p, buf, n) /* read n bytes from position p */
    int fd, n;
    long p;
    char *buf;
{
    lseek(fd, p, SEEK_SET);  /* move to p */
    return(read(fd, buf, n));
}
```

File and Record Locking

Mandatory and advisory file and record locking both are available on current releases of the UNIX system. The intent of this capability to is provide a synchronization mechanism for programs accessing the same stores of data simultaneously. Such processing is characteristic of many multiuser applications, and the need for a standard method of dealing with the problem has been recognized by standards advocates like /usr/group, an organization of UNIX system users from businesses and campuses across the country.

Advisory file and record locking can be used to coordinate self-synchronizing processes. In mandatory locking, the standard I/O subroutines and I/O system calls enforce the locking protocol. In this way, at the cost of a little efficiency, mandatory locking double checks the programs against accessing the data out of sequence.

The remainder of this chapter describes how file and record locking capabilities can be used. Examples are given for the correct use of record locking. Misconceptions about the amount of protection that record locking affords are dispelled. Record locking should be viewed as a synchronization mechanism, not a security mechanism.

The manual pages for the fcntl(2) system call, the lockf(3) library function, and fcntl(5) data structures and commands are referred to throughout this section. You should read them before continuing.

Terminology

Before discussing how to use record locking, let us first define a few terms.

Record
> A contiguous set of bytes in a file. The UNIX operating system does not impose any record structure on files. This may be done by the programs that use the files.

Cooperating Processes
> Processes that work together in some well-defined fashion to accomplish the tasks at hand. Processes that share files must request permission to access the files before using them. File access permissions must be carefully set to restrict noncooperating processes from accessing those files. The term process will be used interchangeably with cooperating process to refer to a task obeying such protocols.

Read (Share) Locks

> These are used to gain limited access to sections of files. When a read lock is put on a record, other processes may also read lock that record, in whole or in part. No other process, however, may have or obtain a write lock on an overlapping section of the file. If a process holds a read lock it may assume that no other process will be writing or updating that record at the same time. This access method also lets many processes read the given record. This might be necessary when searching a file, without the contention involved if a write or exclusive lock were used.

Write (Exclusive) Locks

> These are used to gain complete control over sections of files. When a write lock is put on a record, no other process may read or write lock that record, in whole or in part. If a process holds a write lock it may assume that no other process will be reading or writing that record at the same time.

Advisory Locking

> A form of record locking that does not interact with the I/O subsystem. Advisory locking is not enforced, for example, by creat(2), open(2), read(2), or write(2). The control over records is accomplished by requiring an appropriate record lock request before I/O operations. If appropriate requests are always made by all processes accessing the file, then the accessibility of the file will be controlled by the interaction of these requests. Advisory locking depends on the individual processes to enforce the record locking protocol; it does not require an accessibility check at the time of each I/O request.

Mandatory Locking

> A form of record locking that does interact with the I/O subsystem. Access to locked records is enforced by the creat, open, read, and write(2) system calls. If a record is locked, then access of that record by any other process is restricted according to the type of lock on the record. The control over records should still be performed explicitly by requesting an appropriate record lock before I/O operations, but an additional check is made by the system before each I/O operation to ensure the record locking protocol is being honored. Mandatory locking offers an extra synchronization check, but at the cost of some additional system overhead.

File Protection

There are access permissions for UNIX system files to control who may read, write, or execute such a file. These access permissions may only be set by the owner of the file or by the superuser. The permissions of the directory in which the file resides can also affect the ultimate disposition of a file. Note that if the directory permissions allow anyone to write in it, then files within the directory may be removed, even if those files do not have read, write or execute permission for that user. Any information that is worth protecting, is worth protecting properly. If your application warrants the use of record locking, make sure that the permissions on your files and directories are set properly. A record lock, even a mandatory record lock, will only protect the portions of the files that are locked. Other parts of these files might be corrupted if proper precautions are not taken.

Only a known set of programs and/or administrators should be able to read or write a data base. This can be done easily by setting the set-group-ID bit of the data base accessing programs; see chmod(1). The files can then be accessed by a known set of programs that obey the record locking protocol. An example of such file protection, although record locking is not used, is the mail(1) command. In that command only the particular user and the mail command can read and write in the unread mail files.

Opening a File for Record Locking

The first requirement for locking a file or segment of a file is having a valid open file descriptor. The file must be opened with at least read accessibility if read locks are to be done, and with write accessibility for write locks.

 NOTE Mapped files cannot be locked: if a file has been mapped, any attempt to use file or record locking on the file fails. See mmap(2).

For our example we will open our file for both read and write access:

```
#include <stdio.h>
#include <errno.h>
#include <fcntl.h>

int fd;              /* file descriptor */
char *filename;

main(argc, argv)
int argc;
char *argv[];
{
     extern void exit(), perror();

     /* get data base file name from command line and open the
      * file for read and write access.
      */
     if (argc < 2) {
         (void) fprintf(stderr, "usage: %s filename\n", argv[0]);
         exit(2);
         }
     filename = argv[1];
     fd = open(filename, O_RDWR);
     if (fd < 0) {
         perror(filename);
         exit(2);
         }
     .
     .
     .
```

The file is now open for us to perform both locking and I/O functions. We then
proceed with the task of setting a lock.

Setting a File Lock

There are several ways for us to set a lock on a file. In part, these methods
depend on how the lock interacts with the rest of the program. There are also
questions of performance as well as portability. Two methods will be given
here, one using the fcntl(2) system call, the other using the /usr/group standards compatible lockf library function call.

Locking an entire file is just a special case of record locking. For both these methods the concept and the effect of the lock are the same. The file is locked starting at a byte offset of zero (0) until the end of the maximum file size. This point extends beyond any real end of the file so that no lock can be placed on this file beyond this point. To do this the value of the size of the lock is set to zero. The code using the fcntl system call is as follows:

```
#include <fcntl.h>
#define MAX_TRY     10
int try;
struct flock lck;

try = 0;

/* set up the record locking structure, the address of which
 * is passed to the fcntl system call.
 */
lck.l_type = F_WRLCK;    /* setting a write lock */
lck.l_whence = 0;        /* offset l_start from beginning of file */
lck.l_start = 0L;
lck.l_len = 0L;          /* until the end of the file address space */

/* Attempt locking MAX_TRY times before giving up.
 */
while (fcntl(fd, F_SETLK, &lck) < 0) {
        if (errno == EAGAIN || errno == EACCES) {
                /* there might be other errors cases in which
                 * you might try again.
                 */
                if (++try < MAX_TRY) {
                        (void) sleep(2);
                        continue;
                }
                (void) fprintf(stderr,"File busy try again later!\n");
                return;
        }
        perror("fcntl");
        exit(2);
}
        .
        .
        .
```

This portion of code tries to lock a file. This is attempted several times until one of the following things happens:

- the file is locked

- an error occurs

- it gives up trying because MAX_TRY has been exceeded

To perform the same task using the `lockf` function, the code is as follows:

```
#include <unistd.h>
#define MAX_TRY    10
int try;
try = 0;

/* make sure the file pointer
 * is at the beginning of the file.
 */
lseek(fd, 0L, 0);

/* Attempt locking MAX_TRY times before giving up.
 */
while (lockf(fd, F_TLOCK, 0L) < 0) {
        if (errno == EAGAIN || errno == EACCES) {
                /* there might be other errors cases in which
                 * you might try again.
                 */
                if (++try < MAX_TRY) {
                        sleep(2);
                        continue;
                }
                (void) fprintf(stderr,"File busy try again later!\n");
                return;
        }
        perror("lockf");
        exit(2);
}
        .
        .
        .
```

It should be noted that the `lockf` example appears to be simpler, but the `fcntl(2)` example exhibits additional flexibility. Using the `fcntl(2)` method, it is possible to set the type and start of the lock request simply by setting a few structure variables. `lockf` merely sets write (exclusive) locks; an additional system call, `lseek`, is required to specify the start of the lock.

Setting and Removing Record Locks

Locking a record is done the same way as locking a file except for the differing starting point and length of the lock. We will now try to solve an interesting and real problem. There are two records (these records may be in the same or different file) that must be updated simultaneously so that other processes get a consistent view of this information. (This type of problem comes up, for example, when updating the interrecord pointers in a doubly linked list.) To do this you must decide the following questions:

- What do you want to lock?

- For multiple locks, in what order do you want to lock and unlock the records?

- What do you do if you succeed in getting all the required locks?

- What do you do if you fail to get all the locks?

In managing record locks, you must plan a failure strategy if you cannot obtain all the required locks. It is because of contention for these records that we have decided to use record locking in the first place. Different programs might:

- wait a certain amount of time, and try again

- abort the procedure and warn the user

- let the process sleep until signaled that the lock has been freed

- some combination of the above

Let us now look at our example of inserting an entry into a doubly linked list. For the example, we will assume that the record after which the new record is to be inserted has a read lock on it already. The lock on this record must be changed or promoted to a write lock so that the record may be edited.

Promoting a lock (generally from read lock to write lock) is permitted if no other process is holding a read lock in the same section of the file. If there are processes with pending write locks that are sleeping on the same section of the file, the lock promotion succeeds and the other (sleeping) locks wait. Promoting (or demoting) a write lock to a read lock carries no restrictions. In either case, the lock is merely reset with the new lock type. Because the /usr/group lockf function does not have read locks, lock promotion is not applicable to that call. An example of record locking with lock promotion follows:

Integrated Software Development Guide

```
struct record {
        .
        .               /* data portion of record */
        .
        long prev;   /* index to previous record in the list */
        long next;   /* index to next record in the list */
};

/* Lock promotion using fcntl(2)
 * When this routine is entered it is assumed that there are read
 * locks on "here" and "next".
 * If write locks on "here" and "next" are obtained:
 *     Set a write lock on "this".
 *     Return index to "this" record.
 * If any write lock is not obtained:
 *     Restore read locks on "here" and "next".
 *     Remove all other locks.
 *     Return a -1.
 */
long
set3lock (this, here, next)
long this, here, next;
{
        struct flock lck;

        lck.l_type = F_WRLCK;   /* setting a write lock */
        lck.l_whence = 0;       /* offset l_start from beginning of file */
        lck.l_start = here;
        lck.l_len = sizeof(struct record);

        /* promote lock on "here" to write lock */
        if (fcntl(fd, F_SETLKW, &lck) < 0) {
                return (-1);
        }
        /* lock "this" with write lock */
        lck.l_start = this;
        if (fcntl(fd, F_SETLKW, &lck) < 0) {
                /* Lock on "this" failed;
                 * demote lock on "here" to read lock.
                 */
                lck.l_type = F_RDLCK;
                lck.l_start = here;
                (void) fcntl(fd, F_SETLKW, &lck);
                return (-1);
        }
        /* promote lock on "next" to write lock */
```

(continued on next page)

```
              lck.l_start = next;
              if (fcntl(fd, F_SETLKW, &lck) < 0) {
                      /* Lock on "next" failed;
                       * demote lock on "here" to read lock,
                       */
                      lck.l_type = F_RDLCK;
                        lck.l_start = here;
                      (void) fcntl(fd, F_SETLK, &lck);
                      /* and remove lock on "this".
                       */
                      lck.l_type = F_UNLCK;
                      lck.l_start = this;
                      (void) fcntl(fd, F_SETLK, &lck);
                      return (-1);/* cannot set lock, try again or quit */
              }

              return (this);
      }
```

The locks on these three records were all set to wait (sleep) if another process was blocking them from being set. This was done with the F_SETLKW command. If the F_SETLK command was used instead, the fcntl system calls would fail if blocked. The program would then have to be changed to handle the blocked condition in each of the error return sections.

Let us now look at a similar example using the lockf function. Since there are no read locks, all (write) locks will be referenced generically as locks.

```
/* Lock promotion using lockf(3)
 * When this routine is entered it is assumed that there are
 * no locks on "here" and "next".
 * If locks are obtained:
 *    Set a lock on "this".
 *    Return index to "this" record.
 * If any lock is not obtained:
 *    Remove all other locks.
 *    Return a -1.
 */

#include <unistd.h>

long
set3lock (this, here, next)
long this, here, next;

{

        /* lock "here" */
        (void) lseek(fd, here, 0);
        if (lockf(fd, F_LOCK, sizeof(struct record)) < 0) {
                return (-1);
        }
        /* lock "this" */
        (void) lseek(fd, this, 0);
        if (lockf(fd, F_LOCK, sizeof(struct record)) < 0) {
                /* Lock on "this" failed.
                 * Clear lock on "here".
                 */
                (void) lseek(fd, here, 0);
                (void) lockf(fd, F_ULOCK, sizeof(struct record));
                return (-1);

        }

        /* lock "next" */
        (void) lseek(fd, next, 0);
        if (lockf(fd, F_LOCK, sizeof(struct record)) < 0) {

                /* Lock on "next" failed.
                 * Clear lock on "here",
                 */
                (void) lseek(fd, here, 0);
                (void) lockf(fd, F_ULOCK, sizeof(struct record));
```

(continued on next page)

```
                        /* and remove lock on "this".
                         */
                        (void) lseek(fd, this, 0);
                        (void) lockf(fd, F_ULOCK, sizeof(struct record));
                        return (-1);/* cannot set lock, try again or quit */
                }

            return (this);
    }
```

Locks are removed in the same manner as they are set, only the lock type is different (F_UNLCK or F_ULOCK). An unlock cannot be blocked by another process and will only affect locks that were placed by this process. The unlock only affects the section of the file defined in the previous example by lck. It is possible to unlock or change the type of lock on a subsection of a previously set lock. This may cause an additional lock (two locks for one system call) to be used by the operating system. This occurs if the subsection is from the middle of the previously set lock.

Getting Lock Information

You can determine which processes, if any, are blocking a lock from being set. This can be used as a simple test or as a means to find locks on a file. A lock is set up as in the previous examples and the F_GETLK command is used in the fcntl call. If the lock passed to fcntl would be blocked, the first blocking lock is returned to the process through the structure passed to fcntl. That is, the lock data passed to fcntl is overwritten by blocking lock information. This information includes two pieces of data that have not been discussed yet, l_pid and l_sysid, that are only used by F_GETLK. (For systems that do not support a distributed architecture the value in l_sysid should be ignored.) These fields uniquely identify the process holding the lock.

If a lock passed to fcntl using the F_GETLK command would not be blocked by another process's lock, then the l_type field is changed to F_UNLCK and the remaining fields in the structure are unaffected. Let us use this capability to print all the segments locked by other processes. Note that if there are several read locks over the same segment only one of these will be found.

```
struct flock lck;

/* Find and print "write lock" blocked segments of this file. */
        (void) printf("sysid   pid type    start   length\n");
        lck.l_whence = 0;
        lck.l_start = 0L;
        lck.l_len = 0L;
        do {
                lck.l_type = F_WRLCK;
                (void) fcntl(fd, F_GETLK, &lck);
                if (lck.l_type != F_UNLCK) {
                        (void) printf("%5d %5d   %c  %8d %8d\n",
                                      lck.l_sysid,
                                      lck.l_pid,
                                      (lck.l_type == F_WRLCK) ? 'W' : 'R',
                                      lck.l_start,
                                      lck.l_len);
                        /* if this lock goes to the end of the address
                         * space, no need to look further, so break out.
                         */
                        if (lck.l_len == 0)
                                break;
                        /* otherwise, look for new lock after the one
                         * just found.
                         */
                        lck.l_start += lck.l_len;
                }
        } while (lck.l_type != F_UNLCK);
```

fcntl with the F_GETLK command will always return correctly (that is, it will not sleep or fail) if the values passed to it as arguments are valid.

The lockf function with the F_TEST command can also be used to test if there is a process blocking a lock. This function does not, however, return the information about where the lock actually is and which process owns the lock. A routine using lockf to test for a lock on a file follows:

```
/* find a blocked record. */
/* seek to beginning of file */
(void) lseek(fd, 0, 0L);
/* set the size of the test region to zero (0)
 * to test until the end of the file address space.
 */
if (lockf(fd, F_TEST, 0L) < 0) {
        switch (errno) {
                case EACCES:
                case EAGAIN:
                (void) printf("file is locked by another process\n");
                break;
                case EBADF:
                /* bad argument passed to lockf */
                perror("lockf");
                break;
                default:
                (void) printf("lockf: unknown error <%d>\n", errno);
                break;
                }
        }
```

When a process forks, the child receives a copy of the file descriptors that the
parent has opened. The parent and child also share a common file pointer for
each file. If the parent were to seek to a point in the file, the child's file pointer
would also be at that location. This feature has important implications when
using record locking. The current value of the file pointer is used as the reference for the offset of the beginning of the lock, as described by l_start, when
using a l_whence value of 1. If both the parent and child process set locks on
the same file, there is a possibility that a lock will be set using a file pointer that
was reset by the other process. This problem appears in the lockf(3) function
call as well and is a result of the /usr/group requirements for record locking.
If forking is used in a record locking program, the child process should close
and reopen the file if either locking method is used. This will result in the creation of a new and separate file pointer that can be manipulated without this
problem occurring. Another solution is to use the fcntl system call with a
l_whence value of 0 or 2. This makes the locking function atomic, so that even
processes sharing file pointers can be locked without difficulty.

Deadlock Handling

There is a certain level of deadlock detection/avoidance built into the record
locking facility. This deadlock handling provides the same level of protection
granted by the /usr/group standard lockf call. This deadlock detection is
only valid for processes that are locking files or records on a single system.
Deadlocks can only potentially occur when the system is about to put a record
locking system call to sleep. A search is made for constraint loops of processes
that would cause the system call to sleep indefinitely. If such a situation is
found, the locking system call will fail and set errno to the deadlock error
number. If a process wishes to avoid the use of the systems deadlock detection
it should set its locks using F_GETLK instead of F_GETLKW.

Selecting Advisory or Mandatory Locking

The use of mandatory locking is not recommended for reasons that will be
made clear in a subsequent section. Whether or not locks are enforced by the
I/O system calls is determined at the time the calls are made by the permissions
on the file; see chmod(2). For locks to be under mandatory enforcement, the file
must be a regular file with the set-group-ID bit on and the group execute permission off. If either condition fails, all record locks are advisory. Mandatory
enforcement can be assured by the following code:

```
#include <sys/types.h>
#include <sys/stat.h>

int mode;
struct stat buf;
                     .
                     .
                     .
        if (stat(filename, &buf) < 0) {
                perror("program");
                exit (2);
        }
        /* get currently set mode */
        mode = buf.st_mode;
        /* remove group execute permission from mode */
        mode &= ~(S_IEXEC>>3);
        /* set 'set group id bit' in mode */
        mode |= S_ISGID;
        if· (chmod(filename, mode) < 0) {
                perror("program");
                exit(2);
        }
                     .
                     .
                     .
```

Files that are to be record locked should never have any type of execute permission set on them. This is because the operating system does not obey the record locking protocol when executing a file.

The chmod(1) command can also be easily used to set a file to have mandatory locking. This can be done with the command:

    chmod +1 *file*

The ls(1) command shows this setting when you ask for the long listing format:

    ls -1 *file*

causes the following to be printed:

    -rw---l---   1   *user*   *group*   *size*   *mod_time*   *file*

Integrated Software Development Guide

Caveat Emptor—Mandatory Locking

- Mandatory locking only protects those portions of a file that are locked. Other portions of the file that are not locked may be accessed according to normal UNIX system file permissions.

- If multiple reads or writes are necessary for an atomic transaction, the process should explicitly lock all such pieces before any I/O begins. Thus advisory enforcement is sufficient for all programs that perform in this way.

- As stated earlier, arbitrary programs should not have unrestricted access permission to files that are important enough to record lock.

- Advisory locking is more efficient because a record lock check does not have to be performed for every I/O request.

Record Locking and Future Releases of the UNIX System

Provisions have been made for file and record locking in a UNIX system environment. In such an environment the system on which the locking process resides may be remote from the system on which the file and record locks reside. In this way multiple processes on different systems may put locks upon a single file that resides on one of these or yet another system. The record locks for a file reside on the system that maintains the file. It is also important to note that deadlock detection/avoidance is only determined by the record locks being held by and for a single system. Therefore, it is necessary that a process only hold record locks on a single system at any given time for the deadlock mechanism to be effective. If a process needs to maintain locks over several systems, it is suggested that the process avoid the sleep-when-blocked features of fcntl or lockf and that the process maintain its own deadlock detection. If the process uses the sleep-when-blocked feature, then a timeout mechanism should be provided by the process so that it does not hang waiting for a lock to be cleared.

Memory Management

Memory Management Facilities

The UNIX system provides a complete set of memory management mechanisms, providing applications complete control over the construction of their address space and permitting a wide variety of operations on both process address spaces and the variety of memory objects in the system. Process address spaces are composed of a vector of memory pages, each of which can be independently mapped and manipulated. Typically, the system presents the user with mappings that simulate the traditional UNIX process memory environment, but other views of memory are useful as well.

The UNIX memory-management facilities:

- Unify the system's operations on memory.

- Provide a set of kernel mechanisms powerful and general enough to support the implementation of fundamental system services without special-purpose kernel support.

- Maintain consistency with the existing environment, in particular using the UNIX file system as the name space for named virtual-memory objects.

Virtual Memory, Address Spaces and Mapping

The system's virtual memory (VM) consists of all available physical memory resources. Examples include local and remote file systems, processor primary memory, swap space, and other random-access devices. Named objects in the virtual memory are referenced though the UNIX file system. However, not all file system objects are in the virtual memory; devices that cannot be treated as storage, such as terminal and network device files, are not in the virtual memory. Some virtual memory objects, such as private process memory and shared memory segments, do not have names.

A process's address space is defined by mappings onto objects in the system's virtual memory (usually files). Each mapping is constrained to be sized and aligned with the page boundaries of the system on which the process is executing. Each page may be mapped (or not) independently. Only process addresses which are mapped to some system object are valid, for there is no memory associated with processes themselves—all memory is represented by objects in the system's virtual memory.

Each object in the virtual memory has an object address space defined by some physical storage. A reference to an object address accesses the physical storage that implements the address within the object. The virtual memory's associated physical storage is thus accessed by transforming process addresses to object addresses, and then to the physical store.

A given process page may map to only one object, although a given object address may be the subject of many process mappings. An important characteristic of a mapping is that the object to which the mapping is made is not affected by the mere existence of the mapping. Thus, it cannot, in general, be expected that an object has an "awareness" of having been mapped, or of which portions of its address space are accessed by mappings; in particular, the notion of a "page" is not a property of the object. Establishing a mapping to an object simply provides the potential for a process to access or change the object's contents.

The establishment of mappings provides an access method that renders an object directly addressable by a process. Applications may find it advantageous to access the storage resources they use directly rather than indirectly through `read` and `write`. Potential advantages include efficiency (elimination of unnecessary data copying) and reduced complexity (single-step updates rather than the `read`, modify buffer, `write` cycle). The ability to access an object and have it retain its identity over the course of the access is unique to this access method, and facilitates the sharing of common code and data.

Networking, Heterogeneity and Integrity

VM is designed to fit well with the larger UNIX heterogeneous environment. This environment makes extensive use of networking to access file systems—file systems that are now part of the system's virtual memory. Networks are not constrained to consist of similar hardware or to be based upon a common operating system; in fact, the opposite is encouraged, for such constraints create serious barriers to accommodating heterogeneity. While a given set of processes may apply a set of mechanisms to establish and maintain the properties of various system objects—properties such as page sizes and the ability of objects to synchronize their own use—a given operating system should not impose such mechanisms on the rest of the network.

As it stands, the access method view of a virtual memory maintains the potential for a given object (say a text file) to be mapped by systems running the UNIX memory management system and also to be accessed by systems for which virtual memory and storage management techniques such as paging are totally foreign, such as PC-DOS. Such systems can continue to share access to the object, each using and providing its programs with the access method appropriate to that system. The unacceptable alternative would be to prohibit access to the object by less capable systems.

Another consideration arises when applications use an object as a communications channel, or otherwise try to access it simultaneously. In both cases, the object is shared; thus, applications must use some synchronization mechanism to maintain the integrity of their actions on it. The scope and nature of the synchronization mechanism depends on the application. For example, file access on systems which do not support virtual memory access methods must be indirect, by way of `read` and `write`. Applications sharing files on such systems must coordinate their access using semaphores, file locking, or some application-specific protocols. What is required in an environment where mapping replaces `read` and `write` as the access method is an operation, such as `fsync`, that supports atomic update operations.

The nature and scope of synchronization over shared objects must remain application-defined. If the system tried to impose automatic semantics for sharing, it might prohibit other useful forms of mapped access that have nothing to do with communication or sharing. By providing the mechanism to support integrity, and leaving it to cooperating applications to apply the mechanism, the needs of applications are met without eliminating diversity. Note that this design does not prohibit the creation of libraries that provide abstractions for common application needs. Not all abstractions on which an application builds need be supplied by the "operating system."

Memory Management Interfaces

The applications programmer gains access to VM facilities through several sets of system calls. The next sections summarize these calls, and provide examples of their use. For details, see the *Programmer's Reference Manual*.

Creating and Using Mappings

```
caddr_t
mmap(caddr_t addr, size_t len, int prot, int flags, int fd, off_t off);
```

mmap establishes a mapping between a process's address space and an object in the system's virtual memory. All other system functions that contribute to the definition of an address space are built from mmap, the system's most fundamental function for defining the contents of an address space. The format of an mmap call is:

```
paddr = mmap(addr, len, prot, flags, fd, off);
```

mmap establishes a mapping from the process's address space at address *paddr* for *len* bytes to the object specified by *fd* at offset *off* for *len* bytes. A successful call to mmap returns *paddr* as its result, which is an implementation-dependent function of the parameter *addr* and the setting of the MAP_FIXED bit of *flags*, as described below. The address range *[paddr, paddr + len)* must be valid for the address space of the process and the range *[off, off + len)* must be valid for the virtual memory object. (The notation *[start, end)* denotes the interval from *start* to *end*, including *start* but excluding *end*.)

 NOTE The mapping established by mmap replaces any previous mappings for the process's pages in the range *[paddr, paddr + len)*.

The parameter *prot* determines whether read, execute, write or some combination of accesses are permitted to the pages being mapped. To deny all access, set *prot* to PROT_NONE. Otherwise, specify permissions by an OR of PROT_READ, PROT_EXECUTE, and PROT_WRITE.

A write access must fail if `PROT_WRITE` has not been set, though the behavior of the write can be influenced by setting `MAP_PRIVATE` in the *flags* parameter, which provides other information about the handling of mapped pages, as described below:

- `MAP_SHARED` and `MAP_PRIVATE` specify the mapping type, and one of them must be specified. The mapping type describes the disposition of store operations made by this process into the address range defined by the mapping operation. If `MAP_SHARED` is specified, write references will modify the mapped object. No further operations on the object are necessary to effect a change — the act of storing into a `MAP_SHARED` mapping is equivalent to doing a `write` system call.

 NOTE The private copy is not created until the first write; until then, other users who have the object mapped `MAP_SHARED` can change the object. That is, if one user has an object mapped `MAP_PRIVATE` and another user has the same object mapped `MAP_SHARED`, and the `MAP_SHARED` user changes the object before the `MAP_PRIVATE` user does the first write, then the changes appear in the `MAP_PRIVATE` user's copy that the system makes on the first write. If an application needs isolation from changes made by other processes, it should use `read` to make a copy of the data it wishes to keep isolated.

On the other hand, if `MAP_PRIVATE` is specified, an initial write reference to a page in the mapped area will create a copy of that page and redirect the initial and successive write references to that copy. This operation is sometimes referred to as copy-on-write and occurs invisibly to the process causing the store. Only pages actually modified have copies made in this manner. `MAP_PRIVATE` mappings are used by system functions such as exec(2) when mapping files containing programs for execution. This permits operations by programs such as debuggers to modify the "text" (code) of the program without affecting the file from which the program is obtained.

The mapping type is retained across a `fork`.

■ MAP_FIXED informs the system that the value returned by mmap must be *addr*, exactly. The use of MAP_FIXED is discouraged, as it may prevent an implementation from making the most effective use of system resources. When MAP_FIXED is not set, the system uses *addr* as a hint to arrive at *paddr*. The *paddr* so chosen is an area of the address space that the system deems suitable for a mapping of *len* bytes to the specified object. An *addr* value of zero grants the system complete freedom in selecting *paddr*, subject to constraints described below. A non-zero value of *addr* is taken as a suggestion of a process address near which the mapping should be placed. When the system selects a value for *paddr*, it never places a mapping at address 0, nor replaces any extant mapping, nor maps into areas considered part of the potential data or stack "segments." The system strives to choose alignments for mappings that maximize the performance of the its hardware resources.

The file descriptor used in a mmap call need not be kept open after the mapping is established. If it is closed, the mapping will remain until such time as it is replaced by another call to mmap that explicitly specifies the addresses occupied by this mapping; or until the mapping is removed either by process termination or a call to munmap. Although the mapping endures independent of the existence of a file descriptor, changes to the file can influence accesses to the mapped area, even if they do not affect the mapping itself. For instance, should a file be shortened by a call to truncate, such that the mapping now "overhangs" the end of the file, then accesses to that area of the file which "does not exist" will result in SIGBUS signals. It is possible to create the mapping in the first place such that it "overhangs" the end of the file — the only requirement when creating a mapping is that the addresses, lengths, and offsets specified in the operation be possible (i.e., within the range permitted for the object in question), not that they exist at the time the mapping is created (or subsequently.)

Similarly, if a program accesses an address in a manner inconsistently with how it has been mapped (for instance, by attempting a store operation into a mapping that was established with only PROT_READ access), then a SIGSEGV signal will result. SIGSEGV signals will also result on any attempt to reference an address not defined by any mapping.

In general, if a program makes a reference to an address that is inconsistent with the mapping (or lack of a mapping) established at that address, the system will respond with a SIGSEGV violation. However, if a program makes a reference to an address consistent with how the address is mapped, but that address does not evaluate at the time of the access to allocated storage in the object being mapped, then the system will respond with a SIGBUS violation. In this manner a program (or user) can distinguish between whether it is the mapping or the object that is inconsistent with the access, and take appropriate remedial action.

Using mmap to access system memory objects can simplify programs in a variety of ways. Keeping in mind that mmap can really be viewed as just a means to access memory objects, it is possible to program using mmap in many cases where you might program with read or write. However, it is important to realize that mmap can only be used to gain access to memory objects — those objects that can be thought of as randomly accessible storage. Thus, terminals and network connections cannot be accessed with mmap because they are not "memory." Magnetic tapes, even though they are memory devices, can not be accessed with mmap because storage locations on the tape can only be addressed sequentially. Some examples of situations which can be thought of as candidates for use of mmap over more traditional methods of file access include:

- Random access operations — either map the entire file into memory or, if the address space can not accommodate the file or if the file size is variable, create "windows" of mappings to the object.

- Efficiency — even in situations where access is sequential, if the object being accessed can be accessed via mmap, an efficiency gain may be obtained by avoiding the copying operations inherent in accesses via read or write.

- Structured storage — if the storage being accessed is collected as tables or data structures, algorithms can be more conveniently written if access to the file is treated just as though the tables were in memory. Previously, programs could not simply alter storage or tables in memory and save them for access in subsequent runs; however, when the addresses of a table are defined by mappings to a file, then changes to that storage are changes to the file, and are thus automatically recorded in it.

■ Scattered storage — if a program requires scattered regions of storage, such as multiple heaps or stack areas, such areas can be defined by mapping operations during program operation.

The remainder of this section will illustrate some other concepts surrounding mapping creation and use.

Mapping /dev/zero gives the calling program a block of zero-filled virtual memory of the size specified in the call to mmap. /dev/zero is a special device, that responds to read as an infinite source of bytes with the value 0, but when mapped creates an unnamed object to back the mapped region of memory. The following code fragment demonstrates a use of this to create a block of scratch storage in a program, at an address of the system's choosing.

```
/*
 * Function to allocate a block of zeroed storage.  Parameter
 * is the number of bytes desired.  The storage is mapped as
 * MAP_SHARED, so that if a fork occurs, the child process
 * will be able to access and modify the storage.  If we wished
 * to cause the child's modifications (as well as those by the
 * parent) to be invisible to the ancestry of processes, we
 * would use MAP_PRIVATE.
 */
caddr_t
get_zero_storage(int len);
{
        int fd;
        caddr_t result;

        if ((fd = open("/dev/zero", O_RDWR)) == -1)
            return ((caddr_t)-1);
        result = mmap(0, len, PROT_READ|PROT_WRITE, MAP_SHARED, fd, 0);
        (void) close(fd);
        return (result);
}
```

As written, this function permits a hierarchy of processes to use the area of allocated storage as a region of communication (for implicit interprocess communication purposes). Later in this chapter we will describe a set of system facilities that provide a similar function packaged for accomplishing the same purpose without requiring that the processes be in a parent-child hierarchy.

In some cases, devices or files are only useful if accessed via mapping. An example of this is frame buffer devices used to support bit-mapped displays, where display management algorithms function best if they can operate randomly on the addresses of the display directly.

Finally, it is important to remember that mappings can be operated upon at the granularity of a single page. Even though a mapping operation may define multiple pages of an address space, there is absolutely no restriction that subsequent operations on those addresses must operate on the same number of pages. For instance, an mmap operation defining ten pages of an address space may be followed by subsequent munmap (see below) operations that remove every other page from the address space, leaving five mapped pages each followed by an unmapped page. Those unmapped pages may subsequently be mapped to different locations in the same or different objects, or the whole range of pages (or any partition, superset, or subset of the pages) used in other mmap or other memory management operations. Further, it must be noted that any mapping operation that operates on more than a single page can "partially succeed" in that some parts of the address range can be affected even though the call returns a failure. Thus, an mmap operation that replaces another mapping, if it fails, may have deleted the previous mapping and failed to replace it. Similarly, other operations (unless specifically stated otherwise) may process some pages in the range successfully before operating on a page where the operation fails.

Not all device drivers support memory mapping. mmap fails if you try to map a device that does not support mapping.

Removing Mappings

```
int
munmap(caddr_t addr, size_t len);
```

munmap removes all mappings for pages in the range [addr, addr + len) from the address space of the calling process. It is not an error to remove mappings from addresses that do not have them, and any mapping, no matter how it was established, can be removed with munmap. munmap does not in any way affect the objects that were mapped at those addresses.

Cache Control

The UNIX memory management system can be thought of as a form of "cache management", in which a processor's primary memory is used as a cache for pages from objects from the system's virtual memory. Thus, there are a number of operations which control or interrogate the status of this "cache", as described in this section.

Memory Cache Control

```
int
memcntl(caddr_t addr, size_t len, int cmd, caddr_t arg, int attr, int mask);
```

memcntl provides several control operations over mappings in the range *[addr, addr + len)*, including locking pages into physical memory, unlocking them, and writing pages to secondary storage. The functions described in the rest of this section offer simplified interfaces to the memcntl operations.

Memory Page Locking

```
int
mlock(caddr_t addr, size_t len);

int
munlock(caddr_t addr, size_t len);
```

mlock causes the pages referenced by the mapping in the range *[addr, addr + len)* to be locked in physical memory. References to those pages (through other mappings in this or other processes) will not result in page faults that require an I/O operation to obtain the data needed to satisfy the reference. Because this operation ties up physical system resources, and has the potential to disrupt normal system operation, use of this facility is restricted to the superuser. The system prohibits more than a configuration-dependent limit of pages to be locked in memory simultaneously, the call to mlock will fail if this limit is exceeded.

`munlock` releases the locks on physical pages. If multiple `mlock` calls are made through the same mapping, only a single `munlock` call will be required to release the locks (in other words, locks on a given mapping do not nest.) However, if different mappings to the same pages are processed with `mlock`, then the pages will stay locked until the locks on all the mappings are released.

Locks are also released when a mapping is removed, either through being replaced with an `mmap` operation or removed explicitly with `munmap`. A lock will be transferred between pages on the "copy-on-write" event associated with a `MAP_PRIVATE` mapping, thus locks on an address range that includes `MAP_PRIVATE` mappings will be retained transparently along with the copy-on-write redirection (see `mmap` above for a discussion of this redirection).

Address Space Locking

```
int
mlockall(int flags);

int
munlockall(void);
```

`mlockall` and `munlockall` are similar in purpose and restriction to `mlock` and `munlock`, except that they operate on entire address spaces. `mlockall` accepts a *flags* argument built as a bit-field of values from the set:

> `MCL_CURRENT` Current mappings
> `MCL_FUTURE` Future mappings

If *flags* is `MCL_CURRENT`, the lock is to affect everything currently in the address space. If *flags* is `MCL_FUTURE`, the lock is to affect everything added in the future. If *flags* is `(MCL_CURRENT | MCL_FUTURE)`, the lock is to affect both current and future mappings.

`munlockall` removes all locks on all pages in the address space, whether established by `mlock` or `mlockall`.

Memory Cache Synchronization

```
int
msync(caddr_t addr, size_t len, int flags);
```

msync supports applications which require assertions about the integrity of data in the storage backing their mapping, either for correctness or for coherent communications in a distributed environment. msync causes all modified copies of pages over the range *[addr, addr + len)* to be flushed to the objects mapped by those addresses. In the cache analogy discussed previously, msync is the cache "write-back," or flush, operation. It is similar in purpose to the fsync operation for files.

msync optionally invalidates such cache entries so that further references to the pages cause the system to obtain them from their permanent storage locations.

The *flags* argument provides a bit-field of values that influences the behavior of msync. The bit names and their interpretations are:

MS_SYNC	synchronized write
MS_ASYNC	return immediately
MS_INVALIDATE	invalidate caches

MS_SYNC causes msync to return only after all I/O operations are complete. MS_ASYNC causes msync to return immediately once all I/O operations are scheduled. MS_INVALIDATE causes all cached copies of data from mapped objects to be invalidated, requiring them to be reobtained from the object's storage upon the next reference.

Memory Page Residency

```
int
mincore(caddr_t addr, size_t len, char *vec);
```

`mincore` determines the residency of the memory pages in the address space covered by mappings in the range *[addr, addr + len)*. Using the "cache concept" described earlier, this function can be viewed as an operation that interrogates the status of the cache, and returns an indication of what is currently resident in the cache. The status is returned as a char-per-page in the character array referenced by *vec* (which the system assumes to be large enough to encompass all the pages in the address range). Each character contains either a "1" (indicating that the page is resident in the system's primary storage), or a "0" (indicating that the page is not resident in primary storage.) Other bits in the character are reserved for possible future expansion — therefore, programs testing residency should test only the least significant bit of each character.

`mincore` returns residency information that is accurate at an instant in time. Because the system may frequently adjust the set of pages in memory, this information may quickly be outdated. Only locked pages are guaranteed to remain in memory.

Other Mapping Functions

```
long
sysconf(PAGESIZE);
```

`sysconf` returns the system-dependent size of a memory page. For portability, applications should not embed any constants specifying the size of a page, and instead should make use of `sysconf` to obtain that information. Note that it is not unusual for page sizes to vary even among implementations of the same instruction set, increasing the importance of using this function for portability.

```
int
mprotect(caddr_t addr, size_t len, int prot);
```

mprotect has the effect of assigning protection *prot* to all pages in the range
[addr, addr + len). The protection assigned can not exceed the permissions
allowed on the underlying object. For instance, a read-only mapping to a file
that was opened for read-only access can not be set to be writable with mprotect (unless the mapping is of the MAP_PRIVATE type, in which case the write
access is permitted since the writes will modify copies of pages from the object,
and not the object itself).

Address Space Layout

Traditionally, the address space of a UNIX process has consisted of exactly three
segments: one each for write-protected program code (text), a heap of dynamically allocated storage (data), and the process's stack. Text is read-only and
shared, while the data and stack segments are private to the process.

System V Release 4 still uses text, data, and stack segments, though these should
be thought of as constructs provided by the programming environment rather
than by the operating system. As such, it is possible to construct processes that
have multiple segments of each "type," or of types of arbitrary semantic value
— no longer are programs restricted to being built only from objects the system
was capable of representing directly. For instance, a process's address space
may contain multiple text and data segments, some belonging to specific programs and some shared among multiple programs. Text segments from shared
libraries, for example, typically appear in the address spaces of many processes.
A process's address space is simply a vector of pages, and there is no necessary
division between different address-space segments. Process text and data spaces
are simply groups of pages mapped in ways appropriate to the function they
provide the program.

While the system may have multiple areas that can be considered "data" segments, for programming convenience the system maintains operations to operate on an area of storage associated with a process's initial "heap storage area." A process can manipulate this area by calling `brk` and `sbrk`:

```
caddr_t
brk(caddr_t addr);

caddr_t
sbrk(int incr);
```

`brk` sets the system's idea of the lowest data segment location not used by the caller to *addr* (rounded up to the next multiple of the system's page size).

`sbrk`, the alternate function, adds *incr* bytes to the caller's data space and returns a pointer to the start of the new data area.

A process's address space is usually sparsely populated, with data and text pages intermingled. The precise mechanics of the management of stack space is machine-dependent. By convention, page 0 is not used. Process address spaces are often constructed through dynamic linking when a program is `exec`'ed. Operations such as `exec` and dynamic linking build upon the mapping operations described previously. Dynamic linking is described further in the *Programmer's Guide: ANSI C and Programming Support Tools*.

3 Process Management

3. PROCESS MANAGEMENT

3. PROCESS MANAGEMENT

Introduction

A process is the execution of a program; most UNIX System V commands execute as separate processes. Each process is a distinct entity, able to execute and terminate independently of all other processes. Each user can have many processes in the system simultaneously. In fact, it is not always necessary for the user to be logged into the system while those processes are executing.

Whenever you execute a command in the UNIX system you are initiating a process that is numbered and tracked by the operating system. A flexible feature of the UNIX system is that processes can be generated by other processes. This happens more than you might ever be aware of. For example, when you log in to your system you are running a process, very probably the shell. If you then use an editor such as vi, take the option of invoking the shell from vi, and execute the ps command, you will see a display something like the one in the following figure (which shows the results of a ps -f command):

Figure 3-1: Process Status

```
UID    PID     PPID    C    STIME      TTY     TIME   COMD
abc    24210   1       0    06:13:14   tty29   0:05   -sh
abc    24631   24210   0    06:59:07   tty29   0:13   vi c2.uli
abc    28441   28358   80   09:17:22   tty29   0:01   ps -f
abc    28358   24631   2    09:15:14   tty29   0:01   sh -i
```

As you can see, user abc (who went through the steps described above) now has four processes active. It is an interesting exercise to trace the chain that is shown in the Process ID (PID) and Parent Process ID (PPID) columns. The shell that was started when user abc logged on is process 24210; its parent is the initialization process (process ID 1). Process 24210 is the parent of process 24631, and so on.

The four processes in the example above are all UNIX system shell-level commands, but you can spawn new processes from your own program. You might think, "Well, it's one thing to switch from one program to another when I'm at my terminal working interactively with the computer; but why would a program want to run other programs, and if one does, why wouldn't I just put everything together into one big executable module?"

Overlooking the case where your program is itself an interactive application with diverse choices for the user, your program may need to run one or more other programs based on conditions it encounters in its own processing. (If it's the end of the month, go do a trial balance, for example.) The usual reasons why it might not be practical to create one large executable are:

- The load module may get too big to fit in the maximum process size for your system.

- You may not have control over the object code of all the other modules you want to include.

Suffice it to say, there are legitimate reasons why this creation of new processes might need to be done. There are two ways to do it:

- exec(2)—stop this process and start another

- fork(2)—start an additional copy of this process

Program Execution & Process Creation

Program Execution – execl and execv

Overlays, performed by the family of `exec` system-calls, can change the executing program, but can not create new processes. Processes are created (or spawned) by the system-call `fork`, which is discussed later.

`exec` is the name of a family of functions that includes `execl`, `execv`, `execle`, `execve`, `execlp`, and `execvp`. They all have the function of transforming the calling process into a new process. The reason for the variety is to provide different ways of pulling together and presenting the arguments of the function. An example of one version (`execl`) might be:

```
execl("/usr/bin/prog2", "prog", progarg1, progarg2, (char *)0);
```

For `execl` the argument list is

`/usr/bin/prog2`	path name of the new process file
`prog`	the name the new process gets in its `argv[0]`
`progarg1,` `progarg2`	arguments to `prog2` as `char*`'s
`(char *)0`	a null `char` pointer to mark the end of the arguments

Check the `exec(2)` manual page in the *Programmer's Reference Manual* for the rest of the details. The key point of the `exec` family is that there is no return from a successful execution: the new process overlays the process that makes the `exec` system call. The new process also takes over the Process ID and other attributes of the old process. If the call to `exec` is unsuccessful, control is returned to your program with a return value of −1. You can check `errno` to learn why it failed.

The system-call `execl` executes another program, *without returning*; thus, to print the date as the last action of a running program, use:

```
execl("/bin/date", "date", NULL);
```

The first argument to `execl` is the *file-name* of the command; you have to know where it is found in the file-system. The second argument is conventionally the program name (that is, the last component of the file-name), but this is seldom used except as a place-holder. If the command takes arguments, they are strung out after this; the end of the list is marked by a NULL argument.

The execl call overlays the existing program with the new one, runs that, then exits, without returning to the original program.

More realistically, a program might fall into two or more phases that communicate only through temporary files. Here it is natural to make the second pass simply an execl call from the first.

The one exception to the rule that the original program never gets control back occurs when there is an error, for example if the file can't be found or is not executable. If you don't know where date is located, say:

```
execl("/bin/date", "date", NULL);
execl("/usr/bin/date", "date", NULL);
printf(stderr, "Someone stole 'date'\n");
```

A variant of execl called execv is useful when you don't know in advance how many arguments there are going to be. The call is:

```
execv(filename, argp);
```

Where argp is an array of pointers to the arguments; the last pointer in the array must be NULL so execv can tell where the list ends. As with execl, filename is the file in which the program is found, and argp[0] is the name of the program. (This arrangement is identical to the argv array for C program arguments.)

Neither of these functions provides the niceties of normal command execution. There is no automatic search of multiple directories – you have to know precisely where the command is located. Nor do you get the expansion of meta-characters like "<", ">", "*", "?" and "[]" in the argument list. If you want these, use execl to invoke the shell sh, which then does all the work. Construct a string cmdline that contains the complete command as it would have been typed at the terminal, then say:

```
execl("/bin/sh", "sh", "-c", cmdline, NULL);
```

The shell is assumed to be at a fixed place, /bin/sh. Its argument -c says to treat the next argument as a whole command line, so it does just what you want. The only problem is in constructing the right information in cmdline.

Unless we can regain control after running a program with execl or execv, what we've talked about so far isn't really all that useful. Any process may exec (cause execution of) a file. Doing an exec does not change the process-id; the process that did the exec persists, but after the exec it is executing a different program. Files that were open before the exec remain open afterwards. If a program (for example, the first pass of a compiler) wishes to overlay itself with another program (for example, the second pass), then it simply execs the second program. This is analogous to a "goto" in programming.

Process Creation – fork

If a process wishes to regain control after exec-ing a second program, it should fork a child-process, have the child exec the second program, and the parent wait for the child. This is analogous to a "call." The following figure depicts what is involved in executing a program with a typical fork as the first step:

Figure 3-2: Process Primitives

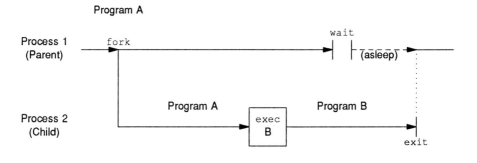

Because the exec functions simply overlay the new program on the old one, to save the old one requires that it first be split into two copies; one of these can be overlaid, while the other waits for the new overlaying program to finish.

The system-call `fork` does the splitting as in the following call:

```
proc_id = fork();
```

The newly created process, known as the "child-process," is a copy of the image of the original process, called the "parent-process." The system-call `fork` splits the program into two copies, both of which continue to run, and which differ only in the value of the "process-id" kept in `proc_id`. In the child-process, `proc_id` equals zero; in the parent-process, `proc_id` equals a non-zero value that is the process number of the child-process. Thus, the basic way to call, and return from, another program is:

```
if (fork() == 0)    /* in child */
    execl("/bin/sh", "sh", "-c", cmd, NULL);
```

And in fact, except for handling errors, this is sufficient. The `fork` is zero, so it calls `execl` which does the `cmd` and then dies. In the parent, `fork` returns non-zero so it skips the `execl`. (If there is any error, `fork` returns −1).

A child inherits its parent's permissions, working-directory, root-directory, open files, etc. This mechanism permits processes to share common input streams in various ways. Files that were open before the `fork` are shared after the `fork`. The processes are informed through the return value of `fork` as to which is the parent and which is the child. In any case the child and parent differ in three important ways:

- The child has a different process-id.
- The child has a different parent-process-id.
- All accounting variables are reset to appropriate values in the child.

The `fork` system-call creates a child-process with code and data copied from the parent-process that created the child-process. Once the copying is completed, the new (child) process is placed on the runnable queue to be scheduled. Each child-process executes independently of its parent-process, although the parent may explicitly wait for the termination of that child or any of its children. Usually the parent waits for the death of its child at some point, since this `wait` call is used to free the process-table entry used by the child. See the discussion under "Process Termination" for more detail.

Calling `fork` creates a new process that is an exact copy of the calling process. If the idea of having two identical processes seems a little funny, consider this:

- Because the return value is different between the child-process and the parent, the program can contain the logic to determine different paths.

- The child-process could say, "Okay, I'm the child; I'm supposed to issue an `exec` for an entirely different program."

- The parent-process could say, "My child is going to `exec` a new program; I'll issue a `wait` until I get word that the new process is finished."

Your code might include statements like the following:

Figure 3-3: Example of `fork`

```
#include <errno.h>

pid_t ch_pid;
int ch_stat, status;
char *p_arg1, *p_arg2;
void exit();
extern int errno;

    if ((ch_pid = fork()) < 0) {
        /*
         * Could not fork... check errno
         */
    }
    else if (ch_pid == 0) {              /* child */
        (void)execl("/usr/bin/prog2", "prog", p_arg1, p_arg2, (char *)NULL);
        exit(2);    /* execl() failed */
    }
    else {                  /* parent */
        while ((status = wait(&ch_stat)) != ch_pid) {
            if (status < 0 && errno == ECHILD)
                break;
            errno = 0;
        }
    }
```

Because the new exec'd process takes over the child-process ID, the parent knows the ID. What this boils down to is a way of leaving one program to run another, returning to the point in the first program where processing left off.

Keep in mind that the fragment of code above includes minimal checking for error conditions, and has potential for confusion about open files and which program is writing to a file. Leaving out the possibility of named files, the new process created by the fork or exec has the three standard files that are automatically opened: stdin, stdout, and stderr. If the parent has buffered output that should appear before output from the child, the buffers must be flushed before the fork. Also, if the parent and the child-process both read input from a stream, whatever is read by one process will be lost to the other. That is, once something has been delivered from the input buffer to a process the pointer has moved on.

Process-creation is essential to the basic operation of UNIX System V because each command run by the Shell executes in its own process. In fact, execution of a Shell command or Shell procedure involves both a fork and an overlay. This scheme makes a number services easy to provide. I/O redirection, for example, is basically a simple operation; it is performed entirely in the child-process that executes the command, and thus no memory in the Shell parent-process is required to rescind the change in standard input and output. Background processes likewise require no new mechanism; the Shell merely refrains from waiting for commands executing in the background to complete. Finally, recursive use of the Shell to interpret a sequence of commands stored in a file is in no way a special operation.

Control of Processes – fork and wait

A parent-process can suspend its execution to wait for termination of a child-process with wait or waitpid. More often, the parent wants to wait for the child to terminate before continuing itself as follows:

```
int status;

if (fork() == 0)
    execl( ... );
wait(&status);
```

The previous code fragment avoids handling any abnormal conditions, such as a failure of the execl or fork, or the possibility that there might be more than one child running simultaneously. (The function wait returns the process-id of the terminated child, which can be checked against the value returned by fork.) In addition, this fragment avoids dealing with any funny behavior on the part of the child (which is reported in status).

The low-order eight bits of the value returned by wait encodes the termination status of the child-process; 0 signifies normal termination and non-zero to signify various kinds of abnormalities. The next higher eight bits are taken from the argument of the call to exit which caused a normal termination of the child-process. It is good coding practice for all programs to return meaningful status.

When a program is called by the shell, the three file-descriptors are available for use. When this program calls another one, correct etiquette suggest making sure the same conditions hold. Neither fork nor the exec calls affects open files in any way. If the parent is buffering output that must come out before output from the child, the parent must flush its buffers before the execl. Conversely, if a caller buffers an input stream, the called program loses any information that has been read by the caller.

Process Termination

Processes terminate in one of two ways:

- Normal Termination occurs by a return from main or when requested by an explicit call to exit or _exit.

- Abnormal Termination occurs as the default action of a signal or when requested by abort.

On receiving a signal, a process looks for a signal-handling function. Failure to find a signal-handling function forces the process to call exit, and therefore to terminate. The functions _exit, exit and abort terminate a process with the same effects except that abort makes available to wait or waitpid the status of a process terminated by the signal SIGABRT [see exit(2) and abort(2)].

As a process terminates, it can set an eight-bit exit status code available to its parent. Usually, this code indicates success (zero) or failure (non-zero), but it can be used in any manner the user wishes. If a signal terminated the process, the system first tries to dump an image of core, then modifies the exit code to indicate which signal terminated the process and whether core was dumped. Next, all signals are set to be ignored, and resources owned by the process are released, including open files and the working directory. The terminating process is now a "zombie" process, with only its process-table entry remaining; and that is unavailable for use until the process has finally terminated. Next, the process-table is searched for any child or zombie processes belonging to the terminating process. Those children are then adopted by `init` by changing their parent-process-id to `1`). This is necessary since there must be a parent to record the death of the child. The last actions of `exit` are to record the accounting information and exit code for the terminated process in the zombie process-table entry and to send the parent the death-of-child signal, `SIGCHLD`.

If the parent wants to wait until a child terminates before continuing execution, the parent can call `wait`, which causes the parent to sleep until a child zombie is found (meaning the child terminated). When the child terminates, the death-of-child signal is sent to the parent although the parent normally ignores this signal. The search for child zombies continues until the terminated child is found; at which time, the child's exit status and accounting information is reported to the parent (remember the call to `exit` in the child put this information in the child's process-table entry) and the zombie process-table entry is freed. Now the parent can wake up and continue executing.

The Process Scheduler

The UNIX system scheduler determines when processes run. It maintains process priorities based on configuration parameters, process behavior, and user requests; it uses these priorities to assign processes to the CPU.

UNIX System V Release 4 gives users absolute control over the order in which certain processes run and the amount of time each process may use the CPU before another process gets a chance.

By default, the Release 4 scheduler uses a time-sharing policy like the policy used in previous releases. A time-sharing policy adjusts process priorities dynamically in an attempt to provide good response time to interactive processes and good throughput to processes that use a lot of CPU time.

The UNIX System V Release 4 scheduler offers a real-time scheduling policy as well as a time-sharing policy. Real-time scheduling allows users to set fixed priorities on a per-process basis. The highest-priority real-time user process always gets the CPU as soon as it is runnable, even if system processes are runnable. An application can therefore specify the exact order in which processes run. An application may also be written so that its real-time processes have a guaranteed response time from the system.

For most UNIX environments, the default scheduler configuration works well and no real-time processes are needed: administrators should not change configuration parameters and users should not change scheduler properties of their processes. However, when the requirements for an application include strict timing constraints, real-time processes sometimes provide the only way to satisfy those constraints.

 NOTE Real-time processes used carelessly can have a dramatic negative effect on the performance of time-sharing processes.

This chapter is addressed to programmers who need more control over order of process execution than they get using default scheduler parameters.

Because changes in scheduler administration can affect scheduler behavior, programmers may also need to know something about scheduler administration. For administrative information on the scheduler, see the *System Administrator's Guide*. There are also a few reference manual entries with information on scheduler administration:

- dispadmin(1M) tells how to change scheduler configuration in a running system.

- ts_dptbl(4) and rt_dptbl(4) describe the time-sharing and real-time parameter tables that are used to configure the scheduler.

The rest of this chapter is organized as follows:

- "How the Process Scheduler Works" tells what the scheduler does and how it does it. It also introduces scheduler classes.

- "Commands and Function Calls" describes and gives examples of the priocntl(1) command and the priocntl(2) and priocntlset(2) system calls, the user interface to scheduler services. The priocntl functions allow you to retrieve scheduler configuration information and to get or set scheduler parameters for a process or a set of processes.

- "Interaction with Other Functions" describes the interactions between the scheduler and related functions.

- "Performance" discusses scheduler latencies that some applications must be aware of and mentions some considerations other than the scheduler that application designers must take into account to ensure that their requirements are met.

How the Process Scheduler Works

The following figure shows how the UNIX System V Release 4 process
scheduler works:

Figure 3-4: The UNIX System V Release 4 Process Scheduler

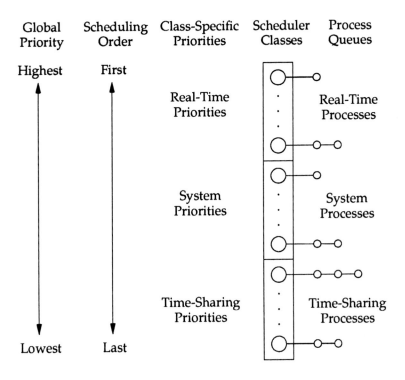

When a process is created, it inherits its scheduler parameters, including
scheduler class and a priority within that class. A process changes class only as
a result of a user request. The system manages the priority of a process based
on user requests and a policy associated with the scheduler class of the process.

In the default configuration, the initialization process belongs to the time-sharing class. Because processes inherit their scheduler parameters, all user login shells begin as time-sharing processes in the default configuration.

The scheduler converts class-specific priorities into global priorities. The global priority of a process determines when it runs—the scheduler always runs the runnable process with highest global priority. Numerically higher priorities run first. Once the scheduler assigns a process to the CPU, the process runs until it uses up its time slice, sleeps, or is preempted by a higher-priority process. Processes with the same priority run round-robin.

Administrators specify default time slices in the configuration tables, but users may assign per-process time slices to real-time processes.

You can display the global priority of a process with the −cl options of the ps(1) command. You can display configuration information about class-specific priorities with the priocntl(1) command and the dispadmin(1M) command.

By default, all real-time processes have higher priorities than any kernel process, and all kernel processes have higher priorities than any time-sharing process.

| NOTE | As long as there is a runnable real-time process, no kernel process and no time-sharing process runs. |

The next sections describe scheduling policies of three default classes.

Time-Sharing Class

The goal of the time-sharing policy is to provide good response time to interactive processes and good throughput to CPU-bound processes. The scheduler switches CPU allocation frequently enough to provide good response time, but not so frequently that it spends too much time doing the switching. Time slices are typically on the order of a few hundred milliseconds.

The time-sharing policy changes priorities dynamically and assigns time slices of different lengths. The scheduler raises the priority of a process that sleeps after only a little CPU use (a process sleeps, for example, when it starts an I/O operation such as a terminal read or a disk read); frequent sleeps are characteristic of interactive tasks such as editing and running simple shell commands. On the other hand, the time-sharing policy lowers the priority of a process that uses the CPU for long periods without sleeping.

The default time-sharing policy gives larger time slices to processes with lower priorities. A process with a low priority is likely to be CPU-bound. Other processes get the CPU first, but when a low-priority process finally gets the CPU, it gets a bigger chunk of time. If a higher-priority process becomes runnable during a time slice, however, it preempts the running process.

The scheduler manages time-sharing processes using configurable parameters in the time-sharing parameter table ts_dptbl. This table contains information specific to the time-sharing class.

System Class

The system class uses a fixed-priority policy to run kernel processes such as servers and housekeeping processes like the paging demon. The system class is reserved for use by the kernel; users may neither add nor remove a process from the system class. Priorities for system class processes are set up in the kernel code for those processes; once established, the priorities of system processes do not change. (User processes running in kernel mode are not in the system class.)

Real-Time Class

The real-time class uses a fixed-priority scheduling policy so that critical processes can run in predetermined order. Real-time priorities never change except when a user requests a change. Contrast this fixed-priority policy with the time-sharing policy, in which the system changes priorities in order to provide good interactive response time.

Privileged users can use the priocntl command or the priocntl system call to assign real-time priorities.

The scheduler manages real-time processes using configurable parameters in the real-time parameter table rt_dptbl. This table contains information specific to the real-time class.

Scheduler Commands and Function Calls

Here is a programmer's view of default process priorities:

Figure 3-5: Process Priorities (Programmer View)

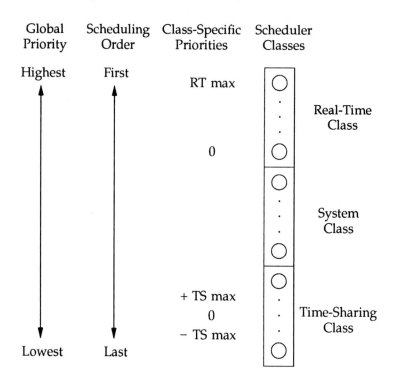

From a user or programmer's point of view, a process priority has meaning only in the context of a scheduler class. You specify a process priority by specifying a class and a class-specific priority value. The class and class-specific value are mapped by the system into a global priority that the system uses to schedule processes.

■ Real-time priorities run from zero to a configuration-dependent max-imum. The system maps them directly into global priorities. They never change except when a user changes them.

■ System priorities are controlled entirely in the kernel. Users cannot affect them.

■ Time-sharing priorities have a user-controlled component (the "user prior-ity") and a component controlled by the system. The system does not change the user priority except as the result of a user request. The system changes the system-controlled component dynamically on a per-process basis in order to provide good overall system performance; users cannot affect the system-controlled component. The scheduler combines these two components to get the process global priority.

The user priority runs from the negative of a configuration-dependent maximum to the positive of that maximum. A process inherits its user priority. Zero is the default initial user priority.

The "user priority limit" is the configuration-dependent maximum value of the user priority. You may set a user priority to any value below the user priority limit. With appropriate permission, you may raise the user priority limit. Zero is the default user priority limit.

You may lower the user priority of a process to give the process reduced access to the CPU or, with the appropriate permission, raise the user prior-ity to get better service. Because you cannot set the user priority above the user priority limit, you must raise the user priority limit before you raise the user priority if both have their default values of zero.

An administrator configures the maximum user priority independent of global time-sharing priorities. In the default configuration, for example, a user may set a user priority only in the range from −20 to +20, but 60 time-sharing global priorities are configured.

A system administrator's view of priorities is different from that of a user or programmer. When configuring scheduler classes, an administrator deals directly with global priorities. The system maps priorities supplied by users into these global priorities. See the *System Administrator's Guide.*

The `ps -cel` command reports global priorities for all active processes. The `priocntl` command reports the class-specific priorities that users and programmers use.

 NOTE Global process priorities and user-supplied priorities are in ascending order: numerically higher priorities run first.

The `priocntl`(1) command and the `priocntl`(2) and `priocntlset`(2) system calls set or retrieve scheduler parameters for processes. The basic idea for setting priorities is the same for all three functions:

- Specify the target processes.
- Specify the scheduler parameters you want for those processes.
- Do the command or system call to set the parameters for the processes.

You specify the target processes using an ID type and an ID. The ID type tells how to interpret the ID. [This concept of a set of processes applies to signals as well as to the scheduler; see `sigsend`(2).] The following table lists the valid ID types that you may specify.

`priocntl` ID types
process ID
parent-process ID
process group ID
session ID
class ID
effective user ID
effective group ID
all processes

These IDs are basic properties of UNIX processes. [See `intro`(2).] The class ID refers to the scheduler class of the process. `priocntl` works only for the time-sharing and the real-time classes, not for the system class. Processes in the system class have fixed priorities assigned when they are started by the kernel.

The priocntl command

The `priocntl` command comes in four forms:

- `priocntl -l` displays configuration information.

- `priocntl -d` displays the scheduler parameters of processes.

- `priocntl -s` sets the scheduler parameters of processes.

- `priocntl -e` executes a command with the specified scheduler parameters.

1. Here is the output of the `-l` option for the default configuration.

```
$ priocntl -l
CONFIGURED CLASSES
==================

SYS (System Class)

TS (Time Sharing)
        Configured TS User Priority Range: -20 through 20

RT (Real Time)
        Maximum Configured RT Priority: 59
```

2. The `-d` option displays the scheduler parameters of a process or a set of processes. The syntax for this option is

> `priocntl -d -i` *idtype idlist*

idtype tells what kind of IDs are in *idlist*. *idlist* is a list of IDs separated by white space. Here are the valid values for *idtype* and their corresponding ID types in *idlist*:

idtype	*idlist*
pid	process IDs
ppid	parent-process IDs
pgid	process group IDs
sid	session IDs
class	class names (TS or RT)
uid	effective user IDs
gid	effective group IDs
all	

Here are some examples of the −d option of priocntl:

```
$ # display info on all processes
$ priocntl -d -i all
        .
        .
        .

$ # display info on all time-sharing processes:
$ priocntl -d -i class TS
        .
        .
        .

$ # display info on all processes with user ID 103 or 6626
$ priocntl -d -i uid 103 6626
        .
        .
        .
```

3. The −s option sets scheduler parameters for a process or a set of processes. The syntax for this option is

> priocntl -s -c *class* *class_options* -i *idtype* *idlist*

idtype and *idlist* are the same as for the −d option described above.

class is TS for time-sharing or RT for real-time. You must be superuser to create a real-time process, to raise a time-sharing user priority above a per-process limit, or to raise the per-process limit above zero. Class options are class-specific:

Class-specific options for `priocntl`			
class	-c *class*	options	meaning
real-time	RT	-p *pri*	priority
		-t *tslc*	time slice
		-r *res*	resolution
time-sharing	TS	-p *upri*	user priority
		-m *uprilim*	user priority limit

For a real-time process you may assign a priority and a time slice.

- The priority is a number from 0 to the real-time maximum as reported by `priocntl -l`; the default maximum is 59.

- You specify the time slice as a number of clock intervals and the resolution of the interval. Resolution is specified in intervals per second. The time slice, therefore, is *tslc/res* seconds. To specify a time slice of one-tenth of a second, for example, you could specify a *tslc* of 1 and a *res* of 10. If you specify a time slice without specifying a resolution, millisecond resolution (a *res* of 1000) is assumed.

If you change a time-sharing process into a real-time process, it gets a default priority and time slice if you don't specify one. If you wish to change only the priority of a real-time process and leave its time slice unchanged, omit the -t option. If you wish to change only the time slice of a real-time process and leave its priority unchanged, omit the -p option.

For a time-sharing process you may assign a user priority and a user priority limit.

- The user priority is the user-controlled component of a time-sharing priority. The scheduler calculates the global priority of a time-sharing process by combining this user priority with a system-controlled component that depends on process behavior. The user priority has the same effect as a value set by nice (except that nice uses higher numbers for lower priority).

- The user priority limit is the maximum user priority a process may set for itself without being superuser. By default, the user priority limit is 0; you must be superuser to set a user priority limit above 0.

Both the user priority and the user priority limit must be within the user priority range reported by the `priocntl -l` command. The default range is −20 to +20.

A process may lower and raise its user priority as often as it wishes, as long as the value is below its user priority limit. It is a courtesy to other users to lower your user priority for big chunks of low-priority work. On the other hand, if you lower your user priority limit, you must be superuser to raise it. A typical use of the user priority limit is to reduce permanently the priority of child-processes or of some other set of low-priority processes.

The user priority can never be greater than the user priority limit. If you set the user priority limit below the user priority, the user priority is lowered to the new user priority limit. If you attempt to set the user priority above the user priority limit, the user priority is set to the user priority limit.

Here are some examples of the `-s` option of `priocntl`:

```
# # make process with ID 24668 a real-time process with default parameters:
# priocntl -s -c RT -i pid 24668

# # make 3608 RT with priority 55 and a one-fifth second time slice:
# priocntl -s -c RT -p 55 -t 1 -r 5 -i pid 3608

# # change all processes into time-sharing processes:
# priocntl -s -c TS -i all

# # for uid 1122, reduce TS user priority and user priority limit to -10:
# priocntl -s -c TS -p -10 -m -10 -i uid 1122
```

4. The `-e` option sets scheduler parameters for a specified command and executes the command. The syntax for this option is

> `priocntl -e -c` *class class_options command [command arguments]*

The class and class options are the same as for the `-s` option described above.

```
# # start a real-time shell with default real-time priority:
# priocntl -e -c RT /bin/sh

$ # run make with a time-sharing  user priority of -10:
$ priocntl -e -c TS -p -10 make bigprog
```

The `priocntl` command subsumes the function of `nice`, which continues to work as in previous releases. `nice` works only on time-sharing processes and uses higher numbers to assign lower priorities. The final example above is equivalent to using `nice` to set an "increment" of 10:

```
nice -10 make bigprog
```

The priocntl system call

```
#include      <sys/types.h>
#include      <sys/procset.h>
#include      <sys/priocntl.h>
#include      <sys/rtpriocntl.h>
#include      <sys/tspriocntl.h>

long priocntl(idtype_t idtype, id_t id, int cmd,
      cmd_struct arg);
```

The `priocntl` system call gets or sets scheduler parameters of a set of processes. The input arguments:

- `idtype` is the type of ID you are specifying.

- `id` is the ID.

- `cmd` specifies which `priocntl` function to perform. The functions are listed in the table below.

- `arg` is a pointer to a structure that depends on `cmd`.

Here are the valid values for *idtype*, which are defined in `priocntl.h`, and their corresponding ID types in *id*:

idtype	Interpretation of id
P_PID	process ID (of a single process)
P_PPID	parent-process ID
P_PGID	process group ID
P_SID	session ID
P_CID	class ID
P_UID	effective user ID
P_GID	effective group ID
P_ALL	all processes

Here are the valid values for `cmd`, their meanings, and the type of `arg`:

priocntl Commands		
cmd	arg Type	Function
PC_GETCID	pcinfo_t	get class ID and attributes
PC_GETCLINFO	pcinfo_t	get class name and attributes
PC_SETPARMS	pcparms_t	set class and scheduling parameters
PC_GETPARMS	pcparms_t	get class and scheduling parameters

Here are the values `priocntl` returns on success:

- The GETCID and GETCLINFO commands return the number of configured scheduler classes.

- PC_SETPARMS returns 0.

- PC_GETPARMS returns the process ID of the process whose scheduler properties it is returning.

On failure, `priocntl` returns −1 and sets `errno` to indicate the reason for the failure. See `priocntl`(2) for the complete list of error conditions.

PC_GETCID, PC_GETCLINFO

The PC_GETCID and PC_GETCLINFO commands retrieve scheduler parameters
for a class based on the class ID or class name. Both commands use the pcinfo
structure to send arguments and receive return values:

```
typedef struct pcinfo {
    id_t  pc_cid;                       /* class id */
    char  pc_clname[PC_CLNMSZ];         /* class name */
    long  pc_clinfo[PC_CLINFOSZ];       /* class information */
} pcinfo_t;
```

The PC_GETCID command gets scheduler class ID and parameters given the
class name. The class ID is used in some of the other priocntl commands to
specify a scheduler class. The valid class names are TS for time-sharing and RT
for real-time.

For the real-time class, pc_clinfo contains an rtinfo structure, which holds
rt_maxpri, the maximum valid real-time priority; in the default configuration,
this is the highest priority any process can have. The minimum valid real-time
priority is zero. rt_maxpri is a configurable value; the *System Administrator's
Guide* tells how to configure process priorities.

```
typedef struct rtinfo {
    short  rt_maxpri;  /* maximum real-time priority */
} rtinfo_t;
```

For the time-sharing class, pc_clinfo contains a tsinfo structure, which
holds ts_maxupri, the maximum time-sharing user priority. The minimum
time-sharing user priority is – ts_maxupri. ts_maxupri is also a
configurable value.

```
typedef struct tsinfo {
    short  ts_maxupri;  /* limits of user priority range */
} tsinfo_t;
```

The following program is a cheap substitute for priocntl –l; it gets and
prints the range of valid priorities for the time-sharing and real-time scheduler
classes.

```
/*
 *  Get scheduler class IDs and priority ranges.
 */

#include <sys/types.h>
#include <sys/priocntl.h>
#include <sys/rtpriocntl.h>
#include <sys/tspriocntl.h>
#include <stdio.h>
#include <string.h>
#include <stdlib.h>
#include <errno.h>

main ()
{
        pcinfo_t        pcinfo;
        tsinfo_t        *tsinfop;
        rtinfo_t        *rtinfop;
        short           maxtsupri, maxrtpri;

    /* time sharing */
        (void) strcpy (pcinfo.pc_clname, "TS");
        if (priocntl (0L, 0L, PC_GETCID, &pcinfo) == -1L) {
                perror ("PC_GETCID failed for time-sharing class");
                exit (1);
        }
        tsinfop = (struct tsinfo *) pcinfo.pc_clinfo;
        maxtsupri = tsinfop->ts_maxupri;
        (void) printf("Time sharing: ID %ld, priority range -%d through %d\n",
                pcinfo.pc_cid, maxtsupri, maxtsupri);

    /* real time */
        (void) strcpy(pcinfo.pc_clname, "RT");
        if (priocntl (0L, 0L, PC_GETCID, &pcinfo) == -1L) {
                perror ("PC_GETCID failed for real-time class");
                exit (2);
        }
        rtinfop = (struct rtinfo *) pcinfo.pc_clinfo;
        maxrtpri = rtinfop->rt_maxpri;
        (void) printf("Real time:    ID %ld, priority range 0 through %d\n",
                pcinfo.pc_cid, maxrtpri);
        return (0);
}
```

The following screen shows the output of this program, called `getcid` in this example.

```
$ getcid
Time sharing: ID 1, priority range -20 through 20
Real time:    ID 2, priority range 0 through 59
```

The following function is useful in the examples below. Given a class name, it uses `PC_GETCID` to return the class ID and maximum priority in the class.

 NOTE All the following examples omit the lines that include header files. The examples compile with the same header files as in the first example above.

```
/*
 *  Return class ID and maximum priority.
 *  Input argument name is class name.
 *  Maximum priority is returned in *maxpri.
 */

id_t
schedinfo (name, maxpri)
        char *name;
        short *maxpri;
{
        pcinfo_t        info;
        tsinfo_t        *tsinfop;
        rtinfo_t        *rtinfop;

        (void) strcpy(info.pc_clname, name);
        if (priocntl (0L, 0L, PC_GETCID, &info) == -1L) {
                return (-1);
        }
        if (strcmp(name, "TS") == 0) {
                tsinfop = (struct tsinfo *) info.pc_clinfo;
                *maxpri = tsinfop->ts_maxupri;
        } else if (strcmp(name, "RT") == 0) {
                rtinfop = (struct rtinfo *) info.pc_clinfo;
                *maxpri = rtinfop->rt_maxpri;
        } else {
                return (-1);
        }
        return (info.pc_cid);
}
```

The PC_GETCLINFO command gets a scheduler class name and parameters given the class ID. This command makes it easy to write applications that make no assumptions about what classes are configured.

The following program uses PC_GETCLINFO to get the class name of a process based on the process ID. This program assumes the existence of a function getclassID, which retrieves the class ID of a process given the process ID; this function is given in the following section.

```
/* Get scheduler class name given process ID. */

main (argc, argv)
        int argc;
        char *argv[];
{
        pcinfo_t        pcinfo;
        id_t            pid, classID;
        id_t            getclassID();

        if ((pid = atoi(argv[1])) <= 0) {
                perror ("bad pid");
                exit (1);
        }
        if ((classID = getclassID(pid)) == -1) {
                perror ("unknown class ID");
                exit (2);
        }
        pcinfo.pc_cid = classID;
        if (priocntl (0L, 0L, PC_GETCLINFO, &pcinfo) == -1L) {
                perror ("PC_GETCLINFO failed");
                exit (3);
        }
        (void) printf("process ID %d, class %s\n", pid, pcinfo.pc_clname);
}
```

PC_GETPARMS, PC_SETPARMS

The PC_GETPARMS command gets and the PC_SETPARMS command sets
scheduler parameters for processes. Both commands use the pcparms structure
to send arguments or receive return values:

```
typedef struct pcparms {
    id_t  pc_cid;                       /* process class */
    long  pc_clparms[PC_CLPARMSZ];      /* class specific */
} pcparms_t;
```

Ignoring class-specific information for the moment, we can write a simple function for returning the scheduler class ID of a process, as promised in the previous section.

```
/*
 *  Return scheduler class ID of process with ID pid.
 */

getclassID (pid)
        id_t pid;
{
        pcparms_t        pcparms;

        pcparms.pc_cid = PC_CLNULL;
        if (priocntl(P_PID, pid, PC_GETPARMS, &pcparms) == -1) {
                return (-1);
        }
        return (pcparms.pc_cid);
}
```

For the real-time class, pc_clparms contains an rtparms structure. rtparms holds scheduler parameters specific to the real-time class:

```
typedef struct rtparms {
    short   rt_pri;      /* real-time priority */
    ulong   rt_tqsecs;   /* seconds in time quantum */
    long    rt_tqnsecs;  /* additional nsecs in quantum */
} rtparms_t;
```

rt_pri is the real-time priority; rt_tqsecs is the number of seconds and rt_tqnsecs is the number of additional nanoseconds in a time slice. That is, rt_tqsecs seconds plus rt_tqnsecs nanoseconds is the interval a process may use the CPU without sleeping before the scheduler gives another process a chance at the CPU.

For the time-sharing class, pc_clparms contains a tsparms structure. tsparms holds the scheduler parameter specific to the time-sharing class:

```
typedef struct tsparms {
    short   ts_uprilim;  /* user priority limit */
    short   ts_upri;     /* user priority */
} tsparms_t;
```

ts_upri is the user priority, the user-controlled component of a time-sharing priority. ts_uprilim is the user priority limit, the maximum user priority a process may set for itself without being superuser. These values are described above in the discussion of the -s option of the priocntl command. Both the user priority and the user priority limit must be within the range reported by the priocntl -l command; this range is also reported by the PC_GETCID and PC_GETCLINFO commands to the priocntl system call.

The PC_GETPARMS command gets the scheduler class and parameters of a single process. The return value of the priocntl is the process ID of the process whose parameters are returned in the pcparms structure. The process chosen depends on the idtype and id arguments to priocntl and on the value of pcparms.pc_cid, which contains PC_CLNULL or a class ID returned by PC_GETCID:

Figure 3-6: What Gets Returned by PC_GETPARMS

Number of Processes Selected by idtype and id	pc_cid		
	RT class ID	TS class ID	PC_CLNULL
1	RT parameters of process selected	TS parameters of process selected	class and parameters of process selected
More than 1	RT parameters of highest-priority RT process	TS parameters of process with highest user priority	(error)

If idtype and id select a single process and pc_cid does not conflict with the class of that process, priocntl returns the scheduler parameters of the process. If they select more than one process of a single scheduler class, priocntl returns parameters using class-specific criteria as shown in the table. priocntl returns an error in the following cases:

- idtype and id select one or more processes and none is in the class specified by pc_cid.

- idtype and id select more than one process process and pc_cid is PC_CLNULL.

- idtype and id select no processes.

The following program takes a process ID as its input and prints the scheduler class and class-specific parameters of that process:

```
/*
 *   Get scheduler class and parameters of
 *   process whose pid is input argument.
 */

main (argc, argv)
        int argc;
        char *argv[];
{
        pcparms_t       pcparms;
        rtparms_t       *rtparmsp;
        tsparms_t       *tsparmsp;
        id_t            pid, rtID, tsID;
        id_t            schedinfo();
        short           priority, tsmaxpri, rtmaxpri;
        ulong           secs;
        long            nsecs;

        pcparms.pc_cid = PC_CLNULL;
        rtparmsp = (rtparms_t *) pcparms.pc_clparms;
        tsparmsp = (tsparms_t *) pcparms.pc_clparms;
        if ((pid = atoi(argv[1])) <= 0) {
                perror ("bad pid");
                exit (1);
        }

/* get scheduler properties for this pid */
        if (priocntl(P_PID, pid, PC_GETPARMS, &pcparms) == -1) {
                perror ("GETPARMS failed");
                exit (2);
        }

/* get class IDs and maximum priorities for TS and RT */
        if ((tsID = schedinfo ("TS", &tsmaxpri)) == -1) {
                perror ("schedinfo failed for TS");
                exit (3);
        }
```

(continued on next page)

```
         if ((rtID = schedinfo ("RT", &rtmaxpri)) == -1) {
                 perror ("schedinfo failed for RT");
                 exit (4);
         }

   /* print results */
      if (pcparms.pc_cid == rtID) {
              priority = rtparmsp->rt_pri;
              secs = rtparmsp->rt_tqsecs;
              nsecs =  rtparmsp->rt_tqnsecs;
              (void) printf ("process %d: RT priority %d\n",
                      pid, priority);
              (void) printf ("  time slice %ld secs, %ld nsecs\n",
                      secs, nsecs);
      } else if (pcparms.pc_cid == tsID) {
              priority = tsparmsp->ts_upri;
              (void) printf ("process %d: TS priority %d\n",
                      pid, priority);
      } else {
              printf ("Unknown scheduler class %d\n",
                      pcparms.pc_cid);
              exit (5);
      }
      return (0);
}
```

The PC_SETPARMS command sets the scheduler class and parameters of a set of
processes. The idtype and id input arguments specify the processes to be
changed. The pcparms structure contains the new parameters: pc_cid contains the ID of the scheduler class to which the processes are to be assigned, as
returned by PC_GETCID; pc_clparms contains the class-specific parameters:

- If pc_cid is the real-time class ID, pc_clparms contains an rtparms
  structure in which rt_pri contains the real-time priority and
  rt_tqsecs plus rt_tqnsecs contains the time slice to be assigned to
  the processes.

- If pc_cid is the time-sharing class ID, pc_clparms contains a tsparms
  structure in which ts_uprilim contains the user priority limit and
  ts_upri contains the user priority to be assigned to the processes.

The following program takes a process ID as input, makes the process a real-time process with the highest valid priority minus 1, and gives it the default time slice for that priority. The program calls the schedinfo function listed above to get the real-time class ID and maximum priority.

```
/*
 *  Input arg is proc ID.  Make process a real-time
 *  process with highest priority minus 1.
 */

main (argc, argv)
        int argc;
        char *argv[];
{
        pcparms_t       pcparms;
        rtparms_t       *rtparmsp;
        id_t            pid, rtID;
        id_t            schedinfo();
        short           maxrtpri;

        if ((pid = atoi(argv[1])) <= 0) {
                perror ("bad pid");
                exit (1);
        }

    /* Get highest valid RT priority. */
        if ((rtID = schedinfo ("RT", &maxrtpri)) == -1) {
                perror ("schedinfo failed for RT");
                exit (2);
        }

    /*  Change proc to RT, highest prio - 1, default time slice */
        pcparms.pc_cid = rtID;
        rtparmsp = (struct rtparms *) pcparms.pc_clparms;
        rtparmsp->rt_pri = maxrtpri - 1;
        rtparmsp->rt_tqnsecs = RT_TQDEF;

        if (priocntl(P_PID, pid, PC_SETPARMS, &pcparms) == -1) {
                perror ("PC_SETPARMS failed");
                exit (3);
        }
}
```

The following table lists the special values rt_tqnsecs can take when
PC_SETPARMS is used on real-time processes. When any of these is used,
rt_tqsecs is ignored. These values are defined in the header file
rtpriocntl.h:

rt_tqnsecs	Time Slice
RT_TQINF	infinite
RT_TQDEF	default
RT_NOCHANGE	unchanged

RT_TQINF specifies an infinite time slice. RT_TQDEF specifies the default time
slice configured for the real-time priority being set with the SETPARMS call.
RT_NOCHANGE specifies no change from the current time slice; this value is useful, for example, when you change process priority but do not wish to change
the time slice. (You can also use RT_NOCHANGE in the rt_pri field to change a
time slice without changing the priority.)

The priocntlset system call

```
#include     <sys/types.h>
#include     <sys/signal.h>
#include     <sys/procset.h>
#include     <sys/priocntl.h>
#include     <sys/rtpriocntl.h>
#include     <sys/tspriocntl.h>

long priocntlset(procset_t *psp, int cmd,
     cmd_struct arg);
```

The priocntlset system call changes scheduler parameters of a set of
processes, just like priocntl. priocntlset has the same command set as
priocntl; the cmd and arg input arguments are the same. But while
priocntl applies to a set of processes specified by a single idtype/id pair,
priocntlset applies to a set of processes that results from a logical combination of two idtype/id pairs. The input argument psp points to a procset
structure that specifies the two idtype/id pairs and the logical operation to
perform. This structure is defined in procset.h:

```
typedef struct procset {
        idop_t    p_op;              /* operator connecting */
                                     /* left and right sets */
    /* left set:  */
        idtype_t  p_lidtype;         /* left ID type */
        id_t      p_lid;             /* left ID */

    /* right set:  */
        idtype_t  p_ridtype;         /* right ID type */
        id_t      p_rid;             /* right ID */
} procset_t;
```

p_lidtype and p_lid specify the ID type and ID of one ("left") set of processes; p_ridtype and p_rid specify the ID type and ID of a second ("right") set of processes. p_op specifies the operation to perform on the two sets of processes to get the set of processes to operate on. The valid values for p_op and the processes they specify are:

- POP_DIFF: set difference—processes in left set and not in right set

- POP_AND: set intersection—processes in both left and right sets

- POP_OR: set union—processes in either left or right sets or both

- POP_XOR: set exclusive-or—processes in left or right set but not in both

The following macro, also defined in procset.h, offers a convenient way to initialize a procset structure :

```
#define setprocset(psp, op, ltype, lid, rtype, rid) \
            (psp)->p_op       = (op); \
            (psp)->p_lidtype  = (ltype); \
            (psp)->p_lid      = (lid); \
            (psp)->p_ridtype  = (rtype); \
            (psp)->p_rid      = (rid);
```

Here is a situation where priocntlset would be useful: suppose an application had both real-time and time-sharing processes that ran under a single user ID. If the application wanted to change the priority of only its real-time processes without changing the time-sharing processes to real-time processes, it could do so as follows. (This example uses the function schedinfo, which is defined above in the section on PC_GETCID.)

```
/*
 *  Change real-time priorities of this uid
 *  to highest real-time priority minus 1.
 */
main (argc, argv)
        int argc;
        char *argv[];
{
        procset_t       procset;
        pcparms_t       pcparms;
        struct rtparms  *rtparmsp;
        id_t            rtclassID;
        id_t            schedinfo();
        short           maxrtpri;
    /* left set: select processes with same uid as this process */
        procset.p_lidtype = P_UID;
        procset.p_lid = getuid();

    /* get info on real-time class */
        if ((rtclassID = schedinfo ("RT", &maxrtpri)) == -1) {
                perror ("schedinfo failed");
                exit (1);
        }

    /* right set: select real-time processes */
        procset.p_ridtype = P_CID;
        procset.p_rid = rtclassID;

    /* select only my RT processes */
        procset.p_op = POP_AND;

    /* specify new scheduler parameters */
        pcparms.pc_cid = rtclassID;
        rtparmsp = (struct rtparms *) pcparms.pc_clparms;
        rtparmsp->rt_pri = maxrtpri - 1;
        rtparmsp->rt_tqnsecs = RT_NOCHANGE;
        if (priocntlset (&procset, PC_SETPARMS, &pcparms) == -1) {
                perror ("priocntlset failed");
                exit (2);
        }
}
```

`priocntl` offers a simple scheduler interface that is adequate for many applications; applications that need a more powerful way to specify sets of processes can use `priocntlset`.

Scheduler Interaction with Other Functions

Kernel Processes

The kernel assigns its demon and housekeeping processes to the system scheduler class. Users may neither add processes to nor remove processes from this class, nor may they change the priorities of these processes. The command ps -cel lists the scheduler class of all processes. Processes in the system class are identified by a SYS entry in the CLS column.

If the workload on a machine contains real-time processes that use too much CPU, they can lock out system processes, which can lead to all sorts of trouble. Real-time applications must ensure that they leave some CPU time for system and other processes.

fork, exec

Scheduler class, priority, and other scheduler parameters are inherited across the fork(2) and exec(2) system calls.

nice

The nice(1) command and the nice(2) system call work as in previous versions of the UNIX system. They allow you to change the priority of only a time-sharing process. You still use use lower numeric values to assign higher time-sharing priorities with these functions.

To change the scheduler class of a process or to specify a real-time priority, you must use one of the priocntl functions. You use higher numeric values to assign higher priorities with the priocntl functions.

init

The init process is treated as a special case by the scheduler. To change the scheduler properties of init, init must be the only process specified by idtype and id or by the procset structure.

Scheduler Performance

Because the scheduler determines when and for how long processes run, it has an overriding importance in the performance and perceived performance of a system.

By default, all processes are time-sharing processes. A process changes class only as a result of one of the `priocntl` functions.

In the default configuration, all real-time process priorities are above any time-sharing process priority. This implies that as long as any real-time process is runnable, no time-sharing process or system process ever runs. So if a real-time application is not written carefully, it can completely lock out users and essential kernel housekeeping.

Besides controlling process class and priorities, a real-time application must also control several other factors that influence its performance. The most important factors in performance are CPU power, amount of primary memory, and I/O throughput. These factors interact in complex ways. For more information, see the chapter on performance management in the *System Administrator's Guide*. In particular, the `sar`(1) command has options for reporting on all the factors discussed in this section.

Process State Transition

Applications that have strict real-time constraints may need to prevent processes from being swapped or paged out to secondary memory. Here's a simplified overview of UNIX process states and the transitions between states:

Figure 3-7: Process State Transition Diagram

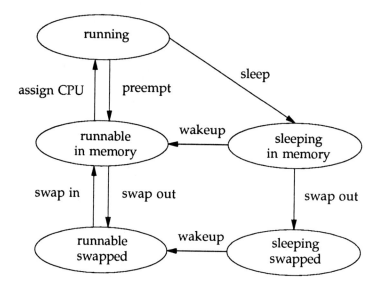

An active process is normally in one of the five states in the diagram. The arrows show how it changes states.

■ A process is running if it is assigned to a CPU. A process is preempted—that is, removed from the running state—by the scheduler if a process with a higher priority becomes runnable. A process is also preempted if it consumes its entire time slice and a process of equal priority is runnable.

■ A process is runnable in memory if it is in primary memory and ready to run, but is not assigned to a CPU.

■ A process is sleeping in memory if it is in primary memory but is waiting for a specific event before it can continue execution. For example, a process is sleeping if it is waiting for an I/O operation to complete, for a locked resource to be unlocked, or for a timer to expire. When the event occurs, the process is sent a wakeup; if the reason for its sleep is gone, the process becomes runnable.

■ A process is runnable and swapped if it is not waiting for a specific event but has had its whole address space written to secondary memory to make room in primary memory for other processes.

■ A process is sleeping and swapped if it is both waiting for a specific event and has had its whole address space written to secondary memory to make room in primary memory for other processes.

If a machine does not have enough primary memory to hold all its active processes, it must page or swap some address space to secondary memory:

■ When the system is short of primary memory, it writes individual pages of some processes to secondary memory but still leaves those processes runnable. When a process runs, if it accesses those pages, it must sleep while the pages are read back into primary memory.

■ When the system gets into a more serious shortage of primary memory, it writes all the pages of some processes to secondary memory and marks those processes as swapped. Such processes get back into a schedulable state only by being chosen by the system scheduler demon process, then read back into memory.

Both paging and swapping, and especially swapping, introduce delay when a process is ready to run again. For processes that have strict timing requirements, this delay can be unacceptable. To avoid swapping delays, real-time processes are never swapped, though parts of them may be paged. An application can prevent paging and swapping by locking its text and data into primary memory. For more information see memcntl(2) in the *Programmer's Reference Manual*. Of course, how much can be locked is limited by how much memory is configured. Also, locking too much can cause intolerable delays to processes that do not have their text and data locked into memory. Tradeoffs between performance of real-time processes and performance of other processes depend on local needs. On some systems, process locking may be required to guarantee the necessary real-time response.

Software Latencies

Designers of some real-time applications must have information on software latencies to analyze the performance characteristics of their applications and to predict whether performance constraints can be met. These latencies depend on kernel implementation and on system hardware, so it is not practical to list the latencies. It is useful, however, to describe some of the most important latencies. Consider the following time-line:

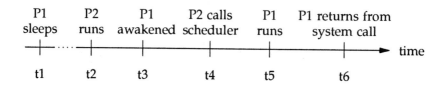

P1 and P2 represent processes; t1 through t6 represent points in time. Suppose that P1 has a higher priority than all other active processes, including P2. P1 runs and does a system call that causes it to sleep at time t1, waiting for I/O. P2 runs. The I/O device interrupts, resulting in a wakeup at time t3 that makes P1 runnable. If P2 is running in user mode at time t3, it is preempted immediately and the interval (t4 − t3) is, for practical purposes, zero. If P2 is running in kernel mode at time t3, it is preempted as soon as it gets to a kernel preemption point, a point in kernel code where data structures are in a consistent state and where the state of the current process (P2 in this example) may be saved and a different process run. Therefore, if P2 is running in kernel mode at time t3, the interval (t4 − t3) depends on kernel preemption points, which are spread throughout the kernel. It is useful to know both a typical time to preemption and a maximum time to preemption; these times depend on kernel implementation and on hardware. Eventually, the scheduler runs (at time t4), finds that a higher-priority process P1 is runnable, and runs it. We refer to the interval (t5 − t4) as the software switch latency of the system. This latency is, for practical purposes, a constant; again it is an implementation-dependent value. At time t6, P1 returns to the user program from the system call that put it to sleep at time t1. For simplicity, suppose that the program is getting only a few bytes of data from the I/O device. In this simple case, the interval (t6 − t5) consists basically of the overhead of getting out of the system call. We refer to the interval (t6 − t3) as the software wakeup latency of the system; this is the interval from the I/O device interrupt until the user process returns to application level to deal with the interrupt (assuming that it is the highest priority process). So the software wakeup latency is composed of a preemption latency, context-switch time, and a part of system call overhead. Of course, the latency increases as the system call asks for more data.

This discussion of latencies assumes that the text and data of the processes are in primary memory. An application may have to use process locking to guarantee that its processes do not get swapped or paged out of primary memory. See the discussion in the previous section.

Signals

A signal is an asynchronous notification of an event, and is the most frequently used means for one process to indicate the occurrence of some event that may have an impact on another process. Process signalling involves two specific functions:

- the function `kill` which sends a signal.

- the function `sigaction` which establishes how to handle a signal.

A signal is said to be "generated for" (or "sent to") a process when the event that causes the signal first occurs. Examples of such events include hardware-faults, timer-expiration and terminal-activity as well as any call to `kill` [see `kill`(2) in the *Programmer's Reference Manual*]. In some circumstances, the same event generates signals for multiple processes.

There are two categories of signals, those generated externally, such as a break from a terminal, and those generated internally (a process fault). Both types are treated identically. There are several ways a signal can be generated, some of which are:

- A user-mode attempting to write into protected memory.

- An error during a system-call.

- Some condition raised at the controlling-terminal of a process (such as break or hangup).

- An explicit system-call to `kill`.

- Expiration of the alarm clock timer or the generation of the trap signal during process tracing.

Signals interrupt the normal flow of control in a process. Signals do not directly affect the execution of a process; but rather, request that the process take some action. Each process has established actions to take in response to signals [see "Signal Actions" in `siginfo`(5)].

A signal is said to be "delivered" to a process when the process receives the signal and takes the action established for it. Signal delivery resembles the occurrence of a hardware interrupt: the signal is normally blocked from further occurrence, the current process context is saved, and a new one is built. A process may specify the handler to which a signal is delivered, or specify that the signal is to be blocked or ignored. A process may also specify that a default action is to be taken when signals occur.

Some signals will cause a process to exit when they are not caught. This may be accompanied by creation of a `core` image file, containing the current memory image of the process for use in post-mortem debugging. A process may choose to have signals delivered on a special stack, so that sophisticated software stack manipulations are possible.

All signals have the same priority. If multiple signals are pending simultaneously, the order in which they are delivered to a process is implementation specific. Signal routines normally execute with the signal that caused their invocation to be blocked, but other signals may yet occur. Mechanisms are provided whereby critical sections of code may protect themselves against the occurrence of specified signals.

Protecting Critical Sections

To block a section of code against one or more signals, a `sigprocmask` call may be used to add a set of signals to the existing mask, and return the old mask:

```
sigprocmask(SIG_BLOCK, mask, omask);
    sigset_t *mask;
    sigset_t *omask;
```

The old mask can then be restored later with `sigprocmask`,

```
sigprocmask(SIG_UNBLOCK, mask, omask);
    sigset_t *mask;
    sigset_t *omask;
```

The `sigprocmask` call can be used to read the current mask without changing it by specifying null pointer as its second argument.

It is possible to check conditions with some signals blocked, and then to pause waiting for a signal and restoring the mask, by using:

```
sigsuspend(mask);
    sigset_t *mask;
```

Signal Types

The signals defined by the system fall into one of five classes: hardware conditions, software conditions, input/output notification, process control, or resource control. The file /usr/include/signal.h defines the set of signals that may be delivered to a process.

Hardware signals are derived from exceptional conditions which may occur during execution. Such signals include SIGFPE representing floating point and other arithmetic exceptions, SIGILL for illegal instruction execution, SIGSEGV for addresses outside the currently assigned area of memory or for accesses that violate memory protection constraints and SIGBUS for accesses that result in hardware related errors. Other, more CPU-specific hardware signals exist, such as SIGABRT, SIGEMT, and SIGTRAP.

Software signals reflect interrupts generated by user request: SIGINT for the normal interrupt signal; SIGQUIT for the more powerful quit signal, that normally causes a core image to be generated; SIGHUP and SIGTERM that cause graceful process termination, either because a user has hung up, or by user or program request; and SIGKILL, a more powerful termination signal which a process cannot catch or ignore. Programs may define their own asynchronous events using SIGUSR1 and SIGUSR2. Other software signals (SIGALRM, SIGVTALRM, SIGPROF) indicate the expiration of interval timers.

A process can request notification via a SIGPOLL signal when input or output is possible on a descriptor, or when a non-blocking operation completes. A process may request to receive a SIGURG signal when an urgent condition arises.

A process may be stopped by a signal sent to it or the members of its process group. The SIGSTOP signal is a powerful stop signal, because it cannot be caught. Other stop signals SIGTSTP, SIGTTIN, and SIGTTOU are used when a user request, input request, or output request respectively is the reason for stopping the process. A SIGCONT signal is sent to a process when it is continued from a stopped state. Processes may receive notification with a SIGCHLD signal when a child-process changes state, either by stopping or by terminating.

Exceeding resource limits may cause signals to be generated. SIGXCPU occurs when a process nears its CPU time limit and SIGXFSZ warns that the limit on file size creation has been reached.

Signal Handlers

For each signal, the `<signal.h>` header file establishes the default signal-action to be one of the following:

Abort   On receipt of the signal, the receiving-process terminates abnormally with all the consequences outlined in exit.

Exit   On receipt of the signal, the receiving-process terminates normally with all the consequences outlined in exit.

Stop   On receipt of the signal, the receiving-process stops.

Ignore   On receipt of the signal, the receiving-process ignores it.

As the default action for a signal typically is to terminate a process, a process must use `sigaction` to alter the default action for a signal and to prearrange how it will handle the signal. The function `sigaction` takes three arguments:

■ the first argument specifies the signal.

■ the second argument specifies how to handle it.

■ the third argument returns the previous signal-action.

The first argument to `sigaction` is just an integer code number that represents a signal. The second and third arguments designate one of three types of actions that can be established for a signal:

1. to take the default action for the signal — `SIG_DFL`

2. to ignore the signal — `SIG_IGN`

3. to catch the signal by calling a function — *a pointer to a signal-action*

The `<signal.h>` header file defines the special values used to request that the default action for the signal be taken (`SIG_DFL`) or that the signal be ignored (`SIG_IGN`) as well as the structure `sigaction` used to specify a signal-handling function. The second and third arguments to the function `sigaction` are pointers to the structure `sigaction` defined by the `<signal.h>` header file. The `<signal.h>` header file also defines symbolic names for the signal-numbers and must always be included when signals are used.

To control the way a signal is delivered, a process calls `sigaction` to associate a handler with that signal. The call

```
#include <signal.h>

struct sigaction {
        void        (*sa_handler)();
        sigset_t    sa_mask;
        int         sa_flags;
};

sigaction(signo, sa, osa)
        int signo;
        struct sigaction *sa;
        struct sigaction *osa;
```

assigns interrupt handler address `sa_handler` to signal `signo`. If `osa` is nonzero, the previous signal action is returned.

Each handler address specifies either an interrupt routine for the signal, that the signal is to be ignored, or that a default action (usually process termination) is to occur if the signal occurs. The constants `SIG_IGN` and `SIG_DFL` used as values for `sa_handler` cause ignoring or defaulting of a condition.

 NOTE There are two things that must be done to reset a signal handler from within a signal handler. Resetting the routine that catches the signal [`signal(n, SIG_DFL);`] is only the first. It's also necessary to unblock the blocked signal, which is done with `sigprocmask`.

`sa_mask` specifies the set of signals to be masked when the handler is invoked; it implicitly includes the signal which invoked the handler. Five operations are permitted on signal sets.

1. A call to `sigemptyset` empties a set.

2. A call to `sigfillset` fills a set with every signal currently supported.

3. A call to `sigaddset` adds specified signals to a set.

4. A call to `sigdelset` deletes specified signals from a set.

5. A call to `sigismember` tests membership in a set.

Signals sets should always be initialized with a call to `sigemptyset` or `sig-fillset`.

`sa_flags` specifies special properties of the signal, such as whether system calls should be restarted if the signal handler returns, if the signal action should be reset to `SIG_DFL` when it is caught, and whether the handler should operate on the normal run-time stack or a special signal stack (see "Signal Stacks" below).

When a signal condition arises for a process, the signal is added to a set of signals pending for the process. If the signal is not currently blocked by the process then it will be delivered. The process of signal delivery adds the signal to be delivered and those signals specified in the associated signal handler's `sa_mask` to a set of those masked for the process, saves the current process context, and places the process in the context of the signal handling routine. The call is arranged so that if the signal handling routine exits normally the signal mask will be restored and the process will resume execution in the original context. If the process wishes to resume in a different context, then it must arrange to restore the signal mask itself.

The mask of blocked signals is independent of handlers for delays. It delays the delivery of signals much as a raised hardware interrupt priority level delays hardware interrupts. Preventing an interrupt from occurring by changing the handler is analogous to disabling a device from further interrupts.

The signal handling routine `sa_handler` is called by a C call of the form

```
(*sa_handler)(signo, infop, ucp);
        int signo;
        siginfo_t *infop;
        ucontext_t *ucp;
```

`signo` gives the number of the signal that occurred. `infop` is either equal to 0, or points to a structure that contains information detailing the reason why the signal was generated. This information must be explicitly asked for when the signal's action is specified. The `ucp` parameter is a pointer to a structure containing the process's context prior to the delivery of the signal, and will be used to restore the process's context upon return from the signal handler.

In the following example, the first call to sigaction causes interrupts to be ignored; while the second call to sigaction restores the default action for interrupts, which is to terminate the process:

```
main() {
    #include <signal.h>
    struct sigaction new_act, old_act;

    new_act.sa_handler = SIG_IGN;
    sigaction(SIGINT, &new_act, &old_act);

    new_act.sa_handler = SIG_DFL;
    sigaction(SIGINT, &new_act, &old_act);
}
```

In both cases, sigaction returns the previous signal-action in the final argument sig_act.

Initially, all signals are set to SIG_DFL or SIG_IGN prior to entry of the function main [see exec(2) in the *Programmer's Reference Manual*]. Once an action is established for a specific signal, it usually remains established until another action is explicitly established by a call to either signal, sigset, sigignore or sigaction, or until the process execs [see signal(2), sigset(2) and sigaction(2) as well as exec(2) in the *Programmer's Reference Manual*]. When a process execs, all signals set to catch the signal are reset to SIG_DFL. Alternatively, a process may request that the action for a signal automatically be reset to SIG_DFL after catching it [see sigaction(2)].

Instead of the special values SIG_IGN or SIG_DFL, the second argument to sigaction may specify a signal-handling function; in which case, the specified function is called when the signal occurs. Most commonly this facility is used to allow the program to clean up unfinished business before terminating, for example to delete a temporary file, as in the following example:

Figure 3-8: Signal programming example

```
#include <signal.h>

main() {
    struct sigaction new_act, old_act;
    void on_intr();

    new_act.sa_handler = SIG_IGN;
    sigaction(SIGINT, &new_act, &old_act);
    if (old_act.sa_handler != SIG_IGN) {
        new_act.sa_handler = on_intr;
        sigaction(SIGINT, &new_act, &old_act);
    }

    /* do processing */

    exit(0);
}

void on_intr() {
    unlink(tempfile);
    exit(1);
}
```

Before establishing on_intr as the signal-handling function for the interrupt signal SIGINT, the program tests the state of interrupt handling, and continues to ignore interrupts if they are already being ignored. This is needed because signals like interrupt are sent to *all* processes started from a specific terminal. Accordingly, when a program runs as a background-process, without any interaction (started by &), the shell turns off interrupts for it so it won't be stopped by interrupts intended for foreground-processes. If this program began by announcing that all interrupts be caught by the function on_intr regardless, that would undo the shell's efforts to protect it when run in the background.

The solution, shown above, is to call sigaction for SIGINT first to get the signal-action currently established for the interrupt signal, which is returned in the third argument to sigaction. If interrupt signals were already being ignored, the process should continue to ignore them; otherwise, they should be caught. In that case, the second call to sigaction for SIGINT establishes a new signal-action which specifies on_intr as the signal-handling function.

Sending Signals

A signal may be sent to a process by another process, from the terminal or by
the system itself. For most signals, a process can arrange to be terminated on
receipt of a signal, to ignore it completely or to catch it and act on it in some
way defined by the user-process. For example, an INTERRUPT signal may be sent
by depressing an appropriate key on the terminal (*delete, break* or *rubout*). The
action taken depends on the requirements of the specific program being executed. For example:

- The shell invokes most commands in such a way that they stop executing
  immediately (die) when an interrupt is received. For example, the `pr`
  (print) command normally dies, allowing the user to stop unwanted output.

- The shell itself ignores interrupts when reading from the terminal because
  the shell should continue execution even when the user terminates a command like `pr`.

- The editor `ed` chooses to catch interrupts so that it can halt its current
  action (especially printing) without allowing itself to be terminated.

A process can send a signal to another process or group of processes with the
calls:

```
kill(pid, signo);
      int pid, signo;
sigsend(idtype, id, signo);
      idtype_t idtype;
      id_t id;
```

Unless the process sending the signal is privileged, its real or effective user ID
must be equal to the receiving process's real or saved user ID.

Signals can also be sent from from a terminal device to the process group or session leader associated with the terminal. See `termio`(7).

Each type of signal is represented by a specific integer value; for example, the value 1 represents the hangup signal. The signal-number indexes the signal-array of the receiving-process. For each type of signal, the signal-array contains the address of a signal-handling function defined in the user-process. If no function has been defined, the entry is 0 or 1. If the value is 1, the signal is set to be ignored; and if 0, the signal is set to take the default action.

A child-process inherits the actions of the parent for the defaulted and ignored signals. Caught signals are reset to the default action in the child-process. This is necessary since the address linkage for signal-handling functions specified in the parent are no longer appropriate in the child.

Signal Stacks

Applications that maintain complex or fixed size stacks can use the call

```
struct sigaltstack {
        caddr_t      ss_sp;
        int    ss_size;
        int    ss_flags;
};

sigaltstack(ss, oss)
        struct sigaltstack *ss;
        struct sigaltstack *oss;
```

to provide the system with a stack based at ss_sp of size ss_size for delivery of signals. The system automatically adjusts for direction of stack growth. ss_flags indicates whether the process is currently on the signal stack, and whether the signal stack is disabled.

When a signal is to be delivered and the process has requested that it be delivered on the alternate stack (see sigaction above), the system checks whether the process is on a signal stack. If it is not, then the process is switched to the signal stack for delivery, with the return from the signal arranged to restore the previous stack.

If the process wishes to take a non-local exit from the signal routine, or run code from the signal stack that uses a different stack, a sigaltstack call should be used to reset the signal stack.

Basic Interprocess Communication – Pipes

The system-call `pipe` creates a *pipe*, a type of unnamed FIFO (First In First Out) file used as an I/O channel between two cooperating processes: one process writes onto the pipe, while the other reads from it. Most pipes are created by the shell, as in:

```
ls | pr
```

which connects the standard output of `ls` to the standard input of `pr`. Sometimes, however, it is most convenient for a process to set up its own plumbing; this section illustrates how to establish and use the pipe connection.

Since a pipe is both for reading and writing, `pipe` returns two file-descriptors as follows:

```
int   fd[2];
stat = pipe(fd);
if (stat == -1)
    /* there was an error ... */
```

where `fd` is an array of two file-descriptors, with `fd[0]` for the read end of the pipe and `fd[1]` for the write end of the pipe. These may be used in `read`, `write` and `close` calls just like any other file-descriptors.

Implementation of pipes consists of implied `lseek` operations before each `read` or `write` in order to implement first-in-first-out. The system looks after buffering the data and synchronizing the two processes to prevent the writer from grossly out-producing the reader and to prevent the reader from overtaking the writer. If a process reads a pipe which is empty, it will wait until data arrive; if a process writes into a pipe which is full, it will wait until the pipe empties somewhat. If the write end of the pipe is closed, a subsequent `read` will encounter end-of-file.

To illustrate the use of pipes in a realistic setting, consider a function `popen(cmd, mode)`, which creates a process `cmd`, and returns a file-descriptor that will either read or write that process, according to `mode`; thus, the call

```
fout = popen("pr", WRITE);
```

creates a process that executes the `pr` command; subsequent `write` calls using the file-descriptor `fout` send data to that process through the pipe.

Figure 3-9: popen

```
#include <stdio.h>

#define    READ    0
#define    WRITE   1
#define    tst(a, b) (mode == READ ? (b) : (a))
static     int popen_pid;

popen(cmd, mode)
    char *cmd;
    int  mode;
{
    int p[2];

    if (pipe(p) < 0)
        return(NULL);

    if ((popen_pid = fork( )) == 0) {
        close(tst(p[WRITE], p[READ]));
        close(tst(0, 1));
        dup(tst(p[READ], p[WRITE]));
        close(tst(p[READ], p[WRITE]));
        execl("/bin/sh", "sh", "-c", cmd, 0);
        _exit(1) /* disaster occurred if we got here */
    }
    if (popen_pid == -1)
        return(NULL);

    close(tst(p[READ], p[WRITE]));
    return(tst(p[WRITE], p[READ]));
}
```

The function popen first calls pipe to create a pipe, then calls fork to create two copies of itself. The child decides whether it is supposed to read or write, closes the other end of the pipe, then calls the shell (via execl) to run the desired process. The parent likewise closes the end of the pipe it does not use. These close operations are necessary to make end-of-file tests work properly. For example, if a child that intends to read fails to close the write end of the pipe, it will never encounter the end-of-file on the pipe, just because there is one writer potentially active. The sequence of close operations in the child is a bit tricky. Suppose that the task is to create a child-process that will read data from the parent. Then the first close closes the write end of the pipe, leaving the read end open.

To associate a pipe with the standard input of the child, use the following:

```
close(tst(0, 1));
dup(tst(p[READ], p[WRITE]));
```

The `close` call closes file-descriptor 0, the standard input, then the `dup` call returns a duplicate of the open file-descriptor. File-descriptors are assigned in increasing order and `dup` returns the first available one, so the `dup` call effectively copies the file-descriptor for the pipe (read end) to file-descriptor 0 making the read end of the pipe the standard input. (This may seem a bit tricky, but it's a standard idiom.) Finally, the old read end of the pipe is closed. A similar sequence of operations takes place when the child-process must write to the parent-process instead of reading from it.

To finish the job we need a function `pclose` to close a pipe created by `popen`.

Figure 3-10: pclose

```
#include <signal.h>

pclose(fd)       /* close pipe descriptor */
    int fd;
{
    struct sigaction o_act, h_act, i_act, q_act;
    extern pid_t popen_pid;
    pid_t c_pid;
    int   c_stat;

    close(fd);

    sigaction(SIGINT, SIG_IGN, &i_act);
    sigaction(SIGQUIT, SIG_IGN, &q_act);
    sigaction(SIGHUP, SIG_IGN, &h_act);

    while ((c_pid=wait(&c_stat))!=-1 && c_pid!=popen_pid);
    if (c_pid == -1)
       c_stat = -1;

    sigaction(SIGINT, &i_act, &o_act);
    sigaction(SIGQUIT, &q_act, &o_act);
    sigaction(SIGHUP, &h_act, &o_act);

    return(c_stat);
}
```

The main reason for using a separate function rather than close is that it is desirable to wait for the termination of the child-process. First, the return value from pclose indicates whether the process succeeded. Equally important when a process creates several children is that only a bounded number of unwaited-for children can exist, even if some of them have terminated; performing the wait lays the child to rest. The calls to sigaction make sure that no interrupts, etc., interfere with the waiting process [see sigaction(2)].

The routine as written has the limitation that only one pipe may be open at once, because of the single shared variable popen_pid; it really should be an array indexed by file-descriptor. A popen function, with slightly different arguments and return value is available as part of the Standard I/O Library [see stdio(3S)].

4   Interprocess Communication

4. INTERPROCESS COMMUNICATION

Introduction

UNIX System V Release 4.0 provides several mechanisms that allow processes to exchange data and synchronize execution. The simpler of these mechanisms are pipes, named pipes, and signals. These are limited, however, in what they can do. For instance,

- Pipes do not allow unrelated processes to communicate.

- Named pipes allow unrelated processes to communicate, but they cannot provide private channels for pairs of communicating processes; that is, any process with appropriate permission may read from or write to a named pipe.

- Sending signals, via the kill system call, allows arbitrary processes to communicate, but the message consists only of the signal number.

Release 4.0 also provides an InterProcess Communication (IPC) package that supports three, more versatile types of interprocess communication. For example,

- Messages allow processes to send formatted data streams to arbitrary processes.

- Semaphores allow processes to synchronize execution.

- Shared memory allows processes to share parts of their virtual address space.

When implemented as a unit, these three mechanisms share common properties such as

- each mechanism contains a "get" system call to create a new entry or retrieve an existing one

- each mechanism contains a "control" system call to query the status of an entry, to set status information, or to remove the entry from the system

- each mechanism contains an "operations" system call to perform various operations on an entry

This chapter describes the system calls for each of these three forms of IPC.

This information is for programmers who write multiprocess applications. These programmers should have a general understanding of what semaphores are and how they are used.

Information from other sources would also be helpful. See the `ipcs`(1) and `ipcrm`(1) manual pages in the *User's Reference Manual* and the following manual pages in the *Programmer's Reference Manual*:

`intro`(2)		
`msgget`(2)	`msgctl`(2)	`msgop`(2)
`semget`(2)	`semctl`(2)	`semop`(2)
`shmget`(2)	`shmctl`(2)	`shmop`(2)

Included in this chapter are several example programs that show the use of these IPC system calls. Since there are many ways to accomplish the same task or requirement, keep in mind that the example programs were written for clarity and not for program efficiency. Usually, system calls are embedded within a larger user-written program that makes use of a particular function provided by the calls.

Messages

The message type of IPC allows processes (executing programs) to communicate through the exchange of data stored in buffers. This data is transmitted between processes in discrete portions called messages. Processes using this type of IPC can send and receive messages.

Before a process can send or receive a message, it must have the UNIX operating system generate the necessary software mechanisms to handle these operations. A process does this using the msgget system call. In doing this, the process becomes the owner/creator of a message queue and specifies the initial operation permissions for all processes, including itself. Subsequently, the owner/creator can relinquish ownership or change the operation permissions using the msgctl system call. However, the creator remains the creator as long as the facility exists. Other processes with permission can use msgctl to perform various other control functions.

Processes which have permission and are attempting to send or receive a message can suspend execution if they are unsuccessful at performing their operation. That is, a process which is attempting to send a message can wait until it becomes possible to post the message to the specified message queue; the receiving process isn't involved (except indirectly, e.g., if the consumer isn't consuming, the queue space will eventually be exhausted) and vice versa. A process which specifies that execution is to be suspended is performing a "blocking message operation." A process which does not allow its execution to be suspended is performing a "nonblocking message operation."

A process performing a blocking message operation can be suspended until one of three conditions occurs:

- It is successful.

- It receives a signal.

- The message queue is removed from the system.

System calls make these message capabilities available to processes. The calling process passes arguments to a system call, and the system call either successfully or unsuccessfully performs its function. If the system call is successful, it performs its function and returns applicable information. Otherwise, a known error code (-1) is returned to the process, and an external error number variable, errno, is set accordingly.

Using Messages

Before a message can be sent or received, a uniquely identified message queue and data structure must be created. The unique identifier is called the message queue identifier (msqid); it is used to identify or refer to the associated message queue and data structure.

The message queue is used to store (header) information about each message being sent or received. This information, which is for internal use by the system, includes the following for each message:

- pointer to the next message on queue
- message type
- message text size
- message text address

There is one associated data structure for the uniquely identified message queue. This data structure contains the following information related to the message queue:

- operation permissions data (operation permission structure)
- pointer to first message on the queue
- pointer to last message on the queue
- current number of bytes on the queue
- number of messages on the queue
- maximum number of bytes on the queue
- process identification (PID) of last message sender
- PID of last message receiver
- last message send time
- last message receive time
- last change time

The structure definition for the associated data structure is as follows:

```
struct msqid_ds
{
        struct ipc_perm  msg_perm;     /* operation permission struct */
        struct msg       *msg_first;   /* ptr to first message on q */
        struct msg       *msg_last;    /* ptr to last message on q */
        ulong            msg_cbytes;   /* current # bytes on q */
        ulong            msg_qnum;     /* # of messages on q */
        ulong            msg_qbytes;   /* max # of bytes on q */
        pid_t            msg_lspid;    /* pid of last msgsnd */
        pid_t            msg_lrpid;    /* pid of last msgrcv */
        time_t           msg_stime;    /* last msgsnd time */
        long             msg_pad1;     /* reserved for time_t expansion */
        time_t           msg_rtime;    /* last msgrcv time */
        long             msg_pad2;     /* time_t expansion */
        time_t           msg_ctime;    /* last change time */
        long             msg_pad3;     /* time expansion */
        long             msg_pad4[4];  /* reserve area*/
};
```

It is located in the <sys/msg.h> header file. Note that the msg_perm member of this structure uses ipc_perm as a template. Figure 4-1 shows the breakout for the operation permissions data structure.

The definition of the ipc_perm data structure is as follows:

Figure 4-1: `ipc_perm` **Data Structure**

```
struct ipc_perm
{
        uid_t    uid;       /* owner's user id */
        gid_t    gid;       /* owner's group id */
        uid_t    cuid;      /* creator's user id */
        gid_t    cgid;      /* creator's group id */
        mode_t   mode;      /* access modes */
        ulong    seq;       /* slot usage sequence number */
        key_t    key;       /* key */
        long     pad[4];    /*reserve area */
};
```

It is located in the `<sys/ipc.h>` header file and is common to all IPC facilities.

The `msgget` system call is used to perform one of two tasks:

- to get a new message queue identifier and create an associated message queue and data structure for it

- to return an existing message queue identifier that already has an associated message queue and data structure

Both tasks require a `key` argument passed to the `msgget` system call. For the first task, if the `key` is not already in use for an existing message queue identifier , a new identifier is returned with an associated message queue and data structure created for the `key`. This occurs as long as no system-tunable parameters would be exceeded and a control command `IPC_CREAT` is specified in the `msgflg` argument passed in the system call.

There is also a provision for specifying a `key` of value zero, known as the private `key` (`IPC_PRIVATE`). When specified, a new identifier is always returned with an associated message queue and data structure created for it unless a system-tunable parameter would be exceeded. The `ipcs` command will show the KEY field for the `msqid` as all zeros.

For the second task, if a message queue identifier exists for the `key` specified, the value of the existing identifier is returned. If you do not want to have an existing message queue identifier returned, a control command (`IPC_EXCL`) can be specified (set) in the `msgflg` argument passed to the system call. ("Using `msgget`" describes how to use this system call.)

When performing the first task, the process that calls `msgget` becomes the owner/creator, and the associated data structure is initialized accordingly. Remember, ownership can be changed but the creating process always remains the creator. The message queue creator also determines the initial operation permissions for it.

Once a uniquely identified message queue and data structure are created, `msgop` (message operations) and `msgctl` (message control) can be used.

Message operations, as mentioned before, consist of sending and receiving messages. The `msgsnd` and `msgrcv` system calls are provided for each of these operations. See "Operations for Messages" for `msgsnd` and `msgrcv` system call details.

The `msgctl` system call permits you to control the message facility in the following ways:

- by retrieving the data structure associated with a message queue identifier (`IPC_STAT`)

- by changing operation permissions for a message queue (`IPC_SET`)

- by changing the size (`msg_qbytes`) of the message queue for a particular message queue identifier (`IPC_SET`)

- by removing a particular message queue identifier from the UNIX operating system along with its associated message queue and data structure (`IPC_RMID`)

See "Controlling Message Queues" for `msgctl` system call details.

Getting Message Queues

This section describes how to use the msgget system call. The accompanying program illustrates its use.

Using msgget

The synopsis found in the msgget(2) entry in the *Programmer's Reference Manual* is as follows:

```
#include  <sys/types.h>
#include  <sys/ipc.h>
#include  <sys/msg.h>

int  msgget (key, msgflg)
key_t  key;
int msgflg;
```

All of these include files are located in the /usr/include/sys directory of the UNIX operating system.

The following line in the synopsis:

```
int msgget (key, msgflg)
```

informs you that msgget is a function with two formal arguments that returns an integer-type value. The next two lines:

```
key_t   key;
int msgflg;
```

declare the types of the formal arguments. key_t is defined by a typedef in the <sys/types.h> header file to be an integral type.

The integer returned from this function upon successful completion is the message queue identifier that was discussed earlier. Upon failure, the external variable errno is set to indicate the reason for failure, and the value -1 (which is not a valid msqid) is returned.

As declared, the process calling the msgget system call must supply two arguments to be passed to the formal key and msgflg arguments.

A new msqid with an associated message queue and data structure is provided if either

- key is equal to IPC_PRIVATE,

or

- key is a unique integer and the control command IPC_CREAT is specified in the msgflg argument.

The value passed to the msgflg argument must be an integer-type value that will specify the following:

- operations permissions
- control fields (commands)

Operation permissions determine the operations that processes are permitted to perform on the associated message queue. "Read" permission is necessary for receiving messages or for determining queue status by means of a msgctl IPC_STAT operation. "Write" permission is necessary for sending messages. Figure 4-2 reflects the numeric values (expressed in octal notation) for the valid operation permissions codes.

Figure 4-2: Operation Permissions Codes

Operation Permissions	Octal Value
Read by User	00400
Write by User	00200
Read by Group	00040
Write by Group	00020
Read by Others	00004
Write by Others	00002

A specific value is derived by adding or bitwise ORing the octal values for the operation permissions wanted. That is, if read by user and read/write by others is desired, the code value would be 00406 (00400 plus 00006). There are constants located in the <sys/msg.h> header file which can be used for the user operations permissions. They are as follows:

```
MSG_W 0200  /* write permissions by owner */

MSG_R 0400  /* read permissions by owner */
```

Control flags are predefined constants (represented by all uppercase letters). The flags which apply to the `msgget` system call are `IPC_CREAT` and `IPC_EXCL` and are defined in the `<sys/ipc.h>` header file.

The value for `msgflg` is therefore a combination of operation permissions and control commands. After determining the value for the operation permissions as previously described, the desired flag(s) can be specified. This is accomplished by adding or bitwise ORing (|) them with the operation permissions; the bit positions and values for the control commands in relation to those of the operation permissions make this possible.

The `msgflg` value can easily be set by using the flag names in conjunction with the octal operation permissions value:

```
msqid = msgget (key, (IPC_CREAT | 0400));

msqid = msgget (key, (IPC_CREAT | IPC_EXCL | 0400));
```

As specified by the `msgget`(2) page in the *Programmer's Reference Manual*, success or failure of this system call depends upon the argument values for `key` and `msgflg` or system-tunable parameters. The system call will attempt to return a new message queue identifier if one of the following conditions is true:

- `key` is equal to `IPC_PRIVATE`
- `key` does not already have a message queue identifier associated with it and (`msgflg` and `IPC_CREAT`) is "true" (not zero).

The `key` argument can be set to `IPC_PRIVATE` like this:

```
msqid = msgget (IPC_PRIVATE, msgflg);
```

The system call will always be attempted. Exceeding the `MSGMNI` system-tunable parameter always causes a failure. The `MSGMNI` system-tunable parameter determines the systemwide number of unique message queues that may be in use at any given time.

IPC_EXCL is another control command used in conjunction with IPC_CREAT. It will cause the system call to return an error if a message queue identifier already exists for the specified key. This is necessary to prevent the process from thinking that it has received a new identifier when it has not. In other words, when both IPC_CREAT and IPC_EXCL are specified, a new message queue identifier is returned if the system call is successful.

Refer to the msgget(2) page in the *Programmer's Reference Manual* for specific, associated data structure initialization for successful completion. The specific failure conditions and their error names are contained there also.

Example Program

Figure 4-3 is a menu-driven program. It allows all possible combinations of using the msgget system call to be exercised.

From studying this program, you can observe the method of passing arguments and receiving return values. The user-written program requirements are pointed out.

This program begins (lines 4-8) by including the required header files as specified by the msgget(2) entry in the *Programmer's Reference Manual*. Note that the <sys/errno.h> header file is included as opposed to declaring errno as an external variable; either method will work.

Variable names have been chosen to be as close as possible to those in the synopsis for the system call. Their declarations are self explanatory. These names make the programs more readable are perfectly legal since they are local to the program. The variables declared for this program and what they are used for are as follows:

key   used to pass the value for the desired key

opperm   used to store the desired operation permissions

flags   used to store the desired control commands (flags)

opperm_flags
         used to store the combination from the logical ORing of the opperm and flags variables; it is then used in the system call to pass the msgflg argument

msqid   used for returning the message queue identification number
                        for a successful system call or the error code (-1) for an
                        unsuccessful one.

The program begins by prompting for a hexadecimal key, an octal operation
permissions code, and finally for the control command combinations (flags)
which are selected from a menu (lines 15-32). All possible combinations are
allowed even though they might not be viable. This allows errors to be
observed for illegal combinations.

Next, the menu selection for the flags is combined with the operation permissions, and the result is stored in the opperm_flags variable (lines 36-51).

The system call is made next, and the result is stored in the msqid variable (line
53).

Since the msqid variable now contains a valid message queue identifier or the
error code (-1), it is tested to see if an error occurred (line 55). If msqid equals
-1, a message indicates that an error resulted, and the external errno variable
is displayed (line 57).

If no error occurred, the returned message queue identifier is displayed (line
61).

The example program for the msgget system call follows. We suggest you
name the program file msgget.c and the executable file msgget.

Figure 4-3: msgget **System Call Example**

```
1     /*This is a program to illustrate
2     **the message get, msgget(),
3     **system call capabilities.*/

4     #include    <stdio.h>
5     #include    <sys/types.h>
6     #include    <sys/ipc.h>
7     #include    <sys/msg.h>
8     #include    <errno.h>

9     /*Start of main C language program*/
10    main()
11    {
12        key_t key;
13        int opperm, flags;
14        int msqid, opperm_flags;
15        /*Enter the desired key*/
16        printf("Enter the desired key in hex = ");
17        scanf("%x", &key);


18        /*Enter the desired octal operation
19          permissions.*/
20        printf("\nEnter the operation\n");
21        printf("permissions in octal = ");
22        scanf("%o", &opperm);

23        /*Set the desired flags.*/
24        printf("\nEnter corresponding number to\n");
25        printf("set the desired flags:\n");
26        printf("No flags                = 0\n");
27        printf("IPC_CREAT               = 1\n");
28        printf("IPC_EXCL                = 2\n");
29        printf("IPC_CREAT and IPC_EXCL  = 3\n");
30        printf("            Flags       = ");

31        /*Get the flag(s) to be set.*/
32        scanf("%d", &flags);

33        /*Check the values.*/
34        printf ("\nkey =0x%x, opperm = 0%o, flags = 0%o\n",
35            key, opperm, flags);

36        /*Incorporate the control fields (flags) with
37          the operation permissions*/
```

(continued on next page)

Figure 4-3: msgget **System Call Example** (continued)

```
38        switch (flags)
39        {
40        case 0:    /*No flags are to be set.*/
41             opperm_flags = (opperm | 0);
42             break;
43        case 1:    /*Set the IPC_CREAT flag.*/
44             opperm_flags = (opperm | IPC_CREAT);
45             break;
46        case 2:    /*Set the IPC_EXCL flag.*/
47             opperm_flags = (opperm | IPC_EXCL);
48             break;
49        case 3:    /*Set the IPC_CREAT and IPC_EXCL flags.*/
50             opperm_flags = (opperm | IPC_CREAT | IPC_EXCL);
51        }

52        /*Call the msgget system call.*/
53        msqid = msgget (key, opperm_flags);

54        /*Perform the following if the call is unsuccessful.*/
55        if(msqid == -1)
56        {
57             printf ("\nThe msgget call failed, error number = %d\n", errno);
58        }
59        /*Return the msqid upon successful completion.*/
60        else
61             printf ("\nThe msqid = %d\n", msqid);
62        exit(0);
63    }
```

Controlling Message Queues

This section describes how to use the msgctl system call. The accompanying program illustrates its use.

Using msgctl

The synopsis found in the `msgctl`(2) entry in the *Programmer's Reference Manual* is as follows:

```
#include <sys/types.h>
#include <sys/ipc.h>
#include <sys/msg.h>

int msgctl (msqid, cmd, buf)
int msqid, cmd;
struct msqid_ds *buf;
```

The `msgctl` system call requires three arguments to be passed to it; it returns an integer-type value.

When successful, it returns a zero value; when unsuccessful, it returns a -1.

The `msqid` variable must be a valid, non-negative, integer value. In other words, it must have already been created by using the `msgget` system call.

The `cmd` argument can be any one of the following values:

IPC_STAT   return the status information contained in the associated data structure for the specified message queue identifier, and place it in the data structure pointed to by the `buf` pointer in the user memory area.

IPC_SET   for the specified message queue identifier, set the effective user and group identification, operation permissions, and the number of bytes for the message queue to the values contained in the data structure pointed to by the `buf` pointer in the user memory area.

IPC_RMID   remove the specified message queue identifier along with its associated message queue and data structure.

A process must have an effective user identification of OWNER/CREATOR or superuser to perform an IPC_SET or IPC_RMID control command. Read permission is required to perform the IPC_STAT control command.

The details of this system call are discussed in the following example program. If you need more information on the logic manipulations in this program, read the msgget(2) section of the *Programmer's Reference Manual*; it goes into more detail than would be practical for this document.

Example Program

Figure 4-4 is a menu-driven program. It allows all possible combinations of using the msgctl system call to be exercised.

From studying this program, you can observe the method of passing arguments and receiving return values. The user-written program requirements are pointed out.

This program begins (lines 5-9) by including the required header files as specified by the msgctl(2) entry in the *Programmer's Reference Manual*. Note in this program that errno is declared as an external variable, and therefore, the <sys/errno.h> header file does not have to be included.

Variable and structure names have been chosen to be as close as possible to those in the synopsis for the system call. Their declarations are self explanatory. These names make the program more readable and are perfectly legal since they are local to the program. The variables declared for this program and what they are used for are as follows:

uid	used to store the IPC_SET value for the effective user identification
gid	used to store the IPC_SET value for the effective group identification
mode	used to store the IPC_SET value for the operation permissions
bytes	used to store the IPC_SET value for the number of bytes in the message queue (msg_qbytes)
rtrn	used to store the return integer value from the system call
msqid	used to store and pass the message queue identifier to the system call

command   used to store the code for the desired control command so that subsequent processing can be performed on it

choice   used to determine which member is to be changed for the IPC_SET control command

msqid_ds   used to receive the specified message queue identifier's data structure when an IPC_STAT control command is performed

buf   a pointer passed to the system call which locates the data structure in the user memory area where the IPC_STAT control command is to place its return values or where the IPC_SET command gets the values to set

Note that the msqid_ds data structure in this program (line 16) uses the data structure, located in the <sys/msg.h> header file of the same name, as a template for its declaration.

The next important thing to observe is that although the buf pointer is declared to be a pointer to a data structure of the msqid_ds type, it must also be initialized to contain the address of the user memory area data structure (line 17). Now that all of the required declarations have been explained for this program, this is how it works.

First, the program prompts for a valid message queue identifier which is stored in the msqid variable (lines 19, 20). This is required for every msgctl system call.

Then the code for the desired control command must be entered (lines 21-27) and stored in the command variable. The code is tested to determine the control command for subsequent processing.

If the IPC_STAT control command is selected (code 1), the system call is performed (lines 37, 38) and the status information returned is printed out (lines 39-46); only the members that can be set are printed out in this program. Note that if the system call is unsuccessful (line 106), the status information of the last successful call is printed out. In addition, an error message is displayed and the errno variable is printed out (line 108). If the system call is successful, a message indicates this along with the message queue identifier used (lines 110-113).

If the IPC_SET control command is selected (code 2), the first thing is to get the current status information for the message queue identifier specified (lines 50-52). This is necessary because this example program provides for changing only one member at a time, and the system call changes all of them. Also, if an

invalid value happened to be stored in the user memory area for one of these
members, it would cause repetitive failures for this control command until
corrected. The next thing the program does is to prompt for a code corresponding to the member to be changed (lines 53-59). This code is stored in the choice
variable (line 60). Now, depending upon the member picked, the program
prompts for the new value (lines 66-95). The value is placed into the appropriate member in the user memory area data structure, and the system call is made
(lines 96-98). Depending upon success or failure, the program returns the same
messages as for IPC_STAT above.

If the IPC_RMID control command (code 3) is selected, the system call is performed (lines 100-103), and the msqid along with its associated message queue
and data structure are removed from the UNIX operating system. Note that the
buf pointer is ignored in performing this control command, and its value can
be zero or NULL. Depending upon the success or failure, the program returns
the same messages as for the other control commands.

The example program for the msgctl system call follows. We suggest that you
name the source program file msgctl.c and the executable file msgctl.

Figure 4-4: msgctl **System Call Example**

```
 1    /*This is a program to illustrate
 2    **the message control, msgctl(),
 3    **system call capabilities.
 4    */

 5    /*Include necessary header files.*/
 6    #include    <stdio.h>
 7    #include    <sys/types.h>
 8    #include    <sys/ipc.h>
 9    #include    <sys/msg.h>

10    /*Start of main C language program*/
11    main()
12    {
13        extern int errno;
14        int uid, gid, mode, bytes;
15        int rtrn, msqid, command, choice;
16        struct msqid_ds msqid_ds, *buf;
17        buf = &msqid_ds;
```

(continued on next page)

Figure 4-4: `msgctl` **System Call Example** (continued)

```
18        /*Get the msqid, and command.*/
19        printf("Enter the msqid = ");
20        scanf("%d", &msqid);
21        printf("\nEnter the number for\n");
22        printf("the desired command:\n");
23        printf("IPC_STAT    = 1\n");
24        printf("IPC_SET     = 2\n");
25        printf("IPC_RMID    = 3\n");
26        printf("Entry       = ");
27        scanf("%d", &command);

28        /*Check the values.*/
29        printf ("\nmsqid =%d, command = %d\n",
30            msqid, command);

31        switch (command)
32        {
33        case 1:    /*Use msgctl() to duplicate
34            the data structure for
35                    msqid in the msqid_ds area pointed
36                    to by buf and then print it out.*/
37            rtrn = msgctl(msqid, IPC_STAT,
38                buf);
39            printf ("\nThe USER ID = %d\n",
40                buf->msg_perm.uid);
41            printf ("The GROUP ID = %d\n",
42                buf->msg_perm.gid);
43            printf ("The operation permissions = 0%o\n",
44                buf->msg_perm.mode);
45            printf ("The msg_qbytes = %d\n",
46                buf->msg_qbytes);
47            break;
48        case 2:    /*Select and change the desired
49                    member(s) of the data structure.*/
50            /*Get the original data for this msqid
51                data structure first.*/
52            rtrn = msgctl(msqid, IPC_STAT, buf);
53            printf("\nEnter the number for the\n");
54            printf("member to be changed:\n");
55            printf("msg_perm.uid   = 1\n");
56            printf("msg_perm.gid   = 2\n");
57            printf("msg_perm.mode  = 3\n");
58            printf("msg_qbytes     = 4\n");
```

(continued on next page)

Figure 4-4: msgctl **System Call Example** (continued)

```
59          printf("Entry          = ");

60          scanf("%d", &choice);
61          /*Only one choice is allowed per
62            pass as an illegal entry will
63                cause repetitive failures until
64            msqid_ds is updated with
65                IPC_STAT.*/

66          switch(choice){
67          case 1:
68              printf("\nEnter USER ID = ");
69              scanf ("%ld", &uid);
70              buf->msg_perm.uid =(uid_t)uid;
71              printf("\nUSER ID = %d\n",
72                  buf->msg_perm.uid);
73              break;
74          case 2:
75              printf("\nEnter GROUP ID = ");
76              scanf("%d", &gid);
77              buf->msg_perm.gid = gid;
78              printf("\nGROUP ID = %d\n",
79                  buf->msg_perm.gid);
80              break;
81          case 3:
82              printf("\nEnter MODE = ");
83              scanf("%o", &mode);
84              buf->msg_perm.mode = mode;
85              printf("\nMODE = 0%o\n",
86                  buf->msg_perm.mode);
87              break;
88          case 4:
89              printf("\nEnter msg_bytes = ");
90              scanf("%d", &bytes);
91              buf->msg_qbytes = bytes;
92              printf("\nmsg_qbytes = %d\n",
93                  buf->msg_qbytes);
94              break;
95          }

96          /*Do the change.*/
97          rtrn = msgctl(msqid, IPC_SET,
98              buf);
99          break;
```

(continued on next page)

Figure 4-4: `msgctl` **System Call Example** (continued)

```
100        case 3:    /*Remove the msqid along with its
101                        associated message queue
102                        and data structure.*/
103            rtrn = msgctl(msqid, IPC_RMID, (struct msqid_ds *) NULL);
104        }
105        /*Perform the following if the call is unsuccessful.*/
106        if(rtrn == -1)
107        {
108            printf ("\nThe msgctl call failed, error number = %d\n", errno);
109        }
110        /*Return the msqid upon successful completion.*/
111        else
112            printf ("\nMsgctl was successful for msqid = %d\n",
113                msqid);
114        exit (0);
115    }
```

Operations for Messages

This section describes how to use the `msgsnd` and `msgrcv` system calls. The accompanying program illustrates their use.

Using msgop

The synopsis found in the `msgop(2)` entry in the *Programmer's Reference Manual* is as follows:

```
#include <sys/types.h>
#include <sys/ipc.h>
#include <sys/msg.h>

int msgsnd (msqid, msgp, msgsz, msgflg)
int msqid;
struct msgbuf *msgp;
int msgsz, msgflg;

int msgrcv (msqid, msgp, msgsz, msgtyp, msgflg)
int msqid;
struct msgbuf *msgp;
int msgsz;
long msgtyp;
int msgflg;
```

Sending a Message

The msgsnd system call requires four arguments to be passed to it. It returns an integer value.

When successful, it returns a zero value; when unsuccessful, msgsnd returns a −1.

The msqid argument must be a valid, non-negative, integer value. In other words, it must have already been created by using the msgget system call.

The msgp argument is a pointer to a structure in the user memory area that contains the type of the message and the message to be sent.

The msgsz argument specifies the length of the character array in the data structure pointed to by the msgp argument. This is the length of the message. The maximum size of this array is determined by the MSGMAX system-tunable parameter.

The msgflg argument allows the "blocking message operation" to be performed if the IPC_NOWAIT flag is not set ((msgflg and IPC_NOWAIT)= = 0); the operation would block if the total number of bytes allowed on the specified message queue.are in use (msg_qbytes or MSGMNB), or the total system-wide number of messages on all queues is equal to the system- imposed limit (MSGTQL). If the IPC_NOWAIT flag is set, the system call will fail and return a −1.

The msg_qbytes data structure member can be lowered from MSGMNB by using the msgctl IPC_SET control command, but only the superuser can raise it afterwards.

Further details of this system call are discussed in the following program. If you need more information on the logic manipulations in this program, read "Using msgget". It goes into more detail than would be practical for every system call.

Receiving Messages

The msgrcv system call requires five arguments to be passed to it; it returns an integer value.

When successful, it returns a value equal to the number of bytes received; when unsuccessful it returns a -1.

The msqid argument must be a valid, non-negative, integer value. In other words, it must have already been created by using the msgget system call.

The msgp argument is a pointer to a structure in the user memory area that will receive the message type and the message text.

The msgsz argument specifies the length of the message to be received. If its value is less than the message in the array, an error can be returned if desired (see the msgflg argument below).

The msgtyp argument is used to pick the first message on the message queue of the particular type specified. If it is equal to zero, the first message on the queue is received; if it is greater than zero, the first message of the same type is received; if it is less than zero, the lowest type that is less than or equal to its absolute value is received.

The msgflg argument allows the "blocking message operation" to be performed if the IPC_NOWAIT flag is not set ((msgflg and IPC_NOWAIT) == 0); the operation would block if there is not a message on the message queue of the desired type (msgtyp) to be received. If the IPC_NOWAIT flag is set, the system call will fail immediately when there is not a message of the desired type on the queue. msgflg can also specify that the system call fail if the message is longer than the size to be received; this is done by not setting the MSG_NOERROR flag in the msgflg argument ((msgflg and MSG_NOERROR)) == 0). If the MSG_NOERROR flag is set, the message is truncated to the length specified by the msgsz argument of msgrcv.

Further details of this system call are discussed in the following program. If you need more information on the logic manipulations in this program read "Using msgget". It goes into more detail than would be practical for every system call.

Example Program

Figure 4-5 is a menu-driven program. It allows all possible combinations of using the msgsnd and msgrcv system calls to be exercised.

From studying this program, you can observe the method of passing arguments and receiving return values. The user-written program requirements are pointed out.

This program begins (lines 5-9) by including the required header files as specified by the msgop(2) entry in the *Programmer's Reference Manual*. Note that in this program errno is declared as an external variable; therefore, the <sys/errno.h> header file does not have to be included.

Variable and structure names have been chosen to be as close as possible to those in the synopsis. Their declarations are self explanatory. These names make the program more readable and are perfectly legal since they are local to the program. The variables declared for this program and what they are used for are as follows:

sndbuf   used as a buffer to contain a message to be sent (line 13); it uses the msgbuf1 data structure as a template (lines 10-13). The msgbuf1 structure (lines 10-13) is a duplicate of the msgbuf structure contained in the <sys/msg.h> header file, except that the size of the character array for mtext is tailored to fit this application. The msgbuf structure should not be used directly because mtext has only one element that would limit the size of each message to one character. Instead, declare your own structure. It should be identical to msgbuf except that the size of the mtext array should fit your application.

rcvbuf   used as a buffer to receive a message (line 13); it uses the msgbuf1 data structure as a template (lines 10-13)

msgp	used as a pointer (line 13) to both the sndbuf and rcvbuf buffers
i	used as a counter for inputting characters from the keyboard, storing them in the array, and keeping track of the message length for the msgsnd system call; it is also used as a counter to output the received message for the msgrcv system call
c	used to receive the input character from the getchar function (line 50)
flag	used to store the code of IPC_NOWAIT for the msgsnd system call (line 61)
flags	used to store the code of the IPC_NOWAIT or MSG_NOERROR flags for the msgrcv system call (line 117)
choice	used to store the code for sending or receiving (line 30)
rtrn	used to store the return values from all system calls
msqid	used to store and pass the desired message queue identifier for both system calls
msgsz	used to store and pass the size of the message to be sent or received
msgflg	used to pass the value of flag for sending or the value of flags for receiving
msgtyp	used for specifying the message type for sending or for picking a message type for receiving.

Note that a msqid_ds data structure is set up in the program (line 21) with a pointer initialized to point to it (line 22); this will allow the data structure members affected by message operations to be observed. They are observed by using the msgctl (IPC_STAT) system call to get them for the program to print them out (lines 80-92 and lines 160-167).

The first thing the program prompts for is whether to send or receive a message. A corresponding code must be entered for the desired operation; it is stored in the choice variable (lines 23-30). Depending upon the code, the program proceeds as in the following msgsnd or msgrcv sections.

msgsnd

When the code is to send a message, the msgp pointer is initialized (line 33) to the address of the send data structure, sndbuf. Next, a message type must be entered for the message; it is stored in the variable msgtyp (line 42), and then (line 43) it is put into the mtype member of the data structure pointed to by msgp.

The program now prompts for a message to be entered from the keyboard and enters a loop of getting and storing into the mtext array of the data structure (lines 48-51). This will continue until an end-of-file is recognized which, for the getchar function, is a control-D (CTRL-D) immediately following a carriage return (<CR>).

The message is immediately echoed from the mtext array of the sndbuf data structure to provide feedback (lines 54-56).

The next and final thing that must be decided is whether to set the IPC_NOWAIT flag. The program does this by requesting that a code of a 1 be entered for yes or anything else for no (lines 57-65). It is stored in the flag variable. If a 1 is entered, IPC_NOWAIT is logically ORed with msgflg; otherwise, msgflg is set to zero.

The msgsnd system call is performed (line 69). If it is unsuccessful, a failure message is displayed along with the error number (lines 70-72). If it is successful, the returned value is printed and should be zero (lines 73-76).

Every time a message is successfully sent, three members of the associated data structure are updated. They are:

msg_qnum   represents the total number of messages on the message queue; it is incremented by one.

msg_lspid   contains the process identification (PID) number of the last process sending a message; it is set accordingly.

msg_stime   contains the time in seconds since January 1, 1970, Greenwich Mean Time (GMT) of the last message sent; it is set accordingly.

These members are displayed after every successful message send operation (lines 79-92).

msgrcv

When the code is to receive a message, the program continues execution as in the following paragraphs.

The msgp pointer is initialized to the rcvbuf data structure (line 99).

Next, the message queue identifier of the message queue from which to receive the message is requested; it is stored in msqid (lines 100-103).

The message type is requested; it is stored in msgtyp (lines 104-107).

The code for the desired combination of control flags is requested next; it is stored in flags (lines 108-117). Depending upon the selected combination, msgflg is set accordingly (lines 118-131).

Finally, the number of bytes to be received is requested; it is stored in msgsz (lines 132-135).

The msgrcv system call is performed (line 142). If it is unsuccessful, a message and error number is displayed (lines 143-145). If successful, a message indicates so, and the number of bytes returned and the msg type returned (because the value returned may be different from the value requested) is displayed followed by the received message (lines 150-156).

When a message is successfully received, three members of the associated data structure are updated. They are:

msg_qnum   contains the number of messages on the message queue; it is decremented by one.

msg_lrpid   contains the PID of the last process receiving a message; it is set accordingly.

msg_rtime   contains the time in seconds since January 1, 1970, Greenwich Mean Time (GMT) that the last process received a message; it is set accordingly.

Figure 4-5 shows the msgop system calls. We suggest that you put the program into a source file called msgop.c and then compile it into an executable file called msgop.

Figure 4-5: `msgop` **System Call Example**

```
 1    /*This is a program to illustrate
 2    **the message operations, msgop(),
 3    **system call capabilities.
 4    */

 5    /*Include necessary header files.*/
 6    #include    <stdio.h>
 7    #include    <sys/types.h>
 8    #include    <sys/ipc.h>
 9    #include    <sys/msg.h>

10    struct msgbuf1 {
11        long    mtype;
12        char    mtext[8192];
13    } sndbuf, rcvbuf, *msgp;

14    /*Start of main C language program*/
15    main()
16    {
17        extern int errno;
18        int i, c, flag, flags, choice;
19        int rtrn, msqid, msgsz, msgflg;
20        long mtype, msgtyp;
21        struct msqid_ds msqid_ds, *buf;
22        buf = &msqid_ds;

23        /*Select the desired operation.*/
24        printf("Enter the corresponding\n");
25        printf("code to send or\n");
26        printf("receive a message:\n");
27        printf("Send          =   1\n");
28        printf("Receive       =   2\n");
29        printf("Entry         =   ");
30        scanf("%d", &choice);

31        if(choice == 1) /*Send a message.*/
32        {
33            msgp = &sndbuf; /*Point to user send structure.*/

34            printf("\nEnter the msqid of\n");
35            printf("the message queue to\n");
36            printf("handle the message = ");
37            scanf("%d", &msqid);
```

(continued on next page)

Figure 4-5: `msgop` **System Call Example** (continued)

```
38              /*Set the message type.*/
39              printf("\nEnter a positive integer\n");
40              printf("message type (long) for the\n");
41              printf("message = ");
42              scanf("%ld", &msgtyp);
43              msgp->mtype = msgtyp;

44              /*Enter the message to send.*/
45              printf("\nEnter a message: \n");

46              /*A control-d (^d) terminates as
47                EOF.*/

48              /*Get each character of the message
49                and put it in the mtext array.*/
50              for(i = 0; ((c = getchar()) != EOF); i++)
51                  sndbuf.mtext[i] = c;

52              /*Determine the message size.*/
53              msgsz = i;

54              /*Echo the message to send.*/
55              for(i = 0; i < msgsz; i++)
56                  putchar(sndbuf.mtext[i]);

57              /*Set the IPC_NOWAIT flag if
58                desired.*/
59              printf("\nEnter a 1 if you want \n");
60              printf("the IPC_NOWAIT flag set:  ");
61              scanf("%d", &flag);
62              if(flag == 1)
63                  msgflg = IPC_NOWAIT;
64              else
65                  msgflg = 0;

66              /*Check the msgflg.*/
67              printf("\nmsgflg = 0%o\n", msgflg);

68              /*Send the message.*/
69              rtrn = msgsnd(msqid, msgp, msgsz, msgflg);
70              if(rtrn == -1)
71              printf("\nMsgsnd failed.  Error = %d\n",
72                      errno);
73              else {
```

(continued on next page)

Figure 4-5: msgop **System Call Example** (continued)

```
74              /*Print the value of test which
75                   should be zero for successful.*/
76              printf("\nValue returned = %d\n", rtrn);

77              /*Print the size of the message
78                sent.*/
79              printf("\nMsgsz = %d\n", msgsz);

80              /*Check the data structure update.*/
81              msgctl(msqid, IPC_STAT, buf);

82              /*Print out the affected members.*/

83              /*Print the incremented number of
84                messages on the queue.*/
85              printf("\nThe msg_qnum = %d\n",
86                  buf->msg_qnum);
87              /*Print the process id of the last sender.*/
88              printf("The msg_lspid = %d\n",
89                  buf->msg_lspid);
90              /*Print the last send time.*/
91              printf("The msg_stime = %d\n",
92                  buf->msg_stime);
93          }
94      }

95      if(choice == 2)   /*Receive a message.*/
96      {
97          /*Initialize the message pointer
98            to the receive buffer.*/
99          msgp = &rcvbuf;

100         /*Specify the message queue which contains
101              the desired message.*/
102         printf("\nEnter the msqid = ");
103         scanf("%d", &msqid);

104         /*Specify the specific message on the queue
105              by using its type.*/
106         printf("\nEnter the msgtyp = ");
107         scanf("%ld", &msgtyp);

108         /*Configure the control flags for the
109              desired actions.*/
```

(continued on next page)

Figure 4-5: msgop **System Call Example** (continued)

```
110         printf("\nEnter the corresponding code\n");
111         printf("to select the desired flags: \n");
112         printf("No flags                     = 0\n");
113         printf("MSG_NOERROR                  = 1\n");
114         printf("IPC_NOWAIT                   = 2\n");
115         printf("MSG_NOERROR and IPC_NOWAIT   = 3\n");
116         printf("              Flags          = ");
117         scanf("%d", &flags);

118         switch(flags) {
119         case 0:
120             msgflg = 0;
121             break;
122         case 1:
123             msgflg = MSG_NOERROR;
124             break;
125         case 2:
126             msgflg = IPC_NOWAIT;
127             break;
128         case 3:
129             msgflg = MSG_NOERROR | IPC_NOWAIT;
130             break;
131         }

132         /*Specify the number of bytes to receive.*/
133         printf("\nEnter the number of bytes\n");
134         printf("to receive (msgsz) = ");
135         scanf("%d", &msgsz);

136         /*Check the values for the arguments.*/
137         printf("\nmsqid =%d\n", msqid);
138         printf("\nmsgtyp = %ld\n", msgtyp);
139         printf("\nmsgsz = %d\n", msgsz);
140         printf("\nmsgflg = 0%o\n", msgflg);

141         /*Call msgrcv to receive the message.*/
142         rtrn = msgrcv(msqid, msgp, msgsz, msgtyp, msgflg);

143         if(rtrn == -1)  {
144             printf("\nMsgrcv failed., Error = %d\n", errno);
145         }
146         else {
147             printf ("\nMsgctl was successful\n");
148             printf("for msqid = %d\n",
```

(continued on next page)

Figure 4-5: msgop **System Call Example** (continued)

```
149                    msqid);

150               /*Print the number of bytes received,
151                 it is equal to the return
152                 value.*/
153               printf("Bytes received = %d\n", rtrn);

154               /*Print the received message.*/
155               for(i = 0; i<rtrn; i++)
156                    putchar(rcvbuf.mtext[i]);
157          }
158          /*Check the associated data structure.*/
159          msgctl(msqid, IPC_STAT, buf);
160          /*Print the decremented number of messages.*/
161          printf("\nThe msg_qnum = %d\n", buf->msg_qnum);
162          /*Print the process id of the last receiver.*/
163          printf("The msg_lrpid = %d\n", buf->msg_lrpid);
164          /*Print the last message receive time*/
165          printf("The msg_rtime = %d\n", buf->msg_rtime);
166     }
167  }
```

Semaphores

The semaphore type of IPC allows processes (executing programs) to communicate through the exchange of semaphore values. Since many applications require the use of more than one semaphore, the UNIX operating system has the ability to create sets or arrays of semaphores. A semaphore set can contain one or more semaphores up to a limit set by the system administrator. The tunable parameter, SEMMSL, has a default value of 25. Semaphore sets are created by using the semget (semaphore get) system call.

The process performing the semget system call becomes the owner/creator, determines how many semaphores are in the set, and sets the initial operation permissions for all processes, including itself. This process can subsequently relinquish ownership of the set or change the operation permissions using the semctl(semaphore control) system call. The creating process always remains the creator as long as the facility exists. Other processes with permission can use semctl to perform other control functions.

Any process can manipulate the semaphore(s) if the owner of the semaphore grants permission. Each semaphore within a set can be incremented and decremented with the semop(2) system call (documented in the *Programmer's Reference Manual*).

To increment a semaphore, an integer value of the desired magnitude is passed to the semop system call. To decrement a semaphore, a minus (−) value of the desired magnitude is passed.

The UNIX operating system ensures that only one process can manipulate a semaphore set at any given time. Simultaneous requests are performed sequentially in an arbitrary manner.

A process can test for a semaphore value to be greater than a certain value by attempting to decrement the semaphore by one more than that value. If the process is successful, then the semaphore value is greater than that certain value. Otherwise, the semaphore value is not. While doing this, the process can have its execution suspended (IPC_NOWAIT flag not set) until the semaphore value would permit the operation (other processes increment the semaphore), or the semaphore facility is removed.

The ability to suspend execution is called a "blocking semaphore operation." This ability is also available for a process which is testing for a semaphore equal to zero; only read permission is required for this test; it is accomplished by passing a value of zero to the semop (semaphore operation) system call.

On the other hand, if the process is not successful and did not request to have its execution suspended, it is called a "nonblocking semaphore operation." In this case, the process is returned a known error code (-1), and the external errno variable is set accordingly.

The blocking semaphore operation allows processes to communicate based on the values of semaphores at different points in time. Remember also that IPC facilities remain in the UNIX operating system until removed by a permitted process or until the system is reinitialized.

Operating on a semaphore set is done by using the semop system call.

When a set of semaphores is created, the first semaphore in the set is semaphore number zero. The last semaphore number in the set is numbered one less than the total in the set.

A single system call can be used to perform a sequence of these "blocking/nonblocking operations" on a set of semaphores. When performing a sequence of operations, the blocking/nonblocking operations can be applied to any or all of the semaphores in the set. Also, the operations can be applied in any order of semaphore number. However, no operations are done until they can all be done successfully. For example, if the first three of six operations on a set of ten semaphores could be completed successfully, but the fourth operation would be blocked, no changes are made to the set until all six operations can be performed without blocking. Either the operations are successful and the semaphores are changed, or one ("nonblocking") operation is unsuccessful and none are changed. In short, the operations are "atomically performed."

Remember, any unsuccessful nonblocking operation for a single semaphore or a set of semaphores causes immediate return with no operations performed at all. When this occurs, an error code (-1) is returned to the process, and the external variable errno is set accordingly.

System calls (documented in the *Programmer's Reference Manual*) make these semaphore capabilities available to processes. The calling process passes arguments to a system call, and the system call either successfully or unsuccessfully performs its function. If the system call is successful, it performs its function and returns the appropriate information. Otherwise, a known error code (-1) is returned to the process, and the external variable errno is set accordingly.

Using Semaphores

Before semaphores can be used (operated on or controlled) a uniquely identified data structure and semaphore set (array) must be created. The unique identifier is called the semaphore set identifier (semid); it is used to identify or refer to a particular data structure and semaphore set.

The semaphore set contains a predefined number of structures in an array, one structure for each semaphore in the set. The number of semaphores (nsems) in a semaphore set is user selectable. The following members are in each structure within a semaphore set:

- semaphore value
- PID performing last operation
- number of processes waiting for the semaphore value to become greater than its current value
- number of processes waiting for the semaphore value to equal zero

There is one associated data structure for the uniquely identified semaphore set. This data structure contains the following information related to the semaphore set:

- operation permissions data (operation permissions structure)
- pointer to first semaphore in the set (array)
- number of semaphores in the set
- last semaphore operation time
- last semaphore change time

The C programming language data structure definition for the semaphore set (array member) is as follows:

```
struct sem
{
        ushort  semval;        /* semaphore value */
        pid_t   sempid;        /* pid of last operation */
        ushort  semncnt;       /* # awaiting semval > cval */
        ushort  semzcnt;       /* # awaiting semval = 0 */
};
```

It is located in the `<sys/sem.h>` header file.

Likewise, the structure definition for the associated semaphore data structure is as follows:

```
struct semid_ds
{
        struct ipc_perm sem_perm;    /* operation permission struct */
        struct sem      *sem_base;   /* ptr to first semaphore in set */
        ushort          sem_nsems;   /* # of semaphores in set */
        time_t          sem_otime;   /* last semop time */
        long            sem_pad1;    /* reserved for time_t expansion */
        time_t          sem_ctime;   /* last change time */
        long            sem_pad2;    /*time_t expansion */
        long            sem_pad3[4]; /* reserve area */
};
```

It is also located in the `<sys/sem.h>` header file. Note that the `sem_perm` member of this structure uses `ipc_perm` as a template. Figure 4-1 shows the breakout for the operation permissions data structure.

The `ipc_perm` data structure is the same for all IPC facilities; it is located in the `<sys/ipc.h>` header file and is shown in the "Messages" section.

The semget system call is used to perform two tasks:

- to get a new semaphore set identifier and create an associated data structure and semaphore set for it

- to return an existing semaphore set identifier that already has an associated data structure and semaphore set

The task performed is determined by the value of the key argument passed to the semget system call. For the first task, if the key is not already in use for an existing semid and the IPC_CREAT flag is set, a new semid is returned with an associated data structure and semaphore set created for it provided no system tunable parameter would be exceeded.

There is also a provision for specifying a key of value zero (0), which is known as the private key (IPC_PRIVATE). When specified, a new identifier is always returned with an associated data structure and semaphore set created for it, unless a system-tunable parameter would be exceeded. The ipcs command will show the key field for the semid as all zeros.

When performing the first task, the process which calls semget becomes the owner/creator, and the associated data structure is initialized accordingly. Remember, ownership can be changed, but the creating process always remains the creator (see "Controlling Semaphores"). The creator of the semaphore set also determines the initial operation permissions for the facility.

For the second task, if a semaphore set identifier exists for the key specified, the value of the existing identifier is returned. If you do not want to have an existing semaphore set identifier returned, a control command (IPC_EXCL) can be specified (set) in the semflg argument passed to the system call. The system call will fail if it is passed a value for the number of semaphores (nsems) that is greater than the number actually in the set; if you do not know how many semaphores are in the set, use 0 for nsems. ("Using semget" describes how to use this system call.)

Once a uniquely identified semaphore set and data structure are created, semop (semaphore operations) and semctl (semaphore control) can be used.

Semaphore operations consist of incrementing, decrementing, and testing for zero. The semop system call is used to perform these operations. See "Operations on Semaphores" for semop system call details.

The semctl system call permits you to control the semaphore facility in the following ways:

- by returning the value of a semaphore (GETVAL)

- by setting the value of a semaphore (SETVAL)

- by returning the PID of the last process performing an operation on a semaphore set (GETPID)

- by returning the number of processes waiting for a semaphore value to become greater than its current value (GETNCNT)

- by returning the number of processes waiting for a semaphore value to equal zero (GETZCNT)

- by getting all semaphore values in a set and placing them in an array in user memory (GETALL)

- by setting all semaphore values in a semaphore set from an array of values in user memory (SETALL)

- by retrieving the data structure associated with a semaphore set (IPC_STAT)

- by changing operation permissions for a semaphore set (IPC_SET)

- by removing a particular semaphore set identifier from the UNIX operating system along with its associated data structure and semaphore set (IPC_RMID)

See "Controlling Semaphores" for semctl system call details.

Getting Semaphores

This section describes how to use the semget system call. The accompanying program illustrates its use.

Using semget

The synopsis found in the semget(2) entry in the *Programmer's Reference Manual* is as follows:

```
#include  <sys/types.h>
#include  <sys/ipc.h>
#include  <sys/sem.h>

int   semget (key, nsems, semflag)
key_t  key;
int nsems, semflag;
```

The following line in the synopsis:

```
int semget (key, nsems, semflg)
```

informs you that semget is a function with three formal arguments that returns an integer-type value. The next two lines:

```
key_t  key;
int nsems, semflg;
```

declare the types of the formal arguments. key_t is defined by a typedef in the <sys/types.h> header file to be an integer.

The integer returned from this system call upon successful completion is the semaphore set identifier that was discussed above.

The process calling the semget system call must supply three actual arguments to be passed to the formal key, nsems, and semflg arguments.

A new `semid` with an associated semaphore set and data structure is created if either

■ `key` is equal to `IPC_PRIVATE`,

or

■ `key` is a unique integer and `semflg` ANDed with `IPC_CREAT` is "true."

The value passed to the `semflg` argument must be an integer that will specify the following:

■ operation permissions
■ control fields (commands)

Figure 4-6 reflects the numeric values (expressed in octal notation) for the valid operation permissions codes.

Figure 4-6: Operation Permissions Codes

Operation Permissions	Octal Value
Read by User	00400
Alter by User	00200
Read by Group	00040
Alter by Group	00020
Read by Others	00004
Alter by Others	00002

A specific value is derived by adding or bitwise ORing the values for the operation permissions wanted. That is, if read by user and read/alter by others is desired, the code value would be 00406 (00400 plus 00006). There are constants #define'd in the `<sys/sem.h>` header file which can be used for the user (OWNER). They are as follows:

```
SEM_A    0200    /* alter permission by owner */
SEM_R    0400    /* read permission by owner */
```

Control flags are predefined constants (represented by all uppercase letters). The flags that apply to the `semget` system call are `IPC_CREAT` and `IPC_EXCL` and are defined in the `<sys/ipc.h>` header file.

The value for semflg is, therefore, a combination of operation permissions and control commands. After determining the value for the operation permissions as previously described, the desired flag(s) can be specified. This specification is accomplished by adding or bitwise ORing (|) them with the operation permissions; the bit positions and values for the control commands in relation to those of the operation permissions make this possible.

The semflg value can easily be set by using the flag names in conjunction with the octal operation permissions value:

```
semid = semget (key, nsems, (IPC_CREAT | 0400));
semid = semget (key, nsems, (IPC_CREAT | IPC_EXCL | 0400));
```

As specified by the semget(2) entry in the *Programmer's Reference Manual*, success or failure of this system call depends upon the actual argument values for key, nsems, and semflg, and system-tunable parameters. The system call will attempt to return a new semaphore set identifier if one of the following conditions is true:

- key is equal to IPC_PRIVATE

- key does not already have a semaphore set identifier associated with it and (semflg & IPC_CREAT) is "true" (not zero).

The key argument can be set to IPC_PRIVATE like this:

```
semid = semget(IPC_PRIVATE, nsems, semflg);
```

Exceeding the SEMMNI, SEMMNS, or SEMMSL system-tunable parameters will always cause a failure. The SEMMNI system-tunable parameter determines the maximum number of unique semaphore sets (semid's) that may be in use at any given time. The SEMMNS system-tunable parameter determines the maximum number of semaphores in all semaphore sets system wide. The SEMMSL system-tunable parameter determines the maximum number of semaphores in each semaphore set.

IPC_EXCL is another control command used in conjunction with IPC_CREAT. It will cause the system call to return an error if a semaphore set identifier already exists for the specified key provided. This is necessary to prevent the process from thinking that it has received a new (unique) identifier when it has not. In other words, when both IPC_CREAT and IPC_EXCL are specified, a new semaphore set identifier is returned if the system call is successful. Any

value for `semflg` returns a new identifier if the key equals zero
(`IPC_PRIVATE`) and no system- tunable parameters are exceeded.

Refer to the `semget`(2) manual page in the *Programmer's Reference Manual* for
specific associated data structure initialization for successful completion. The
specific failure conditions and their error names are contained there also.

Example Program

Figure 4-7 is a menu-driven program. It allows all possible combinations of
using the `semget` system call to be exercised.

From studying this program, you can observe the method of passing arguments
and receiving return values. The user-written program requirements are
pointed out.

This program begins (lines 4-8) by including the required header files as
specified by the `semget`(2) entry in the *Programmer's Reference Manual*. Note
that the `<sys/errno.h>` header file is included as opposed to declaring `errno`
as an external variable; either method will work.

Variable names have been chosen to be as close as possible to those in the
synopsis. Their declarations are self explanatory. These names make the program more readable and are perfectly legal since they are local to the program.
The variables declared for this program and what they are used for are as follows:

`key`	used to pass the value for the desired key
`opperm`	used to store the desired operation permissions
`flags`	used to store the desired control commands (flags)
`opperm_flags`	used to store the combination from the logical ORing of the `opperm` and `flags` variables; it is then used in the system call to pass the `semflg` argument
`semid`	used for returning the semaphore set identification number for a successful system call or the error code (−1) for an unsuccessful one.

The program begins by prompting for a hexadecimal `key`, an octal operation permissions code, and the control command combinations (flags) which are selected from a menu (lines 15-32). All possible combinations are allowed even though they might not be viable. This allows observing the errors for illegal combinations.

Next, the menu selection for the flags is combined with the operation permissions; the result is stored in `opperm_flags` (lines 36-52).

Then, the number of semaphores for the set is requested (lines 53-57); its value is stored in `nsems`.

The system call is made next; the result is stored in the `semid` (lines 60, 61).

Since the `semid` variable now contains a valid semaphore set identifier or the error code (-1), it is tested to see if an error occurred (line 63). If `semid` equals -1, a message indicates that an error resulted and the external `errno` variable is displayed (line 65). Remember that the external `errno` variable is only set when a system call fails; it should only be examined immediately following system calls.

If no error occurred, the returned semaphore set identifier is displayed (line 69).

The example program for the `semget` system call follows. We suggest that you name the source program file `semget.c` and the executable file `semget`.

Figure 4-7: semget **System Call Example**

```
1    /*This is a program to illustrate
2    **the semaphore get, semget(),
3    **system call capabilities.*/

4    #include    <stdio.h>
5    #include    <sys/types.h>
6    #include    <sys/ipc.h>
7    #include    <sys/sem.h>
8    #include    <errno.h>

9    /*Start of main C language program*/
10   main()
11   {
12       key_t key;      /*declare as long integer*/
13       int opperm, flags, nsems;
14       int semid, opperm_flags;

15       /*Enter the desired key*/
16       printf("\nEnter the desired key in hex = ");
17       scanf("%x", &key);

18       /*Enter the desired octal operation
19            permissions.*/
20       printf("\nEnter the operation\n");
21       printf("permissions in octal = ");
22       scanf("%o", &opperm);

23       /*Set the desired flags.*/
24       printf("\nEnter corresponding number to\n");
25       printf("set the desired flags:\n");
26       printf("No flags                = 0\n");
27       printf("IPC_CREAT               = 1\n");
28       printf("IPC_EXCL                = 2\n");
29       printf("IPC_CREAT and IPC_EXCL  = 3\n");
30       printf("       Flags            = ");
31       /*Get the flags to be set.*/
32       scanf("%d", &flags);

33       /*Error checking (debugging)*/
34       printf ("\nkey =0x%x, opperm = 0%o, flags = %d\n",
35           key, opperm, flags);
36       /*Incorporate the control fields (flags) with
37            the operation permissions.*/
38       switch (flags)
```

(continued on next page)

Figure 4-7: semget **System Call Example** (continued)

```
39      {
40      case 0:    /*No flags are to be set.*/
41          opperm_flags = (opperm | 0);
42          break;
43      case 1:    /*Set the IPC_CREAT flag.*/
44          opperm_flags = (opperm | IPC_CREAT);
45          break;
46      case 2:    /*Set the IPC_EXCL flag.*/
47          opperm_flags = (opperm | IPC_EXCL);
48          break;
49      case 3: /*Set the IPC_CREAT and IPC_EXCL
50                  flags.*/
51          opperm_flags = (opperm | IPC_CREAT | IPC_EXCL);
52      }

53      /*Get the number of semaphores for this set.*/
54      printf("\nEnter the number of\n");
55      printf("desired semaphores for\n");
56      printf("this set (25 max) = ");
57      scanf("%d", &nsems);

58      /*Check the entry.*/
59      printf("\nNsems = %d\n", nsems);

60      /*Call the semget system call.*/
61      semid = semget(key, nsems, opperm_flags);

62      /*Perform the following if the call is unsuccessful.*/
63      if(semid == -1)
64      {
65          printf("The semget call failed, error number = %d\n", errno);
66      }
67      /*Return the semid upon successful completion.*/
68      else
69          printf("\nThe semid = %d\n", semid);
70      exit(0);
71  }
```

Controlling Semaphores

This section describes how to use the semctl system call. The accompanying program illustrates its use.

Using semctl

The synopsis found in the semctl(2) entry in the *Programmer's Reference Manual* is as follows:

```
#include <sys/types.h>
#include <sys/ipc.h>
#include <sys/sem.h>

int semctl (semid, semnum, cmd, arg)
int semid, cmd;
int semnum;
union semun
{
        int val;
        struct semid_ds *buf;
        ushort *array;
} arg;
```

The semctl system call requires four arguments to be passed to it, and it returns an integer value.

The semid argument must be a valid, non-negative, integer value that has already been created by using the semget system call.

The semnum argument is used to select a semaphore by its number. This relates to sequences of operations (atomically performed) on the set. When a set of semaphores is created, the first semaphore is number 0, and the last semaphore is numbered one less than the total in the set.

The cmd argument can be replaced by one of the following values:

GETVAL   return the value of a single semaphore within a semaphore
                set

SETVAL	set the value of a single semaphore within a semaphore set
GETPID	return the PID of the process that performed the last operation on the semaphore within a semaphore set
GETNCNT	return the number of processes waiting for the value of a particular semaphore to become greater than its current value
GETZCNT	return the number of processes waiting for the value of a particular semaphore to be equal to zero
GETALL	return the value for all semaphores in a semaphore set
SETALL	set all semaphore values in a semaphore set
IPC_STAT	return the status information contained in the associated data structure for the specified semid, and place it in the data structure pointed to by the buf pointer in the user memory area; arg.buf is the union member that contains pointer
IPC_SET	for the specified semaphore set (semid), set the effective user/group identification and operation permissions
IPC_RMID	remove the specified semaphore set (semid) along with its associated data structure.

A process must have an effective user identification of OWNER/CREATOR or superuser to perform an IPC_SET or IPC_RMID control command. Read/alter permission is required as applicable for the other control commands.

The arg argument is used to pass the system call the appropriate union member for the control command to be performed. For some of the control commands, the arg argument is not required and is simply ignored.

- arg.val required: SETVAL
- arg.buf required: IPC_STAT, IPC_SET
- arg.array required: GETALL, SETALL
- arg ignored: GETVAL, GETPID, GETNCNT, GETZCNT, IPC_RMID

The details of this system call are discussed in the following program. If you need more information on the logic manipulations in this program, read "Using semget". It goes into more detail than would be practical to do for every system call.

Example Program

Figure 4-8 is a menu-driven program. It allows all possible combinations of using the semctl system call to be exercised.

From studying this program, you can observe the method of passing arguments and receiving return values. The user-written program requirements are pointed out.

This program begins (lines 5-9) by including the required header files as specified by the semctl(2) entry in the *Programmer's Reference Manual*. Note that in this program errno is declared as an external variable, and therefore the <sys/errno.h> header file does not have to be included.

Variable, structure, and union names have been chosen to be as close as possible to those in the synopsis. Their declarations are self explanatory. These names make the program more readable and are perfectly legal since they are local to the program. Those declared for this program and what they are used for are as follows:

semid_ds	used to receive the specified semaphore set identifier's data structure when an IPC_STAT control command is performed
c	used to receive the input values from the scanf function (line 119) when performing a SETALL control command
i	used as a counter to increment through the union arg.array when displaying the semaphore values for a GETALL (lines 98-100) control command, and when initializing the arg.array when performing a SETALL (lines 117-121) control command
length	used as a variable to test for the number of semaphores in a set against the i counter variable (lines 98, 117)
uid	used to store the IPC_SET value for the user identification

gid	used to store the IPC_SET value for the group identification
mode	used to store the IPC_SET value for the operation permissions
retrn	used to store the return value from the system call
semid	used to store and pass the semaphore set identifier to the system call
semnum	used to store and pass the semaphore number to the system call
cmd	used to store the code for the desired control command so that subsequent processing can be performed on it
choice	used to determine which member (uid, gid, mode) for the IPC_SET control command is to be changed
semvals[]	used to store the set of semaphore values when getting (GETALL) or initializing (SETALL)
arg.val	used to pass the system call a value to set, or to store a value returned from the system call, for a single semaphore (union member)
arg.buf	a pointer passed to the system call which locates the data structure in the user memory area where the IPC_STAT control command is to place its return values, or where the IPC_SET command gets the values to set (union member)
arg.array	a pointer passed to the system call which locates the array in the user memory where the GETALL control command is to place its return values, or when the SETALL command gets the values to set (union member)

Note that the semid_ds data structure in this program (line 14) uses the data structure located in the <sys/sem.h> header file of the same name as a template for its declaration.

Note that the semvals array is declared to have 25 elements (0 through 24). This number corresponds to the maximum number of semaphores allowed per set (SEMMSL), a system-tunable parameter.

Now that all of the required declarations have been presented for this program, this is how it works.

First, the program prompts for a valid semaphore set identifier, which is stored in the semid variable (lines 24-26). This is required for all semctl system calls.

Then, the code for the desired control command must be entered (lines 17-42), and the code is stored in the cmd variable. The code is tested to determine the control command for subsequent processing.

If the GETVAL control command is selected (code 1), a message prompting for a semaphore number is displayed (lines 48, 49). When it is entered, it is stored in the semnum variable (line 50). Then, the system call is performed, and the semaphore value is displayed (lines 51-54). Note that the arg argument is not required in this case, and the system call will simply ignore it. If the system call is successful, a message indicates this along with the semaphore set identifier used (lines 197, 198); if the system call is unsuccessful, an error message is displayed along with the value of the external errno variable (lines 194, 195).

If the SETVAL control command is selected (code 2), a message prompting for a semaphore number is displayed (lines 55, 56). When it is entered, it is stored in the semnum variable (line 57). Next, a message prompts for the value to which the semaphore is to be set; it is stored as the arg.val member of the union (lines 58, 59). Then, the system call is performed (lines 60, 62). Depending upon success or failure, the program returns the same messages as for GETVAL above.

If the GETPID control command is selected (code 3), the system call is made immediately since all required arguments are known (lines 63-66), and the PID of the process performing the last operation is displayed. Note that the arg argument is not required in this case, and the system call will simply ignore it. Depending upon success or failure, the program returns the same messages as for GETVAL above.

If the GETNCNT control command is selected (code 4), a message prompting for a semaphore number is displayed (lines 67-71). When entered, it is stored in the semnum variable (line 73). Then, the system call is performed and the number of processes waiting for the semaphore to become greater than its current value is displayed (lines 73-76). Note that the arg argument is not required in this case, and the system call will simply ignore it. Depending upon success or failure, the program returns the same messages as for GETVAL above.

If the GETZCNT control command is selected (code 5), a message prompting for a semaphore number is displayed (lines 77-80). When it is entered, it is stored in the semnum variable (line 81). Then the system call is performed and the number of processes waiting for the semaphore value to become equal to zero is displayed (lines 82-85). Depending upon success or failure, the program returns the same messages as for GETVAL above.

If the GETALL control command is selected (code 6), the program first performs an IPC_STAT control command to determine the number of semaphores in the set (lines 87-93). The length variable is set to the number of semaphores in the set (line 93). The arg.array union member is set to point to the semvals array where the system call is to store the values of the semaphore set (line 96). Now, a loop is entered which displays each element of the arg.array from zero to one less than the value of length (lines 98-104). The semaphores in the set are displayed on a single line, separated by a space. Depending upon success or failure, the program returns the same messages as for GETVAL above.

If the SETALL control command is selected (code 7), the program first performs an IPC_STAT control command to determine the number of semaphores in the set (lines 107-110). The length variable is set to the number of semaphores in the set (line 113). Next, the program prompts for the values to be set and enters a loop which takes values from the keyboard and initializes the semvals array to contain the desired values of the semaphore set (lines 115-121). The loop puts the first entry into the array position for semaphore number zero and ends when the semaphore number that is filled in the array equals one less than the value of length. The arg.array union member is set to point to the semvals array from which the system call is to obtain the semaphore values. The system call is then made (lines 122-125). Depending upon success or failure, the program returns the same messages as for GETVAL above.

If the IPC_STAT control command is selected (code 8), the system call is performed (line 129), and the status information returned is printed out (lines 130-141); only the members that can be set are printed out in this program. Note that if the system call is unsuccessful, the status information of the last successful one is printed out. In addition, an error message is displayed, and the errno variable is printed out (line 194).

If the IPC_SET control command is selected (code 9), the program gets the current status information for the semaphore set identifier specified (lines 145-149). This is necessary because this example program provides for changing only one member at a time, and the semctl system call changes all of them. Also, if an invalid value happened to be stored in the user memory area for one of these members, it would cause repetitive failures for this control command until corrected. The next thing the program does is to prompt for a code corresponding to the member to be changed (lines 150-156). This code is stored in the choice variable (line 157). Now, depending upon the member picked, the program prompts for the new value (lines 158-181). The value is placed into the appropriate member in the user memory area data structure, and the system call is made (line 184). Depending upon success or failure, the program returns the same messages as for GETVAL above.

If the IPC_RMID control command (code 10) is selected, the system call is performed (lines 186-188). The semaphore set identifier along with its associated data structure and semaphore set is removed from the UNIX operating system. Depending upon success or failure, the program returns the same messages as for the other control commands.

The example program for the semctl system call follows. We suggest that you name the source program file semctl.c and the executable file semctl.

Figure 4-8: semctl **System Call Example**

```
 1    /*This is a program to illustrate
 2    **the semaphore control, semctl(),
 3    **system call capabilities.
 4    */

 5    /*Include necessary header files.*/
 6    #include    <stdio.h>
 7    #include    <sys/types.h>
 8    #include    <sys/ipc.h>
 9    #include    <sys/sem.h>

10    /*Start of main C language program*/
11    main()
12    {
13        extern int errno;
14        struct semid_ds semid_ds;
15        int c, i, length;
16        int uid, gid, mode;
17        int retrn, semid, semnum, cmd, choice;
18        ushort semvals[25];
19        union semun {
20            int val;
```

(continued on next page)

Figure 4-8: `semctl` **System Call Example** (continued)

```
21            struct semid_ds *buf;
22            ushort *array;
23        } arg;

24        /*Enter the semaphore ID.*/
25        printf("Enter the semid = ");
26        scanf("%d", &semid);

27        /*Choose the desired command.*/
28        printf("\nEnter the number for\n");
29        printf("the desired cmd:\n");
30        printf("GETVAL       = 1\n");
31        printf("SETVAL       = 2\n");
32        printf("GETPID       = 3\n");
33        printf("GETNCNT      = 4\n");
34        printf("GETZCNT      = 5\n");
35        printf("GETALL       = 6\n");
36        printf("SETALL       = 7\n");
37        printf("IPC_STAT     = 8\n");
38        printf("IPC_SET      = 9\n");
39        printf("IPC_RMID     = 10\n");
40        printf("Entry        = ");
41        scanf("%d", &cmd);

42        /*Check entries.*/
43        printf ("\nsemid =%d, cmd = %d\n\n",
44            semid, cmd);

45        /*Set the command and do the call.*/
46        switch (cmd)
47        {

48        case 1: /*Get a specified value.*/
49            printf("\nEnter the semnum = ");
50            scanf("%d", &semnum);
51            /*Do the system call.*/
52            retrn = semctl(semid, semnum, GETVAL, arg);
53            printf("\nThe semval = %d", retrn);
54            break;
55        case 2: /*Set a specified value.*/
56            printf("\nEnter the semnum = ");
57            scanf("%d", &semnum);
58            printf("\nEnter the value = ");
59            scanf("%d", &arg.val);
```

(continued on next page)

Figure 4-8: `semctl` **System Call Example** (continued)

```
60              /*Do the system call.*/
61              retrn = semctl(semid, semnum, SETVAL, arg);
62              break;
63          case 3: /*Get the process ID.*/
64              retrn = semctl(semid, 0, GETPID, arg);
65              printf("\nThe sempid = %d", retrn);
66              break;
67          case 4: /*Get the number of processes
68              waiting for the semaphore to
69              become greater than its current
70              value.*/
71              printf("\nEnter the semnum = ");
72              scanf("%d", &semnum);
73              /*Do the system call.*/
74              retrn = semctl(semid, semnum, GETNCNT, arg);
75              printf("\nThe semncnt = %d", retrn);
76              break;

77          case 5: /*Get the number of processes
78              waiting for the semaphore
79              value to become zero.*/
80              printf("\nEnter the semnum = ");
81              scanf("%d", &semnum);
82              /*Do the system call.*/
83              retrn = semctl(semid, semnum, GETZCNT, arg);
84              printf("\nThe semzcnt = %d", retrn);
85              break;

86          case 6: /*Get all of the semaphores.*/
87              /*Get the number of semaphores in
88                the semaphore set.*/
89              arg.buf = &semid_ds;
90              retrn = semctl(semid, 0, IPC_STAT, arg);
91              if(retrn == -1)
92                  goto ERROR;
93              length = arg.buf->sem_nsems;
94              /*Get and print all semaphores in the
95                specified set.*/
96              arg.array = semvals;
97              retrn = semctl(semid, 0, GETALL, arg);
98              for (i = 0; i < length; i++)
99              {
100                 printf("%d", semvals[i]);
101                 /*Separate each
```

(continued on next page)

Figure 4-8: `semctl` **System Call Example** (continued)

```
102                semaphore.*/
103            printf(" ");
104            }
105            break;

106        case 7: /*Set all semaphores in the set.*/
107            /*Get the number of semaphores in
108              the set.*/
109            arg.buf = &semid_ds;
110            retrn = semctl(semid, 0, IPC_STAT, arg);
111            if(retrn == -1)
112                goto ERROR;
113            length = arg.buf->sem_nsems;
114            printf("Length = %d\n", length);
115            /*Set the semaphore set values.*/
116            printf("\nEnter each value:\n");
117            for(i = 0; i < length ; i++)
118            {
119                scanf("%d", &c);
120                semvals[i] = c;
121            }
122            /*Do the system call.*/
123            arg.array = semvals;
124            retrn = semctl(semid, 0, SETALL, arg);
125            break;

126        case 8: /*Get the status for the semaphore set.*/
127            /*Get and print the current status values.*/
128            arg.buf = &semid_ds;
129            retrn = semctl(semid, 0, IPC_STAT, arg);
130            printf ("\nThe USER ID = %d\n",
131                arg.buf->sem_perm.uid);
132            printf ("The GROUP ID = %d\n",
133                arg.buf->sem_perm.gid);
134            printf ("The operation permissions = 0%o\n",
135                arg.buf->sem_perm.mode);
136            printf ("The number of semaphores in set = %d\n",
137                arg.buf->sem_nsems);
138            printf ("The last semop time = %d\n",
139                arg.buf->sem_otime);
140            printf ("The last change time  = %d\n",
141                arg.buf->sem_ctime);
142            break;
```

(continued on next page)

Figure 4-8: `semctl` **System Call Example** (continued)

```
143        case 9:    /*Select and change the desired
144                       member of the data structure.*/
145            /*Get the current status values.*/
146            arg.buf = &semid_ds;
147            retrn = semctl(semid, 0, IPC_STAT, arg.buf);
148            if(retrn == -1)
149                goto ERROR;
150            /*Select the member to change.*/
151            printf("\nEnter the number for the\n");
152            printf("member to be changed:\n");
153            printf("sem_perm.uid  = 1\n");
154            printf("sem_perm.gid  = 2\n");
155            printf("sem_perm.mode = 3\n");
156            printf("Entry         = ");
157            scanf("%d", &choice);
158            switch(choice){

159            case 1: /*Change the user ID.*/
160                printf("\nEnter USER ID = ");
161                scanf ("%d", &uid);
162                arg.buf->sem_perm.uid = uid;
163                printf("\nUSER ID = %d\n",
164                     arg.buf->sem_perm.uid);
165                break;

166            case 2: /*Change the group ID.*/
167                printf("\nEnter GROUP ID = ");
168                scanf("%d", &gid);
169                arg.buf->sem_perm.gid = gid;
170                printf("\nGROUP ID = %d\n",
171                     arg.buf->sem_perm.gid);
172                break;

173            case 3: /*Change the mode portion of
174                 the operation
175                          permissions.*/
176                printf("\nEnter MODE in octal = ");
177                scanf("%o", &mode);
178                arg.buf->sem_perm.mode = mode;
179                printf("\nMODE = 0%o\n",
180                     arg.buf->sem_perm.mode);
181                break;
182            }
183            /*Do the change.*/
```

(continued on next page)

Figure 4-8: `semctl` **System Call Example** (continued)

```
184            retrn = semctl(semid, 0, IPC_SET, arg);
185            break;
186        case 10:   /*Remove the semid along with its
187                      data structure.*/
188            retrn = semctl(semid, 0, IPC_RMID, arg);
189        }
190        /*Perform the following if the call is unsuccessful.*/
1911     if(retrn == -1)
192        {
193    ERROR:
194            printf ("\nThe semctl call failed!, error number =  %d\n", errno);
195            exit(0);
196        }
197        printf ("\n\nThe semctl system call was successful\n");
198        printf ("for semid = %d\n", semid);
199        exit (0);
200    }
```

Operations on Semaphores

This section describes how to use the `semop` system call. The accompanying program illustrates its use.

Using semop

The synopsis found in the `semop`(2) entry in the *Programmer's Reference Manual* is as follows:

```
#include <sys/types.h>
#include <sys/ipc.h>
#include <sys/sem.h>

int semop (semid, sops, nsops)
int semid;
struct sembuf *sops;
unsigned nsops;
```

The semop system call requires three arguments to be passed to it and returns an integer value which will be zero for successful completion or -1 otherwise.

The semid argument must be a valid, non-negative, integer value. In other words, it must have already been created by using the semget system call.

The sops argument points to an array of structures in the user memory area that contains the following for each semaphore to be changed:

- the semaphore number (sem_num)

- the operation to be performed (sem_op)

- the control flags (sem_flg)

The *sops declaration means that either an array name (which is the address of the first element of the array) or a pointer to the array can be used. sembuf is the *tag* name of the data structure used as the template for the structure members in the array; it is located in the <sys/sem.h> header file.

The nsops argument specifies the length of the array (the number of structures in the array). The maximum size of this array is determined by the SEMOPM system-tunable parameter. Therefore, a maximum of SEMOPM operations can be performed for each semop system call.

The semaphore number (sem_num) determines the particular semaphore within the set on which the operation is to be performed.

The operation to be performed is determined by the following:

- if sem_op is positive, the semaphore value is incremented by the value of sem_op

- if sem_op is negative, the semaphore value is decremented by the absolute value of sem_op

- if sem_op is zero, the semaphore value is tested for equality to zero

The following operation commands (flags) can be used:

- IPC_NOWAIT—this operation command can be set for any operations in the array. The system call will return unsuccessfully without changing any semaphore values at all if any operation for which IPC_NOWAIT is set cannot be performed successfully. The system call will be unsuccessful when trying to decrement a semaphore more than its current value, or when testing for a semaphore to be equal to zero when it is not.

- SEM_UNDO—this operation command is used to tell the system to undo the process's semaphore changes automatically when the process exits; it allows processes to avoid deadlock problems. To implement this feature, the system maintains a table with an entry for every process in the system. Each entry points to a set of undo structures, one for each semaphore used by the process. The system records the net change.

Example Program

Figure 4-9 is a menu-driven program. It allows all possible combinations of using the semop system call to be exercised.

From studying this program, you can observe the method of passing arguments and receiving return values. The user-written program requirements are pointed out.

This program begins (lines 5-9) by including the required header files as specified by the shmop(2) entry in the *Programmer's Reference Manual*. Note that in this program errno is declared as an external variable; therefore, the <sys/errno.h> header file does not have to be included.

Variable and structure names have been chosen to be as close as possible to those in the synopsis. Their declarations are self explanatory. These names make the program more readable and are perfectly legal since the declarations are local to the program. The variables declared for this program and what they are used for are as follows:

sembuf[10]	used as an array buffer (line 14) to contain a maximum of ten sembuf type structures; ten is the standard value of the tunable parameter SEMOPM, the maximum number of operations on a semaphore set for each semop system call
sops	used as a pointer (line 14) to the sembuf array for the system call and for accessing the structure members within the array
string[8]	used as a character buffer to hold a number entered by the user
rtrn	used to store the return value from the system call
flags	used to store the code of the IPC_NOWAIT or SEM_UNDO flags for the semop system call (line 59)
sem_num	used to store the semaphore number entered by the user for each semaphore operation in the array
i	used as a counter (line 31) for initializing the structure members in the array, and used to print out each structure in the array (line 78)
semid	used to store the desired semaphore set identifier for the system call
nsops	used to specify the number of semaphore operations for the system call; must be less than or equal to SEMOPM

First, the program prompts for a semaphore set identifier that the system call is to perform operations on (lines 18-21). semid is stored in the semid variable (line 22).

A message is displayed requesting the number of operations to be performed on this set (lines 24-26). The number of operations is stored in the nsops variable (line 27).

Next, a loop is entered to initialize the array of structures (lines 29-76). The semaphore number, operation, and operation command (flags) are entered for each structure in the array. The number of structures equals the number of semaphore operations (nsops) to be performed for the system call, so nsops is tested against the i counter for loop control. Note that sops is used as a pointer to each element (structure) in the array, and sops is incremented just like i. sops is then used to point to each member in the structure for setting them.

After the array is initialized, all of its elements are printed out for feedback (lines 77-84).

The sops pointer is set to the address of the array (lines 85, 86). sembuf could be used directly, if desired, instead of sops in the system call.

The system call is made (line 88), and depending upon success or failure, a corresponding message is displayed. The results of the operation(s) can be viewed by using the semctl GETALL control command.

The example program for the semop system call follows. We suggest that you name the source program file semop.c and the executable file semop.

Figure 4-9: semop **System Call Example**

```
1       /*This is a program to illustrate
2       **the semaphore operations, semop(),
3       **system call capabilities.
4       */

5       /*Include necessary header files.*/
6       #include    <stdio.h>
7       #include    <sys/types.h>
8       #include    <sys/ipc.h>
9       #include    <sys/sem.h>
10      /*Start of main C language program*/
11      main()
12      {
13          extern int errno;
14          struct sembuf sembuf[10], *sops;
15          char string[8];
16          int retrn, flags, sem_num, i, semid;
17          unsigned nsops;

18          /*Enter the semaphore ID.*/
19          printf("\nEnter the semid of\n");
20          printf("the semaphore set to\n");
21          printf("be operated on = ");
22          scanf("%d", &semid);
23          printf("\nsemid = %d", semid);

24          /*Enter the number of operations.*/
```

(continued on next page)

Figure 4-9: semop **System Call Example** (continued)

```
25          printf("\nEnter the number of semaphore\n");
26          printf("operations for this set = ");
27          scanf("%d", &nsops);
28          printf("\nsops = %d", nsops);

29          /*Initialize the array for the
30            number of operations to be performed.*/
31          for(i = 0, sops = sembuf; i < nsops; i++, sops++)
32          {

33              /*This determines the semaphore in
34                the semaphore set.*/
35              printf("\nEnter the semaphore\n");
36              printf("number (sem_num) = ");
37              scanf("%d", &sem_num);
38              sops->sem_num = sem_num;
39              printf("\nThe sem_num = %d", sops->sem_num);

40              /*Enter a (-)number to decrement,
41                an unsigned number (no +) to increment,
42                or zero to test for zero.  These values
43                are entered into a string and converted
44                to integer values.*/
45              printf("\nEnter the operation for\n");
46              printf("the semaphore (sem_op) = ");
47              scanf("%s", string);
48              sops->sem_op = atoi(string);
49              printf("\nsem_op = %d\n", sops->sem_op);

50              /*Specify the desired flags.*/
51              printf("\nEnter the corresponding\n");
52              printf("number for the desired\n");
53              printf("flags:\n");
54              printf("No flags                 = 0\n");
55              printf("IPC_NOWAIT               = 1\n");
56              printf("SEM_UNDO                 = 2\n");
57              printf("IPC_NOWAIT and SEM_UNDO  = 3\n");
58              printf("          Flags          = ");
59              scanf("%d", &flags);

60              switch(flags)
61              {
62              case 0:
63                  sops->sem_flg = 0;
```

(continued on next page)

Integrated Software Development Guide

Figure 4-9: semop **System Call Example** (continued)

```
64              break;
65          case 1:
66              sops->sem_flg = IPC_NOWAIT;
67              break;
68          case 2:
69              sops->sem_flg = SEM_UNDO;
70              break;
71          case 3:
72              sops->sem_flg = IPC_NOWAIT | SEM_UNDO;
73              break;
74          }
75          printf("\nFlags = 0%o\n", sops->sem_flg);
76      }

77      /*Print out each structure in the array.*/
78      for(i = 0; i < nsops; i++)
79      {
80          printf("\nsem_num = %d\n", sembuf[i].sem_num);
81          printf("sem_op = %d\n", sembuf[i].sem_op);
82          printf("sem_flg = 0%o\n", sembuf[i].sem_flg);
83          printf(" ");
84      }

85      sops = sembuf; /*Reset the pointer to
86                          sembuf[0].*/

87      /*Do the semop system call.*/
88      retrn = semop(semid, sops, nsops);
89      if(retrn == -1)  {
90          printf("\nSemop failed, error = %d\n", errno);
91      }
92      else {
93          printf ("\nSemop was successful\n");
94          printf("for semid = %d\n", semid);

95          printf("Value returned = %d\n", retrn);
96      }
97  }
```

Shared Memory

The shared memory type of IPC allows two or more processes (executing programs) to share memory and, consequently, the data contained there. This is done by allowing processes to set up access to a common virtual memory address space. This sharing occurs on a segment basis, which is memory management hardware-dependent.

This sharing of memory provides the fastest means of exchanging data between processes. However, processes that reference a shared memory segment must reside on one processor. Consequently, processes running on different processors (such as in an Remote File Sharing (RFS) network or a multiprocessing environment) may not be able to use shared memory segments.

A process initially creates a shared memory segment facility using the shmget system call. Upon creation, this process sets the overall operation permissions for the shared memory segment facility, sets its size in bytes, and can specify that the shared memory segment is for reference only (read-only) upon attachment. If the memory segment is not specified to be for reference only, all other processes with appropriate operation permissions can read from or write to the memory segment.

shmat (shared memory attach) and shmdt (shared memory detach) can be performed on a shared memory segment.

shmat allows processes to associate themselves with the shared memory segment if they have permission. They can then read or write as allowed.

shmdt allows processes to disassociate themselves from a shared memory segment. Therefore, they lose the ability to read from or write to the shared memory segment.

The original owner/creator of a shared memory segment can relinquish ownership to another process using the shmctl system call. However, the creating process remains the creator until the facility is removed or the system is reinitialized. Other processes with permission can perform other functions on the shared memory segment using the shmctl system call.

System calls (documented in the *Programmer's Reference Manual*) make these shared memory capabilities available to processes. The calling process passes arguments to a system call, and the system call either successfully or unsuccessfully performs its function. If the system call is successful, it performs its function and returns the appropriate information. Otherwise, a known error code (-1) is returned to the process, and the external variable errno is set accordingly.

Using Shared Memory

Sharing memory between processes occurs on a virtual segment basis. There is only one copy of each individual shared memory segment existing in the UNIX operating system at any point in time.

Before sharing of memory can be realized, a uniquely identified shared memory segment and data structure must be created. The unique identifier created is called the shared memory identifier (shmid); it is used to identify or refer to the associated data structure. The data structure includes the following for each shared memory segment:

- operation permissions
- segment size
- segment descriptor (for internal system use only)
- PID performing last operation
- PID of creator
- current number of processes attached
- last attach time
- last detach time
- last change time

The C programming language data structure definition for the shared memory segment data structure is located in the <sys/shm.h> header file. It is as follows:

```
/*
**      There is a shared mem id data structure for
**      each segment in the system.
*/

struct shmid_ds {
    struct ipc_perm    shm_perm;       /* operation permission struct */
    int                shm_segsz;      /* segment size */
    struct region      *shm_reg;       /* ptr to region structure */
    char               pad[4];         /* for swap compatibility */
    pid_t              shm_lpid;       /* pid of last shmop */
    pid_t              shm_cpid;       /* pid of creator */
    ushort             shm_nattch;     /* used only for shminfo */
    ushort             shm_cnattch;    /* used only for shminfo */
    time_t             shm_atime;      /* last shmat time */
    time_t             shm_dtime;      /* last shmdt time */
    time_t             shm_ctime;      /* last change time */
};
```

Note that the shm_perm member of this structure uses ipc_perm as a template.

The ipc_perm data structure is the same for all IPC facilities; is it located in the <sys/ipc.h> header file and shown in Figure 4-1.

The shmget system call performs two tasks:

- it gets a new shared memory identifier and creates an associated shared memory segment data structure for it

- it returns an existing shared memory identifier that already has an associated shared memory segment data structure

The task performed is determined by the value of the key argument passed to the shmget system call. For the first task, if the key is not already in use for an existing shared memory identifier and the IPC_CREAT flag is set in shmflg, a new identifier is returned with an associated shared memory segment data structure created for it provided no system-tunable parameters would be exceeded.

There is also a provision for specifying a key of value zero which is known as the private key (IPC_PRIVATE); when specified, a new shmid is always returned with an associated shared memory segment data structure created for it unless a system-tunable parameter would be exceeded. The ipcs command will show the key field for the shmid as all zeros.

For the second task, if a shmid exists for the key specified, the value of the existing shmid is returned. If it is not desired to have an existing shmid returned, a control command (IPC_EXCL) can be specified (set) in the shmflg argument passed to the system call. "Using shmget" discusses how to use this system call.

When performing the first task, the process that calls shmget becomes the owner/creator, and the associated data structure is initialized accordingly. Remember, ownership can be changed, but the creating process always remains the creator (see "Controlling Shared Memory"). The creator of the shared memory segment also determines the initial operation permissions for it.

Once a uniquely identified shared memory segment data structure is created, shmop (shared memory segment operations) and shmctl (shared memory control) can be used.

Shared memory segment operations consist of attaching and detaching shared memory segments. shmat and shmdt are provided for each of these operations. See "Operations for Shared Memory" for shmat and shmdt system call details.

The shmctl system call permits you to control the shared memory facility in the following ways:

■ by retrieving the data structure associated with a shared memory segment (IPC_STAT)

■ by changing operation permissions for a shared memory segment (IPC_SET)

■ by removing a particular shared memory segment from the UNIX operating system along with its associated shared memory segment data structure (IPC_RMID)

■ by locking a shared memory segment in memory (SHM_LOCK)

■ by unlocking a shared memory segment (SHM_UNLOCK)

See "Controlling Shared Memory" for shmctl system call details.

Getting Shared Memory Segments

This section describes how to use the shmget system call. The accompanying program illustrates its use.

Using shmget

The synopsis found in the shmget(2) entry in the *Programmer's Reference Manual* is as follows:

```
#include  <sys/types.h>
#include  <sys/ipc.h>
#include  <sys/shm.h>

int  shmget (key, size, shmflg)
key_t  key;
int size, shmflg;
```

All of these include files are located in the /usr/include/sys directory of the UNIX operating system. The following line in the synopsis:

```
int shmget (key, size, shmflg)
```

informs you that shmget is a function with three formal arguments that returns an integer-type value. The next two lines:

```
key_t  key;
int size, shmflg;
```

declare the types of the formal arguments. key_t is defined by a typedef in the <sys/types.h> header file to be an integer.

The integer returned from this function (upon successful completion) is the shared memory identifier (shmid) that was discussed earlier.

As declared, the process calling the shmget system call must supply three arguments to be passed to the formal key, size, and shmflg arguments.

A new shmid with an associated shared memory data structure is provided if
either

■ key is equal to IPC_PRIVATE,

or

■ key is a unique integer and shmflg ANDed with IPC_CREAT is "true"
(not zero).

The value passed to the shmflg argument must be an integer-type value and
will specify the following:

■ operations permissions

■ control fields (commands)

Access permissions determine the read/write attributes and modes determine
the user/group/other attributes of the shmflg argument. They are collectively
referred to as "operation permissions." Figure 4-10 reflects the numeric values
(expressed in octal notation) for the valid operation permissions codes.

Figure 4-10: Operation Permissions Codes

Operation Permissions	Octal Value
Read by User	00400
Write by User	00200
Read by Group	00040
Write by Group	00020
Read by Others	00004
Write by Others	00002

A specific octal value is derived by adding or bitwise ORing the octal values for
the operation permissions desired. That is, if read by user and read/write by
others is desired, the code value would be 00406 (00400 plus 00006). There are
constants located in the <sys/shm.h> header file which can be used for the
user (OWNER). They are:

```
SHM_R 0400
SHM_W 0200
```

Control flags are predefined constants (represented by all uppercase letters). The flags that apply to the `shmget` system call are `IPC_CREAT` and `IPC_EXCL` and are defined in the `<sys/ipc.h>` header file.

The value for `shmflg` is, therefore, a combination of operation permissions and control commands. After determining the value for the operation permissions as previously described, the desired flag(s) can be specified. This is accomplished by adding or bitwise ORing (|) them with the operation permissions; the bit positions and values for the control commands in relation to those of the operation permissions make this possible.

The `shmflg` value can easily be set by using the names of the flags in conjunction with the octal operation permissions value:

```
shmid = shmget (key, size, (IPC_CREAT | 0400));

shmid = shmget (key, size, (IPC_CREAT | IPC_EXCL | 0400));
```

As specified by the `shmget`(2) entry in the *Programmer's Reference Manual*, success or failure of this system call depends upon the argument values for `key`, `size`, and `shmflg`, and system-tunable parameters. The system call will attempt to return a new `shmid` if one of the following conditions is true:

- `key` is equal to `IPC_PRIVATE` .

- `key` does not already have a `shmid` associated with it and (`shmflg` & `IPC_CREAT`) is "true" (not zero).

The `key` argument can be set to `IPC_PRIVATE` like this:

```
shmid = shmget(IPC_PRIVATE, size, shmflg);
```

The `SHMMNI` system-tunable parameter determines the maximum number of unique shared memory segments (`shmids`) that may be in use at any given time. If the maximum number of shared memory segments is already in use, an attempt to create an additional segment will fail.

`IPC_EXCL` is another control command used in conjunction with `IPC_CREAT`.

It will cause the system call to retrieve an error if a shared memory identifier exists for the specified `key` provided. This is necessary to prevent the process from thinking that it has received a new (unique) `shmid` when it has not. In other words, when both `PC_CREAT` and `IPC_EXCL` are specified, a unique shared memory identifier is returned if the system call is successful. Any value for `shmflg` returns a new identifier if the `key` equals zero (`IPC_PRIVATE`) and no system-tunable parameters are exceeded.

The system call will fail if the value for the `size` argument is less than `SHMMIN` or greater than `SHMMAX`. These tunable parameters specify the minimum and maximum shared memory segment sizes.

Refer to the `shmget`(2) manual page in the *Programmer's Reference Manual* for specific associated data structure initialization for successful completion. The specific failure conditions and their error names are contained there also.

Example Program

Figure 4-11 is a menu-driven program. It allows all possible combinations of using the `shmget` system call to be exercised.

From studying this program, you can observe the method of passing arguments and receiving return values. The user-written program requirements are pointed out.

This program begins (lines 4-7) by including the required header files as specified by the `shmget`(2) entry in the *Programmer's Reference Manual*. Note that the `<sys/errno.h>` header file is included as opposed to declaring `errno` as an external variable; either method will work.

Variable names have been chosen to be as close as possible to those in the synopsis for the system call. Their declarations are self explanatory. These names make the program more readable and are perfectly legal since they are local to the program. The variables declared for this program and what they are used for are as follows:

`key`	used to pass the value for the desired `key`
`opperm`	used to store the desired operation permissions
`flags`	used to store the desired control commands (flags)
`shmid`	used for returning the message queue identification number for a successful system call or the error code (-1) for an unsuccessful one

size   used to specify the shared memory segment size

opperm_flags   used to store the combination from the logical ORing of the opperm and flags variables; it is then used in the system call to pass the shmflg argument

The program begins by prompting for a hexadecimal key, an octal operation permissions code, and finally for the control command combinations (flags) which are selected from a menu (lines 14-31). All possible combinations are allowed even though they might not be viable. This allows observing the errors for illegal combinations.

Next, the menu selection for the flags is combined with the operation permissions; the result is stored in the opperm_flags variable (lines 35-50).

A display then prompts for the size of the shared memory segment; it is stored in the size variable (lines 51-54).

The system call is made next; the result is stored in the shmid variable (line 56).

Since the shmid variable now contains a valid message queue identifier or the error code (-1), it is tested to see if an error occurred (line 58). If shmid equals -1, a message indicates that an error resulted and the external errno variable is displayed (line 60).

If no error occurred, the returned shared memory segment identifier is displayed (line 64).

The example program for the shmget system call follows. We suggest that you name the source program file shmget.c and the executable file shmget.

Figure 4-11: shmget **System Call Example**

```
1    /*This is a program to illustrate
2    **the shared memory get, shmget(),
3    **system call capabilities.*/
4    #include    <sys/types.h>
5    #include    <sys/ipc.h>
6    #include    <sys/shm.h>
7    #include    <errno.h>
8    /*Start of main C language program*/
9    main()
10   {
11       key_t key;              /*declare as long integer*/
12       int opperm, flags;
13       int shmid, size, opperm_flags;
14       /*Enter the desired key*/
15       printf("Enter the desired key in hex = ");
16       scanf("%x", &key);
17       /*Enter the desired octal operation
18         permissions.*/
19       printf("\nEnter the operation\n");
20       printf("permissions in octal = ");
21       scanf("%o", &opperm);
22       /*Set the desired flags.*/
23       printf("\nEnter corresponding number to\n");
24       printf("set the desired flags:\n");
25       printf("No flags                 = 0\n");
26       printf("IPC_CREAT                = 1\n");
27       printf("IPC_EXCL                 = 2\n");
28       printf("IPC_CREAT and IPC_EXCL   = 3\n");
29       printf("            Flags        = ");
30       /*Get the flag(s) to be set.*/
31       scanf("%d", &flags);
32       /*Check the values.*/
33       printf ("\nkey =0x%x, opperm = 0%o, flags = %d\n",
34           key, opperm, flags);
35       /*Incorporate the control fields (flags) with
36         the operation permissions*/
37       switch (flags)
38       {
39       case 0:    /*No flags are to be set.*/
40           opperm_flags = (opperm | 0);
41           break;
42       case 1:    /*Set the IPC_CREAT flag.*/
```

(continued on next page)

Figure 4-11: shmget **System Call Example** (continued)

```
43              opperm_flags = (opperm | IPC_CREAT);
44              break;
45        case 2:    /*Set the IPC_EXCL flag.*/
46              opperm_flags = (opperm | IPC_EXCL);
47              break;
48        case 3:    /*Set the IPC_CREAT and IPC_EXCL flags.*/
49              opperm_flags = (opperm | IPC_CREAT | IPC_EXCL);
50        }
51        /*Get the size of the segment in bytes.*/
52        printf ("\nEnter the segment");
53        printf ("\nsize in bytes = ");
54        scanf ("%d", &size);
55        /*Call the shmget system call.*/
56        shmid = shmget (key, size, opperm_flags);
57        /*Perform the following if the call is unsuccessful.*/
58        if(shmid == -1)
59        {
60            printf ("\nThe shmget call failed, error number = %d\n", errno);
61        }
62        /*Return the shmid upon successful completion.*/
63        else
64            printf ("\nThe shmid = %d\n", shmid);
65        exit(0);
66    }
```

Controlling Shared Memory

This section describes how to use the shmctl system call. The accompanying program illustrates its use.

Using shmctl

The synopsis found in the shmctl(2) entry in the *Programmer's Reference Manual* is as follows:

```
#include <sys/types.h>
#include <sys/ipc.h>
#include <sys/shm.h>

int shmctl (shmid, cmd, buf)
int shmid, cmd;
struct shmid_ds *buf;
```

The shmctl system call requires three arguments to be passed to it. It returns an integer value which will be zero for successful completion or -1 otherwise.

The shmid variable must be a valid, non-negative, integer value. In other words, it must have already been created by using the shmget system call.

The cmd argument can be replaced by one of following values:

IPC_STAT	return the status information contained in the associated data structure for the specified shmid and place it in the data structure pointed to by the buf pointer in the user memory area
IPC_SET	for the specified shmid, set the effective user and group identification, and operation permissions
IPC_RMID	remove the specified shmid with its associated shared memory segment data structure
SHM_LOCK	lock the specified shared memory segment in memory; must be superuser to perform this operation
SHM_LOCK	lock the shared memory segment from memory; must be superuser to perform this operation

A process must have an effective user identification of OWNER/CREATOR or superuser to perform an IPC_SET or IPC_RMID control command. Only the superuser can perform a SHM_LOCK or SHM_UNLOCK control command. A process must have read permission to perform the IPC_STAT control command.

The details of this system call are discussed in the example program. If you need more information on the logic manipulations in this program, read "Using shmget". It goes into more detail than what would be practical for every system call.

Example Program

Figure 4-12 is a menu-driven program. It allows all possible combinations of using the shmctl system call to be exercised.

From studying this program, you can observe the method of passing arguments and receiving return values. The user-written program requirements are pointed out.

This program begins (lines 5-9) by including the required header files as specified by the shmctl(2) entry in the *Programmer's Reference Manual*. Note that in this program errno is declared as an external variable, and therefore, the <sys/errno.h> header file does not have to be included.

Variable and structure names have been chosen to be as close as possible to those in the synopsis for the system call. Their declarations are self explanatory. These names make the program more readable and are perfectly legal since they are local to the program. The variables declared for this program and what they are used for are as follows:

uid	used to store the IPC_SET value for the user identification
gid	used to store the IPC_SET value for the group identification
mode	used to store the IPC_SET value for the operation permissions
rtrn	used to store the return integer value from the system call
shmid	used to store and pass the shared memory segment identifier to the system call
command	used to store the code for the desired control command so that subsequent processing can be performed on it
choice	used to determine which member for the IPC_SET control command is to be changed

shmid_ds   used to receive the specified shared memory segment identifier's data structure when an IPC_STAT control command is performed

buf   a pointer passed to the system call which locates the data structure in the user memory area where the IPC_STAT control command is to place its return values or where the IPC_SET command gets the values to set.

Note that the shmid_ds data structure in this program (line 16) uses the data structure of the same name located in the <sys/shm.h> header file as a template for its declaration.

The next important thing to observe is that although the buf pointer is declared to be a pointer to a data structure of the shmid_ds type, it must also be initialized to contain the address of the user memory area data structure (line 17).

Now that all of the required declarations have been explained for this program, this is how it works.

First, the program prompts for a valid shared memory segment identifier which is stored in the shmid variable (lines 18-20). This is required for every shmctl system call.

Then, the code for the desired control command must be entered (lines 21-29); it is stored in the command variable. The code is tested to determine the control command for subsequent processing.

If the IPC_STAT control command is selected (code 1), the system call is performed (lines 39, 40) and the status information returned is printed out (lines 41-71). Note that if the system call is unsuccessful (line 139), the status information of the last successful call is printed out. In addition, an error message is displayed and the errno variable is printed out (lines 141). If the system call is successful, a message indicates this along with the shared memory segment identifier used (lines 143-147).

If the IPC_SET control command is selected (code 2), the first thing done is to get the current status information for the shared memory identifier specified (lines 88-90). This is necessary because this example program provides for changing only one member at a time, and the system call changes all of them. Also, if an invalid value happened to be stored in the user memory area for one of these members, it would cause repetitive failures for this control command until corrected. The next thing the program does is to prompt for a code corresponding to the member to be changed (lines 91-96). This code is stored in the choice variable (line 97). Now, depending upon the member picked, the program prompts for the new value (lines 98-120). The value is placed in the appropriate member in the user memory area data structure, and the system call is made (lines 121-128). Depending upon success or failure, the program returns the same messages as for IPC_STAT above.

If the IPC_RMID control command (code 3) is selected, the system call is performed (lines 125-128), and the shmid along with its associated message queue and data structure are removed from the UNIX operating system. Note that the buf pointer is ignored in performing this control command and its value can be zero or NULL. Depending upon the success or failure, the program returns the same messages as for the other control commands.

If the SHM_LOCK control command (code 4) is selected, the system call is performed (lines 130,131). Depending upon the success or failure, the program returns the same messages as for the other control commands.

If the SHM_UNLOCK control command (code 5) is selected, the system call is performed (lines 133-135). Depending upon the success or failure, the program returns the same messages as for the other control commands.

The example program for the shmctl system call follows. We suggest that you name the source program file shmctl.c and the executable file shmctl.

Figure 4-12: `shmctl` **System Call Example**

```
1      /*This is a program to illustrate
2      **the shared memory control, shmctl(),
3      **system call capabilities.
4      */

5      /*Include necessary header files.*/
6      #include    <stdio.h>
7      #include    <sys/types.h>
8      #include    <sys/ipc.h>
9      #include    <sys/shm.h>

10     /*Start of main C language program*/
11     main()
12     {
13         extern int errno;
14         int uid, gid, mode;
15         int rtrn, shmid, command, choice;
16         struct shmid_ds shmid_ds, *buf;
17         buf = &shmid_ds;

18         /*Get the shmid, and command.*/
19         printf("Enter the shmid = ");
20         scanf("%d", &shmid);
21         printf("\nEnter the number for\n");
22         printf("the desired command:\n");

23         printf("IPC_STAT    = 1\n");
24         printf("IPC_SET     = 2\n");
25         printf("IPC_RMID    = 3\n");
26         printf("SHM_LOCK    = 4\n");
27         printf("SHM_UNLOCK  = 5\n");
28         printf("Entry       = ");
29         scanf("%d", &command);

30         /*Check the values.*/
31         printf ("\nshmid =%d, command = %d\n",
32             shmid, command);

33         switch (command)
34         {
35         case 1:    /*Use shmctl() to get
36                    the data structure for
37                    shmid in the shmid_ds area pointed
38                    to by buf and then print it out.*/
```

(continued on next page)

Figure 4-12: shmctl **System Call Example** (continued)

```
39              rtrn = shmctl(shmid, IPC_STAT,
40                  buf);
41              printf ("\nThe USER ID = %d\n",
42                  buf->shm_perm.uid);
43              printf ("The GROUP ID = %d\n",
44                  buf->shm_perm.gid);
45              printf ("The creator's ID = %d\n",
46                  buf->shm_perm.cuid);
47              printf ("The creator's group ID = %d\n",
48                  buf->shm_perm.cgid);
49              printf ("The operation permissions = 0%o\n",
50                  buf->shm_perm.mode);
51              printf ("The slot usage sequence\n");
52              printf ("number = 0%x\n",
53                  buf->shm_perm.seq);
54              printf ("The key= 0%x\n",
55                  buf->shm_perm.key);
56              printf ("The segment size = %d\n",
57                  buf->shm_segsz);
58              printf ("The pid of last shmop = %d\n",
59                  buf->shm_lpid);
60              printf ("The pid of creator = %d\n",
61                  buf->shm_cpid);
62              printf ("The current # attached = %d\n",
63                  buf->shm_nattch);
64              printf("The last shmat time = %ld\n",
65                  buf->shm_atime);
66              printf("The last shmdt time = %ld\n",
67                  buf->shm_dtime);
68              printf("The last change time = %ld\n",
69                  buf->shm_ctime);
70              break;

                /* Lines 71 - 85 deleted */

86      case 2:   /*Select and change the desired
87                   member(s) of the data structure.*/

88              /*Get the original data for this shmid
89                  data structure first.*/
90              rtrn = shmctl(shmid, IPC_STAT, buf);

91              printf("\nEnter the number for the\n");
92              printf("member to be changed:\n");
```

(continued on next page)

Figure 4-12: shmctl **System Call Example** (continued)

```
93              printf("shm_perm.uid   = 1\n");
94              printf("shm_perm.gid   = 2\n");
95              printf("shm_perm.mode  = 3\n");
96              printf("Entry          = ");
97              scanf("%d", &choice);

98              switch(choice){
99              case 1:
100                 printf("\nEnter USER ID = ");
101                 scanf ("%d", &uid);
102                 buf->shm_perm.uid = uid;
103                 printf("\nUSER ID = %d\n",
104                     buf->shm_perm.uid);
105                 break;

106             case 2:
107                 printf("\nEnter GROUP ID = ");
108                 scanf("%d", &gid);
109                 buf->shm_perm.gid = gid;
110                 printf("\nGROUP ID = %d\n",
111                     buf->shm_perm.gid);
112                 break;

113             case 3:
114                 printf("\nEnter MODE in octal = ");
115                 scanf("%o", &mode);
116                 buf->shm_perm.mode = mode;
117                 printf("\nMODE = 0%o\n",
118                     buf->shm_perm.mode);
119                 break;
120             }
121             /*Do the change.*/
122             rtrn = shmctl(shmid, IPC_SET,
123                 buf);
124             break;

125         case 3:    /*Remove the shmid along with its
126                         associated
127                         data structure.*/
128             rtrn = shmctl(shmid, IPC_RMID, (struct shmid_ds *) NULL);
129             break;

130         case 4: /*Lock the shared memory segment*/
131             rtrn = shmctl(shmid, SHM_LOCK, (struct shmid_ds *) NULL);
```

(continued on next page)

Interprocess Communication

Figure 4-12: shmctl **System Call Example** (continued)

```
132          break;
133     case 5: /*Unlock the shared memory
134               segment.*/
135          rtrn = shmctl(shmid, SHM_UNLOCK, (struct shmid_ds *) NULL);
136          break;
137     }
138     /*Perform the following if the call is unsuccessful.*/
139     if(rtrn == -1)
140     {
41          printf ("\nThe shmctl call failed, error number = %d\n", errno);
142     }
143     /*Return the shmid upon successful completion.*/
144     else
145          printf ("\nShmctl was successful for shmid = %d\n",
146               shmid);
147     exit (0);
148     }
```

Operations for Shared Memory

This section describes how to use the shmat and shmdt system calls. The accompanying program illustrates their use.

Using shmop

The synopsis found in the shmop(2) entry in the *Programmer's Reference Manual* is as follows:

```
#include <sys/types.h>
#include <sys/ipc.h>
#include <sys/shm.h>

char *shmat (shmid, shmaddr, shmflg)
int shmid;
char *shmaddr;
int shmflg;

int shmdt (shmaddr)
char *shmaddr;
```

Attaching a Shared Memory Segment

The shmat system call requires three arguments to be passed to it. It returns a character pointer value. Upon successful completion, this value will be the address in memory where the process is attached to the shared memory segment and when unsuccessful the value will be -1.

The shmid argument must be a valid, non-negative, integer value. In other words, it must have already been created by using the shmget system call.

The shmaddr argument can be zero or user supplied when passed to the shmat system call. If it is zero, the UNIX operating system picks the address where the shared memory segment will be attached. If it is user supplied, the address must be a valid address that the UNIX operating system would pick. The following illustrates some typical address ranges.

> 0xc00c0000
> 0xc00e0000
> 0xc0100000
> 0xc0120000

Note that these addresses are in chunks of 20,000 hexadecimal. It would be wise to let the operating system pick addresses so as to improve portability.

The shmflg argument is used to pass the SHM_RND and SHM_RDONLY flags to the shmat system call.

Detaching Shared Memory Segments

The shmdt system call requires one argument to be passed to it. It returns an integer value which will be zero for successful completion or -1 otherwise.

Further details on shmat and shmdt are discussed in the example program. If you need more information on the logic manipulations in this program, read "Using shmget". It goes into more detail than would be practical to do for every system call.

Example Program

Figure 4-13 is a menu-driven program. It allows all possible combinations of using the shmat and shmdt system calls to be exercised.

From studying this program, you can observe the method of passing arguments and receiving return values. The user-written program requirements are pointed out.

This program begins (lines 5-9) by including the required header files as specified by the shmop(2) entry in the *Programmer's Reference Manual*. Note that in this program errno is declared as an external variable; therefore, the <sys/errno.h> header file does not have to be included.

Variable and structure names have been chosen to be as close as possible to those in the synopsis. Their declarations are self explanatory. These names make the program more readable and are perfectly legal since they are local to the program. The variables declared for this program and what they are used for are as follows:

addr	used to store the address of the shared memory segment for the shmat and shmdt system calls and to receive the return value from the shmat system call
laddr	used to store the desired attach/detach address entered by the user
flags	used to store the codes of the SHM_RND or SHM_RDONLY flags for the shmat system call
i	used as a loop counter for attaching and detaching

`attach`	used to store the desired number of attach operations
`shmid`	used to store and pass the desired shared memory segment identifier
`shmflg`	used to pass the value of flags to the `shmat` system call
`retrn`	used to store the return values from the `shmdt` system call
`detach`	used to store the desired number of detach operations

This example program combines both the `shmat` and `shmdt` system calls. The program prompts for the number of attachments and enters a loop until they are done for the specified shared memory identifiers. Then, the program prompts for the number of detachments to be performed and enters a loop until they are done for the specified shared memory segment addresses.

shmat

The program prompts for the number of attachments to be performed, and the value is stored at the address of the attach variable (lines 19-23).

A loop is entered using the attach variable and the i counter (lines 23-72) to perform the specified number of attachments.

In this loop, the program prompts for a shared memory segment identifier (lines 26-29); it is stored in the `shmid` variable (line 30). Next, the program prompts for the address where the segment is to be attached (lines 32-36); it is stored in the `laddr` variable (line 37) and converted to a pointer (line 39). Then, the program prompts for the desired flags to be used for the attachment (lines 40-47), and the code representing the flags is stored in the `flags` variable (line 48). The `flags` variable is tested to determine the code to be stored for the `shmflg` variable used to pass them to the `shmat` system call (lines 49-60). The system call is executed (line 63). If successful, a message stating so is displayed along with the attach address (lines 68-70). If unsuccessful, a message stating so is displayed and the error code is displayed (line 65). The loop then continues until it finishes.

shmdt

After the attach loop completes, the program prompts for the number of detach operations to be performed (lines 73-77) and the value is stored in the detach variable (line 76).

A loop is entered using the detach variable and the i counter (lines 80-98) to perform the specified number of detachments.

In this loop, the program prompts for the address of the shared memory segment to be detached (lines 81-85); it is stored in the laddr variable (line 86) and converted to a pointer (line 88). Then, the shmdt system call is performed (line 89). If successful, a message stating so is displayed along with the address that the segment was detached from (lines 95, 96). If unsuccessful, the error number is displayed (line 92). The loop continues until it finishes.

The example program for the shmop system calls follows. We suggest that you name the source program file shmop.c and the executable file shmop.

Figure 4-13: shmop **System Call Example**

```
 1    /*This is a program to illustrate
 2    **the shared memory operations, shmop(),
 3    **system call capabilities.
 4    */

 5    /*Include necessary header files.*/
 6    #include    <stdio.h>
 7    #include    <sys/types.h>
 8    #include    <sys/ipc.h>
 9    #include    <sys/shm.h>
10    /*Start of main C language program*/
11    main()
12    {
13        extern int errno;
14        char *addr;
15        long laddr;
16        int flags, i, attach;
17        int shmid, shmflg, retrn, detach;

18        /*Loop for attachments by this process.*/
19        printf("Enter the number of\n");
20        printf("attachments for this\n");
21        printf("process (1-4).\n");
22        printf("       Attachments = ");

23        scanf("%d", &attach);
24        printf("Number of attaches = %d\n", attach);
```

(continued on next page)

Figure 4-13: shmop **System Call Example** (continued)

```
25          for(i = 1; i <= attach; i++) {
26              /*Enter the shared memory ID.*/
27              printf("\nEnter the shmid of\n");
28              printf("the shared memory segment to\n");
29              printf("be operated on = ");
30              scanf("%d", &shmid);
31              printf("\nshmid = %d\n", shmid);


32              /*Enter the value for shmaddr.*/
33              printf("\nEnter the value for\n");
34              printf("the shared memory address\n");
35              printf("in hexadecimal:\n");
36              printf("          Shmaddr = ");
37              scanf("%lx", &laddr);
38              addr = (char*) laddr;
39              printf("The desired address = 0x%lx\n", (long)addr);

40              /*Specify the desired flags.*/
41              printf("\nEnter the corresponding\n");
422              printf("number for the desired\n");
43              printf("flags:\n");
44              printf("SHM_RND               = 1\n");
45              printf("SHM_RDONLY            = 2\n");
46              printf("SHM_RND and SHM_RDONLY = 3\n");
47              printf("          Flags    = ");
48              scanf("%d", &flags);

49              switch(flags)
50              {
51              case 1:
52                  shmflg = SHM_RND;
53                  break;
54              case 2:
55                  shmflg = SHM_RDONLY;
56                  break;
57              case 3:
58                  shmflg = SHM_RND | SHM_RDONLY;
59                  break;
60              }
61              printf("\nFlags = 0%o\n", shmflg);

62              /*Do the shmat system call.*/
63              addr = shmat(shmid, addr, shmflg);
```

(continued on next page)

Figure 4-13: shmop **System Call Example** (continued)

```
64          if(addr == (char*) -1) {
65              printf("\nShmat failed, error = %d\n", errno);
66          }
67          else {
68              printf ("\nShmat was successful\n");
69              printf("for shmid = %d\n", shmid);
70              printf("The address = 0x%lx\n", (long)addr);
71          }
72      }

73      /*Loop for detachments by this process.*/
74      printf("Enter the number of\n");
75      printf("detachments for this\n");
76      printf("process (1-4).\n");
77      printf("      Detachments = ");

78      scanf("%d", &detach);
79      printf("Number of attaches = %d\n", detach);
80      for(i = 1; i <= detach; i++) {

81          /*Enter the value for shmaddr.*/
82          printf("\nEnter the value for\n");
83          printf("the shared memory address\n");
84          printf("in hexadecimal:\n");
85          printf("            Shmaddr = ");
86          scanf("%lx", &laddr);
87          addr = (char*)laddr;
88          printf("The desired address = 0x%lx\n", (long)addr);

89          /*Do the shmdt system call.*/
90          retrn = shmdt(addr);
91          if(retrn == -1)  {
92              printf("Error = %d\n", errno);
93          }
94          else {
95              printf ("\nShmdt was successful\n");
96              printf("for address  = 0x%lx\n", (long)addr);

97          }
98      }
99  }
```

IPC Programming Example

To illustrate the use of UNIX system programming tools in the development of an application, we are going to pretend we are engaged in the development of a computer system for a library. The system is known as liber. The early stages of system development, we assume, have already been completed; feasibility studies have been done, the preliminary design is described in the coming paragraphs. We are going to stop short of producing a complete detailed design and module specifications for our system. You will have to accept that these exist. In using portions of the system for examples of the topics covered in this chapter, we will work from these virtual specifications.

We make no claim as to the efficacy of this design. It is the way it is only in order to provide some passably realistic examples of UNIX system programming tools in use. It is not an application, but rather is code fragments only.

liber is a system for keeping track of the books in a library. The hardware consists of a single computer with terminals throughout the library. One terminal is used for adding new books to the data base. Others are used for checking out books and as electronic card catalogs.

The design of the system calls for it to be brought up at the beginning of the day and remain running while the library is in operation. Associated with each terminal is a program specific to the function of that terminal, each running as a separate UNIX process. The system has one master index that contains the unique identifier of each title in the library. When the system is running the index is mapped into the address space of each process. Semaphores are used to synchronize access to the index. In the pages that follow fragments of some of the system's programs are shown to illustrate the way they work together. The startup program performs the system initialization; opening the semaphores and the index file; mapping the index file into memory; and kicking off the other programs. The id numbers for the semaphores (wrtsem, and rdsem) are written to a file during initialization, this file is then read by all the subsidiary programs so that all use the same semaphores.

All the programs share access to the index file. They gain access to it with the following code:

```
/*
 * Gain access to the index file, map it in.
 * After mapping, free the file descriptor so
 * that it will be available for other uses --
 * the mapping will remain until the program
 * exits, or until the mapping is removed either
 * by munmap() or by mapping over top of this one
 * with another call to mmap().  Note the use of
 * the read/write open mode -- all programs but
 * "add-books" should open just for read-only.
 */
if ((index_fd = open("index.file", O_RDWR)) == -1)
{
        (void) fprintf(stderr, "index open failed: %d\n", errno);
        exit(1);
}
/*
 * Establish the mapping.  As with the call to
 * open(), all programs but "add-books" should
 * map with PROT_READ for read-only access.
 */
if ((int)(index = (INDEX *)mmap(0, sizeof (INDEX), PROT_READ|PROT_WRITE,
    MAP_SHARED, index_fd, 0) == -1)
{
        (void) fprintf(stderr, "shmat failed: %d\n", errno);
        exit(1);
}
(void) close(index_fd);
```

The preceding code fragment establishes a mapping to the index file in the
address space of the program. Access to the addresses at which the file is
mapped affect the file directly, no further file operations are required. For
instance, if the access deposits data at the accessed address, then the file will be
modified by operation. If the access examines data, then the file will be
accessed. In either case, the portion of the file containing the information will
be obtained or restored to secondary storage automatically by the system and
transparently to the application.

Of the programs shown, add-books is the only one that alters the index. The
semaphores are used to ensure that no other programs will try to read the index
while add-books is altering it. The checkout program locks the file record for
the book, so that each copy being checked out is recorded separately and the
book cannot be checked out at two different checkout stations at the same time.

The program fragments do not provide any details on the structure of the index or the book records in the data base.

```
                        /* liber.h - header file for the
                         *          library system.
                         */
typedef ... INDEX;       /* data structure for book file index */
typedef struct {         /* type of records in book file */
       char title[30];
       char author[30];
         .
         .
         .
} BOOK;
int index_fd;
int wrtsem;
int rdsem;
INDEX *index;

int book_file;
BOOK book_buf;

/*      startup program  */

/*
 * 1. Open index file and map it in.
 * 2. Open two semaphores for providing exclusive write access to index.
 * 3. Stash id's for shared memory segment and semaphores in a file
 *    where they can be accessed by the programs.
 * 4. Start programs:  add-books, card-catalog, and checkout running
 *    on the various terminals throughout the library.
 */

#include    <stdio.h>
#include    <sys/types.h>
#include    <sys/ipc.h>
#include    <sys/shm.h>
#include    <sys/sem.h>
#include    "liber.h"

void exit();
extern int errno;

key_t key;
int shmid;
int wrtsem;
```

(continued on next page)

```
int rdsem;
FILE *ipc_file;

main()
{
     .
     .
     .
     /*
      * Open index file and map it.
      */

     /* See previous example */

     /*
      * Get the read/write semaphores.
      */
     if ((wrtsem = semget(key, 1, IPC_CREAT | 0666)) == -1)
     {
          (void) fprintf(stderr, "startup: semget failed: errno=%d\n", errno);
          exit(1);
     }

     if ((rdsem = semget(key, 1, IPC_CREAT | 0666)) == -1)
     {
          (void) fprintf(stderr, "startup: semget failed: errno=%d\n", errno);
          exit(1);
     }
     (void) fprintf(ipc_file, "%d\n%d\n", wrtsem, rdsem);

     /*
      * Start the add-books program running on the terminal in the
      * basement.  Start the checkout and card-catalog programs
      * running on the various other terminals throughout the library.
      */
     .
     .
     .
}

/*     card-catalog program*/

/*
 * 1. Read screen for author and title.
 * 2. Use semaphores to prevent reading index while it is being written.
 * 3. Use index to get position of book record in book file.
```

(continued on next page)

```
* 4. Print book record on screen or indicate book was not found.
* 5. Go to 1.
*/

#include        <stdio.h>
#include        <sys/types.h>
#include        <sys/ipc.h>
#include        <sys/sem.h>
#include    <fcntl.h>
#include    "liber.h"

void exit();
extern int errno;
struct sembuf sop[1];

main() {
    .
    .
    .

    while (1)
    {
        /*
         * Read author/title/subject information from screen.
         */

        /*
         * Wait for write semaphore to reach 0 (index not being written).
         */
        sop[0].sem_op = 1;
        if (semop(wrtsem, sop, 1) == -1)
        {
                (void) fprintf(stderr, "semop failed: %d\n", errno);
                exit(1);
        }
        /*
         * Increment read semaphore so potential writer will wait
         * for us to finish reading the index.
         */
        sop[0].sem_op = 0;
        if (semop(rdsem, sop, 1) == -1)
        {
                (void) fprintf(stderr, "semop failed: %d\n", errno);
                exit(1);
        }
```

(continued on next page)

```
              /* Use index to find file pointer(s) for book(s) */

              /* Decrement read semaphore */
              sop[0].sem_op = -1;
              if (semop(rdsem, sop, 1) == -1)
              {
                      (void) fprintf(stderr, "semop failed: %d\n", errno);
                      exit(1);
              }

              /*
               * Now we use the file pointers found in the index to
               * read the book file.  Then we print the information
               * on the book(s) to the screen.
               */

              /*
               * Note design alternatives for this portion of the
               * the code: the book file could be accessed by
               * lseek()s to the portion of the file containing
               * the record, and then read() could be used to
               * obtain the file information.  Alternatively, the
               * entire book file could be mapped into memory, and the
               * the record accessed directly without further
               * file operations, or the area of the file containing
               * the book record could just be mapped and then unmapped
               * when the access is complete.
               */
               .
               .
               .

       } /* while */
}
/*    checkout program */

/*
 * 1. Read screen for Dewey Decimal number of book to be checked out.
 * 2. Use semaphores to prevent reading index while it is being written.
 * 3. Use index to get position of book record in book file.
 * 4. If book not found print message on screen, otherwise lock
 *    book record and read.
 * 5. If book already checked out print message on screen, otherwise
 *    mark record "checked out" and write back to book file.
 * 6. Unlock book record.
 * 7. Go to 1.
```

(continued on next page)

```
    */

#include        <stdio.h>
#include        <sys/types.h>
#include        <sys/ipc.h>
#include        <sys/sem.h>
#include     <fcntl.h>
#include     "liber.h"

void exit();
long lseek();
extern int errno;
struct flock flk;
struct sembuf sop[1];
long bookpos;

main()
{
    .
    .
    .
    while (1)
    {
        /*
         * Read Dewey Decimal number from screen.
         */

        /*
         * Wait for write semaphore to reach 0 (index not being written).
         */
        sop[0].sem_flg = 0;
        sop[0].sem_op = 0;
        if (semop(wrtsem, sop, 1) == -1)
        {
                (void) fprintf(stderr, "semop failed: %d\n", errno);
                exit(1);
        }
        /*
         * Increment read semaphore so potential writer will wait
         * for us to finish reading the index.
         */
        sop[0].sem_op = 1;
        if (semop(rdsem, sop, 1) == -1)
        {
                (void) fprintf(stderr, "semop failed: %d\n", errno);
                exit(1);
```

(continued on next page)

```
        }
        /*
         * Now we can use the index to find the book's record position.
         * Assign this value to "bookpos".
         */

        /* Decrement read semaphore */
        sop[0].sem_op = -1;
        if (semop(rdsem, sop, 1) == -1)
        {
                (void) fprintf(stderr, "semop failed: %d\n", errno);
                exit(1);
        }

        /*
         * Lock the book's record in book file, read the record.
         * Here again we have the design option of deciding to
         * access and update the database through the use of
         * seeks, read()s and write()s; or file mapping can
         * be used to access the file.  File mapping has the
         * disadvantage that it does not interact well with
         * enforcement-mode locking, although semaphores
         * could be used as an alternative synchronization
         * mechanism to file locking.  File mapping would have
         * potential efficiency advantages, eliminating the need
         * for repetitive file access operations and attendant
         * data copying.  For this example, however, we choose
         * not to use mapping to demonstrate the use of other
         * system facilities.
         */
        flk.l_type = F_WRLCK;
        flk.l_whence = 0;
        flk.l_start = bookpos;
        flk.l_len = sizeof(BOOK);
        if (fcntl(book_file, F_SETLKW, &flk) == -1)

        {
                (void) fprintf(stderr, "trouble locking: %d\n", errno);
                exit(1);
        }
        if (lseek(book_file, bookpos, 0) == -1)
        {
                (Error processing for lseek);
        }
        if (read(book_file, &book_buf, sizeof(BOOK)) == -1)
```

(continued on next page)

```
                {
                        (Error processing for read);
                }

                /*
                 * If the book is checked out inform the client, otherwise
                 * mark the book's record as checked out and write it
                 * back into the book file.
                 */

                /* Unlock the book's record in book file. */
                flk.l_type = F_UNLCK;
                if (fcntl(book_file, F_SETLK, &flk) == -1)
                {
                        (void) fprintf(stderr, "trouble unlocking: %d\n", errno);
                        exit(1);
                }
        } /* while */
}

/*      add-books program*/

/*
 * 1. Read a new book entry from screen.
 * 2. Insert book in book file.
 * 3. Use semaphore "wrtsem" to block new readers.
 * 4. Wait for semaphore "rdsem" to reach 0.
 * 5. Insert book into index.
 * 6. Decrement wrtsem.
 * 7. Go to 1.
 */

#include <stdio.h>
#include    <sys/types.h>
#include    <sys/ipc.h>
#include    <sys/sem.h>
#include    "liber.h"

void exit();
extern int errno;
struct sembuf sop[1];
BOOK bookbuf;

main()
{
```

(continued on next page)

```
.
.
.
for (;;)
{

      /*
       * Read information on new book from screen.
       */

      addscr(&bookbuf);

      /* write new record at the end of the bookfile.
       * Code not shown, but
       * addscr() returns a 1 if title information has
       * been entered, 0 if not.
       */

      /*
       * Increment write semaphore, blocking new readers from
       * accessing the index.
       */
      sop[0].sem_flg = 0;
      sop[0].sem_op = 1;
      if (semop(wrtsem, sop, 1) == -1)
      {
                (void) fprintf(stderr, "semop failed: %d\n", errno);
                exit(1);
      }

      /*
       * Wait for read semaphore to reach 0 (all readers to finish
       * using the index).
       */
      sop[0].sem_op = 0;
      if (semop(rdsem, sop, 1) == -1)
      {
                (void) fprintf(stderr, "semop failed: %d\n", errno);
                exit(1);
      }
      /*
       * Now that we have exclusive access to the index we
       * insert our new book with its file pointer.
       */

      /* Decrement write semaphore, permitting readers to read index. */
      sop[0].sem_op = -1;
```

(continued on next page)

```
        if (semop(wrtsem, sop, 1) == -1)
        {
                (void) fprintf(stderr, "semop failed: %d\n", errno);
                exit(1);
        }
  } /* for */
  .
  .
  .
}
```

The example following, addscr, illustrates two significant points about curses screens:

1. Information read in from a curses window can be stored in fields that are part of a structure defined in the header file for the application.

2. The address of the structure can be passed from another function where the record is processed.

```
                        /*  addscr is called from add-books.
                         *  The user is prompted for title
                         *  information.
                         */
#include <curses.h>

WINDOW *cmdwin;

addscr(bb)
struct BOOK *bb;
{
      int c;

      initscr();
      nonl();
      noecho();
      cbreak();                    .

      cmdwin = newwin(6, 40, 3, 20);
      mvprintw(0, 0, "This screen is for adding titles to the data base");
      mvprintw(1, 0, "Enter  a  to add;  q  to quit: ");
      refresh();
      for (;;)
      {
            refresh();
            c = getch();
            switch (c) {
              case 'a':
                        werase(cmdwin);
                        box(cmdwin, '|', '-');
                        mvwprintw(cmdwin, 1, 1, "Enter title: ");
                        wmove(cmdwin, 2, 1);
                        echo();
                        wrefresh(cmdwin);
                        wgetstr(cmdwin, bb->title);
                        noecho();
                        werase(cmdwin);
                        box(cmdwin, '|', '-');
                        mvwprintw(cmdwin, 1, 1, "Enter author: ");
                        wmove(cmdwin, 2, 1);
                        echo();
                        wrefresh(cmdwin);
                        wgetstr(cmdwin, bb->author);
                        noecho();
                        werase(cmdwin);
                        wrefresh(cmdwin);
```

(continued on next page)

```
                        endwin();
                        return(1);
                case 'q':
                        erase();
                        endwin();
                        return(0);
                }
        }
}


#
# Makefile for liber library system
#

CC = cc
CFLAGS = -O
all: startup add-books checkout card-catalog

startup: liber.h startup.c
     $(CC) $(CFLAGS) -o startup startup.c

add-books: add-books.o addscr.o
     $(CC) $(CFLAGS) -o add-books add-books.o addscr.o

add-books.o: liber.h

checkout: liber.h checkout.c
     $(CC) $(CFLAGS) -o checkout checkout.c

card-catalog: liber.h card-catalog.c
     $(CC) $(CFLAGS) -o card-catalog card-catalog.c
```

5 Directory and File Management

5. DIRECTORY AND FILE MANAGEMENT

Summary of UNIX System Files & Directories

5. DIRECTORY AND FILE MANAGEMENT

Integrated Software Development Guide

Introduction

UNIX System V File System functions create and remove files and directories, and inspect and modify their characteristics. Processes use these functions to access files and directories for subsequent I/O operations. One of the most important services provided by an operating system is to maintain a consistent, orderly and easily accessed file-system. The UNIX System V file-system contains directories of files arranged in a tree-like structure. The UNIX System V file-system is simple in structure; nevertheless, it is more powerful and general than those often found even in considerably larger operating systems.

All UNIX System V files have a consistent structure to conceal physical properties of the device storing the file, such as the size of a disk track. It is not necessary, nor even possible, to preallocate space for a file. The size of a file is the number of bytes in it, with the last byte determined by the high-water mark of writes to the file. UNIX System V presents each file as a featureless, randomly addressable sequence of bytes arranged as a one-dimensional array of bytes ending with EOF.

The UNIX System V file-system organizes files and directories into a tree-like structure of directories with files attached anywhere (and possibly multiply) into this hierarchy of directories. Files can be accessed by a "full-path-name" or "relative-path-name", have independent protection modes, are automatically allocated and de-allocated, and can be linked across directories.

In the hierarchically arranged directory tree-structure, each directory contains a list of names (character strings) and the associated file index, which implicitly refers to the same device as does the directory. Because directories are themselves files, the naming structure is potentially an arbitrary directed graph. Administrative rules restrict it to have the form of a tree, except that non-directory-files may have several names (entries in various directories).

The same non-directory-file may appear in several directories under possibly different names. This feature is called *linking*; a directory-entry for a file is sometimes called a *link*. UNIX System V differs from other systems in which linking is permitted in that all links to a file have equal status. That is, a file does not exist within a particular directory; the directory-entry for a file consists merely of its name and a pointer to the information actually describing the file. Thus, a file exists independently of any directory-entry, although in practice a file is removed along with the last link to it.

Structure of the File System

Types of Files

From the point of view of the user, there are three types of files:

1. regular-files.

2. directory-files.

3. special-files.

The user and user application programs access all three types of files simply as a string of bytes, and must interpret the file appropriately. In UNIX System V, files normally reside on a disk.

Regular Files

Regular-files contain whatever information users write onto them (e.g., character data, source programs or binary objects). Any file other than a special-file or a directory-file is a regular-file. Every file is a (one-dimensional) array of bytes; UNIX System V imposes no further structure on the contents of files. A file of text consists simply of a string of characters, with the new-line character delimiting lines. Binary files are sequences of words as they appear in memory when the file executes. Some programs operate on files with more structure; for example, the assembler generates, and the loader expects, object files in a specific format. The programs that use files dictate their structure, not the system.

Directory Files

Directory-files (also called "directories") provide the mapping (paths) between the names of files and the files themselves. Directories induce a tree-like structure on the file-system as a whole to create a hierarchical system of files with directories as the nodes in the hierarchy. A directory is a file that catalogs the files, including directories (sub-directories), directly beneath it in the hierarchy.

Each user owns a directory of files, and may also create sub-directories to contain groups of files conveniently treated together. A directory behaves exactly like a regular-file except that only the operating system can write onto it. UNIX System V controls the contents of directories; however, users with permission may read a directory just like any other file.

Integrated Software Development Guide

The operating system maintains several directories for its own use. One of these is the *root-directory*. Each file in the file-system can be found by tracing a path from the root-directory through a chain of directories until the desired file is reached. Other system directories contain any programs provided for general use; that is, all *commands*; however, it is by no means necessary that a program reside in one of these directories for it to be executed.

Entries in a directory-file are called *links*. A link associates a file-identifier with a file-name. Each directory has at least two links, " . " (*dot*) and " . . " (*dot-dot*). The link *dot* refers to the directory itself; while *dot-dot* refers to the parent of the directory in which *dot-dot* appears. Programs may read the current-directory using " . " without knowing its complete path-name.

The root-directory, which is the top-most node of the hierarchy, has itself as its parent-directory; thus, " / " is the path-name of both the root-directory and the parent-directory of the root-directory.

The directory structure is constrained to have the form of a rooted tree. Except for the special entries " . " and " . . ", each directory must appear as an entry in exactly one other directory, which is its parent. The reason for this is to simplify the writing of programs that visit sub-trees of the directory structure, and more important, to avoid the separation of portions of the hierarchy. If arbitrary links to directories were permitted, it would be quite difficult to detect when the last connection from the root-directory to a directory was severed.

Special Files

Special files constitute the most unusual feature of the UNIX System V file-system. Each supported I/O device is associated with at least one special file. Special files are read and written just like regular-files, but requests to read or write result in activation of the associated device-handler (driver) rather than the normal file mechanism.

An entry for each special-file resides under the directory " /dev", although a link may be made to one of these files just as it may to a regular-file. For example, to write on magnetic tape one may write on the file " /dev/mt ". Special files exist for peripheral devices such as terminal ports, communication links, disk drives, tape drives and for physical main memory. Of course, the active disks and memory special-files are protected from indiscriminate access by appropriate *read* and *write* permissions.

There are several advantages to treating I/O devices this way:

- file and device I/O are as similar as possible; all I/O is treated uniformly, and the same system calls work on all types of files.

- file and device names have the same syntax and meaning, so that a program expecting a file-name as a parameter can be passed a device name.

- the same protection mechanism works on special-files, directory-files and regular-files.

Organization of Files

The file system is made up of a set of regular files, special files, symbolic links, and directories. These components provide a way to organize, retrieve, and manage information electronically. Chapter 2 on "File and Device Input/Output" introduced some of the properties of directories and files; this section will review them briefly before discussing how to use them.

- A regular file is a collection of characters stored on a disk. It may contain text for a report or code for a program.

- A special file represents a physical device, such as a terminal or disk.

- A symbolic link is a file that points to another file.

- A directory is a collection of files and other directories (sometimes called subdirectories). Use directories to group files together on the basis of any criteria you choose. For example, you might create a directory for each product that your company sells or for each of your student's records.

The set of all the directories and files is organized into a tree shaped structure. Figure 5-1 shows a sample file structure with a directory called root (/) as its source. By moving down the branches extending from root, you can reach several other major system directories. By branching down from these, you can, in turn, reach all the directories and files in the file system.

Figure 5-1: A Sample File System

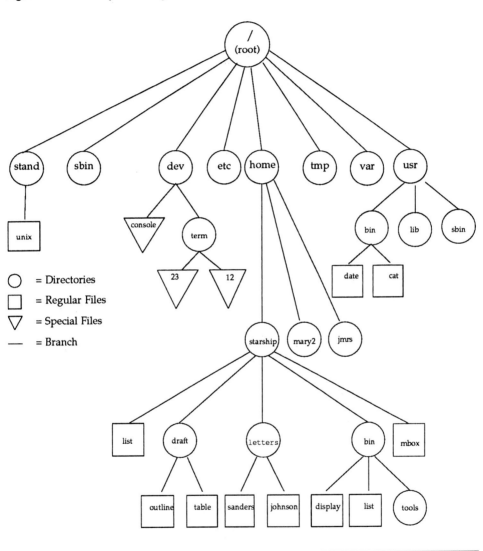

In this hierarchy, files and directories that are subordinate to a directory have what is called a parent/child relationship. This type of relationship is possible for many layers of files and directories. In fact, there is no limit to the number of files and directories you may create in any directory that you own. Neither is there a limit to the number of layers of directories that you may create. Thus you have the capability to organize your files in a variety of ways, as shown in the preceding figure.

File Naming

Strings of 1 to {NAME_MAX} characters may be used to name a regular-file, directory-file or special-file. {NAME_MAX} must be at least 14, and the characters may be any from the set of all character values excluding *null* and *slash*, " / ". The following are examples of legal directory or file names:

```
memo        MEMO        section2    ref:list
file.d      chap3+4     item1-10    outline
```

A regular-file, special-file or directory may have any name that conforms to the following rules:

- All characters other than / are legal.

- Non-printing characters including space, tab and backspace, are best avoided. If you use a space or tab in a directory or file-name, you must enclose the name in quotation-marks on the command-line.

- Note that it is generally unwise to use " * ", " ? ", " ! ", " [" or "] " as part of file-names because of the special meaning given these characters for file-name expansion by the command interpreter [see system(2)]. Other characters to avoid are the hyphen, " < ", " > ", backslash, single and double quotes, accent grave, vertical bar, caret, curly braces and parentheses.

- Avoid using a +, - or . as the first character in a file-name.

- Upper case and lower case characters are distinct to the UNIX system. For example, the system considers a directory (or file) named draft to be different from one named DRAFT.

Path Names

The name of a file may take the form of a *path-name*, which is a sequence of directory names separated from one another by " / " and ending in a file-name. In a program, a path-name is a null-terminated character-string starting with an optional slash, " / ", followed by zero or more directory-names separated by slashes and optionally followed by a file-name.

More precisely, a path-name is a null-terminated character-string as follows:

```
<path_name> ::= <file_name> | <path_prefix><file_name> | / | . | . .
<path_prefix> ::= <rtprefix> | /<rtprefix> | empty
<rtprefix> ::= <dirname> / | <rtprefix><dirname> /
```

where <file_name> is a string of 1 to {NAME_MAX} significant characters (other than slash and null), and <dirname> is a string of 1 to {NAME_MAX} significant characters (other than slash and null) that names a directory. The result of names not produced by the grammar are undefined. A null string is undefined and may be considered an error. As a limiting case, the path-name " / " refers to the root-directory itself. An attempt to create or delete the path-name slash by itself is undefined and may be considered an error. The meanings of " . " and " . . " are defined earlier under the heading "Directory Files".

The sequence of directories preceding the file-name is called a *path-prefix*, and if the path-prefix begins with a slash, the search begins in the root-directory. This is called a *full-path-name*.

Full Path Names

A full path name (sometimes called an "absolute path name") starts in the root directory and leads down through a unique sequence of directories to a particular directory or file. Because a full path name always starts at the root of the file system, its leading character is always a / (slash). The final name in a full path name can be either a file name or a directory name. All other names in the path must be directories. You can use a full path name to reach any file or directory in the UNIX system in which you are working.

To understand how a full path name is constructed and how it directs you, consider the following example. Suppose you are working in the starship directory, located in /home. You issue the pwd command and the system responds by printing the full path name of your working directory: /home/starship.

The following figure and key diagrams the elements of this path name:

Figure 5-2: Diagram of a Full Path-Name

/ (leading)	= the slash that appears as the first character in the path name is the root of the file system
home	= system directory one level below root in the hierarchy to which root points or branches
/ (subsequent)	= the next slash separates or delimits the directory names home and starship
starship	= current working directory

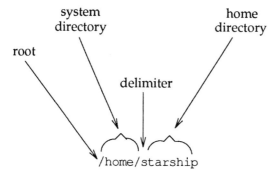

The following path-name:

    /usr/bin/send

causes a search of the root-directory for directory "usr", then a search of "usr" for "bin", finally to find "send" in "bin". The file "send" may be a directory, regular or special-file. A null-prefix (or for that matter, any path-prefix without an initial " / ") causes the search to begin in the current-directory of the user. Thus, the simplest form of path-name, "alpha", refers to a file found in the current-directory, and the path-name "alpha/beta" specifies the file named "beta" in sub-directory "alpha" of the current-directory. This *relative-path-name* allows a user to quickly specify a sub-directory without needing to know (or input) the full-path-name.

The dashed lines in Figure 5-3 trace the full path to /home/starship.

Figure 5-3: Full Path-Name of the /home/starship Directory

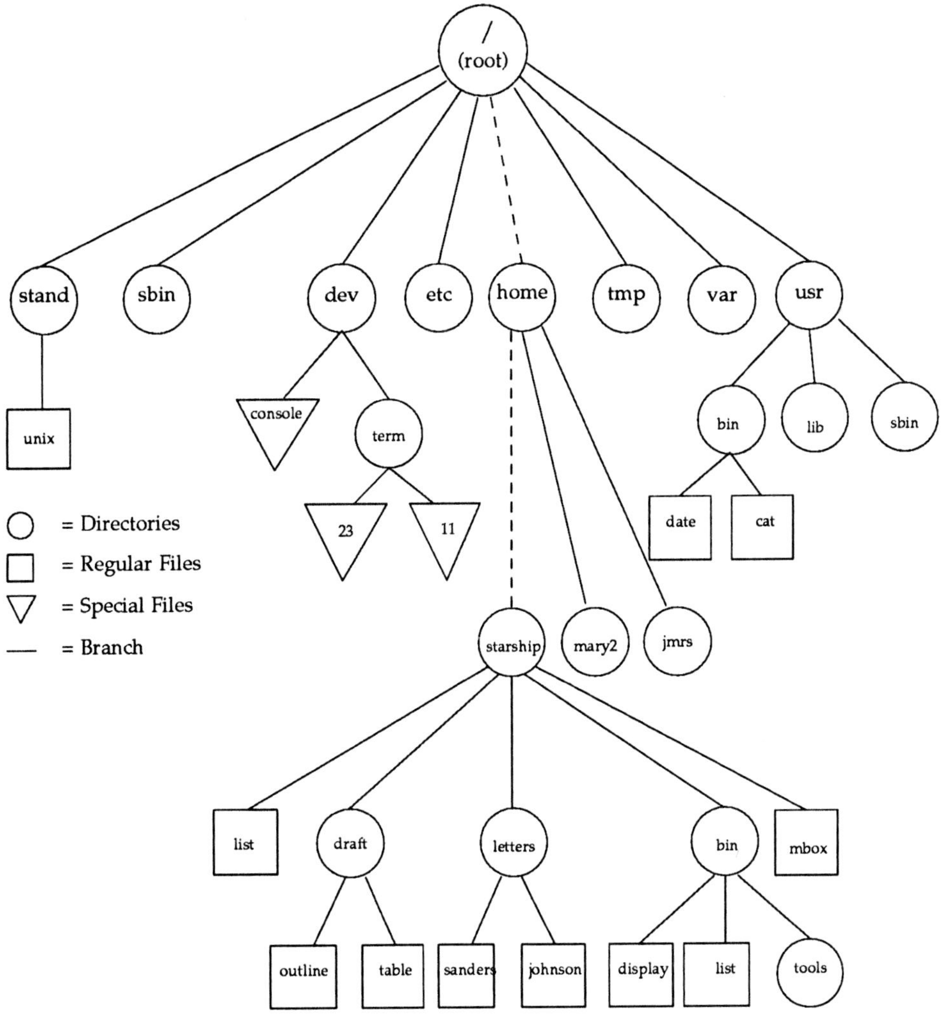

Relative Path Names

A relative path name gives directions that start in your current working directory and lead you up or down through a series of directories to a particular file or directory. By moving down from your current directory, you can access files and directories you own.

For example, suppose you are in the directory starship in the sample system and starship contains directories named draft, letters, and bin and a file named mbox. The relative path name to any of these is simply its name, such as draft or mbox. Figure 5-4 traces the relative path from starship to draft.

Figure 5-4: Relative Path-Name of the draft Directory

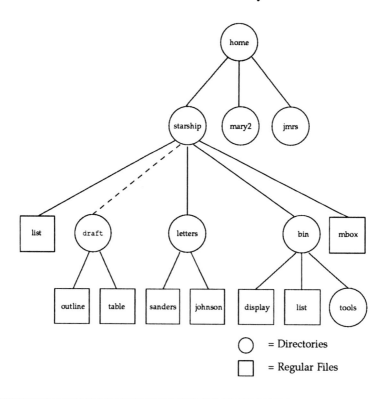

The draft directory belonging to starship contains the files outline and table. The relative path name from starship to the file outline is draft/outline.

Figure 5-5 traces this relative path. Notice that the slash in this path name separates the directory named draft from the file named outline. Here, the slash is a delimiter showing that outline is subordinate to draft; that is, outline is a child of its parent, draft.

Figure 5-5: Relative Path-Name from starship to outline

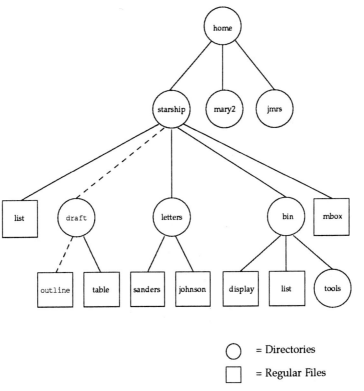

So far, the discussion of relative path-names has covered how to specify names of files and directories that belong to, or are children of, the current directory. You can move down the system hierarchy level by level until you reach your destination. You can also, however, ascend the levels in the system structure or ascend and subsequently descend into other files and directories.

By moving up from your current directory, you pass through layers of parent directories to the grandparent of all system directories, root. From there you can move anywhere in the file system.

The relative-path-name is just one of the mechanisms built into the file-system to alleviate the need to use full-path-names. By convention, the path-prefix " .. " refers to the parent-directory (i.e., the directory containing the current-directory), and the path-prefix " . " refers to the current-directory.

A relative path-name begins with one of the following: a directory or file name; a " . " (pronounced dot), which is a shorthand notation for your current directory; or a " .. " (pronounced dot dot), which is a shorthand notation for the directory immediately above your current directory in the file system hierarchy. The directory represented by " .. " (dot dot) is called the parent directory of . (your current directory).

To ascend to the parent of your current directory, you can use the " .. " notation. This means that if you are in the directory named "draft" in the sample file system, " .. " is the path-name to "starship", and " ../.. " is the path-name to "starship"'s parent directory, "home".

From "draft", you can also trace a path to the file "sanders" by using the path name " ../letters/sanders". The " .. " brings you up to "starship". Then the names "letters" and "sanders" take you down through the "letters" directory to the "sanders" file.

Keep in mind that you can always use a full path-name in place of a relative one.

Figure 5-6 shows some examples of full and relative path names.

Figure 5-6: Example Path-Names

Path Name	Meaning
/	full path name of the root directory
/usr/bin	full path name of the bin directory that belongs to the usr directory that belongs to root (contains most executable programs and utilities)
/home/starship/bin/tools	full path name of the tools directory belonging to the bin directory that belongs to the starship directory belonging to home that belongs to root
bin/tools	relative path name to the file or directory tools in the directory bin
	If the current directory is /, then the UNIX system searches for /usr/bin/tools. However, if the current directory is starship, then the system searches the full path /home/starship/bin/tools.
tools	relative path name of a file or directory tools in the current directory.

Moving files to the directory " . " moves them into the current-directory. In addition, files can be linked across directories. Linking a file to the current-directory obviates the need to supply a path-prefix when accessing the file. When created, a process has one current-directory and one root-directory associated with it, which can differ for other processes. See the chapter entitled "Process Management" for more detail on processes.

File Types

When the `ls -l` command displays the contents of a directory, the first column of output describes the "mode" of the file. This information tells you not only what type of file it is, but who has permission to access it. This first field is 10 characters long. The first character defines the file type and can be one of the following types:

Figure 5-7: File Types

Type	Symbol
Text, programs, etc.	–
Directories	d
Character special	c
Block special	b
FIFO (named pipe) special	p
Symbolic links	l

Using this key to interpret the previous screen, you can see that the `starship` directory contains three directories and two regular disk files.

The next several characters, which are either letters or hyphens, identify who has permission to read and use the file or directory. (Permissions are discussed in the description of the `chmod` function under "Accessing and Manipulating Files" later in this chapter.)

The following number is the link count. For a file, this equals the number of users linked to that file. For a directory, this number shows the number of directories immediately under it plus two (for the directory itself and its parent directory).

Next, the login name of the file's owner appears (here it is `starship`), followed by the group name of the file or directory (`project`).

The following number shows the length of the file or directory entry measured in units of information (or memory) called bytes. The month, day, and time that the file was last modified is given next. Finally, the last column shows the name of the directory or file.

Figure 5-8 identifies each column in the rows of output from the ls -l command.

Figure 5-8: Description of Output Produced by the ls -l Command

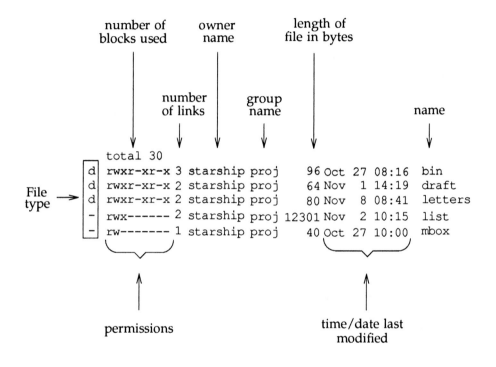

File Protection

Because the UNIX operating system is a multi-user system, you usually do not work alone in the file system. System users can follow pathnames to various directories and read and use files belonging to one another, as long as they have permission to do so.

If you own a file, you can decide who has the right to read it, write in it (make changes to it), or, if it is a program, to execute it. You can also restrict permissions for directories. When you grant execute permission for a directory, you allow the specified users to change directory to it and list its contents with the ls(1) command. Only the owner or a privileged user can define the following:

- which users have permission to access data

- which types of permission they have (that is, how they are allowed to use the data)

This section introduces access-permissions for files and discusses file protection.

File Permissions

UNIX System V defines access-control and privilege mechanisms to allow for extended-security-controls that implement security policies different from those in UNIX System V, but which avoid altering or overriding the defined semantics of any functions in UNIX System V. Although quite simple, the access-control scheme has some unusual features. Each UNIX System V user has a unique user-identification (user-id) number, as well as a shared group-identification (group-id) number. A file is tagged with the user-id and group-id of its owner, and a set of access-permission-bits when created by open, creat, mkdir and mkfifo [see open(2), creat(2), mkdir(2) and mkfifo(2)]. UNIX System V file-access-control uses the access-permission-bits to specify independent *read*, *write* and *execute* permissions for the *owner* of the file, for any members of the owner's *group* and for any *other* users. For directories, *execute* permission means *search* permission. These access-permission-bits are changed by chmod, and are read by stat and fstat [see chmod(2), stat(2) and fstat(2)].

When a process requests file-access-permission for *read*, *write* or *execute/search*, access is determined as follows:

1. If the effective-user-id of the process is a user with appropriate access-permissions (such as a super-user).

    a. If *read, write* or directory *search* permission is requested, access is granted.

    b. If *execute* permission is requested, access is granted if *execute* permission is granted to at least one user by the file-permission-bits or by an alternate-access-control mechanism; otherwise, access is denied.

2. Otherwise:

    a. The *read, write* and *execute/search* access-permissions on a file are granted to a process if one or more of the following are true [see chmod(2)]:

        ■ The appropriate access-permission-bit of the *owner* portion of the file-mode is set and the effective-user-id of the process matches the user-id of the owner of the file

        ■ The appropriate access-permission-bit of the *group* portion of the file-mode is set, the effective-group-id of the process matches the group-id of the file and the effective-user-id of the process fails to match the user-id of the owner of the file.

        ■ The appropriate access-permission-bit of the *other* portion of the file-mode is set, the effective-group-id of the process fails to match the group-id of the file and the effective-user-id of the process fails to match the user-id of the owner of the file.

    Otherwise, the corresponding access-permissions on a file are denied to the process.

    b. Access is granted if an alternate-access-control mechanism is not enabled and the requested access-permission-bit is set for the class to which the process belongs, or if an alternate-access-control mechanism is enabled and it allows the requested access; otherwise, access is denied.

Implementations may provide additional-file-access-control or alternate-file-access-control mechanisms, or both. An additional-access-control mechanism only further restricts the file-access-permissions defined by the file-permission-bits. An alternate-access-control mechanism shall:

1. specify file-permission-bits for the file-owner-class, file-group-class and file-other-class of the file, corresponding to the access-permissions, that stat and fstat return.

2. Be enabled only by explicit user action, on a per-file basis by the file-owner or a user with the appropriate-privilege.

3. Be disabled for a file after the file-permission-bits are changed for that file with chmod. The disabling of the alternate mechanism need not disable any additional mechanisms defined by an implementation.

UNIX System V recognizes one particular user-id, the "super-user", as exempt from the usual constraints on file access; thus, for example, programs may be written to dump and reload the file-system without unwanted interference from the protection system. A process is recognized as a super-user process and is granted special privileges if its effective-user-id is 0.

Setting Default Permissions

When a file is created its default permissions are set. These default settings may be changed by placing an appropriate umask command in the system profile (/etc/profile).

Figure 5-9: umask(1) Settings for Different Security Levels

Level of Security	umask	Disallows
Permissive	0002	w for others
Moderate	0027	w for group, rwx for others
Severe	0077	rwx for group and others

How to Determine Existing Permissions

You can determine what permissions are currently in effect on a file or a directory by using ls -l to produce a long listing of a directory's contents.

In the first field of the ls -l output, the next nine characters are interpreted as three sets of three bits each. The first set refers to the owner's permissions; the next to permissions of members in the file's group; and the last to all others. Within each set, the three characters show permission to read, to write, and to execute the file as a program, respectively. For a directory, "execute" permission is interpreted to mean permission to search the directory for a specified file. For example, typing ls -l while in the directory named starship/bin in the sample file-system produces the following output:

```
$ ls -l
total 35
-rwxr-xr-x   1 starship     project       9346  Nov 1  08:06  display
-rw-r--r--   1 starship     project       6428  Dec 2  10:24  list
drwx--x--x   2 starship     project         32  Nov 8  15:32  tools
$
```

Permissions for the display and list files and the tools directory are shown on the left of the screen under the line total 35, and appear in this format:

> -rwxr-xr-x   (for the display file)
> -rw-r--r--   (for the list file))
> drwx--x--x   (for the tools directory)

After the initial character, which describes the file type (for example, a - (dash) symbolizes a regular file and a d a directory), the other nine characters that set the permissions comprise three sets of three characters. The first set refers to permissions for the *owner*, the second set to permissions for *group* members, and the last set to permissions for all *other* system users. Within each set of characters, the r, w, and x show the permissions currently granted to each category. If a dash appears instead of an r, w, or x, permission to read, write, or execute is denied.

The following diagram summarizes this breakdown for the file named `display`.

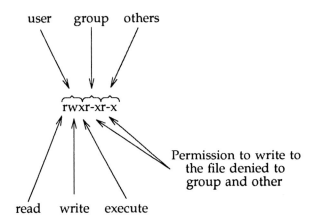

As you can see, the owner has `r`, `w`, and `x` permissions and members of the group and other system users have `r` and `x` permissions.

There are two exceptions to this notation system. Occasionally the letter s or the letter l may appear in the permissions line, instead of an `r`, `w` or `x`. The letter s (short for set user ID or set group ID) represents a special type of permission to execute a file. It appears where you normally see an `x` (or −) for the user or group (the first and second sets of permissions). From a user's point of view it is equivalent to an `x` in the same position; it implies that execute permission exists. It is significant only for programmers and system administrators. (See the *System Administrator's Guide* for details about setting the user or group ID.) The letter l indicates that locking will occur when the file is accessed. It does not mean that the file has been locked.

The permissions are as follows:

Figure 5-10: File Access Permissions

Symbol	Explanation
r	The file is readable.
w	The file is writable.
x	The file is executable.
–	This permission is *not* granted.
l	Mandatory locking will occur during access. (The set-group-ID bit is on and the *group* execution bit is off.)
s	The set-user-ID or set-group-ID bit is on, and the corresponding *user* or *group* execution bit is also on.
S	The set-user-ID bit is on and the *user* execution bit is off.
t	The sticky and the execution bits for *other* are on.
T	The sticky bit is turned on, and the execution bit for *other* is off.

Figure 5-11: Directory Access Permissions

Symbol	Explanation
r	The directory is readable.
w	The directory may be altered (files may be added or removed).
x	The directory may be searched. (This permission is required to cd to the directory.)
t	File removal from a writable directory is limited to the owner of the directory or file unless the file is writable.

How to Change Existing Permissions

After you have determined what permissions are in effect, you can change them by calling the chmod command in the following format:

> chmod *who+permission file(s)*

or

> chmod *who=permission file(s)*

The following list defines each component of this command line.

chmod	name of the program
who	one of three user groups (u, g, or o) u = user g = group o = others
+ or -	instruction that grants (+) or denies (-) permission
permission	any combination of three authorizations (r, w, and x) r = read w = write x = execute
file(s)	file (or directory) name(s) listed; assumed to be branches from your current directory, unless you use full pathnames.

NOTE The chmod command will not work if you type a space(s) between *who*, the instruction that gives (+) or denies (-) permission, and the *permission*.

The following examples show a few possible ways to use the chmod command. As the owner of display, you can read, write, and run this executable file. You can protect the file against being accidentally changed by denying yourself write (w) permission. To do this, type the command line:

> chmod u-w display

After receiving the prompt, type ls -l and press the RETURN key to verify that this permission has been changed, as shown in the following screen.

Integrated Software Development Guide

```
$ chmod u-w display
$ ls -l
total 35
-r-xr-xr-x    1 starship      project         9346  Nov 1  08:06  display
rw-r--r--     1 starship      project         6428  Dec 2  10:24  list
drwx--x--x    2 starship      project           32  Nov 8  15:32  tools
$
```

As you can see, you no longer have permission to write changes into the file.
You will not be able to change this file until you restore *write* permission for
yourself.

Now consider another example. Notice that permission to write into the file
display has been denied to members of your group and other system users.
However, they do have read permission. This means they can copy the file into
their own directories and then make changes to it. To prevent all system users
from copying this file, you can deny them read permission by typing:

    chmod go-r display

The g and o stand for group members and all other system users, respectively,
and the -r denies them permission to read or copy the file. Check the results
with the ls -l command.

```
$ chmod go-r display
$ ls -l
total 35
-rwx--x--x    1 starship      project         9346  Nov 1  08:06  display
rw-r--r--     1 starship      project         6428  Dec 2  10:24  list
drwx--x--x    2 starship      project           32  Nov 8  15:32  tools
$
```

For more information, refer to ls(1) and chmod(1) in the *User's Reference
Manual*.

A Note on Permissions and Directories

You can use the chmod command to grant or deny permission for directories as well as files. Simply specify a directory name instead of a file name on the command line.

However, consider the impact on various system users of changing permissions for directories. For example, suppose you grant read permission for a directory to yourself (u), members of your group (g), and other system users (o). Every user who has access to the system will be able to read the names of the files contained in that directory by running the ls -l command. Similarly, granting write permission allows the designated users to create new files in the directory and remove existing ones. Granting permission to execute the directory allows designated users to move to that directory (and make it their current directory) by using the cd command.

An Alternative Method

There are two methods by which the chmod command can be executed. The method described above, in which symbols such as r, w, and x are used to specify permissions, is called the symbolic method.

An alternative method is the octal method. Its format requires you to specify permissions using three octal numbers, ranging from 0 to 7. (The octal number system is different from the decimal system that we typically use on a day-to-day basis.) To learn how to use the octal method, see the chmod(1) entry in the *User's Reference Manual*.

Symbolic Links

A symbolic link is a special type of file that represents another file. The data in a symbolic link consists of the path name of a file or directory to which the symbolic link file is linked. The link that is formed is called symbolic to distinguish it from a regular (also called a hard) link such as can be created by using the ln(1) command. A symbolic link differs functionally from a regular link in three major ways: files from different file systems may be linked together; directories as well as regular files may be symbolically linked by any user; and a symbolic link can be created even if the file it represents does not exist.

In order to understand how a symbolic link works, it is necessary to understand how the UNIX operating system views files. (The following description pertains to files that belong to the standard System V file system type.) The internal representation of a file is contained in an inode, which contains a description of the layout of the file data on disk as well as information about the file, such as the file owner, the access permissions, and the access times. Every file has one inode, but a file may have several names, all of which point to the inode. Each name is called a regular (or hard) link.

When a file is created, an inode is allocated for it, the file contents are stored in data blocks, and an entry is created in a directory. A directory is a file whose data is a sequence of entries, each consisting of an inode number and the name of a file. The inode initially has a link count of one, which means that this file has one name (or one link to it).

We are now in a position to understand the difference between the creation of a regular and a symbolic link. When a user creates a regular link to a file with the ln(1) command, a new directory entry is created containing a new file name and the inode number of an existing file. The link count of the file is incremented.

In contrast, when a user creates a symbolic link both a new directory entry and a new inode are created. A data block is allocated to contain the path name of the file to which the symbolic link refers. The link count of the referenced file is not incremented.

Symbolic links can be used to solve a variety of common problems. For example, it frequently happens that a disk partition (such as root) runs out of disk space. With symbolic links, an administrator can create a link from a directory on that file system to a directory on another file system. Such a link provides extra disk space and is, in most cases, transparent to both users and programs.

Symbolic links can also help deal with the built-in path names that appear in the code of many commands. Changing the path names would require changing the programs and recompiling them. With symbolic links, the path names can effectively be changed by making the original files symbolic links that point to new files.

In a shared resource environment like RFS, symbolic links can be very useful. For example, if it is important to have a single copy of certain administrative files, symbolic links can be used to help share them. Symbolic links can also be used to share resources selectively. Suppose a system administrator wants to do a remote mount of a directory that contains sharable devices. These devices must be in /dev on the client system, but this system has devices of its own so the administrator does not want to mount the directory onto /dev. Rather than do this, the administrator can mount the directory at a location other than /dev and then use symbolic links in the /dev directory to refer to these remote devices. (This is similar to the problem of built-in path names since it is normally assumed that devices reside in the /dev directory.)

Finally, symbolic links can be valuable within the context of the virtual file system (VFS) architecture. With VFS new services, such as higher performance files, events, and network IPC, may be provided on a file system basis. Symbolic links can be used to link these services to home directories or to places that make more sense to the application or user. Thus one might create a database index file in a RAM-based file system type and symbolically link it to the place where the database server expects it and manages it.

NOTE The phrases "following symbolic links" and "not following symbolic links" as they are used in this document refer to the evaluation of the last component of a path name. In the evaluation of a path name, if any component other than the last is a symbolic link, the symbolic link is followed and the referenced file is used in the path name evaluation. However, if the last component of a path name is a symbolic link, the link may or may not be followed.

Properties of Symbolic Links

As we have seen above, a symbolic link is a new type of file that represents another file. The file to which it refers may be of any type; a regular file, a directory, a character-special, block-special, or FIFO-special file, or another symbolic link. The file may be on the local system or on a remote system. In fact, the file to which a symbolic link refers does not even have to exist. In particular, the file does not have to exist when the symbolic link is created or when it is removed.

Creation and removal of a symbolic link follow the same rules that apply to any file. To do either, the user must have write permission in the directory that contains the symbolic link. The ownership and the access permissions (mode) of the symbolic link are ignored for all accesses of the symbolic link. It is the ownership and access permissions of the referenced file that are used. A symbolic link cannot be opened or closed and its contents cannot be changed once it has been created.

If `/usr/jan/junk` is a symbolic link to the file `/etc/passwd`, in effect the file name `/etc/passwd` is substituted for `junk` so that when the user executes

        cat /usr/jan/junk

it is the contents of the file `/etc/passwd` that are printed.

Similarly, if `/usr/jan/junk` is a symbolic link to the file `../junk2`, executing

        cat /usr/jan/junk

is the same as executing

        cat /usr/jan/../junk2

or

        cat /usr/junk2

When a symbolic link is followed and brings a user to a different part of the file tree, we may distinguish between where the user really is (the physical path) and how the user got there (the virtual path). The behavior of `/usr/bin/pwd`, the shell built-in `pwd`, and `..` are all based on the physical path. In practical terms this means that there is no way for the user to retrace the path which brought the user to the current position in the file tree.

Other shells may use the virtual path. For example, by default the Korn shell pwd uses the virtual path, though there is an option allowing the user to make it use the physical path.

Figure 5-12: File Tree with Symbolic Link

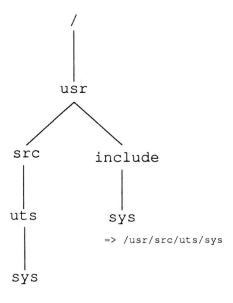

Consider the case shown in Figure 5-12 where /usr/include/sys is a symbolic link to /usr/src/uts/sys. Here if a user enters

cd /usr/include/sys

and then enters pwd, the result is

/usr/src/uts/sys

If the user then enters   cd .. followed by pwd, the result is

/usr/src/uts

Using Symbolic Links

Creating Symbolic Links

Syntax and Semantics

To create a symbolic link, the new system call symlink(2) is used and the owner must have write permission in the directory where the link will reside. The file is created with the user's user-id and group-id but these are subsequently ignored. The mode of the file is created as 0777.

> **CAUTION** No checking is done when a symbolic link is created. There is nothing to stop a user from creating a symbolic link that refers to itself or to an ancestor of itself or several links that loop around among themselves. Therefore, when evaluating a path name, it is important to put a limit on the number of symbolic links that may be encountered in case the evaluation encounters a loop. The variable MAXSYMLINKS is used to force the error ELOOP after MAXSYMLINKS symbolic links have been encountered. The value of MAXSYMLINKS should be at least 20.

To create a symbolic link, the ln(1) command is used with the −s option. If the −s option is not used and a user tries to create a link to a file on another file system, a symbolic link will not be created and the command will fail.

The syntax for creating symbolic links is as follows:

> ln −s *sourcefile1* [*sourcefile2* ...] *target*

With two arguments:

- *sourcefile1* may be any path name and need not exist.

- *target* may be an existing directory or a non-existent file.

- If *target* is an existing directory, a file is created in directory *target* whose name is the last component of *sourcefile1* ('basename *sourcefile1*'). This file is a symbolic link that references *sourcefile1*.

- If *target* does not exist, a file with name *target* is created and it is a symbolic link that references *sourcefile1*.

- If *target* already exists and is not a directory, an error is returned.

- *sourcefile1* and *target* may reside on different file systems.

With more than two arguments:

- For each *sourcefile*, a file is created in *target* whose name is *sourcefile* or its last component ('basename *sourcefile*') and is a symbolic link to *sourcefile*.

- If *target* is not an existing directory, an error is returned.

- Each *sourcefile* and *target* may reside on different file systems.

Examples

The following examples show how symbolic links may be created.

```
ln -s /usr/src/uts/sys  /usr/include/sys
```

In this example /usr/include is an existing directory. But file sys does not exist so it will be created as a symbolic link that refers to /usr/src/uts/sys. The result is that when file /usr/include/sys/x is accessed, the file /usr/src/uts/sys/x will actually be accessed.

This kind of symbolic link may be used when files exist in the directory /usr/src/uts/sys but programs often refer to files in /usr/include/sys. Rather than creating corresponding files in /usr/include/sys that are hard links to files in /usr/src/uts/sys, one symbolic link can be used to link the two directories. In this example /usr/include/sys becomes a symbolic link that links the former /usr/include/sys directory to the /usr/src/uts/sys directory.

```
ln -s /etc/group  .
```

In this example the *target* is a directory (the current directory), so a file called group ('basename /etc/group') is created in the current directory that is a symbolic link to /etc/group.

```
ln -s /fs1/jan/abc  /var/spool/abc
```

In this example we imagine that /fs1/jan/abc does not exist at the time the command is issued. Nevertheless, the file /var/spool/abc is created as a symbolic link to /fs1/jan/abc. Later, /fs1/jan/abc may be created as a directory, regular file, or any other file type.

The following example illustrates the use of more than two arguments:

```
ln -s /etc/group /etc/passwd  .
```

The user would like to have the group and passwd files in the current directory but cannot use hard links because /etc is a different file system. When more than two arguments are used, the last argument must be a directory; here it is the current directory. Two files, group and passwd, are created in the current directory, each a symbolic link to the associated file in /etc.

Removing Symbolic Links

Normally, when accessing a symbolic link, one follows the link and actually accesses the referenced file. However, this is not the case when one attempts to remove a symbolic link. When the rm(1) command is executed and the argument is a symbolic link, it is the symbolic link that is removed; the referenced file is not touched.

Accessing Symbolic Links

Suppose abc is a symbolic link to file def. When a user accesses the symbolic link abc, it is the file permissions (ownership and access) of file def that are actually used; the permissions of abc are always ignored. If file def is not accessible (i.e., either it does not exist or it exists but is not accessible to the user because of access permissions) and a user tries to access the symbolic link abc, the error message will refer to abc, not file def.

Copying Symbolic Links

This section describes the behavior of the cp(1) command when one or more arguments are symbolic links. With the cp(1) command, if any argument is a symbolic link, that link is followed. Then the semantics of the command are as described in the *User's Reference Manual*. Suppose the command line is

```
cp sym file3
```

where sym is a symbolic link that references a regular file test1 and file3 is a regular file. After execution of the command, file3 gets overwritten with the contents of the file test1.

If the last argument is a symbolic link that references a directory, then files are copied to that directory. Suppose the command line is

```
cp file1 sym symd
```

where file1 is a regular file, sym is a symbolic link that references a regular file test1, and symd is a symbolic link that references a directory DIR. After execution of the command, there will be two new files, DIR/file1 and DIR/sym that have the same contents as file1 and test1.

Linking Symbolic Links

This section describes the behavior of the ln(1) command when one or more arguments are symbolic links. To understand the difference in behavior between this and the cp(1) command, it is useful to think of a copy operation as dealing with the contents of a file while the link operation deals with the name of a file.

If the first argument to ln(1) is a symbolic link it is not followed, and a hard link is made to the symbolic link. With the last argument, a stat(2) is done to see if it is a directory; if it is, files are linked in that directory. Otherwise, if the last argument is an existing file, it is overwritten. This means that if the last argument is a symbolic link to a directory, it is followed but if it is a symbolic link to a regular file, the symbolic link is overwritten.

For example, if the command line is

        ln sym file1

where sym is a symbolic link that references a regular file foo, and file1 is a regular file, file1 is overwritten and hard-linked to sym, i.e., file1 becomes a symbolic link that references foo. Thus a hard link has been created to a symbolic link.

If the command is

        ln file1 sym

where the files are the same as in the first example, sym is overwritten and hard-linked to file1.

When the last argument is a directory as in

        ln file1 sym symd

where symd is a symbolic link to a directory DIR, the file DIR/file1 is hard-linked to file1 and DIR/sym is hard-linked to sym.

Moving Symbolic Links

This section describes the behavior of the mv(1) command. Like the ln(1) command, mv(1) deals with file names rather than file contents. With two arguments, a user invokes the mv(1) command to rename a file. Therefore, one would not want to follow the first argument if it is a symbolic link because it is the name of the file that is to be changed rather than the file contents. Suppose that sym is a symbolic link to /etc/passwd and abc is a regular file. If the command

        mv sym abc

is executed, the file sym is renamed abc and is still a symbolic link to /etc/passwd. If abc existed (as a regular file or a symbolic link to a regular file) before the command was executed, it is overwritten.

Suppose the command is

        mv sym1 file1 symd

where sym1 is a symbolic link to a regular file foo, file1 is a regular file, and symd is a symbolic link that references a directory DIR. When the command is executed, the files sym1 and file1 are moved from the current directory to the DIR directory so that there are two new files, DIR/sym1, which is still a symbolic link to foo, and DIR/file1.

In SVR4.0, the rename(2) system call will be used by the mv(1) command. If the first argument to rename(2) is a symbolic link, rename(2) does not follow it; instead it renames the symbolic link itself. Prior to SVR4.0 a file was moved using the link(2) system call followed by the unlink(2) system call. Since link(2) and unlink(2) do not follow symbolic links, the result of those two operations is the same as the result of a call to rename(2).

File Ownership and Permissions

The system-calls chmod and chown are used to change the mode and ownership of a file. If the argument to chmod or chown is a symbolic link, the mode and ownership of the referenced file rather than of the symbolic link itself will be changed. (See the section on "Symbolic Links" that follows in this chapter). In such cases, the link is followed.

Once a symbolic link has been created, its permissions cannot be changed. By default, the chown(1) and chgrp(1) commands change the owner and group of the referenced file. However, a new -h option enables the user to change the owner and group of the symbolic link itself. This is useful for removing files from sticky directories.

Using Symbolic Links with RFS

 To use symbolic links on two systems running RFS, both systems must be running SVR4.0. In cases where the server is an SVR4.0 system but the client is not, errors will be generated when the client encounters a symbolic link.

When using symbolic links in an RFS environment, it is important to understand how pathnames are evaluated. The rule by which evaluations are performed is simple. Symbolic links that a client encounters on the server are interpreted in accordance with the client's view of the file tree.

Users on a server system must keep this rule in mind when they create symbolic links in order to avoid problems. The examples that follow illustrate situations in which failure to consider the client's view of the file tree can lead to problems.

Figure 5-13: Symbolic Links with RFS: Example 1

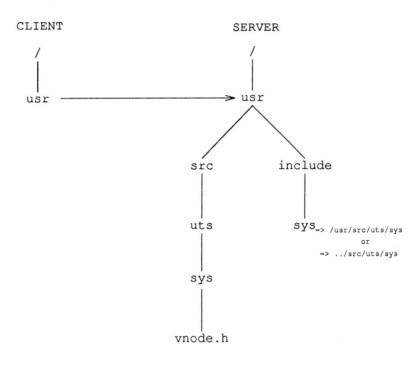

In the example shown in Figure 5-13, the server advertises its /usr file system as USR. If the server creates the symbolic link /usr/include/sys as an absolute pathname to /usr/src/uts/sys, evaluation of the link will work as intended as long as a client mounts USR as /usr. Another way of saying this is that if the file tree naming conventions are the same on the client and the server, things will work as intended. However, if the client mounts USR as /mnt/usr, when the symbolic link /usr/src/uts/sys is evaluated, the evaluation will be done with respect to the client's view of the file tree and will not cross the mount point back to the server but will remain on the client. Thus the client will not access the file intended. In this situation the server should create the symbolic link as a relative path name, ../src/uts/sys, so that evaluation will produce the desired results regardless of where the client mounts USR.

Figure 5-14: Symbolic Links with RFS: Example 2

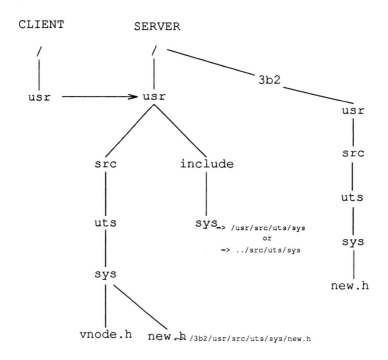

Figure 5-14 shows another potential problem situation in which the server advertises its /usr file system as USR. But in this case the server has a symbolic link from /usr/src/uts/sys/new.h to /3b2/usr/src/uts/sys/new.h. Because the referenced file, /3b2/usr/src/uts/sys/new.h, is outside of the advertised resource, users on the server can access this file but users on the client cannot. In this example, it would make no difference if the symbolic link was a relative rather than an absolute pathname, because the directory /3b2 on the server is not part of the client's name space. When the system evaluates the symbolic link, it will look for the file on the client and will not follow the link as intended.

Archiving Commands

The cpio(1) command copies file archives usually to or from a storage medium such as tape, disk, or diskette. By default, cpio does not follow symbolic links. However, a new −L option used with the −o and -p options indicates that symbolic links should be followed. This option is *not* valid with the −i option.

Normally, a user invokes the find(1) command to produce a list of filenames and pipes this into the cpio(1) command to create an archive of the files listed. The find(1) command also has a new option −follow to indicate that symbolic links should be followed. If a user invokes find(1) with the −follow option, then cpio(1) must also be invoked with its new option −L to indicate that it too should follow symbolic links.

Whether symbolic links are followed makes a difference in evaluating the output of find(1) only on encountering a symbolic link to a directory. For example, if /usr/jan/symd is a symbolic link to the directory ../joe/test and files test1 and test2 are in directory /usr/joe/test, the output of a find starting from /usr/jan includes the file /usr/jan/symd if symbolic links are not followed, but includes /usr/jan/symd as well as /usr/jan/symd/test1 and /usr/jan/syd/test2 if symbolic links are followed.

If the user wants to preserve the structure of the directories being archived, it is recommended that symbolic links not be followed on both commands. (This is the default.) When this is done symbolic links will be preserved and the directory hierarchy will be duplicated as it was.

If the user is more concerned that the contents of the files be saved, then the user should use the −L option to cpio(1) and the −follow option to find(1) to follow symbolic links.

 The user should take care not to mix modes, that is, the user should either follow or not follow symbolic links for both cpio(1) and find(1). If modes are mixed, an archive will be created but the resulting hierarchy created by cpio −i may exhibit unexpected and undesirable results.

Copying in using the −i option to cpio(1) copies symbolic links as is. If a user is creating an archive to be read in on a pre-SVR4.0 system, it may be more useful to follow symbolic links because systems prior to SVR4.0 do not understand symbolic links and the result of copying in a symbolic link will be a regular file whose contents are the path name of the referenced file.

Summary of UNIX System Files & Directories

UNIX system files are organized in a hierarchy; their structure is often described as an inverted tree. At the top of this tree is the root directory, the source of the entire file system. It is designated by a / (slash). All other directories and files descend and branch out from root, as shown in the following figure:

Figure 5-15: Directory Tree from root

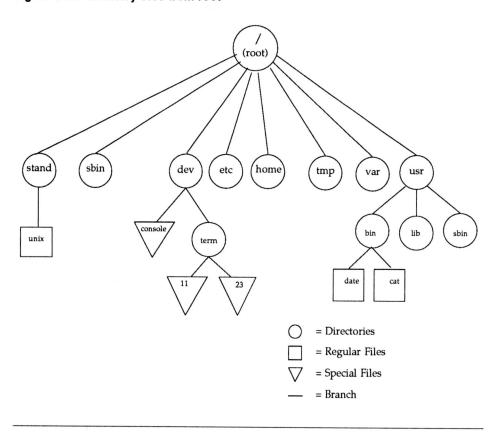

The following section provides brief descriptions of the root directory and the system directories under it, as shown in earlier figure.

UNIX System Directories

/	the source of the file system (called the root directory)
/stand	contains programs and data files used in the booting process
/sbin	contains essential executables used in the booting process and in manual system recovery
/dev	contains special files that represent peripheral devices, such as:

console	console
lp	line printer
term/*	user terminal(s)
dsk/*	disks

/etc	contains machine-specific administrative configuration files and system administration databases
/home	the root of a subtree for user directories
/tmp	contains temporary files, such as the buffers created for editing a file
/var	the root of a subtree for varying files such as log files
/usr	contains other directories, including lib and bin
/usr/bin	contains many executable programs and utilities, including the following:

```
cat
date
login
grep
mkdir
who
```

/usr/lib	contains libraries for programs and languages

Directories and Files

This section describes:

- Directories and files that are important for administering a system
- Directories that are new for this software release
- The reorganization of the directory structure introduced in this release
- The new organization of the root file system, and significant directories mounted on root

 WARNING   To maintain a secure environment, do not change the file or directory permissions from those assigned at the time of installation.

Directory and File Relocations

For this software release, many commands and directories have been relocated. This section lists the commands that have been moved, the locations of these commands in UNIX System V Release 4, and the locations of the same commands in earlier releases of the UNIX system. UNIX System V Release 4.0 provides symbolic links between the old and new locations. However, in future software releases, these links may be removed. The asterisk (*) means that all files in the directory indicated have been moved to the new location.

Pre-Release 4 Location	Release 4 Location
/bin/*	/usr/bin/*
/etc/bcheckrc	/sbin/bcheckrc
/etc/chroot	/usr/sbin/chroot
/etc/ckbupscd	/usr/sbin/ckbupscd
/etc/crash	/usr/sbin/crash
/etc/cron	/usr/sbin/cron
/etc/dcopy	/usr/sbin/dcopy
/etc/devnm	/usr/sbin/devnm
/etc/dfsck	/usr/sbin/dfsck
/etc/disks	/sbin/disks
/etc/drvinstall	/usr/sbin/drvinstall
/etc/editsa	/usr/sbin/editsa
/etc/edittbl	/usr/sbin/edittbl
/etc/errdump	/usr/sbin/errdump
/etc/ff	/usr/sbin/ff
/etc/finc	/usr/sbin/finc
/etc/fmtflop	/usr/sbin/fmtflop
/etc/fmthard	/sbin/fmthard
/etc/frec	/usr/sbin/frec
/etc/fsck	/sbin/fsck
/etc/fsdb	/sbin/fsdb
/etc/fsstat	/sbin/fsstat
/etc/fstyp	/sbin/fstyp
/etc/fuser	/usr/sbin/fuser

Pre-Release 4 Location	Release 4 Location
/etc/getmajor	/usr/sbin/getmajor
/etc/getty	/usr/lib/saf/ttymon
/etc/grpck	/usr/sbin/grpck
/etc/hdeadd	/usr/sbin/hdeadd
/etc/hdefix	/sbin/hdefix
/etc/hdelogger	/usr/sbin/hdelogger
/etc/init	/sbin/init
/etc/install	/usr/sbin/install
/etc/killall	/usr/sbin/killall
/etc/labelit	/sbin/labelit
/etc/ldsysdump	/usr/sbin/ldsysdump
/etc/led	/sbin/led
/etc/link	/usr/sbin/link
/etc/log/*	/var/adm/log/*
/etc/mkboot	/usr/sbin/mkboot
/etc/mkfs	/sbin/mkfs
/etc/mknod	/sbin/mknod
/etc/mount	/sbin/mount
/etc/mountall	/sbin/mountall
/etc/mvdir	/usr/sbin/mvdir
/etc/ncheck	/usr/sbin/ncheck
/etc/npump	/sbin/npump
/etc/ports	/sbin/ports
/etc/prfdc	/usr/sbin/prfdc
/etc/prfld	/usr/sbin/prfld
/etc/prfpr	/usr/sbin/prfpr
/etc/prfsnap	/usr/sbin/prfsnap
/etc/prfstat	/usr/sbin/prfstat
/etc/prtconf	/usr/sbin/prtconf
/etc/prtvtoc	/sbin/prtvtoc
/etc/pump	/sbin/pump
/etc/pwck	/usr/sbin/pwck
/etc/rc0	/sbin/rc0
/etc/rc1	/sbin/rc1
/etc/rc2	/sbin/rc2

Pre-Release 4 Location	Release 4 Location
/etc/rc3	/sbin/rc3
/etc/rc6	/sbin/rc6
/etc/rmount	/usr/sbin/rmount
/etc/rmountall	/usr/sbin/rmountall
/etc/rumountall	/usr/sbin/rumountall
/etc/savecpio	/usr/sbin/savecpio
/etc/setclk	/sbin/setclk
/etc/setmnt	/sbin/setmnt
/etc/shutdown	/sbin/shutdown
/etc/swap	/usr/sbin/swap
/etc/sysdef	/usr/sbin/sysdef
/etc/system	/stand/system
/etc/telinit	/sbin/init
/etc/termcap	/usr/share/lib/termcap
/etc/uadmin	/sbin/uadmin
/etc/umount	/sbin/umount
/etc/umountall	/sbin/umountall
/etc/unlink	/usr/sbin/unlink
/etc/utmp	/var/adm/utmp
/etc/volcopy	/usr/sbin/volcopy
/etc/wall	/usr/sbin/wall
/etc/whodo	/usr/sbin/whodo
/etc/wtmp	/var/adm/wtmp
/lib/*	/usr/lib/*
/shlib/*	/usr/lib/*
/unix	/stand/unix
/usr/adm/*	/var/adm/*
/usr/bin/fumount	/usr/sbin/fumount
/usr/bin/fusage	/usr/sbin/fusage
/usr/bin/mountfsys	/usr/sbin/mountfsys

Pre-Release 4 Location	Release 4 Location
/usr/bin/nlsadmin	/usr/sbin/nlsadmin
/usr/bin/powerdown	/usr/sbin/powerdown
/usr/bin/sadp	/usr/sbin/sadp
/usr/bin/strace	/usr/sbin/strace
/usr/bin/strclean	/usr/sbin/strclean
/usr/bin/strerr	/usr/sbin/strerr
/usr/bin/umountfsys	/usr/sbin/umountfsys
/usr/lib/cron/.proto	/etc/cron.d/.proto
/usr/lib/cron/at.allow	/etc/cron.d/at.allow
/usr/lib/cron/cron.allow	/etc/cron.d/cron.allow
/usr/lib/cron/logchecker	/etc/cron.d/logchecker
/usr/lib/cron/queuedefs	/etc/cron.d/queuedefs
/usr/lib/font/*	/usr/share/lib/font/*
/usr/lib/lex/*	/usr/ccs/lib/lex/*
/usr/lib/macros/*	/usr/share/lib/macros/*
/usr/lib/spell/spellhist	/var/adm/spellhist
/usr/lib/spell/compress	/usr/share/lib/spell/compress
/usr/lib/spell/hlista	/usr/share/lib/spell/hlista
/usr/lib/spell/hlistb	/usr/share/lib/spell/hlistb
/usr/lib/spell/hstop	/usr/share/lib/spell/hstop
/usr/share/lib/terminfo/*	/usr/share/lib/terminfo/*
/usr/lib/tmac/*	/usr/share/lib/tmac/*
/usr/lib/uucp/Devconfig	/etc/uucp/Devconfig
/usr/lib/uucp/Devices	/etc/uucp/Devices
/usr/lib/uucp/Dialcodes	/etc/uucp/Dialcodes
/usr/lib/uucp/Dialers	/etc/uucp/Dialers
/usr/lib/uucp/Permissions	/etc/uucp/Permissions
/usr/lib/uucp/Poll	/etc/uucp/Poll
/usr/lib/uucp/Sysfiles	/etc/uucp/Sysfiles
/usr/lib/uucp/Systems	/etc/uucp/Systems
/usr/mail/*	/var/mail/*
/usr/man/*	/usr/share/man/*
/usr/net/nls/dbfconv	/usr/lib/saf/dbfconv
/usr/net/nls/listen	/usr/lib/saf/listen

Pre-Release 4 Location	Release 4 Location
`/usr/nserve/*`	`/etc/rfs/*`
`/usr/nserve/nserve`	`/usr/lib/rfs/nserve`
`/usr/nserve/rfudaemon`	`/usr/lib/rfs/rfudaemon`
`/usr/nserve/TPnserve`	`/usr/lib/rfs/TPnserve`
`/usr/pub/*`	`/usr/share/lib/*`
`/usr/spool/*`	`/var/spool/*`
`/usr/tmp/*`	`/var/tmp/*`

There are some additional directories in root that did not appear in previous software releases. These directories are:

```
/export   /opt    /sbin   /stand   /var
/home     /proc
```

The root directories are explained in the next section. Important administrative files and subdirectories are explained later.

Directories in root

The / (root) file system contains executables and other files necessary to boot and run the system. The directories of the root file system are explained next.

/bck

The /bck directory is used to mount a backup file system for restoring files.

/boot

The /boot directory contains configurable object files created by the /usr/sbin/mkboot program (see mkboot(1M)).

/config

The /config directory contains files needed and produced by the user-level configuration program cunix (see cunix(1M)).

/dev

The /dev directory contains block and character special files that are usually associated with hardware devices or STREAMS drivers.

/dgn

The /dgn directory contains diagnostic programs.

/etc

The /etc directory contains machine-specific configuration files and system administration databases.

/export

The /export directory contains the default root of the exported file system tree.

/home

The /home directory contains user directories.

/install

The /install directory is used by the sysadm command to mount utilities packages for installation and removal (/install file system).

`/lost+found`

The `/lost+found` directory is used by `fsck` to save disconnected files and directories.

`/mnt`

The `/mnt` directory is used to mount file systems for temporary use.

`/opt`

The `/opt` directory is the mount point from which add-on application packages are installed.

`/proc`

The `/proc` directory is the mount point of the `proc` file system which provides information on the system's processes.

`/save`

The `/save` directory is used by `sysadm` for saving data on floppy diskettes.

`/sbin`

The `/sbin` directory contains executables used in the booting process and in manual recovery from a system failure.

`/stand`

The `/stand` directory is used as the mount point for the boot file system, which contains the standalone (bootable) programs and data files necessary for the system boot procedure.

`/tmp`

The `/tmp` directory contains temporary files.

`/usr`

The `/usr` directory is the mount point of the `usr` file system.

`/var`

The `/var` directory is the mount point of the `var` file system. It contains those files and directories that vary from machine to machine, such as `tmp`, `spool`, and `mail`. The `/var` file system also contains administrative directories such as `/var/adm` and `/var/opt`, the latter is installed by application packages.

Directories in /etc

This section describes the directories under the /etc directory, which contain machine-specific configuration files and system administration databases.

/etc/bkup

This directory contains machine-specific files and directories for backup and restore operations. Also contained here are files and directories that allow restore operations to be performed from single-user mode (system state 1).

/etc/bkup/method

This directory contains files that describe all backup and restore methods currently used on your computer.

/etc/cron.d

This directory contains administrative files for controlling and monitoring cron activities.

/etc/default

This directory contains files that assign default values to certain system parameters.

/etc/init.d

This directory contains executable files used in upward and downward transitions to all system states. These files are linked to files beginning with S (start) or K (stop) in /etc/rcn.d, where *n* is the appropriate system state. Files are executed from the /etc/rcn.d directories.

/etc/lp

This directory contains the configuration files and interface programs for the LP print service.

/etc/mail

This directory contains files used in administering the electronic mail system.

/etc/mail/lists

This directory contains files, each of which contains a mail alias. The name of each file is the name of the mail alias that it contains. (See the mailx(1) command for a description of the mail alias format.)

`/etc/master.d`

This directory contains files that define the configuration of hardware devices, software drivers, system parameters, and aliases. The files are used by `/usr/sbin/mkboot` to obtain device information for the generation of device driver and configurable module files. The `/usr/sbin/sysdef` program uses the `master.d` files to get the names of supported devices. The first step in reconfiguring the system to run with different tunable parameters is to edit the appropriate files in the `/etc/master.d` directory. (See `master`(4) in the *System Files and Devices Reference Manual*.)

`/etc/rc.d`

This directory contains executable files that perform the various functions needed to initialize the system to system state 2. The files are executed when `/usr/sbin/rc2` is run. (Files contained in this directory before UNIX System V Release 3.0 were moved to `/etc/rc2.d`. This directory is maintained only for compatibility reasons.)

`/etc/rc0.d`

This directory contains files executed by `/usr/sbin/rc0` for transitions to system states 0, 5, and 6. Files in this directory are linked from the `/etc/init.d` directory, and begin with either a K or an S. K shows processes that are stopped, and S shows processes that are started when entering system states 0, 5, or 6.

`/etc/rc1.d`

This directory contains files executed by `/usr/sbin/rc1` for transitions to system state 1. Files in this directory are linked from the `/etc/init.d` directory, and begin with either a K or an S. K shows processes that should be stopped, and S shows processes that should be started when entering system state 1.

`/etc/rc2.d`

This directory contains files executed by `/usr/sbin/rc2` for transitions to system state 2. Files in this directory are linked from the `/etc/init.d` directory, and begin with either a K or an S. K shows processes that should be stopped, and S shows processes that should be started when entering system state 2.

/etc/rc3.d

This directory contains files executed by /usr/sbin/rc3 for transitions to system state 3 (multi-user mode). Files in this directory are linked from the /etc/init.d directory, and begin with either a K or an S. K shows processes that should be stopped, and S shows processes that should be started when entering system state 3.

/etc/saf

This directory contains files and subdirectories used by the Service Access Facility. The following commands in /usr/sbin use /etc/saf subdirectories for data storage and retrieval: nlsadmin, pmadm, and sacadm. The following files are included:

_sactab	A list of port monitors to be started by the Service Access Controller (SAC). Each port monitor listed in this table has a _pmtab file in the /etc/saf/*pmtag* directory, where *pmtag* is the tag of this port monitor (such as /etc/saf/starlan for the starlan port monitor).
_sysconfig	The configuration script used to modify the environment for the Service Access Facility.

/etc/save.d

This directory contains files used by the sysadm command for backing up data on floppy diskettes. The following files are included:

except	A list of the directories and files that should not be copied as part of a backup is maintained in this file.
timestamp/ . . .	The date and time of the last backup (volume or incremental) is maintained for each file system in the /etc/save.d/timestamp directory.

/etc/shutdown.d

This directory is maintained only for compatibility reasons. The files contained in this directory prior to UNIX System V Release 3.0 were executable files that invoked the various functions required during the transition to the single-user mode (system states 1, s, or S). These files are now located in /etc/rc0.d.

Integrated Software Development Guide

Files in /etc

The following files are used in machine-specific configuration and system administration databases.

/etc/bkup/bkexcept.tab

This file contains a list of files to be excluded from an incremental backup.

/etc/bkup/bkhist.tab

This file contains information about the success of all backup attempts.

/etc/bkup/bkreg.tab

This file contains instructions to the system for performing backup operations on your computer.

/etc/bkup/bkstatus.tab

This file contains the status of backup operations currently taking place.

/etc/bkup/rsmethod.tab

This file contains descriptions of the types of objects that may be restored using the full or partial restore method.

/etc/bkup/rsnotify.tab

This file contains the electronic mail address of the operator to be notified whenever restore requests require operator intervention.

/etc/bkup/rsstatus.tab

This file contains a list of all restore requests made by users of your computer.

/etc/bkup/rsstrat.tab

This file specifies a strategy for selecting archives when handling restore requests. In completing restore operations for these requests, the backup history log is used to navigate through the backup tape to find the desired files and or directories.

/etc/boot_tab

This file contains a list of the file systems mounted during the configuring of a new bootable operating system (system configuration). It is used by the /sbin/buildsys script, along with the /etc/vfstab file, to mount necessary file systems. You should not need to change this file.

`/etc/d_passwd`

This file contains a list of programs that will require dial-up passwords when run from `login`. Each line in the file is formatted as

> *program* : *encrypted_password* :

where *program* is the full path to any programs into which a user can log in and run. The password referred to in the *encrypted_password* is the one that will be used by the dial-up password program. This password must be entered before the user is given the login prompt. It is used in conjunction with the file `/etc/dialups`.

`/etc/default/cron`

This file contains the default status (`enable` or `disable`) for the `CRONLOG` operation.

`/etc/default/login`

This file may contain the following parameters that define a user's login environment:

ALTSHELL	Alternate shell status available to users (`yes` or `no`).
CONSOLE	Root login allowed only at the console terminal.
HZ	Number of clock ticks per second.
IDLEWEEKS	Number of weeks a password may remain unchanged before the user is denied access to the system.
PASSREQ	Password requirement on logins (`yes` or `no`).
PATH	User's default `PATH`.
SUPATH	Root's default `PATH`.
TIMEOUT	Number of seconds allowed for logging in before a timeout occurs.
TIMEZONE	Time zone used within the user's environment.
ULIMIT	File size limit (`ulimit`).
UMASK	User's value for `umask`.

`/etc/default/passwd`

This file contains the following information about the length and aging of user passwords:

MINWEEKS	Minimum number of weeks before a password can be changed.
MAXWEEKS	Maximum number of weeks a password can be unchanged.
PASSLENGTH	Minimum number of characters in a password.
WARNWEEKS	Number of weeks before a password expires that the user is to be warned.

`/etc/default/su`

This file contains values for the following parameters affecting the work of super users:

SULOG	A pathname that identifies a file in which a log of all su attempts may be created.
CONSOLE	Pathnames of the console on which are broadcast messages notifying you whenever someone attempts to su root.
PATH	PATH used for su users.
SUPATH	PATH used for su root users.

`/etc/device.tab`

This file is the device table. It lists the device alias, path to the vnode, and special attributes of every device connected to the computer.

`/etc/devlock.tab`

This file is created at run time and lists the reserved (locked) devices. Device reservations do not remain intact across system reboots.

`/etc/saf/`*pmtag*`/_config`

This file contains a configuration script used to customize the environment for the port monitor tagged as *pmtag* (such as `/etc/saf/starlan/_config` for the starlan port monitor). Port monitor configuration scripts are optional.

`/etc/dgroup.tab`

This file lists the group or groups to which a device belongs.

`/etc/dialups`

This file contains a list of terminal devices that cannot be accessed without a dial-up password. It is used in conjunction with the file `/etc/d_passwd`.

`/etc/group`

This file describes each user group to the system. An entry is added for each new group with the `groupadd` command.

`/etc/inittab`

This file contains instructions for the `/sbin/init` command. The instructions define the processes created or stopped for each initialization state. Initialization states are called system states or run states. By convention, system state 1 (or S or s) is single-user mode; system states 2 and 3 are multi-user modes. (See `inittab`(4) in the *System Files and Devices Reference Manual* for additional information.)

`/etc/mail/mailcnfg`

This file permits per-site customizing of the mail subsystem. See the `mailcnfg`(4) manual page in the *System Files and Devices Reference Manual* and "Administering the Mail Subsystem" in this guide.

`/etc/mail/mailsurr`

This file lists actions to be taken when mail containing particular patterns is processed by `mail`. This can include routing translations and logging. See the `mailsurr`(4) manual page in the *System Files and Devices Reference Manual*.

`/etc/mail/mailx.rc`

This file contains defaults for the `mailx` program. It may be added by the system administrator. See `mailx`(1).

`/etc/mail/notify` and `/etc/mail/notify.sys`

These files are used by the `notify` program to determine the location of users in a networked environment and to establish systems to use in case of file error.

`/etc/motd`

This file contains the message of the day. The message of the day is displayed on a user's screen after that user has successfully logged in. (The commands that produce this output on the screen are in the `/etc/profile` file.) This message should be kept short and to the point. The `/var/news` files should be used for lengthy messages.

`/etc/passwd`

This file identifies each user to the system. An entry is automatically added for each new user with the `useradd` command, removed with the `userdel` command, and modified with the `usermod` command.

`/etc/profile`

This file contains the default profile for all users. The standard (default) environment for all users is established by the instructions in the `/etc/profile` file. The system administrator can change this file to set options for the `root` login. For example, the six lines of code shown in Figure 5-16 can be added to the `/etc/profile`. This code defines the erase character, automatically identifies the terminal type, and sets the TERM variable when the login ID is `root`.

Figure 5-16: Excerpt from `/etc/profile`

```
1   if [ ${LOGNAME} = root ]
2       then
3           stty echoe
4           echo "Terminal: 5          export TERM
6       fi
```

`/etc/rfs/rmnttab`

This file is created by the `rmount`(1M) command. This file contains a listing of unsuccessfully mounted resources or disconnected resources. These resources are polled by the `rmnttry`(1M) `cron` entry.

`/etc/dfs/dfstab`

This file specifies the Remote File Sharing resources from your machine that are automatically shared to remote machines when entering RFS mode (system state 3). Each entry in this file should be a `share`(1M) command line.

`/etc/saf/`*pmtag*`/_pmtab`

This is the administrative file for the port monitor tagged as *pmtag*. It contains an entry for each service available through the *pmtag* port monitor.

`/etc/saf/_sactab`

This file contains information about all port monitors for which the Service Access Controller (SAC) is responsible.

`/etc/saf/_sysconfig`

This file contains a configuration script to customize the environments for all port monitors on the system. This per-system configuration file is optional.

`/etc/TIMEZONE`

This file sets the time zone shell variable `TZ`. The `TZ` variable is initially established for the system via the `sysadm setup` command. The `TZ` variable in the `TIMEZONE` file is changed by the `sysadm timezone` command. The `TZ` variable can be redefined on a user (login) basis by setting the variable in the associated `.profile`. The `TIMEZONE` file is executed by `/usr/sbin/rc2`. (See `timezone`(4) in the *System Files and Devices Reference Manual* for more information.)

`/etc/ttydefs`

This file contains information used by ttymon port monitor to set the terminal modes and baud rate for a TTY port.

`/etc/vfstab`

This file provides default values for file systems and remote resources. The following information can be stored in this file:

- The block and character devices on which file systems reside

- The resource name

- The location where a file system is usually mounted

- The file system type

- Information on special mounting procedures

These defaults do not override command line arguments that have been entered manually. (See `mountall`(1M) in the *System Administrator's Reference Manual* for additional information.) Figure 5-17 shows a sample of this file.

Figure 5-17: Sample `/etc/vfstab` **File**

```
1  #special          fsckdev           mountp    fstype fsckpass automnt mntflags
2  /dev/SA/diskette1 /dev/rdiskette    /install  s5     -        no      -
3  /dev/diskette     /dev/rdiskette    /install  s5     -        no      -
4  /dev/dsk/c1d0s3   /dev/rdsk/c1d0s3  /stand    bfs    1        yes     -
5  /dev/dsk/c1d0s8   /dev/rdsk/c1d0s8  /usr2     s5     1        yes     -
6  /dev/dsk/c1d1s2   /dev/rdsk/c1d1s2  /usr      s5     1        yes     -
7  /dev/dsk/c1d1s8   /dev/rdsk/c1d1s8  /home     s5     1        yes     -
8  /dev/root         /dev/root         -         s5     -        no      -
9  /proc             -                 /proc     proc   -        no      -
```

Directories in /usr

This section describes the directories in the /usr file system. The /usr file system contains architecture-dependent and architecture-independent files and system administration databases that can be shared.

/usr/bin

This directory contains public commands and system utilities.

/usr/include

This directory contains public header files for C programs.

/usr/lib

This directory contains public libraries, daemons, and architecture dependent databases.

/usr/lib/lp

This directory contains the directories and files used in processing requests to the LP print service.

/usr/lib/mail

This directory contains directories and files used in processing mail.

/usr/lib/mail/surrcmd

This directory contains programs necessary for mail surrogate processing.

/usr/sadm/bkup

This directory contains executables for the backup and restore services.

/usr/sbin

This directory contains executables used for system administration.

/usr/share

This directory contains architecture independent files that can be shared.

/usr/share/lib

This directory contains architecture independent databases.

`/usr/sadm/skel`

This directory contains the files and directories built when using the `useradd` command with the `-m` argument. All directories and files under this location are built under the `$HOME` location for the new user.

`/usr/ucb`

This directory contains binaries from the BSD Compatibility Package.

`/usr/ucbinclude`

This directory contains header files from the BSD Compatibility Package.

`/usr/ucblib`

This directory contains libraries from the BSD Compatibility Package.

Files in /usr

This section describes the files in the /usr directories, which contain architecture-dependent and architecture-independent files and system administrative databases that can be shared.

/usr/sbin/rc0

This file contains a shell script executed by /usr/sbin/shutdown for transitions to single-user state, and by /sbin/init for transitions to system states 0, 5, and 6. Files in the /etc/shutdown.d and /etc/rc0.d directories are executed when /usr/sbin/rc0 is run. The file K00ANNOUNCE in /etc/rc0.d prints the message System services are now being stopped. Any task that you want executed when the system is taken to system states 0, s, 5, or 6 is done by adding a file to the /etc/rc0.d directory.

/usr/sbin/rc1

This file contains a shell script executed by /sbin/init for transitions to system state 1 (single-user state). Executable files in the /etc/rc.d directory and any executable files beginning with S or K in the /etc/rc1.d directories are executed when /usr/sbin/rc1 is run. All files in rc1.d are linked from files in the /etc/init.d directory. Other files may be added to the /etc/rc1.d directory as a function of adding hardware or software to the system.

/usr/sbin/rc2

This file contains a shell script executed by /sbin/init for transitions to system state 2 (multi-user state). Executable files in the /etc/rc.d directory and any executable files beginning with S or K in the /etc/rc2.d directories are executed when /usr/sbin/rc2 is run. All files in rc2.d are linked from files in the /etc/init.d directory. Other files may be added to the /etc/rc2.d directory as a function of adding hardware or software to the system.

/usr/sbin/rc3

This file is executed by /sbin/init. It executes the shell scripts in /etc/rc3.d for transitions to RFS mode (system state 3).

/usr/sbin/rc6

This shell script is run for transitions to system state 6 (for example, using shutdown -i6). If the kernel needs reconfiguring, the /sbin/buildsys script is run. If reconfiguration succeeds, /usr/sbin/rc6 reboots without running diagnostics. If reconfiguration fails, it spawns a shell.

`/usr/sbin/shutdown`

This file contains a shell script to shut down the system gracefully in preparation for a system backup or scheduled downtime. After stopping all nonessential processes, the `shutdown` script executes files in the `/etc/shutdown.d` directory by calling `/usr/sbin/rc0` for transitions to system state 1 (single-user state). For transitions to other system states, the `shutdown` script calls `/sbin/init`.

`/usr/share/lib/mailx/mailx.help` and
`/usr/share/lib/mailx/mailx.help`.

Help files for `mailx`. The file `mailx.help.~` contains help messages for `mailx`'s tilde commands. See `mailx`(1) in the *User's Reference Manual*.

Directories in /var

This section describes the directories of the /var directory, which contain files and directories that vary from machine to machine.

/var/adm

This directory contains system logging and accounting files.

/var/cron

This directory contains the cron log file.

/var/lp

This directory contains log files for the LP print service.

/var/mail

This directory contains subdirectories and mail files that users access with the mail(1) and mailx(1) commands.

/var/mail/:saved

This directory contains temporary storage for mail messages while mail is running. Files are named with the user's ID while they are in /var/mail.

/var/news

This directory contains news files. The file names are descriptive of the contents of the files; they are analogous to headlines. When a user reads the news, using the news command, an empty file named .news_time is created in his or her login directory. The date (time) of this file is used by the news command to determine if a user has read the latest news file(s).

/var/opt

This directory is created and used by application packages.

/var/options

This directory contains a file (or symbolic link to a file) that identifies each utility installed on the system. This directory also contains information created and used by application packages (such as temporary files and logs).

`/var/preserve`

This directory contains backup files for `vi` and `ex`.

`/var/sadm`

This directory contains logging and accounting files for the backup and restore services, software installation utilities, and package management facilities.

`/var/sadm/pkg`

This directory contains data directories for installed software packages.

`/var/saf`

This directory contains log files for the Service Access Facility.

`/var/spool`

This directory contains temporary spool files.

`/var/spool/cron/crontabs`

This directory contains `crontab` files for the `adm`, `root`, and `sys` logins. Users whose login IDs are in the `/etc/cron.d/cron.allow` file can establish their own `crontab` file using the `crontab` command. If the `cron.allow` file does not exist, the `/etc/cron.d/cron.deny` file is checked to determine if the user should be denied the use of the `crontab` command.

As `root`, you can use the `crontab` command to make the desired entries. Revisions to the file take effect at the next reboot. The file entries support the `calendar` reminder service and the Basic Networking Utilities. Remember, you can use the `cron` function to decrease the number of tasks you perform with the `sysadm` command; include recurring and habitual tasks in your `crontab` file. (See `crontab`(1) in the *User's Reference Manual* for additional information.)

`/var/spool/lp`

This directory contains temporary print job files.

`/var/spool/smtpq`

This directory contains Simple Mail Transfer Protocol (SMTP) directories and log files. Directories named *host* contain messages spooled to be sent to that host. Files named LOG.*n* contain the logs from the past seven days (Sunday's log is called `log.0`). The current day's log is simply LOG.

`/var/spool/uucp`

This directory contains files to be sent by `uucp`.

`/var/spool/uucppublic`

This directory contains files received by `uucp`.

`/var/tmp`

This directory contains temporary files.

`/var/uucp`

This directory contains logging and accounting files for `uucp`.

Files in /var

This section describes the files in the /var directories, which contain information that varies from machine to machine.

/var/adm/spellhist

If the Spell Utility is installed, this file contains a history of all words that the spell command fails to match. Periodically, this file should be reviewed for words that you can add to the dictionary. Clear the spellhist file after reviewing it. (Refer to spell(1) in the *User's Reference Manual* for information on adding words to the dictionary, cleaning up the spellhist file, and other commands that can be used with the Spell Utility.)

/var/adm/utmp

This file contains information on the current system state. This information is accessed with the who command.

/var/adm/utmpx

This file contains information similar to that in the /var/adm/utmp file, along with a record of the remote host.

/var/adm/wtmp

This file contains a history of system logins. The owner and group of this file must be adm, and the access permissions must be 664. Each time login is run this file is updated. As the system is accessed, this file increases in size. Periodically, this file should be cleared or truncated. The command line >/var/adm/wtmp when executed by root creates the file with nothing in it. The following command lines limit the size of the /var/adm/wtmp file to the last 3600 characters in the file:

```
# tail -3600c /var/adm/wtmp > /var/tmp/wtmp
# mv /var/tmp/wtmp /var/adm/wtmp
#
```

The /usr/sbin/cron, /usr/sbin/rc0, or /usr/sbin/rc2 command can be used to clean up the wtmp file. You can add the appropriate command lines to the /var/spool/cron/crontabs/root file or add shell command lines to directories such as /etc/rc2.d, /etc/rc3.d, and so on.

`/var/adm/wtmpx`

This file contains information similar to that in the `/var/adm/wtmp` file, along with a record of the remote host.

`/var/adm/loginlog`

If this file exists, it is a text file that contains one entry for each group of five consecutive unsuccessful attempts to log in to the system.

`/var/adm/sulog`

This file contains a history of substitute user (`su`) command usage. As a security measure, this file should not be readable by `others`. The `/var/adm/sulog` file should be truncated periodically to keep the size of the file within a reasonable limit. The `/usr/sbin/cron`, the `/usr/sbin/rc0`, or the `/usr/sbin/rc2` command can be used to clean up the `sulog` file. You can add the appropriate command lines to the `/var/spool/cron/crontabs/root` file or add shell command lines to directories such as `/etc/rc2.d`, `/etc/rc3.d`, and so on. The following command lines limit the size of the log file to the last 100 lines in the file:

```
# tail -100 /var/adm/sulog > /var/tmp/sulog
# mv /var/tmp/sulog /var/adm/sulog
#
```

`/var/cron/log`

This file contains a history of all actions taken by `/usr/sbin/cron`. The `/var/cron/log` file should be truncated periodically to keep the size of the file within a reasonable limit. The `/usr/sbin/cron`, `/usr/sbin/rc0`, or `/usr/sbin/rc2` command can be used to clean up the `/var/cron/log` file. You can add the appropriate command lines to the `/var/spool/cron/crontabs/root` file or add shell command lines in the following directories (as applicable): /etc/rc2.d, /etc/rc3.d, (and so on). The following command lines limit the size of the log file to the last 100 lines in the file:

```
# tail -100 /var/cron/log > /var/tmp/log
# mv /var/tmp/log /var/cron/log
#
```

/var/sadm/bkup/logs/bklog

This file contains a process log used when troubleshooting a backup operation.

/var/sadm/bkup/logs/bkrs

This file contains a process log used when troubleshooting a backup or restore operation for which a method was not specified.

/var/sadm/bkup/logs/rslog

This file contains a process log used when troubleshooting a restore operation.

/var/sadm/bkup/toc

This file contains table of contents entries created by a backup method.

6 Keyboard and Display Input/Output

Vertical left margin text:

6. KEYBOARD AND DISPLAY INPUT/OUTPUT

Introduction

This chapter describes how to manage text and graphics output on UNIX System V Release 4 for the Intel386 and compatible architectures. Most of the content is also applicable to Release 3.2.

This chapter is intended primarily for programmers concerned with developing low-level graphics applications. The aim of the chapter is to enable you to get at the internal hardware controls necessary to make effective use of the video adapters; it is not concerned with higher level graphics concerns such as shading or rotating images.

While it would be useful to have some familiarity with the PC AT architecture and understand the basics of video programming, it is not necessary. You should, however, be knowledgeable of UNIX System V Release 4 for the Intel386 Architecture and the C programming language, since all examples are written in C.

The chapter is divided into several distinct sections. The first sections present both a conceptual and technical overview of developing programs that make full use of the text and graphics facilities. The next sections present the same material from a more specific technical viewpoint and provide annotated programming examples. They describe the specific requirements for text mode programming, the use of video memory, and graphics mode programming, including specific requirements for programming the video control registers.

One of the significant features of the video interface is its Virtual Terminal Capability. This capability extends the notion of windowing to the next level and allows for controlling several independent windowing applications. After presenting the initial view of graphics programming, there is an extensive section that describes the Virtual Terminal Capability and provides extensive programming examples of how to make effective use of that capability.

The last sections present various miscellaneous features, including Setting Borders, Keyboard Operations, Sound Control, Font Operations and Programming the Mouse. The final sections provide useful supplementary information such as tables that summarize the various graphics and text modes.

This chapter should be viewed as a supplement to the reference manual. It is not a tutorial; rather it summarizes and organizes the most common and frequently used technical information and provides extensive examples demonstrating the use of the video capabilities of the video interface.

The primary source of information on programming the video interface is:

- The display(7) and keyboard(7) man pages, either on-line or in the UNIX System V/386 Release 4 Administrator's Reference Manual.

The display(7) manual page describes both text and graphics control of the display. For text output, the manual pages present the effect of different output character sequences on the display. For graphic control, the manual pages describe the function call details of the ioctl system routine [see ioctl(2) in the *Programmer's Reference Manual*] that provides the graphics interface to the display and to the keyboard/display (kd) driver known as the kd driver. Both the display(7) and keyboard(7) man pages (in the *System Administrtor's Reference Manual*) include necessary information for using and controlling Virtual Terminals.

You should refer to the manuals that come with the video board you are using for information on the hardware layout, the differences among different video boards, the memory maps, and video registers.

Overview of Video Display Programming

Before you start you will need to become familiar with the `ioctl(2)` system call and the header file, `/usr/include/sys/kd.h`. The header file defines the display vocabulary (i.e. the complete set of `#defines`) that you need in order to use the `ioctl(2)` system call. It also contains the definitions of those structures that allow you to read and write the control registers.

The other `#include` files that you will require are `/usr/include/sys/types.h` and `/usr/include/sys/at_ansi.h`.

Aside from normal design considerations, the two most important decisions you must make before you start are:

- Will I be in text mode or graphics mode?

- What board should I program for; more specifically, what resolution should I program for?

Text Mode and Graphics Mode

A critical aspect to video display programming is the distinction between text mode and graphics mode. The two modes are mutually exclusive; an adapter can only be in one of those two modes, not both. Thus, a programmer can produce either a graphics display or a text display, but not both at the same time.

Text Mode

Under text mode, you can specify the text format and character set; you can display foreground and background colors; you can control cursor movement and can even control character mapping. In text mode, the display resolution is considered in terms of characters; for example an 80 x 25 resolution screen can hold 80 characters across the width of the screen and 25 lines down the screen. Text mode is the default mode.

There are several different character sets to choose from. Some of these sets provide "graphic" characters, for example arrows, lines, corners, etc. Because text mode is both faster and easier to use than graphics mode, you should consider whether it makes sense to do your application entirely in text mode.

There are three kinds of output possible in text mode. These can be loosely characterized as "standard character output", "non-standard character output" and "escape code sequences".

- In standard output you "see what you say"; that is, the characters "XYZ" appear on the display if a program says `printf("XYZ");`

- Non-standard output describes what happens when you output the non-printing characters such as LF, FF, CR, BEL, etc. The `display`(7) manual pages describe the action that occurs when each of these characters is output. For example, outputting FF will clear the screen and put the cursor at line 1, column 1.

- Escape sequences allow you to control the cursor movement, perform screen editing, assign values to function keys, and specify attributes of each character. Escape sequences also let you manage screen input as well as output. For example, you can program the effect of function keys on the display, lock and unlock the keyboard, etc. The Escape sequences are also described in detail in the `display`(7) manual page. Several of the Escape sequences are used as examples in the next section.

For a program to run in text mode, you must take the following steps:

- Create a set of `#defines` for the escape sequences you will use. This is not a programming requirement, but it is good programming practice and results in more readable and maintainable code.

- Open the `kd` driver.

- Determine which adapter board is attached.

- Establish the text mode, if you do not intend to use the default mode.

- Clear the screen (output the sequence ESCc, i.e., `printf("\033c");`).

- Output the text.

There are two general ways to output text. The first is by using straightforward output functions, such as `printf`. In this mode, the escape sequences are used to control foreground and background color as well as other text attributes, such as blink or underscore.

The second is by writing directly to the video memory. You can actually work with several screenloads at once. The amount of memory available to the video adapter is a multiple of 16K bytes, depending on which adapter is used. The amount used for a text screen is either 2K or 4K, depending on the mode selected. This means that there can be at least 4 to 8 text screens stored simultaneously. You control which of those screens is currently displayed and you can switch the displays instantaneously (at least from the viewpoint of the end-user).

Graphics Mode

In graphics mode, the display is viewed as consisting of addressable points called picture elements (or pixels). The combination of the adapter board and the display mode establish a screen resolution and color capability. You can address each pixel of the display and specify the color of each display pixel.

In both text and graphics mode, you can read and set video hardware registers, and create Virtual Terminals.

The adapters respond to additional commands that allow you to read and set the keyboard LEDs, generate sounds and tones, and perform other miscellaneous functions.

In order to be effective in using graphics mode, you must develop a basic library of primitive routines. All graphics programming is a function of writing to memory and mapping the memory to the display screen.

The getting started steps are the same for graphics mode as for text mode and consist of:

- Open the kd driver.

- Determine the adapter board.

- Establish the Graphic Mode (a combination of number of colors and resolution).

- Clear the screen.

  This consists of writing the appropriate foreground/background pixel value into all of video memory. The actual value written depends on the background attribute.

- Get to work.

The section entitled "Comprehensive Video Programming Example" at the end of this chapter presents a complete graphics programming example.

Video Adapter Boards

The video display is physically controlled by hardware boards called video adapters. The video adapters essentially determine the resolution and color possibilities of the display image in both text and graphics modes. Adapters will differ in the number of colors that are possible and the maximum possible screen resolution.

The first step in video display programming, then, is to determine the specific adapter board (sometimes called an adapter card) that is being used. It is possible to develop programs for the lowest level board, in which case this step is not necessary. In most cases, however, you would want to make use of the maximum capabilities of the board, to have the highest possible screen resolution, in which case it is essential that you know the board you are using.

There are many standard video adapters widely used in the PC marketplace. These include:

■ The MDA (Monochrome Display Adapter) is a basic 2 color display, i.e. black and one other. It has a resolution of 720 pixels across by 350 pixels down.

■ The CGA (Color Graphics Adapter) provides 4 colors, with a 320 x 200 resolution, or 2 colors, with a 640 x 200 resolution.

■ The EGA (Enhanced Graphics Adapter) provides 16 colors and 640 x 350 pixel resolution.

■ The VGA (Video Graphics Adapter) provides 16 colors, with 640 x 480 pixel resolution and 256 colors at 320 x 200 pixel resolution.

You may also use a Hercules monochrome graphics adapter and other commonly available graphics adapters. Each controller/adapter has different capabilities, registers, and memory mapping. The section entitled "Graphics Modes" at the end of this chapter summarizes the characteristics of each of the graphics modes that are available.

Determining the Adapter

Accessing the VDC requires two programming steps:

- Opening the Device
- Getting the Adapter Information

Like all devices in Release 4.0 Version 1.0, the adapter is opened as if it were a file. A specific statement to use is:

```
disp = open("/dev/video", O_RDWR);
```

The expectation in opening /dev/video is that the controlling tty is a Virtual Terminal. The open will fail if the device is connected via a serial terminal port. If the device cannot be opened, the error return is a negative number. The ioctl(2) system call is used to gather information, set modes, issue miscellaneous commands, etc. Because of the historical evolution of UNIX System V, there are several different versions of the ioctl(2) system call that either can be used or have to be used, depending on the specific information required. The techniques used in the examples are recommended. They provide a cleaner interface to the driver code and are essential for the effective use of Virtual Terminals. These calls and variations are:

- ioctl(fd, KIOCINFO, 0);

  This call is used to determine if the file description given by fd is for a device that can be controlled by the kd driver. If it is, the return will be ('k'<<8 | 'd').

- ioctl(disp, KDVDCTYPE, &disp_info);

  The argument, &disp_info, is the address of a structure that is filled by the called routine. For example, it may be defined by:

  ```
  struct kd_vdctype    disp_info;
  ```

  On return from the ioctl routine, the structure will contain the controller type and the display type. The mnemonics used are defined in /usr/include/sys/kd.h.

Return values for the controller field are:

Return	Adapter Type
KD_MONO	IBM monochrome display adapter.
KD_HERCULES	Hercules monochrome adapter
KD_CGA	IBM colorgraphics adapter
KD_EGA	IBM enhanced graphics adapter
KD_VGA	IBM video graphics adapter
KD_VDC400	AT&T VDC 400 adapter
KD_VDC750	AT&T VDC 750 adapter
KD_VDC600	AT&T VDC 600 adapter

And the standard returns for the monitor type are:

Return	Monitor Type
KD_UNKNOWN	Unknown monitor type
KD_STAND_M	Standard monochrome monitor
KD_STAND_C	Standard color monitor
KD_MULTI_M	Multi-mode monochrome monitor
KD_MULTI_C	Multi-mode color monitor

If the ioctl(2) system call function returns a value of -1, a data transfer error occurred.

The following code fragment illustrates how to find the adapter type:

```
{
    ...
    struct kd_vdctype vdcinfo;
    ...
    /*issue the ioctl to get the VDC type */
    if (ioctl(disp, KDVDCTYPE, &vdcinfo) < 0) {
        fprintf(stderr, "KDVDCTYPE failed");
        exit(1);
    }
    /* LOOK AT THE ADAPTER TYPE */
    switch (vdcinfo.cntlr) {  /* switch on the adapter type */
    case KD_EGA:
        printf("EGA Compatible Adapter Unit \n");
        break;
    case KD_VGA:
        printf("VGA Compatible Adapter Unit \n");
        break;
    default:
        printf("This application will only run on systems\n");
        printf("configured with EGA or VGA compatible controllers\n");
        exit(1);
    }
    /* LOOK AT THE MONITOR TYPE */
    switch (vdcinfo.disply) {  /* switch on monitor type  */
    case KD_STAND_M:
    case KD_MULTI_M:
        printf("Warning: This application requires a color\n");
        printf("monitor for some of the options.\n");
        break;
    case KD_STAND_C:
    case KD_MULTI_C:
        printf("Color Monitor \n");
        break;
    default:
        printf("Warning: Unknown monitor type.\n");
        break;
    }
    ...
}
```

Getting and Setting the Mode

The mnemonics for setting the adapter mode are of the form SW_type, where "type" indicates the combination of adapter and mode. For example, SW_C80x25 is used to set the mode to CGA text, 80 x 25 while SW_VDC640x400V selects the 640 x 400 graphics mode.

The mode is set by calling the routine:

```
ioctl(disp, SW_type, 0);
```

A negative return indicates an error.

The CONS_GET routine is used to determine the current adapter mode. It returns the mode using the mnemonic DM_type, where "type" is as above. The mode is obtained by calling:

```
ioctl(disp, CONS_GET, 0);
```

The return is the current mode setting, or a value less than zero if there was an error.

The relationship between the mode as gotten and the mode to be set is:

```
SW_type = DM_type | MODESWITCH;
```

That is, the value used to set the mode can be obtained by or-ing a previously gotten and saved mode value with MODESWITCH.

A call to `ioctl(disp, KDSETMODE, KD_TEXT);` sets the adapter from whatever its current mode is to the default text mode and also clears the screen.

One reason for having to save and restore adapter modes is that a video application may be invoked within other video applications, such as OPEN LOOK.

The example below illustrates the operation just described. The code fragment opens the device in one mode; gets and saves that mode; switches modes and then restores the original mode. Prudent programming will also catch all catchable signals in order to restore the initial settings.

```
# include <stdio.h>
# include <fcntl.h>
# include <sys/kd.h>
# include <errno.h>
main()
{
        int     disp, save_mode;

        if ((disp = open("/dev/video", O_RDWR)) < 0) {
             fprintf(stderr, "Cannot open /dev/video, errno %d\n", errno);
             exit(1);
        }
        /* set the mode to wide text and print something out */
        if (ioctl(disp, SW_C40x25, 0) < 0) {
             fprintf(stderr, "SW_C40x25 ioctl failed\n");
             exit(1);
        }
        printf("Testing SW_C40x25 ioctl\n");
        sleep(2);

        /* Save that mode */

        if ((save_mode = ioctl(disp, CONS_GET, 0)) < 0) {
             fprintf(stderr, "CONS_GET failed");
             exit(1);
        }
        /* Clear the screen and reset the display back to the default text mode: */

        if (ioctl(disp, KDSETMODE, KD_TEXT) < 0) {
                fprintf(stderr, "Unable to reset display, error: %d\n", errno);
                exit(1);
        }
        /* Show normal text */
        printf("Now in normal narrow text mode ");
        sleep(2);
        /* Return to wide text */
        if (ioctl(disp, MODESWITCH | save_mode, 0) < 0) {
             fprintf(stderr, "Unable to reset display, mode: %x\n", save_mode);
             exit(1);
        }
        exit(0);
}
```

Memory

All access to physical hardware is regulated by the UNIX system kernel and device drivers. In the case of the console video graphics controller, the kd display driver is charged with this responsibility.

To provide a reasonable level of protection, most of the common controller operations are supported via the ioctl(2) UNIX system call interface. Examples of such operations include: video mode selects, controller status, I/O operations to the controller, and get/set screen attributes. In addition to these operations for interacting with the controller, one additional important feature is provided; the ability to map video memory into your address space.

From a programmer's viewpoint, the adapter card can be considered to be directly linked to memory locations within the computer. Changing the contents of the memory immediately changes the content of the display. An essential element of programming the video display, then, is understanding exactly how the memory corresponds to the output. The specific way in which memory must be laid out is a function of the adapter card and the mode with which that adapter is being used. The specific layout and mapping of memory are described in subsequent sections.

Registers

The actual operation of the adapter is controlled by certain registers on the adapter.

In the UNIX System V Release 4, the kd driver does all the basic video register setup at the time you select the graphics mode. The driver has been designed to provide good performance while maintaining a safe user level interface. The driver does not fully protect you against programming mistakes. On the contrary, you are specifically allowed to read and write the video hardware registers directly. Some of these registers should not be directly written unless you are fully aware of the consequences and have taken steps to ensure the correctness of the operation.

Programming in Text Mode

How Text is Stored

In text mode, each character is stored in memory as two data bytes. The first one is for the character itself and the second one is for its attributes. A character's attributes specify the foreground and background colors, as well as whether that character is to be highlighted, underlined, or blinking. These characteristics differ somewhat, depending on the video mode and the adapter, and also on whether the display screen is monochrome or color.

Bits 0 - 3 affect the Foreground Color; bits 4 - 7 affect the Background Color.

Character Sets

The adapters provide alternate character sets. We recommend that you run a simple program that exercises the different character set options. The following code fragment is illustrative:

```
{
        NOTE: Escape (ESC) is octal 33

        /* Clear the screen and select 1st alt char set. */
        printf("\033c\033[11m");
        for (i = 0; i < 255; i++)
                printf("%c", (char)i);

        /* Select 2nd alt char set. */
        printf("\n\n\033[12m");
        for (i = 0; i < 255; i++)
                printf("%c", (char)i);

        /* Restore the primary character set. */
        printf("\033[10m");
}
```

Many video display controllers allow additional character sets or text fonts to be created locally by an application programmer. For example, some VDCs allow 16 such fonts and others may allow 8 such fonts. Each character set is stored in a fixed section of memory and is selected by setting the Expanded Character Select Register. Register programming will be described in a subsequent section.

Selecting the Text Mode

Each of the adapters allows several possible text modes.

- One approach to selecting a mode is to choose the highest resolution mode available on the adapter.

- If compatibility is an issue, select the mode that will work on the lowest common adapter that the application will run on.

Assuming an 80 column width, the difference between text modes on the same adapter is that the actual characters can be displayed with different resolutions. For example, a VDC that can operate compatibly with CGA, EGA or VGA applications can display characters in 3 different 80 x 25 character modes.

- VGA mode 2 displays characters in a 9 x 16 box (144 pixels),

- EGA mode 2 displays characters in an 8 x 14 box (112 pixels).

- CGA mode 2 displays characters in an 8 x 8 box (64 pixels).

The VGA and EGA's higher resolutions produce characters that are crisper and easier to read.

The section entitled "Text and Graphics IOCTLs" summarizes all text and graphics modes. It lists the defined mnemonic used in the ioctl(2) system call and the adapter type it can work on.

Escape Sequences

Escape sequences are used for three purposes:

- To change the characteristics of the text to be displayed.

   These characteristics can also be altered by directly addressing the video memory. This aspect of video programming is discussed in the next sub-section.

- To program some of the Video Registers and affect the overall display.

   For example, Escape sequences can modify those registers that select the character set, move the cursor, erase all or part of the screen, etc.

■ To issue some miscellaneous commands.

> For example, you can issue an escape sequence (ESC[1k) that pro-
> duces a "click" each time the user presses a key. The sequence
> ESC[0k disables that feature.

The Escape sequences can be issued at the command level; in particular, they
can be embedded in shell scripts that are integral to an application system. For
example, including the following within a user's .profile displays the primary prompt as the machine name in cyan:

```
UNAME=`uname`
PS1=`echo "\033[36m$UNAME: \033[37m"`
```

The Escape sequences adhere to the ANSI X3.64 standard for ASCII terminals,
with a few extensions for color and enabling the key-click feature. The complete
list of escape commands is included in the display(7) documentation.

The following C program displays the characters of the alphabet in different
foreground and background colors:

```
main ()
{
        int i, j;
        char *string = "abcdefghijklmnopqrstuvwxyz"
        for (i = 30; i < 38; i++)
                for (j = 40; j < 48; j++)
                        printf("\033[%d;%dm%s\n", i, j, string);

        /* Restore the default white on black display colors: */
        printf("\033[0m\n");
}
```

Example of Text Mode Programming

The following program opens the video adapter and displays the printable character set under whatever text modes are valid on that adapter. Note that not all monitors will support all modes.

```
#include <stdio.h>
#include <fcntl.h>
#include <sys/types.h>
#include <sys/at_ansi.h>
#include <sys/kd.h>
#include <errno.h>

struct {
        unchar  m_name[20];   /* ioctl name */
        int     m_value;      /* ioctl value */
} modes[] = {
        { "SW_B40x25",        SW_B40x25 },
        { "SW_C40x25",        SW_C40x25 },
        { "SW_B80x25",        SW_B80x25 },
        { "SW_C80x25",        SW_C80x25 },
        { "SW_ENHB40x25",     SW_ENHB40x25 },
        { "SW_ENHC40x25",     SW_ENHC40x25 },
        { "SW_ENHB80x25",     SW_ENHB80x25 },
        { "SW_ENHC80x25",     SW_ENHC80x25 },
        { "SW_EGAMONO80x25",  SW_EGAMONO80x25 },
        { "SW_ENHB80x43",     SW_ENHB80x43 },
        { "SW_ENHC80x43",     SW_ENHC80x43 },
        { "SW_VGAC40x25",     SW_VGAC40x25 },
        { "SW_VGAC80x25",     SW_VGAC80x25 },
        { "SW_VGAMONO80x25",  SW_VGAMONO80x25 }
};

main()
{
        int     i, j;
        int     disp;

        /* Standard form for opening the driver. If the open is
        successful, the controlling tty is, in fact, a valid
        display device. */

        if ((disp = open("/dev/video", O_RDWR)) < 0) {
                fprintf(stderr, "Cannot open /dev/video, error: %d\n",
                        errno);
                exit(1);
        }
```

(continued on next page)

Integrated Software Development Guide

```
/*Try to set every possible text mode.  Only the valid modes will work. */
for (i = 0; i < 14; i++) {
        if (ioctl(disp, modes[i].m_value, 0) < 0) {
                printf("\033c%s not supported.", modes[i].m_name);
                fflush(stdout);
        } else {
                /* For every valid mode, output every printable character. */
                printf("\033c%s\n", modes[i].m_name);
                for (j = 0x21; j < 0x7f; j++) {
                        printf("%c", j);
                        if (!((j - 0x20) % 24))
                                printf("\n");
                }
                fflush(stdout);
        }
        sleep(1);
}
/* Clear the screen and reset the display back to the default text mode: */
if (ioctl(disp, KDSETMODE, KD_TEXT) < 0) {
        fprintf(stderr, "Unable to reset display, error: %d\n",
                errno);
        exit(1);
}
}
```

Text Programming Memory Management

The ability to access video memory is a necessary feature for developing high performance graphics applications. The information that appears on the screen is directly correlated to a block of memory. Writing to memory directly is faster than going through intermediate routines. And changing video memory produces instant change on the screen.

In text mode you can store several screen loads in video memory at the same time. This gives you the ability to write to one screen without disturbing what the end user sees and then switching to a new, full screen's worth of data. There is a tradeoff in using this particular technique. Its downside is that using memory switching bypasses the kd driver control which means that switching Virtual Terminals may not be effective. This means you would have to seize the screen during the operation (by entering VT_PROCESS mode, which is described later).

Memory Layout

The specific layout of video memory is a function of the type of display and the video mode that is being used. The combination of the video mode and the display controller type determine both the amount of memory that needs to be mapped as well as where within video memory a particular screen's display data exists.

The table below describes the various video text modes and identifies the adapters that support each mode. The list is not exhaustive in that EGA and VGA adapters do support variations of the CGA modes. As an example, the mode 0 text mode for a VGA adapter has the ability to support the 40x25 character set in higher resolution (320 x 350 and 320 x 400) as opposed to the CGA's 320 x 200 pixel resolution.

Video Text Modes for CGA/EGA/VGA					
Video Mode	Type	Resolution	Colors	Start Address	Cont Type
0	Text	40 x 25	16 grey	0xB8000	CGA
1	Text	40 x 25	16f, 8b	0xB8000	CGA
2	Text	80 x 25	16 grey	0xB8000	CGA
3	Text	80 x 25	16f, 8b	0xB8000	CGA
7	Text	80 x 25	b/w	0xB0000	MDA

Addressing of video memory in text mode is identical for all standard video systems (CGA, EGA, VGA). Two bytes of data are required for each character represented on the display screen. The first byte contains the ASCII character to be displayed and the second byte contains the attributes of that character.

For example, the memory required to display a single screen's data for a CGA 80 x 25 color adapter (mode 3) would be 25 rows * 80 lines * 2 bytes or 4000 bytes.

The attribute byte indicates the foreground/background colors, intensity, and underline. Consider the following memory dump for a single page:

Contents of Memory

```
                                                              displayed
           0   1   2   3   4   5   6   7   8   9   A   B   C   D   E   F    Data
0xB8000   30  07  31  07  32  07  33  07  34  07  35  07  36  07  37  07   01234567
0xB8010   38  07  39  07  3a  07  3b  07  3c  07  3d  07  3e  07  3f  07   89:;<=>?
0xB8020   20  07  20  07  20  07  20  07  20  07  20  07  20  07  20  07
0xB8F90   20  07  20  07  20  07  20  07  20  07  20  07  20  07  20  07
```

Actual Screen display

```
       Column   10           20          30          40                    80
                |            |           |           |                      |
       12345678901234567890123456789012345678890......1234567890
       _____......_____
Row  |                                                                      |
 1   |0123456789:;<=>?                                                      |
 2   |                                                                      |
 3   |                                                                      |
 4   |                                                                      |
 5   |                                                                      |
 6   |                                                                      | display
 .   .                                                                      . Screen
 .   .                                                                      .
 .   .                                                                      .
25   |                                                                      |
       _____
```

The even-numbered bytes hold the character representation and the odd-numbered bytes hold the attributes. The attribute bytes (in this case the "07"s) are not displayed; rather these are used by the controller to determine how to display the data. In this case the attribute being called for is simply white on a black background.

The layout of the attribute byte is a function of the adapter. In this case, mode 3, the layout is:

Color Attribute (mode 3)	
Bit	
7	Blinking foreground component
6	Red background component
5	Green background component
4	Blue background component
3	Intensity
2	Red foreground component
1	Green foreground component
0	Blue foreground component

Since (in this case) only 4000 characters are needed to represent an entire screen within memory, then the video memory within a CGA compatible controller is not being fully used. The remaining memory however, need not be wasted. It is possible to make use of the remaining video buffer for storing more than one screen's data at a time. This feature allows a programmer to switch what is currently displayed on the screen quickly simply by redirecting where the controller begins addressing. Writing an entire screen of data into video memory is much slower than redirecting the controller's address register.

NOTE If you are doing this, you are bypassing the kd driver control. Because of this, switching Virtual Terminals may not be effective. To ensure that it is you need to enter VT_PROCESS mode (described later in the chapter on Virtual Terminals).

Because the CGA controller supports 16K RAM (16384 bytes), there is the possibility of storing 4 screens of data in video mode 3 (8 in video modes 0 and 1). With a screen using 4000 bytes however, four screens of memory will consume only 16000 bytes of the 16384 available. Each screen of data is aligned on a 4K (4096) byte boundary and thus there are 96 bytes at the end of each screen of video memory that is not used. See the following diagram:

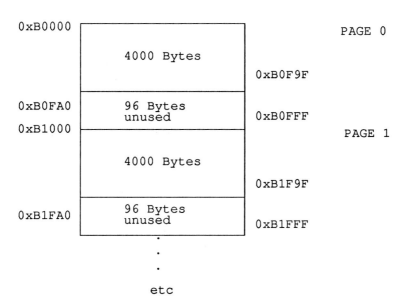

The following formula provides one method of directly associating a byte position on the screen with an address in video memory:

video buffer address = video_memory_start + 2 * (80 * row + column)

The video_memory_start is the start of the video buffer for the video mode we are using. The factor of two is necessary because of the attribute byte associated with each screen location. As an example, if we are using video mode 3 and wish to access the data and attribute for screen location row = 3, column = 30, then the video buffer address would be

0xB0000 + 2 * (80 * 3 + 30) = 0xB021C

B021C would be the address for the data byte and B021D would correspond to the attribute byte for location 3, 30 in page 0. If on the other hand we wished to address row 3, column 30 in page 1, 0x1000 would be added to this value producing 0xB121C. The same types of calculations are applicable to other video text modes. The above calculations are based on the assumption that the upper left corner of the screen, i.e., the origin, is (0, 0) and not (1, 1).

High speed interactions with the end-user can be accomplished:

- Read the current cursor position by reading the high/low cursor registers (see the section on Register Programming).

- Read the data at the cursor position by reading memory.

- Write data to the cursor position by writing memory.

- Use Escape Sequences to reposition the cursor.

These four capabilities allow you to develop completely interactive full screen sessions.

Programming Access to Video Memory

Gaining access to video memory is identical in both text and graphics mode. It is essentially a three-step process:

1. Open the kd driver. The kd driver is opened as the file /dev/video.

2. Get the physical address of the display in memory.

3. Map the display memory into an area of your program's address space.

Getting the Physical Address

Use the KDDISPTYPE ioctl to retrieve the display memory start address. The way to use this ioctl(2) system call is to define a structure that the driver will fill. In using KDDISPTYPE, the argument passed in the call is a pointer to the structure. The structure used by KDDISPTYPE is:

```
struct kd_disparam {
     long type;                    /* display type */
     char *physaddr;               /* display memory address */
     ushort ioaddr[MKDIOADDR];     /* valid I/O addresses */
};
```

The structure element type becomes the type of display (CGA, EGA, VGA, ...).

 NOTE While this call works on all adapters and modes, not all display types are returned. The return types are limited to KD_MONO, KD_HERCULES, KD_CGA, KD_EGA and KD_VGA.

The desired physical address is returned in physaddr (e.g. 0xB8000 for CGA).

The third element is an array of I/O addresses that the driver will allow operations on. These addresses are I/O port addresses on the video display controller. Some possible values that one might find here are 0x3B4, 0x3B5, 0x3D4 and 0x3D5.

Mapping the Video Memory

To access the video buffer you must request that the physical memory obtained by calling KDDISPTYPE be mapped into your address space. This is accomplished with the display driver ioctl(2) system call, KDMAPDISP. In using KDMAPDISP, the argument passed in the call is a pointer to the structure:

```
struct kd_memloc {
    char   *vaddr;      /* virtual address to map to */
    char   *physaddr;   /* physical address to map from */
    long   length;      /* size in bytes to map */
    long   ioflg;       /* enable i/o addresses if set */
};
```

The first element of the array, vaddr, must be a page aligned pointer to a physical area of memory. This will point to the area of memory within your address space where the video buffer will be made accessible to you. You must use malloc, or another allocation routine to obtain this memory space.

The physical address, physaddr, is passed as input to KDMAPDISP. This is the address returned by the previous call to KDDISPTYPE.

Mapping Example

To illustrate the mapping concept, consider the following code fragment:

```
/* The assumption here is that vaddr is a pointer to an array at least
 * 4096 bytes larger than needed to hold the mapped data.  The reason
 * for this is to ensure that when the pointer is page aligned that
 * the entire mapped area is addressable.  NOTE: The desired area
 * could also be allocated using the alloc() functions. */

char scrmem[16384 + 4096];             /* define the memory array */

map_memory()
{
        struct kd_disparam parm_area, *kdp;
        struct kd_memloc map;
        char *vaddr;
        int disp;

        kdp = &parm_area;
        vaddr = scrmem;

        if((disp = open("/dev/video", O_RDWR | O_NDELAY)) < 0) {
                fprintf(stderr,"driver open failed, errno = %d\n, errno);
                exit(-1);
        }
        if(ioctl(disp, KD_DISPTYPE, kdp) < 0) {
                fprintf(stderr,"KD_DISPTYPE failed, errno = %d\n", errno);
                exit(1);
        }
        map.physaddr = kdp->addr;      /* set the video address  */
        vaddr = (vaddr + 4095) & 4095; /* page align the address */
        map.vaddr = vaddr;             /* set the address        */
        map.length = 16384;            /* set the screen size    */
        map.ioflg = 1;                 /* enable io addresses     */

        if(ioctl(disp, KDMAPDISP, &map) < 0)
        {
                fprintf(stderr,"KDMAPDISP failed, errno = %d\n",errno);
                exit(-1);
        }
}
```

Upon return from KDMAPDISP, `vaddr` points to an area of the mapped video buffer. Reads and writes to the memory at `vaddr` directly affect the information displayed on the screen.

To unmap the display buffer from user memory, the KDUNMAPDISP `ioctl` is provided. There are no arguments to KDUNMAPDISP and it may be called as follows:

```
if(ioctl(disp, KDUNMAPDISP, 0) < 0) {
        fprintf(stderr, "KDUNMAPDISP failed, errno = %d\n",
                errno);
        exit(-1);
}
```

The section entitled "Comprehensive Video Programming Example" at the end of this chapter contains additional examples of accessing video memory. The routine `get_display_info` illustrates the use of KDDISPTYPE. The routine `map_video_screen` similarly illustrates the use of KDMAPDISP.

Relationship to MAPCONS

An investigation of the list of `ioctl`(2) system calls show several alternative ways to do a number of the functions. Some of the calls exist to allow compatibility with programs previously written for XENIX. A specific question may arise here regarding the use of the MAPCONS call (i.e. `ioctl(disp, MAP-CONS, 0);`). The MAPCONS call establishes a direct pointer to video memory and seems easier to use than the method described here which requires allocating the memory in your own program space.

However, the use of MAPCONS locks the Virtual Terminals and the end-user cannot switch Virtual Terminals until you specifically exit your application and free up the terminal.

Using KDMAPDISP in conjunction with process mode (see following sections), keeps your application well-behaved in a Virtual Terminal environment.

Graphics Mode

Addressing Graphics Mode Video Memory

Memory allocation for each of the adapters, when used in graphics mode, is displayed in the following table:

Video Modes for CGA/EGA/VGA					
4	Graphics	320 x 200	4	0xB8000	CGA
5	Graphics	320 x 200	4 grey	0xB8000	CGA
6	Graphics	640 x 200	2	0xB8000	CGA
D	Graphics	320 x 200	16	0xA0000	EGA
E	Graphics	640 x 200	16	0xA0000	EGA
F	Graphics	640 x 350	2	0xA0000	EGA
10	Graphics	640 x 350	4	0xA0000	EGA
10	Graphics	640 x 350	16	0xA0000	VGA
11	Graphics	640 x 480	2	0xA0000	VGA
12	Graphics	640 x 480	16	0xA0000	VGA
13	Graphics	320 x 200	256	0xA0000	VGA

Accessing the video buffer when in graphics modes differs significantly from the mechanism used in text mode. In text mode characters displayed on the screen are stored in the video buffer as a data byte and an associated attribute byte; two bytes correspond to a single fixed screen position. Accessing this information is fairly simple.

Graphics modes do not operate on a character level, but on a pixel level. Graphics screen addressability is on a row/column basis; however, the row and column correspond to the pixel coordinates on the displayed screen. As an example, consider a resolution of 320x200. This resolution implies that there are 200 rows of 320 columns.

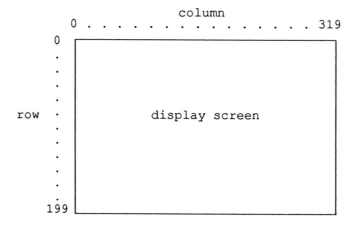

Accessing a pixel within the video RAM is not as straight forward as characters in text modes. As graphics modes vary, so do the ways that the information is stored within memory. A four color graphics mode requires two bits to store the four discrete color values. The remaining six bits within a byte are available to store pixel values for other screen locations. In this way, a single byte can store four pixel's worth of data in four color graphics modes. As the number of available colors increases, so does the memory required to store the additional information.

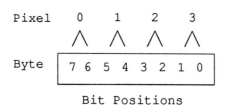

A programmer needs to be concerned not only with pixel addressing within a byte, but also with which screen row is being addressed. In CGA graphics modes for instance, even rows (scan lines) are within one area of memory (0xB8000) and odd scan lines start at 0xB8000 + 0x2000, or 0xBA000.

Putting both concepts together, the following address map results:

```
 display  │ Pixels (0 1 2 3)
  addr    ↓
```

0xB8000	·················· Line 0 ·················
0xB8050	·················· Line 2 ·················

.
.
.

0xB9EA0	·················· Line 196 ·············
0xB9EF0	·················· Line 198 ·············
0xB9F40	Unused Space 192 bytes (0xB9F40 - 0xB9FFE)
0xBA000	·················· Line 1 ·················
0xBA050	·················· Line 3 ·················

.
.
.

0xBBEA0	·················· Line 197 ·············
0xBBEF0	·················· Line 199 ·············
0xBBF40	Unused Space 192 bytes (0xBBF40 - 0xBBFFE)

The above map shows that there is an area of memory at 0xB9f40 and 0xBAF40 that is unused. This is because only 8000 bytes are needed to represent 100 scans lines (80 bytes per row * 100 rows). Because 0x2000 bytes are allocated for this area (8192 bytes), this leaves 8192 - 8000 = 192 bytes of unused space.

To properly access a particular byte within mapped memory (for modes 4 & 5), the following formula could be used:

$$\text{address} = 0xB8000 + 0x2000 * \text{row} \% 2 + \text{row}/2 * 0x50 + \text{column}/4$$

 NOTE It is important to note that this discussion is limited to CGA modes 4 and 5. After this section we will give examples for EGA addressing. These should give you a sufficient basis for developing your own memory addressing algorithms.

To access the last pixel within the last row of the above display (row = 199, column = 319) the formula above would yield

$0xB8000 + 0x2000 * 0xC7 \% 2 + 0xC7 / 2 * 0x50 + 0x13F / 4 = 0xBA000 + 0x1EF0 + 0x4F = 0xBBF3F$

Since the pixel is embedded within the byte at 0xBBF3F an additional step is necessary to extract the value. This could be accomplished by masking out the required bits within the byte. One method for accomplishing this would be as follows:

```
value =  byte & (0xA0 >> (column % 4) * 2)
```

In the above case, the formula would yield

```
value = byte & (0xA0 >> (319 % 4) * 2)
```

or

```
value = byte & (0xA0 >> 6)  = byte & 0x3
```

This is exactly what we want since column 319 should be in the lower two bits of the byte at 0xBBF3F.

The following programming example illustrates one method of writing a pixel of information. It accepts arguments: row, col and color. It is assumed that the driver has already been opened and that `screen` is a page aligned pointer to an already mapped video buffer.

```
/* mask and shift defines.  These are needed to place the color
 * information into the correct place within the written byte.
 */
unsigned int bmask[4] = {0xff3f, 0xffcf, 0xfff3, 0xfffc};
int color_shift[4] = {6, 4, 2, 0};

int write_pixel(row, col, color)
int row, col, color;
{
    int      index;          /* screen byte index */
    unsigned int mask;
    char *sptr;              /* screen memory pointer */

    sptr = screen;           /* set pointer to screen area */

    /* Find the correct position in the screen memory
     * The video memory is set up with odd/even
     * rows residing at different (non)contiguous memory addresses.
     * Because of this, we need to ensure that the starting address
     * of the byte we need to access is indeed correct.
     */
    index = row * 40 + col/4;

    /* Now decide whether the row was even or odd.  If the row
     * is odd, use (0xB8000 + index + 8152).  If the row
     * is even, use (0xB8000 + index).  This means
     * that the first odd row starts at (0xB8000 + 40 + 8152 = 0xBA000)
     * In short, the calculations ensure that the 8192 byte offset
     * between 0xb8000 and 0xBA000 is handled correctly.
     */
    if(row % 2)
        index += 8152;       /* bank 2 if odd */

    color <<= color_shift[col % 4];   /* shift color information */
    mask = bmask[col % 4];            /* select the right mask */
                                      /* buffer write */
    *(sptr + index) = color | *(sptr + index) & mask;

    return(SUCCESS);
}
```

Addressing Video Memory in EGA Graphics Modes

EGA supports additional modes with higher resolution than those of CGA. To support the additional modes more video memory is needed to store the pixel values. An EGA video controller supports up to 256KB of video buffer. (This is also the case for the VGA). This buffer is physically addressable within the address spectrum as a single 64KB block of physical memory. This is accomplished by overlaying the four 64KB blocks (planes) of memory at the same physical address. Selection of a plane is controlled by registers within the video controller.

As an example, consider a resolution of 320 x 200 with 16 colors. This would require 64Kb * 4bits or 32KB of RAM. The pixels are situated within a byte such that each physical pixel location on the screen maps to one bit within an addressed byte. This however, would only allow two colors to be displayed. To support 16 colors, four bits are needed. All four bits are mapped to the same location in a different plane. One way to access all four bits of color data for a selected pixel location might be to read the same location in video memory four consecutive times while selecting the appropriate plane within the video controller (using the "Read Map Select Register" command). A graphic example is provided below:

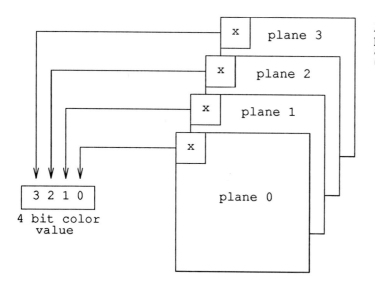

The above 4 bit color value would be used by the video controller hardware to represent the 16 colors for a selected pixel.

Mode F (640x350, two color) requires two bits to store a single pixel's worth of data. The first bit is the video bit (on/off) and the second bit is really an attribute (intensity). This information is stored in two memory planes; plane 0 and 2. As with all native EGA modes, pixels are stored consecutively within memory in a manner similar to alphanumeric modes for CGA. To access the pixel data for a particular x/y coordinate, the offset is a linear index from the start of the video buffer.

As an example, consider y = 0, x = 30. The index from the start of video RAM for this would be 0xA0003. This is computed by taking the start of the video buffer (0xA0000), adding the row displacement (80 bytes per row - here it is 0) and finally adding the x coordinate divided by the number of bits per byte.

This can be summarized by the following computation:

```
0xA0000 + y * BYTES_PER_LINE + BYTES_OFF_SET_WITHIN_LINE
```

or

```
0xA0000 + y * 80 + (30 Bytes/8 Bits Per byte)
```

or

```
0xA0000 + 0 + 3 = 0xA0003
```

Two things to remember are that the x coordinate in this example after the division is the integer value 3. The remainder (6) is the bit offset within the addressed byte. This implies a masking operation to extract the desired bit. The second thing to remember is that the intensity bit still needs to be retrieved from bit plane number 2 (at the same address).

VGA Only Addressing Modes

Modes D, E and F are VGA only modes. Addressing of video memory in these modes differs only because of the hardware differences in the video controller. The driver interface to VGA video hardware is identical to that for CGA and EGA. Rather than duplicate what has already been described for CGA and EGA, the reader is referred to readily available VGA reference manuals for information specific to VGA addressing and operation.

Mode Switching

Changing from text mode to graphics mode is a simple ioctl(2) system call. For example, the following will change the display from text mode to 320 columns x 200 rows CGA graphics Mode 5:

```
{
...
        if ((disp = open("/dev/video", O_RDWR)) < 0) {
                fprintf(stderr, "Cannot open /dev/video, errno: %d\n", errno);
                exit(1)
        }

        if (ioctl(disp, SW_CG320, 0) != 1) {
                fprintf("stderr, "Unable to select SW_CG320 graphics mode,\
                        errno: %d\n",errno);
                exit(1)
        }
...
}
```

The video display buffer is accessed by opening /dev/video.

Use the KDSETMODE ioctl to reset the display back to text mode when done:

```
        if (ioctl (disp, KDSETMODE, KD_TEXT) < 0) {
                fprintf(stderr, "KDSETMODE failed, errno: %d\n",errno);
        }
```

Accessing Video Controller Registers

Control Register programming is valuable in both text and graphics modes. In text mode, for example, it allows you to select alternate character sets.

To access the CRT controller registers, a two step procedure is needed. During the first step, an I/O location is written with a value corresponding to the controller register desired. For example, 0x3D4 is one of these 'key' I/O locations. Some VDCs have more than one such location and the location to use may differ for monochrome and color adapters. Because of this, you should use the outb function call to access the register. The step of writing to this location tells the controller hardware which register's contents to make ready. To read the desired controller register, a second I/O operation (read) is directed to another location, typically 0x3D5. The byte of data returned is the value of the register requested. The following table lists some of the registers and the values that are used to select them. The example below (and the more extensive example in the section entitled "Comprehensive Video Programming Example" at the end of this chapter) illustrates performing such an operation.

Note that in conditions in which a VGA card is doing monochrome emulation, use of the 3d4/3d5 registers should be replaced by 3b4/3b5. An application can determine whether to use 3d or 3b with the following code:

```
int regbase = 0x3b0;    /* default to 3b0 */
if (inb(0x3cc)&0x01)
    regbase = 0x3d0;    /* 3cc is CRT status byte. The */
                        /* least significant bit is set if VGA */
                        /* is in  color mode and not mono- */
                        /* chrome emulation */
```

VGA CRT CONTROLLER REGISTERS	
Register	Register Name
0x00	Horizontal Total
0x01	Horizontal displayed End
0x02	Start Horizontal Blank
0x03	End Horizontal Blank
0x04	Start Horizontal Retrace
0x05	End Horizontal Retrace
0x06	Vertical Total
0x07	Overflow
0x08	Preset Row Scan
0x09	Maximum Scan Line Address
0x0A	Cursor Start
0x0B	Cursor End
0x0C	Start High Address
0x0D	Start Low Address
0x0E	Cursor Location High
0x0F	Cursor Location Low
0x10	Vertical Retrace Start
0x11	Vertical Retrace Low
0x12	Vertical display End
0x13	Offset
0x14	Underline Location
0x15	Start Vertical Blanking
0x16	End Vertical Blanking
0x17	Mode Control
0x18	Line Compare

NOTE All of the registers above are read/write in a VGA based video system. In EGA and CGA systems, not all registers are both read and write; refer to a video technical reference manual for details.

Using Registers for Efficiency

Many applications will need more efficient ways of quickly filling the video buffer than the byte by byte method used in the examples. These applications will use the most efficient hardware read and write modes when updating the display. Doing so requires setting up certain hardware registers described in the Hardware Technical Reference Manual. Before these hardware registers may be accessed, an internal I/O flag must be set. One way is to set the ioflg variable of a kd_memloc structure to 1 before mapping the display using KDMAPDISP. An equivalent way is to explicitly set the I/O enable flag via the KDENABIO ioctl(2) system call. Once the flag is set, data may be moved in and out of the registers a byte at a time by using the inb and outb subroutines defined in the header file /usr/include/sys/inline.h. The first argument of the call is the hardware register address. The second is the data byte to be moved into or out of the register.

To prevent errant or malicious programs from leaving a shared display in an inconsistent state upon exit, the KDDELIO ioctl is provided. It restricts access to the specified hardware registers by removing them from an internal list of valid register port addresses. It is ordinarily used by the system administrator and requires superuser privileges. These registers may later be restored to the list by using the KDADDIO ioctl.

Register Programming Example

The following code fragment demonstrates how to make use of the ioctl(2) system call interface to change the shape of the cursor. This example is only illustrative; you can change the cursor shape simply by issuing an escape sequence: ESC [c0 changes the shape to an underscore; ESC [c1 changes it to a block.

```
#include <stdio.h>
#include <fcntl.h>
#include <sys/types.h>
#include <sys/at_ansi.h>
#include <sys/kd.h>
#include <sys/inline.h>
#include <errno.h>

int       disp;
/* This program tests the KDENABIO and KDDISABIO ioctl(2) system call.
   In order to have an easily visible result, the test changes the cursor.
   Depending on the current cursor type, the cursor will shift between an
   underscore and a block.  This test should only be run on an EGA or VGA
   controller. */

main()
{
        struct kd_vdctype vdcinfo;
        unchar  cur_start, cur_end, new_val;
        int regbase = 0x3b0;

        printf("\033c");
        fflush(stdout);

        if (ioctl(0, KIOCINFO, 0) != (('k' << 8) | 'd')) {
                fprintf(stderr, "These tests are meaningless if run on");
                fprintf(stderr, "a TTY other than a graphics display!!\n");
                exit(1);
        }
        if ((disp = open("/dev/video", O_RDWR)) < 0) {
                fprintf(stderr, "Cannot open /dev/video, errno %d\n\n",
                        errno);
                exit(1);
        }
        if (ioctl(disp, KDENABIO, 0) < 0) {
                fprintf(stderr, "KDENABIO failed: errno %d\n\n", errno);
                exit(1);
        }
        if (ioctl(disp, KDVDCTYPE, &vdcinfo) < 0) {
           /* code for error processing */
        }
        if (vdcinfo.cntlr == KD_VGA || (inb(0x3cc)&0x01))
                regbase = 0x3d0;
     /* Inform the adapter that you will read register 0x0a (Cursor Start) */
        outb(regbase+4, 0x0a);

     /* And read it */
        cur_start = inb(regbase+5);
```

(continued on next page)

```
/* Similarly, read Cursor End */
outb(regbase+4, 0x0b);
cur_end = inb(regbase+5);

if (cur_start == (cur_end - 1)) {          /* line cursor */
        printf("The cursor is an under-score ");
        fflush(stdout);
        new_val = 0x00;          /* set value for block */
}
else {                                     /* assume block */
        printf("The cursor is a block ");
        fflush(stdout);
        new_val = cur_end - 1; /* and set value for line */
}
sleep(5);
printf("\nChanging the cursor now ");
fflush(stdout);
/* Change the Cursor Shape */
outb(regbase+4, 0x0a);
outb(regbase+5, new_val);
sleep(5);
outb(regbase+4, 0x0a);
outb(regbase+5, cur_start);
errno = 0;
if (ioctl(disp, KDDISABIO, 0) < 0) {
        fprintf(stderr, "KDDISABIO failed: errno %d\n\n", errno);
        exit(1);
}
printf("\n\nThis test fails if the cursor did not change.\n");
exit(0);
}
```

The example illustrates the sequence of steps necessary to access video controller registers. Such an example may be extended to include access to other registers within the video controller. The section entitled "Comprehensive Video Programming Example" at the end of this chapter presents a more complete example in terms of how an actual program might be structured.

The `ioctl` command KDENABIO tells the driver to allow the user program to do I/O to the video controller; KDDISABIO tells the driver to disable this I/O capability. Two more `ioctl` commands, KDADDIO and KDDELIO, are provided for adding and deleting video controller addresses from the allowable I/O list maintained within the driver. The first one adds an address to the allowable I/O port list and the second removes an address. For instance, these commands could be used to add/delete I/O addresses 0x3C4 and 0x3C5, which correspond to the EGA/VGA sequencer registers. Once a user program adds these addresses, it can use them to access the 6 sequencer registers. The following example illustrates how to use the KDADDIO and KDDELIO ioctls.

```
extern int disp;   /* driver file descriptor */

{
        if(ioctl(disp, KDADDIO, (unsigned short) 0x3C4) < 0) {
                fprintf(stderr,"KDADDIO failed, errno = %d\n, errno);
                exit(-1);
        }

        if(ioctl(disp, KDADDIO, (unsigned short) 0x3C5) < 0) {
                fprintf(stderr,"KDADDIO failed, errno = %d\n, errno);
                exit(-1);
        }
}
```

Deletion of addressable ports is similar and is demonstrated below:

```
extern int disp;   /* driver file descriptor */

{
        if(ioctl(disp, KDDELIO, (unsigned short) 0x3C4) < 0) {
                fprintf(stderr,"KDDELIO failed, errno = %d\n, errno);
                exit(-1);
        }

        if(ioctl(disp, KDDELIO, (unsigned short) 0x3C5) < 0) {
                fprintf(stderr,"KDDELIO failed, errno = %d\n, errno);
                exit(-1);
        }
}
```

Using Virtual Terminals

Introduction

Virtual Terminals (VTs) are designed to enhance the interfacing capabilities of UNIX System V/386. They represent the next evolutionary step in the use of terminals for graphics applications. The first advance was allowing a single user to develop a graphics application. Over the last few years, windowing systems have become widely available. In these systems, several users can develop graphics applications under the control of a windowing system such as AT&T's OPEN LOOK. The UNIX System V Release 4 allows several windowing systems to operate simultaneously. It is not necessary to stop one application before another starts.

In this respect the Virtual Terminal capability of the UNIX System V Release 4 analogous to your television set; changing Virtual Terminals is like switching channels. The programs continue on the other channels and you tune in to them. The analogy breaks down in several very important aspects:

- In a VT environment, a program that is switched away can put itself to sleep so that nothing happens until it is again activated (i.e., there is no chance that the user can miss any output).

- A program can hog the system and insist that it not be switched away.

- An application program can create and manage Virtual Terminals independent of the end-user. That is, the application can switch terminals based on purely functional requirements.

This section describes how to use Virtual Terminals in these respects:

- Use by End-Users.

- Writing Graphics Applications that are "aware" of VTs and are well-behaved.

- Writing VT management applications.

Use of Virtual Terminals

New virtual terminals are created by a particular "hot key" sequence once vtlmgr has been specifically invoked [see vtlmgr(1M) in the *User's Reference Manual*]:

     ALT - SYS-REQ *key*

where *key* is either a function key whose number corresponds to the number of the VT to switch into (F1, F2, ...) or, if virtual terminals have already been created with vtlmgr or newvt; one of the following letters [see newvt(1M) in the *User's Reference Manual*].

Key	Interpretation
h	home VT
n	next VT
p	previous VT
f	force a switch to a VT

The f key is used only when a user discovers that the current VT is essentially locked up or stuck in graphics mode. This will cause the kd driver to reset the VT to a sane text state and kill all processes associated with the VT.

The user can control how many VTs are available by setting a parameter in the file /etc/default/workstations. VT 0 - 8 are configured by default and the default keyboard map makes up to 13 VTs available (i.e., the user can readily define an additional 4 VTs within the default settings). The default VTs are the home terminal and one corresponding to each function key. An application can make two more available to the end-user (by reprogramming the keyboard map), or can reserve the last two for programmatic use only, making 15 VTs in all.

The end-user also needs to be aware that processes that are no longer visible may still be running. Standard output is directed to the current VT screen. For example, a user can issue a cat command on one VT and then switch to another VT to start an application. A third VT can be opened to do an edit. The cat output can be lost unless the user initially redirects that output to a file (if the virtual terminal scrolls the data off the screen).

Programming Features

VTs are a kernel maintained resource. The kernel keeps all VTs for a particular terminal on a circular queue. The zeroth VT is special and is activated if all other VTs on that device are closed. Any process desiring Virtual Terminals must compete with all other processes using a Virtual Terminal associated with the same minor device.

Programs that use VTs must include the header file /usr/include/sys/vt.h. The kd driver supports the Virtual Terminal feature in the following ways:

- It allows switching between open Virtual Terminals.

- It maintains the file /dev/vtmon for signalling user requests for VT activation,

- It responds to a series of controlling ioctl commands.

The ioctl commands used to control VT operation are:

Command	Function
VT_SETMODE	Sets the VT mode to automatic or process controlled.
VT_GETMODE	Gets the current VT mode.
VT_RELDISP	Releases, refuses to release, or acquires the display.
VT_WAITACTIVE	Waits until the specified VT becomes active.
VT_OPENQRY	Returns the number of the next available VT.
VT_ACTIVATE	Activates the specified VT.
VT_GETSTATE	Returns the active VT number and list of open VTs,
VT_SENDSIG	Sends a specified signal to open VTs owned by the process.

The first four commands are required for the development of well-behaved graphics applications. The remaining four commands are only required when you want to develop an application that manages multiple VTs.

`ioctls` done in the background on a VT may cause the process to block.

VT Modes of Operation

There are two modes of operation for Virtual Terminals. The first mode is the automatic mode (VT_AUTO) of operation. This is the simplest case and the default case. In automatic mode the application is not made aware of the end-user's requests to switch away from or back to the current VT. This means that any output in process while the user is switched away may be lost. The only option at your disposal is to issue the VT_WAITACTIVE command before every output statement. This command causes the program to suspend operation until it is using the currently active VT. This is, at best, tedious.

The second mode is the process control mode, or *process mode*, VT_PROCESS. This mode allows you to synchronize your application with other processes that are using VTs. When you set the mode to VT_PROCESS you assume the responsibility of accepting and relinquishing use of the VT.

Writing Well-Behaved Programs

The most common circumstance is that you want to develop a graphics application that will run in a VT environment. You want to be responsible for its running in that environment and you want to take minimal responsibility for that aspect of your program.

This is how to set-up your program to run in this manner:

1. Make sure you use the KDMAPDISP command to manage your use of display memory.

2. When you are ready to initiate the use of the terminal, issue a VT_GETMODE command. This command passes a structure to the driver. The driver fills the structure with information, but you are only interested in the current mode. If the mode is already VT_PROCESS, there is an error condition. You cannot go into process mode from process mode.

3. Assuming you can continue, issue a VT_SETMODE command. This command passes the mode structure into the driver. The VT_SETMODE command accomplishes three things:

   ■ It establishes VT_PROCESS mode.

   ■ It defines the signal to be received when the end-user requests to switch to another VT.

   ■ Normally, when your VT is not active your program can continue to execute. You can specify in this command that even though your program can continue to execute, it will not perform any output until the VT is again active. That is, it will hang when it encounters an output instruction.

4. Write signal processing routines to process each of the signals defined by VT_SETMODE.

   ■ Relinquishing Control

     Once a request to switch out of your VT has been issued, you must respond within ten seconds. The VT_RELDISP command is the response vehicle. If you issue the command with an argument of zero, you are refusing to give up control (and the end-user will get a "beep" at the terminal). A non-zero argument says "okay to switch now." Before you authorize the switch, you need to save the display mode (unless you explicitly know it), restore the adapter to the default text mode, and save the status of any registers you have explicitly changed. You also issue a KDUNMAPDISP to cut the linkage between the video memory and your memory. The last thing you do is issue the VT_RELDISP command.

   ■ Regaining Control

     When the signal indicates that you have regained control you do the opposite tasks; you first issue the VT_RELDISP command with an argument of VT_ACKACQ (ACKnowledge ACQuisition); then reinitialize the adapter mode; re-modify any specially set registers and re-establish the connection between your memory and the video memory.

Example of a Well-Behaved Graphics Application

The example that follows illustrates the techniques to develop a well-behaved graphics application.

```
#include <stdio.h>
#include <fcntl.h>
#include <sys/types.h>
#include <sys/at_ansi.h>
#include <sys/kd.h>
#include <sys/vt.h>
#include <sys/signal.h>
#include <sys/inline.h>
#include <errno.h>

unchar    *Tdisplay,
          *Display;

int disp;

struct kd_memloc   memloc;
struct kd_disparam kd_param;

struct modes {
        char      m_name[20];       /* mode name */
        int       m_value,          /* ioctl value */
                  m_layout,         /* memory layout */
                  m_cnt,            /* count for drawing */
                  m_len;            /* length of memory to map */
} Modes = {
          "SW_CG320",
          SW_CG320,
          1,
          8000,
          16384
};
```

```
/*
This routine fills the screen with a simple pattern.  CGA mode was chosen
because it is common to all of the color adapters.
*/
redraw_scrn()
{
        int cnt1;
        if (!Modes.m_layout)
                return(0);
        errno = 0;

        for (cnt1 = 0; cnt1 < Modes.m_cnt; cnt1++) {
                *(Display + cnt1) = 0xa5 ;     /* 0xa5 is random pattern */
                *(Display + 8192 + cnt1) = 0xa5;
        }
}
```

```
/*
This routine is entered when the user terminates the session.  It unmaps the
display and resets the mode before exiting.
*/
sigintr()
{
        if (ioctl (disp, KDUNMAPDISP, 0) == -1) {
                fprintf(stderr, "KDUNMAPDISP failed, errno %d\n", errno);
                exit(1);
        }
        if (ioctl (disp, KDSETMODE, KD_TEXT) == -1) {
                fprintf(stderr, "KDSETMODE failed, errno %d\n", errno);
                exit(1);
        }
        exit(0);
}
```

```
/* This routine is entered when there is a request to switch to another Virtual Terminal.
   The process is to unmap the display, restore the adapter to text mode and then allow the switch. */
sigusr1()
{
        if (ioctl (disp, KDUNMAPDISP, 0) == -1) {
                fprintf(stderr, "KDUNMAPDISP failed, errno %d\n", errno);
                return(0);
        }
        if (ioctl (disp, KDSETMODE, KD_TEXT) == -1) {
                fprintf(stderr, "KDSETMODE failed, errno %d\n", errno);
                return(0);
        }
        if (ioctl (disp, VT_RELDISP, 1) == -1) {
                fprintf(stderr, "VT_RELDISP failed, errno %d\n", errno);
                return(0);
        }
        sigrelse(SIGUSR1);
}
```

```
/* This routine is entered when the user re-activates this VT.  The RELDISP is
   issued first, to acknowledge that the program is back.  You then set graphics
   mode and re-map display memory. */
sigusr2()
{
        if (ioctl (disp, VT_RELDISP, VT_ACKACQ) == -1) {
                fprintf(stderr, "VT_RELDISP ack failed, errno %d\n", errno);
                return(0);
        }
        if (ioctl (disp, SW_CG320, 0) == -1) {
                fprintf(stderr, "SW_CG320 failed, errno %d\n", errno);
                return(0);
        }
        if (ioctl(disp, KDMAPDISP, &memloc) < 0) {
                fprintf(stderr, "KDMAPDISP failed, errno %d\n", errno);
                return(0);
        }
        redraw_scrn();
        sigrelse(SIGUSR2);
}
```

```
/*The main program sets up the interrupt signal routines and draws the
  initial screen.*/

main()
{
        int             cnt, ch, mask = 0;
        struct vt_mode  vtmode;


        if (ioctl(0, KIOCINFO, 0) < 0) {
                fprintf(stderr, "These tests are meaningless if run on");
                fprintf(stderr, "a TTY other than a graphics display!!\n");
                exit(1);
        }
        if ((disp = open("/dev/video", O_RDWR)) < 0) {
                fprintf(stderr, "Cannot open /dev/video, errno %d\n\n",
                        errno);
                exit(1);
        }

        fprintf(stdout,"This VT will be put into graphics mode,\n");
        fprintf(stdout,"a picture will be drawn. We also put the VT\n");
        fprintf(stdout,"in process mode, so you can VT switch to other\n");
        fprintf(stdout,"VTs. Upon switching back, the screen should\n");
        fprintf(stdout,"be repainted.  This tests VT_SETMODE, KDDISPTYPE,\n");
        fprintf(stdout,"KDMAP/UNMAP/DISP,VT_RELDISP,SW_320CG graphics mode.\n");
        fprintf(stdout," and text mode\n\nThis test should fail if you\n");
        fprintf(stdout,"do not have a CGA/EGA/VGA adapter\n\n");
        fprintf(stdout,"Hit [DEL] to quit.\n\n");
        sleep(10);

        /* Make sure allocated memory is page-aligned. */
        Tdisplay = (unchar *)malloc(64 * 1024 + 4096);
        Display = (unsigned char *)((unsigned)(Tdisplay + 4095) &  4095);

        /* Make sure we are not already in process mode. */
        if (ioctl(disp, VT_GETMODE, &vtmode) < 0) {
                fprintf(stderr, "VT_GETMODE failed: errno %d\n", errno);
                exit(1);
        }
        if (vtmode.mode == VT_PROCESS) {
                fprintf(stderr, "VT is already in VT_PROCESS mode\n");
                exit(1);
        }
        /* Set up process mode and set up the interrupt handling structure.
        In this case, forced switch behavior will be the same as normal
```

(continued on next page)

```
release behavior. */
vtmode.mode = VT_PROCESS;
vtmode.relsig = SIGUSR1;
vtmode.frsig  = SIGUSR1;
vtmode.acqsig = SIGUSR2;
if (ioctl(disp, VT_SETMODE, &vtmode) < 0) {
        fprintf(stderr, "VT_SETMODE failed: errno %d\n", errno);
        exit(1);
}
/* Set the display type to CGA for widest applicability. */
if (ioctl (disp, SW_CG320, 0) == -1) {
        fprintf(stderr, "SW_CG320 failed, errno %d\n", errno);
        return(0);
}
/* Get the memory address of the display. */
errno = 0;
if (ioctl(disp, KDDISPTYPE, &kd_param) == -1) {
        fprintf(stderr, "KDDISPTYPE failed, errno %d\n", errno);
        return(0);
}
/* Set up the structure for the KDMAPDISP command. */
memloc.vaddr = (char *)Display;
memloc.physaddr = kd_param.addr;
memloc.length = Modes.m_len;
memloc.ioflg = 1;

/* Map the Display. */
if (ioctl(disp, KDMAPDISP, &memloc) < 0) {
        fprintf(stderr, "KDMAPDISP failed, errno %d\n", errno);
        return(0);
}
/* Draw the screen.  Set up the signals and wait. */
redraw_scrn();
sigset(SIGUSR1,sigusr1);
sigset(SIGUSR2,sigusr2);
sigset(SIGINT,sigintr);

/* User must hit break (e.g., 'DEL') to interrupt the infinite loop. */
while (1)
        ;

}
```

Programming to Manage Virtual Terminal Use

The next sub-sections illustrate different aspects of a single process managing other processes that use VTs.

Suppose a process needs to respond to given events in an indeterminate fashion. By choosing a Virtual Terminal the process can handle just about any I/O requirements. By setting VT_PROCESS and spawning event handling processes attached to the VTs that are waiting upon VT activation (either because they issued a VT_WAITACTIVATE command or because they issued a VT_SETMODE requesting a hangup on output), the server process can act as an event gateway relinquishing access to the VT to the associated event handling client and regaining access when it is through.

The following is a simple shell level command that kills all of the active processes associated with the Virtual Terminals. The program examines the Virtual Terminals and based on their state, individually sends a SIGKILL to each open VT. It illustrates the use of the `ioctl` request VT_SENDSIG.

VT_SENDSIG allows a process to send a particular signal to any combination of Virtual Terminals. This is a powerful feature extending the standard UNIX operating System's signal handling capabilities, creating a user definable Virtual Terminal group that can collectively or selectively act upon any given signal. A controlling process can exploit this during initialization, error recovery and synchronization.

```
#include <stdio.h>
#include <string.h>
#include <sys/types.h>
#include <signal.h>
#include <fcntl.h>
#include <sys/at_ansi.h>
#include <sys/kd.h>
#include <sys/vt.h>
#include <sys/termio.h>
#include <sys/stat.h>
#include <errno.h>
#include <varargs.h>

#define KD_DRIVER 0x6b64    /* "kd" */
#define FOS_DRIVER 0x73   /* Fiber Optic Station driver */
#define EQUAL 0

char      vtname[20];

main(argc, argv)
int       argc;
char      **argv;
{
        int i, disp, ttype, activeVTs, vtActive;
        struct vt_stat  vtinfo;

        /*Determine what type of terminal we are on.  This must be
        a graphics terminal such as the console. */

        ttype = ioctl(0, KIOCINFO, 0);

        if ((ttype != KD_DRIVER) && ((ttype & 0xff00) >> 8) != FOS_DRIVER){
                fprintf(stderr, "Must be run on a graphics display.\n");
                exit(1);
        }
        /* Open the driver. */

        if ((disp = open("/dev/video", O_RDWR)) < 0) {
                printf("Cannot open /dev/video\n");
                exit(1);
        }
        /* Get the state information from the driver.  This will tell us
         * which VT is the active one as well as the signal states and
         * allocated VTs. */

        ioctl(disp, VT_GETSTATE, &vtinfo);
        activeVTs = vtinfo.v_state;
        vtinfo.v_signal = SIGKILL;   /* select kill signal */
```

(continued on next page)

Integrated Software Development Guide

```
        /* Now check the state of all VTs and only kill those
         * that are truly active. */

        for (i = 0; i < 15; i++) {
                printf("        /dev/vt%.2d ", i);

                /* Note that a single bit within "v_state" is
                 * being set for the ioctl(VT_SENDSIG).  This
                 * is acceptable since we have saved the active VT
                 * value in "activeVTs". */

                if (vtinfo.v_state = activeVTs & (1 << i))  {
                        if (i == vtinfo.v_active)  {

                                /* The physically active VT will be
                                 * killed last; therefore save the
                                 * VT number in vtActive. */

                                printf("will be killed last.\n");
                                vtActive = i;
                                continue;
                        }
                        /* This VT is allocated; therefore, send
                         * it a kill signal.  This has been selected
                         * by setting the signal type in the structure
                         * pointed to by vtinfo. */

                        printf("...killing.\n");
                        ioctl(disp, VT_SENDSIG, &vtinfo);
                }
                else
                        printf("not in use.\n");
        }
        /* Now we need to kill the physically active VT,
         * the number of which has been saved in "vtActive". */

        if (vtActive)  {   /* not the console */
                printf("\t/dev/vt%.2d will be killed now", vtActive);
                sleep(3);
                vtinfo.v_state = activeVTs & (1 << vtActive);
                ioctl(disp, VT_SENDSIG, &vtinfo);
        }
        exit(0);
}
```

Virtual Terminal Creation and Application

The following example is a program to create new Virtual Terminal shells. When executed, the program spawns a new process which then becomes another instance of the user's login session. Once such a session is established, the user may switch between the different shells using the keyboard driver CTL-ALT-SYSREQ key sequences. This would allow a user to have multiple login sessions active on a single physical terminal (system console). Because the functionality of Virtual Terminals is part of the keyboard driver, this functionality is not supported on remote terminals.

The kd ioctls used within the application are: KIOCINFO, VT_OPENQRY and VT_ACTIVATE. KIOCINFO is used to ensure that the controlling driver for the terminal is the keyboard driver. Such a test is necessary because remote terminal drivers do not possess Virtual Terminal capability.

VT_OPENQRY is used to ask the driver for an available VT slot. This slot allows the kd driver to associate a virtual screen with a process. All screen input and output from a process must be directed to an area of memory within the driver until that screen's contents are mapped to the physical display terminal. VT_OPENQRY returns a slot number that also corresponds to the VT id used to build the pathname for the terminal special device (i.e. /dev/vt01, /dev/vt02,...).

VT_ACTIVATE, allows you to specify the VT to be mapped to the physical display device. The VT number to be mapped is passed as an argument in the VT_ACTIVATE ioctl. This is one way to have the application control which screen to switch to. This functionality could be embedded as a menu item within a screen menu for instance.

```
#include <stdio.h>
#include <sys/types.h>
#include <string.h>
#include <signal.h>
#include <fcntl.h>
#include <ctype.h>
#include <sys/at_ansi.h>
#include <sys/kd.h>
#include <sys/vt.h>
#include <sys/termio.h>
#include <errno.h>

extern int errno;

main(argc, argv)
int argc;
char *argv[];
{
        int     fd, disp;
        long    vtno;                   /* Virtual Terminal id */
        char    prompt[11];             /* prompt string */
        char    vtname[VTNAMESZ];       /* vt name character string */
        ushort  ttype;                  /* driver identification */
        struct  termio     term;        /* termio terminal parameters */

        /* Open the controlling terminal for the device. */

        if ((fd = open("/dev/video", O_RDONLY)) == -1)
                exit(1);

        /* Determine the special device name for the terminal.
         * The returned value should be "kd" for keyboard driver.  This is
         * to ensure that the user is executing on the console and not on
         * a remote terminal. */

        if((ttype = ioctl(fd, KIOCINFO, 0)) == (ushort)-1) {
                fprintf(stderr, "KIOCINFO failed, errno = %d\n",errno);
                exit(1);
        }
        if(ttype != 0x6b64) {           /* "kd" */
                fprintf(stderr, "cannot execute %s on remote terminals",
                        argv[0]);
                exit(1);
        }

        /* Get the terminal parameters for this terminal.  see termio(7) */
```

(continued on next page)

```
if(ioctl(fd, TCGETA, &term) < 0) {
        fprintf(stderr, "TCGETA failed, errno = %d\n", errno);
        exit(1);
}
/* The VT_OPENQRY ioctl will ask the driver for the next
 * available Virtual Terminal port, i.e., (00, 01, 02, ...); */

if(ioctl(fd, VT_OPENQRY, &vtno) < 0) {
        fprintf(stderr, "VT_OPENQRY failed, errno = %d\n", errno);
        exit(1);
}
if (vtno < 0) {
        fprintf(stderr, "No vts available, errno = %d\n", errno);
        exit(1);
}
sprintf(vtname, "/dev/vt%02d", vtno); /* setup vt path */

close(fd);
close(2); /* close stderr */
close(1); /* close stdout */
close(0); /* close stdin  */

/* Now the program will fork a child.  The child process will
 * inherit the new Virtual Terminal.  Once the fork succeeds,
 * the parent program can terminate since its job is done.  The
 * child will continue with its environment setup.  */

if (fork())
        exit(0); /* parent exits */

setpgrp();                      /* set group id to uid */

/* Now open the Virtual Terminal as stderr.  The Virtual Terminal
 * name will correspond to one of the special device files:
 *
 * /dev/vt01, /dev/vt02, ...       */

if (open(vtname, O_RDWR) == -1)
        exit(1);

ioctl(0, TCSETA, &term);     /* restore terminal parameters */
```

(continued on next page)

```
        /* Re-establish stdout, stderr. */

        dup(0);
        dup(0);
        if ((disp = open("/dev/video", O_RDWR)) == -1)
                exit(1);

        /* Set Virtual Terminal's prompt variable PS1 to make easier identification
         * for the user. */

        sprintf(prompt,"PS1=VT %d> ", vtno);
        putenv(prompt);

        /* Clear the screen. */

        fputs(" 33c", stdout);

        signal(SIGINT, SIG_DFL);    /* ignore interrupts */
        signal(SIGQUIT, SIG_DFL);   /* ignore quit */

        /* The following ioctl will activate the new vt so that the display
         * will be refreshed with the new VT's virtual screen. */
        if(ioctl(disp, VT_ACTIVATE, vtno) < 0) {
                fprintf(stderr,"VT_ACTIVATE failed\n");
                /* Continue (this should not happen but is not fatal) */
        }
        /* This will spawn a new shell for the Virtual Terminal.  In some
         * applications this could be an exec of application program. */

        if (execl("/bin/sh", "sh", 0) == -1)
                fprintf(stderr, "exec of /bin/sh failed, errno = %d\n",
                        errno);

        /* Should only get here if the execl fails.  In this case sleep 5 seconds
         * to let the user see the error on the new Virtual Terminal. */

        sleep(5);
        exit(1);
}
```

Determining VT State

An interesting aspect of the VT feature is that you can gain access to the state information of active VT sessions. For instance, you may wish to know which VTs are allocated and which VT is currently controlling the display screen. The following example demonstrates the use of the VT_GETSTATE `ioctl` and the information it returns.

The example provided first opens the controlling tty to return a file descriptor for the console driver. This implies that the command can only run from the console in its current incarnation. Once a connection to the driver has been established, the VT_GETSTATE `ioctl` is invoked and a structure containing three items is populated by the console driver. The remainder of the program then individually examines each bit in the `v_state` element to determine the state of each of the 15 possible VTs.

```
#include <stdio.h>
#include <fcntl.h>
#include <sys/types.h>
#include <sys/at_ansi.h>
#include <sys/kd.h>
#include <sys/vt.h>
#include <errno.h>

int       disp;

main(argc, argv)
int       argc;
char      *argv[];
{
        int       cnt;
        struct vt_stat   vtinfo;   /* structure for VT_GETSTATE */

        /* Open the controlling terminal.  If this is successful, the device
         * is automatically a proper controlling tty. */

        if((disp = open("/dev/video", O_RDONLY)) < 0) {
                fprintf(stderr, "Cannot open /dev/video, errno %d\n",
                                errno);
                exit(1);
        }

        /* Get the video state information.   */

        if (ioctl(disp, VT_GETSTATE, &vtinfo) < 0) {
                fprintf(stderr, "VT_GETSTATE failed: errno %d\n", errno);
                exit(1);
        }
```

```
/*
        * Print the contents of the vtinfo structure. v_active
        * is the number of the active Virtual Terminal. v_signal
        * is the signal state of the process controlling the
        * terminal and v_state is the a bit field where each of the
        * lower 16 bits correspond to 16 possible combinations of
        * terminals. The following is the bit layout of v_state:
        *
        * |-------------|-----------|-----------|---------|
        * | 15 14 13 12 | 11 10 9 8 | 7 6 5 6 4 | 3 2 1 0 |
        * |-------------|-----------|-----------|---------|
        *                                        ^  ^
        *                                        |  |
        *                                        |  | VT 0
        *·                                       |
        *                                        |- VT 1
        */
        printf("The active vt is %x\n", vtinfo.v_active);
        printf("The signal state is %x\n", vtinfo.v_signal);
        printf("The vt state is %x\n", vtinfo.v_state);

        /* Now let's print out the state of all the Virtual Terminals.
         * This can be accomplished by looking at the v_state and
         * v_active structure elements. */

        for (cnt = 0; cnt < 15; cnt++) {
                printf("      /dev/vt%.2d is ", cnt);
                if (cnt == vtinfo.v_active)
                        printf("active.\n");
                else if (vtinfo.v_state & (1 << cnt))
                        printf("open.\n");
                else
                        printf("not in use.\n");
        }
        exit(0);
}
```

Virtual Terminal Control

In the section on writing well-behaved programs, the commands
VT_GETMODE, VT_SETMODE and VT_RELDISP were used to synchronize a
program with the end-user's VT switching activity. In this section we use the
same commands to coordinate VT usage at the application-controlled level.

VT_GETMODE and VT_SETMODE are used to enable/disable the way the
switching of the VTs takes place. The default action is to have the driver perform the switching function upon receipt of the appropriate keyboard sequence.

VT_GETMODE returns a structure of type "vt_mode". This structure defines
the current VT switching state (VT_AUTO or VT_PROCESS) as well as signal
and control information. Recall that VT_AUTO is the default mode and that
VT_PROCESS allows you to take responsibility for managing the switching process and to take additional control of the switching mechanism.

The example provides two programs to demonstrate the functionality provided
when a process chooses to manage VT switching.

The first program requests that a particular VT be activated. This is accomplished when the program executes the VT_ACTIVATE ioctl.
VT_ACTIVATE informs kd that a program wishes to make a new VT be the
active VT. This is the same as an end-user executing a hot-key sequence.

Before performing the switch, the driver sends a signal to the program that
currently owns the active VT to request that it relinquish control. When the
controlling VT receives the signal, it should execute the VT_RELDISP ioctl to
inform the driver to proceed. Once this takes place, the driver performs the
actual VT switch.

This provides a mechanism for cooperation between the various programs controlling their VTs. Not only can a controlling display agree to relinquish the
active VT slot, but it can also refuse (by using a 0 argument in the
VT_RELDISP ioctl). In this example, the programs cooperate.

The test program is implemented by initiating two new virtual terminals manually (VT1 and VT2). Next, the "acquire 1" command is invoked on VT1.
Immediately (within 10 seconds), the user should manually switch to VT2 and
execute the "release" program. The reason for this contortion is once the release
program is executed on VT2, the user's ability to make use of the automatic
(VT_AUTO) VT switching capability is disabled. So, the release program starts
first and sleeps to give the user time to manually switch VTs to VT2.

The following diagram illustrates the sequence of steps necessary to run the program.

VT1	User Operation	VT2	Result
release 1			VT1 program sleeps 10 secs
	switch to VT2		VT2 displayed
		acquire	VT2 program waits for release request from VT1
signal sent to VT2 by "release" program			VT1 "acquire" program releases the active slot; Driver does the switch.
			VT1 is the actively displayed VT. VT2 program continues execution after handling the release signal. VT1 "release" terminates.

The result of the above efforts are that VT2 will be switched backed to VT1 as a result of program control instead of a manual keystroke.

```
/*********************************************************************
 * release allows the Virtual Terminal to be manually
 * released under program control.  It is used in conjunction
 * with "acquire" to demonstrate the VT_PROCESS VT mode.
 *********************************************************************/
#include <stdio.h>
#include <fcntl.h>
#include <sys/types.h>
#include <signal.h>
#include <sys/at_ansi.h>
#include <sys/kd.h>
#include <sys/vt.h>
#include <errno.h>

int      disp;

main()
{
        int      cnt, i;
        int release(), acquire();

        struct vt_stat      vtinfo;
        struct vt_mode      vtmode;  /* structure for VT_GETMODE */

        /* Open the controlling terminal.  If successful, the device is an
         * appropriate Virtual Terminal. */

        if((disp = open("/dev/video", O_RDONLY)) < 0) {
                fprintf(stderr, "Cannot open /dev/video, errno %d\n",
                        errno);
                exit(1);
        }
        /* Get the video mode information.   */

        if (ioctl(disp, VT_GETMODE, &vtmode) < 0) {
                fprintf(stderr, "VT_GETMODE failed: errno %d\n",
                        errno);
                exit(1);
        }
        printf("mode is %x\n", vtmode.mode);      /* VT_AUTO or VT_PROCESS */
        printf("waitv is %x\n", vtmode.waitv);    /* Hang on writes */
        printf("relsig is %x\n", vtmode.relsig);  /* release signal type */
        printf("acqsig is %x\n", vtmode.acqsig);  /* acquire signal type */
        printf("frsig is %x\n", vtmode.frsig);    /* forced signal type */
        /* Now that we have acquired the vt_mode structure,
         * let's change the way we switch VTs.
         * Instead of having it done automatically by the driver,
         * we can request to do this within the application program.
```

(continued on next page)

```
              * The release and acquire signals are by default set
              * to SIGUSR1 and SIGUSR2; we will not change them. */
         vtmode.mode = VT_PROCESS;     /* select application process control */

         if (ioctl(disp, VT_SETMODE, &vtmode) < 0) {
                  fprintf(stderr, "VT_SETMODE failed: errno %d\n", errno);
                  exit(1);
         }
         /* Set up to catch SIGUSR1 and SIGUSR2 */
         signal(SIGUSR1, release);
         signal(SIGUSR2, acquire);
          /* For simplicity, assume that we are on vt02 and this is the active session.
           * Furthermore we wish to now handle requests from other processes that
           * want to activate VTs other than our active session "vt02".
           *
           * The release happens when our process receives a SIGUSR1.  When this
           * occurs, we know that some other process has made a request to the
           * driver to activate a VT.  release() will get control and do an
           * ioctl to the driver to give up control. The driver will then switch
           * VTs */
         while(1) {            /* loop forever */
                  sleep(5); /* sleep 5 seconds */
                  fprintf(stderr,"Alive message # %d\n",i++);
         }
}

release()
{
         signal(SIGUSR1, release);

         if(ioctl(disp, VT_RELDISP, 1) < 0) {
                  fprintf(stderr, "VT_RELDISP (1) failed, errno = %d\n",
                           errno);
                  exit(1);
         }
}
/*
 * Provided for completeness; however, this function will not be
 * called.  It is used in combination with the waitv structure element
 * in combination with VT_GETMODE for additional process handshaking.
 */
acquire()
{
         signal(SIGUSR2, acquire);

         if(ioctl(disp, VT_RELDISP, VT_ACKACQ) < 0) {
```

(continued on next page)

```
                        fprintf(stderr, "VT_RELDISP(VT_ACKACQ) failed, errno = %d\n",
                                errno);
                        exit(1);
                }
}
/***************************************************************
 * This is the acquire command.  It is used to request a particular
 * VT be made active.  Its syntax is
 *
 *        acquire VT_NUMBER
 ***************************************************************/
#include <stdio.h>
#include <fcntl.h>
#include <sys/types.h>
#include <signal.h>
#include <sys/at_ansi.h>
#include <sys/kd.h>
#include <sys/vt.h>
#include <errno.h>

int     disp;

main(argc, argv)
int     argc;
char    *argv[];
{
        int             cnt, nuvt, i;
        struct vt_stat  vtinfo;

        if(argc != 2){
                fprintf(stderr, "usage: %s vt_num\n", argv[0]);
                exit(1);
        }
        nuvt = atoi(argv[1]);

        if((nuvt < 1) || (nuvt > 16)) {
                fprintf(stderr, "usage: %s vt_num\n", argv[0]);
                exit(1);
        }
        /* Wait for the process on the other VT to be manually started. */
        sleep(10);
        /* Open /dev/video. */
        if((disp = open("/dev/video", O_RDONLY)) < 0) {
                fprintf(stderr, "Cannot open /dev/video, errno %d\n",
                        errno);
                exit(1);
```

(continued on next page)

```
        }
        if (ioctl(disp, VT_ACTIVATE, nuvt) < 0) {
                fprintf(stderr, "VT_ACTIVATE failed: errno %d\n",
                        errno);
                exit(1);
        }
        sleep(5); /* sleep 5 seconds */
}
```

Miscellaneous Capabilities

Setting Borders

An application may set an EGA or VGA monitor to one of 63 different border colors by using the KDSBORDER `ioctl`. Bits 0 - 5 of the argument correspond to the colors blue, green, red, secondary blue, secondary green, and secondary red. These colors may be combined to generate different shades. An argument of 0 will turn off the border.

Keyboard Operations

The KDGKBTYPE `ioctl` can be used to determine the type of keyboard attached to the system. The return value of this `ioctl` specifies whether an 84 key, 101 key, or unknown keyboard is attached.

The application can set and read the current "Num Lock", "Caps Lock" and "Scroll Lock" LED settings on the keyboard by using the KDSETLED and KDGETLED `ioctl`s. Note that setting the "Num Lock" and "Caps Lock" LEDs via the KDSETLED `ioctl` will have exactly the same effect as if you had depressed those keys manually. That is not the case when setting the "Scroll Lock" LED via software. Doing so will not suspend output to the screen as might be expected.

Sound Effects

Use the KIOCSOUND and KDMKTONE `ioctl`s to add sound effects to an application. KIOCSOUND generates the same tone until called again either with a new argument for a new tone or a zero argument to turn off the tone altogether. KDMKTONE is similar except that the argument specifies the tone frequency as well as its duration.

Font Operations

Applications can change the displayed text font. The default font information is stored in ROM and does not consume system memory. Modifications to the font, therefore, cannot be overlaid but rather require use of kernel memory resources. For this reason, changing the font information is a capability that should be used only when necessary since storing a new font consumes additional system resources. A well-behaved application will restore the font information to its original state before exiting.

There are two different font programming interfaces. Both change the font not only for the active Virtual Terminal but for the other VTs as well. The first interface replaces the entire font, while the second interface allows particular characters within a font to be modified. In both cases, access is through an open file descriptor to /dev/video. Use of one interface to change the font information undoes the changes made by use of the other interface, so the two interfaces cannot be used together.

Replacing the Entire Font

The first interface uses the PIO_FONT8x8, PIO_FONT8x14, PIO_FONT8x16, GIO_FONT8x8, GIO_FONT8x14 and GIO_FONT8x16 ioctls. The GIO_ ioctls obtain the current font information from the KD driver, and the PIO_ ioctls download the new font information to the video adapter.

Each of the GIO_ and PIO_ ioctl requests apply to a specific character box size (8x8, 8x14 and 8x16). The character box size is related to the current CGA/EGA/VGA text mode. To display a character in an 8x14 font requires 14 bytes of information. Each byte corresponds to one horizontal line of the font. Each bit within the byte corresponds to a pixel on that line, and the value of the bit is the pixel's on/off state. There are 256 characters per font, so an 8x14 font requires 14*256 = 3,584 bytes of storage. Similar logic applies to 8x16 and 8x8 fonts.

For both the PIO_ and GIO_ ioctls, the *arg* should be a pointer to an array of unsigned characters, the size of which is dependent on the character box size. The font information obtained by the GIO_ ioctls or downloaded by the PIO_ ioctls is of the same format as is used by the vidi command [see vidi(1M) in the *System Administrator's Reference Manual*]. If a NULL pointer is supplied as the argument to the PIO_ ioctls, the font is reset to the default system font.

Replacing Characters Within a Font

The second interface consists of one `ioctl`: `WS_PIO_ROMFONT`. It is used to change the font information for any number of characters but does not require replacing the entire font. Rather, the changes are overlaid on top of the font information in the ROM. This interface is also different from the interface above in that changing the font information for a character cannot be done for just one character box size. Instead, the font information is supplied for each character box size: 8x8, 8x14, 8x16 and 9x16 (essentially the same as 8x16). The argument of the `ioctl` is a pointer to a `rom_font_t` structure (defined in `/usr/include/sys/kd.h`). This structure contains the number of font entries being changed and the font information for each entry. An argument value of NULL restores the font information to the ROM font.

Programming the Mouse

Most graphics applications assume that the end-user is using a mouse to move through the screen. The UNIX System V/386 Release 4 Mouse Driver Package provides the system and command-level support for the operation of three types of mice. Information about how to install and configure support for mice is documented in the *System Administrator's Guide*, and programming information beyond what is discussed here is available in the `mouse`(7) manual page (in the *System Administrator's Reference Manual*).

An application program's access to the mouse is the same regardless of the type of mouse (although a particular mouse may have special commands available to it). For most applications, interacting with a mouse involves:

- opening the mouse

- receiving mouse inputs for motion and button presses

- updating the screen to reflect the change in mouse state (including the display of the mouse cursor on the screen)

- repeating the previous two steps until the application is ready to release access to the mouse

- closing the mouse

The mouse is opened by opening the special file /dev/mouse. If an error
value is returned, there are three possible reasons:

1. The mouse is not attached or is not working.

2. The mouse has not been configured in the system and assigned a display
   terminal [see mouseadmin(1M)].

3. The controlling TTY of the process opening the mouse is not a virtual terminal to which a mouse has been assigned.

As was the case with the special file /dev/video, access to /dev/mouse
requires that the controlling TTY of the process be a Virtual Terminal.

Using the ioctl command MOUSEIOCREAD, ioctl(2) will obtain the
current mouse state, The system fills in a mouseinfo structure with the current
mouse status information. The value of MOUSEIOCREAD and the definition of
the mouseinfo structure are both in the file /usr/include/sys/mouse.h,
which should be included by applications using the mouse.

NOTE The read(2) and write(2) system calls are meaningless on the file
/dev/mouse.

The mouseinfo structure is defined as follows:

```
struct mouseinfo {
        unsigned char      status;
        char   xmotion,  ymotion;
};
```

status contains the information about the current button state. Bit 0 (least
significant) is 1 if mouse button 3 is depressed. Bits 1 and 2 similarly relate the
button state of buttons 2 and 1, respectively. The x and y motion members
reflect the *change* in movement that occurred since the last MOUSEIOCTREAD
ioctl, not the absolute x,y coordinates. The units of motion are 200 per inch.
It is the program's responsibility to scale the change in mouse movement to a
visual change in the mouse cursor's location on the screen. Larger scales
require less mouse motion to traverse the screen but reduce the granularity of
pointing.

In a Virtual Terminal environment, it is important that the application cease using MOUSEIOCREAD to process mouse events while its Virtual Terminal is not active. Otherwise, mouse events are potentially "stolen" from an application that is running in the active Virtual Terminal.

The following application uses the MOUSEIOCREAD ioctl to track mouse movement and also prints the current button status. It also uses the VT_SETMODE ioctl to put the Virtual Terminal in process mode, and demonstrates how to appropriately share the mouse in a virtual terminal environment. Screen control is done by using libcurses routines (see the *Programmer's Guide: Character User Interface* for a description of libcurses):

```
#include <fcntl.h>
#include <sys/kd.h>
#include <sys/vt.h>
#include <errno.h>
#include <signal.h>
#include <curses.h>
#include <sys/mouse.h>

extern int errno;

int xscale = 10;
int yscale = 10;

int disp; /* video file descriptor */
int mouse_is_on = 0; /* should we MOUSEIOCREAD or not? */


cleanup () {
        endwin ();
        exit ();
}
/*
 * VT release signal handler. Turn mouse off as part of releasing VT
 */
sigusr1()
{
        if (ioctl (disp, VT_RELDISP, 1) == -1) {
                fprintf(stderr, "VT_RELDISP failed, errno %d\n",
                        errno);
                return(0);
        }
        mouse_is_on = 0;
```

(continued on next page)

```
                sigrelse(SIGUSR1);
        }
        /*
         * VT acquire signal handler. Turn mouse on as part of acquiring VT
         */
        sigusr2()
        {
                if (ioctl (disp, VT_RELDISP, VT_ACKACQ) == -1) {
                        fprintf(stderr, "VT_RELDISP ack failed, errno %d\n",
                                errno);
                        return(0);
                }
                mouse_is_on = 1;
                sigrelse(SIGUSR2);
        }
        /*
         * invoke as mtracki <number>.
         * Mouse motions and button presses will be tracked.
         */

        main (ac, av)
        int ac;
        char *av[];
        {
                int msefd, x, y, sx, sy, old_sx, old_sy, sleep_time;
                struct mouseinfo m;
                struct vt_mode vtmode;

                if (ac != 2) {
                        fprintf (stderr, "Usage: %s <sleep_time>\n", av[0]);
                        exit (1);
                }
                sleep_time = atoi (av[0]);

                if ((disp = open("/dev/video",O_RDWR)) < 0) {
                        fprintf (stderr, "%s: can't open /dev/video; errno = %d\n",
                                av[0], errno);
                        exit (1);
                }
                /* set signal handlers for VT process mode */
                signal (SIGINT, cleanup);
                signal (SIGUSR1, sigusr1);
                signal (SIGUSR2, sigusr2);


                /* set up for VT_SETMODE ioctl */
```

(continued on next page)

```
vtmode.mode = VT_PROCESS;
vtmode.relsig = SIGUSR1;
vtmode.acqsig = SIGUSR2;
vtmode.frsig = SIGUSR1; /* treat forced release same as release */
vtmode.waitv = 0;
errno = 0;

/* go into process mode */
if (ioctl(disp, VT_SETMODE, &vtmode) < 0) {
        fprintf(stderr, "VT_SETMODE failed: errno %d\n", errno);
        exit(1);
}
/* open the mouse */
if ((msefd = open ("/dev/mouse", O_RDONLY)) < 0) {
        fprintf (stderr, "%s: can't open /dev/mouse; errno = %d\n",
                    av[0], errno);
        exit (1);
}
mouse_is_on = 1;

/* initialize screen output using curses(3x) routines */
initscr ();
mvaddstr(LINES - 1, 0, "Mouse tracking with ioctl's");
refresh();

/* set scale and initialize mouse positions */
old_sx = sx = old_sy = sy = 0;
x = COLS / 2 * xscale;
y = LINES / 2 * yscale;

/* loop doing MOUSEIOCREAD ioctl. VT_WAITACTIVE ioctl will
 * cause the process to sleep until its VT becomes active
 * again. Whether the VT is active or not is controlled by
 * mouse_is_on
 */
while (1) {
        if (sleep_time > 0)
                sleep(sleep_time);
        if (!mouse_is_on && (ioctl(disp,VT_WAITACTIVE,0) < 0)) {
                fprintf (stderr, "%s: can't VT_WAITACTIVE; errno = %d\n",
                            av[0], errno);
                refresh ();
                exit (1);
        }
        if (ioctl (msefd, MOUSEIOCREAD, &m) == -1) {
                fprintf (stderr, "can't ioctl; errno = %d\n",
```

(continued on next page)

```
                             av[0], errno);
                refresh ();
                exit (1);
        }
        /* update mouse cursor position */
        x += m.xmotion;
        y += m.ymotion;

        /* erase current cursor */
        mvaddch (old_sy, old_sx, (int) ' ');

        /* comput new x,y location */
        if ((sx = x / xscale) < 0)
                x = sx = 0;
        else if (sx >= COLS)
                x = (sx = COLS - 1) * xscale;
        if ((sy = y / yscale) < 0)
                y = sy = 0;
        else if (sy >= LINES - 1)
                y = (sy = LINES - 2) * yscale;

        /* draw new mouse cursor */
        mvaddch (sy, sx, (int) 'M');
        old_sy = sy;
        old_sx = sx;

        /* display button status. Defines are in mouse.h */
        mvprintw (0, 0, "Status: %02X\n", m.status);
        printw ("Buttons:  1 %s   2 %s   3 %s",
                m.status & BUT1STAT ? "DN" : "UP",
                m.status & BUT2STAT ? "DN" : "UP",
                m.status & BUT3STAT ? "DN" : "UP");

        /* beep if the button state changed */
        if (m.status & BUTCHNGMASK)
                beep ();
        refresh ();
    }
}
```

Comprehensive Video Programming Example

```
----------------------- main.c -----------------------------

#include <stdio.h>
#include <fcntl.h>
#include <sys/types.h>
#include <sys/at_ansi.h>
#include <sys/kd.h>
#include <sys/signal.h>
#include "vutil.h"

extern FILE                *logfp;          /* logfile pointer */
extern char                *disptypes[];
extern struct kd_disparam  parms;
extern struct kd_memloc    map;
extern char                scrmem[];
extern char                *screen;
extern int                 disp;
extern int                 errno;
extern int                 save_mode;

main(argc,argv)
int argc;
char *argv[];
{
        void            *signal();
        void            sigtrap();
        int             i;
        int             indata;
        extern long int end;
        int fd;

          /* Open the kd driver                              */
        if(open_driver() != SUCCESS) {
                vreset();
                exit(1);
        }
        /* Catch program termination signals and clean up */
        signal(SIGHUP,sigtrap);        /* 01 hang up */
        signal(SIGINT,sigtrap);        /* 02 interrupt */
        signal(SIGBUS,sigtrap);        /* 10 bus error */
        signal(SIGSEGV,sigtrap);       /* 11 seg violation */

        /* Set the video mode to CGA 320x200 */
        if(set_video_mode(disp, SW_CG320) != SUCCESS) {
                vreset();
```

(continued on next page)

```
            exit (1) ;
    }
    /* Retrieve the current display type, video memory
        address,etc */
    if (get_display_info(&parms) != SUCCESS) {
            vreset () ;
            exit (1) ;
    }
    if (print_display_info(&parms) != SUCCESS) {
            vreset () ;
            exit (1) ;

    }
    /* Map the display area into user address space. */
    if (map_video_screen(CGA_SCREEN_SIZE, 1) != SUCCESS) {
            vreset () ;
            exit (1) ;

    }
    /* Paint the entire screen with given color */
    loadmem(screen, (unsigned char) 0x00,CGA_SCREEN_SIZE); /*black*/
    sleep(2);      /* let the user see it */
    loadmem(screen, (unsigned char) 0x55,CGA_SCREEN_SIZE); /*cyan*/
    sleep(2);
    loadmem(screen, (unsigned char) 0xaa,CGA_SCREEN_SIZE); /*magenta*/
    sleep(2);
    loadmem(screen, (unsigned char) 0xff,CGA_SCREEN_SIZE); /*white*/
    sleep(2);

    clearmem(screen,CGA_SCREEN_SIZE);         /* clear the display */

    line(0, 0, 100, 100, 0x2);                /* draw a line */
    box(120, 120, 190, 190, 0x2);             /* draw a box */
    shade_box(120, 120, 190, 190, 0x2);       /* fill it in */
    circle(70, 220, 50, 0x01);                /* draw a circle */
    shade_circle(70, 220, 50, 0x01);          /* fill it in */

    /* Dump the screen buffer to the file "memdump"   */
    disp_dump(screen, CGA_SCREEN_SIZE);
    sleep(2);

    /* Note that it is ESSENTIAL to unmap and reset the display prior to
    * exiting the program.  Otherwise the display is left in an
    * unusable state. */

    vreset () ;
}
```

(continued on next page)

```
/*----------------------- util.c ----------------------------*/
#include <stdio.h>
#include <fcntl.h>
#include <sys/types.h>
#include <sys/at_ansi.h>
#include <sys/kd.h>
#include <sys/signal.h>

#define VGA_SCREEN_SIZE         (1024 * 64)
#define EGA_SCREEN_SIZE         (1024 * 32)
#define CGA_SCREEN_SIZE         (1024 * 16)

#define SUCCESS         1
#define FAIL            0
#define YES             1
#define NO              0

int save_mode;
struct kd_disparam      parms;
char                    *screen, *Tscreen;
int                     Vinit = NO;         /* initialization flag */
int                     map_flag = 0;
int                     disp;               /* console file descriptor */
FILE                    *logfp;
extern                  errno;

log(format,arg)
char *format;
int arg;
{
        fprintf(logfp,format,arg);
        fflush(logfp);
        return(SUCCESS);
}
/* sigtrap() is to protect against a signal terminating the process
 * and leaving the video display in an inconsistent state.
 */
void sigtrap(sig)
int sig;
{
        log("Trapped signal = %x, exiting...0,sig);
        vreset();
        fclose(logfp);
        exit(0);
}
```

(continued on next page)

```
vreset ()
{
        if (map_flag) {
                if (unmap_video_screen() != SUCCESS) {
                        log ("ERROR: Unmap_video_screen() failed\n");
                        vreset ();
                        return (FAIL);
                }
                map_flag = 0;
        }
        if (save_mode)   /* Reset to original display mode: */
                if (ioctl (disp, MODESWITCH | save_mode, 0) < 0) {
                        log ("ERROR: Unable to reset, mode: %x\n",
                                        save_mode);
                        return (FAIL);
                }
        else /* Reset to default text mode: */
                if (ioctl (disp, KDSETMODE, KD_TEXT) < 0) {
                        log ("Unable to reset display to text mode\n");
                        return (FAIL);
                }
        return (SUCCESS);
}
/*
 * This subroutine will open the log file and console driver and will save
 * the current display mode settings for later reset.  It must be
 * executed before attempting any access of the video driver functions.
 */
open_driver ()
{
        Vinit = 1;        /* set the initialization flag */

        if ((logfp = fopen ("video_log","w+")) < 0) {
                log ("ERROR: could not open logfile\n");
                exit (1);
        }
        log ("Opened logfile\n");

        if ((disp = open ("/dev/console", (O_RDWR | O_NDELAY))) < 0) {
                log ("ERROR: open (dev/console) failed, errno = $%d\n",
                                errno);
                return (FAIL);
        }
        if ((save_mode = ioctl (disp, CONS_GET, 0)) < 0) {
                log ("CONS_GET failed\n");
                return (FAIL);
```

(continued on next page)

```
        }
        return(SUCCESS);
}
/*
 * This routine will retrieve display parameters from the video driver.
 * Specifically, the display type, video memory address and valid I/O addresses.
 */
get_display_info(kdp)
struct kd_disparam *kdp;
{/*
        * ioctl(KDDISPTYPE) will return a structure populated with
        * the type of display, the physical memory location of the
        * screen memory and valid I/O port addresses.
        *
        * struct kd_disparam {
        *     long type;
        *     char *addr;
        *     ushort ioaddr[MKDIOADDR];
        * };
        */
        if(ioctl(disp, KDDISPTYPE, kdp) < 0) {
                log("ERROR: ioctl(KDDISPTYPE) failed, errno = $%d\n",
                                 errno);
                return(FAIL);
        }
        return(SUCCESS);
}
/* This function will print the kd_disparam structure contents to the logfile.
 * Call get_display_info() first.
 */
print_display_info(kdp)
struct kd_disparam *kdp;
{
        int i;
        char *type;

        switch (kdp->type) {
                case KD_MONO:          type="MONOCHROME";  break;
                case KD_HERCULES:      type="HERCULES";    break;
                case KD_CGA:           type="CGA";         break;
                case KD_EGA:           type="EGA";         break;
                case KD_VGA:           type="VGA";         break;
                default:               type="Invalid type";break;
        }
        log("display type  = %s\n", type);
        log("Video Address = 0x%lx\n", kdp->addr);
```

(continued on next page)

```
        for (i = 0; i < MKDBASEIO; i++) {
                log("0x%.3x\n",kdp->ioaddr[i]);
        }
        return(SUCCESS);
}
/* set_video_mode() will accept a passed argument and set the video mode accordingly.
 */
set_video_mode(fd,mode)
int fd;
int mode;
{
        if(ioctl(fd, mode) < 0) {
            log("ERROR: set_video_mode: ioctl(%x) failed, errno = $%d\n",
                    mode, errno);
            return(FAIL);
        }
        return(SUCCESS);
}
/*
 * map_video_screen() will map the video memory into thee user's address space.
 * The arguments to this function are:
 * Length of memory to map,      - 16K for CGA mode 5
 * I/O address enable flag.      - Needed to do inp/outp
 */
map_video_screen(length,ioflg)
long length;
long ioflg;
{
        struct kd_disparam      kd_param;
        struct kd_memloc        map;

        Tscreen = (char *)malloc(length + 4096);
        screen = (char *)((unsigned)(Tscreen + 4095) &  4095);

        if (ioctl(disp, KDDISPTYPE, &kd_param) == -1) {
                log("KDDISPTYPE failed, errno: %d\n", errno);
                return(FAIL);
        }
        map.physaddr = kd_param.addr;   /* set the video address */
        map.vaddr = screen;             /* set the virtual address */
        map.length = length;            /* set the screen size */
        map.ioflg = ioflg;              /* enable i/o addresses */

        if(ioctl(disp, KDMAPDISP, &map) < 0) {
                log("ERROR: KDMAPDISP failed, errno = %d\n",errno);
```

(continued on next page)

```
                        return(FAIL);
                }
        map_flag = 1;
        return(SUCCESS);
}
/*
 * unmap_video_screen() will release the mapped memory.  This should
 * be called before exit by the program that called map_video_screen().
 * It releases the video screen so that other programs can map it.
 */
unmap_video_screen()
{
        if (map_flag) {
                if(ioctl(disp, KDUNMAPDISP) < 0) {
                        log("ERROR: ioctl(KDUNMAPDISP) failed, errno = %d\n",
                                   errno);
                        return(FAIL);
                }
        } else  {
                log("ERROR: unmap_video_screen: display not mapped.\n");
                return(FAIL);
        }
        map_flag = 0;
        return(SUCCESS);
}
/*
 * disp_dump will dump the contents of the video screen to disk in a file called
 * "memdump".  Useful for debugging.
 */
disp_dump(addr,dsize)
char *addr;
int dsize;
{
        int fd;
        if((fd = open("memdump",O_CREAT | O_WRONLY, 0644)) < 0) {
                log("ERROR: open(memdump) failed, errno = %d\n",errno);
                return(FAIL);
        }
        if(write(fd, addr, dsize) < 0) {
                log("ERROR: write(memdump) failed, errno = %d\n",errno);
                return(FAIL);
        }
        close(fd);
}
/*
 * loadmem() will clear the screen to a selected color attribute based on
```

(continued on next page)

```
 * the passed in variable color.
 */
loadmem(ptr,color,count)
char *ptr;
unsigned char color;
int count;
{
        int i;

        for(i = 0; i<count; i++) {
                *ptr++ = color;
        }
        return(SUCCESS);
}
/*
 * This function does a clear of the entire screen.
 * It sets the color to background (black).
 */
clearmem(ptr,count)
char *ptr;
int count;
{
        loadmem(ptr, (unsigned char) 0x00,count);
        return(SUCCESS);
}
/*
 * This routine will write one screen point in 320x200 color
 * mode.  The bit layout for video memory in this mode is
 *
 *      byte
 * ------------
 * 7 6 5 4 3 2 1 0
 *
 *
 *      pixel
 * ------------
 * 00  11  22  33     <- byte 0
 * 44  55  66  77     <- byte 1
 *
 * Start Address = 0xB8000 for even rows
 *
 * Start Address = 0xB8000 + 8192 = BA000 for odd rows
 *
 *
 * Each byte of screen memory holds 4 screen points worth of data.  There
 * are 2 bits per screen pixel to allow color representation (00,01,10,11).
```

(continued on next page)

```
 * The video memory is segmented into segments where the even rows
 * start at address 0xB8000 and the odd rows at 0xB8000 + 8192.  Therefore
 * to write the first 4 pixels on the screen, it would be necessary to
 * write the first byte at 0xB8000.  To write to the next 4 points on the
 * first line, the first byte at 0xB8000 + 1 would have to be written.
 * To write the first 4 pixels on the 2nd screen line, the address to
 * be written must be (0xB8000 + 8192 = 0xBA000).
 *
 *
 * This function is specific to CGA but can be modified to work with
 * EGA and VGA.
 */

unsigned int bmask[4] = {0xff3f, 0xffcf, 0xfff3, 0xfffc};
int color_shift[4] = {6, 4, 2, 0};


int write_pixel(row,col,color)
int row, col, color;
{
    int     index;          /* screen byte index */
    unsigned int mask;
    char *sptr;             /* screen memory pointer */

    sptr = screen;          /* set pointer to screen area */

    color <<= color_shift[col % 4];
    mask = bmask[col % 4];
    /*
     * Find the correct position in the screen memory.
     * The video memory is set up with odd/even rows residing at different
     * (non)contiguous memory addresses.
     * Because of this, we need to ensure that the starting address of the
     * byte we need to access is indeed correct.
     */
    index = row * 40 + col/4;
    /*
     * Now decide whether the row was even or odd.  If the row
     * is odd, use (B8000 + index + 8152).  If the row
     * is even, use (B8000 + index).  This means
     * that the first odd row starts at (B8000 + 40 + 8152 = BA000)
     */
    if(row % 2) index += 8152;      /* bank 2 if odd */

    *(sptr + index) = color | *(sptr + index) & mask;
```

(continued on next page)

```
        return(SUCCESS);
}
/*
 * This function will draw a line in a specified color.
 */
line(start_row, start_col, end_row, end_col, color)
int     start_row,
        start_col,
        end_row,
        end_col,
        color;
{
        register int    i,
                        length;
        int             ydiff,
                        xdiff,
                        inc_row,
                        inc_col;
    /*
     * Determine which way the line is sloping and the appropriate directional
     * increment.

     * Now determine the row and column increment value
         */
        if((ydiff = end_row - start_row) > 0)
                inc_row = 1;
        else if(ydiff == 0)
                inc_row = 0;
        else
                inc_row = -1;

        if((xdiff = end_col - start_col) > 0)
                inc_col = 1;
        else if(xdiff == 0)
                inc_col = 0;
        else
                inc_col = -1;
    /*
     * Determine which length is greater
     */
        if(abs(ydiff) > abs(xdiff))
                length = abs(ydiff);
        else
                length = abs(xdiff);
    /*
     * Now draw the line.
```

(continued on next page)

```
        */
        for(i = 0; i<= length; i++) {
                write_pixel(start_row, start_col, color);
                start_row += inc_row;
                start_col += inc_col;
        }
        return(SUCCESS);
}
/*
 * This function will draw a box.  It makes use of line() which
 * then makes use of write_pixel().
 */
box(start_row, start_col, end_row, end_col, color)
int     start_row,
        start_col,
        end_row,
        end_col,
        color;
{
        if(line(start_row, start_col, end_row, start_col,color) != SUCCESS)
                return(FAIL);
        if(line(start_row, start_col, start_row, end_col,color) != SUCCESS)
                return(FAIL);
        if(line(start_row, end_col, end_row, end_col,color) != SUCCESS)
                return(FAIL);
        if(line(end_row, start_col, end_row, end_col,color) != SUCCESS)
                return(FAIL);
        return(SUCCESS);
}
/*
 * This function will shade a box.  This is another function being provided
 * to demonstrate the graphics capabilities that could be implemented
 * with this interface.  It works by using line() to shade in the
 * previously created box.
 */
shade_box(start_row, start_col, end_row, end_col, color)
int     start_row,
        start_col,
        end_row,
        end_col,
        color;
{
        register int    i,
                        start,
                        end;
```

(continued on next page)

```
            if(start_row < end_row) {
                    start = start_row;
                    end = end_row;
            }
            else {
                    start = end_row;
                    end = start_row;
            }
        for(i = start; i <= end; i++) {
                if(line(i, start_col, i, end_col, color) != SUCCESS)
                        return(FAIL);
        }
        return(SUCCESS);
}
/*
 * This routine will draw a circle
 */
circle(xlocus, ylocus, radius, color)
int   xlocus,
      ylocus,
      radius,
      color;
{
     register int x, diff;

     diff = radius/2;

     for(x = 0; x < radius; x++) {
            write_pixel(radius + xlocus, x + ylocus, color);
            write_pixel(xlocus - radius, x + ylocus, color);
            write_pixel(radius + xlocus, ylocus - x, color);
            write_pixel(xlocus - radius, ylocus - x, color);

            write_pixel(x + xlocus, radius + ylocus, color);
            write_pixel(xlocus - x, radius + ylocus, color);
            write_pixel(x + xlocus, ylocus - radius, color);
            write_pixel(xlocus - x, ylocus - radius, color);

            if(diff < 0)
                diff +=  radius-- - x;
            else
                diff -= x;
     }
     if(radius) {
            write_pixel(radius + xlocus, x + ylocus, color);
            write_pixel(xlocus - radius, x + ylocus, color);
```

(continued on next page)

```
                write_pixel(radius + xlocus, ylocus - x, color);
                write_pixel(xlocus - radius, ylocus - x, color);

                write_pixel(x + xlocus, radius + ylocus, color);
                write_pixel(xlocus - x, radius + ylocus, color);
                write_pixel(x + xlocus, ylocus - radius, color);
                write_pixel(xlocus - x, ylocus - radius, color);
        }
        return(SUCCESS);
}
/*
 * this will fill in a circle by calling circle() repeatedly
 * with smaller circle values.
 */
shade_circle(a, b, c, d)
int     a, b, c, d;
{
        while(c--)
                circle(a,b,c,d);
        return(SUCCESS);
}

/*--------------------- vtutil.h ---------------------*/

#define VGA_SCREEN_SIZE         (1024 * 64)
#define EGA_SCREEN_SIZE         (1024 * 32)
#define CGA_SCREEN_SIZE         (1024 * 16)

#define SUCCESS         1
#define FAIL            0
#define YES             1
#define NO              0
```

Graphics Modes

SW_BG320

Description: 320x200 Black & White Graphics Mode
Mode: CGA Mode 4
Memory requirements: 8K per page (2 pages)
Map 0: B8000 - B9F3F
Pixel layout: One bit per pixel

SW_CG320

Description: 320x200, 4 Color
Mode: CGA Mode 5
Memory map requirements: 16K per page (2 pages)
Map 0: B8000, B8002, ... B9F3E (even scans); BA000, BA002, ... BBF3E (odd scans)
Map 1: B8001, B8003, ... B9F3F (even scans); BA001, BA003, ... BBF3F (odd scans)
Pixel layout: 2 bits per pixel as follows:

```
   --------------------------------
   |  P0   |   P1   |   P2   |   P3   |
   --------------------------------
     7  6    5  4    3  2    1  0
```

Pixel byte mapping alternates between Map 0 and Map 1. Byte B8000 contains first 4 pixels in upper left hand corner of display. Byte B8001 contains the next 4 in that first row, etc. Addresses B8000 - B9F3F map all the pixels in the even scan lines, while addresses BA000 - BBF3F map all the pixels in the odd scan lines.

Color selection:

>   0 0 : Black
>   0 1 : Light Cyan
>   1 0 : Light Magenta
>   1 1 : Intense White

SW_BG640

Description: 640x200, 2 Color
Mode: CGA Mode 6
Memory map requirements: 16K per page (2 pages)

This mode has the same mapping and addressing scheme as SW_CG320 above, except the data format layout is 1 bit per pixel as follows:

```
------------------------------------------
| P0 | P1 | P2 | P3 | P4 | P5 | P6 | P7 |
------------------------------------------
  7    6    5    4    3    2    1    0
```

Color selection:

> 0 : Black
> 1 : Intense White

SW_CG320_D

Description: 320 x 200, 16 Color
Mode: EGA Mode D
Memory requirements: 8K per page (8 pages)
Map 0: A0000 - A1F3F, blue bit plane (C0)
Map 1: A0000 - A1F3F, green bit plane (C1)
Map 2: A0000 - A1F3F, red bit plane (C2)
Map 3: A0000 - A1F3F, intensity bit plane (C3)
Pixel layout: 4 bits per pixel as follows:

C3: $P0_{[3]}$| $P1_{[3]}$| $P2_{[3]}$| $P3_{[3]}$| $P4_{[3]}$| $P5_{[3]}$| $P6_{[3]}$| $P7_{[3]}$|
C2: $P0_{[2]}$| $P1_{[2]}$| $P2_{[2]}$| $P3_{[2]}$| $P4_{[2]}$| $P5_{[2]}$| $P6_{[2]}$| $P7_{[2]}$|
C1: $P0_{[1]}$| $P1_{[1]}$| $P2_{[1]}$| $P3_{[1]}$| $P4_{[1]}$| $P5_{[1]}$| $P6_{[1]}$| $P7_{[1]}$|
C0: $P0_{[0]}$| $P1_{[0]}$| $P2_{[0]}$| $P3_{[0]}$| $P4_{[0]}$| $P5_{[0]}$| $P6_{[0]}$| $P7_{[0]}$|
     7   6   5   4   3   2   1   0

Each of the 4 maps provide one bit of a pixel's color.

Color selection:

C3	C2	C1	C0	Color
0	0	0	0	Black
0	0	0	1	Blue
0	0	1	0	Green
0	0	1	1	Cyan
0	1	0	0	Red
0	1	0	1	Magenta
0	1	1	0	Brown
0	1	1	1	White
1	0	0	0	Dark Gray
1	0	0	1	Light Blue
1	0	1	0	Light Green
1	0	1	1	Light Cyan
1	1	0	0	Light Red
1	1	0	1	Light Magenta
1	1	1	0	Yellow
1	1	1	1	Intense White

SW_CG640_E

Description: 640 x 200, 16 Color
Mode: EGA Mode E
Memory requirements: 16K per page (4 pages)
Map 0: A0000 - A3E7F, blue bit plane (C0)
Map 1: A0000 - A3E7F, green bit plane (C0)
Map 2: A0000 - A3E7F, red bit plane (C0)
Map 3: A0000 - A3E7F, intensity bit plane (C0)
Pixel layout and color selection are identical to that of SW_CG320_D.

SW_CG640x350

Description: 640 x 350, 4 Color (Valid only for EGA systems with 64K video RAM)
Mode: EGA Mode 10
Memory requirements: 32K per page (2 pages)
Map 0: A0000 - A6D5F, blue bit plane (C0)
Map 1: A0000 - A6D5F, green bit plane (C1)
Map 2: A0000 - A6D5F, red bit plane (C2)
Map 3: A0000 - A6D5F, intensity bit plane (C3)
Pixel layout and color selection are identical to that of SW_CG320_D except that
Maps 0 and 2 are chained together to provide a 4 bit color code for pixels at
even addresses, and Maps 1 and 3 are chained together to provide 4 bit color
codes for pixels at odd addresses.

SW_ENH_CG640

Description: 640 x 350 16 Color (Valid only for EGA systems with 128K video RAM)
Mode: EGA Mode 10*
Memory requirements: 128K
Map 0: A0000 - A6D5F, blue bit plane (C0)
Map 1: A0000 - A6D5F, green blue bit plane (C1)
Map 2: A0000 - A6D5F, red bit plane (C2)
Map 3: A0000 - A6D5F, intensity bit plane (C3)
Pixel layout and color selection are identical to that of SW_CG320_D.

This `ioctl(2)` system call is the same as SW_CG640x350, except it is used for
systems configured with a mininum of 128K bytes of video memory.

SW_VGA640x480C

Description: 640 x 480, 2 color
Mode: VGA Mode 11
Memory requirements: 64K per page (1 page)
Map 0: A0000 - A95FF
Pixel layout:

```
-------------------------------------------
| P0  | P1  | P2  | P3  | P4  | P5  | P6  | P7|
-------------------------------------------
   7     6     5     4     3     2     1     0
```

Color selection:

> 0 : Black
> 1 : Intense White

SW_VGA640x480E

Description: 640 x 480, 16 Color from 256K
Mode: VGA Mode 12
Memory requirements: 64K - 1 page
Map 0: A0000 - A95FF, blue bit plane (C0)
Map 1: A0000 - A95FF, green bit plane (C1)
Map 2: A0000 - A95FF, red bit plane (C2)
Map 3: A0000 - A95FF, intensity bit plane (C3)
Pixel layout and color selection are identical to that of SW_CG320_D.

SW_VGA320x200

Description: 320x200, 256 colors
Mode: VGA Mode 13
Memory requirements: 64K - 1 page
Map 0: A0000, A0004, A0008, ... AF9FC
Map 1: A0001, A0005, A0009, ... AF9FD
Map 2: A0002, A0006, A000A, ... AF9FE
Map 3: A0003, A0007, A000B, ... AF9FF
Pixel layout: 8 bits per pixel (1 pixel per byte)

Color selection:

8 bits select one out of a possible 256 color registers. Each color register has 3 components, corresponding to a value for RED, GREEN and BLUE. Each component is represented by 6 bits:

```
          6 bits      6 bits      6 bits
      -----------------------------------
      |    RED    |  GREEN   |   BLUE   |    Color Register
      |_____|
```

SW_ATT640

Description: AT&T Enhancement - 640 x 400, 16 colors
Mode: AT&T enhancement
Memory requirements: 64K
Map 0: A0000 - A7DFF, blue bit plane (C0)
Map 1: A0000 - A7DFF, blue bit plane (C1)
Map 2: A0000 - A7DFF, blue bit plane (C2)
Map 3: A0000 - A7DFF, blue bit plane (C3)
Pixel layout and color layout identical to SW_C6320_D.

SW_VDC800x600E

Description: AT&T enhancement- 800 x 600, 16 colors from 256K
Mode: EGA Mode 12
Memory requirements: 64K
Map 0: A0000 - AEA5F, blue bit plane (C0)
Map 1: A0000 - AEA5F, green bit plane (C1)
Map 2: A0000 - AEA5F, red bit plane (C2)
Map 3: A0000 - AEA5F, intensity bit plane (C3)
Pixel layout and color selection are identical to that of SW_C6320_D.

SW_VDC640x400V

Description: AT&T Enhancement - 640 x 400, 256 colors from 256K
Mode: AT&T enhancement
Memory Requirements:
64K
Map 0: A0000 - AF9FF(1st Quadrant)
Map 1: A0000 - AF9FF(2nd Quadrant)
Map 2: A0000 - AF9FF(3rd Quadrant)
Map 3: A0000 - AF9FF(4th Quadrant)
Pixel layout and color selection are identical to that of SW_VGA320x200

Text and Graphics Mode IOCTLs

Text Mode Selection IOCTLs

Description	Note	Adapter	IOCTL
40x25 B&W		VGA, EGA & CGA	SW_B40x25
40x25 Color	CGA Mode 1		SW_C40x25
80x25 B&W			SW_B80x25
80x25 Color	CGA Mode 3	SW_C80x25	
40x25 B&W		VGA & EGA	SW_ENHB40x25
40x25 Color	EGA Mode 0,1		SW_ENHC40x25
80x25 B&W			SW_ENHB80x25
80x25 Color	EGA Mode 2,3		SW_ENHC80x25
80x25 Mono	EGA Mode 7		SW_EGAMONO80x25
80x43 B&W		EGA only	SW_ENHB80x43
80x43 Color		EGA only	SW_ENHC80x43
40x25 Color	VGA Mode 0,1	VGA only	SW_VGAC40x25
80x25 Color	VGA Mode 2,3		SW_VGAC80x25
80x25 Mono	VGA Mode 7		SW_VGAMONO80x25

Graphics Mode Selection IOCTLs

Description	Note	Adapter	IOCTL
320x200 B&W	CGA Mode 4	VGA, EGA & CGA	SW_BG320
320x200 4 Color	CGA Mode 5		SW_CG320
640x200 B&W	CGA Mode 6		SW_BG640
320x200 16 Color	EGA Mode D	VGA & EGA	SW_CG320_D
640x200 16 Color	EGA Mode E		SW_CG640_E
640x350 Mono	EGA Mode F		SW_EGAMONOAPA
640x350 Mono	EGA Mode F*		SW_ENH_MONOAPA2
640x350 4 Color	EGA Mode 10		SW_CG640x350
640x350 16 Color	EGA Mode 10*		SW_ENH_CG640
640x480 2 Color	VGA Mode 11	VGA only	SW_VGA640x480C
640x480 16 Color	VGA Mode 12		SW_VGA640x480E
320x200 256 Color	VGA Mode 13		SW_VGA320x200
640x400 16 Color		AT&T VDC 750, 600	SW_ATT640
800x600 16 Color		AT&T VDC 600	SW_VDC800x600E
600x400 256 Color		AT&T VDC 600	SW_VDC640x400V

display(7) Ioctl Summary

Ioctl	Description	Arguments	Return Value
*KIOCINFO	Identifies driver	none	if KD driver, returns (('k'<<8)|'d')

KDDISPTYPE	Display info	(struct kd_disparam *) arg	`struct kd_disparam {`
			`    long type;`
			`    char *addr;`
			`    ushort ioaddr[MKDIOADDR];`
			`}`
			Valid values for type field
			`KD_MONO`
			`KD_HERCULES`
			`KD_CGA`
			`KD_EGA`
			`KD_VGA`

KDVDCTYPE	Adapter info	(struct kd_vdctype *) arg	`struct kd_vdctype {`
			`    long cntlr;`
			`    long disply;`
			`    long rsrvd;`
			`}`
			
			Valid Cntrlr Values / **Valid Display Values**
			`KD_MONO` — `KD_UNKNOWN`
			`KD_HERCULES` — `KD_STAND_M`
			`KD_CGA` — `KD_STAND_C`
			`KD_EGA` — `KD_MULTI_M`
			`KD_VGA` — `KD_MULTI_C`
			`KD_VDC400`
			`KD_VDC750`
			`KD_VDC600`

Ioctl	Description	Arguments	Return Value

KDGKBTYPE	Keyboard type	`(char *)`
		       `arg`
			`KD_84    /*84 Key Keyboard*/`
			`KD_101   /*101 Key Keyboard*/`
			`KB_OTHER`

KDGETMODE	Display mode	`(int *)`
		       `arg`
			`KD_TEXT     /*clear screen*/`
			`KD_TEXT1    /*don't clear*/`
			`KD_GRAPHICS /*Graphics mode*/`

KDSETMODE	Set mode	`(int) arg`	
CONS_GET	Get mode	none	decode for specific mode,e.g. `SW_CG320, SW_ENHC80x25,...`
GIO_ATTR	Get attributes	none	decode for FG and BG color
KDSBORDER	Set border	`(char) arg`	

KDMAPDISP	Maps memory	`(struct`
		  `kd_memloc *)`
		       `arg`
			`struct kd_memloc {`
			    `char *vaddr; /*map TO*/`
			    `char *physaddr; /*FROM*/`
			    `long length; /* # to map*/`
			    `long ioflg; /*enable I/O*/`
			`}`

KDUNMAPDISP	Unmap memory	none	
KDENABIO	Enable Video I/O	none	
KDDISABIO	Disable Video I/O	none	
KDADDIO	Add I/O port	`(unsigned short) arg`	
KDDELIO	Delete I/O port	`(unsigned short) arg`	

Ioctl	Description	Arguments	Return Value

KDQUEMODE	Enable/disable queue	`(struct`
		`    kd_quemode *)`
		`                arg`
			`struct kd_quemode {`
			`    int qsize; /* # in q*/`
			`    int signo; /*sig to send*/`
			`    char *qaddr; /*vaddr of q*/`
			`}`

KDGETLED	Get LED status	`(char *) arg`	`LED_SCR`
			`LED_CAP`
			`LED_NUM`

KDSETLED	Set LED status	`(char *) arg`	
KIOCSOUND	Generate sound	`(int) arg`	
KDMKTONE	Generate tone	`(int) arg`	
*VT_OPENQRY	Find VT	`(long *) arg`	first available VT #

VT_GETMODE	Get VT mode	`(struct`
		`    vt_mode *)`
		`            arg`
			`struct vt_mode {`
			`    char mode;`
			`    char waitv;`
			`    short relsig;`
			`    short acqsig;`
			`    short frsig;`
			`}`
			mode field values
			`VT_AUTO    /*auto switch*/`
			`VT_PROCESS /*process switch*/`

VT_SETMODE	Set VT mode	`(struct`
		`    vt_mode *)`
		`            arg`	

Ioctl	Description	Arguments	Return Value
VT_RELDISP	Release status	`(int) arg`	
VT_ACTIVATE	Make VT active	`(int) arg`	
VT_WAITACTIVE	Wait until VT active	none	

NOTE

Entries marked by "∗" are not applicable when the application opens `/dev/video`. For these ioctls, use a file descriptor to the Virtual Terminal itself.

7 Driver Software Development

7. DRIVER SOFTWARE DEVELOPMENT

Introduction

This chapter defines procedures for writing and packaging a device driver for Release 4.0 of UNIX System V/386, the implementation of UNIX System V for the Intel386 and compatible processor architectures. It contains general information common to device drivers for UNIX System V Release 4.0 implementations on any hardware platform as well as information specific to UNIX System V for the Intel386 and compatible architectures. Also described is the Installable Driver (ID) scheme for Release 4.0 of UNIX System V/386. ID allows users to add peripheral devices using a floppy diskette or cartridge tape containing a Driver Software Package (DSP). Users will install and remove DSPs by using the pkgadd and pkgrm commands. Additional DSP reference material can be found in the UNIX System V/386 Release 4.0 *System Administrator's Reference Manual* and *System Files and Devices Reference Manual*.

This chapter also provides the implementation-dependent information for UNIX System V Release 4.0 for Intel386 and compatible processor architectures, including UNIX System V Release 4.0 Multi-Processor enhancements. The UNIX System V Release 4.0 Multi-Processor operating system extends the UNIX System V Release 4.0 operating system functionality from a uniprocessor environment to multiprocessor environments. Users upgrading to Release 4.0 Multi-Processor should read this chapter for a description of new device driver related features added to support multiprocessor environments. Additional device driver reference material can be found in the UNIX System V/386 Release 4.0 *Device Driver Interface/Driver-Kernel Interface (DDI/DKI) Reference Manual*.

In this chapter, the phrase "uniprocessor releases" refers to releases of UNIX System V which run only on uniprocessor systems; while the phrase "multiprocessor releases" refers to UNIX System V Release 4.0 Multi-Processor, which can run on either uniprocessor or multiprocessor systems. While UNIX System V/386 Release 4.0 Multi-Processor (MP) maintains all pre-MP DDI/DKI routines for compatibility, some of them are obsolete on multiprocessors and should be avoided. The text uses the phrase "in uniprocessor releases" to identify device driver interfaces and behavior that is obsolete in UNIX System V Release 4.0 Multi-Processor. The text uses the phrase "multiprocessor releases" to identify new device driver interfaces and behavior which UNIX System V Release 4.0 Multi-Processor introduces and which earlier uniprocessor releases never implemented. Describing device driver interfaces and behavior both for uniprocessor releases and for multiprocessor releases should help programmers to migrate existing driver software to the new multiprocessor relases as well as to develop new driver software that works equally well on uniprocessor and multiprocessor systems.

Multiprocessor Enhancements to UNIX System V

Several features have been added or modified for the multiprocessor version of the UNIX System V Release 4.0 operating system. These include:

- Locking mechanisms - Release 4.0 Multi-Processor enhances the Device Driver Interface/Driver-Kernel Interface (DDI/DKI) to support device drivers in multiprocessor environments. Because more than one processor at a time can access the same driver data, locking functions must be used to serialize access to data structures. For this purpose, Release 4.0 Multi-Processor adds locking primitives to the DDI/DKI. The three locking mechanisms: the basic lock, the read/write lock, and the sleep lock, ensure that only one processor operates on a set of data at any one time.

- Synchronization variables - Release 4.0 Multi-Processor adds a synchronization variable (SV) mechanism to coordinate driver activities with events. The "SV_" functions SV_ALLOC, SV_DEALLOC, SV_BROADCAST, SV_SIGNAL, SV_WAIT and SV_WAIT_SIG replace the sleep and wakeup mechanisms used in uniprocessor releases of UNIX System V.

- itimeout routine - Release 4.0 Multi-Processor replaces timeout with itimeout, which executes a function after a given length of time.

- Kernel Debugger - Release 4.0 Multi-Processor adds a new multiprocessor kernel debugger that allows memory examination and modification, disassembly of instructions, program downloading and execution, breakpoint setting and single-step instruction execution in a multiprocessor environment. The new multiprocessor kernel debugger works on all online processors in real-time.

Target Audience

It is assumed that the reader has user-level experience with the UNIX system, some general knowledge of UNIX system concepts, and the ability to write sophisticated C language programs. Writing a device driver carries a heavy responsibility. As part of the UNIX operating system kernel, a device driver is assumed to always take the correct action. Few limits are placed on the driver by the other parts of the kernel, and the driver must be written to never compromise the system's stability.

What Is a Device Driver?

The UNIX operating system kernel can be divided into two parts: the first part manages the file system and processes, and the second part manages physical devices, such as terminals, disks, tape drives, and network media. To simplify the terminology, this chapter refers to the first part as "the kernel", (although strictly speaking, drivers are part of the kernel too), and refers to the second part, which contains the drivers, as "the I/O subsystem".

Associated with each physical device is a piece of code, called the device driver, which manages the device hardware. The device driver brings the device into and out of service, sets hardware parameters in the device, transmits data from the kernel to the device, receives data from the device and passes it back to the kernel, and handles device errors.

Although device drivers are normally associated with hardware devices, some drivers may have no hardware counterpart. These devices are often referred to as *pseudo*-devices. For example, a trace driver may log certain classes of events. User programs write to the driver to record the events and read from the driver to recall the information. A trace driver has internal mechanisms for formatting and storing the data. No hardware is associated with the driver, and the driver interfaces with software only. The section entitled "A Trace Driver Implementation" contains a sample trace driver as a device driver model. You may actually use this driver to help debug the driver you are developing.

One strength of the UNIX system is the ease with which new hardware can be integrated with existing software. The integration process is simple because the operating system architecture provides a uniform software interface to every device. Processes use the same model when communicating with disks, terminals, printers or even "pseudo" devices that exist only in software. Every device on a UNIX system looks like a file. In fact, the user-level interface to the device is called a "special file".

Special Files

The UNIX system treats a device as if it were a file; that is, when a user program wishes to access a device, it accesses the file associated with that device. These special files are also called *nodes* or *device nodes*. The system calls `open`, `close`, `read`, `write`, and `ioctl` that access regular UNIX system files (such as /etc/passwd) are the same calls that access devices (such as /dev/console). The section "Driver Entry Point Routines" later in this chapter describes in detail the system calls at the driver level.

The /dev Directory

A device file may exist anywhere in the file system, but by convention, all device files are contained in the directory /dev. The names of the files are generally derived from the names of the hardware, a convention that allows users to know what the device is by looking at the file-name. Part of the name of the device file usually corresponds to the unit number of the device to be accessed via the file or, specifically, the minor number. (For example, it would be confusing if the file /dev/tty were a disk.)

The device special files reside in the /dev directory, and a simple ls will tell you quite a bit about the device. For example, the command "ls -l /dev/lp" yields the following on UNIX System V Release 4.0:

```
crw-rw-rw  1 root  root    7,  1  Nov 26 12:33  lp
```

This says that the "lp" (line printer) is a character type device (the first letter of the file mode field is "c") and that major number 7, minor device 1 is assigned to the device. More will be said about device types, and both major and minor numbers, later.

A new convention of Release 4.0 of UNIX System V across all processor architectures is that /dev can contain subdirectories that hold the nodes for all the subdevices of a particular type. This reduces the clutter in the /dev directory. For example, /dev/dsk contains all the "block special" files for the floppy and hard disks; /dev/rdsk contains all the "character special" files for the diskette and hard disks.

The device file may exist in the file system even though the device is not configured in the running system. If a user attempts to access the device, or more specifically, the file, an error results on the system call. Conversely, the device may be configured into the running operating system without the device file in the file system (in which case, the device is inaccessible).

Types of Devices

There are two classes of devices: block and character. Block devices are addressable, and as the term implies, the data on the device are formatted and addressed in "blocks". The term "character device" is a misnomer that should be "raw device," implying that the data being read are raw or unformatted; the device drivers and user programs, not the file system, assign semantics to the data. A device can be both a block and character device in a system configuration, implying that the system can access the device in two ways.

Major and Minor Numbers

Major numbers are used by the system to determine which device driver to execute when a user reads or writes from/to the special file. The system maintains two tables for mapping I/O requests to the drivers: one table for "character special" and the other for "block special". There are two sets of major numbers, one for character devices and one for block devices. Both start at zero and are numbered up to the last used major number (with an upper limit of 64 for character devices and a limit of 32 block devices for UNIX System V/386 Release 4.0 and Release 4.0 Multi-Processor). If you do an "ls -l /dev", you may find that two very different devices have the same major number. One is probably a "block special" device, using the block major number, and the other is a "character special" device, using the character major number. For those drivers that are both block and character devices, such as the floppy driver, one major number of each type must be assigned. In this case, the actual numbers may be different and, in fact, often are different.

Minor numbers are entirely under control of the driver writer and usually refer to "subdevices" of the device. These subdevices may be separate units attached to a controller. A disk device driver, for example, may talk to a hardware controller (the device) to which several disk drives (subdevices) may be attached. The UNIX system accesses different subdevices using different minor numbers.

In traditional UNIX systems, major numbers were assigned by the driver writer or the system administrator. The mknod command was then used to create the files (or nodes) to be associated with the device. In contrast, the UNIX System V/386 Release 4.0 Installable Driver (ID) feature assigns the major number when the DSP is loaded by the user.

The Structure of Driver Source Files

The Master and System Files

Associated with device drivers are two device configuration files: the `master` file and the `system` file (also known as the `dfile`). The device driver portions of the traditional master file are in a file named `mdevice` for Release 4.0 of UNIX System V/386. The device driver portions of the system files are in a file called `sdevice`. See the UNIX System V/386 Release 4.0 *System Administrator's Reference Manual* and `mdevice`(4) and `sdevice`(4) in the UNIX System V/386 Release 4.0 *System Files and Devices Reference Manual* for information describing the `mdevice` and `sdevice` file format.

The `mdevice` file contains the device name (15 characters or less), the definition of the functions the device supports (second column has an "`r`" if `read` is implemented, a "`w`" if `write` is implemented, and so forth), the block and/or character major number, and other descriptive information about the driver.

The `sdevice` file contains information on how the device is installed in the system, that is, the number of units (subdevices), interrupt vector number (IVN) used, and other local information.

Include Files

Every file in the operating system source code includes header files containing declarations of global data structures. The source code for device drivers need not be contained in a single file; therefore, programmers should subdivide the driver among several files if it is large. Even if the driver is contained in a single file, programmers should follow convention and declare the driver data structures in new driver-specific header (" .h") files. The definition of the data structures (the place in the source code where the compiler allocates memory storage) should be of the form `extern`, in a " .c" file, usually the driver source file. The only data structures that should be defined outside the driver are those that are configuration-dependent; that is, if the driver needs to allocate storage for each subdevice, a method is needed to allocate based on the number configured. The file `Space.c` is used to allocate configuration-dependent data for use by device drivers in Release 4.0 of UNIX System V/386.

For instance, if a system is configured for four trace devices, the file `Space.c` includes a line as follows:

```
struct trace tr_data[TR_UNITS];
```

and the `include` file for the trace driver contains the declaration of the `trace` structure. The configuration process that ID executes sets `TR_UNITS` equal to 4 based on the `unit` parameter (column 3) of the System file.

The driver source code file should "include" the new header files. Driver file names conventionally contain the device name as part of their names.

As an example, consider a driver for a new networking device called `nnet`. Assume the driver consists of two ".c" files, `nnet.c` and `nnetprot.c`, and one header file, `nnet.h`. The names suggest that the files are associated with the new `nnet` device and that the `nnetprot.c` file contains a protocol for the device. The header file may contain a declaration such as

```
struct nnet {
        char     nn_state;
        char     nn_flags;
        int      nn_port;
        int      nn_chan;
        struct   nn_queue    *nn_qptr;
};
```

and the ".c" files should contain the line

```
#include          "sys/nnet.h"
```

General System Data Structures

Driver programmers must not change standard system header files, such as the `proc` file, the `user` file, or the `inode` file. Since the drivers are a separate part of the system, it is unacceptable to introduce new data structures and new "hooks" into standard system data structures to accommodate a private driver. In addition, changing system data structures can cause user-level programs to work incorrectly if they rely on the system data structure. For example, changes to the process table usually require recompilation of the `ps` command. Driver programmers should likewise refrain from tampering with kernel source files.

Usually, driver source code must contain some standard "include" files that allow the driver access to system utilities and data structures commonly used to return information to the kernel. The description of each kernel utility function in the DDI/DKI indicates which header files must be included in a driver that uses that function.

The list below identifies a few of the more commonly used include files:

- /usr/include/sys/types.h – basic system data types

- /usr/include/sys/param.h – fundamental system parameters

- /usr/include/sys/signal.h – system signals

  If the driver sends signals to user processes, it must include this file.

- /usr/include/sys/conf.h – device switch tables

  This file is needed for the driver to define its devflag value.

- /usr/include/sys/file.h – file structures

  This file is needed if the driver uses control flags such as "no delay" (-FNDELAY).

- /usr/include/sys/buf.h – the buf (system buffer) structure

  This file is needed if the driver uses the system buffer pool (see the section "Buffer Pool" later in this chapter).

- /usr/include/sys/kmem.h – the Kernel Memory Allocator

  This file is needed if the driver allocates memory for buffers out of the common memory pool.

- /usr/include/sys/ksynch.h – kernel synchronization structures (locks).

  This file is needed if the driver uses the multiprocessor locks described in the section "Kernel Utility Routines" later in this chapter.

- /usr/include/sys/ddi.h – Device Driver Interface (DDI) routines.

  Note that this header file must come last in the list of included header files.

Driver-Specific Data Structures

Naming Conventions

The names of driver data structures and variables should have the driver name in the prefix to ease program readability and debugging and to avoid conflict with other variables in the system with the same name. For example, in the section entitled "A Trace Driver Implementation", the trace driver contains the variable `tr_cnt` and the data structure `tr_data`. Both names are private to the trace driver, and the prefix "`tr_`" identifies them as part of the trace driver.

Unit Numbers

A single driver may often "drive" several hardware units. One terminal driver can "drive" many terminals; each terminal has a unit number corresponding to the minor number of the device file. Many drivers use a data structure with a flag field to record the device status, such as open, sleeping, waiting for data to drain, and so forth. Apart from a flag field, the data structure is device-dependent, so no recommendation can be made. However, there should be one entry per unit, defined in the driver file and declared in the header file. Each `nnet` device should have one of the `nnet` data structures described earlier.

devflag

Each driver should define a `devflag` variable so that the kernel knows the characteristics of the driver. For the `nnet` device, the `devflag` declaration is:

```
int nnetdevflag = val;
```

val may be a combination of flags. Each flag defines a special feature of the driver. For example, `D_DMA` should be set if the driver does DMA. If no flags are needed, *val* should be 0. The different flag values are identified on the manual page `devflag`(D1D) in the UNIX System V/386 Release 4.0 *Device Driver Interface/Driver-Kernel Interface (DDI/DKI) Reference Manual*.

To maintain compatibility with existing SVR3.2-based or older drivers, ID assumes by default that all drivers are "old-style" drivers that use the SVR3.2 block and character device driver interfaces. Drivers written to use the new device driver interfaces defined in the UNIX System V Release 4.0 *Device Driver Interface/Driver-Kernel Interface (DDI/DKI) Reference Manual* must include an "f" in the "characteristic field" (third field) of the `mdevice` entry to identify it as a "new-style" driver. This convention is new for ID in SVR4.0, and signifies that the driver defined a `devflag` variable. The `d_flag` field for older type block devices is set by ID to point to a kernel defined integer variable `nodevflag`, which the kernel initializes as `D_OLD`. Failing to include an "`f`" will not prevent a new-style driver from being successfully linked into the kernel, but may result in the driver operating incorrectly.

Driver Activities and Responsibilities

A user process runs in a space isolated from critical system data and other programs, protecting the system and other programs from its mistakes. In contrast,
a driver executes in kernel mode, placing few limits on its freedom of action; the
driver is simply assumed to be correct and responsible.

This level of responsibility and reliability cannot be avoided. A driver must be
part of the kernel to service interrupts and access device hardware. The
existence of the driver is one of the major factors that permits the kernel to
present a uniform interface for all devices and to protect processes from some
kinds of errors.

The importance of reliable driver code is clear. The driver must not make mistakes that hurt any portion of the system, and should process interrupts
efficiently to preserve the scheduler's ability to balance demands on the system.
For instance, the driver should use system buffers responsibly to avoid degrad-
ing system performance or requiring that more space be devoted to buffers than
is really needed.

The following subsection provides a broad overview of what device drivers do
inside the kernel. The specific details are provided later. The purpose of this
overview is to introduce issues of significance and establish a common language
for further discussion. Experienced driver developers will be familiar with
much of the information, but those new to UNIX system device drivers may
find the implications of a multitasking environment more complex than
expected.

Data Transfer Between System and User Space

The kernel instruction and data spaces are strictly segregated from those of user
processes. The need for the kernel to protect itself is obvious. This protection
creates the need for a way to transfer information from user space to kernel
space and back.

Several routines transfer data across the user/system boundary. Some transfer
bytes, some transfer words, and others transfer arbitrary size buffers. Each type
of operation implies a pair of routines: one for transfers from user space to system space and one for those in the opposite direction.

Consider a representative I/O operation and the information transfer across the user/kernel boundary it generates. As an example, take a request from a process to write a buffer on the disk. The function `write` takes the file descriptor, the buffer address in user space, and the length of the data in the buffer as parameters.

The system call causes the processor to transfer from user to kernel mode, and to execute the write routine in the generic file interface. When `write` realizes that the file is "special" (a device), it uses the appropriate switch table (defined in the section "Major and Minor Numbers") to select the corresponding routine associated with the device.

The device driver's `write` routine is then faced with a decision. Because the disk is a shared resource, the device driver may not find it convenient or possible to do the requested write just when it is requested. However, when the system call returns, the process assumes that the operation is complete and may do whatever it wishes with its buffer. If the kernel wishes to defer the write to disk, it must take a copy of the information from user space, keeping it in system space until the write can be done.

Allocating Buffer Space

A feature common to most drivers is their use of buffers. As the discussion on the driver `read` and `write` routines noted, drivers may require buffers for passing data around. A standard UNIX System V Release 4.0 kernel has three types of buffers:

1. Kernel Memory Allocator buffers.

2. STREAMS message buffers.

3. system buffers.

Each buffer differs greatly in size and structure and fulfills different needs.

All of the above types of buffers are commonly used UNIX system resources. Every driver should be written with the finite nature of the machine in mind; intense buffer use by a driver can reduce the performance of other drivers or require more memory be devoted to buffers. When more memory or space is allocated to buffers, the memory or space available for user processes is correspondingly decreased.

Kernel Memory Allocator Buffers

Kernel Memory Allocator (KMA) buffers are "borrowed" by the driver from a common memory pool used by all parts of the kernel. All types of drivers may use them. When drivers allocate their own data areas or independent buffer pools, this increases the size of the driver, and thus the size of the kernel.

UNIX System V/386 Release 4.0 provides routines to allocate and release kernel memory – `kmem_alloc` and `kmem_free` – which can be used by drivers. Refer to the UNIX System V/386 Release 4.0 *Device Driver Interface/Driver-Kernel Interface (DDI/DKI) Reference Manual* for more information on these kernel memory allocator routines.

STREAMS Message Buffers

STREAMS messages are for use by drivers written to the STREAMS interface. They are allocated for the driver through the kernel utilities, so the driver need not allocate a pool of its own messages.

UNIX System V/386 Release 4.0 allocates and releases buffers that the STREAMS I/O mechanism uses to hold the messages that STREAMS modules send to one another. Refer to the UNIX System V/386 Release 4.0 *Programmer's Guide: STREAMS* for more information on these STREAMS message buffers.

System Buffer Pool

System buffers are the size of a file system block, and the size of the file system block depends on the type of the file system. File system sizes can vary anywhere from 1K to 16K depending on the file system type. This buffer pool primarily supports disk I/O operations.

UNIX System V provides a set of buffers that are normally used for file system I/O, but they can be "borrowed" by drivers if they follow the rules outlined here. The driver must include the header file `sys/buf.h`. The size of a buffer is 1024 bytes.

The functions that drivers may use to manipulate the buffers are as follows:

1. `struct buf *geteblk(void);`

   Allocates a buffer big enough to hold 1024 bytes, and returns a pointer to a buffer header that, in turn, points to the data buffer.

2. `struct buf *ngeteblk(size_t n);`

   Allocates a buffer big enough to hold *n* bytes and returns a pointer to a buffer header that, in turn, points to the data buffer.

3. `brelse(struct buf *bp);`

   Releases a previously allocated buffer.

4. `struct buf *getrbuf(long flag);`

   Allocates a buffer header only. The caller must supply a data buffer and set the data pointer in the buffer header to point to it.

5. `freerbuf(struct fub *bp);`

   Releases a buffer that was previously allocated with `getrbuf`.

6. `biowait(struct buf *bp);`

   Sleeps on the buffer awaiting an event, such as completion of I/O.

7. `biodone(struct buf *bp);`

   Awakens a process sleeping via `biowait`.

8. `bioerror(struct buf *bp, int err);`

   Sets the error number associated with a buffer.

9. `geterror(struct buf *bp);`

   Returns the error number associated with a buffer.

10. `clrbuf(struct buf *bp);`

    Clears the contents of the buffer (sets every byte in the buffer to 0) whose header is the pointer `bp`.

Here is an example of the use of buffers in a tape driver:

```
taperewind(dev, flag)
{
        register struct buf *bp;
        register int rcode;

        bp = geteblk();
        if (flag == FNDELAY)
                /*
                 * Set iodone function so buffer
                 * will be released when done.
                 */
                bp->b_iodone = brelse;
        bp->b_dev = dev;
        /*
         * tapestrategy recognizes blkno == -1
         * as a request to rewind.
         */
        bp->b_blkno = -1;
        tapestrategy(bp);
        if (flag == FNDELAY) {
                /* Don't wait for completion */
                rcode = 0;
        } else {
                /* Wait for completion. */
                biowait(bp);
                rcode = geterror(bp);
                brelse(bp);
        }
        return(rcode);
}
```

Sleeping and Waking Processes

A process might have to wait for the requested information to be read or written from/to the disk before continuing. Consider a read operation in greater detail. When the request is made, the driver has calculations and setup to do. After these are complete, the request for the data can be made, but there is a short delay before the data are available. The delay, at a minimum, is due to the retrieval time for the disk; although, the delay can be longer if other requests are queued ahead of this one.

Because UNIX System V is a multiuser, multitasking operating system, it is possible that another job is ready to run and waiting for a chance to use the machine. One process should not keep the machine idle while another process is ready to run, so some way must be found to have the first process wait until its information is available.

In the case of disk access, the read routine in the disk's driver set issues a request for the data and puts the process to "sleep". Processes can coordinate their actions with events using sleep and wakeup in uniprocessor releases, or through the "SV_" (synchronization variable) calls in multiprocessor releases. For more information on the sleep and wakeup functions as well as the "-SV_" functions, see the individual manual pages in the uniprocessor and multiprocessor parts of the UNIX System V/386 Release 4.0 *Device Driver Interface/Driver-Kernel Interface (DDI/DKI) Reference Manual* and the section entitled "Kernel Utility Routines" in this book.

A sleeping process regarded as an active process but is kept on a queue of jobs whose execution is suspended while they wait for a particular event. When the process sleeps, it specifies the event that must occur before it may continue its task. This event is represented by the synchronization variable associated with the transition. The sleep call in uniprocessor releases and the SV_WAIT call in multiprocessor releases each record the process number and the event, then place it on the list of sleeping processes. Control then transfers to the highest priority runnable process.

When the data transfer completes, the disk posts an interrupt, which activates the interrupt routine in the driver. The interrupt routine does whatever it must to service the device properly, and in uniprocessor releases calls wakeup, but in multiprocessor releases calls SV_SIGNAL. It must know what synchronization variable was used by the process as the sleeping event to wake it. This scenario for coordinating asynchronous events appears in many drivers.

This discussion is purely illustrative. In actual practice, block drivers do not use **SV_WAIT**, **SV_WAIT_SIG**, and **SV_BROADCAST**, but rather **biowait** and **biodone**. Refer to "**biowait**/**biodone** – Block Driver Event Synchronization" in the section entitled, "Kernel Utility Routines", later in this chapter for further information.

Synchronous and Interrupt Sections of a Driver

Drivers provide the connection between two frames of reference: the process and real-time realms.

The portion of the driver that deals with real-time events is driven by interrupts from devices, and is thus called the interrupt section. The rest of the driver executes only when the process talking to the driver is the active process. The execution of this part of the driver is synchronized with the process it serves and is called the synchronous portion of the driver.

Because the synchronous portion of the driver has the proper process context, it is responsible for organizing the information required for the requested operation and for any transfer of information across the user/system boundary. If the request was properly submitted, the synchronous portion of the driver can do nothing but wait until the requested operation is complete, so it sleeps.

The interrupt driven section of the driver responds to the demands of the device as they come. The synchronous part must leave enough information in common data structures to permit the interrupt routine to figure out what is happening.

 The terms "interrupt section," "interrupt portion," and "interrupt driven section" are interchangeable.

The interrupt routine is called as a result of a change in the state of the hardware, i.e. completion of a hardware operation, receipt of data, and so forth. It is responsible for servicing the device and awakening the process waiting on the event. Note that the interrupt routine can be called at any time and in the context of any process. It cannot engage in any activity that depends on process context.

Interrupt Processing

When a device requests some software service, it generates an "interrupt". Each device can interrupt the system at a specific "priority level". If the currently executing code has not blocked interrupts at that level, it immediately saves its status and "traps" to an interrupt handler. The interrupt routine in the driver must determine the cause of the interrupt and take appropriate action. If the synchronous portion of the driver is waiting for this event, the interrupt routine should issue a call to SV_BROADCAST or SV_SIGNAL in multiprocessor releases, or to wakeup in uniprocessor releases.

Critical Sections of the Driver

The discussion so far has centered on the case of a single interrupt, occurring in isolation. Though helpful, this view is unrealistic and potentially misleading. Interrupts from all devices on the system can occur at any time, and the implications of this are important. The relationship between the synchronous and interrupt portions of the driver are affected, as are those between drivers sharing data.

When two sections of kernel code have a common interest in specific data, they must be careful to coordinate their efforts. If an interrupt switches control of the system to the interrupt driven portion of the driver, then manipulation of the common data may be caught in the midst of its work, rendering the information invalid and inconsistent.

These concerns are grouped under the general heading *critical sections*. The importance of the issue is clear; the integrity and accuracy of the data used by drivers is at stake. The word *sections* refers to the portions of code that manipulate the common data, rather than the data itself. Thus, a *critical section* of code is one that manipulates data that is of concern to another piece of code capable of interrupting the first.

A routine in the kernel that has a critical section must protect itself from being interrupted when manipulating critical data. A set of subroutines that permit code to Set the Priority Level (spl) of the processor solve the problem and are described in the section entitled "Setting Processor Priority Levels". A clear understanding of the need for these routines can be achieved only by examining a detailed scenario.

Imagine a section of code in the synchronous portion of a driver that manipulates status flags. Such flags are frequently used to communicate between the synchronous and interrupt portions of a driver. Consider also that the interrupt portion has code that manipulates those flags, and that these manipulations do not take place in a single machine operation.

Consider what happens if the synchronous portion of the driver receives a request that requires it to manipulate the values of several flags, but in the midst of the manipulation, the device gives an interrupt, transferring control to the interrupt portion of the driver. The interrupt routine decides that it must consult the flag values to make some decision and then set them to new values.

The flags are in the incorrect state because the synchronous routine has only half finished changing them when the interrupt routine took over. This may cause the interrupt routine to behave unpredictably, or it may simply make an innocuous but incorrect decision. Assume that the interrupt routine simply looks at the flags, makes decisions, and changes a couple of flag values. Then, when the interrupt returns, the synchronous portion of the code, unaware that it was interrupted, finishes the changes it started.

Whether the data manipulated in a critical section is changed by the interrupting routine is unimportant. The fact that the interrupting routine uses it is sufficient, proving any portion of code that can be interrupted and that also manipulates data of interest to the interrupting code is a *critical section*. When a critical section is identified, it can be protected from interruption in uniprocessor releases by a call to an `spl` routine of the appropriate level.

Multiprocessor Critical Sections

In a multiprocessor environment, an additional, different type of critical section concerns the driver writer. The critical sections mentioned earlier arise when an interrupt routine uses the same data structures that are used by code that may be interrupted. With multiprocessors, two pieces of code may be using the same data structure at the same instant on two different processors. This can occur even when no interrupt routines are involved.

Ordinarily, critical sections are handled by blocking certain interrupts during the critical section with one of the `spl` functions. Multiprocessor critical sections are handled by using one of the multiprocessor locking functions. The simplest of the locking primitives, LOCK, allows only one processor at a time to acquire the lock, preventing two or more processors from accessing a data item at the same time. A data item that is accessed only while a lock is held is said to be protected by that lock. It is very important to note that every data item (other than automatic stack variables) accessed by a multithreaded driver must be protected by a lock. For further information, see the section on "Locking" in "Kernel Utility Routines", later in this chapter, and the UNIX System V/386 Release 4.0 Multi-Processor *Device Driver Interface/Driver-Kernel Interface (DDI/DKI) Reference Manual*.

How Data Moves Between the Kernel and the Device

The discussions above assume data moves magically between memory accessed by the kernel and the device itself. This detail is machine-dependent, but it is instructive to examine how this is done. Some machines require the processor to execute special I/O instructions to move data between a device register and addressable memory or to set up a block transfer between the I/O device and memory, a method called Direct Memory Access (DMA). Another scheme, known as memory mapped I/O, implements the device interface as one or more locations in the memory address space. UNIX System V/386 Release 4.0 uses all of these schemes, but most commonly uses I/O instructions.

Kernel I/O Functions

UNIX System V provides functions that let drivers transfer data onto and from an I/O port or device in a general way. The syntax of these data transfer functions is shown below. Example drivers in this chapter use some of these calls.

The function inb reads a single byte from and outb writes a single byte on port, an I/O address. The functions inw and outw transfer 16-bit words, while inl and outl move 32-bit words ("long"s).

```
uchar_t inb(int port);

outb(int port, uchar_t data);

ushort_t inw(int port)

outw(int port, ushort_t data)

long inl(int port)

outl(int port, ulong_t data)
```

The functions `repinsb`, `repinsw` and `repinsd` input a stream of bytes, 16-bit and 32-bit words, respectively, from an I/O port to kernel memory.

```
repinsb(int port, char *addr, int cnt)

repinsw(int port, short *addr, int cnt)

repinsd(int port, long *addr, int cnt)
```

The functions `repoutsb`, `repoutsw` and `repoutsd` output a stream of bytes, 16-bit and 32-bit words, respectively, from kernel memory to an I/O port.

```
repoutsb(int port, char *addr, int cnt)

repoutsw(int port, short *addr, int cnt)

repoutsd(int port, long *addr, int cnt)
```

As described earlier, it is the driver's job to copy data between the kernel's address space and the user program's address space whenever the user makes a `read` or `write` system call.

DMA Allocation Routines

Direct Memory Access (DMA) controllers are accessed through a collection of control registers mapped to I/O (port) addresses. The DMA control registers define the DMA start address and word count that the driver must manipulate. The number of DMA channels is hardware-dependent. Some channels are reserved for invisible housekeeping such as screen refresh and cannot be reallocated. The file `dma.h` defines the names of the various channels. (See the subsection entitled "DMA Controller Operations" in the section on "Controller Interface Basics" later in this chapter for further information.) Your Hardware Reference Manual should describe the DMA controller hardware.

Low-level programming for DMA is done through DMA allocation routines. The DMA interface functions and their parameters are described in the UNIX System V/386 Release 4.0 *Device Driver Interface/Driver-Kernel Interface (DDI/DKI) Reference Manual* for Intel Processors and for Intel Multi-Processors. Use of the DMA routines found in the DDI/DKI allow drivers to be independent of DMA procedures. These routines allow DMA usage to be locked against DMA requests by other drivers. Not all devices use DMA, but those that do must have exclusive access to their DMA channel for the duration of the transfer.

The DMA chips on some machines malfunction when more than one allocated channel is used simultaneously. To allow installation on these machines, the dma_single flag is set by default. On machines without this deficiency, clear the dma_single flag to allow simultaneous DMA on multiple channels. This can be done using the idtune(1M) command to set DMAEXCL to 0 (legal values are 0 and 1). For more information on using the idtune(1M) command, see the UNIX System V/386 Release 4.0 *System Administrator's Reference Manual*.

Driver Entry Point Routines

This section describes the functions that form the driver interface to the kernel. For a block device, they are `init`, `start`, `halt`, `open`, `close`, `strategy` and `intr`. For a raw (character) device, they are `init`, `start`, `halt`, `open`, `close`, `read`, `write`, `ioctl`, `chpoll` and `intr`. A driver may omit some routines if they are irrelevant (a line printer driver usually has no `read` routine). If a device is both raw and block, the driver must contain all approriate routines. For more information on all driver entry point routines, refer to the UNIX System V/386 Release 4.0 *Device Driver Interface/Driver-Kernel Interface (DDI/DKI) Reference Manual*.

Function Naming Conventions

The names of the driver `init`, `start`, `halt`, `open`, `close`, `read`, `write`, `ioctl`, `chpoll`, `strategy` and interrupt routines must be prefaced by the generic driver name, which is specified in the driver's `mdevice` file. For example, the names of the `nnet` driver routines are `nnetopen`, `nnetclose`, `nnetread`, `nnetwrite`, `nnetioctl` and `nnetintr`. Other functions in the driver have no restrictions on names, but it is best to preface the function names with the driver name for identification purposes, to avoid mistakenly using a function name already defined in other parts of the operating system.

poll

The routine `poll`, if present, is called by the system clock at `splhi` during every clock tick, which is useful for repriming devices that constantly lose interrupts or that do not interrupt at all.

 NOTE The **poll** entry point is specific to UNIX System V/386 Release 4.0 its use reduces the portability of a device driver, so it should be used only when absolutely necessary. **poll** is not included in the UNIX System V/386 Release 4.0 Multi-Processor DDI/DKI.

For the `nnet` device, the function `poll` prototype looks like:

```
nnetpoll(pl_t ps)
```

The parameter `ps` is an integer that indicates the previous processor priority level before it was interrupted by the system clock.

Interrupt Handler

Hardware interrupts cause the processor to stop its current execution stream and to start executing an instruction stream that services the interrupt. The system identifies the device causing the interrupt and accesses a table of interrupt vectors to transfer control to the interrupt handler for the device.

The exact mechanism of associating interrupt vectors with interrupt handlers varies on different UNIX systems. The discussion here assumes the system finds the correct interrupt routine on receipt of the device interrupt, and that the system executes the interrupt routine at a processor execution level high enough to prevent more interrupts of that type. UNIX System V/386 Release 4.0 has a limited number of available interrupts. For more information on this and other machine-dependent aspects of the interrupt structure of Release 4.0 of UNIX System V/386, see the subsection entitled "Interrupts" in the section on "Controller Interface Basics" later in this chapter.

The device interrupt handler routines handle device interrupts, which are the device responses to data transfers and requests. System software cannot predict when a device will interrupt the system. Typically, a system call blocks, that is, sleeps on an event, awaiting the device to interrupt. The device interrupt causes the system to invoke the interrupt handler which, in turn, awakens the blocked system call. For instance, device open routines may block until the device interrupts and "announces" its connection; or device read routines may block until the device interrupts and "announces" that data has arrived and can be read into the system.

Upon receipt of the interrupt, the kernel calls the driver interrupt handler. For the nnet device, the interrupt handler function prototype looks like:

```
nnetintr(int ivn)
```

where ivn indicates the interrupt number associated with the interrupt, which is determined by the jumper setting on the particular controller board. The vector field in the sdevice file for that controller board must also contain the interrupt vector number.

If the system is configured with two peripheral interrupt controllers (PICS), ivn can be 0, 1, 3 − 15. The values reflect the 15 available interrupt lines on the two PICs combined. (Interrupt vector 2 is unavailable because it is used to wire the second PIC to the first PIC.)

The `ivn` argument can determine which controller interrupted in cases where the driver supports multiple instances of a controller (each controller set at a different `ivn`).

The interrupt handler must identify the reason for the interrupt (device connect, write acknowledge, data available), and set or clear device status bits as appropriate. It can also awaken sleeping processes, waiting for the event corresponding to the interrupt (see the section entitled "Sleeping and Waking"). Interrupt handlers must not call `SV_WAIT` or any other function that may sleep. For further information on sleep functions, see the UNIX System V/386 Release 4.0 Multi-Processor *Device Driver Interface/Driver-Kernel Interface (DDI/DKI) Reference Manual*.

Sharing Interrupts and DMA Channels

The Installable Driver (ID) scheme of UNIX System V/386 Release 4.0 allows for the sharing of interrupt lines and DMA channels among device drivers. When an interrupt occurs, the interrupt handler for each device sharing the interrupt is called. Each interrupt routine must first poll its device to see if the interrupt belongs to them. If not, they must return immediately with no processing so that the correct interrupt routine can execute. The default kernel configuration is to disallow devices that share interrupts. This prevents inadvertent re-use of interrupts or new drivers from sharing interrupts with old drivers expecting the interrupt to themselves.

To indicate that a device can share its interrupt, column 5 of the `sdevice` (*type* field) entry must include a "3". All devices sharing this interrupt must also have a "3" in this field. If it does not, an error results during kernel configuration. See the UNIX System V/386 Release 4.0 *System Files and Devices Reference Manual* for the `sdevice`(4) manual page describing the `sdevice` file format.

To indicate that a device can share its DMA channel, column 3 of the `mdevice` (the "characteristic field") entry must include a "D" identifier. If they do not, an error results during kernel configuration. See the UNIX System V/386 Release 4.0 *System Files and Devices Reference Manual* for the `mdevice`(4) manual page describing the `mdevice` file format.

Controller Interface Basics

I/O devices connect to controllers that reside either on the Intel386 processor motherboard or on a peripheral board. The controller interface generally requires

- An interrupt line designated by an interrupt vector number (IVN).

- A Direct Memory Access (DMA) channel number (if used by peripheral).

- An I/O Address (IOA) range for a port through which the processor and device can communicate.

- An optional Controller Memory Address (CMA) range that references memory (usually dual-port RAM) on the controller board.

Interrupts

Most Intel386 processor-based computer systems are outfitted with two Intel 8259 peripheral interrupt controllers (PICs), each with eight interrupt lines. The 16 interrupt ports of the controller are assigned as follows:

interrupt number	bus pin	common name	devices on Intel386 systems using interrupt
0	—	clock	1/100 second timer
1	—	keyboard	keyboard
2	—	game port	expansion PIC (see IVN 9)
3	IRQ3	com2	serial port 2
4	IRQ4	com1	serial port 1
5	IRQ5	hard disk	not used
6	IRQ6	floppy	integral floppy controller
7	IRQ7	printer	integral parallel port
8	IRQ8	—	real time clock
9	IRQ2	—	not used (wired to IVN 2)
10	IRQ10	—	not used
11	IRQ11	—	not used
12	IRQ12	—	not used
13	IRQ13	—	iAPX387 math co-processor
14	IRQ14	—	integral hard disk controller
15	IRQ15	—	not used

In the above table, IVN 0 through 7 have a "common name" that is derived from the PC/XT architecture. Most Intel386 processor-based computer systems have a PC/AT architecture with 15 available interrupts. IVN 2 is used to connect the second PIC; however, peripheral boards that use IRQ 2 can still be used by configuring the device driver to expect IVN 9. Note that with the expansion PIC installed, the hard disk is moved to IRQ14, freeing up IRQ 5 for PC/XT add-on devices.

Most devices that require an interrupt are hardware strappable to two or more different interrupts to allow the user some flexibility in installation.

Number of Installed Drivers

Due to limited available interrupts, there is a limit to the number of conventional peripheral devices that can be installed on Release 4.0 of UNIX System V/386. Additional drivers could, however, be installed for devices not requiring interrupts, for software pseudo-devices, or for devices sharing interrupts. (See the section entitled "Sharing Interrupts and DMA Channels" earlier in this chapter.)

As the table above shows, several AT-type and a few XT-type interrupts are available. In that list, IVN3 is assigned to the add-on serial port (COM2), and IVN 7 is assigned to the integral parallel port (line printer interface). If you are installing hardware/driver software on a system that does not have a COM2 interface configured or does not use a line printer, it is possible to unconfigure one of those devices, thus freeing the respective IVN.

I/O Addresses and Controller Memory Addresses

Each controller requires an IOA and possibly a CMA. These address regions must be unique and not overlap with any other device's address regions. Refer to your Hardware Technical Reference Manual for the IOA and CMA addresses that are permanently assigned to the above list of devices and to some optional peripheral devices. If a device on the parent board is not configured into a kernel, the interrupt is freed up, but the IOA and CMA remain assigned to that device and should not be used by any new device.

A quick look at the file `/etc/conf/cf.d/sdevice` shows assignments for the base system. For UNIX System V/386 Release 4.0, the IVN, starting and ending IOA and CMA addresses without any added peripheral boards, is as follows (IOA and CMA values are in hexadecimal):

Device	Prefix	IVN	SIOA	EIOA	SCMA	ECMA
Serial ports	asy	4	3f8	3ff	0	0
	asy	3	2f8	2ff	0	0
Floppy Disk	fd	6	3f0	3f7	0	0
Co-processor:	fp	13	0	0	0	0
Hard Disk:	hd	14	320	32f	0	0
Keyboard:	kd	1	60	64	0	0
	kd	1	64	64	0	0
Parallel Port:	lp	7	378	37f	0	0
Real Time Clk.:	rtc	8	0	0	0	0

DMA Controller Operations

Most Intel386 processor-based computer systems have two Intel 8237A DMA controllers, which provide seven channels to transfer data directly to and from memory without CPU involvement. The following table summarizes DMA channels and their usage in the Base System.

```
Ch 0: spare
Ch 1: spare
Ch 2: floppy
Ch 3: spare
Ch 4: unusable - cascade from chip 1
Ch 5: spare
Ch 6: spare
Ch 7: spare
```

Examine the file /usr/include/sys/dma.h for additional information on control register locations used to initiate DMA.

Kernel Utility Routines

UNIX system device drivers call kernel utility routines to perform system-level functions, many of which were introduced in the section "Driver Activities and Responsibilities". The following section describes the syntax and use of these kernel functions.

This section addresses issues relevant to drivers on any UNIX system. Throughout this section, references are made to how things work on a "generic" or traditional UNIX system, along with some specific details on how UNIX System V Release 4.0 for the Intel386 and compatible architectures is implemented. Device interrupts and priority levels in particular are heavily machine-dependent and reflect the implementation of UNIX System V Release 4.0 for the Intel386 and compatible architectures.

Although UNIX system device drivers for different computer systems have many identical characteristics, one driver may be very different from another, even on the same machine, because of the wide spectrum of functions that drivers perform. The section will first discuss some design issues and examine the common features.

 Not all portions of this section are appropriate for STREAMS drivers and modules. Programmers are encouraged to use the UNIX System V Release 4.0 *Programmer's Guide: STREAMS for Intel Processors* as a principal reference and use only those parts of this section that pertain to machine specifics and driver installation.

Setting Processor Priority Levels

As described in the section entitled "Critical Sections of the Driver", if a device interrupts the processor, the integrity of driver data structures might be destroyed if they are manipulated by an interrupt handler of the interrupted code. To prevent such problems, the system has special functions that set the processor execution level to prohibit interrupts below certain levels. These interfaces allow the driver to block certain levels of interrupts during critical sections.

Setting Priority Levels in Uniprocessor Releases

The functions used to Set the Priority Level of the processor are the splN functions, where N ranges between 0 and 7 and corresponds to the priority level in the kernel. While spl0 allows all interrupts to occur; spl7 allows none. Most UNIX systems have an splhi function to set the processor execution level to the highest value, which is spl7 for UNIX System V/386.

All splN functions return the previous priority level. When setting a given priority level, the previous level (returned by the spl function) should be saved and the splx function should be used to restore the previous level at the end of the critical section. When the driver is ready to lower the priority level, it should not lower it all the way to 0 but rather to the old priority level. Consider the following code:

```
register pl_t pl;
...
pl = splhi();    /* Block interrupts */
/*
 * Critical section of code that manipulates data that is
 * also referenced or manipulated by the interrupt handler.
 */
(void) splx(pl);  /* Allow interrupts */
```

Note that at the end of the critical section the level is lowered to the previous level and not below that level.

In uniprocessor releases, it is sufficient to block interrupt handlers with the spl(D3D) interfaces described in the UNIX System V/386 Release 4.0 *Device Driver Interface/Driver-Kernel Interface (DDI/DKI) Reference Manual*. Each spl function is defined to block a certain type of interrupt along with any interrupts that might come in at lower levels, however the total ordering of the levels may not be identical on all systems. The DDI/DKI reference manual pages for multiprocessing releases define a partial ordering of priority levels, and, in order to be fully portable, a driver should not depend on any ordering beyond what the DDI/DKI defines.

Interrupt Priority Level

Another kernel characteristic, Interrupt Priority Level (IPL), interacts with the spl$N$ functions. Some processor architectures have a hardware priority scheme that defines a hierarchy of which devices can interrupt others. Because the Intel386 processor lacks such a scheme, UNIX System V/386 Release 4.0 has assignable priority levels that simulate hardware priority levels. By defining an IPL in the sdevice file, we can protect a driver's critical regions at the appropriate level. IPL8 is the highest level and is reserved for the internal clock. Drivers at this level cannot be interrupted by other devices (their interrupt routines execute at splhi). A device at IPL6 can be interrupted by a device at IPL7 or IPL8. For the Intel386 processor, the base system device drivers in UNIX System V Release 4.0 use the following IPL levels:

DEV	IPL	Device attached
clock	8	UNIX System Clock
asy	7	Serial Ports
fd	6	Floppy Disk
hd	5	Hard Disk
kd	6	Keyboard
lp	3	Line printer (Parallel Port)
rtc	5	Real Time Clock

This shows that the serial ports run at the highest priority to prevent loss of data. The line printer is more safely interrupted and is given a low IPL. See the section entitled "Controller Interface Basics" for a complete definition of the device configuration assignments.

NOTE Do not overstate the device interrupt priority and be sure to limit the amount of time spent at high levels. For example, if any driver elevates to **splhi** for more than a few milliseconds, loss of UNIX system clock time may result.

The mapping of IPL to device shown above is an example only, and is extremely platform specific. In order to be portable, drivers should not depend on IPL mapping, but rather the semantics defined for the spl functions defined by the DDI/DKI (for example, in multiprocessing releases spldisk blocks disk interrupts). In addition, drivers should not be dependent on any ordering of the spl or pl levels beyond those defined by the DDI/DKI, if you want them to be widely portable.

Setting Priority Levels in Multiprocessor Releases

As discussed in the section "Multi-Processor Critical Sections", blocking interrupts using a spl function may not be sufficient to protect a critical section in a multiprocessor driver. Such critical sections must be protected using a locking primitive. Data that may be manipulated at the interrupt level must be protected by a basic or read/write lock. Both of these types of locks allow the caller to specify a processor priority level that will be set at the time the lock is acquired. The priority levels that may be set during lock acquisition are the same as those that can be set using the spl interface. The valid arguments to set the various levels are listed under the LOCK_ALLOC(D3DK) interface in the UNIX System V/386 Release 4.0 Multi-Processor *Device Driver Interface/Driver-Kernel Interface (DDI/DKI) Reference Manual*. As with the spl interface, portable drivers using basic or read/write locks should not depend on any ordering of priority levels beyond those defined by the DDI/DKI.

When acquiring any basic or read/write lock, the priority level set during lock acquisition must be sufficient to block out any interrupt handler that might attempt to acquire the same lock in order to prevent deadlock. In addition, potential deadlock problems involving multiple locks must be considered when determining the priority level to block while holding a lock. For example, assume locks A and B may be held simultaneously and the normal order of acquisition is to acquire lock A first, followed by lock B. In this case, the priority level set when acquiring lock B must always be high enough to block any interrupt handler that might attempt to acquire either lock A or lock B.

As with the spl functions, the previous processor priority level (returned by the call to acquire the lock) should be saved and passed to the function called to release the lock (for example UNLOCK) so that the previous level is properly restored at the end of the critical section.

Locking

As discussed in the section on "Multi-Processor Critical Sections", a multiprocessor environment raises new concerns about more than one processor accessing the same data at the same time. To solve these problems, a set of locking
functions is provided to serialize access to a data structure; that is, to ensure
that only one processor is operating on a set of data at any one time. However,
these functions are closely connected with the new functions to suspend a process. In general, the locking primitives should not be thought of as useful only
on multiprocessor systems, but should be considered as the basic means of
ensuring data integrity on any system.

There are three types of locks: basic locks, read/write locks, and sleep locks,
each with an associated set of functions. The choice of lock depends on the way
the data is accessed, the contention for the data (that is, how often it is
accessed), and the duration that the lock must be held.

Basic Locks

The first type of lock is the basic lock. The function to acquire a basic lock is
simply:

```
pl_t LOCK(lock_t *lock, pl_t pl)
```

The first argument is a pointer to a `lock_t` structure, which must have been
previously allocated by `LOCK_ALLOC`. The second argument is a processor
priority level (see "Setting Processor Priority Levels" below for more details).
The processor priority level is set to the specified level, and the old processor
priority level is returned from `LOCK`.

The function to release a lock is

```
void UNLOCK(lock_t *lock, pl_t pl)
```

The first argument is a pointer to `lock_t`, which is to be unlocked. The
second argument is the priority level to be restored, typically the old processor
priority level that was returned from the `LOCK` call.

When `LOCK` is called, if the lock is available (not held by another processor), the
`lock_t` is marked as acquired and the function returns. If the lock is not available, the processor busy-waits until the lock becomes available. This ensures
that only one processor is executing the critical section of code between `LOCK`
and `UNLOCK`.

As an example, this code fragment searches a table for a slot containing 0, and inserts the variable `entry` into the slot. Without the protection of the lock, two processors may both find the same slot to be unused and try to put different entries into the same slot.

```
s = LOCK(lock, plstr);
for (i = 0;  i < SIZE;  i++)
     if (table[i] == 0)
          break;
if (i >= SIZE)
     goto error;
table[i] = entry;
UNLOCK(lock, s);
```

NOTE It is assumed that the error-handling code at the **error** label performs an **UNLOCK**.

Read/Write Locks

The second type of lock is the read/write lock. In some cases, a set of data is frequently accessed (read), but infrequently modified (written). In this case, a read/write lock can be used to allow several processors to read the data at the same time, but ensure that only one processor is writing the data at any one time. If a processor is writing the data, no other processors may be reading or writing the data. The functions to acquire a read/write lock are

```
pl_t RW_RDLOCK(rwlock_t *lock, pl_t pl);

pl_t RW_WRLOCK(rwlock_t *lock, pl_t pl);
```

Unlike the basic `LOCK`, there are two functions, one to acquire the lock in read mode, and one to acquire the lock in write mode. When `RW_RDLOCK` returns, the calling processor has acquired the lock in read mode. Other processors may also acquire the lock in read mode, but no other processors may have the lock in write mode. When `RW_WRLOCK` returns, the calling processor has acquired the lock in write mode; no other processors may have the lock in read or write mode.

There is a single unlock function:

```
void RW_UNLOCK(rwlock_t *lock, pl_t pl);
```

A modification of the previous example shows how read/write locks are used:

```
s = RW_RDLOCK(lock, plstr);
found = 0;
for (i = 0;  i < SIZE;  i++)
        if (table[i] == entry) {
                found = 1;
                break;
        }
RW_UNLOCK(lock, s);


        ...


s = RW_WRLOCK(lock, plstr);
for (i = 0;  i < SIZE;  i++)
        if (table[i] == 0)
                break;
if (i >= SIZE)
        goto error;
table[i] = entry;
RW_UNLOCK(lock, s);
```

In this example, the first code fragment merely looks through the table to determine if a specific value is in the table. Because it does not modify the data structure protected by the lock, the lock is acquired in read mode, allowing other processors to execute the same section of code at the same time. The second fragment is similar to the previous example; it inserts a new value into the table. Because it modifies the data structures, the lock is acquired in write mode to prevent other processors from reading or writing the data structure while the insert operation is in progress.

In the first code fragment, after the lock is unlocked, the variable found only indicates whether the entry was in the table at the time it was searched. As soon as the lock is unlocked, another processor is free to modify the table, adding or deleting entries. Care must be taken to ensure that a lock protects data for the entire duration that the data must remain unchanged.

Sleep Locks

The third type of lock is the sleep lock, which is similar to the basic LOCK. However, if the lock is not available when an attempt to acquire it is made, the process attempting to acquire it goes to sleep rather than spinning. The process wakes up when it acquires the lock. Sleep locks must be acquired from process context; they cannot be called from the interrupt level. A held sleep lock is associated with a process, while a held basic LOCK or read/write lock is associated with a processor.

Multiple Locks

Sometimes it is useful for a driver to have more than one lock. Suppose there are several data structures that are accessed more or less independently. One single lock could control access to all of the data structures, but it would be more efficient to have a different lock for each data structure. This allows several processors to access different data structures at the same time. The tradeoff is that more lock/unlock functions are called.

If more than one lock exists, it may be desired to acquire more than one lock at one time. That is, the driver may wish to acquire a lock, and then acquire another lock without unlocking the first lock. This can be done, but there are some restrictions.

First, when a basic or read/write lock is held, sleep locks may not be acquired. However, when a basic or read/write lock is held, other basic and read/write locks may be acquired. When a sleep lock is held, other sleep, basic, or read/write locks may be acquired.

Second, there must be an ordering to the locks, so that a sequence of locks are always acquired in the same order. This ordering is often called a lock hierarchy. To see why this is necessary, suppose that two locks, A and B, could be acquired in any order. Then, suppose process X acquires lock A and process Y acquires lock B. Next, process X attempts to acquire lock B. Because B is held by Y, process X spins waiting for process Y to release the lock. If process Y attempts to acquire lock A, which is held by process X, the two processes are permanently deadlocked, and each is spinning waiting for the other to release a lock. The lock hierarchy prevents this type of deadlock by forcing locks to be acquired in a specific order.

Sleeping and Waking

Drivers sometimes must suspend or block their execution to await certain events, where an event is a change in the state of system hardware or software. Suspending execution of a process is called "sleeping". In uniprocessor releases, calling the function `sleep` puts the driver to sleep. In multiprocessor releases, the driver sleeps by calling the `SV_WAIT` or `SV_WAIT_SIG` function. These sleep functions cause the system to do a context switch and schedule another process to run.

 NOTE Block drivers use **biowait** to sleep instead of **sleep** or **SV_WAIT** and **SV_WAIT_SIG**. For further information, refer to the section "**biowait**/- **biodone** – Block Driver Event Synchronization".

A driver that is sleeping remains sleeping until an interrupt handler or another process executes a call to `wakeup` in uniprocessor releases or a call to `SV_SIGNAL` or `SV_BROADCAST` in multiprocessor releases. This causes the sleeping process to become runnable, and as soon as the system schedules it on a processor, it resumes running. The act of calling a function to bring a process out of the sleeping state is called "waking up" the process.

sleep / wakeup

The `sleep` function takes two parameters: a synchronization variable (an address used to signify an event) on which the process sleeps and a priority value that is assigned to the process when it is awakened:

```
sleep(caddr_t addr, int pri)
```

The synchronization variable used for sleeping is an arbitrary address that lacks any meaning except to the corresponding `wakeup` function call. The sleep addresses are usually taken from the entry in the device data structure of the device the process is accessing to guarantee uniqueness across the system. When a process goes to sleep awaiting an event, the driver should set a flag in the device data structure indicating the reason to sleep:

```
driver.state |= cond_flg;
sleep(&driver.state, PRIORITY);
```

Later, either an interrupt handler or another process calls `wakeup` to awaken the sleeping process.

The code calling `wakeup` should check for a particular flag bit, indicating the reason the process is sleeping. The driver then calls `wakeup` with one parameter, the address where a process may be sleeping.

```
wakeup(caddr_t addr)
```

Particularly nasty race conditions can occur if spl*N* functions are not used with the `sleep` function. For example, the code segment

```
while (driver.state & cond_flg)
        sleep(&driver.state, PRIORITY);
```

causes the process to sleep if the `cond_flg` bit is set in the field `driver.state`. (As processes can sleep on the address for several events, the `sleep` call is enclosed in the `while` loop so the code, when awakened, again checks that `cond_flg` is indeed no longer set. This is one reason it is best to sleep on different address values for different sleep reasons.) Without using the spl*N* function, the process could check the `cond_flg` bit, find it set, and try to call `sleep`. But if an interrupt occurred before the process called `sleep` and the interrupt handler checked the `cond_flg` bit to determine if a process was sleeping, it would assume the process was asleep and call `wakeup` to awaken it. Consider the following code:

```
driver.state &= ~cond_flg;
wakeup(&driver.state);
```

By the time the interrupted process calls `sleep`, it will have missed the `wakeup` call, and another one may never come. By bracketing the calls to `sleep` with spl*N* function calls, the driver prevents the race condition:

```
register int oldpri;
...
oldpri = spl5();
while (driver.state & cond_flg)
        sleep(&driver.state, PRIORITY);
splx(oldpri);
```

SV_WAIT and SV_WAIT_SIG

In multiprocessing releases, the two functions cause a process to sleep:

- `SV_WAIT`

- `SV_WAIT_SIG`

The `SV_WAIT` and `SV_WAIT_SIG` functions behave differently if the process receives a signal while it is sleeping. ("Signal" refers to UNIX system signals, such as `SIGINT` and `SIGHUP`, not the `SV_SIGNAL` function.)

- If a process sleeps due to `SV_WAIT`, signals do not cause the process to wake up. Signals for the process are saved and may be processed after `SV_SIGNAL` or `SV_BROADCAST` wakes up the process normally.

- If a process sleeps due to `SV_WAIT_SIG`, signals cause the process to wake up. Receipt of a signal by the process causes an immediate return from the `SV_WAIT_SIG` call, even if no call to `SV_BROADCAST` or `SV_SIGNAL` occurred. `SV_WAIT_SIG` returns zero if it returns due to a signal, and non-zero if it returns due to a normal wakeup.

The driver usually treats a return due to a signal as an abnormal termination and would "clean up" and return. Typical items that need cleaning up are locked data structures that should be unlocked when the system call completes. The error number `EINTR` is often used to indicate that a driver operation was aborted by a signal:

```
if (SV_WAIT_SIG(sv, pritty, lock) == 0) {
    /*
     * driver state cleanup
     */
    return(EINTR);
}
```

Before calling `SV_WAIT` or `SV_WAIT_SIG`, a driver almost always should check some condition to see if it is appropriate to sleep. A driver may check a status variable to see if a device controller is ready and sleep if it is not, or may check a variable to see if an I/O operation is done and sleep until it is. Because one processor can change the condition while another processor checks the condition, the code that checks the condition is a multiprocessor critical section. To protect the multiprocessor critical section, a lock must be released before the process goes to sleep, otherwise problems may occur.

In the following example, the accesses to `driver.state` and `driver.inuse` are unprotected:

```
while (driver.state != READY || driver.inuse) {
    .SV_WAIT(driver.cond, … );
}
```

One processor may be manipulating this data at the same time another processor is examining it. A first attempt to fix this may be the following:

```
s = LOCK(driver.lock, pldisk);
while (driver.state != READY || driver.inuse) {
    UNLOCK(driver.lock, s);
    SV_WAIT(driver.cond, … );
    s = LOCK(driver.lock, pldisk);
}
UNLOCK(driver.lock, s);
```

Here the driver writer is careful to unlock the lock before calling `SV_WAIT`, because `SV_WAIT` cannot be called with locks held. If this driver goes to sleep with `driver.lock` locked and another processor tries to lock `driver.lock`, the other processor will spin until this process is rescheduled and unlocks the lock. This prevents the spinning processor from doing any useful work for what may be a long period of time, which could seriously degrade system performance.

However, another problem is when some other processor wishes to set `driver.state` to `READY` immediately after `driver.lock` is unlocked. It may execute this code:

```
s = LOCK(driver.lock, pldisk);
driver.state = READY;
SV_BROADCAST(driver.lock, 0);
UNLOCK(driver.lock, s);
```

If the other processor executes `SV_BROADCAST` before the first processor executes `SV_WAIT`, the first processor effectively misses the wakeup unless the unlock and the act of going to sleep occur atomically, that is, uninterruptibly, to prevent any wakeups occurring between the unlock and the sleep. To achieve this, one of the arguments to `SV_WAIT` and `SV_WAIT_SIG` is the address of a lock which they atomically unlock when they put the process to sleep.

Because the operation of unlocking the lock then putting the process to sleep is atomic, the driver writer need not worry that any wakeups might occur between the two events, and the driver need not unlock the lock before calling SV_WAIT. It merely passes a pointer to the lock into SV_WAIT and the lock automatically unlocks before the process sleeps. Thus, the correct code for the earlier case becomes the following:

```
s = LOCK(driver.lock, pldisk);
while (driver.state != READY || driver.inuse) {
        SV_WAIT(driver.cond, pridisk, driver.lock);
        s = LOCK(driver.lock, pldisk);
}
UNLOCK(driver.lock, s);
```

Synchronization Variables

To wake up all processes sleeping on a particular synchronization variable, enabling them to execute when the scheduler chooses them, use wakeup in uniprocessor releases and SV_BROADCAST in multiprocessor releases. If no process is sleeping on the synchronization variable when a wakeup function such as wakeup on uniprocessors or SV_BROADCAST on multiprocessors is called, the function returns without bad side-effects. It is best for code readability and for efficiency to have a one-to-one correspondence between events and synchronization variables avoid using one synchronization variable to sleep on two different events.

When SV_BROADCAST is used, each process that wakes up must usually recheck the sleep-condition, in case some other process woke up first and changed the sleep-condition. In the example above, the while loop causes the sleep-condition to be rechecked. SV_BROADCAST can be an expensive operation if a large number of processes are sleeping on a synchronization variable. In the example above, although all the sleeping processes will wake up and check their sleep-condition; only one will proceed while the others go back to sleep (sometimes called the "thundering herd" problem). This uses up a large amount of processor time.

When SV_SIGNAL is used, only one of the processes sleeping on a synchronization variable wakes up. The driver writer must make sure the other sleeping processes are properly awakened, usually by having each process complete the work it must do, then call SV_SIGNAL to wake up the next sleeping process.

It is invalid to call sleep functions such as SV_WAIT, SV_WAIT_SIG or sleep when handling an interrupt because a process independent of the device could have been executing when the device interrupted. If the interrupt handler goes to sleep, the interrupted process is effectively put to sleep for reasons beyond its control. But second and far more important, sleeping in an interrupt handler can cause the system to crash in some UNIX system implementations because of the interdependency of the process context switch mechanism and interrupt levels. The interrupt handler must, therefore, not invoke any function that could lead to a context switch. Such functions are identified in the UNIX System V/386 Release 4.0 Multi-Processor *Device Driver Interface/Driver-Kernel Interface (DDI/DKI) Reference Manual*.

Sleep Priorities

The second parameter to sleep is a scheduling parameter used when the process wakes up. This parameter, called the "sleep priority", takes a value ranging from 0 (highest priority) to the constant PSLEP (lowest system priority, usually 39). The sleep priority controls how the sleeping process reacts to signals. If the value is lower than the manifest constant PZERO (25 on most systems), the priority is higher than PZERO (lower value priority levels mean higher priority in the UNIX system) and the system will not wake up sleeping processes on receipt of a signal, but if the value is higher than PZERO (the priority is lower than PZERO), the system can "prematurely" wake up sleeping processes on receipt of a signal.

In uniprocessor releases, sleep calls the longjmp function. Executing longjmp bypasses the conventional C function call/return sequence by resetting the program counter, stack pointer, and data registers to the values they had when the most recent setjmp call was done, usually at one of the higher levels in the system that caused the device driver routine to be invoked. The implication for the driver calling sleep is that the sleep call never seems to return. For instance, a driver entry point routine will end immediately without returning to the code that called sleep if a process receives a signal while sleeping in the following sleep call:

```
sleep((caddr_t)&tp->t_rawq, PZERO + 5);
```

Drivers that allow this behavior must make sure that memory and hardware resources allocated by the driver before calling sleep are freed up and made available again.

Drivers must occasionally "clean up" on receipt of a signal while sleeping before returning to upper levels. Because the longjmp call, as discussed so far, takes place directly from the sleep call, the priority parameter to the sleep call has additional meaning: if the priority parameter is OR'ed with the manifest constant PCATCH, the sleep call returns 1 if awakened on receipt of a signal. But if the sleeping process is awakened by an explicit wakeup call rather than by a signal, then the sleep call returns 0. If the PCATCH bit is clear (not set), the process immediately finishes the driver entry point routine, that is, it executes a longjmp out of the driver. The following code sequence allows the driver to clean up before returning:

```
if (sleep(sleep_address, cond_flg | PCATCH)) {
    /*
     * driver code cleanup
     */
    return(EINTR);
}
```

Typical items that need cleaning up are locked data structures that should be unlocked when the system call completes.

```
tp->t_state |= TLOCK;    /* locks the driver unit */
...
tp->t_state |= TSLEEP;
if (sleep((caddr_t) &tp->t_state, TPRI | PCATCH)) {
    tp->t_state &= ~(TLOCK | TSLEEP);
    return(EINTR);
}
/* somebody woke up driver...
 * continue normally here */
```

The functions SV_WAIT and SV_WAIT_SIG also take a priority argument, but this is merely a hint to the process scheduler as to what the relative priority of the process should be when it wakes up. Use a higher relative priority when the caller sleeps waiting for a highly contended resource, or when the caller is already holding one or more locks or other kernel resources when it goes to sleep. In such cases, it is important to schedule this process to run quickly so that it can finish its work and release the resources it is holding. If the process is not holding any critical resources, it can be assigned a lower relative priority.

The priority values that can be used are listed in the description of SV_WAIT and SV_WAIT_SIG in the UNIX System V/386 Release 4.0 Multi-Processor *Device Driver Interface/Driver-Kernel Interface (DDI/DKI) Reference Manual*.

If a driver must call a sleep function, how should the driver programmer determine the sleep priority? The first decision is whether the process should ignore the receipt of signals or not. To ignore signals in uniprocessor releases, a driver must sleep at a priority greater than PZERO (numerically less than PZERO); to ignore signals in multiprocessor releases, a driver must use SV_WAIT instead of SV_WAIT_SIG. When deciding whether the process should ignore signals or not, the programmer must choose the priority values so as not to affect process scheduling adversely. The system should be benchmarked using several sleep priority values to tune system performance with the new driver.

The driver may ignore signals if it puts the process to sleep for an event that is "sure" to happen. An example of an event that is "sure" to happen is waiting for a locked data structure to be unlocked. The following example uses sleep to wait for a locked data structure to be unlocked:

```
if (tp->t_state & T_LOCKED)
        sleep(&tp->t_state, PZERO - 5);
```

The following example uses SV_WAIT to wait for a locked data structure to be unlocked:

```
s = LOCK(lock, plstr);
while (tp->t_state & T_LOCKED)
        SV_WAIT(tp->t_sync, pritty, lock);
        s = LOCK(lock, plstr);
}
UNLOCK(lock, s);
```

In both examples, another process locked the data structure, may have gone to sleep, but left the data structure locked, thereby blocking changes by other processs until it wakes up. Unless the driver has a bug, the first process eventually unlocks the data structure then awakens all other processes waiting for the T_LOCKED bit (the lock) to clear; therefore, the event announcing the unlock is "sure" to happen either through a call to wakeup in uniprocessor releases or through a call to SV_BROADCAST in multiprocessor releases.

If the driver puts a process to sleep while it awaits an event that may not happen, the process must sleep interruptibly. To sleep interruptibly in uniprocessor releases, a driver must sleep at a priority less than PZERO (numerically greater than PZERO); to sleep interruptibly in multiprocessor releases, a driver must use SV_WAIT_SIG instead of SV_WAIT. An example of an event that may not happen is waiting for data to arrive from a remote device. For example, when the system reads data from a terminal, the read system call sleeps in the terminal driver waiting for data to arrive from the terminal. If data never arrives, the read sleeps indefinitely.

When a user at the terminal presses the interrupt key or disconnects, the terminal driver interrupt handler sends a signal to the reading process that is still sleeping, and the signal causes the reading process to wake up and finish the system call without reading any data. If the driver sleeps ignoring signals, either by sleeping at a priority level that ignores signals in uniprocessor releases or by using SV_WAIT in multiprocessor releases, the process can awaken only by an explicit call to wakeup in uniprocessor releases or to SV_SIGNAL or SV_BROADCAST in multiprocessor releases. If that call never happens (for example, if the user disconnects the terminal), then the process sleeps forever, clearly an undesirable characteristic.

biowait / biodone – Block Driver Event Synchronization

Block-access drivers using the buffer header scheme use the function pair biowait/biodone when waiting for an I/O event instead of using synchronization functions such as sleep/wakeup in uniprocessor releases or SV_WAIT/SV_BROADCAST in multiprocessor releases.

The biowait function can put a block driver to sleep until the I/O operation is complete; biowait sleeps uninterruptibly. Because it operates on an I/O buffer header, it is not used by a character device; although it is used by block devices doing raw I/O through physio.

In UNIX System V/386 Release 4.0, biowait does not set b_flags. In addition, biodone calls brelse, which automatically releases either 1K or 2K buffers to the free list.

Kernel Timers

Sometimes, a driver arrives at a state where it wishes to re-enter itself after a specified time. In uniprocessor releases, the driver uses the `timeout` function for this purpose. In multiprocessor releases, the driver uses the `itimeout` function for this purpose.

timeout – Uniprocessor Kernel Timers

In uniprocessor releases, the function `timeout` is available for a driver to make sure that it is awakened after a maximum period, for those situations where a limit must be placed on how long a process will sleep. The function `timeout` takes three parameters:

1. the function to be invoked when the time increment expires.

2. the value of a parameter with which the function should be called.

3. the number of clock cycles to wait before the function is called.

The third argument to `timeout` is an integer value specifying the period of time in "ticks". The function `drv_usectohz` can convert a period of time in microseconds to the equivalent number of ticks. When this period of time has passed, the function pointed to by the first argument to `timeout` is called with the second argument as its parameter.

A sample `timeout` call is

```
timeout(repeat, n, count);
```

where `n` is the parameter to the function `repeat`, to be called after `count` clock ticks. If `count` is 100 and if the clock interrupts the processor 100 times a second, the system executes the function `repeat` in one second of real time as a result of the above `timeout` call.

A driver can ensure that it can resume its execution (even if no call to `wakeup` is made) by first calling `timeout` and then `sleep`. This should be done, however, only if truly necessary, as it carries some heavy processing requirements. When the call to `timeout` is made, it inserts the specified event into the callout table, which is a list of events.

If the sleeping process is not awakened before the "timeout" event, the specified function will be called. The second argument to the timeout routine could be the event the driver was about to sleep on. When the function is called, it can use this information to call wakeup to wake the driver. The function called from the callout table should also set some internal flag to permit the driver to distinguish between the two ways it can be awakened.

The exact time until the timeout takes effect may not be precise because of the interaction of other parts of the system.

A call to timeout returns a numeric "timeout-ID" which the driver should save. A driver uses this timeout-ID when it has scheduled a timeout which it later would like to cancel because, for example, it received a normal wakeup from sleeping and therefore does not need the timeout event to occur. The ID returned by the call to timeout is passed to the function untimeout to prevent the timeout from occurring.

itimeout − Multiprocessor Kernel Timer

In multiprocessor releases, the function itimeout is available for a driver must be sure that it is awakened after a maximum period, for those situations where a limit must be placed on how long a process will sleep. itimeout takes four parameters:

1. the function to be invoked when the time increment expires.

2. the value of a parameter with which the function should be called.

3. the number of clock cycles to wait before the function is called.

4. the priority level at which the function should be called.

The third argument to itimeout is an integer value specifying the period of time in "ticks". The function drv_usectohz can convert a period of time in microseconds to the equivalent number of ticks. When this period of time has passed, the function pointed to by the first argument to itimeout is called with the second argument as its parameter. The function is called with the processor priority level set to the value specified as the fourth argument to itimeout.

A sample `itimeout` call is

```
itimeout(repeat, n, count, pldisk);
```

where `n` is the parameter to the function `repeat`, to be called after `count` clock ticks. The function `drv_usectohz` can be used to convert a time interval expressed in microseconds to the equivalent number of clock ticks.

A driver can ensure that it can resume its execution (even if no call to `SV_SIGNAL` or `SV_BROADCAST` is made) by first calling `itimeout` before sleeping. This should be done, however, only if truly necessary, as it carries some heavy processing requirements. When the call to `itimeout` is made, it records some information in the callout table, which can be a fairly time-consuming operation.

If the sleeping process is not awakened before the "timeout" event, the specified function will be called. The second argument to the `itimeout` routine could be the event the driver was about to sleep on. When the function is called, it can use this information to call `SV_SIGNAL` or `SV_BROADCAST` to wake the driver. The function called from the callout table should also set some internal flag to permit the driver to distinguish between the two ways it can be awakened.

The exact time until the timeout takes effect may not be precise because of the interaction of other parts of the system.

`itimeout` returns an ID value that can later be used in a call to `untimeout` to cancel the timeout before it takes effect. For example, any outstanding timeouts should be canceled in a driver's `close` routine. Otherwise, driver code is executed after the driver is closed, possibly resulting in unpredictable results.

`untimeout` can be called from an interrupt routine as long as the interrupt priority level associated with the interrupt routine is less than or equal to the level specified in the `itimeout`.

Another type of timeout, `dtimeout`, may be used to cause a timeout function to be run on a specific processor. Otherwise, it is similar to `itimeout`. This timeout is most often used on machine architectures where some processors do not have access to some I/O devices.

delay

This function stops execution of the current process for a given period of time. Drivers can use the function delay instead of the time-out functions, timeout and itimeout, to instruct the driver to sleep for a specified amount of time and then wake up. To use delay, specify the amount of time to wait. In uniprocessor releases, delay automatically calls wakeup to resume execution.

The following piece of code illustrates the use of delay. This code is from a driver for a line printer. Before allocating buffers and storing data in them, the driver checks the status of the device. If the printer needs to have paper loaded, it displays a message on the system console. If the driver called a sleep function directly, the operator has to signal when the paper loaded. By using delay, the driver waits one minute and tries again. If paper is loaded, processing resumes automatically.

```
while (rp->status & NOPAPER) /* while printer is out of paper */
{           /* display message & ring bell on system console */
        cmn_err(CE_WARN, "xx_write: NO PAPER in printer %d 07", (dev&0xf));
        ticks = drv_usectohz(60 * 1000000);
        delay(ticks);           /* wait one minute & try again */
}           /* endwhile */
```

Error Reporting

One of the most important aspects of writing a device driver is the correct handling of errors. Driver code must handle any error condition, or the consequences may be severe. For example, a stray interrupt should be a trivial event, but could panic the system if the driver is not prepared to handle it. For instance the panic could cause data corruption and physically damage the system.

When an error occurs, the driver can do one or more of the following:

- Write the error condition to a structure so the driver knows about it. At base level, the error is stored in a state structure and returned to the caller. At the interrupt or base level, errors on block devices can be recorded in the `b_error` member of the `buf` structure by calling `bioerror`.

- Retry the process. The error may be a transient problem. Some hardware device boards have retry capabilities; let these boards do the retry. But if the error is software-related, the driver must decide how many times to retry.

- Report the error to a system error log. If the error is severe, take the faulty hardware out of service to minimize the damage and keep the system running normally.

- Report the error to the system administrator, either by printing it on the system console, or by writing it to `putbuf`, or both (see `cmn_err` in the section entitled "Driver Debugging Techniques").

- Send a signal to a user process.

- Panic the operating system.

Driver Debugging Techniques

Kernel Print Statements

There are, of course, limitations in debugging and testing device drivers. In the absence of a kernel debugging tool, print statements inside the driver are the primary method used. Because the print statements are written by the kernel, there is no way to redirect the output to a file or to a remote terminal. Using print statements also modifies the timing of driver code execution, which may change the behavior of problems you are investigating. Print statements in the driver can be made more efficient by using an `ioctl` to set one or more levels of debugging output. This way you can write a simple user program to turn the print output on or off as needed. Sometimes kernel print statements scroll by too quickly to read. There is a limited kernel buffer called `putbuf` that records all kernel print calls. There are several ways to retrieve this data later:

1. Use the `crash` command.

   After executing `/etc/crash`, try the following command:

   ```
   od -a putbuf 2000
   ```

   You can examine the `crash`(1M) manual page in the UNIX System V/386 Release 4.0 *System Administrator's Reference Manual* for more information.

2. Use the built-in kernel console monitor `/dev/osm`.

   If the base system does not have preconfigured `/dev/osm` device nodes, you should make one by:

   a. Creating a file named `/etc/conf/node.d/osm` that contains the following:

      ```
      osm osm0 c 0
      ```

   b. Executing the `/etc/conf/bin/idmknod` command.

   c. Using `cat` or `tail` to examine `/dev/osm0`.

Note that `cmn_err` has the same syntax as `printf`, but only supports print options byte, hexadecimal, character, decimal, unsigned decimal, octal, hexadecimal and string (option variables `b`, `c`, `d`, `u`, `o`, `x` and `s`). See the UNIX System V/386 Release 4.0 *Device Driver Interface/Driver-Kernel Interface (DDI/DKI) Reference Manual* for more information on `cmn_err`.

In Release 4.0 of UNIX System V/386, cmn_err calls made inside the kernel appear on the monitor (/dev/console). The cmn_err has an option of putting the character data only in putbuf and not having the data appear on the console at all. This is done by preceding the text string with an exclamation mark (" ! "). For example:

```
cmn_err(CE_NOTE,"!this driver print statement will only go
into putbuf, not onto the screen.");
```

The Trace Driver

Another useful way to observe driver behavior is by using a trace driver. Such a driver can be called by your driver to log data. A user program can then be written to read the trace driver either in real-time or as a postmortem analysis. The section entitled "A Trace Driver Implementation" provides the source code for such a driver which logs data presented to it by trsave calls made from other drivers. The trace driver uses clists to save these traces. Although this driver isn't delivered with the UNIX System V/386 Release 4.0 base, you can compile and link edit the driver into your system from the source code presented in the section entitled "A Trace Driver Implementation". Not only will /dev/trace0 be useful for your debugging, but it may help you better understand how the Installable Driver (ID) facility works before you actually write your driver.

System Panics

If the programmer expects that the driver could enter a state that is illegal, the driver can halt the system by using the cmn_err function with a panic flag set. For example, if the driver expects one of three specific cases in a switch statement, the driver can add a fourth default case that calls the cmn_err function. The system will dump an image of memory for later analysis. If the error is recoverable, the driver should not panic the system. An example of panicking using cmn_err is

```
cmn_err(CE_PANIC,"Your system has panicked, DEV_NAME error!");
```

Taking a System Dump

In the event a `panic` occurs, there may be some value in examining the dump produced by the system. Because UNIX System V/386 Release 4.0 uses the same physical hard disk partition for both "swap" and "dump", it is important that you do not reboot to the multiuser state before examining the dump. If the system reaches multiuser state, the dump may be overwritten by system paging.

To examine the dump, the dump image must be saved. If the `root` partition does not have enough space to save the crash dump, the following message will appear:

```
Need nnnnK to save crash dump.
Root has only xxxxK free.
F - write to floppy disk
T - write to tape
S - spawn a shell
X - skip it
```

You may then proceed in whatever manner you prefer.

NOTE We recommend that you write your crash dump to tape.

When the system reboots and detects a dump image, it will copy the dump image from the `swap/dump` area to the file `crash.MMDD` in the `/crash` directory; where `MM` is the month, and `DD` is the day. If a crash file already exists in the `/crash` directory, another crash file is created with a `.1`, `.2`, `.3`, and so forth appended to the file name. A corresponding symbol file, `sym.MMDD` is also saved in the `/crash` directory.

Before the dump image is saved, the following message appears on the console:

```
Saving nnnnK crash dump in crash.MMDD
```

where `nnnn` is the size of the dump in KB. After the dump image is saved, the console displays the following message, `Done`, and the system continues its start-up procedure.

You can use the `crash` command to examine the dump as follows:

>   crash -d *dumpfile* -n *symbolfile*

or you can use the `kcrash` command to examine the dump as follows:

>   kcrash *dumpfile symbolfile*

Consult the `crash`(1M) and `kcrash`(1M) manual pages in the UNIX System V/386 Release 4.0 *System Administrator's Reference Manual* for information on how to use `crash` and `kcrash` to examine the UNIX operating system kernel and user process status at the time of the `panic`. To retrieve the `panic` printout and any other kernel messages that have made their way into `putbuf`, use the following `crash` command:

>   od -a putbuf *count*

where *count* is the length of the `putbuf` data you wish to examine.

You could also use the following `kcrash` command:

>   dl putbuf

Note that the procedures to examine a memory dump only apply to UNIX systems that have completed the dump sequence, usually in response to a `panic`. The prompt that you may see after an improper shutdown only indicates that the system was not properly brought down and a dump may exist. If the system is inadvertently powered down or reset, or if your device driver causes the kernel to hang or go berserk without ever executing a `panic`, no dump will have been taken. Remember, the system will only do a dump when you have properly detected an error and executed the `panic` function inside your driver or when your driver has caused a system error detected by the kernel or some other driver causing it to `panic`.

At this point, it might be well to repeat the advice stated in the introduction:

Writing a device driver carries a heavy responsibility. As part of the UNIX system kernel it is assumed to always take the correct action. Few limits are placed on the driver by the other parts of the kernel, and the driver must be written to never compromise the system's stability.

Kernel Debugger

An extremely useful tool for debugging device drivers is the multiprocessor kernel debugger (kdb), which allows you to examine and modify memory, disassemble instructions, set breakpoints, and single-step instructions on all the online processors in the running UNIX kernel. Refer to the kdb(1) manual page in the UNIX System V Release 4.0 *User's Reference Manual* for more detail and a complete list of commands for the kdb utility.

kdb is an extremely powerful tool, and should be used carefully to avoid accidental corruption of kernel data structures, which could lead to a system crash. kdb has few provisions for preventing programmer error.

NOTE   The kernel debugger is not meant for debugging user programs. Use an appropriate user-level debugger such as adb(1) or sdb(1) for that purpose.

kdb must exist in your kernel before you can use it (just like any device driver).

kdb prints and accepts address inputs symbolically, using kernel procedure and variable names instead of hexadecimal numbers, but you must load the debugger with the kernel's symbols after the debugger itself has been installed into the kernel. You can do this by using the dbsym command, which loads the symbols into the kernel executable file after building it and before booting it. For more information, refer to the dbsym(1) manual page in the UNIX System V Release 4.0 *User's Reference Manual*. This has the advantage that you need to load the symbols only once per kernel build.

NOTE   The symbols must be loaded before the system panics (or you enter the kernel debugger for some other reason) for them to be useful. You cannot load the kernel symbols while in the debugger.

The following sections assume that you have both kdb and the symbol table loaded into your kernel.

Debugging Crashed Drivers

kdb, like the `crash` utility, allows postmortem analysis of system crashes. Unlike `crash`, kdb allows you to examine the failure without having to reboot the machine and perform a crash dump. When the system panics, it prints the panic message and enters the kernel debugger before dumping the core image. This gives you the opportunity to examine the system immediately.

If you want to continue with the normal crash dump, continue execution with the kdb command `go`.

You should first investigate where the panic occurred. Panics unrelated to your driver should be brought to the attention of your system administrator.

Sometimes panics occur because of an unexpected fault, and the panic message is unhelpful (for example, `PANIC: Trap type 0xE in kernel mode`). When this happens, you can backtrace the kernel's execution stack to see where the panic occurred with the kdb command `bt`. `bt` displays the function name and an offset into the function where the call occurred followed by the arguments with which the procedure was called. kdb allows you to backtrace over interrupts and traps as well as normal procedure calls within the kernel. Sometimes the backtrace becomes confused by a procedure that does not set up a normal C stack frame. You can see what procedure was omitted in the backtrace by disassembling the call instruction in the calling procedure.

While backtracing, you should look for procedure calls within your driver or addresses of data for which your driver is responsible. When you see one of these, you should examine the registers (debugger `dr` and `dR` commands) and memory (debugger `dl` and `dy` commands, for example) to determine the nature of the problem within your driver.

Crashed Driver Example

The kernel crashes with the message

```
PANIC: usrxmemflt: no as allocated: 0000000C
```

and enters the kernel debugger.

This message indicates that an attempt was made to access kernel virtual memory location `0xC`. This address is invalid in kernel mode. All kernel virtual addresses are above `0xC0000000`; all user virtual addresses are below `0xC0000000`. The most likely cause of this problem is a structure dereference from a null pointer. That is, some C code uses a pointer type variable to point to some data, the pointer is 0, and the code attempts to dereference the pointer anyway.

To solve this problem, you should change the C code to check for the null pointer-case and handle it appropriately. In multiprocessor code, you might also want to place locks around the use of the pointer.

The real problem is finding the right place in the assembler code and recognizing where that is in the C code. A good course of action would be to do the following:

1. Backtrace (bt) the kernel stack on the processor that panicked. In this specific case, you should see several procedure calls on the stack above the actual faulting instruction (for example, cmn_err, usrxmemflt, k_trap, and cmntrap).

2. Find the first frame that is not part of the fault-handling code (probably immediately below cmntrap).

3. Disassemble the instruction with di at the address printed in the backtrace. It should be a memory reference instruction, in this case, most likely a movl to or from offset 0xC from some register (for example, movl %eax, C(%edi)). Now you know that register %edi, at that instruction, is the null pointer to blame.

4. Disassemble backwards (using the – subcommand of the di command to step backward one instruction at a time) to find where the value in %edi came from. It was probably set from some global data structure, or from an argument to the procedure. It helps to look at the C code and match it with the assembler code.

5. Change the procedure to handle the null pointer-case gracefully, or eliminate the race condition that allowed the pointer to be zeroed out on one processor and subsequently used on another.

6. Recompile.

Debugging Active Drivers

kdb can be invoked at any time during normal kernel execution to help identify device driver bugs. The ability to debug during run-time is the main advantage of using the kernel debugger instead of a post-crash analyzer utility. In addition to the commands described above, while the kernel is still running normally you can do the following to help you better understand the nature of a driver error:

- Single-step through your driver (tr and to)
- Set instruction and chip breakpoints (br and ur)
- Modify data (ml), instructions (mi), and registers (mr and mR)
- Read and write I/O ports (in and ou)
- Call procedures with any arguments and see the return value (call)

Some guidelines and tips when using kdb commands on an active kernel are as follows:

- Be careful not to damage the kernel and cause a crash.
- Never set instruction breakpoints in kernel debugger procedures, nor chip breakpoints on kernel debugger data. Entering the debugger while already in the debugger (breaking this rule, for example, or the call restrictions below) may cause it to malfunction.
- Never modify kernel debugger data.
- Never modify instructions in procedures the kernel debugger calls.
- Set breakpoints in procedures after the initial few instructions that create a new stack frame, so backtracing will work properly. Do not set them at the very beginning of the procedures.
- Clear breakpoints (bc and uc) when you no longer need them so you do not have to keep typing go.
- Note that reading and writing I/O ports may not function properly on some processors, depending on your multiprocessor hardware.

- Beware of reading I/O ports that change value because they have been read.

- Beware of writing I/O ports that could reset the system.

- Never `call` procedures that might sleep or context switch.

- Never `call` procedures in which you have set instruction breakpoints, or that use data on which you have set chip breakpoints, or that call the `calldebug` macro.

- Beware of `calling` procedures that require kernel-level or driver locks to be held when called.

Some typical ways to enter the kernel debugger while the system is running are the following:

- Typing CTL-ALT-D on the console.

- Using the macro `calldebug` (in `<sys/xdebug.h>`) in your driver.

- Hitting a previously set debugger breakpoint.

You may place a call to the `calldebug` C macro or set a debugger breakpoint at any point in your driver, even in interrupt-level routines. The call or breakpoint will enter the debugger and return normally when you resume execution using the `go` command. This allows you to stop the system from running at specific points in your driver and examine its state.

Active Driver Examples

If your driver has a problem that shows up only intermittently after long periods of successful execution, post-panic debugging will reveal corrupted driver-global data that caused the actual panic, but you may not know how the data became corrupted. To identify this problem, use the chip breakpoint features of the kernel debugger as follows:

1. Reboot the system.

2. Enter the kernel debugger by typing CTL-ALT-D on the console.

3. Verify that the data is currently correct. (If it is not, try placing a `calldebug` statement in your driver's `start` routine; if the data is incorrect even that early, perhaps it is being initialized improperly.)

4. Set a chip breakpoint (ur) for a write to the address that becomes corrupted and resume execution.

Each time the processor writes to that virtual address, it enters the debugger
and you can backtrace to find the error.

NOTE

1. There may be many such writes, only one of which is writing bad data.

2. Chip breakpoints are set on only one processor. If another processor
without the same breakpoints corrupts the data, the breakpoint will not
trigger. Try setting the same chip breakpoints on all the processors to make
sure you find the real problem.

The above example had an easy solution – only use chip breakpoints – because
it involved driver-global data that is always at the same address. The following
is an example of the more difficult problem of having data that becomes corrupt
in a dynamically allocated (see kmem_alloc) data structure. In this example,
the address is an argument to the function that panicked and is different every
time the procedure is called.

■ Set breakpoints at all the instructions that write to the field of the structure that becomes corrupted. For example,

1. Search through your driver code for all the places where the particular structure field in question is assigned.

2. Find the corresponding assembly code locations for these sections in the debugger.

3. Set breakpoints at those instructions.

If none of the breakpoints trigger on a write of the bad data, yet the data
still becomes corrupted, double check all your structure assignments,
bcopy routine calls, and other places where the data could be implicitly
written.

Integrated Software Development Guide

Multi-Processor kdb Features

kdb allows you to control and perform all of the above commands on each online processor independently. To see which processors are currently online and in the debugger, use the ss debugger command. You can switch from one processor to another using the cpu command. Because each processor has its own execution stack, registers, and processor private data area, each processor's view of the system may be slightly different. It is helpful to backtrace all the processors to determine if your multiprocessor driver has a race condition (for example by seeing if the processors are sharing some data at a particular address). For more information on the kernel debugger, see Chapter 4, "Kernel Debugging" and the kdb(1) manual page in UNIX System V Release 4.0 *User's Reference Manual*.

kdb Macros and User-Defined Variables

Another kernel debugger feature is the ability to define and execute macros, which are essentially programs consisting of debugger commands. Macros are very handy for displaying complex data and can very easily improve readability over a command, such as the dl command, which just spews hexadecimal numbers. Using macros, you can iterate to follow linked-list data structures and call other macros to print embedded structures.

It is possible to define macros directly from the debugger prompt, but as there is no editing facility in the debugger, this is tedious. You may, however, define macros outside the debugger and load them into the debugger similar to the same way you load kernel symbols into the debugger, using the dbcmd. For more information, refer to the dbcmd(1) manual page in the UNIX System V Release 4.0 *User's Reference Manual*.

Two shell scripts accompany the kernel debugger to ease macro development. One compiles symbolic kernel debugger macros into pure macros, which you may then load into the debugger. This allows you to use structure field names instead of offsets, for example. The other creates symbolic macros from C header files, so you can create instant macros for data structures directly from their C definitions.

The debugger also supports user-defined variables, which are variables internal to the debugger only and not accessible by the system at all. They are especially useful in conjunction with macros for maintaining state information, and also for assigning a symbolic name to an otherwise unmemorable piece of data. For example, instead of trying to remember that the address D102E7B0 points to some driver data, you could assign it the name `badptr`.

Analyzing Crash Dumps with kdb

The kernel debugger is also available as a postmortem crash dump analyzer utility. For more information, see the `kcrash`(1M) manual page in the UNIX System V Release 4.0 *System Administrator's Reference Manual*. `kcrash` uses exactly the same commands and syntax, and provides much the same functionality as the kernel debugger, including macros, (except for execution control commands and breakpoints, among others.)

Converting XENIX System V/386 Drivers to UNIX System V/386 Release 4

This section describes how to convert XENIX System V/386 device drivers to work on Release 4.0 of UNIX System V/386.

In Release 4.0 of UNIX System V/386, the COFF and x.out 286 binaries are supported by the /bin/i286emul and /bin/x286emul user-level emulators. i286emul and x286emul trap system calls issued by an Intel286 program and either handle the system calls internally or perform necessary argument conversions before issuing an Intel386 system call. Therefore, the XENIX System V/386 device driver code that was used to support system calls from a 286 binary is no longer necessary.

> **NOTE** In Release 3.2 of UNIX System V/386, the kernel supports routines available for device drivers handling 286 system calls (for example, **ldtalloc**, **ldtfree**, **cvtoint**, and **cvtoaddr**) are provided as stubs to help facilitate compilation. Version 1.0 of UNIX System V/386 Release 4.0 provides these stubs, but they will be removed in a future version of UNIX System V/386 Release 4.0.

Programmers should keep the following information in mind when converting XENIX System V/386 device drivers to work on UNIX System V/386.

- All XENIX System V/386 include lines that use the form

      #include "../h/<file>"

  must be changed to

      #include "sys/<file>"

- The UNIX System V/386 Release 4.0 Software Generation System (SGS) does not define the M_I8086, M_I286, or M_I386 symbols. Instead, the i8086, i286, and i386 symbols can be used for native development.

- UNIX System V/386 Release 4.0 does not support the near and far keywords; thus, all references to near and far should be removed.

- UNIX System V/386 Release 4.0 replaces the b_paddr field with the b_un.b_addr field, which stores an address as a kernel virtual address. In XENIX System V/386, the b_paddr field of the buf structure stores an address as a physical address. All references to b_paddr should be changed to b_un.b_addr. Where appropriate, the ktop macro should be used to convert the address stored in b_un.b_addr to a physical address.

- In UNIX System V/386 Release 4.0, the `b_blkno` field of the `buf` structure stores block numbers in units of 512 bytes; while in XENIX System V/386, `b_blkno` stores blocks in units of 1024 bytes. Be sure to examine and convert all references of `b_blkno` to the units expected by your device driver.

- In UNIX System V/386 Release 4.0, all block devices must have a *xx*-`print` routine. The following example shows a *xx*`print` routine for a floppy diskette device driver:

```
flprint (dev, str)
dev_t dev;
char *str;
{
        cmm_err (CE_NOTE, "%s on floppy diskette unit %d,
        minor %d", str, unitbits (dev), minor(dev));
}
```

- In UNIX System V/386 Release 4.0, the user structure no longer contains the `u_cpu` field; instead, a new field in the user structure, `u_renv`, contains the same information as `u_cpu` in bits 16-23.

- UNIX System V/386 Release 4.0 calls the `open`, `close`, `read`, `write` and `ioctl` routines with the entire device number. XENIX System V/386 calls these routines with the minor device number. When converting XENIX System V/386 device drivers, be sure to mask off the major portion of the device number only if the minor number is desired. This can be done with the `minor` macro.

- After all device driver `halt` routines are called (those defined in the array `io_halt[]`), interrupts may be turned on again. In UNIX System V/386 Release 4.0, if the device driver is used to control hardware, its `halt` routine should ensure that no interrupt is pending.

- In UNIX System V/386 Release 4.0, the `disksort` routine uses the `b_sector` field of the `buf` structure to sort requests. In XENIX System V/386, `disksort` uses the `b_cylin` field of the `buf` structure to sort requests. By using the `b_sector` field (which is a 32-bit field) better resolution can be obtained over the `b_cylin` field (which is a 16-bit field).

- All XENIX System V/386 device driver references to the cmos.h include file should be changed to sys/cram.h.

- The use of the physio routine in UNIX System V/386 Release 4.0 is slightly different than in XENIX System V/386. In UNIX System V/386 Release 4.0, the read and write routines first call the phyck routine to validate the requested transfer; physio is then called with a pointer to the device driver's *xx*breakup routine. *xx*breakup then calls the system breakup routine (either dma_breakup or pio_breakup) with a pointer to the device driver's *xx*strategy routine. In XENIX System V/386, a driver's read and write routines call the physio routine with a pointer to the driver's strategy routine (possibly with B_TAPE set).

The following example illustrates the UNIX system calling convention. Please note that this code uses a Release 3.2 style driver interface, not the Release 4.0 interfaces defined in the Device Driver Interface/Driver-Kernel Interface (DDI/DKI).

```
flbreakup(bp)
struct buf          *bp;
{
int        flstrategy;

        dma_breakup(flstrategy, bp);
}

flread(dev)
dev_t dev;
{
        register int size;

        size = flblktosec(flsize[sizeindx(dev)]);
        /* size in sectors */
        if (physck(size, B_READ))
                physio(flbreakup, NULL, dev, B_READ);
}
```

■ UNIX System V/386 Release 4.0 does not support the XENIX System V/386 mapptov routine. Instead, the mappages routine should be used. The mappages interface is shown below:

```
mappages (begmapaddr, length, begphysaddr)
caddr_t begmapaddr;
int length;
paddr_t begphysaddr;
```

Often, XENIX system programmers did not use the **ktop** macro to convert virtual addresses to physical addresses (for example, in the first call to **copyio**, which expects a physical address) because in the XENIX system physical addresses are equivalent to virtual addresses. In UNIX System V/386 Release 4.0, programmers cannot make this assumption; they must use a physical or virtual address where needed, using the proper conversion macro, where appropriate.

Driver Programming Examples

This section presents examples that illustrate the techniques for programming and packaging device driver software discussed in the preceding sections of this chapter. Real examples provide the kind of information that explanation alone never adequately conveys. The following examples of device driver programming should help complete your understanding of how to develop installable driver software for UNIX System V Release 4.0 on the Intel386 processor and compatible architectures:

- The Trace Driver Implementation
- A Prototype Floppy Disk Driver
- A Multithreaded Hard Disk Driver

The Trace Driver Implementation

The trace driver is a pseudo-device that allows the UNIX System V kernel or other device drivers to report debugging information without using console printfs. The basic mechanism uses trsave calls to the trace driver to store short bursts of trace data in system character buffers (clists). These data items are retrieved from the clists and are reported to a user process by reading /dev/trace0. This driver uses some additional calls common to other drivers, specifically, sleep, wakeup, and the clist handling routines.

In addition to providing the driver source code, other files needed to actually compile and use the trace device are provided:

> Space.c – The DSP's memory allocation file
> trace.c – The driver source code
> trace.h – The driver header file
> trsav.c – A user program to read the trace device and redirect
>   output to a disk file
> trfmt.c – A user program to print the trace information

If you wish to key this source code into your system, you can make use of this trace driver to debug a driver that you are writing.

The following notes help explain some of the driver source (trace.c) code:

- Lines 1-121:
  Represent the inclusion of system header files and define the open, close, and ioctl functions. The code is self-explanatory.

- Lines 122-149:
  The trace driver read routine. The driver blocks (waits) until data is available via the sleep function call. The read will block until the Kernel or some other driver issues a call to trsave. When a trsave call is made, trace data is put into a clist and a wakeup is issued. The read awakens and transfers the trace data to the user process executing the read and releases the clist. Note the use of the internal trace driver address as the sleep event (&tr_p->tr_rcnt).

  Since trsave calls can be done at interrupt level by other drivers, and since the trsave function and the trread function both manipulate the queue of clists, the read function surrounds its manipulation of the clist structures with splN calls.

- lines 150-179:
  Data from other drivers is put into clists. Note that trsave accesses the system time counter (lbolt), which represents time in ticks (1/100th of a second on the 386 System) since the system was booted. This places a time stamp on the trace event.

Figure 7-1: Intel386 Trace Driver Program Example – `Space.c` File

```
1    /* Copyright (c) 1987 AT&T                                        */
2    /* Copyright (c) 1991 UNIX System Laboratories, Inc.              */
3    /*    All Rights Reserved                                         */
4    /*                                                                */
5    /*              Space.c file for 386unix trace driver.            */
6    /*                                                                */
7    /* The trace structure defined here provides storage on a         */
8    /* per-subdevice basis. That is, one trace structure will be      */
9    /* allocated for each sub-device. The variable TR_UNITS           */
10   /* is a #define created by the idconfig program. It represents    */
11   /* the number of trace subdevices for the trace driver. It is     */
12   /* derived from field 3 of the "System" entry for the device.     */
13   /*                                                                */
14   /* To locate TR_UNITS, this file should include config.h. This    */
15   /* header file is created by the reconfiguration process and      */
16   /* resides in the local directory of the reconfiguration          */
17   /* process (note use of double quotes around config.h).           */
18   /*                                                                */
19   #include "sys/types.h"
20   #include "sys/tty.h"
21   #include "sys/trace.h"
22   #include "config.h"
23
24   struct trace tr_data[TR_UNITS];
25   int tr_cnt=TR_UNITS;
```

Figure 7-2: Intel386 Trace Driver Program Example – Program Code

```
26   /*              Copyright (c) 1987 AT&T              */
27   /*  Copyright (c) 1991 UNIX System Laboratories, Inc.*/
28   /*              All Rights Reserved  */
29   /*            386unix Trace Driver
30    *
31    * The trace driver is a pseudo-device that allows
32    * the UNIX Kernel or other device drivers to report debugging
33    * information without the use of console printf's.
34    * The basic mechanism used is that calls to the trace driver
35    * (via trsave()) will store short bursts of trace data in system
36    * character buffers (clists). These data items are retrieved from the
37    * clists and are reported to a user process by reading /dev/trace.
38    *
39    */
40
41   #include "sys/types.h"
42   #include "sys/signal.h"
43   #include "sys/errno.h"
44   #include "sys/param.h"
45   #include "sys/dir.h"
46   #include "sys/user.h"
47   #include "sys/page.h"
48   #include "sys/systm.h"
49   #include "sys/tty.h"
50   #include "sys/sysmacros.h"
51   #include "sys/trace.h"
52
53   #define OPEN  01
54   #define TRSLEEP                             04
55   #define TRQMAX                              1024
56   #define NIL   0377
57   #define TRPRI (PZERO + 3)
58
59   extern int tr_cnt;
60   extern struct trace tr_data[ ];
61
62   tropen(dev)
63   {
64           int chan;
65           register struct trace *tr_p;
66
67           chan=minor(dev);
68           if (chan >= tr_cnt) {
69                   u.u_error = ENXIO;
```

(continued on next page)

Figure 7-2: Intel386 Trace Driver Program Example – Program Code (continued)

```
70                              return;
71                      }
72                      tr_p = &tr_data[chan];
73                      if (tr_p->tr_state&OPEN) {
74                              u.u_error = EACCES;
75                              return;
76                      }
77                      tr_p->tr_chno = NIL;
78                      tr_p->tr_state |= OPEN;
79      }
80
81      trioctl(dev, cmd, arg, mode)
82      {
83                      register struct trace *tr_p;
84                      int chan;
85
86                      chan=minor(dev);
87                      tr_p = &tr_data[chan];
88                      switch(cmd) {
89                      case TRACRCO:
90                              tr_p->tr_chbits |= (01<<(int)arg);
91                              return;
92                      case TRAGETC:
93                              arg = tr_p->tr_chbits;
94                              return;
95                      case TRASETC:
96                              tr_p->tr_chbits |= arg;
97                              return;
98                      case TRACLRC:
99                              tr_p->tr_chbits &= ~(short)arg;
100                             return;
101                     default:
102                             u.u_error = EINVAL;
103                             return;
104                     }
105     }
106
107     trclose(dev)
108     {
109                     register struct trace *tr_p;
110                     int chan;
111
112                     chan=minor(dev);
113                     tr_p = &tr_data[chan];
```

(continued on next page)

Figure 7-2: Intel386 Trace Driver Program Example – Program Code (continued)

```
114                     tr_p->tr_chbits = 0;
115                     tr_p->tr_ct = 0;
116                     tr_p->tr_chno = 0;
117                     tr_p->tr_rcnt = 0;
118                     while (getc(&tr_p->tr_outq)>=0);
119                     tr_p->tr_state = 0;
120     }
121
122     trread(dev)
123     {
124                     register struct trace *tr_p;
125                     int chan;
126
127                     chan=minor(dev);
128                     tr_p = &tr_data[chan];
129                     spl5();
130                     tr_p->tr_state |= TRSLEEP;
131                     while (tr_p->tr_rcnt == 0)
132                             sleep((caddr_t)&tr_p->tr_rcnt, TRPRI);
133                     spl0();
134                     while (u.u_count && tr_p->tr_rcnt) {
135                             if (tr_p->tr_chno == NIL) {
136                                     tr_p->tr_chno = getc(&tr_p->tr_outq);
137                                     tr_p->tr_ct = getc(&tr_p->tr_outq);
138                             }
139                             if (u.u_count < (tr_p->tr_ct + 2))
140                                     return;
141                             passc(tr_p->tr_chno);
142                             passc(tr_p->tr_ct);
143                             while (tr_p->tr_ct--)
144                                     passc(getc(&tr_p->tr_outq));
145                             tr_p->tr_chno = NIL;
146                             tr_p->tr_rcnt--;
147                     }
148     }
149
150     trsave(dev, chno, buf, ct)
151     int dev, chno, ct;
152     char *buf;
153     {
154
155                     register struct trace *tr_p;
156                     register int n;
157                     register char *cpt;
```

(continued on next page)

Figure 7-2: Intel386 Trace Driver Program Example – Program Code (continued)

```
158
159                 if (dev >= tr_cnt)
160                         return;
161             tr_p = &tr_data[dev];
162             ct &= 0377;
163             if ((tr_p->tr_chbits&(1<<chno)) == 0)
164                         return;
165             if ((tr_p->tr_outq.c_cc + ct + 2 + sizeof(lbolt)) >TRQMAX)
166                         return;
167             putc(chno, &tr_p->tr_outq);
168             putc(ct + sizeof(lbolt), &tr_p->tr_outq);
169             cpt = (char *)&lbolt;
170             for (n = 0; n < sizeof(lbolt); ++n)
171                         putc(*cpt++, &tr_p->tr_outq);
172             for (n=0;n<ct;n++)
173                         putc(buf[n], &tr_p->tr_outq);
174             tr_p->tr_rcnt++;
175             if (tr_p->tr_state&TRSLEEP) {
176                         tr_p->tr_state &= ~TRSLEEP;
177                         wakeup((caddr_t)&tr_p->tr_rcnt);
178             }
179     }
```

Figure 7-3: Intel386 Trace Driver Program Example – `trsav` Command

```
180  /*  Copyright (c) 1985 AT&T                                        */
181  /*  Copyright (c) 1991 UNIX System Laboratories, Inc.             */
182  /*     All Rights Reserved                                        */
184  /*                                                                */
185  /*                 trsav - save 386unix event traces             */
185  /*                                                                */
186  /*  usage: trsav mask device                                      */
187  /*                                                                */
188  /*  Invoking trsav opens the minor device of the trace driver specified */
189  /*  by "device," enables the channels specified by "mask" (octal), and  */
190  /*  then reads event records and writes them to its standard output     */
191  /*  (unformatted) until killed.  Bit 0 of mask enables channel zero,    */
192  /*  bit 1 channel one, and so forth                               */
193  /*                                                                */
194  /*  For example, to enable saving of trace channel 0 from minor   */
195  /*  device 0 of the trace driver and save the output in a file in */
196  /*  use the following command:  trsav 1 /dev/trace0 > /tmp/temp.file */
197  /*                                                                */
199  #include <stdio.h>
200  #include "sys/types.h"
201  #include "sys/tty.h"
202  #include "sys/trace.h"
203
204  char ev[512];
205  main(argc, argv)
206  char *argv[ ];
207  {
208          int fd, n, k, seqno, chbits;
209          if (argc != 3) {
210                  fprintf(stderr, "Incorrect number of arguments0);
211                  fprintf(stderr, "Usage: trsav mask device0);
212                  exit(1);
213          }
214          if ((fd = open(argv[2], 2)) < 0) {
215                  perror("trsav open:");
216                  exit(2);
217          }
218          setbuf(stdout, NULL);
219          sscanf(argv[1], "%6o", &chbits);
220          if ((k = ioctl(fd, TRASETC, chbits)) < 0) {
221                  perror("trsav ioctl:");
222                  exit(3);
223          }
224          seqno = 1;
```

(continued on next page)

Figure 7-3: Intel386 Trace Driver Program Example – trsav Command (continued)

```
225             for (;;) {
226                     if ((n = read(fd, ev, 512)) < 0) {
227                             perror("trsav read:");
228                             exit(4);
229                     }
230                     if (write(1, ev, n) < 0) {
231                             perror("trsav write:");
232                             exit(5);
233                     }
234             }
235     }
```

Figure 7-4: Intel386 Trace Driver Program Example – Header File

```
236  /*  Copyright (c) 1985 AT&T                                     */
237  /*  Copyright (c) 1991 UNIX System Laboratories, Inc.           */
238  /*    All Rights Reserved                                       */
239  /*                                                              */
240  /*               386unix trace.h driver header file.            */
241  /*                                                              */
242  /*  When the IOCTL defines are provided in a .h file,           */
243  /*  both the driver and any user programs that need the IOCTL   */
244  /*  values can work from the same set of #defines.              */
245  /*                                                              */
246  /*                                                              */
247  /* IOCTL defines */
248  #define TRAC                     ('T'<<8)
249  #define TRACMD                   (TRAC|8)
250  #define TRAERRS                  (TRAC|9)
251  #define TRARPT                   (TRAC|10)
252  #define TRASDEV                  (TRAC|11)
253  #define TRAATTACH                (TRAC|11)
254  #define TRADETACH                (TRAC|31)
255  #define TRAERRSET                (TRAC|32)
256  #define TRAERRGET                (TRAC|34)
257  #define TRAOPTS                  (TRAC|33)
258  #define TRAPCDOPTS               (TRAC|35)
259  #define TRACRCO                  (TRAC|16)
260  #define TRAGETC                  (TRAC|17)
261  #define TRASETC                  (TRAC|18)
262  #define TRACLRC                  (TRAC|19)
263  #define TRASTAT                  (TRAC|36)
264
265  /*
266  * Per trace structure
267  */
268  struct trace {
269               struct           clist tr_outq;
270               short            tr_state;
271               short            tr_chbits;
272               short            tr_rcnt;
273               unsigned char    tr_chno;
274               char             tr_ct;
275  };
```

Figure 7-5: Intel386 Trace Driver Program Example – `trfmt` Command

```
276  /*  Copyright (c) 1987 AT&T                                    */
277  /*  Copyright (c) 1991 UNIX System Laboratories, Inc.          */
278  /*    All Rights Reserved                                      */
279  /*                                                             */
280  /*              trfmt - print 386unix event traces            */
281  /*                                                             */
282  /*    Trfmt reads its standard input, which it assumes was     */
283  /*    generated by trsav, and prints it (formatted) to         */
284  /*    standard output until killed. Trfmt can read a file      */
285  /*    written by trsav or except pipe output as follows:       */
286  /*                                                             */
287
288  /*              trfmt < /tmp/temp.file           */
289  /*                       or                      */
290  /*              trsav mask device | trfmt        */
291  /*                                                             */
292  /*    This version will format and print predefined lines of text */
293  /*    for only a few types of typical driver traces: O is "open," */
294  /*    C is "close," etc. If you wish to use other trace points in  */
295  /*    your driver, define your own trace identifiers and add them  */
296  /*    to the case statement below.                             */
297  /*                                                             */
298  /*                                                             */
299
300  #include <stdio.h>
301
302  #define     MASK16            0177777
303  #define     SSTOL(x, y)       (((((long)x)<<16)|(((long)y)&MASK16)))
304
305  struct event {
306              unsigned short    lbolt1;
307              unsigned short    lbolt2;
308              unsigned short    seq;
309              unsigned char     typ;
310              unsigned char     dev;
311              unsigned short    wd1;
312              unsigned short    wd2;
313  } ev;
314  main(argc, argv)
315  char *argv[ ];
316  {
317              extern int optind;
318              int x, fd, k, n, seqno, con;
319              char *type;
```

(continued on next page)

Figure 7-5: Intel386 Trace Driver Program Example – **trfmt** Command (continued)

```
320             long time1;
321             char xxx;
322
323  setbuf(stdout,NULL);
324             seqno = 1;
325             for (;;) {
326                     x = getchar();
327                     n = getchar();
328                     if ((k=fread((char *)&ev, sizeof(xxx), n, stdin))< 0){
329                             perror();
330                             exit(3);
331                     }
332                     if (k == 0) {
333                             clearerr(stdin);
334                             sleep(1);
335                             continue;
336                     }
337                     if (ev.seq != seqno)
338                             printf("**%d event records lost**0,
339                                     ev.seq - seqno);
340                     seqno = ev.seq + 1;
341                     if (k == 12) {
342                             time1 = SSTOL(ev.lbolt2, ev.lbolt1);
343                             printf(" %10lu%6d", time1, ev.seq);
344                             switch((int)ev.typ){
345                             case 'W':
346                                     type = "write";
347                                     printf(" %-8s %2o%6o%6o", type, ev.dev,
348                                     ev.wd1, ev.wd2);
349                                     break;
350                             case 'R':
351                                     type = "read";
352                                     printf(" %-8s %2o%6o%6o", type, ev.dev,
353                                     ev.wd1, ev.wd2);
354                                     break;
355                             case 'O':
356                                     type = "open";
357                                     printf(" %-8s %2o%6o%6o", type, ev.dev,
358                                     ev.wd1, ev.wd2);
359                                     break;
360                             case 'C':
361                                     type = "close";
362                                     printf(" %-8s %2o%6o%6o", type, ev.dev,
363                                     ev.wd1, ev.wd2);
```

(continued on next page)

Figure 7-5: Intel386 Trace Driver Program Example – `trfmt` Command (continued)

```
364                          break;
365              case 'I':
366                      type = "ioctl";
367                      printf(" %-8s %2o%7o%7o",type,ev.dev,
368                      ev.wd1, ev.wd2);
369                      break;
370              /*
371              case '?':
372              * Place custom driver reports here.
373              * Drivers or Kernel functions which call
374              * trsave() can use any type definitions
375              * and/or print formats deemed appropriate.
376              */
377              default:
378                      printf(" %-10c%2o%7o%6o", ev.typ,
379                      ev.dev, ev.wd1, ev.wd2);
380              }
381              printf("\n");
382          }
383      }
384  }
```

A Prototype Floppy Disk Driver

The attached source code presents some selected portions of a prototype PC floppy disk device driver. This is not the entire source file, and some aspects of this driver are not representative of more general drivers. For example, since the floppy driver contains many data structures that are similar or identical to a companion hard disk driver, some common data structures are shared by the two device drivers, and the block major device number is used to access the floppy and hard disk portions of those data structures. Additionally, some of the function calls made inside the floppy driver are to functions that have been deleted for brevity or are functions defined in other source files. Despite these restrictions, the floppy device driver is a good example of a rather complex driver.

This driver also shows how a driver can implement both block and character (raw) device I/O. As a block device driver, the UNIX File System accesses the device through the driver `strategy` routine (see `PCf_strategy` on line 211). Since the floppy driver also acts as a character device, the "raw" I/O driver entry points (`PCf_read` on line 369 and `PCf_write` on line 390) are also provided. You can see that the `PCf_read` and `PCf_write` routines make use of `physio`, which, in turn, calls the floppy `strategy` routine.

Figure 7-6: Floppy Disk Driver Program Example

```
 1  /*  Copyright (c) 1987 AT&T
 2   *  Copyright (c) 1991 UNIX System Laboratories, Inc.
 3   *  All Rights Reserved
 4   *
 5   *  These procedures define portions of a Prototype PC floppy disk driver:
 6   *
 7   *  NOTE: THIS IS NOT THE COMPLETE DRIVER SOURCE CODE; ONLY REPRESENTATIVE
 8   *  SECTIONS ARE INCLUDED AS EXAMPLES.
 9   *
10   *  PCf_open:  Opens a unit by setting flags, initializing variables and structures
11   *  PCf_close: Closes a unit by resetting flags or flushing buffers or queues
12   *  PCf_strategy: Validates requests, queues it on device queue, tries to start I/O
13   *  PCf_intr:  Handles interrupts such as access completion, seek end, and others
14   *  PCf_read:  Performs raw read (uses physio routine)
15   *  PCf_write: Performs raw write (uses physio routine)
16   *  PCf_ioctl: Special functions - format, etc.
17   *
18   *  Internal routines:
19   *
20   *  PCf_init:  Internal routine to initialize device at boot time
21   *
22   *  (Other internal routines have been deleted for brevity)
23   */
24  #include <sys/signal.h>
25  #include <sys/types.h>
26  #include <sys/sysmacros.h>
27  #include <sys/param.h>
28  #include <sys/systm.h>
29  #include <sys/buf.h>
30  #include <sys/iobuf.h>
31  #include <sys/conf.h>
32  #include <sys/dir.h>
33  #include <sys/user.h>
34  #include <sys/errno.h>
35  #include <sys/elog.h>
36  #include <sys/open.h>
37  #include <sys/file.h>
38  #include "sys/PCf_disk.h"
39
40  #define FMAJ 1          /* MAJOR DEVICE-used in minor device macros */
41                          /* Floppy assigned Block Major=1; needed since  */
42                          /* floppy and wini(hard disk) share data structures */
43  char S5fraw_buf[512];
44  long Fmt_sec;
```

(continued on next page)

Figure 7-6: Floppy Disk Driver Program Example (continued)

```
45 long physaddr();
46 extern struct  PCd_dev   PCf_dev[];              /* device-data-structures */
47 extern struct  iobuf     PCf_tab[];              /* buffer header */
48 extern struct  PCd_dev   *PCf_i_tab[];           /* intr -> device mapping */
49 extern struct  buf       PCf_rbuf[];             /* raw buffer header */
50 extern struct  PCd_cdrt  PCdf[F_NDRTAB];     /* drtabs */
51 extern struct  fparm_tab ibmf512[];           /* floppy disk parameter table */
52 extern struct  PCd_minor PCd_major[][F_MAXMINOR]; /* major/minor number bit map */
53 extern int     fcntr_state;   /* current state of controller*/
54 extern int     activefloppy;  /* active floppy I/O */
55 extern long    ftransvector;  /* base address of memory transfer area */
56 extern int     ftrans_cnt;    /* # of sectors being transferred */
57 extern int     fsec_cnt;      /* total # sectors transferred so */
                                 /* far for a buf structure */
58 struct iotime   PCfstat[F_NPER_CONTR];
59 extern char     Flastdev[F_NPER_CONTR];
60 extern char     Ftryflop[F_NPER_CONTR];
61
62 PCf_tmout()
63 {
64        /* Stub for timeout routine */
65 }
66
67 /*
68  * PCf_init
69  *    Call at boot time to init device.
70  *    This routine sets up the mmu and intr tables for the ROM based
71  *    disk routines.  Recalibration will be done by boot strap loader.
72  */
73 PCf_init()
74 {
75        int i;
76        struct iobuf *iobuf;
77        char arg;
78
79        /* Initialize data structure constants */
80        for(i=0; i < F_NPER_CONTR; i++) {
81        PCf_dev[i].d_state.s_bufh = &PCf_tab[i];    /* buffer header */
82        PCf_dev[i].d_state.s_devcode = i;           /* device code */
83        PCf_dev[i].d_state.s_level = F_INTLVL;      /* local copy */
84        PCf_dev[i].d_state.s_active = IO_IDLE;      /*active flag */
85        fcntr_state = IO_IDLE;
86        iobuf = &PCf_tab[i];
87        iobuf->b_forw = (struct buf *)iobuf;        /* initialize buffer */
```

(continued on next page)

Driver Software Development

Figure 7-6: Floppy Disk Driver Program Example (continued)

```
88          iobuf->b_back = (struct buf *)iobuf;
89          iobuf->b_actf = (struct buf *)iobuf;        /* headers as in 310 */
90          iobuf->b_actl = (struct buf *)iobuf;
91          Flastdev[i] = F96DEV;
92          Ftryflop[0] = 0;
93          Ftryflop[1] = 0;
94          }
95          timeout(PCf_tmout,&arg,3*HZ);
96  }
97
98  /*
99   * PCf_open
100  *    Open a unit.
101  *
102  * Sets up given partition as open.
103  */
104 PCf_open(dev, flag, otyp)
105 dev_t dev;
106 int   flag;
107 unsigned otyp;
108 {
109         register struct PCd_dev *dd;
110         register struct iobuf*bufh;
111         register struct buf *bp;
112         register unsigned board;
113         unsigned unit, x;
114         static int firsttime = 1;
115         char *dp;
116         int i, fret;
117
118         if(getminor(dev) > F_MAXMINOR) {
119                         u.u_error = ENXIO;
120                         return;
121         }
122         /*
123          * if this is the first open ever then initialize
124          */
125         if (firsttime) {
126                         firsttime--;
127                         PCf_init();
128         }
129         board = UNIT(FMAJ,dev);
130         dd = &PCf_dev[board];
131         bufh = dd->d_state.s_bufh;
```

(continued on next page)

Figure 7-6: Floppy Disk Driver Program Example (continued)

```
132        if ((dd->d_state.s_flags & SF_OPEN) == 0) {
133                bp = &PCf_rbuf[UNIT(FMAJ,dev)];
134                x = spl5();
135                while (bp->b_flags&B_BUSY) {
136                    bp->b_flags |= B_WANTED;
137                    sleep((caddr_t)bp,PRIBIO);
138                }
139                bp->b_flags = B_BUSY | B_READ;
140                splx(x);
141                if ((dd->d_state.s_flags & SF_OPEN) == 0) {
142                    dd->d_state.s_flags = SF_OPEN | SF_READY | RESETING;
143                    bufh->b_active = IO_BUSY;
144                    u.u_error = PCf_sweep(dd, dev, flag, bp);
145                    bp->b_flags &= ~(B_BUSY | B_READ);
146                    if (bp->b_flags&B_WANTED)
147                        wakeup((caddr_t)bp);
148                    if (u.u_error == 0)
149                        dd->d_state.s_flags = SF_OPEN|SF_READY;
150                    else {
151                        dd->d_state.s_flags = 0;
152                        return;
153                    }
154                    for ( i=0; i<OTYPCNT; i++ )
155                        dd->d_state.s_popen[i] = 0;
156                    PCf_start(dd);
157                }
158        }
159        dp = &dd->d_state.s_popen[0];
160        if ( otyp == OTYP_LYR )
161                ++dp[OTYP_LYR];
162        else if ( otyp < OTYPCNT )
163                dp[otyp] |= (1 << PARTITION(FMAJ,dev));
164 }
165
166 /*
167  * PCf_close
168  * Close a unit.
169  *
170  * Called on last close of a partition; thus, "close" the partition.
171  * If this was last partition, make the unit closed & not-ready.
172  * In this case, next open will re-initialize.
173  */
174 PCf_close(dev, flag, otyp)
175 register dev_t dev;
```

(continued on next page)

Figure 7-6: Floppy Disk Driver Program Example (continued)

```
176 int flag;
177 unsigned otyp;
178 {
179     register struct PCd_dev          *dd;
180     extern          dev_t            rootdev;
181     struct buf                       *bufh;
182     char *dp;
183     int i;
184
185     if (dev == rootdev)
186             return;                  /* never close rootdev */
187     dd = &PCf_dev[UNIT(FMAJ,dev)];
188     /*
189      * Close the partition. If last partition, close the unit.
190      */
191     dp = &dd->d_state.s_popen[0];
192     if ( otyp == OTYP_LYR )
193             --dp[OTYP_LYR];
194     else if ( otyp < OTYPCNT )
195             dp[otyp] &= ~(1 << PARTITION(FMAJ,dev));
196     for ( i=0; i<OTYPCNT && dp[i]==0; i++ );
197     if ( i == OTYPCNT ) /* only close if closed for all types of open */
198             dd->d_state.s_flags = 0;
199 }
200
201 /*
202  * PCf_strategy
203  * Queue an I/O Request, and start it if not busy already.
204  *
205  * Check legality, and adjust for partitions.
206  * Reject request if unit is not-ready.
207  * Note: The partition-check algorithm insists that requests must not cross
208  *       a sector boundary.  If partition size is not a multiple of BSIZE,
209  *       the last few sectors in the partition are not accessible.
210  */
211 PCf_strategy(bp)
212 register struct buf *bp;
213 {
214     register struct PCd_dev     *dd;
215     register struct PCd_drtab *dr;
216     register struct PCd_cdrt    *cdr;
217     register struct PCd_part    *p;
218     struct    iobuf      *bufh;
219     struct    buf        *ap;
```

(continued on next page)

Integrated Software Development Guide

Figure 7-6: Floppy Disk Driver Program Example (continued)

```
220        daddr_t           secno;
221        unsigned          x;
222        char drive;
223
224        drive = UNIT(FMAJ,bp->b_dev);
225        dd = &PCf_dev[drive];
226        dr = &dd->d_drtab;
227        p = &dr->dr_part[PARTITION(FMAJ,bp->b_dev)];
228        PCfstat[drive].io_bcnt += btoc(bp->b_bcount);
229        bp->b_start = lbolt;
230        /*
231         * Figure "secno" from b_blkno. Check if ready,
232                  and see if fits in partition.
           * Adjust sector # for partition.
233         *
234         * Note: if format, b_blkno is already the correct sector number.
235         */
236        secno = bp->b_blkno;
237        if ( Ftryflop[drive] ) {
238            if ( secno >= p->p_nsec ||
239            (secno+(bp->b_bcount+dr->dr_secsiz-1)/dr->dr_secsiz) > p->p_nsec){
240                    if ( Flastdev[drive] == F96DEV ) {
241                            cdr = &PCdf[F48DEV];
242                            Flastdev[drive] = F48DEV;
243                    }
244                    else {
245                            cdr = &PCdf[F96DEV];
246
247                            Flastdev[drive] = F96DEV;
248                    }
249                    dr->dr_ncyl = cdr->cdr_ncyl;
250                    dr->dr_nhead = cdr->cdr_nhead;
251                    dr->dr_nsec = cdr->cdr_nsec;
252                    dr->dr_spc = dr->dr_nhead * dr->dr_nsec;
253                    dr->dr_secsiz = cdr->cdr_secsiz;
254                    dr->dr_part = cdr->cdr_part;
255                    p = &dr->dr_part[PARTITION(FMAJ,bp->b_dev)];
256            }
257        }
258        if (((dd->d_state.s_flags & SF_READY) == 0)
259            || (secno > p->p_nsec)) {
260                    /* not ready or off end */
261                    bp->b_flags |= B_ERROR;
262                    bp->b_error = ENXIO;       /* bad block */
```

(continued on next page)

Driver Software Development

Figure 7-6: Floppy Disk Driver Program Example (continued)

```
263                    x = spl5();
264                    biodone(bp);              /* return buffer */
265                    splx(x);
266                    return;
267              }
268         if (secno == p->p_nsec) {
269              if (bp->b_flags & B_READ)
270                   bp->b_resid = bp->b_bcount;
271              else {
272                   bp->b_error = ENXIO;
273                   bp->b_flags |= B_ERROR;
274              }
275              x = spl5();
276              biodone(bp);
277              splx(x);
278              return;
279         }
280         if ((secno+(bp->b_bcount+dr->dr_secsiz-1)/dr->dr_secsiz) > p->p_nsec) {
281              /* just asked to read last one. Send EOF */
282              bp->b_resid = bp->b_bcount;
283              x = spl5();
284              biodone(bp);
285              splx(x);
286              return;
287         }
288         secno += p->p_fsec;
289         bp->b_resid = p->p_fsec/dr->dr_spc;/* starting cylinder of slice */
290         /*
291          * Add request to queue, & (maybe) start it.
292          */
293         x = spl5();
294         bufh = dd->d_state.s_bufh;
295         ap = bufh->b_forw;
296         /*
297          * find right place to put this buffer in the list by cylinder number
298          */
299         while (ap != bufh->b_back) {
300              if (
                        (bp->b_blkno+(bp->b_resid*dr->dr_spc))
                   <
                        (ap->b_blkno+(ap->b_resid*dr->dr_spc))
                   )
301                   break;
302              else
```

(continued on next page)

Integrated Software Development Guide

Figure 7-6: Floppy Disk Driver Program Example (continued)

```
303                 ap = ap->av_forw;
304         }
305     if ( ap == (struct buf *)bufh ) {
306         /* no list currently exists - start one */
307         bufh->b_actf = bp;
308         bufh->b_forw = bp;
309         bufh->b_back = bp;
310         bp->av_forw = bp;
311         bp->av_back = bp;
312     }
313     else if ( ap == bufh->b_back ) {
314             if (
                    (bp->b_blkno+(bp->b_resid*dr->dr_spc))
                    <
                    (ap->b_blkno+(ap->b_resid*dr->dr_spc))
                    ) {
315             bp->av_back = ap->av_back;
316             ap->av_back->av_forw = bp;
317             bp->av_forw = ap;
318             ap->av_back = bp;
319             if ( bufh->b_forw == ap )
320                 bufh->b_forw = bp;
321             }
322         else {
323             ap->av_forw->av_back = bp;
324             bp->av_forw = ap->av_forw;
325             ap->av_forw = bp;
326             bp->av_back = ap;
327             bufh->b_back = bp;
328             }
329     }
330     else {
331         bp->av_back = ap->av_back;
332         ap->av_back->av_forw = bp;
333         bp->av_forw = ap;
334         ap->av_back = bp;
335         if ( bufh->b_forw == ap )
336         bufh->b_forw = bp;
337     }
338     if (fcntr_state == IO_IDLE)
339         PCf_start(dd,x);
340     splx(x);
341 }
342
```

(continued on next page)

Figure 7-6: Floppy Disk Driver Program Example (continued)

```
343 PCf_intr(dev)
344 int   dev;
345 {
346      extern char seek_status;
347      register struct PCd_dev *dd;
348      struct iobuf  *bufh;
349      unsigned int x;
350      static int save_state=0;
351
352      seek_status |= 0x80;
353      dd = &PCf_dev[activefloppy];
354      bufh = dd->d_state.s_bufh;/* get buf-header, too */
355      if(dd->d_state.s_active == IO_BUSY)
356           /* call BIOS Hardware Interrupt service routine */
357           flpy_hwintr();
358      else
359           save_state=dd->d_state.s_active;
360 }
361
362 /*
363  * PCf_read
364  * "Raw" read.  Use physio().
365  *
366  * Calls:
367  * PCf_strategy (indirectly, thru physio)
368  */
369 PCf_read(dev)
370 dev_t dev;
371 {
372      register struct PCd_dev *dd;
373      register struct PCd_drtab *dr;
374      register struct PCd_part *p;
375
376      dd = &PCf_dev[UNIT(FMAJ,dev)];
377      dr = &dd->d_drtab;
378      p = &dr->dr_part[PARTITION(FMAJ,dev)];
379      if ( physck(p->p_nsec,B_READ) )
380      physio(PCf_strategy, &PCf_rbuf[UNIT(FMAJ,dev)], dev, B_READ);
381 }
382
383 /*
384  * PCf_write
385  * "Raw" write.  Use physio().
386  *
```

(continued on next page)

Figure 7-6: Floppy Disk Driver Program Example (continued)

```
387  * Calls:
388  * PCf_strategy (indirectly, thru physio)
389  */
390  PCf_write(dev)
391  dev_t dev;
392  {
393       register struct PCd_dev *dd;
394       register struct PCd_drtab *dr;
395       register struct PCd_part *p;
396
397       dd = &PCf_dev[UNIT(FMAJ,dev)];
398       dr = &dd->d_drtab;
399       p = &dr->dr_part[PARTITION(FMAJ,dev)];
400       if ( physck(p->p_nsec,B_WRITE) )
401           physio(PCf_strategy, &PCf_rbuf[UNIT(FMAJ,dev)], dev, B_WRITE);
402  }
403
404  /*
405   * PCf_ioctl
406   */
407  PCf_ioctl(dev, cmd, cmdarg, flag)
408  dev_t dev;
409  int   cmd;
410  char *cmdarg;
411  int   flag;
412  {
413       register struct buf *bp;
414       register struct PCd_dev *dd;
415       register struct PCd_drtab *dr;
416       register struct PCd_part *p;
417       unsigned        x;
418       char j, k, *tblptr;
419       int *cmdint;
420
421       dd = &PCf_dev[UNIT(FMAJ,dev)];
422       dr = &dd->d_drtab;
423       bp = &PCf_rbuf[UNIT(FMAJ,dev)];
424       p = &dr->dr_part[PARTITION(FMAJ,dev)];
425
426       switch (cmd) {
427       case FMTFLPY:
428                       /* ....
429                       .... Specific ioctl code deleted
430                       ....
```

(continued on next page)

Figure 7-6: Floppy Disk Driver Program Example (continued)

```
431                         break;
432     case ....
433                         ....
434                         .... Specific ioctl code deleted
435                         ....
436                         break;*/
437     default:
438                     u.u_error = ENXIO;
439                     return;
440         }
441 }
442
```

Integrated Software Development Guide

Figure 7-7: Floppy Disk Driver Program Example

```
443
444 /*    Copyright (c) 1984 AT&T                                      */
445 /*    Copyright (c) 1991 UNIX System Laboratories, Inc.            */
446 /*    All Rights Reserved                                          */
447
448
449 /*    @(#)1.3.1.6*/
450
451 /*
452 * disk.h
453 */
454 #include "sys/open.h"
455
456 /***********************************************/
457 /********    MCS ADDED FOR VTOC STUFF*******/
458 #define MAXBAD99
459 #define UNIXOS99/* system indicator for UNIX partition */
460 #defineALTMGK10x55
461 #define ALTMGK20xAA
462
463 /*** DEFINES TO SUPPORT THE VARIABLE SIZE OF ALTERNATE TRACKS ***/
464 #define MAXUPTO40      64 /* Max # of bad tracks for disks of 40 MB or less   */
465 #define MAXOVER40      99 /* Max # of bad tracks for disks greater than 40 MB */
466 #define NSECINA40   85000 /* Number of sectors in a 40 MB disk */
467                           /* 83385 sectors for a 40MB with 981 cyl & 5 heads  */
468                           /* 83640 sectors for a 40MB with 820 cyl & 6 heads  */
469 /** FLAGS FOR PCW_io ROUTINES ***************/
470
471 #define B_FMTBAD    020000          /* must NOT overlap see buf.h! */
472 #define B_FMTTRK    030000          /* must NOT overlap see buf.h! */
473 #define B_RECOVR    060000          /* as above - used for recovery io */
474 #define B_FMTMSK    070000          /* mask for above */
475
476 /*** DEFINES FOR CASE STATEMENTS IN IOCTL ROUTINES ************/
477
478 #define RDDPARM                0
479 #define FMTBAD                 1
480 #define FMTVERIFY              2
481 #define FMTFLPY                3
482 #define RDPARTBL               4
483 #define WRPARTBL               5
484 #define WRALTBL                6
485 #define WRBOOT                 7
486 #define DOFMT                  8
```

(continued on next page)

Figure 7-7: Floppy Disk Driver Program Example (continued)

```
487 #define DOVRFY                 9
488 #define W_RECOVER              10
489 #define RDALTBL                11
490 #define FMTEND                 -1
491
492 /*** DEFINES FOR WINI VTOC ********************/
493
494 #define VSANITY                0xAA55
495 #define VVERSION               1
496 #define WSECSIZ                512
497 #define SEC_TRK                17
498 #define VNOWRITE               0
499 #define VNORM                  1
500
501 /***********************************************/
502 #define FDUALDEV    2           /* drtab of either 96 or 48tpi floppy */
503 #define F48DEV      4           /* drtab for 48tpi, 9 sec/trk     */
504 #define F96DEV      3           /* drtab for 96tpi, 15 sec/trk    */
505
506 #define F_NDRTAB    5
507 #define F_NPART     2
508 #define F_NPER_CONTR  2         /* number of drivers per controller */
509 #define F_MAXMINOR    F_NDRTAB*F_NPART*F_NPER_CONTR
510     /* maximum minor # for floppy driver */
511 #define W_NDRTAB    1
512 #define W_NPART     5
513 #define W_NPER_CONTR  2         /* number of drivers per controller */
514 #define W_MAXMINOR    F_MAXMINOR /* maximum minor # for wini driver */
515     /* assumes more or equal floppy devs.*/
516 #define FBADSPEED   0x0200    /* wrong floppy speed error return */
517 #define FCMDERROR   0x0100    /* wrong floppy type error return */
518 #define FWRPROT     0x0300    /* write protect floppy error return */
519 #define WBADTRK     0x0B00    /* Wini bad track */
520 #define WUNERR      0x1000    /* Wini unrecoverable error */
521 #define WADRMRK     0x0200    /* Wini address mark not found */
522 #define WECCERR     0x1100    /* corrected ecc error */
523 #define WSEEKERR    0x4000    /* seek error */
524 #define DOS_SLICE   4         /* Major Minor of E drive */
525 #define S5WRETRY    5         /* wini retry count */
526 #define S5FRETRY    25        /* floppy retry count */
527 #define F_INTLVL    6         /* floppy interrupt level */
528 #define W_INTLVL    5         /* wini  interrupt level */
529
530 structPCd_minor {
```

(continued on next page)

Figure 7-7: Floppy Disk Driver Program Example (continued)

```
531      unsigned partition: 4;                /* partition number */
532      unsigned drtab:4;                     /* alternate drtab's */
533      unsigned unit: 4;                     /* unit number */
534 };
535
536 #define      UNIT(maj,dev)       (PCd_major[maj][getminor(dev)].unit)
537      /* dev -> unit# map I003 */
538 #define      DRTAB(maj,dev)      (PCd_major[maj][getminor(dev)].drtab)
539      /* dev -> drtab-index map I003 */
540 #define      PARTITION(maj,dev)      (PCd_major[maj][getminor(dev)].partition)
541      /* dev -> partition-index map I003 */
542 #define S5D_MINOR(unum,drnum,panum)  ((unum<<8)|(drnum<<4)|panum)
543      /* I003 used in c215.c */
544
545
546 #define LHWORD(secnum)   (LOW(secnum),HIGH(secnum))
547      /* I004 c order problem fix for user ease in c215.c */
548 #define      LOW(x)   ((x)&0xFF)         /* "low" byte */
549 #define      HIGH(x)  (((x)>>8)&0xFF)    /* "high" byte */
550
551 /* Gives offset and selector for a pointer   dab */
552 #define SELECTOR(x)  ((unsigned int)(((long)(x))>>16))
553 #define OFFSET(x)  ((unsigned int)(((long)(x))&0xffff))
554
555 /* Whole disk partition table */
556 struct PCpart {
557      unsigned char bootind;
558      unsigned char bhead;
559      unsigned char b_psec;
560      unsigned char b_pcyl;
561      unsigned char sysind;
562      unsigned char ehead;
563      unsigned char e_psec;
564      unsigned char e_pcyl;
565      long relsec;
566      long numsec;
567 };
568
569 /*
570  * Winchester Drive Parameter Table
571  */
572
573 struct wparm_tab {
574      unsigned char cyls1;                  /* number of cylinders */
```

(continued on next page)

Figure 7-7: Floppy Disk Driver Program Example (continued)

```
575        unsigned char cyls2;
576        char heads;              /* number of heads */
577        char write2_cur;         /* reduced write current */
578        char write1_cur;
579        char precomp1;           /* write precompensation */
580        char precomp2;
581        char ecc_len;            /* max. ecc burst length */
582        char control_byte;       /* enable retry, enable ecc, 70 usec steps */
583        char timeout;            /* standard timeout */
584        char fmt_timeout;        /* timeout for format drive */
585        char drvdiag_timeout;    /* timeout for test drive ready */
586        long zzj;
587        };
588
589 /*
590  * Floppy Drive Parameter Table
591  */
592
593 struct fparm_tab {
594        char spec1;          /* first spec byte */
595        char spec2;          /* second spec byte */
596        char optim;          /* wait after opn til motor off */
597        char bps;            /* bytes per sector */
598        char gap;            /* gap length */
599        char dtl;            /* DTL */
600        char gapformat;      /* gap length for format */
601        char fillbyte;       /* fill byte for format */
602        char hdsettle;       /* head settle time */
603        char motorstime;     /* motor start time */
604        };
605
606 /*
607  * Floppy Drive Parameter Table
608  */
609
610 /*
611  * Partition structure.  One per floppy drtab[] entry.
612  */
613
614 struct        PCd_part {
615     ushort    p_flag;                    /* permission flag */
616     daddr_t   p_fsec;                    /* first sector */
617     daddr_t   p_nsec;                    /* number sectors */
618 };
```

(continued on next page)

Figure 7-7: Floppy Disk Driver Program Example (continued)

```
619
620 /*
621  * VTOC structure for hard disk - one per wini drtab[] entry.
622  */
623
624 struct PCd_vtoc {
625      ushort v_sanity;                   /* magic to verify vtoc */
626      ushort v_version;                  /* layout version */
627      char v_volume[8];                  /* volume name */
628      ushort v_sectorsz;                 /* sector size */
629      ushort v_nparts;                   /* number of partitions per volume */
630      unsigned long v_reserved[10];      /* free space */
631      struct PCd_part pw[W_NPART];       /* wini partitions */
632 };
633 /*
634  * Per-board configuration.
635  */
636
637 /*
638  * Per-board driver "dynamic" data.
639  */
640
641 struct     PCd_state {
642     char        s_active;       /* the state of the controller */
                                    /* - IDLE or BUSY */
643     char        s_state;        /* what just finished (for interrupt) */
644     char        s_level;        /* what interrupt level (for PCd_io) */
645     char        s_flags;        /* flags per spindle; see below */
646     char        s_popen[OTYPCNT]; /* bit[i] ==> partition[i] open */
647     char        s_init;         /* status from init operation */
648     char        s_devcode;      /* device-code */
649     struct iobuf *s_bufh;       /* -> buffer header */
650     unsigned    s_hcyl;         /* hold cylinder # during restore */
651 };
652
653 /*
654  * State Flags.
655  */
656
657 #define SF_OPEN           0x01    /* unit is open */
658 #define SF_READY          0x02    /* unit is ready; reset by media-change */
659 #define RESETING          0x04    /* unit is resetting */
660 #define STATUSCK          0x08    /* checking status of disk operation */
661 #define INDIRECT          0x10    /* indirect disk operation (data copied */
```

(continued on next page)

Figure 7-7: Floppy Disk Driver Program Example (continued)

```
                                /* to/from low memory) */
662
663
664  /*
665   * Macros to make things easier to read/code/maintain/etc...
666   */
667
668  #defineIO_OP(bp)((bp->b_flags&B_READ) ? DSK_READ :
669  ((bp->b_flags&B_FORMAT) ? DSK_FORMAT : DSK_WRITE))
670
671  /* ALTERNATE TRACKING TABLE */
672  struct alt_tbl {                        /* needs to be defined */
673      ushort    a_numbad; /* number of bad tracks                    */
674      ushort    a_fstalt; /* first track of alternate area           */
675      ushort    a_lstalt; /* last track of alternate area            */
676      ushort    a_maxbad; /* total number of allowable bad tracks    */
677      struct alt {
678      ushort          a_btrk;       /* packed bad track       */
679      ushort          a_gtrk;       /* packed good track      */
680      } a_alt[MAXBAD];
681  };
682
683  struct      PCd_drtab {
684      unsigned        dr_ncyl;    /* # cylinders */
685      char            dr_nhead;   /* # heads */
686      char            dr_nsec;    /* # sectors per track */
687      struct alt_tbl *dr_altptr;  /* alternate track table pointer */
688      /* if floppy, 0==FM, 1==MFM */
689      unsigned        dr_spc;     /* actual sectors/cylinder */
690      unsigned        dr_spb;     /* sectors/block */
691      unsigned        dr_secsiz;  /* sector-size (bytes) */
692      struct PCd_part *dr_part;   /* partition table pointer */
693  };
694
695  struct      PCd_cdrt {
696      unsigned        cdr_ncyl;   /* # cylinders */
697      char            cdr_nhead;  /* # heads */
698      char            cdr_nsec;   /* # sectors per track */
699      unsigned        cdr_secsiz; /* sector-size */
700      struct PCd_part *cdr_part;  /* partition table pointer */
701  };
702
703  /*
704   * Device-Data.  One per board (declared in driver).
```

(continued on next page)

Figure 7-7: Floppy Disk Driver Program Example (continued)

```
705  */
706
707 struct        PCd_dev {
708     struct   PCd_state        d_state;
709     struct   PCd_drtab        d_drtab;
710 };
711
712 /*
713  * Values of buffer-header b_active, used for mutual-exclusion of
714  * opens and other IO requests.
715  */
716
717 #define       IO_IDLE          0            /* idle -- anything goes */
718 #define       IO_OPEN_WAIT     1            /* open waiting */
719 #define       IO_BUSY          2            /* something going on */
720 #define       IOC_WAIT         3            /* waiting for the device */
721
722 /*
723  * Values of PCd_state.s_devcode, internal driver state.
724  */
725 #define FLPY       0x00    /* BIOS floppy disk selector */
726 #define WINI       0x00    /* BIOS winchester selector */
727
728 /*
729  * Floppy FM/MFM codes for drtab[*].nalt.
730  */
731
732 #define FLPY_FM     0      /* FM -- single density */
733 #define FLPY_MFM    1      /* MFM -- double density */
734
735 #define FDESCR      8      /* Floppy workspace descriptor */
736 #define WDESCR      9      /* Wini workspace descriptor */
737
738 #define NWCONFIG    32     /* number of Wini parameter tables */
739
740 /*
741 ********************************************************************************
742  * Parameters common to Fdisk.c and Format.c in regard to the whole disk
743  * partition table
744 ********************************************************************************
745  */
746
747 #define PARENT      4      /* Number of entries within the partition table */
748      /* maximum four entries on whole disk */
```

(continued on next page)

Figure 7-7: Floppy Disk Driver Program Example (continued)

```
749 #define UNIXOS      99      /* UNIX + DOS (merged) partition */
750 #define DOSOS       1       /* DOS only partition */
751 #define DOSOS16     4       /* DOS only partition (16-bit FAT) */
752 #define DOSDATA     86      /* DOS-DATA partition */
753 #define ACTIVE      128     /* Current partition is active */
                                /* (only 1 per drive is allowed) */
754 #define EMPTY       100     /* No partition (partition slot unoccupied) */
755 #define MIN_USIZ    19      /* Min size (cylinders) for UNIX partition */
756 #define MAXDOS      65535L   /* Max size (sectors) for a DOS partition */
757
758 /*********************************************************************/
```

Multithreading Hard Disk Drivers

Introduction

This section describes how the AT hard disk driver was multithreaded for UNIX System V Release 4 Multi-Processor for Intel Processors. It contains multiprocessor-specific information on how the AT driver splits the handling of I/O requests.

As part of the UNIX operating system kernel, the hard disk driver splits the handling of I/O requests. The multithreaded hard disk driver must allow some processors to queue disk requests while the other processors are busy processing requests at the front of the queue. To this end, three locks have been implemented to multithread the AT hard disk driver. These are the hardware lock, the queue lock, and the active lock, which are described in this chapter, "Multithreading Hard Disk Drivers."

Like the rest of this manual, it is assumed that the reader has user-level experience with the UNIX system, some general knowledge of UNIX system concepts, and the ability to write sophisticated C language programs.

Handling I/O Requests

The AT hard disk driver splits the handling of I/O requests into two parts: queuing a request, and processing the request on the front of the queue. A multithreaded hard disk driver allows some processors to queue disk requests while others are busy processing requests on the front of the queue. This minimizes the amount of processor time wasted waiting for ownership of the hard disk controller.

With only one hard disk controller it is not possible for more than one processor to perform physical I/O transfers at the same time. Commands to the disk controller consist of sequences of I/O reads and writes (inb and outb instructions) that the multithreaded driver serializes to ensure controller integrity. The multithreaded driver uses a single lock to protect the controller. This controller lock serializes programming the controller and maintains the data structures associated with the controller.

Because each request queue requires one lock, one processor can queue a request while another deals with the controller, although two processors can not queue requests on the same queue at exactly the same time. Queuing requests insures that no processor waits for the queue lock for a long time.

Multithreading the Hard Disk Driver

Each AT driver supports one controller and two drives, with one lock proving sufficient for all the hardware. Because each drive owns its own queue, each drive can own its own lock. However, this method does not prove optimal for the driver mechanism. The driver maintains many other data structures parallel with the request queue, some of which are not drive-specific.

There is a high degree of recursion within the driver. The hdstrategy routine is an entry point from the kernel for block device transfers. It is also called indirectly from the hdread, hdwrite, hdopen, and hdioctl routines. The hdstrategy routine calls _hdstrategy, which takes an extra argument indicating whether or not it should perform locking. Calls from within the driver were changed to call _hdstrategy, with the new argument indicating that it should not perform locking.

The first step is to find all the places that touch the hardware disk controller directly using inbs and outbs. Although ownership of the hardware lock is necessary during these sections, it is not necessarily sufficient. Sequences of controller commands must be serialized, as well as consistent.

The scope of the lock was expanded bottom-up to cover all the code that assumed consistency in the uniprocessor driver. For example, acquiring the lock just before calling ATout (which calls inb directly) is certainly possible, but it is not early enough to ensure consistency within the driver. hdintr reads the controller status using ATstatus and then decides what action is necessary. Eventually, it may call ATout, but doing so is not correct unless the state of the controller is what hdintr expects it to be—hence hdintr must hold the hardware lock for the duration.

Most of the driver must execute while holding the hardware lock, simply to ensure consistency. It is possible to minimize the driver's scope by splitting the locking of pieces of structures. Data structures are treated as single objects, always using the same lock for all the elements. Some benefit is gained by investigating the locking requirements of each structure element, including whether it is worthwhile to use shared and exclusive locks instead of purely exclusive locks, and using the appropriate lock in each case.

Once the hardware lock has stabilized, the scope of the hard disk queue lock can be investigated top-down. The queue lock must be held during direct manipulation of the queue (hdutab[].b_actf). It is also convenient to use the queue lock for other data structures modified at the same time, such as hddrvinfo[].hd_latest and all of hdstat[].

However, several data structures (hddrvinfo[].hd_geom, hdpartinfo[][], and hdwholedisk[][]) are used in the scopes of both hardware and queue locks. It is important to determine which lock should protect the data structures. Using the queue lock would require much of the controller programming and bad block mapping to hold the queue lock, contrary to the goal of simultaneous queuing and request processing. Using the hardware lock necessitates acquiring the hardware lock while queuing a request. Because the hardware lock can be held for relatively long periods, this would effectively eliminate most of the advantages of multithreading the driver. By determining when the data structures changed, and what the effects would be of only partially locking them, it was found that they were modified in only a few well-defined and rarely-used places (opens and ioctls for instance). In these cases, it was acceptable to degrade driver performance in favor of streamlining the heavily-used paths (hdstrategy). Therefore, both locks are used to lock these data structures, creating a shared and exclusive lock out of two separate locks. In the normal case, the information is only read and not modified, while holding either lock is sufficient to protect data from changing. In rare cases, when information is actually modified, both locks are acquired and entirely lock all other processors out of the driver while changing these widely-used data structures.

It is necessary to acquire the hardware lock in hdstrategy before checking hdcst.hd_active and calling hdstart. By that point, the request has been queued and the queue lock has been released, although the processor still must lock the hardware lock to check if it has to call hdstart to initiate the transfer. Because the hardware lock can be held for long periods, spinning on that lock in hdstrategy would waste large quantities of processor time. To remedy this, a third lock, the active lock, was invented to protect just that one variable in the driver. Therefore, after the request has been queued, hdstrategy needs to acquire only a low-contention lock to see if it must call hdstart; if it does, only then does it acquire the hardware lock.

Summary of Locking Strategy

Only three locks were used to multithread the AT driver. This minimal number of locks was used for several reasons.

- There was no appreciable gain from using more than three locks. More processors could have been executing more of the code simultaneously while the amount of code protected by each lock would have been extremely minimal.

- Retaining a tracking mechanism for locks in a driver of such complexity would have been extremely difficult. Locking hierarchies must be adhered to. Switching frequently from the protection of one lock to another for the sole purpose of reading one variable would degrade the driver's performance.

- Locking cannot be separated from the structure of the driver code and since so much of the driver assumes consistency with other parts called much later on, large-scope locks are necessary to preserve the correct behavior.

- Absorbing lightly-used variables into the rules for a lock that is already held during other operations is more convenient than creating a new lock.

The Design

The following table lists the three types of locks and which functions they lock. Note that all three locks are exclusive, meaning that the lock can be acquired and held by only one process at a time.

Lock	Type	Functions Locked
hd_lck	spin, exclusive	controller and associated data
hdq_lck	spin, exclusive	queues and convenient data
hda_lck	spin, exclusive	controller-active flag

The following table lists data objects the hard disk driver uses and which lock protects them.

Type	Data Structure	Locks
char*	hdb_msg[]	(static)
struct hdbadhnd	hdbad	hd_lck
char *	bbh_trkmap[]	hd_lck
char *	bth_trkmap[]	hd_lck
unsigned int	prev_mapsize	hd_lck
struct hdcstat	hdcst	(split)
	.hd active	hda_lck
	(all else)	hd_lck
struct hddrvinfo	hddrvinfo[]	(split)
	.hd_latest	hdq_lck
	.hd_geom	hd_lck + hdq_lck
	(all else)	hd_clk
struct partition	hdpartinfo[][]	hd_lck + hdq_lck
struct partition	hdwholedisk[]	hd_lck + hdq_lck
char	hd_closing[][]	hd_lck
struct alt_info	hdaltinfo[]i	hd_lck
struct iotime	hdstat[]	hdq_lck
struct iobuf	hdutab[]	(split)
	actf	hdq_lck
	(all else)	hdq_lck
char *	ATerrmsg[]	(static)
char	itable[]	hd_lck
int	fmtvfyreq	hdq_lck
char	fmtvfywait	hdq_lck
time_t	vfytime	hd_lck
unsigned short	vfystatus	hd_lck
int	hddebug	none
struct buf	rdalts_buf[]	hd_lck
int	writefault	hd_lck
int	hddevlfag	none
struct cur_req	cur_req	hd_lck
int	Hd_timeout	hd_lck
struct AT_cmd	AT_cmd	hd_lck

The following table lists the routines the hard disk driver uses and designates which locks are already held when the routine is called and/or which locks are acquired from within the routine.

Function	Notes	Locks Held When Called	Locks Acquired
hdinit		(entry point)	hd_lck, hdq_lck
hdsetcont	hardware	hd_lck, hdq_lck	none
hdgetblock	new	hd_lck, hdq_lck	
hdputblock		none	none
hdputblock	new	hd_lck, hdq_lck	none
rdagetblocks		hd_lck, hdq_lck	none
rdarerelease		hd_lck, hdq_lck	none
hdopen		(entry point)	hd_lck, hdg_lck
hdclose		(entry point)	hd_lck, hdq_lck
hdstrategy		(entry point)	hd_lck, hdq_lck
_hdstrategy	new	hd_lck? hdq_lck?	hd_lck? hdq_lck? hda_lck
hdbreakup		none	none
hdread	(entry point)	none	
hdwrite		(entry point)	none
hdstart		hd_lck	hdq_lck? hda_lck
hdio		hd_lck	none
hdxfer		hd_lck	hd_lck, hdq_lck
hdintr	hardware	(entry point)	hd_lck, hdq_lck [
hdioctl		(entry point)	hd_lck, hdq_lck, hda_lck
hddone		hd_lck	none
hderror		hd_lck	none
hderrmsg		hd_lck	none
hdprint		(entry point)	none
ATdocmd	hardware	hd_lck	none
ATiocmd	hardware	hd_lck	none
ATxcmd	hardware	hd_lck	none
ATfmtcmd	hardware	hd_lck	none
ATcmd	hardware	hd_lck	none
ATstatus	hardware	hd_lck	none
ATwait	hardware	hd_lck	none

Function	Notes	Locks Held When Called	Locks Acquired
ATout	hardware	hd_lck	none
ATin	hardware	hd_lck	none
hdb_inunix		hd_lck	none
hdb_sacred		hd_lck	none
hdb_nospar		hd_lck	none
hdb_verify		hd_lck	none
hdb_b2vfy		hd_lck	none
hdb_retry		hd_lck	none
hdb_contvfy		hd_lck	none
hdb_mapblk		hd_lck	none
hdb_blktyp		hd_lck	none
hdb_updtbl		hd_lck	none
hdb_wrttbl		hd_lck	none
hdb_cleanup		hd_lck	none
hdb_wrtsrc		hd_lck	none
hdb_mapbad		hd_lck	none
hdb_err		hd_lck	none
hdb_0mrgflg		hd_lck	none
hdb_0badflg		hd_lck	none
hdsize		(entry point)	hd_lck, hdq_lck
hdtimeout	hardware	hd_lck	hd_lck

Use of Locks

In general use, the hard disk queue lock exclusively protects only the drive queues, one queue-sorting variable, the array of statistics, and (shared) drive and partition information. Enqueuing and dequeuing disk requests is a relatively quick procedure. Most of this locking is done in `_hdstrategy`, `hdstart`, `hdintr`, and `hddone`. In unusual use, the queue lock protects (exclusively, in conjunction with the hardware lock) the drive and partition information, and some state variables.

In general use, the hard disk hardware lock protects (exclusively) all of the bad-block mapping data structures, controller status structure, miscellaneous variables, and (shared) drive and partition information. In unusual use, the hardware lock exclusively protects, in conjunction with the queue lock, the drive and partition information.

The active lock (exclusively) protects only one variable.

There are a few places in the driver where strict locking would have eliminated much of the parallel execution within the driver. These are, for example, `hdread` and `hdwrite`, both of which examine a partition table and pass the data to `physio` routines, which eventually call `hdstrategy`. Technically, either the hardware or the queue lock should be held. However, this would cause hierarchy problems and severely limit parallelism and throughput. Because the partition table information rarely changes, the lock is not held at all until inside `hdstrategy`.

The Results

Stress tests indicate that all three locks have moderate to low contention, and that `hda_lck` and `hdq_lck` execute short to average spin times. (Processors do not waste time spinning on the lock when another processor is holding it.) The hardware lock `hd_lck` has high spin times but extremely low contention.

These results are exactly as desired. The disk queue grows long, but more processor time is available to run other processors instead of being wasted spinning on hard disk locks. And under disk-intensive loads, the hard disk controller is busy nearly 100% of the time; there are no periods during which there are requests queued and the disk is idle.

Hard Disk Driver Program Example

The following figure shows how a hard disk driver can be multithreaded:

Figure 7-8: Multithreaded Hard Disk Driver Program Example

```
#define HD_LOCK_ID 0x54      /*       random id number */
/*
 * hd_lck locks the hard disk hardware and bad block mapping variables
 */
mutex_t hd_lck;
lockinfo_t hd_lkinfo;
#define hd_lock(spxlfunc)            mutex_lock(&hd_lck, L_EXCL, splfunc)
#define hd_unlock(splev)             mutex_unxlock(&hd_lck, splev)
#define hd_is_mine()                       mutex_is_mine(&hd_lck, L_EXCL)
/*
 * hdq_lck locks the hard disk queue
 */
mutex_t hdq_lck;
Lockinfo_t hdq_lkinfo;
#define hdq_lock(splfunc)            mutex_lock(&hdq_lck, L_EXCL, splfunc)
#define hdq_unlock(splev)            mutex_unlock(hdq_lck, splev)
#define hdq_is_mine()                      mutex_is_mine(&hdq_lck, L_EXCL)
/*
 * both hd_lck and hdq_lck lock hddrvinfo, hdpartinfo, and hdwholedisk; that
 * is, both must be held in order to change it, so holding either lock
 * guarantees consistency
 *
 * hda_lck locks the hard-disk active flag (hdcst.hd_active)
 */
mutex_t hdq_lck:

lockinfo_t hdq_lkinfo;
/*
 * Process interrupts.  There are three cases:
 *      1) Restore has completed.  Retry if there was an error, otherwise do
 *          the transfer.
 *      2) Format has completed.  No error reporting is supported.
 *      3) Read/write has completed.  Check for errors and retry command if
 *          error wasn't write fault.  Issue a notice if an error was corrected
 *          by the ECC algorithm, which may indicate that that sector should be
 *          or a command involving bad block mapping, or if we're finished call
 *          hddone.
 */
```

(continued on next page)

Figure 7-8: Multithreaded Hard Disk Driver Program Example (continued)

```
hdintr()
{
        register struct buf *bp;
        register struct hddrvinfo *hdi;
        int   statlow, stathigh, status;
        int   errval, altstatus, errcnt;
        int   track, i;
        daddr_t block;
        ushort  curdrv, blktyp;

#if
        (void) hd_lock(splnull);
#endif
        bp = hdutab[hdcst.hd_curdrv].b_actf;
        hdi = &hddrvinfo[hdcst.hd_curdrv];
        status = ATstatus(hdcst.hd_curdrv);

        if (!(hdi->hd_state & (HD_DO_RST|HD_DO_FMT|HD_DO_VFY))) {
                /* Read or write command has completed */

                                .....
                                .....
                                .....

        }
        else if (hdi->hd_state & HD_DO_VFY)  /* Verify command completed */
        {
                drv_getparm(LBOLT, &vfytime);
                if (status & ERROR)
                        vfystatus = inb(HD0+HD_ERROR);
                hdi->hd_state &= ~HD_DO_VFY;
                wakeup(itable);
        }
        else if (hdi->hd_state & HD_DO_RST)  /* Restore command has completed */
        {
                if (status & ERROR)
                        hderror(bp, RETRY);
                else
                {
                        hdi->hd_state &= ~HD_DO_RST;
                        hdxfer(bp);
                }
        }
        else /* hdi->hd_state & HD_DO_FMT */  /* Format command completed */
        {
```

(continued on next page)

Integrated Software Development Guide

Figure 7-8: Multithreaded Hard Disk Driver Program Example (continued)

```
                        hdi->hd_state &= ~HD_DO_FMT;
                        wakeup(itable);
        }
#if
        hd_unlock(NULLSPL);
#endif

        return(0);
}
/*
 * Queue an I/O request, and start if not busy.
 */
hdstrategy(bp)
struct buf *bp;
{
        return _hdstrategy(bp, 1);
}

_hdstrategy(bp, do_locking)
register struct buf *bp;
int do_locking;
/*
 * do_locking tells whether to grab & release hdq_lck and hd_lck when their
 * times come (we could be called with or without them held, and this tells
 * which).
 */
{
        register struct partition *hdp;
        register struct hddrvinfo *hdi;
        register struct iotime *hdit;
        register struct buf *curbp, *nextbp;
        struct iobuf *hdu;
        int oldpri;
        unsigned unit;

#if
        if (do_locking)
                oldpri = hdq_lock(spl5);
#endif
        /* If a format is waiting, block all other I/O until it's done */
        while (fmtvfyreq)
                sleep((char *)&fmtvfyreq, PRIBIO);

        /* If the requested count to be transferred is zero, we're done. */
```

(continued on next page)

Figure 7-8: Multithreaded Hard Disk Driver Program Example (continued)

```
            if (bp->b_bcount == 0) {
#if
                    if (do_locking)
                            hdq_unlock(oldpri);
#endif
                    iodone(bp);
                    return(0);
            } .

            unit = UNIT(bp->b_edev);
            hdi = &hddrvinfo[unit];
            if (ISABSDEV(bp->b_edev))
                    hdp = &hdwholedisk[unit];
            else
                    hdp = &hdpartinfo[unit][PARTITION(bp->b_edev)];
            /*
             * Check if partition is valid, and for trying to write to a
             * read-only partition if not root.
             */
            if (!(hdp->p_flag & V_VALID) ||
                !(bp->b_flags & B_READ) && (hdp->p_flag & V_RONLY) && drv_priv(u.u_cred)) {
#if
                    if (do_locking)
                            hdq_unlock(oldpri);
#endif
                    bp->b_flags |= B_ERROR;
                    bp->b_error = ENXIO;
                    iodone(bp);
                    return(0);
            }

            if (bp->b_blkno < 0) {
#if
                    if (do_locking)
                            hdq_unlock(oldpri);
#endif
                    bp->b_flags |= B_ERROR;
                    bp->b_error = ENXIO;
                    iodone(bp);
                    return(0);
            }

            if (bp->b_blkno >= hdp->p_size) {
                    if (bp->b_blkno > hdp->p_size || !(bp->b_flags & B_READ)) {
```

(continued on next page)

Figure 7-8: Multithreaded Hard Disk Driver Program Example (continued)

```
                        /* if request is off the end or we're not reading */
                        bp->b_flags |= B_ERROR;
                        bp->b_error = ENXIO;
                }
#if
                if (do_locking)
                        hdq_unlock(oldpri);
#endif
                /* reading last block is allowed: it indicates EOF */
                bp->b_resid = bp->b_bcount;
                iodone(bp);
                return(0);
        }

        /* must not exceed maximum transfer allowed by the controller */
        if (bp->b_bcount > MAXXFER << SCTRSHFT ) {
#if
                if (do_locking)
                        hdq_unlock(oldpri);
#endif
                bp->b_flags |= B_ERROR;
                bp->b_error = ENXIO;
                iodone(bp);
                return(0);
        }
        /* Calculate the physical cylinder number of the request. */
         * ((ushort *)&bp->cylin) = (bp->b_blkno + hdp->p_start) /
            (daddr_t)(hdi->hd_nsecs * hdi->hd_nhds);
        bp->av_forw = NULL;
        drv_getparm(LBOLT, &bp->b_start);  /* time in 1/60 sec. since boot */
        /*
         * Update I/O count statistics
         */
        hdit = &hdstat[unit];
        hdit->io_cnt++;
        hdit->io_bcnt += (bp->b_bcount + NBPSCTR - 1) >> SCTRSHFT;

        /* Put the buffer onto the queue using an elevator algorithm. */
        hdu = &hdutab[unit];
        if (hdu->b_actf == NULL)
                hdu->b_actf = bp;
        else if (hdi->hd_latest &&
                        (ushort)hdi->hd_latest->cylin == (ushort)bp->cylin) {
```

(continued on next page)

Figure 7-8: Multithreaded Hard Disk Driver Program Example (continued)

```
                        bp->av_forw = hdi->hd_latest->av_forw;
                        hdi->hd_latest->av_forw = bp;
                } else {
                        int       s1, s2;

                        for (curbp = hdu->b_actf; nextbp=curbp->av_forw; curbp = nextbp) {
                                if ((s1 = (ushort)curbp->cylin - (ushort)bp->cylin)<0)
                                        s1 = -s1;
                                if ((s2 = (ushort)curbp->cylin- (ushort)nextbp->cylin)<0)
                                        s2 = -s2;
                                if (s1 < s2)
                                        break;
                        }
                        bp->av_forw = nextbp;
                        curbp->av_forw = bp;
                }
                hdi->hd_latest = bp;
#if
                if (do_locking)
                        hdq_unlock(NULLSPL);
                /*
                 * If no requests are in progress, start this one.
                 */
                hda_lock();
                if (hdcst.hd_active == 0) {
                        hdcst.hd_active = 1;
                        hda_unlock();
                        if (do_locking)
                                (void) hd_lock(splnull);
                        hdstart(do_locking);
                        if (do_locking)
                                hd_unlock(NULLSPL);
                } else
                        hda_unlock();
                if (do_locking)
                        splx(oldpri);
#endif
                return(0);
}
```

8 Application Software Packaging

8. APPLICATION SOFTWARE PACKAGING

Sidebar: **8. APPLICATION SOFTWARE PACKAGING**

Package Installation Case Studies

An Overview of Software Packaging

This chapter describes how to package software that will be installed on a computer running UNIX System V Release 4.0 for the Intel386 and compatible architectures. The approach to packaging in such an environment differs from approach used previously. Pre-UNIX System V Release 4.0 packages deliver information to the system through script actions, but a UNIX System V Release 4.0 package for the Intel386 and compatible architectures does this through package information files. A packaging tool, the pkgmk command, is provided to help automate package creation. It gathers the components of a package on the development machine, copies them onto the installation medium, and places them into a structure that pkgadd recognizes.

This chapter also describes the installation tool, the pkgadd command, which copies the package from the installation medium onto a system and performs system housekeeping routines that concern the package. This tool is primarily for the installer but is described here to give you some background on the environment into which your packages will be placed and to help you test-install your packages.

The next two sections describe what a package consists of and gives an overview of the structural life cycle of a package (how its structure on your development machine relates to its structure on the installation medium and on the installation machine).

The remaining sections familiarize you with all of the tools, files, and scripts involved in creating a package, provide suggestions for how to approach software packaging, and describe some specific procedures. At the end of this chapter, you should study the section entitled ''Package Installation Case Studies'' , which provides case studies using the tools and techniques described in this chapter.

All of the commands, files, and functions mentioned in this chapter have manual pages in the *Administrator's Reference Manual*.

Contents of a Package

A software package is made up of a group of components that together create the software. These components naturally include the executables that compose the software, but they also include at least two information files and can optionally include other information files and scripts.

A package's contents fall into three categories:

- required information files(i.e., the pkginfo file, the prototype file, package objects)

- optional package information files (i.e., the compver file, the depend file, the space file, and the copyright file). The prototype file is not part of the package, but is used to create it.

- optional packaging scripts (i.e., the request script, the class action script, and the procedure script)

The Structural Life Cycle of a Package

The material covered in this chapter talks about package object pathnames. While reading, keep in mind that a package object resides in three places while being packaged and installed. To help you avoid confusion, consider which of the three possible locations are being discussed:

- On a development machine

  Packages originate on a development machine. They can be in the same directory structure on your machine as they will be placed on the installation machine. Or pkgmk can locate components on the development machine and give them different pathnames on the installation machine.

- On the installation media

  When pkgmk copies the package components from the development machine to the installation medium, it places them into the structure you have defined in your prototype file and a format that pkgadd recognizes.

■ On the installation machine

pkgadd copies a package from the installation medium and places it in the structure defined in your pkgmap file. Package objects can be defined as relocatable, meaning the installer can define the actual location of these package objects on the installation machine during installation. Objects with fixed locations are copied to their predefined path.

The Packaging Tools

The packaging tools are provided to automate package creation and to remove the burden of packaging from the developer. There are three packaging tools: the pkgmk command, the pkgtrans command, and the pkgproto command. Each of these commands is described in the following text and has a manual page in the *Administrator's Reference Manual*.

The pkgmk Command

This command takes all of the package objects residing on the development machine, and copies them onto removable media or a directory structure in a hard disk. You are not required to know the details of the fixed directory structure since pkgmk takes care of the formatting.

Files can be unstructured on the development machine and pkgmk will structure them correctly on the medium based on information supplied in the prototype file. The installation medium onto which a package is formatted can be what is typically thought of as a medium (a diskette, for example) or it can be a directory on a machine.

pkgmk requires the presence of two information files on the development machine, the prototype and the pkginfo file (other package information files may be present). These will be discussed in the "Package Information Files" section in this chapter.

pkgmk creates the pkgmap file, which is the package contents file on the installation medium, by processing the prototype file and then adding three fields to each entry.

pkgmk follows these steps when processing a package:

1. Processes all of the command lines in the input prototype file.

2. Copies the objects of a package onto the installation medium, using the prototype file as a listing of contents.

3. Puts the package objects into the proper format.

4. Divides a package into pieces and distributes those pieces on multiple volumes, if necessary.

5. Creates the pkgmap file. It is similar to the prototype file except that all command lines are processed, and the volno, size, cksum, and modtime fields are added to each entry.

The pkgtrans Command

This command provides a way to translate the file system to a data stream format for floppy diskettes or cartridge tape. When packages are created with pkgmk the default format for the package is a file system format. It can make the following translations:

- a fixed directory structure to a datastream
- a datastream to a fixed directory structure

Note that a package in a fixed directory structure can be in a directory on disk (for example, in a spooling directory) or on a removable device such as a diskette. A datastream can be on any device; for example, on a diskette or a tape. A thing to note is, fixed directory structure is not supported on cartridge tape.

The pkgproto Command

This command generates a prototype file. It scans the paths specified on the command line and creates description line entries for these paths. If the pathname is a directory, an entry for each object in the directory is generated. You can use the −c option of the pkgproto command to place objects into classes.

The prototype File

This required package information file contains a list of the package contents. The pkgmk command uses the prototype file to identify the contents of a package and their location on the development machine when building the package. This file is used during package creation and installation and is never seen by the end user of the package.

NOTE All package components, including the `pkginfo` file, must be listed in the `prototype` file.

You can create this file in two ways. As with all the package information files, you can use an editor to create a file named `prototype`. It should contain entries following the description given later in this chapter. You can also use the `pkgproto` command to automatically generate the file. To make use of the second method, you must have a copy of your package on your development machine that is structured exactly as you want it structured on the installation machine and all modes and permissions must be correct. If you are not going to use `pkgproto`, you do not need a structured copy of your package.

There are two types of entries in the `prototype` file: description lines and command lines.

The Description Lines

You must create one description line for each deliverable object that consists of several fields describing the object. This entry describes such information as mode, owner, and group for the object. You can also use this entry to accomplish the tasks listed below.

- You can override `pkgmk`'s placement of an object on a multiple-part package. (Refer to the section entitled "Distributing Packages over Multiple Volumes" for more details.)

- You can place objects into classes. (Refer to the section entitled "Placing Your Objects into Classes" for details.)

- You can tell `pkgmk` where to find an object in your development directory structure and map that name to the correct placement on the installation machine. (Refer to the section entitled "Mapping Development Pathnames to Installation Pathnames" for details.)

- You can define an object as relocatable. (Refer to the section entitled "Setting Package Objects as Relocatable" for details.)

- You can define links. (Refer to the section entitled "Creating the `prototype` File" for details.)

The generic format of the descriptive line is:

[part] ftype class pathname [major minor] [mode owner group]

Definitions for each field are as follows:

part
Designates the part in which an object should be placed. A package can be divided into a number of parts. A part is a collection of files and is the atomic unit by which a package is processed. A developer can choose the criteria for grouping files into a part (for example, by class). If not defined, pkgmk decides in which part the object will be placed.

ftype
Designates the file type of an object. Example file types are f (a standard executable or data file), d (a directory), l (a linked file), and i (a package information file). (Refer to the prototype manual page in the *Administrator's Reference Manual* for a complete list of file types.)

class
Defines the class to which an object belongs. All objects must belong to a class. If the object belongs to no special class, this field should be defined as none.

pathname
Defines the pathname which an object should have on the installation machine. If you do not begin this name with a slash, the object is considered to be relocatable. You can use the form path1=path2 to map the location of an object on your development machine to the pathname it should have on the installation machine.

major/minor
Defines the major and minor numbers for a block or character special device.

mode/owner/group
Defines the mode, owner, and group for an object. If not defined, the defaults defined with the default command are assigned. If not defined and there are not defaults, the values 644 root other are used.

Figure 8-1 shows an example of this file with only description lines.

Figure 8-1: Sample #1 `prototype` **File**

```
i pkginfo
i request
d bin nampbin 0755 root other
f bin nampbin/dired=/usr/ncmp/bin/dired 0755 root other
f bin nampbin/less=/usr/ncmp/bin/less 0755 root other
f bin nampbin/ttype=/usr/ncmp/bin/ttype 0755 root other
```

The Command Lines

There are four types of commands that can be embedded in the `prototype` file. They are:

`search` *pathnames* Specifies a list of directories (separated by white space) in which `pkgmk` should search when looking for package objects. *pathnames* is prepended to the basename of each object in the `prototype` file until the object is located.

`include` *filename* Specifies the pathname of another `prototype` file that should be merged into this one during processing. (Note that `search` requests do not span `include` files. Each `prototype` file should have its own `search` command defined, if one is needed.)

`default` *mode owner group*

Defines the default *mode owner group* that should be used if this information is not supplied in a `prototype` entry that requires the information. (The defaults do not apply to entries in any `include` files. Each `prototype` should have its own `default` command defined, if one is needed.)

param=value Places the indicated parameter in the packaging environment. This allows you to expand a variable pathname so that `pkgmk` can locate the object without changing the actual object pathname. (This assignment will not be available in the installation environment.)

A command line must always begin with an exclamation point (!). Commands may have variable substitutions embedded within them.

Figure 8-2 shows an example `prototype` file with both description and command lines.

Figure 8-2: Sample #2 `prototype` **File**

```
!PROJDIR=/usr/myname
!search /usr/myname/bin /usr/myname/src /usr/myname/hdrs
!include $PROJDIR/src/prototype
i pkginfo
i request
d bin ncmpbin 0755 root other
f bin ncmpbin/dired=/usr/ncmp/bin/dired 0755 root other
f bin ncmpbin/less=/usr/ncmp/bin/less 0755 root other
f bin ncmpbin/ttype=/usr/ncmp/bin/ttype 0755 root other
!default 755 root bin
```

The Installation Tools

The IT tools are introduced to you here so that you can understand the environment into which your package will be placed. The installation tools are:

- `pkgadd` installs a package.

 NOTE The major and minor device numbers for block and character special file designations in `pkgmap` and `prototype` will be ignored by `pkgadd`. On AT-based machines, these numbers are generated for each device by the ID/TP tools.

- `pkgrm` removes a package.

- `pkgask` creates a file that contains an installer's response to prompts in the request script. This file is named on the `pkgadd` command line when a package is installed in noninteractive mode. It replaces the output of the request script.

- `pkgchk` checks the content and attribute information for an installed package to ensure that it was not corrupted during installation.

- `pkginfo` and `pkgparam` display information about packages.

The system administrator can set parameters that control various aspects of installation in an administration file called the `admin` file. Refer to the manual pages in the *Administrator's Reference Manual* for more information on these commands and on the `admin` file.

The Package Information Files

`pkgmap` and `pkginfo` are the only two package files that are required in a package. The remaining package files are optional and are necessary only if the package developer wants to take full advantage of the flexibility of the installation tools. Each of the package information files will be described in the following pages. All of these files can be created using any editor. File formats are described in the following text and in full detail in the *Administrator's Reference Manual*.

The package information files are:

- the `pkginfo` file
- the `pkgmap` file
- the `compver` file
- the `depend` file
- the `space` file
- the `copyright` file
- the `request` file

The pkginfo File

This required package information file defines parameter values that describe characteristics of the package, such as the package abbreviation, full package name, package version, and package architecture. This file is used during package creation and installation and is never seen by the end user of the package.

Each entry in the file uses the following format to establish the value of a parameter:

    PARAM="value"

Figure 8-3 shows an example pkginfo file.

Figure 8-3: Sample pkginfo **File**

```
PKG="pkgA"
NAME="My Package A"
ARCH="i386"
RELEASE="4.0"
VERSION="2"
VENDOR="MYCOMPANY"
HOTLINE="1-800-677-BUGS"
VSTOCK="0122c3f5566"
CATEGORY="application"
ISTATES="S 2"
RSTATES="S 2"
```

The pkginfo and pkgparam commands can be used to access information in a pkginfo file.

NOTE Before defining the PKG, ARCH, and VERSION parameters, you need to know how pkgadd defines a package instance and the rules associated with naming a package. Refer to the section entitled ''Defining a Package Instance'' before assigning values to these parameters.

Integrated Software Development Guide

The pkgmap File

This required package information file provides a complete listing of the package content. The pkgmk command creates the pkgmap file when it processes the prototype file. This new file contains all the information in the prototype file plus three new fields for each entry. These fields are size (file size in bytes), cksum (checksum of file), and modtime (last time of modification). All command lines defined in the prototype file are executed as pkgmk creates the pkgmap file. pkgmap is an ASCII file used to specify information required to install object files on a target machine. Each entry in the pkgmap describes a single deliverable object file. A "deliverable object file" includes shell scripts, executables objects, data files, directories, etc. The pkgmap file is placed on the installation medium. The prototype file is not. Refer to the pkgmap manual page in the *Administrator's Reference Manual* for more details about this file.

The compver File

This package information file is an optional file that defines previous (or future) versions of the package that are compatible with this version. compver is generated by an application developer. Each line in the file consists of a string defining a version of the package with which the current version is upward compatible. Since some packages may require installation of a particular version of another software package, compatibility information is extremely crucial. If a package "A" requires version "1.0" of application "B" as a prerequisite, but the customer installing "A" has a new and improved version of "1.3" of "B", the *compver* file for "B" must indicate that the new version is compatible with version "1.0" in order for the customer to install package "A". The string must match the definition of the VERSION parameter in the pkginfo file of the package considered to be compatible. Figure 8-4 shows an example of this file.

Figure 8-4: Sample compver **File**

```
Version 1.3
Version 1.0
```

The depend File

This package information file is an optional file that defines software dependencies associated with the package.

The generic format of a line in this file is:

```
type pkg name
        (arch) version
        (arch) version
```

Definitions for each field are as follows:

type

    P - indicates a prerequisite for installation, i.e referenced package/version(s) must be installed.

    I - indicates existence of indicated package/version(s) implies an incompatibility exists.

    R - indicates a reverse type of dependency. Instead of indicating the package's own dependencies, this designates a package that depends on the present package. It should be used only when an old package does not have a *depend* file but relies on the newer package nontheless. The present package should not be removed if the designated old package is still on the system. If it is removed, the old package will break.

pkg

    Indicates the package abbreviation for the package.

name

    Specifies the full package name (used for display purposes only).

(arch) version

    Defines a particular instance of a package by defining the architecture and version, and is completely optional. If (arch) version is not supplied, it means the entry refers to any version or architecture of the package.

Figure 8-5 shows an example of this file.

Figure 8-5: Sample depend **File**

```
P acu    Advanced C Utilities
         Issue 4 Version 1
P cc     C Programming Language
         Issue 4 Version 1 (386)
R vpkg   Another Vendor Package
```

The space File

This package information file is an optional file that defines disk space requirements for the target environment beyond that which is used by objects defined in the `prototype` file — for example, files that will be dynamically created at installation time. `space` is generated by application developer. It should define the maximum amount of additional space that a package will require. This differs from the pre–UNIX System V 4.0 size file, which reported the total space required for the `root` and `usr` file systems.

The generic format of a line in this file is:

> *pathname blocks inodes*

Definitions for each field are as follows:

`name`   Names a directory in which there are objects that will require additional space. The name may be the mount point for a filesystem. Names that do not begin with a slash (/) indicate relocatable directories.

`blocks`   Defines the number of 512 byte disk blocks required for installation of the files and directory entries contained in the pathname. (Do not include file system dependent disk usage.)

`inodes`   Defines the number of inodes required for installation of the files and directory entries contained in `name`.

Numbers of blocks or inodes can be negative to indicate that the package will ultimately (after processing by scripts, etc.) take up less space than the installation tool would calculate.

Figure 8-6 shows an example of this file.

Figure 8-6: Sample space **File**

```
# extra space required by config data which is
# dynamically loaded onto the system
data   500   1
```

The copyright File

This package information file is an optional file that contains the text of a copyright message that will be printed on the terminal at the time of package installation or removal. The display is exactly as shown in the file. Figure 8-7 shows an example of this file.

Figure 8-7: Sample copyright **File**

```
Copyright (c) 1989 AT&T
All Rights Reserved.


THIS PACKAGE CONTAINS UNPUBLISHED PROPRIETARY SOURCE CODE OF AT&T.

The copyright notice above does not evidence any
actual or intended publication of such source code.
```

The request File

This package information file is an optional file that contains interactive scripts for package installation. The `request` file contains a procedure script for situations that the Installation Tools do not handle. This request script will be described in the "Installation Scripts" section of this chapter.

The Installation Scripts

The pkgadd command automatically performs all of the actions necessary to install a package, using the package information files as input. As a result, you do not have to supply any packaging scripts. However, if you want to customize the installation procedures for your package needs, the following three types of scripts can be used:

request script   Solicits administrator interaction during package installation for the purpose of assigning or redefining environment parameter assignments.

class action scripts   Define an action or set of actions that should be applied to a class of files during installation or removal. You define your own classes or you can use one of three standard classes (sed, awk, and build). See the "Placing Objects into Classes" section for details on how to define a class.

procedure scripts   Specifies a procedure to be invoked before or after the installation or removal of a package. The four procedure scripts are preinstall, postinstall, preremove, and postremove.

> **NOTE**   Scripts provide flexibility for add-on packages that previously used Install and Remove files on UNIX System V Release 4.0 for the Intel386 and compatible architectures. The procedure scripts can be used before or after installation or removal of packages to execute code that was previously included in the Install and Remove files.

You decide which type of script to use based on when you want the script to execute. To help you with this assessment, script processing is discussed next, followed by a description of parameters available to packaging scripts, how to get information about a package for your scripts, and script exit codes. After that, each type of script is described in detail.

> **NOTE**   All installation scripts must be executable by sh (for example, a shell script or a program executable).

Script Processing

You can customize the actions taken during installation by delivering installation scripts with your package. The decision on which type of script to use to meet a need depends upon when the action of the script is needed during the installation process. As a package is installed, `pkgadd` performs the following steps:

- Executes the request script.

  This is the only point at which your package can solicit input from the installer.

- Executes the `preinstall` script.

- Installs the package objects.

  Installation occurs class-by-class and class action scripts are executed accordingly. The list of classes operated upon and the order in which they should be installed is initially defined with the `CLASSES` parameter in your `pkginfo` file. However, your request script can change the value of `CLASSES`.

- Executes the `postinstall` script.

When a package is being removed, `pkgrm` performs these steps:

- Executes the `preremove` script.

- Executes the removal class action scripts.

  Removal also occurs class-by-class. As with the installation class action scripts, if more than one removal script exists, they are processed in the reverse order in which the classes were listed in the `CLASSES` parameter at the time of installation.

- Executes the `postremove` script.

The request script is not processed at the time of package removal. However, its output (a list of parameter values) is saved and so is available to removal scripts.

Installation Parameters

These following four groups of parameters are available to all installation scripts. Some of the parameters can be modified by a request script, others cannot be modified at all.

- The four system parameters that are part of the installation software (see below for a description of these). None of these parameters can be modified by a package.

- The 20 standard installation parameters defined in the pkginfo file. Of these, a package can only modify the CLASSES parameter. (The standard installation parameters are described in detail on the pkginfo manual page in the *Administrator's Reference Manual.*)

- You can define your own installation parameters by assigning a value to them in the pkginfo file. Such a parameter must be alphanumeric with an initial capital letter. Any of these parameters can be changed by a request script.

- Your request script can define new parameters by assigning values to them and placing them into the installation environment, as shown in Figure 8-8.

The four installation parameters that can be accessed by installation scripts are described below:

PATH   Specifies the search list used by sh to find commands; is set to
            /sbin:/usr/sbin:/usr/bin:/usr/sadm/install/bin
            upon script invocation.

UPDATE   Indicates that the current installation is intended to update the
            system. Automatically set to true if the package being
            installed is overwriting a version of itself.

PKGINST   Specifies the instance identifier of the package being installed.
            If another instance of the package is not already installed, the
            value will be the package abbreviation. Otherwise, it is the
            package abbreviation followed by a suffix, such as pkg.1.

            (Multiple variations of the same package can reside simultane-
            ously on the installation medium, as well as on the installation

machine. Each variation is known as a package instance and assigned an instance identifier. See "Defining a Package Instance" for more details.)

PKGSAV   Specifies the directory where files can be saved for use by removal scripts or where previously saved files may be found.

Getting Package Information for a Script

There are two commands that can be used from your scripts to solicit information about a package.

The pkginfo command returns information about software packages, such as the instance identifier and package name.

The pkgparam command returns values only for the parameters requested.

The pkginfo and pkgparam [(1) and (4)] manual pages in the *Administrator's Reference Manual* give details for these tools.

Exit Codes for Scripts

Each script must exit with one of the following exit codes:

0   Successful completion of script.

1   Fatal error. Installation process is terminated at this point.

2   Warning or possible error condition. Installation will continue. A warning message will be displayed at the time of completion.

3   Script was interrupted and possibly left unfinished. Installation terminates at this point.

10   System should be rebooted when installation of all selected packages is completed. (This value should be added to one of the single-digit exit codes described above.)

20   The system should be rebooted immediately upon completing installation of the current package. (This value should be added to one of the single-digit exit codes described above.)

See the Case Studies for examples of exit codes in installation scripts.

The Request Script

The request script solicits interaction during installation and is the only place where your package can interact directly with the installer. It can be used, for example, to ask the installer if optional pieces of a package should be installed.

The output of a request script must be a list of parameters and their values. This list can include any of the parameters you created in the pkginfo file and the CLASSES parameter. The list can also introduce parameters that have not been defined elsewhere.

When your request script assigns values to a parameter, it must then make those values available to the installation environment for use by pkgadd and also by other packaging scripts. The following example shows a request script segment that performs this task for the four parameters CLASSES, NCMPBIN, EMACS, and NCMPMAN.

Figure 8-8: Placing Parameters into the Installation Environment

```
# make parameters available to installation service
# and any other packaging script we might have
cat >$1 <<!
CLASSES=' $CLASSES'
NCMPBIN=' $NCMPBIN'
EMACS=' $EMACS'
NCMPMAN=' $NCMPMAN'
!
```

Request Script Naming Conventions

There can only be one request script per package and it must be named request.

Request Script Usage Rules

1. The request script can not modify any files. It is intended only to interact with users and to create a list of parameter assignments based upon that interaction. (To enforce this restriction, the request script is executed as the nonprivileged user `install`.)

2. `pkgadd` calls the request script with one argument that names the file to which the output of this script will be written.

3. The parameter assignments should be added to the installation environment for use by `pkgadd` and other packaging scripts (as shown in Figure 8-8).

4. System parameters and standard installation parameters, except for the CLASSES parameter, cannot be modified by a request script. Any of the other parameters available can be changed.

5. The format of the output list should be `Parameter = "value"`. For example:

   ```
   CLASSES="none class1"
   ```

6. The list should be written to the file named as the argument to the request script.

7. The user's terminal is defined as standard input to the request script.

8. The request script is not executed during package removal. However, the parameter values assigned in the script are saved and are available during removal.

The Class Action Script

The class action script defines a set of actions to be executed during installation or removal of a package. The actions are performed on a group of pathnames based on their class definition. (See the Case Studies for examples of class action scripts.)

Class Action Script Naming Conventions

The name of a class action script is based on which class it should operate and whether those actions should occur during package installation or removal. The two name formats are:

- i.*class* (operates on pathnames in the indicated class during package installation)

- r.*class* (operates on pathnames in the indicated class during package removal)

For example, the name of the installation script for a class named class1 would be i.class1 and the removal script would be named r.class1.

Class Action Script Usage Rules

1. Class action scripts are executed as uid=root and gid=other.

2. If a package spans more than one volume, the class action script will be executed once for each volume that contains at least one file belonging to the class. Consequently, each script must be "multiply executable." This means that executing a script any number of times with the same input must produce the same results as executing the script only once.

 NOTE   The installation service relies upon this condition being met.

3. The script is executed only if there are files in the given class existing on the current volume.

4. pkgadd (and pkgrm) creates a list of all objects listed in the pkgmap file that belong to the class. As a result, a class action script can only act upon pathnames defined in the pkgmap and belonging to a particular class.

5. A class action script should never add, remove, or modify a pathname or system attribute that does not appear in the list generated by pkgadd unless by use of the installf or removef command. (See the manual pages in the *Administrator's Reference Manual* for details on these two commands and the Case Studies for examples of them in use.)

6. When the class action script executes for the last time (meaning the input pathname is the last path on the last volume containing a file of this class), it is executed with the keyword argument ENDOFCLASS. This flag allows you to include post-processing actions into your script.

Installation of Classes

The following steps outline the system actions that occur when a class is installed. The actions are repeated once for each volume of a package as that volume is being installed.

1. pkgadd creates a pathname list.

   pkgadd creates a list of pathnames upon which the action script will operate. Each line of this list consists of source and destination pathnames, separated by white space. The source pathname indicates where the object to be installed resides on the installation volume and the destination pathname indicates the location on the installation machine where the object should be installed. The contents of the list is restricted by the following criteria:

   - The list contains only pathnames belonging to the associated class.

   - Directories, named pipes, character/block devices, and symbolic links are included in the list with the source pathname set to /dev/null. They are automatically created by pkgadd (if not already in existence) and given proper attributes (mode, owner, group) as defined in the pkgmap file.

   - Linked files are not included in the list, that is, files where ftype is l. (ftype defines the file type and is defined in the prototype file. Links in the given class are created in Step 4.)

   - If a pathname already exists on the target machine and its contents are no different from the one being installed, the pathname will not be included in the list.

     To determine this, pkgadd compares the cksum, modtime, and size fields in the installation software database with the values for those fields in your pkgmap file. If they are the same, it then checks the actual file on the installation machine to be certain it really has those values. If the field values are the same and are correct, the pathname for this object will not be included in the list.

2. If no class action script is provided for installation of a particular class, the pathnames in the generated list will simply be copied from the volume to the appropriate target location.

3. If there is a class action script, the script is executed.

   The class action script is invoked with standard input containing the list generated in Step 1. If this is the last volume of the package and there are no more objects in this class, the script is executed with the single argument of ENDOFCLASS.

4. pkgadd performs a content and attribute audit and creates links.

   After successfully executing Step 2 or 3, an audit of both content and attribute information is performed on the list of pathnames. pkgadd creates the links associated with the class automatically. Detected attribute inconsistencies are corrected for all pathnames in the generated list.

Removal of Classes

Objects are removed class-by-class. Classes that exist for a package, but are not listed in the CLASSES parameter are removed first (for example, an object installed with the installf command). Classes that are listed in the CLASSES parameter are removed in reverse order. The following steps outline the system actions that occur when a class is removed:

1. pkgrm creates a pathname list.

   pkgrm creates a list of installed pathnames that belong to the indicated class. Pathnames referenced by another package are excluded from the list unless their ftype is e (meaning the file should be edited upon installation or removal).

   If a pathname is referenced by another package, it will not be removed from the system. However, it may be modified to remove information placed in it by the package being removed.

2. If there is no class action script, the pathnames are removed.

   If your package has no removal class action script for the class, all of the pathnames in the list generated by pkgrm will be removed.

    NOTE You should always assign a class for files with an ftype of e (editable) and have an associated class action script for that class. Otherwise, they will be removed at this point, even if the pathname is shared with other packages.

3. If there is a class action script, the script is executed.

   pkgrm invokes the class action script with standard input containing the list generated in Step 1.

4. pkgrm performs an audit.

   Upon successful execution of the class action script, knowledge of the pathnames is removed from the system unless a pathname is referenced by another package.

The Special System Classes

The system provides three special classes. They are:

- The sed class (provides a method for using sed instructions to edit files upon installation and removal).

- The awk class (provides a method for using awk instructions to edit files upon installation and removal).

- The build class (provides a method to dynamically construct a file during installation).

The sed Class Script

The sed installation class provides a method of installing and removing objects that require modification to an existing object on the target machine. A sed class action script delivers sed instructions in the format shown in Figure 8-9. You can give instructions that will be executed during either installation or removal. Two commands indicate when instructions should be executed. sed instructions that follow the !install command are executed during package installation and those that follow the !remove command are executed during package removal. It does not matter in which order the commands are used in the file.

The sed class action script executes automatically at installation time if a file belonging to class sed exists. The name of the sed class file should be the same as the name of the file upon which the instructions will be executed.

Figure 8-9: sed Script Format

```
# comment, which may appear on any line in the file
!install
# sed(1) instructions which are to be invoked during
# installation of the object
[address [,address]] function [arguments]
   ...

!remove
# sed(1) instructions to be invoked during the removal process
[address [,address]] function [arguments]
   ...


address, function, and arguments are as defined on the sed manual page
in the User's Reference Manual.
```

See Case Studies 5a and 5b for examples of sed class action scripts.

The awk Class Script

The awk installation class provides a method of installing and removing objects that require modification to an existing object on the target machine. Modifications are delivered as awk instructions in an awk class action script.

The awk class action script executes automatically at the time of installation if a file belonging to class awk exists. Such a file contains instructions for the awk class script in the format shown in Figure 8-10. Two commands indicate when instructions should be executed. awk instructions that follow the !install command are executed during package installation and those that follow the

!remove command are executed during package removal. It does not matter in which order the commands are used in the file.

The name of the awk class file should be the same as the name of the file upon which the instructions will be executed.

Figure 8-10: awk **Script Format**

```
# comment, which may appear on any line in the file
!install
# awk(1) program to install changes
   ... (awk program)

!remove
# awk1(1) program to remove changes
   ... (awk program)
```

The file to be modified is used as input to awk and the output of the script ultimately replaces the original object. Parameters may not be passed to awk using this syntax.

See Case Study 5a for example awk class action scripts.

The build Class Script

The build class installs or removes objects by executing instructions that create or modify the object file. These instructions are delivered as a build class action script.

The name of the instruction file should conform to standard UNIX system naming conventions.

The build class action script executes automatically at installation time if a file belonging to class build exists.

A build script must be executable by sh. The script's output becomes the new version of the file as it is built.

See Case Study 5c for an example `build` class action script.

The Procedure Script

The procedure script gives a set of instructions that are performed at particular points in installation or removal. Four possible procedure scripts are described below. (The Case Studies show examples of procedure scripts.)

Naming Conventions for Procedure Scripts

The four procedure scripts must use one of the names listed below, depending on when these instructions are to be executed.

- `preinstall` (executes before class installation begins)
- `postinstall` (executes after all volumes have been installed)
- `preremove` (executes before class removal begins)
- `postremove` (executes after all classes have been removed)

Procedure Script Usage Rules

1. Procedure scripts are executed as `uid=root` and `gid=other`.

2. Each installation procedure script must use the `installf` command to notify `pkgadd` that it will add or modify a pathname. After all additions or modifications are complete, this command should be invoked with the `-f` option to indicate all additions and modifications are complete. (See the manual page for the `installf` command in the *Administrator's Reference Manual* and the Case Studies for details and examples.)

3. Each removal procedure script must use the `removef` command to notify `pkgrm` that it will remove a pathname. After removal is complete, this command should be invoked with the `-f` option to indicate all removals have been completed. (See the manual page for the `removef` command in the *Administrator's Reference Manual* and the Case Studies for details and examples.)

NOTE The `installf` and `removef` commands must be used because procedure scripts are not automatically associated with any pathnames listed in the `pkgmap` file.

Basic Steps of Packaging

The steps you take to create a package will vary depending on how customized your package will be. Therefore it is difficult to give you a step-by-step guide on how to proceed. Your first step should be to plan your packaging. For example, you must decide on which package information files and scripts your package needs.

The following list outlines some of the steps you might use in a packaging scenario. The remainder of this chapter gives procedural information for each step.

 NOTE This list, and the following procedures, are intended only as guidelines. You still need to read the rest of this chapter to learn what options are available to your package, and do your own individualized planning.

1. Assign a package abbreviation.

2. Define a package instance.

3. Place your objects into classes.

4. Set up a package and its objects as relocatable.

5. Decide which installation scripts your package needs.

6. Define package dependencies

7. Write a copyright message.

8. Create the pkginfo file.

   You must create a pkginfo file before executing pkgmk.

9. Create the prototype file.

   This file is required and must be created before you can execute pkgmk.

10. Distribute packages over multiple volumes.

    You msut decide if you want to leave those calculations up to pkgmk or customize package placement on multiple volumes.

11. Create the package using the pkgmk command.

This is always the last step of packaging, unless you want to create a datastream structure for your package. If so, you must execute pkgtrans after creating a package with pkgmk.

Step 1. Assigning a Package Abbreviation

Each package installed on UNIX System V Release 4.0 for the Intel386 and compatible architectures must have a package abbreviation assigned to it. This abbreviation is defined with the PKG parameter in the pkginfo file.

A valid package abbreviation must meet the criteria defined below:

- It must start with an alphabetic character.

- Additional characters may be alphanumeric and contain the two special characters + and –.

- It cannot be longer than nine characters.

- Reserved names are install, new, and all.

Step 2. Defining a Package Instance

The same software package can differ by version or architecture or both. Multiple variations of the same package can reside simultaneously on the same machine. Each variation is known as a package instance. pkgadd assigns a package identifier to each package instance at the time of installation. The package identifier is the package abbreviation with a numerical suffix. This identifier distinguishes an instance from any other package, including other instances of the same package.

Identifying a Package Instance

Three parameters defined in the pkginfo file combine to uniquely identify each instance. You cannot assign identical values for all three parameters for two instances of the same package installed in the same target environment. These parameters are:

- PKG (defines the software package abbreviation and remains constant for every instance of a package)

- VERSION (defines the software package version)

- ARCH (defines the software package architecture)

For example, you might identify two identical versions of a package that run on different hardware as:

Instance #1	Instance #2
PKG="abbr"	PKG="abbr"
VERSION="release 1"	VERSION="release 1"
ARCH="AT386"	ARCH="AT386"

Two different versions of a package that run on the same hardware might be identified as:

Instance #1	Instance #2
PKG="abbr"	PKG="abbr"
VERSION="release 1"	VERSION="release 2"
ARCH="i386"	ARCH="i386"

The instance identifier, assigned by pkgadd, maps the three pieces of information that identify an instance to one name consisting of the package abbreviation plus a suffix. The first instance of a package installed on a system does not have a suffix and so its instance identifier will be the package abbreviation. Subsequent instances receive a suffix, beginning with .2. An instance is given the lowest integer extension available and so may not correspond to the order in which a package was installed. For example, if mypkg.2 was deleted after mypkg.3 was installed, the next instance to be added will be named mypkg.2. Because the number of instances of a particular package can vary from machine to machine, the instance identifier can also vary.

| NOTE | pkgmk also assigns an instance identifier to a package as it places it on the installation medium if one or more instances of a package already exists. That identifier bears no relationship to the identifier assigned to the same package on the installation machine. |

Accessing the Instance Identifier in Your Scripts

Because the instance identifier is assigned at the time of installation and will differ from machine to machine, you should use the PKGINST system parameter to reference your package in your installation scripts.

Step 3. Placing Objects into Classes

Installation classes allow a series of actions to be performed on a group of package objects at the time of their installation or removal. You place objects into a class in the prototype file. All package objects must be given a class, although the class of none may be used for objects that require no special action.

The installation parameter CLASSES, defined in the pkginfo file, is a list of classes to be installed (including the none class). Objects defined in the prototype file that belong to a class not listed in this parameter will not be installed. The actions to be performed on a class (other than simply copying the components to the installation machine) are defined in a class action script. These scripts are named after the class itself.

For example, to define and install a group of objects belonging to a class named class1, follow these steps:

1. Define the objects belonging to class1 as such in their prototype file entry. For example,

   ```
   f class1 /usr/src/myfile
   f class1 /usr/src/myfile2
   ```

2. Ensure that the CLASSES parameter in the pkginfo file has an entry for class1. For example,

   ```
   CLASSES="class1 class2 none"
   ```

Package objects cannot be removed by class.

3. Ensure that a class action script exists for this class. An installation script for a class named class1 would be named i.class1 and a removal script would be named r.class1.

   If you define a class but do not deliver a class action script, the only action taken for that class will be to copy components from the installation medium to the installation machine.

In addition to the classes that you can define, the system provides three standard classes for your use. The sed class provides a method for using sed instructions to edit files upon package installation and removal. The awk class provides a method for using awk instructions to edit files upon package installation and removal. The build class provides a method to dynamically construct a file during package installation.

Step 4. Making Package Objects Relocatable

Package objects can be delivered either with fixed locations, meaning that their location on the installation machine is defined by the package and cannot be changed, or as relocatable, meaning that they have no absolute location requirements on the installation machine. The location for relocatable package objects is determined during the installation process.

You can define two types of relocatable objects: collectively relocatable and individually relocatable. All collectively relocatable objects are placed relative to the same directory once the relocatable root directory is established. Individually relocatable objects are not restricted to the same directory location as collectively relocatable objects.

Defining Collectively Relocatable Objects

Follow these steps to define package objects as collectively relocatable:

1. Define a value for the BASEDIR parameter.

    Put a definition for the BASEDIR parameter in your pkginfo file. This parameter names a directory where relocatable objects will be placed by default. If you supply no value for BASEDIR, no package objects will be considered as collectively relocatable.

2. Define objects as collectively relocatable in the prototype file.

    An object is defined as collectively relocatable by using a relative pathname in its entry in the prototype file. A relative pathname does not begin with a slash. For example, src/myfile is a relative pathname, while /src/myfile is a fixed pathname.

     NOTE A package can deliver some objects with relocatable locations and others with fixed locations.

All objects defined as collectively relocatable will be put under the same root directory on the installation machine. The root directory value will be one of the following (and in this order):

- the installer's response to pkgadd when asked where relocatable objects should be installed

- the value of BASEDIR as it is defined in the installer's admin file (the BASEDIR value assigned in the admin file overrides the value in the pkginfo file)

- the value of BASEDIR as it is defined in your pkginfo file (this value is used only as a default in case the other two possibilities have not supplied a value)

Defining Individually Relocatable Objects

A package object is defined as individually relocatable by using a variable in its pathname definition in the `prototype` file. Your request script must query the installer on where such an object should be placed and assign the response value to the variable. `pkgadd` will expand the pathname based on the output of your request script at the time of installation. Case Study 1 shows an example of the use of variable pathnames and the request script needed to solicit a value for the base directory.

Step 5. Writing Your Installation Scripts

You should read the section entitled "The Installation Scripts" to learn what types of scripts you can write and how to write them. You can also look at the Case Studies to see how the various scripts can be utilized and to see examples.

Remember, you are not required to write any installation scripts for a UNIX System V Release 4.0 package for the Intel386 and compatible architectures. The `pkgadd` command performs all of the actions necessary to install your package, using the information you supply with the package information files. Any installation script that you write will be used to perform customized actions beyond those executed by `pkgadd`.

 NOTE Be certain that every installation script being delivered with your package has an entry in the `prototype` file. The file type should be `i`.

`pkgadd` assures that there is enough disk space to install your package, based on the object definitions in the `pkgmap` file. However, sometimes your package will require additional disk space beyond that needed by the objects defined in the `pkgmap` file. For example, your package might create a file during installation. `pkgadd` checks for additional space when you deliver a `space` file with your package. Refer to the section entitled "The `space` File" earlier in this chapter or the `space` manual page in the *Administrator's Reference Manual* for details on the format of this file.

Step 6. Defining Package Dependencies

Package dependencies and incompatibilities can be defined with two of the optional package information files. Delivering a `compver` file lets you name versions of your package that are compatible with the one being installed. Delivering a `depend` file lets you define three types of dependencies associated with your package. These dependency types are:

- a prerequisite package (meaning your package depends on the existence of another package)

- a reverse dependency (meaning another package depends on the existence of your package)

 NOTE This type should only be used when a pre-UNIX System V Release 4.0 package for the Intel386 and comatible architectures cannot deliver a depend file but relies on the newer package.

- an incompatible package (meaning your package is incompatible with this one)

Refer to the sections entitled "The `depend` File" and "The `compver` File" earlier in this chapter, or the manual pages `depend` and `compver` in the *Administrator's Reference Manual,* for details on the formats of these files.

 NOTE Be certain that your `depend` and `compver` files have entries in the `proto-type` file. The file type should be `i` (for package information file).

Step 7. Writing a Copyright Message

To deliver a copyright message, you must create a copyright file named `copyright`. The message will be displayed exactly as it appears in the file (no formatting) as the package is being installed and as it is being removed. Refer to the section entitled "The `copyright` File" earlier in this chapter or the `copyright` manual page in the *Administrator's Reference Manual* for more detail.

NOTE Be certain that your `copyright` file has an entry in the `prototype` file. Its file type should be `i` (for package information file).

Step 8. Creating the pkginfo File

The `pkginfo` file establishes values for parameters that describe the package and is a required package component. The format for an entry in this file is:

    PARAM="value"

PARAM can be any of the 19 standard parameters described on the `pkginfo` manual page in the *Administrator's Reference Manual*. You can also create your own package parameters simply by assigning a value to them in this file. Your parameter names must begin with a capital letter followed by either upper or lowercase letters.

The following five parameters are required:

- `PKG` (package abbreviation)
- `NAME` (full package name)
- `ARCH` (package architecture)
- `VERSION` (package version)
- `CATEGORY` (package category)

The `CLASSES` parameter dictates which classes are installed and the order of installation. Although the parameter is not required, no classes will be installed without it. Even if you have no class action scripts, the `none` class must be defined in the `CLASSES` parameter before objects belonging to that class will be installed.

NOTE You can choose to define the value of CLASSES with a request script and not to deliver a value in the pkginfo file.

Step 9. Creating the prototype File

The prototype file is a list of package contents and is a required package component.

You can create the prototype file by using any editor and following the format described in the section entitled "The prototype File" and on the prototype manual page in the *Administrator's Reference Manual*. You can also use the pkgproto command to create one automatically.

Creating the File Manually

While creating the prototype file, you must at the very least supply the following three pieces of information about an object:

- The object's type

  All of the possible object types are defined on the prototype manual page in the *Administrator's Reference Manual*. f (for a data file), l (for a linked file), and d (for a directory) are examples of object types.

- The object's class

  All objects must be assigned a class. If no special handling is required, you can assign the class none.

- The object's pathname

  The pathname can define a fixed pathname such as /mypkg/src/filename, a collectively relocatable pathname such as src/filename, and an individually relocatable pathname such as $BIN/filename or /opt/$PKGINST/filename.

Creating Links

To define links you must do the following in the `prototype` entry for the linked object:

1. Define its `ftype` as `l` (a link) or `s` (a symbolic link).

2. Define its pathname with the format *path1=path2* where *path1* is the destination and *path2* is the source file.

Mapping Development Pathnames to Installation Pathnames

If your development area is in a different structure than you want the package to be in on the installation machine, you can use the `prototype` entry to map one pathname to the other. You use the *path1=path2* format for the pathname as is used to define links. However, if the `ftype` is not defined as `l` or `s`, *path1* is interpreted as the pathname you want the object to have on the installation machine, and *path2* is interpreted as the pathname the object has on your development machine.

For example, your project might require a development structure that includes a project root directory and numerous `src` directories. However, on the installation machine you might want all files to go under a package root directory and for all `src` files to be in one directory. So, a file on your machine might be named `/projdir/srcA/filename`. If you want that file to be named `/pkgroot/src/filename` on the installation machine, your `prototype` entry for this file might look like this:

```
f class1 /pkgroot/src/filename=/projdir/srcA/filename
```

Defining Objects for pkgadd to Create

You can use the `prototype` file to define objects that are not actually delivered on the installation medium. `pkgadd` creates objects with the following `ftypes` if they do not already exist at the time of installation:

- `d` (directories)

- `x` (exclusive directories)

- `l` (linked files)

- s (symbolically linked files)

- p (named pipes)

- c (character special device)

- b (block special device)

To request that one of these objects be created on the installation machine, you should add an entry for it in the `prototype` file using the appropriate `ftype`.

For example, if you want a directory created on the installation machine, but do not want to deliver it on the installation medium, an entry for the directory in the `prototype` file is sufficient. An entry such as the one shown below will cause the directory to be created on the installation machine, even if it does not exist on the installation medium.

```
d none /directoryA 644 root other
```

Using the Command Lines

There are four types of commands that you can put into your `prototype` file. They allow you to do the following:

- Nest `prototype` files (the `include` command)

- Define directories for `pkgmk` to look in when attempting to locate objects as it creates the package (the `search` command)

- Set a default value for `mode owner group` (the `default` command). If all or most of your objects have the same values, using the `default` command will keep you from having to define these values for every entry in the `prototype` file.

- Assign a temporary value for variable pathnames to tell `pkgmk` where to locate these relocatable objects on your machine (with *param=value*)

Creating the File Using pkgproto

The `pkgproto` command scans your directories and generates a `prototype` file. `pkgproto` cannot assign `ftypes` of v (volatile files), e (editable files), or x (exclusive directories). You can edit the `prototype` file and add these `ftypes`, as well as perform any other fine-tuning you require (for example, adding command lines or classes).

pkgproto writes its output to the standard output. To create a file, you should redirect the output to a file. The examples shown in this section do not perform redirection in order to show you what the contents of the file would like.

Creating a Basic prototype

The standard format of pkgproto is

>   pkgproto *path* [...]

where *path* is the name of one or more paths to be included in the prototype file. If *path* is a directory, then entries are created for the contents of that directory as well.

With this form of the command, all objects are placed into the none class and are assigned the same mode owner group as exists on your machine. The following example shows pkgproto being executed to create a file for all objects in the directory /usr/bin:

```
$ pkgproto /usr/bin
d none /usr/bin 755 bin bin
f none /usr/bin/file1 755 bin bin
f none /usr/bin/file2 755 bin bin
f none /usr/bin/file3 755 bin bin
f none /usr/bin/file4 755 bin bin
f none /usr/bin/file5 755 bin bin
$
```

To create a prototype file that contains the output of the example above, you would execute pkgproto /usr/bin > prototype

NOTE If no pathnames are supplied when executing pkgproto, standard in (stdin) is assumed to be a list of paths. Refer to the pkgproto manual page in the *Administrator's Reference Manual* for details on this usage.

Assigning Objects to a Class

You can use the −c *class* option of pkgproto to assign objects to a class other than none. When using this option, you can only name one class. To define multiple classes in a prototype file created by pkgproto, you must edit the file after its creation.

The following example is the same as above except the objects have been assigned to class1.

```
$ pkgproto -c class1 /usr/bin
d class1 /usr/bin 755 bin bin
f class1 /usr/bin/file1 755 bin bin
f class1 /usr/bin/file2 755 bin bin
f class1 /usr/bin/file3 755 bin bin
f class1 /usr/bin/file4 755 bin bin
f class1 /usr/bin/file5 755 bin bin
$
```

Renaming Pathnames with pkgproto

You can use a *path1=path2* format on the pkgproto command line to give an object a different pathname in the prototype file than it has on your machine. You can, for example, use this format to define relocatable objects in a prototype file created by pkgproto.

The following example is like the others shown in this section, except that the objects are now defined as bin (instead of /usr/bin) and are thus relocatable.

```
$ pkgproto -c class1 /usr/bin=bin
d class1 bin 755 bin bin
f class1 bin/file1 755 bin bin
f class1 bin/file2 755 bin bin
f class1 bin/file3 755 bin bin
f class1 bin/file4 755 bin bin
f class1 bin/file5 755 bin bin
$
```

pkgproto and Links

pkgproto detects linked files and creates entries for them in the prototype file. If multiple files are linked together, it considers the first path encountered the source of the link.

If you have symbolic links established on your machine but want to generate an entry for that file with an ftype of f (file), then use the −i option of pkgproto. This option creates a file entry for all symbolic links.

Step 10. Distributing Packages over Multiple Volumes

As packager, you no longer need to worry about placing package components on multiple volumes. pkgmk performs the calculations and actions necessary to organize a multiple volume package. As pkgmk creates your package, it will prompt you to insert a new volume as often as necessary to distribute the complete package over multiple volumes.

However, you can use the optional part field in the prototype file to define in which part you want an object to be placed. A number in this field overrides pkgmk and forces the placement of the component into the part given in the field. Note again that there is a one-to-one correspondence between parts and volumes for removable media formatted as file systems.

Step 11. Creating a Package with pkgmk

To package your software, execute

> pkgmk [−d *device*] [−f *filename*]

You must use the −d option to name the device onto which the package should be placed. *device* can be a directory pathname or the identifier for a disk. The default device is the installation spool directory.

pkgmk looks for a file named prototype. You can use the −f option to specify a package contents file named something other than prototype. This file must be in the prototype format.

For example, executing pkgmk −d /dev/diskette creates a package based on a file named prototype in your current working directory. The package will be formatted and copied to the diskette in the device /dev/diskette.

Creating a Package Instance for pkgmk

pkgmk will create a new instance of a package if one already exists on the device to which it is writing. It will assign the package an instance identifier. Use the −o option of pkgmk to overwrite an existing instance of a package rather than to create a new one.

Helping pkgmk Locate Package Contents

The following list describes situations that might require supplying pkgmk with extra information and an explanation of how to do so:

- Your development area is not structured in the same way that you want your package structured.

  You should use the *path1=path2* pathname format in your prototype file.

- You have relocatable objects in your package.

  You can use the *path1=path2* pathname format in your prototype file, with *path1* as a relocatable name and *path2* a full pathname to that object on your machine.

  You can use the search command in your prototype file to tell pkgmk where to look for objects.

  You can use the −b *basedir* option of pkgmk to define a pathname to prepend to relocatable object names while creating the package. For example, executing

  ```
  pkgmk −d /dev/diskette −b usr2/myhome/reloc
  ```

  would look in the directory /usr2/myhome/reloc for any relocatable object in your package.

- You have variable object names.

  You can use the search command in your prototype file to tell pkgmk where to look for objects.

  You can use the *param="value"* command in your prototype file to give pkgmk a value to use for the object name variables as it creates your package.

You can use the *variable=value* option on the pkgmk command line to
define a temporary value for variable names.

■ The root directory on your machine differs from the root directory
described in the prototype file (and that will be used on the installation
machine).

You can use the −r *rootpath* option to tell pkgmk to ignore the destination
pathnames in the prototype file. Instead, pkgmk prepends *rootpath* to
the source pathnames in order to find objects on your machine.

Step 12. Creating a Package with pkgtrans

To perform one of these translations, execute

        pkgtrans *device1 device2* [*pkg1* [*pkg2* [. . .]]]

where *device1* is the name of the device where the package currently resides,
device2 is the name of the device onto which the translated package will be
placed, and [*pkg1*[*pkg2* [...]]] is one or more package names. If no package
names are given, all packages residing in *device1* will be translated and placed
on *device2*.

| NOTE | If more than one instance of a package resides on *device1*, you must use an instance identifier for *pkg*. |

Creating a Datastream Package

Creating a datastream package requires two steps:

1. Create a package using pkgmk.

   Use the default device (the installation spool directory) or name a directory into which the package should be placed. pkgmk creates a package
   in a fixed directory format.

2. After the software is formatted in fixed directory format and is residing in
   a spool directory, execute pkgtrans.

This command translates the fixed directory format to the datastream format and places the datastream on the specified medium.

For example, the two steps shown below will create a datastream package.

1. pkgmk -d spooldir

   (Formats a package into a fixed directory structure and places it in a directory named spooldir)

2. pkgtrans spooldir 9track package1

   (Translates the fixed directory format of package1 residing in the directory spooldir into a datastream format. Places the datastream package on the medium in a device named 9track.)

   OR

3. pkgtrans -s spooldir diskette package1

   (Similar to number 2 above, except that it places the datastream package on the medium in a device named diskette.)

Translating a Package Instance

When an instance of the package being translated already exists on *device2*, pkgtrans will not perform the translation. You can use the -o option to tell pkgtrans to overwrite any existing instances on the destination device and the -n option to tell it to create a new instance if one already exists.

Package Installation Case Studies

This section presents packaging case study in order to show packaging techniques such as installing objects conditionally, determining at run time how many files to create, and how to modify an existing data file during package installation and removal.

Each case begins with a description of the study, followed by a list of the packaging techniques it uses and a narrative description of the approach taken when using those techniques. After this material, sample files and scripts associated with the case study are shown.

Case #1

This package has three types of objects. The installer may choose which of the three types to install and where to locate the objects on the installation machine.

Techniques

This case study shows examples of the following techniques:

- using variables in object pathnames
- using the request script to solicit input from the installer
- setting conditional values for an installation parameter

Approach

To set up selective installation, you must:

- Define a class for each type of object which can be installed.

  In this case study, the three object types are the package executables, the manual pages, and the emacs executables. Each type has its own class: bin, man, and emacs, respectively. Notice in the prototype file, shown in Figure 8-12, that all of the object files belong to one of these three classes.

- Initialize the CLASSES parameter in the pkginfo file as null.

  Normally when you define a class, you want the CLASSES parameter to list all classes that will be installed. Otherwise, no objects in that class will be installed. For this example, the parameter is initially set to null. CLASSES will be given values by the request script, based on the package pieces chosen by the installer. This way, CLASSES is set to only those object types that the installer wants installed. Figure 8-11 shows the pkginfo file associated with this package. Notice that the CLASSES parameter is set to null.

- Define object pathnames in the prototype file with variables.

  These variables will be set by the request script to the value which the installer provides. pkgadd resolves these variables at installation time and so knows where to install the package.

The three variables used in this example are:

- $NCMPBIN (defines location for object executables)
- $NCMPMAN (defines location for manual pages)
- $EMACS (defines location for emacs executables)

Look at the example prototype file (Figure 8-12) to see how to define the object pathnames with variables.

■ Create a request script to ask the installer which parts of the package should be installed and where they should be placed.

The request script for this package, shown in Figure 8-13, asks two questions:

- Should this part of the package be installed?

   When the answer is yes, then the appropriate class name is added to the CLASSES parameter. For example, when the question "Should the manual pages associated with this package be installed" is answered yes, the class man is added to the CLASSES parameter.

- If so, where should that part of the package be placed?

   The appropriate variable is given the value of the response to this question. In the manual page example, the variable $NCMPMAN is set to this value.

These two questions are repeated for each of the three object types.

At the end of the request script, the parameters are made available to the installation environment for pkgadd and any other packaging scripts. In the case of this example, no other scripts are provided.

When looking at the request script for this example, notice that the questions are generated by the data validation tools ckyorn and ckpath.

Sample Files

Figure 8-11: Case #1 pkginfo **File**

```
PKG='ncmp'
NAME='NCMP Utilities'
CATEGORY='applications,tools'
ARCH='3b2'
VERSION='Release 1.0, Issue 1.0'
CLASSES=''
```

Figure 8-12: Case #1 prototype **File**

```
i pkginfo
i request
x bin $NCMPBIN 0755 root other
f bin $NCMPBIN/dired=/usr/ncmp/bin/dired 0755 root other
f bin $NCMPBIN/less=/usr/ncmp/bin/less 0755 root other
f bin $NCMPBIN/ttype=/usr/ncmp/bin/ttype 0755 root other
f emacs $NCMPBIN/emacs=/usr/ncmp/bin/emacs 0755 root other
x emacs $EMACS 0755 root other
f emacs $EMACS/ansii=/usr/ncmp/lib/emacs/macros/ansii 0644 root other
f emacs $EMACS/box=/usr/ncmp/lib/emacs/macros/box 0644 root other
f emacs $EMACS/crypt=/usr/ncmp/lib/emacs/macros/crypt 0644 root other
f emacs $EMACS/draw=/usr/ncmp/lib/emacs/macros/draw 0644 root other
f emacs $EMACS/mail=/usr/ncmp/lib/emacs/macros/mail 0644 root other
f emacs $NCMPMAN/man1/emacs.1=/usr/ncmp/man/man1/emacs.1 0644 root other
d man $NCMPMAN 0755 root other
d man $NCMPMAN/man1 0755 root other
f man $NCMPMAN/man1/dired.1=/usr/ncmp/man/man1/dired.1 0644 root other
f man $NCMPMAN/man1/ttype.1=/usr/ncmp/man/man1/ttype.1 0644 root other
f man $NCMPMAN/man1/less.1=/usr/ncmp/man/man1/less.1 0644 inixmr other
```

Figure 8-13: Case Study #1 Request Script

```
trap 'exit 3' 15

# determine if and where general executables should be placed
ans=`ckyorn -d y \
        -p "Should executables included in this package be installed"
` || exit $?
if [ "$ans" = y ]
then
        CLASSES="$CLASSES bin"
        NCMPBIN=`ckpath -d /usr/ncmp/bin -aoy \
                -p "Where should executables be installed"
        ` || exit $?
fi

# determine if emacs editor should be installed, and if it should
# where should the associated macros be placed
ans=`ckyorn -d y \
        -p "Should emacs editor included in this package be installed"
` || exit $?
if [ "$ans" = y ]
then
        CLASSES="$CLASSES emacs"
        EMACS=`ckpath -d /usr/ncmp/lib/emacs -aoy \
                -p "Where should emacs macros be installed"
        ` || exit $?
fi

# determine if and where manual pages should be installed
ans=`ckyorn \
        -d y \
        -p "Should manual pages associated with this package be installed"
` || exit $?
if [ "$ans" = y ]
then
        CLASSES="$CLASSES man"
        NCMPMAN=`ckpath -d /usr/ncmp/man -aoy \
                -p "Where should manual pages be installed"
        ` || exit $?
fi

# make parameters available to installation service,
# and so to any other packaging scripts
cat >$1 <<!
CLASSES='$CLASSES'
```

(continued on next page)

Application Software Packaging

Figure 8-13: Case Study #1 Request Script (continued)

```
NCMPBIN=' $NCMPBIN'
EMACS=' $EMACS'
NCMPMAN=' $NCMPMAN'
!

exit 0
```

Case #2

This package installs a driver. A set of device nodes associated with that driver needs to be created, but the installer will decide how many nodes to create. After installation, the system needs to be rebooted so that the driver is properly configured.

Techniques

This case study shows examples of the following techniques:

- installing a driver with a postinstall script

- using an exit code to reboot the system

- allowing the installer to define how many device nodes to create at installation time

Approach

To install a driver at the time of installation, you must:

- Include the object and master files for the driver in the `prototype` file.

  In this example, the object file for the driver is a data file named `qz.o`. This is the file on which the standard UNIX driver install command, `drvinstall`, operates. The `master.d` file is named `qz` and is used by `drvinstall` to help configure the driver.

  Looking at Figure 8-14 (the `prototype` file for this example), notice the following:

  □ Since no special treatment is required for these files, you can put them into the standard `none` class. The `CLASSES` parameter is set to `none` in the `pkginfo` file (Figure 8-15).

  □ The pathname for `qz.o` begins with the variable `$BOOTDIR`. This variable will be set in the request script and allows the administrator to decide where the object file should be installed. The default directory will be `/boot`.

      □ There is an entry for the postinstall script (the script that will per-
        form the driver installation).

■ Create a request script.

The request script, shown in Figure 8-16, has two major functions:

      □ to determine how many device nodes to create for this driver

      This is accomplished by questioning the installer and then assigning
      the answer to the parameter $NDEVICES. Notice that the data vali-
      dation tool ckrange is used and that it limits the response to a
      number between 0 and 32. It sets the default number to 8.

      If the installer chooses not to install any devices, the CLASSES
      parameter is set to null. This means that no classes are defined and
      therefore no objects will be installed.

      □ to determine where the installer wants the driver objects to be
        installed

      This is accomplished by questioning the installer and assigning the
      answer to the $BOOTDIR parameter.

The script ends with a routine to make the three parameters CLASSES,
NDEVICES, and BOOTDIR available to the installation environment and so
to the postinstall script.

■ Create a postinstall script.

The postinstall script, shown in Figure 8-17, actually performs the driver
installation. It is executed after the two files qz and qz.o have been
installed. The postinstall shown for this example performs the following
actions:

      □ checks to see if any devices should be installed (if not, it exits)

      □ creates the /dev/qz directory using the installf command (this
        directory could also be created by putting an entry for it in the pro-
        totype file)

      □ executes the drvinstall command using the two files installed
        with this package (the major number is returned to the script at this
        time)

       □ calculates the minor numbers for installed devices

       □ installs the device using `installf`

       □ creates a link for the device also using `installf`

       □ finalizes the installation using `installf -f`

■ Reboot the system upon installation.

This is accomplished by exiting from the postinstall script with an exit code of 10, meaning that the system should be rebooted upon completing an error-free installation.

Sample Files

Figure 8-14: Case #2 `prototype` **File**

```
i pkginfo
i request
i postinstall
f none $BOOTDIR/qz.o 444 root root
f none /etc/master.d/qz 444 root root
```

Figure 8-15: Case #2 `pkginfo` **File**

```
PKG='qzdev'
NAME='qz Devices'
CATEGORY='system'
ARCH='3b2'
VERSION='Software Issue #19'
CLASSES='none'
```

Figure 8-16: Case #2 Request Script

```
trap 'exit 3' 15

# determine if and where general executables should be placed
NDEVICES=`ckrange -l0 -u32 -d 8 \
        -p "How many qz devices do you want configured"
` || exit $?

# if user chose to install no devices, don't install anything
if [ $NDEVICES -eq 0 ]
then
        CLASSES=
else
        # determine where driver object should be placed; location
        # must be an absolute pathname which is an existing directory
        BOOTDIR=`ckpath -aoy -d /boot \
                -p "Where do you want driver object installed"
        ` || exit $?
fi

# make parameters available to installation service,
# and so to any other packaging scripts
cat >$1 <<!
CLASSES='$CLASSES'
NDEVICES='$NDEVICES'
BOOTDIR='$BOOTDIR'
!
exit 0
```

Figure 8-17: Case #2 Postinstall Script

```
# PKGINST parameter provided by installation service
# NDEVICES parameter provided by 'request' script
# BOOTDIR parameter provided by 'request' script

[ $NDEVICES -eq 0 ] && exit 0

err_code=1  # an error is considered fatal

# need to create the /dev/qz directory
installf $PKGINST /dev/qz d 755 root sys ||
        exit $err_code

# install the driver object and determine major device number
majno='/usr/sbin/drvinstall -m /etc/master.d/qz -d $BOOTDIR/qz.o -v1.0' ||
        exit $err_code

i=00
while [ $i -lt $NDEVICES ]
do
        for j in 0 1 2 3 4 5 6 7
        do
                # calculate minor number based on loop variables
                minno='expr $i \* 8 + $j' || exit $err_code

                # install character device with appropriate major/minor
                # device numbers and correct permissions (installf will
                # do all of work here - you need only provide the info!)
                installf $PKGINST /dev/qz/$i$j c $majno $minno 644 root sys ||
                        exit $err_code

                # create a link from /dev/qz/xx to /dev/qzxx
                installf $PKGINST /dev/qz$i$j=/dev/qz/$i$j ||
                        exit $err_code
        done
        i='expr $i + 1'

        # add leading zero if necessary
        [ $i -le 9 ] && i="0$i"
done

# finalize installation; the installf command will now
# attempt to create the links that was requested above
installf -f $PKGINST || exit $err_code

exit 10  # requests a reboot from user
```

Case #3

This study creates a database file at the time of installation and saves a copy of the database when the package is removed.

Techniques

This case study shows examples of the following techniques:

- using classes and class action scripts to perform special actions on different sets of objects

- using the `space` file to inform `pkgadd` that extra space will be required to install this package properly

- using the `installf` command

Approach

To create a database file at the time of installation and save a copy on removal, you must:

- Create three classes.

    This package requires three classes:

    - the standard class of `none` (contains a set of processes belonging in the subdirectory `bin`)

    - the `admin` class (contains an executable file `config` and a directory containing data files)

    - the `cfgdata` class (contains a directory)

- Make the package collectively relocatable.

    Notice in the `prototype` file (Figure 8-19) that none of the pathnames begin with a slash or a variable. This indicates that they are collectively relocatable.

- Calculate the amount of space the database file will require and create a `space` file to deliver with the package. This file notifies `pkgadd` that this package requires extra space and how much extra space. Figure 8-20 shows the `space` file for this package.

■ Create an installation class action script for the admin class.

The script, shown in Figure 8-21, initializes a database using the data files belonging to the admin class. To perform this task, it:

  □ copies the source data file to its proper destination

  □ creates an empty file named config.data and assigns it to a class of cfgdata

  □ executes the bin/config command (delivered with the package and already installed) to populate the database file config.data using the data files belonging to the admin class

  □ executes installf -f to finalize installation

No special action is required for the admin class at removal time so no removal class action script is created. This means that all files and directories in the admin class will simply be removed from the system.

■ Create a removal class action script for the cfgdata class.

The script, shown in Figure 8-22, makes a copy of the database file before it is deleted during package removal. No special action is required for this class at installation time, so no installation class action script is needed.

Remember that the input to a removal script is a list of pathnames to remove. Pathnames always appear in lexical order with the directories appearing first. This script captures directory names so that they can be acted upon later and copies any files to a directory named /tmp. When all of the pathnames have been processed, the script then goes back and removes all directories and files associated with the cfgdata class.

The outcome of this removal script is to copy config.data to /tmp and then remove the config.data file and the data directory.

Sample Files

Figure 8-18: Case #3 `pkginfo` **File**

```
PKG='krazy'
NAME='KrAzY Applications'
CATEGORY='applications'
ARCH='3b2'
VERSION='Version 1'
CLASSES='none cfgdata admin'
```

Figure 8-19: Case #3 `prototype` **File**

```
i pkginfo
i request
i i.admin
i r.cfgdata
d none bin 555 root sys
f none bin/process1 555 root other
f none bin/process2 555 root other
f none bin/process3 555 root other
f admin bin/config 500 root sys
d admin cfg 555 root sys
f admin cfg/datafile1 444 root sys
f admin cfg/datafile2 444 root sys
f admin cfg/datafile3 444 root sys
f admin cfg/datafile4 444 root sys
d cfgdata data 555 root sys
```

Integrated Software Development Guide

Figure 8-20: **Case #3** space **File**

```
# extra space required by config data which is
# dynamically loaded onto the system
data 500 1
```

Figure 8-21: Case #3 Installation Class Action Script (i.admin)

```
# PKGINST parameter provided by installation service
# BASEDIR parameter provided by installation service

while read src dest
do
        # the installation service provides '/dev/null' as the
        # pathname for directories, pipes, special devices, etc
        # which it knows how to create
        [ "$src" = /dev/null ] && continue

        cp $src $dest || exit 2
done

# if this is the last time this script will
# be executed during the installation, do additional
# processing here
if [ "$1" = ENDOFCLASS ]
then
        # our config process will create a data file based on any changes
        # made by installing files in this class; make sure
        # the data file is in class 'cfgdata' so special rules can apply
        # to it during package removal
        installf -c cfgdata $PKGINST $BASEDIR/data/config.data f 444 root sys ||
                exit 2
        $BASEDIR/bin/config > $BASEDIR/data/config.data ||
                exit 2
        installf -f -c cfgdata $PKGINST ||
                exit 2
fi
exit 0
```

Figure 8-22: Case #3 Removal Class Action Script (r.cfgdata)

```
# the product manager for this package has suggested that
# the configuration data is so valuable that it should be
# backed up to /tmp before it is removed!

while read path
do
        # pathnames appear in lexical order, thus directories
        # will appear first; you can't operate on directories
        # until done, so just keep track of names until
        # later
        if [ -d $path ]
        then
                dirlist="$dirlist $path"
                continue
        fi
        mv $path /tmp || exit 2
done
if [ -n "$dirlist" ]
then
        rm -rf $dirlist || exit 2
fi
exit 0
```

Case #4

This package uses the optional packaging files to define package compatibilities and dependencies and to present a copyright message during installation.

Techniques

This case study shows examples of the following techniques:

- using the `copyright` file
- using the `compver` file
- using the `depend` file

Approach

To meet the requirements in the description, you must:

- Create a `copyright` file.

  A `copyright` file contains the ASCII text of a copyright message. The message shown in Figure 8-24 will be displayed on the screen during package installation (and also during package removal).

- Create a `compver` file.

  The `pkginfo` file shown in Figure 8-23 defines this package version as version 3.0. The `compver` file, shown in Figure 8-25, defines version 3.0 as being compatible with versions 2.3, 2.2, 2.1, 2.1.1, 2.1.3 and 1.7.

- Create a `depend` file.

  Files listed in a `depend` file must already be installed on the system when a package is installed. The example shown in Figure 8-26 has 11 packages which must already be on the system at installation time.

Sample Files

Figure 8-23: **Case #4** pkginfo **File**

```
PKG='case4'
NAME='Case Study #4'
CATEGORY='application'
ARCH='3b2'
VERSION='Version 3.0'
CLASSES='none'
```

Figure 8-24: **Case #4** copyright **File**

```
Copyright (c) 1989 AT&T
All Rights Reserved.

THIS PACKAGE CONTAINS UNPUBLISHED PROPRIETARY SOURCE CODE OF AT&T.

The copyright notice above does not evidence any
actual or intended publication of such source code.
```

Figure 8-25: **Case #4** compver **File**

```
Version 2.3
Version 2.2
Version 2.1
Version 2.1.1
Version 2.1.3
Version 1.7
```

Figure 8-26: Case #4 depend **File**

```
P acu    Advanced C Utilities
         Issue 4 Version 1
P cc     C Programming Language
         Issue 4 Version 1
P dfm    Directory and File Management Utilities
P ed     Editing Utilities
P esg    Extended Software Generation Utilities
         Issue 4 Version 1
P graph  Graphics Utilities
P rfs    Remote File Sharing Utilities
         Issue 1 Version 1
P rx     Remote Execution Utilities
P sgs    Software Generation Utilities
         Issue 4 Version 1
P shell  Shell Programming Utilities
P sys    System Header Files
         Release 3.1
```

Case #5a

This study modifies a file which exists on the installation machine during package installation. It uses one of three modification methods. The other two methods are shown in Cases 5b and 5c. The file modified is /sbin/inittab.

Techniques

This case study shows examples of the following techniques:

- using the sed class
- using a postinstall script

Approach

To modify /sbin/inittab at the time of installation, you must:

- Add the sed class script to the prototype file.

  The name of a script must be the name of the file that will be edited. In this case, the file to be edited is /sbin/inittab and so our sed script is named /sbin/inittab. There are no requirements for the mode owner group of a sed script (represented in the sample prototype by question marks). The file type of the sed script must be e (indicating that it is editable). The prototype file for this case study is shown in Figure 8-27.

- Set the CLASSES parameter to include 4sed.

  In the case of the example shown in Figure 8-28, sed is the only class being installed. However, it could be one of any number of classes.

- Create a sed class action script.

  You cannot deliver a copy of /sbin/inittab that looks the way you need for it to, since /sbin/inittab is a dynamic file and you have no way of knowing how it will look at the time of package installation. Using a sed script allows us to modify the /sbin/inittab file during package installation.

  As already mentioned, the name of a sed script should be the same as the name of the file it will edit. A sed script contains sed commands to remove and add information to the file. See Figure 8-29 for an example sed script.

■ Create a postinstall script.

You need to inform the system that /sbin/inittab has been modified by executing init q. The only place you can perform that action in this example is in a postinstall script. Looking at the example postinstall script, shown in Figure 8-30, you will see that its only purpose is to execute init q.

This approach to editing /sbin/inittab during installation has two drawbacks. First of all, you have to deliver a full script (the postinstall script) simply to perform init q. In addition to that, the package name at the end of each comment line is hardcoded. It would be nice if this value could be based on the package instance so that you could distinguish between the entries you add for each package.

Sample Files

Figure 8-27: Case #5a pkginfo **File**

```
PKG='case5a'
NAME='Case Study #5a'
CATEGORY='applications'
ARCH='3b2'
VERSION='Version 1d05'
CLASSES='sed'
```

Figure 8-28: Case #5a prototype **File**

```
i pkginfo
i postinstall
e sed /sbin/inittab ? ? ?
```

Figure 8-29: Case #5a sed Script (/sbin/inittab)

```
!remove
# remove all entries from the table that are associated
# with this package, though not necessarily just
# with this package instance
/^[^:]*:[^:]*:[^:]*:[^#]*#ROBOT$/d

!install
# remove any previous entry added to the table
# for this particular change
/^[^:]*:[^:]*:[^:]*:[^#]*#ROBOT$/d

# add the needed entry at the end of the table;
# sed(1) does not properly interpret the '$a'
# construct if you previously deleted the last
# line, so the command
#        $a\
#           rb:023456:wait:/usr/robot/bin/setup #ROBOT
# will not work here if the file already contained
# the modification.  Instead, you will settle for
# inserting the entry before the last line!
$i\
rb:023456:wait:/usr/robot/bin/setup #ROBOT
```

Figure 8-30: Case #5a Postinstall Script

```
# make init re-read inittab
/sbin/init q ||
       exit 2
exit 0
```

Case #5b

This study modifies a file which exists on the installation during package installation. It uses one of three modification methods. The other two methods are shown in Cases 5a and 5c. The file modified is /sbin/inittab.

Techniques

This case study shows examples of the following techniques:

- creating classes
- using installation and removal class action scripts

Approach

To modify /sbin/inittab during installation, you must:

- Create a class.

  Create a class called inittab. You must provide an installation and a removal class action script for this class. Define the inittabl class in the CLASSES parameter in the pkginfo file (as shown in Figure 8-31).

- Create an inittab file.

  This file contains the information for the entry that you will add to /sbin/inittab. Notice in the prototype file (Figure 8-32) that inittab is a member of the inittab class and has a file type of e for editable. Figure 8-35 shows what inittab looks like.

- Create an installation class action script.

  Since class action scripts must be multiply executable (meaning you get the same results each time they are executed), you can't just add our text to the end of the file. The script, shown in Figure 8-33, performs the following procedures:

    - checks to see if this entry has been added before
    - if it has, removes any previous versions of the entry

- □ edits the `inittab` file file and adds the comment lines so you know where the entry is from

- □ moves the temporary file back into `/sbin/inittab`

- □ executes `init q` when it receives the end-of-class indicator

  Note that `init q` can be performed by this installation script. A one-line postinstall script is not needed by this approach.

- Create a removal class action script.

  The removal script, shown in Figure 8-34, is very similar to the installation script. The information added by the installation script is removed and `init q` is executed.

This case study resolves the drawbacks to Case 5a. You can support multiple package instances since the comment at the end of the `inittab` entry is now based on package instance. Also, you no longer need a one-line postinstall script. However, this case has a drawback of its own. You must deliver two class action scripts and the `inittab` file to add one line to a file. Case 5c shows a more streamlined approach to editing `/sbin/inittab` during installation.

Sample Files

Figure 8-31: Case #5b `pkginfo` **File**

```
PKG='case5b'
NAME='Case Study #5b'
CATEGORY='applications'
ARCH='3b2'
VERSION='Version 1d05'
CLASSES='inittab'
```

Figure 8-32: Case #5b prototype **File**

```
i pkginfo
i i.inittab
i r.inittab
e inittab /sbin/inittab ? ? ?
```

Figure 8-33: Case #5b Installation Class Action Script (i.inittab)

```
# PKGINST parameter provided by installation service

while read src dest
do
        # remove all entries from the table that
        # associated with this PKGINST
        sed -e "/^[^:]*:[^:]*:[^:]*:[^#]*#$PKGINST$/d" $dest > /tmp/$$itab ||
                exit 2

        sed -e "s/$/#$PKGINST" $src >> /tmp/$$itab ||
                exit 2

        mv /tmp/$$itab $dest ||
                exit 2
done
if [ "$1" = ENDOFCLASS ]
then
        /sbin/init q ||
                exit 2
fi
exit 0
```

Figure 8-34: Case #5b Removal Class Action Script (r.inittab)

```
# PKGINST parameter provided by installation service

while read src dest
do
        # remove all entries from the table that
        # are associated with this PKGINST
        sed -e "/^[^:]*:[^:]*:[^:]*:[^#]*#$PKGINST$/d" $dest > /tmp/$$itab ||
                exit 2

        mv /tmp/$$itab $dest ||
                exit 2
done
/sbin/init q ||
        exit 2
exit 0
```

Figure 8-35: Case #5b `inittab` **File**

```
rb:023456:wait:/usr/robot/bin/setup
```

Case #5c

This study modifies a file which exists on the installation machine during package installation. It uses one of three modification methods. The other two methods are shown in Cases 5a and 5b. The file modified is /sbin/inittab.

Techniques

This case study shows examples of the following technique:

■ using the build class

Approach

This approach to modifying /sbin/inittab uses the build class. A build class file is executed as a shell script and its output becomes the new version of the file being executed. In other words, the data file inittab that is delivered with this package will be executed and the output of that execution will become /sbin/inittab.

The build class file is executed during package installation and package removal. The argument install is passed to the file if it is being executed at installation time. Notice in the sample build file in Figure 8-38 that installation actions are defined by testing for this argument.

To edit /sbin/inittab using the build class, you must:

■ Define the build file in the prototype file.

   The entry for the build file in the prototype file should place it in the build class and define its file type as e. Be certain that the CLASSES parameter in the pkginfo file is defined as build. Figure 8-36 shows the pkginfo file for this example and Figure 8-37 shows the prototype file.

■ Create the build file.

   The build file shown in Figure 8-38 performs the following procedures:

   □ Edits /sbin/inittab to remove any changes already existing for this package. Notice that the filename /sbin/inittab is hard-coded into the sed command.

□ If the package is being installed, adds the new line to the end of /sbin/inittab. A comment tag is included in this new entry to remind us from where that entry came.

□ Executes init q.

This solution addresses the drawbacks in Case Studies 5a and 5b. Only one file is needed (beyond the pkginfo and prototype files), that file is short and simple, it works with multiple instances of a package since the $PKGINST parameter is used, and no postinstall script is required since init q can be executed from the build file.

Sample Files

Figure 8-36: **Case #5c** pkginfo **File**

```
PKG='case5c'
NAME='Case Study #5c'
CATEGORY='applications'
ARCH='3b2'
VERSION='Version 1d05'
CLASSES='build'
```

Figure 8-37: **Case #5c** prototype **File**

```
i pkginfo
e build /sbin/inittab ? ? ?
```

Figure 8-38: Case #5c build **Script (**/sbin/init)

```
# PKGINST parameter provided by installation service

# remove all entries from the existing table that
# are associated with this PKGINST
sed -e "/^[^:]*:[^:]*:[^:]*:[^#]*#$PKGINST$/d" /sbin/inittab ||
        exit 2

if [ "$1" = install ]
then
        # add the following entry to the table
        echo "rb:023456:wait:/usr/robot/bin/setup #$PKGINST" ||
                exit 2
fi
/sbin/init q ||
        exit 2
exit 0
```

Case #6

This case study modifies a number crontab files during package installation.

Techniques

This case study shows examples of the following techniques:

- using classes and class action scripts
- using the crontab command within a class action script

Approach

You could use the build class and follow the approach shown for editing /sbin/inittab in case study 5c except that you want to edit more than one file. If you used the build class approach, you would need to deliver one for each cron file edited. Defining a cron class provides a more general approach. To edit a crontab file with this approach, you must:

- Define the cron files that will be edited in the prototype file.

  Create an entry in the prototype file for each crontab file which will be edited. Define their class as cron and their file type as e. Use the actual name of the file to be edited, as shown in Figure 8-40.

- Create the crontab files that will be delivered with the package.

  These files contain the information you want added to the existing crontab files of the same name. See Figures 8-43 and 8-44 for examples of what these files look like.

- Create an installation class action script for the cron class.

  The i.cron script (Figure 8-41) performs the following procedures:

  - Calculates the user id.

    This is done by setting the variable *user* to the base name of the cron class file being processed. That name equates to the user id. For example, the basename of /var/spool/cron/crontabs/root is root (which is also the user id).

- □ Executes `crontab` using the user id and the `-l` option.

    Using the `-l` options tells `crontab` to send the standard output the contents of the `crontab` for the defined user.

- □ Pipes the output of the `crontab` command to a `sed` script that removes any previous entries that have been added using this installation technique.

- □ Puts the edited output into a temporary file.

- □ Adds the data file for the root user id (that was delivered with the package) to the temporary file and adds a tag so that you will know from where these entries came.

- □ Executes `crontab` with the same user id and give it the temporary file as input.

- ■ Create a removal class action script for the `cron` class.

    The removal script, shown in Figure 8-42, is the same as the installation script except that there is no procedure to add information to the `crontab` file.

These procedures are performed for every file in the `cron` class.

Sample Files

Figure 8-39: Case #3 `pkginfo` **File**

```
PKG='case6'
NAME='Case Study #6'
CATEGORY='application'
ARCH='3b2'
VERSION='Version 1.0'
CLASSES='cron'
```

Figure 8-40: Case #6 prototype **File**

```
i pkginfo
i i.cron
i r.cron
e cron /var/spool/cron/crontabs/root ? ? ?
e cron /var/spool/cron/crontabs/sys ? ? ?
```

Figure 8-41: Case #6 Installation Class Action Script (i.cron)

```
# PKGINST parameter provided by installation service

while read src dest
do
        user=`basename $dest` ||
                exit 2

        (crontab -l $user |
        sed -e "/#$PKGINST$/d" > /tmp/$$crontab) ||
                exit 2

        sed -e "s/$/#$PKGINST/" $src >> /tmp/$$crontab ||
                exit 2

        crontab $user < /tmp/$$crontab ||
                exit 2
        rm -f /tmp/$$crontab
done
exit 0
```

Figure 8-42: Case #6 Removal Class Action Script (r.cron)

```
# PKGINST parameter provided by installation service

while read path
do
        user=`basename $path` ||
                exit 2

        (crontab -l $user |
        sed -e "/#$PKGINST$/d" > /tmp/$$crontab) ||
                exit 2

        crontab $user < /tmp/$$crontab ||
                exit 2
        rm -f /tmp/$$crontab
done
exit 0
```

Figure 8-43: Case #6 Root `crontab` **File (delivered with package)**

```
41,1,21 * * * * /usr/lib/uucp/uudemon.hour > /dev/null
45 23 * * * ulimit 5000; /usr/bin/su uucp -c "/usr/lib/uucp/uudemon.cleanup" >
/dev/null 2>&1
11,31,51 * * * * /usr/lib/uucp/uudemon.poll > /dev/null
```

Figure 8-44: Case #6 Sys `crontab` **File (delivered with package)**

```
0 * * * 0-6 /usr/lib/sa/sa1
20,40 8-17 * * 1-5 /usr/lib/sa/sa1
5 18 * * 1-5 /usr/lib/sa/sa2 -s 8:00 -e 18:01 -i 1200 -A
```

9 Modifying the sysadm Interface

9. MODIFYING THE sysadm INTERFACE

Application and Driver Software Packaging

Overview of sysadm Modification

UNIX System V Release 4 provides a menu interface to the most common administrative procedures. It is invoked by executing sysadm and so is referred to as the sysadm interface. (A complete description of this interface and instructions on how to use it can be found in the *System Administrator's Guide*.)

You can deliver additions or changes to this interface as part of your application software package. Creating the necessary information for an interface modification is a simple process due to the tools provided by SVR4.

This chapter describes these tools, provides all of the needed background information, and details the procedures necessary to design and write your package administration and to package it so that it will become a part of the administration interface on the installation machine.

 This chapter assumes you are familiar with the material covered in the "Packaging Application Software" chapter.

Introduction to the Tools

Two commands can be used to create the files necessary to deliver modifications to the sysadm interface as a part of your package.

- edsysadm creates all of the files needed for your interface modifications to be installed along with your package
- delsysadm deletes menus or tasks from the interface

This chapter also provides an overview of a group of tools known as the data validation tools. You can use them when writing your system administration to simplify and standardize the programming of administrative interaction. The tools are described in detail in the "Data Validation Tools" section of this chapter.

The edsysadm Command

edsysadm, which allows you to make changes or additions to the interface, is an interactive command that functions much like the sysadm command itself. It presents a series of prompts for information. (Which prompt appears depends on your response to the previous prompt.)

After you have responded to all the prompts, edsysadm presents a form that you must fill in with information describing the menu or task being changed or added. This form is called the menu (or task) definition form. If you are changing an existing menu or task entry, the definition form will already be filled in with the current values, which you can edit. If you are adding a new menu or task entry, the form will be empty and you will have to fill it in.

When you follow the procedures in this chapter, edsysadm creates all of the files and directories necessary to deliver your interface modifications as a part of your package. The section entitled "Introduction to the Package Modification Files" describes the three files that edsysadm creates.

edsysadm builds the directory structure required by the sysadm interface. You do not need to know this structure and you are not required to have your work directory organized in any predefined way. When you fill in a menu or task definition form, you supply filenames (for example, a file containing help messages) that edsysadm should use when creating the packaging for your interface modifications. edsysadm creates a prototype file and builds the interface directory format by using the *path1=path2* naming convention. *path2* defines where the files reside on your machine and *path1* defines where they should be placed on the installation machine.

The delsysadm Command

delsysadm removes tasks and menus from the interface. When you deliver your modifications as a part of your package, you do not need to use delsysadm to remove them. Any time an interface modification is delivered as a part of a package, those modifications are automatically removed at the same time as the package. This chapter describes the delsysadm command in case you need to use it on your own machine, for example to remove modifications added for testing.

delsysadm checks for dependencies on the entry being removed before deleting the entry. (A dependency exists if the menu being removed contains an entry placed there by an application package.) If delsysadm discovers a dependency, you are asked whether you want to continue with the removal. (If a dependency is found during an automatic removal, the interface entry is not removed.)

When you delete a menu entry with delsysadm, it must already be empty (contain no other menus or tasks) or you can execute delsysadm with the −r option. This option removes a menu and all its entries at the same time.

 Use delsysadm to remove only those menu or task entries that you have added to an interface.

The Data Validation Tools

The data validation routines help standardize administration interaction in the SVR4 environment and also make development easier. The tools are available as shell commands and as visual modules to be used in a FACE (Framed Access Command Environment) form. The tools perform the following series of tasks:

- prompt a user for a particular type of input
- validate the response
- format and print help and error messages
- return the input if it passes validation

The type of validation performed is defined by the tool itself. For example, the shell command ckyorn prompts for and validates an affirmative or negative response. These tools should be used in your administration programs if they are to be added to the sysadm interface to maintain consistency within the interface. Refer to the section "Data Validation Tools" for full details on these tools and their uses.

Introduction to the Package Modification Files

When you execute edsysadm to define menus and tasks and save those
definitions to be included in your application software package, it creates three
files:

- the package description file

- the menu information file

- the prototype file

The package description file contains information edsysadm uses to change
interface modifications already saved for packaging. When you decide to
change your modifications after already creating the packaging (meaning the
menu information and prototype files are already created), the package
description file provides edsysadm with the information it needs to locate the
other package modification files and to make the changes. Without this file,
edsysadm cannot make such a change. You are asked to supply a name for this
file during the edsysadm interaction and it is created in your current working
directory (unless you supply a full pathname to a different directory with the
name).

The menu information file contains the menu or task name, where it is located
in the interface structure, and, for tasks, what executable to use when the task is
invoked. It tells the interface installation software how to modify the interface
structures to include the new definitions. The file's name is the hour, minute,
second, day-of-year, and year that the file was created, followed by an .mi
suffix. It is created in your current working directory.

The prototype file created by edsysadm contains entries for all of the interface
modification components that must be packaged with your software (for example, the menu information file and, for tasks, the executables). These entries
must be incorporated into your package either by reading the edsysadm-created
file into your package prototype file or by using the include command in the
main prototype file for your package. The prototype file created by edsysadm
is created in your current working directory with the name of prototype.

Overview of the Interface Modification Process

You must take a number of steps to add your package administration to the
sysadm interface. This chapter explains each step in detail. The following steps
are covered:

- planning your package administration (with details on how to decide if
  you should modify the interface and where to place it in the interface
  structure)

- writing your administration actions (with general information on what
  your executables can be)

- writing your help message (with a description of the required help message file)

- packaging your interface modifications (with procedural details on executing edsysadm and what steps must be taken afterwards)

This chapter also includes instructions on executing delsysadm.

Planning Your Interface Modifications

You will need to plan your interface modifications before executing edsysadm. Planning begins with deciding if your administration tasks should become a part of the sysadm interface. If so, you must decide on where your tasks fit into the interface, what to name your tasks, and the full menu structure involved with your administrative tasks.

Deciding if You Should Modify the Interface

Any type of task can be added to the sysadm interface with the following two restrictions:

- Tasks that can be automated should not be added to the interface (for example, procedures that can run automatically as part of system booting or as part of your package installation).

- Tasks that require the system to be in firmware mode can be added to the interface but it is strongly recommended that they not be.

Once you have decided to add your administration tasks to the interface, you must determine where in the interface you want to locate tasks and menus.

Planning the Location of Your Modifications

To plan your modification you must first become familiar with the interface organization. Then you must decide how to organize the tasks you want to add and how to fit your modifications into the overall structure.

An Overview of the Interface Structure

The sysadm interface consists of a hierarchy of menus. At the top of the hierarchy is the main menu (labeled System Administration Menu). It appears on the screen, immediately after sysadm is invoked, as follows:

```
                    System Administration Menu

applications     -  Administration for Available Applications
backup_service   -  Backup Scheduling, Setup, and Control
diagnostics      -  Diagnosing System Problems
file_systems     -  File System Creation, Checking, and Mounting
machine          -  Machine Configuration Display and Powerdown
networks         -  Network Administration
restore_service  -  Restore From Backup Data
software         -  Software Installation and Removal
storage_devices  -  Storage Device Operations and Definitions
system_setup     -  System Name, Date/Time and Initial Password Setup
users            -  User Login and Group Administration
```

NOTE   The `applications` menu will not appear on the main `sysadm` menu until
at least one menu or task has been placed under it.

The main menu consists of a list of function-specific menus. The lefthand
column notes the menu names (such as `machine`) and the righthand column
gives descriptions of these menus. Each menu offers other menus and/or
names of tasks. For example, the `machine` menu, shown below, contains one
menu (`configuration`) and five tasks.

```
                    Machine Management

configuration - System Configuration Display
firmware      - Stop All Running Programs and Enters Firmware Mode
floppy key    - Creates a Floppy Key Removable Diskette
powerdown     - Stops All Running Programs and Turns Off Machine
reboot        - Stops All Running Programs and Reboots Machine
whos on       - Displays List of Users Logged onto Machine
```

Choosing the entry `configuration` from this screen will cause another menu
to be presented. Choosing a task entry, such as `powerdown`, will begin execution of that task.

Planning Your Administration Structure

Planning your administration structure requires three steps:

1. Deciding what tasks to add to the interface.

   You can add any number of tasks. You should have separate entries for each task to be performed. For example, if your administration allowed a log to be changed, added to, and removed, you should create an entry for each task and not combine them into one entry called log administration.

2. Deciding under which menu the tasks should be placed.

   You can create new sysadm menus at any level and you can change or add to any of the original sysadm menus. You should be aware, however, that if you make changes to original menus you might cause problems in the execution of standard sysadm operations. It is therefore recommended (though not mandatory) that you create new menus for your package administration by placing it under the applications menu (located on the main menu) or by creating a new main menu entry.

3. Organizing your tasks.

   You can organize your tasks under one menu or place them in submenu groups. For example, if your package has tasks to be performed daily and weekly, you might create a structure such as the following:

   - Under the applications menu on the main menu, add an entry for your package called pkgAadmin.

   - Under pkgAadmin, add two submenus called daily and weekly.

   - Under the submenu daily, add entries for each of the daily tasks.

   - Under the submenu weekly, add entries for each of the weekly tasks.

It is important that you have your full administrative structure planned before running edsysadm because you must create a menu entry before placing a task or submenu under it.

After you have planned your structure, you should decide on the names for your menus and tasks.

Naming Your Interface Modifications

Naming your interface modifications requires the following three pieces of information described below. This section also details the interface naming requirements and tells you how the system handles naming collisions.

How to Name Your Modifications

When naming your interface modifications, you must decide on these three pieces of information:

Name
: The name of the menu or task as it will appear in the left-hand column of the screen.

Description
: The description of the menu or task as it will appear in the righthand column of the screen.

Location
: The location of a menu or task in the sysadm menu hierarchy. This location is a combination, step-by-step, of all the menu names that must be chosen to reach the menu or task. Each step must already exist when the entry is added. For example, when you add a task with a location of main:applications:mypkg, you must already have created an entry for the menu mypkg.

: All locations begin with main. When defining a location in the procedures that follow, each step should be separated by a colon. For example, the powerdown task is under the menu machine, which, in turn, is under the main menu. Thus, the location of the powerdown task is main:machine.

You will supply these pieces of information on the menu (or task) definition form.

Interface Naming Requirements

A menu or task name should be as short as possible in length but, at the same time, be descriptive. It can contain only lower case letters and underscores and has a maximum length of 16 characters.

The description field can contain any character string and has a maximum length of 58 characters. This description field text for a menu is also used as the title for that menu when it is displayed. Use of standard title capitalization rules is recommended.

How the System Handles Naming Collisions

A naming collision might occur under two circumstances:

- When the package being installed is an update to an existing version.

  The administrator will be asked during installation if this is an update, in which case the existing menus and tasks will be overwritten.

- When two packages have created identical interface modifications.

  The colliding menu or task will be renamed by adding the first available numerical suffix (beginning with 2). For example, if an entry for menuA already exists and a package attempts to add an identical entry, the one being added will be renamed to menuA2.

Writing Your Administration Actions

When you execute `edsysadm` to create packaging for a task entry, you will fill in a task definition form. One of the fields on that form asks for the name of the task action file. The task action file is the executable that will run when your task is selected from the interface. Your administrative task can use more than one executable, but, if so, you must create one that is called when the task is selected and call any other executables associated with the task from within it.

The task action can be one of two types:

- Non-interactive

    A non-interactive task action can be any shell executable.

- Interactive

    An interactive task action must be a FACE form. (Refer to the *Programmer's Guide: Character User Interface (FMLI and ETI)* for instructions on writing a FACE form.)

Use the tools described in the section "Data Validation Tools" whenever possible when writing administrator interaction.

Writing Your Help Messages

You must write help messages to be packaged with every interface modifications. They are delivered in what is called an item help file. This file has text for two types of messages:

- the help message that will be shown when the user requests help from the parent menu
- the help messages that will be shown for each field when your task action is a FACE form

The format of the item help file allows you to create one item help file for each task, combine all of your help messages for multiple tasks into one file, use the same message for multiple FACE forms, and to define a title hierarchy for the help message screens.

The Item Help File

There are no naming restrictions for the item help file that resides on your machine. However, within the interface structure, the item help file must always be named Help. You can use this name if you want to but it is not mandatory since edsysadm uses the *path1=path2* naming convention in the prototype file that it creates to define the directory structure required by the interface. Regardless of what the item help file is named on your machine, *path1* in the prototype file will have the name Help. This means that you can have more than one item help file in your working directory at the same time and edsysadm will handle the details of giving it the correct name.

There are three types of entries in an item help file:

- the menu item help
- the default title (can define both a global default and a form default)
- the field item help

A description of each type of entry and its format follows. All of the entries use the colon (:) as the keyword delimiter.

The Menu Item Help Message Format

The menu item help message will be shown whenever a user requests help on an entry from the parent menu. Menu item help must be written for each menu and task entry being delivered as an interface modification. For example, if your package administration is adding a menu under `main:applications` and that menu has three tasks under it, you will need to deliver four menu item help messages.

The format for the menu item help definition is as follows:

```
[task_name:]ABSTRACT:
     TAB    Line 1 of message text
     TAB    Line 2 of message text
     TAB    Line n of message text
```

task_name defines the task (or menu) entry to which this help message belongs. This name must match the name that you have decided should appear in the lefthand column of the menu screen. (Refer back to "Naming Your Interface Modifications" for more details on this name.) *task_name* is not optional when more than one menu item help definition is defined in the same item help file. This helps to distinguish to which task or menu the message belongs.

The message text should be entered beneath the header line. There can be multiple lines of text with a maximum length of 69 characters per line. Each line must begin with a tab character. Blank lines may be included within the message as long as they also begin with a tab character. An example menu item help definition is shown below.

```
task1:ABSTRACT:
        This is line one of the menu item help message.
        This is a second line of message text.

        The preceding line will appear as a blank line
        when the help message is shown because it begins
        with a tab.
```

The title for a menu item help message is always the description text, as it appears in the lefthand column of the menu display, prepended by the string `Help on`.

The Default Title Format

You can define two types of default titles:

■ a global default title to be used on all of the help messages defined in the item help file

■ a form default title to be used on all of the help messages defined for a particular form in an item help file with messages defined for numerous forms

Defaults can be overridden, as described in the section "The Title Hierarchy." A default title definition is recommended but not required.

The format for the default title definition is as follows:

> [*form_id*:]TITLE:*Title Text*

form_id is the name of the form as it is defined with lininfo in your FACE form definition. When a *form_id* is supplied, this line defines a form default title. When it is not supplied, this line defines a global default title.

The title text defined after the TITLE keyword will have the string HELP on prepended to it when displayed. Keep this in mind when writing the title.

An example form default title definition is shown below.

    task1:TITLE:Package Administration Task1

If task1 had not been added before TITLE, this example would be defining a global default title. The title defined by the example above will be displayed as:

    HELP on Package Administration Task1

The Field Item Help Message Format

The field item help message will be shown whenever a user requests help from within a FACE form. Each field on the form must have a help message defined in the item help file.

The format for the field item help definition is as follows:

[*form_id*:] field_id:[*Title Text*]
```
TAB    Line 1 of message text
TAB    Line 2 of message text
TAB    Line n of message text
```

form_id is the name of the form as it is defined with lininfo in your FACE
form definition. When one item help file contains messages for multiple tasks
(and so multiple forms), it is used to distinguish with which form a field
belongs. It is optional if the file contains messages for only one task.
field_id is the name of the field as it is defined with lininfo in your FACE
form definition. *Title text* defines a title used only with the help message for
this field. As with the default title, the text defined here will have the string
HELP on prepended to it when displayed.

The message text should be entered beneath the header line. There can be multiple lines of text with a maximum length of 69 characters per line. Each line
must begin with a tab character. Blank lines may be included within the message as long as they also begin with a tab character. An example field item help
definition is shown below.

```
task1:fld1:the Name Field
        This is the text for a field item help for a name
        field.

        The preceding line will appear as a blank line
        when the help message is shown because it begins
        with a tab.
```

The title for this field item help message, as defined above, will be HELP on
the Name Field

The Title Hierarchy

You can define a global default title, a form default title, and a field title in the item help file. When all three are defined in the same file, the following rules are followed:

- The global default title is used for any message defined in an item help file that does not have a form default title or field title.

- The form default title is used for any message defined in an item help file and that is associated with the form, unless it has a field title.

- The field title is used only for the one field item help message for which it is defined.

In summary, if no field title is defined, the form default title is used. If no form default title is defined, the global default title is used. You always want at least a global default title defined; otherwise, the string HELP on will be displayed with no descriptive text.

To define a global default title, add a line to your item help file in the following format:

> TITLE : *Title Text*

where *Title Text* is the text for the global default title.

To define a form default title, add a line to your item help file in the following format:

> *form_id* : TITLE : *Title Text*

where *form_id* is the name of form as it is defined with lininfo in your FACE form definition and *Title Text* is the text for the form default title.

To define a field title, use the following format for the field item help header line:

> *form_id* : *field_id* : *Title Text*

where *form_id* is the name of the form as it is defined with lininfo in your FACE form definition, *field_id* is the name of the field as it is defined with lininfo in your FACE form definition and *Title Text* is the text for the field title.

NOTE In all cases, the text defined as *Title Text* is always prepended with the string `HELP on` when displayed to a user.

Setting Up for Item Help in a FACE Object

To help the interface read your item help file and know with which forms and fields a help message is associated, you must define your `help` and `lininfo` descriptors in your FACE object definition as follows:

- The `help` descriptor must be defined exactly as shown on the line below:

      help=OPEN TEXT $INTFBASE/Text.itemhelp $LININFO

- The `lininfo` descriptor for each field must be defined as

      lininfo=[*form_id*:]*field_id*

  where *form_id* and *field_id* are names each no longer than 30 characters. The names defined here as *form_id* and *field_id* must match exactly those used as *form_id* and *field_id* in the item help file.

 NOTE Since you do not create a FACE form definition for a menu entry, you do not need to take any setup actions. However, you should be certain that the *task_name* keyword precedes the ABSTRACT heading line for a menu entry help message.

Example Item Help Files

This section shows two example item help files. Figure 9-1 shows an item help file that defines messages for only one form. Figure 9-2 shows an example of defining messages for multiple forms in one item help file.

Figure 9-1: Item Help File for One Form

```
ABSTRACT:
        The text defined here will be shown to
        users when they request help while
        viewing the parent menu for this
        task.  The task name is "adding users."

TITLE:Adding Users

field1:
        The text defined here will be shown to
        users when they request help from the
        form and the cursor is positioned at
        field1.  The title for this message will
        be ''HELP on Adding Users'' as defined above.

field2:Field 2
        The text defined here will be shown to
        users when they request help from the
        form and the cursor is positioned at
        field2.  The title for this message will
        be ''HELP on Field 2''.
```

Note: The lininfo descriptors in the form definition associated with this file should look like this:

```
        .
        .
        .

lininfo=field1

        .
        .
        .

lininfo=field2
```

Figure 9-2: Item Help File for Multiple Forms

```
add:ABSTRACT:
        The text defined here will be shown to
        users when they request help while
        viewing the parent menu for the task
        named add.

add_user:TITLE:Adding Users

add_user:field1:
        The text defined here will be shown to
        users when they request help from the
        form and the cursor is positioned at
        field1.  The title for this message will
        be ''HELP on Adding Users'' as defined above.

add_user:field2:Field 2
        The text defined here will be shown to
        users when they request help from the
        form and the cursor is positioned at
        field2.  The title for this message will
        be ''HELP on Field 2''.

delete:ABSTRACT:
        The text defined here will be shown to
        users when they request help while
        viewing the parent menu for the task
        named delete.

delete_user:TITLE:Deleting Users

delete_user:field1:
        The text defined here will be shown to
        users when they request help from the
        form and the cursor is positioned at
        field1.  The title for this message will
        be ''HELP on Deleting Users'' as defined above.

delete_user:field2:Field 2
        The text defined here will be shown to
        users when they request help from the
        form and the cursor is positioned at
        field2.  The title for this message will
        be ''HELP on Field 2''.
```

(continued on next page)

Figure 9-2: Item Help File for Multiple Forms (continued)

```
Note:  The lininfo descriptors in the form definition associated with this
file should look like this:

    .
    .
lininfo=add_user:field1
    .
    .
lininfo=add_user:field2
    .
    .
lininfo=delete_user:field1
    .
    .
lininfo=delete_user:field2
```

Packaging Your Interface Modifications

To prepare your interface modifications for installation, you must create the packaging for your menus and tasks by executing edsysadm. The packaging created by edsysadm consists of two files, a prototype file and a menu information file. This section describes the procedures for creating these files and what to do after they have been created. (It also describes how to change the packaging after it has been created.)

NOTE   edsysadm also creates a package description file. edsysadm uses this file during its execution and is not a part of the packaging.

Basic Steps for Packaging Your Modifications

The procedures described next must be repeated for each menu and task entry being added. Begin with creating the menu entry (or entries) because you cannot add tasks or submenus to a menu that does not exist. Be certain that you use the same package description file name for all of the entries belonging to a package.

After running edsysadm, be certain to follow the steps described in "Preparing Your Package" (at the end of this section) to incorporate the modifications into your software package.

For example, if your administration requires the addition of one menu and four tasks, you will need to follow the procedure for creating the packaging for a menu entry, then repeat the procedure for creating the packaging for a task entry four times. Each time, when asked for a package description file name, give the same name to ensure that the packaging created contains all the necessary entries. These procedures will create a menu information file and a prototype file with all of the information necessary to include your interface modifications in your package. The two remaining steps (described in "Preparing Your Package") are to include the edsysadm created prototype file in your package prototype file and to edit the CLASSES parameter in the pkginfo file.

Creating or Changing the Packaging for a Menu Entry

The procedures for creating and changing the packaging for a new menu are similar and both result in the display of a menu definition form. Each procedure is described below, followed by a description of the menu definition form.

Creating the Packaging for a Menu Entry

Before creating the packaging for a new menu entry, you should:

- Select a name and description for the menu.

- Select a location for it in the interface.

- Prepare a help message file for the menu entry (refer to "Writing Your Help Messages" presented earlier in this chapter for instructions).

- Know the name of the package description file to which the information for this menu should be added (if you are adding multiple menus and tasks)

1. Type edsysadm and press RETURN.

 NOTE If you do not execute this command from the directory in which the help message file resides, supply the full pathname when prompted for the name of the help message file.

2. You are asked to choose between a menu and a task. Choose menu and press RETURN.

3. You are asked to choose between adding a new menu or changing an existing one. Choose add and press RETURN.

4. You are given an empty menu definition form. Fill it in and press SAVE. (See "The Menu Definition Form" for descriptions of the fields on this form.)

5. You are asked if you want to test the changes before actually making them. Answer either yes or no and press SAVE. (If you answer yes, refer to the "Testing Your Menu Changes On-Line" section to learn what the test involves.)

6. You are asked if you want to install the modifications into the interface on your machine or save them for a package. Choose `save` and press SAVE.

7. You are asked to supply a file name. Enter a name for the package description file and press SAVE.

8. If the file name given for the package description file already exists, you are asked if you want to overwrite it or add to its contents. Answer `overwrite,` `do not overwrite,` or `add` and press SAVE.

9. If the file name does not already exist (or after you have completed Step 8) you will see a message stating that the menu information file and `prototype` file have been verified and the top-level `prototype` must be edited to include the new `prototype` file. Press CANCEL to return to the menu shown in step 3. Press CONT to return to the form shown in step 4.

Changing the Packaging for a Menu Entry

Before changing the packaging for a menu entry, you should:

- Know the name and description of the menu entry.

- Know its location in the interface.

- Change the associated help message file, if necessary, or create a new one (refer to "Writing Your Help Messages" presented earlier in this chapter for instructions).

- Know the name of the package description file associated with the package being changed (and know that it is available in your current working directory).

1. Type `edsysadm` and press RETURN.

NOTE If you have changed a help message file or created a new one and you do not execute this command from the directory in which the help message file resides, supply the full pathname when asked for the name of the file.

2. You are asked to choose between a menu and a task. Choose menu and press RETURN.

3. You are asked to choose between adding a new menu and changing an existing one. Choose change and press RETURN.

4. You are asked if your change is for an on-line menu or for a menu that has been saved for a package. Choose packaged and press SAVE.

5. You are asked to supply the package description file name for the package beinging changed. Fill in the name of a valid package description file and press SAVE.

6. You are given a menu definition form filled in with the current values for the menu named above. Make the desired changes and press SAVE. (See the "The Menu Definition Form" for descriptions of the fields on this form.)

7. You are asked if you want to test the changes before actually making them. Answer either yes or no and press SAVE. (If you answer yes, refer to the section entitled "Testing Your Menu Changes On-Line" to learn what the test involves.)

8. You are asked if you want to install the modifications into the interface on your machine or save them for a package. Choose save and press SAVE.

9. You are asked to supply a file name. Enter a name for the package description file and press SAVE. (This must be the same package description file named in Step 5.)

10. If the file name given for the package description file already exists, you are asked if you want to overwrite it or add to its contents. Answer overwrite, do not overwrite, or add and press SAVE.

11. If the file name does not already exist (or after you have completed Step 10) you will see a message stating that the menu information file and prototype file have been verified and the top-level prototype must be edited to include the new prototype file. Press CANCEL to return to

the menu shown in step 4. Press CONT to return to the form shown in step 5.

Testing Your Menu Changes On-Line

Before installing your menu changes, you may want to verify that you've added an entry to a menu. The edsysadm command gives you a chance to do this after you fill in the menu definition form. Follow these steps to perform your test.

1. Type yes when edsysadm presents the following prompt:

   ```
   Do you want to test this modification before continuing?
   ```

2. The parent menu (on which your addition or change is listed) is displayed. Check to make sure your modification has been made correctly.

3. Put the cursor on the new or changed menu entry and press the <HELP> key. The text of the help message for that menu entry is displayed so you can check it. (Press CANCEL to return to the menu.)

4. To exit on-line testing, press the CANCEL key.

5. You are returned to the prompt:

   ```
   Do you want to test this modification before continuing?
   ```

   If you want to continue executing the change, type no.

   If you want to make additional modifications to the menu definition form, press CANCEL. You are returned to the form and can make further changes at that time. (Press SAVE when you have finished your editing. You can then retest your changes or continue executing the change.)

The Menu Definition Form

This form contains four fields in which you must provide: a menu name, a menu description, a menu location, and the name of the help message for the menu. Below are descriptions of the information you must provide in each field.

Menu Name
: The name of the new menu (as it should appear in the lefthand column of the screen). This field has a maximum length of 16 alphanumeric characters.

Menu Description
: A description of the new menu (as it should appear in the righthand column of the screen). This field has a maximum length of 58 characters and can consist of any alphanumeric character except the at sign (@), carat (ˆ), tilde (˜), back grave (`), grave (`), and double quotes (").

Menu Location
: The location of the menu in the menu hierarchy, expressed as a menu pathname. The pathname should begin with the main menu followed by all other menus that must be traversed (in the order they are traversed) to access this menu. Each menu name must be separated by colons. For example, the menu location for a menu entry being added to the Applications menu is `main:applications`. *Do not include the menu name in this location definition.* The complete pathname to this menu entry will be the menu location plus the menu name defined at the first prompt.

  This is a scrollable field, showing a maximum of 50 alphanumeric characters at a time.

Menu Help File Name
: Pathname to the item help file for this menu entry. If it resides in the directory from which you invoked `edsysadm`, you do not need to give a full pathname. If you name an item help file that does not exist, you are placed in an editor (as defined by $EDITOR) to create one. The new file is created in the current directory and named `Help`.

The following screen shows a filled-in sample menu definition.

```
              Define A Menu

Name:  msvr
Description:  Menu Description
Location:  main:applications
Help Message:  Help
```

Creating or Changing the Packaging for a Task Entry

The procedures for creating and changing the packaging for a new task are
similar and both result in the display of a task definition form. Each procedure
is described below, followed by a description of the task definition form.

Creating the Packaging for a Task Entry

Before creating the packaging for a task entry, you should:

- Gather all files that will be associated with this task, such as the help file,
  FACE forms , or other executables. All files should already be prepared.

- Decide on the task name and description.

- Decide on its location in the interface.

- Create a help file (refer to "Writing Your Help Messages" presented earlier in this chapter for instructions).

- Know the name of the package description file to which the information
  for this task should be added (if you are adding multiple menus and
  tasks)

1. Type edsysadm and press RETURN.

NOTE If you do not execute this command from the same directory in which the files associated with this task reside, enter full pathnames when supplying file names.

2. You are asked to choose between a menu and a task. Choose `task` and press RETURN.

3. You are asked to choose between adding a new task or changing an existing one. Choose `add` and press RETURN.

4. You are given an empty task definition form. Fill it in and press SAVE. (See "The Task Definition Form" for descriptions of the fields on this form. Be aware that, when you name the menu under which you want this new task to reside, that menu must already be packaged.)

5. You are asked if you want to install the modifications into the interface on your machine or save them for a package. Choose `save` and press SAVE.

6. You are asked to supply a file name. Enter a name for the package description file and press SAVE.

7. If the file name given for the package description file already exists, you are asked if you want to overwrite it or add to its contents. Answer either `overwrite`, `do not overwrite`, or `add` and press SAVE.

8. If the file name does not already exist (or after you have completed Step 7) you see a message stating that the menu information file and `prototype` file have been verified and the top-level `prototype` must be edited to include the new `prototype` file. Press CANCEL to return to the menu shown in step 3. Press CONT to return to the form shown in step 4.

Changing the Packaging for a Task Entry

Before changing the packaging for a task entry, you should:

■ Gather any of the files associated with this task that have been changed or are new. All files should already be prepared or changed.

- Know the menu name and description.

- Know its location in the interface.

- Change the associated help file, if necessary (refer to "Writing Your Help Messages" presented earlier in this chapter for instructions).

- Know the name of the package description file associated with the package being changed (and know that it is available in your current working directory).

1. Type `edsysadm` and press RETURN.

 NOTE   If your change requires new files or changes to existing files and you do not execute this command from the directory in which the files reside, enter full pathnames when supplying file names.

2. You are asked to choose between a menu and a task. Choose `task` and press RETURN.

3. You are asked to choose between adding a new task and changing an existing one. Choose `change` and press RETURN.

4. You are asked if your change is for an on-line task or for a task that has been saved for a package. Choose `packaged` and press SAVE.

5. You are asked to supply the package description file name for the package being changed. Fill in the name of a valid package description file and press SAVE.

6. You are given a task definition form filled in with the current values for the task named above. Make the desired changes and press SAVE. (See "The Task Definition Form" for descriptions of the fields on this form.)

7. You are asked if you want to install the modifications into the interface on your machine or save them for a package. Choose `save` and press SAVE.

8. You are asked to supply a file name. Enter a name for the package description file and press SAVE. (This must be the same package description file named in Step 5.)

9. If the file name given for the package description file already exists, you are asked if you want to overwrite it or add to its contents. Answer either `overwrite`, `do not overwrite`, or `add` and press SAVE.

10. If the file name does not already exist (or after you have completed Step 9) you see a message stating that the menu information file and `proto-type` file have been verified and the top-level `prototype` must be edited to include the new `prototype` file. Press CANCEL to return to the menu shown in step 4. Press CONT to return to the form shown in step 5.

The Task Definition Form

This form contains six fields in which you must provide: a task name, a task description, a task location, the name of a help message for the task, a task action file, and the files associated with the task. Below are descriptions of the information you must provide in each field.

Task Name	The name of the new task (as it should appear in the left-hand column of the screen). This field has a maximum length of 16 alphanumeric characters.
Task Description	A description of the new task (as it should appear in the righthand column of the screen). This field has a maximum length of 58 characters and can consist of any alphanumeric character except the at sign (@), carat (^), tilde (~), back grave ('), grave (`), and double quotes (").
Task Location	The location of the task in the menu hierarchy, expressed as a pathname. The pathname should begin with the main menu followed by all other menus that must be traversed (in the order they are traversed) to access this task. Each menu name must be separated by colons. For example, the task location for a task entry being added to the applications menu is `main:applications`. *Do not include the task name in this location definition.* The complete pathname to this task entry will be the task location as well as the task name defined at the first prompt.
	This is a scrollable field, showing a maximum of 50 alphanumeric characters at a time.

Task Help File
Name

Pathname to the item help file for this
task entry. If it resides in the directory from which you
invoked edsysadm, you do not need to give a full pathname. If you name an item help file that does not exist,
you are placed in an editor (as defined by $EDITOR) to
create one. The new file is created in the current directory and named Help.

Task Action

The FACE form name or executable that will be run
when this task is selected. This is a scrollable field,
showing a maximum of 58 alphanumeric characters at a
time. This pathname can be relative to the current directory as well as absolute. (Refer to the "Writing Your
Administration Actions" section for details.)

Task Files

Any FACE objects or other executables that support the
task action listed above and might be called from within
that action. *Do not include the help file name or the task
action in this list.* Pathnames can be relative to the
current directory as well as absolute. A dot (.) implies
"all files in the current directory" and includes files in
subdirectories.

This is a scrollable field, showing a maximum of 50
alphanumeric characters at a time.

The following screen shows a filled-in sample task definition form.

```
          Define A Task

Name:  msvrtask
Description:  Task Description
Location:  main:applications:msvr
Help Message:  Help
Action:  Form.msvrtask
Task Files:  Form.task2, Text.task2
```

Preparing Your Package

You must perform two steps, after executing edsysadm, to include your interface modification files in your application package.

1. Include the prototype file

    The prototype file that edsysadm creates must become a part of your
    package prototype file structure. This means that you must either read
    it into another prototype file or use the include command in your pri-
    mary prototype file. For example, adding

    ```
    !include /myproject/admsrc/prototype
    ```

    to a prototype file in the /myproject directory ensures that the pro-
    totype file in /myproject/admsrc, and all of the objects it describes,
    will be included when the packaging tool, pkgmk, creates the package.

2. Change your CLASSES parameter in the pkginfo file

    The components defined in the prototype file that edsysadm creates
    are placed into the two special classes: OAMmif and OAMadmin. You
    must edit the pkginfo file for your package and add these to the
    CLASSES parameter definition. For example, a CLASSES definition before
    the change might look like this:

    ```
    CLASSES="class1 class2"
    ```

    It should be changed to look like this:

    ```
    CLASSES="class1 class2 OAMmif OAMadmin"
    ```

Your interface modifications are now ready to be included in your package
when you create your package using pkgmk. (Details on packaging procedures
are discussed in the "Packaging Application Software" chapter.)

Deleting Interface Modifications

Interface modifications can be deleted in two ways. When a package is removed, the modifications installed with the package are removed automatically. Modifications can also be removed online by executing `delsysadm`.

To delete either a menu or task entry online, execute

    delsysadm *name*

where *name* is the location of the task or menu in the interface, followed by the menu or task name. For example, to delete a task named `mytask` with the location `main:application:mymenu`, execute

    delsysadm main:application:mymenu:mytask

Before an entry for a menu can be removed, that menu must be empty (contain no submenus or tasks). If it is not, you must use the `-r` option with `delsysadm`. This option requests that, in addition to the named menu, all submenus and tasks located under that menu be removed. For example, to remove `main:application:mymenu` and all submenus and tasks that reside under it, execute

    delsysadm -r main:application:mymenu

When you use the `-r` option, `delsysadm` checks for dependencies before removing any subentries. (A dependency exists if the menu being removed contains an entry placed there by an application package.) If a dependency is found, you are shown a list of packages that depend on the menu you want to delete and asked whether you want to continue. If you answer yes, the menu and all of its menus and tasks are removed (even those shown to have dependencies). If you answer no, the menu is not deleted.

 Use `delsysadm` to remove only those menu or task entries that you have added to the interface with `edsysadm`.

Data Validation Tools

The data validation tools are a group of shell level commands that serve two purposes:

- standardize the appearance of administration interaction in the SVR4 environment regardless of who writes it
- simplify development of scripts requiring administrator input

Every tool generates a prompt, validates the answer and returns the response. There are no restrictions on when you should use them. It is recommended that you use them every time your application interacts with an administrator. Using the tools at such a time will make all administrator interaction look alike to the user, regardless of the vendor who created the package. You will see, as well, that using these tools makes writing scripts with administrator interaction much simplier, since the tools do the work based on parameters you provide.

At the very least, it is recommended that you use them in your request script (the packaging script from which you can solicit administrator input) and in the executables you deliver when your package administration will be incorporated into the sysadm interface. See "Modifying the sysadm Interface" for details about writing executables for the sysadm interface and "Packaging Application Software" for details on writing a request script.

This section introduces you to the data validation tools and discusses their characteristics. For details on a specific tool, look in the "Reference Manual" part of this guide. The shell commands and corresponding visual tools are provided as Section 1 manual pages.

Types of Tools

There are two types of data validation tools. Both perform the same series of tasks (described later) but are used in different environments. The two types are:

- Shell Commands

  These tools are invoked from the shell level and used in shell scripts.

- Visual Tools

  These tools are invoked from within the field definition in an FMLI form definition. While the shell commands perform all tasks with one command, the visual tools are broken into separate commands for defining help messages, error messages and performing validation.

Characteristics of the Tools

All of the shell commands perform the same series of tasks (the visual tools each perform a subsection of the full series). Those tasks are:

- Prompt a user for input
- Validate the answer
- Format and print a help message when requested
- Format and present an error message when validation fails
- Return the input if it passes validation
- Allow a user to quit the process

The tool itself defines the type of prompt shown and validation performed is defined. For example, the shell command `ckyorn` prompts for a yes or no answer and accepts only a positive or negative response. Some tools allow you to supply input during execution to help customize the validation. For example, `ckrange` prompts for and validates an answer within a given range. The upper and lower limits of the range can be defined when executing `ckrange`.

 Leading and trailing white space is stripped from the input before validation is performed.

The Data Validation Tool Prompts

Each tool has a default prompt that you can use as is, add to, or overwrite. The manual page for each tool (see Appendix A) shows the default prompt text. You must use the -p option of a shell command before the default can be overwritten.

For example, executing `ckyorn` without options produces the following output:

```
Yes or No [y,n,?,q]:
```

The next example shows the use of the -p option and the output that is produced.

```
$ ckyorn -p "Do you want the manual page files installed?"
Do you want the manual page files installed? [y,n,?,q]:
```

The Data Validation Tool Help Messages

Each tool has a default help message that you can use as is, add to, or completely overwrite. The manual page for each tool (see Appendix A) shows the default help message text. You must use the -h option of a shell command before the default can be overwritten.

For example, if you executed ckyorn without options and the user requested a help message by entering ? at the prompt, the following message would be seen:

```
To respond in the affirmative, enter y, yes, Y, or YES.
To respond in the negative, enter n, no, N, or NO.
```

The next example shows the use of the -h option when executing ckyorn. The text defined after the -h will be shown if the user requests a help message.

```
ckyorn -h "Answer yes if you want the manual page files \
installed or no if you do not."
```

If you insert a tilde (˜) at the beginning or end of your definition, the default text will be added at that point. For example,

```
ckyorn -h "The manual page files will be written to your \
system, or not, based on your answer.˜"
```

will produce the help message:

```
The manual page files will be written to your system, or not,
based on your answer.  To respond in the affirmative, enter y,
yes, Y, or YES.  To respond in the negative, enter n, no, N, \
or NO.
```

The Data Validation Tool Error Messages

Each tool has a default error message that you can use as is, add to, or completely overwrite. The manual page for each tool (see Appendix A) shows the default error message text. You must use the −e option of a shell command before the default can be overwritten.

For example, if you executed ckyorn without options, and validation failed, the following message would be seen:

```
ERROR: Please enter yes or no.
```

The next example shows the use of the −e option when executing ckyorn. The text defined after the −e will be prepended with ERROR: and shown if validation fails.

```
ckyorn -e "You did not respond with yes or no."
```

If you insert a tilde (˜) at the beginning or end of your definition, the default text will be added at that point.

Message Formatting

All three message types (prompt, error, and help) are limited in length to 78 characters and are automatically formatted. Regardless of how you define them in your code, any white space used (including newline) is stripped during formatting.

You can use the −W option of a shell command (or the ckwidth variable of a function) to define the line length to which your messages should be formatted.

The Shell Commands

Figure 9-3 lists the shell commands and what they are used for. All of the shell commands perform the same series of tasks, as described previously. The table's "Purpose" column describes the type of prompt and validation with which the command deals. Details for each command can be found on the respective manual page in Appendix A.

Figure 9-3: The Shell Commands

Command (and Function)	Purpose
ckdate	Prompts for and validates that the answer is a date (can define format for date).
ckgid	Prompts for and validates that the answer is a group id.
ckint	Prompts for and validates an integer value (can define base for input).
ckitem	Builds a menu, prompts for and validates a menu item (can define characteristics of the menu).
ckkeywd	Adds keywords to a prompt and validates that the return answer matches a keyword.
ckpath	Prompts for and validates a pathname (can define what type of validation to perform, such as "pathname must be readable").
ckrange	Prompts for and validates an integer within a range (can define the upper and lower limits of the range).
ckstr	Prompts for and validates that the answer is a string (can define a regular expression, in which case the string must match the expression).
cktime	Prompts for and validates that the answer is a time (can define format for time).

Figure 9-3: The Shell Commands (continued)

Command (and Function)	Purpose
ckuid	Prompts for and validates that the answer is a user id.
ckyorn	Prompts for and validates a yes/no answer. Input must be y, yes, Y, YES, n, no, N, or NO.
dispgid	Displays a list of all valid group names.
dispuid	Displays a list of all valid user names.

The Visual Tools

The visual tools are invoked from within the field definition of an FMLI form. Because of the nature of FMLI form definitions, it is necessary to divide the tasks performed by only one shell command into sets. The purpose of a visual tool set parallels the purpose of a shell command. For example, ckdate performs a group of tasks for a prompt whose response should be a date. The same group of tasks requires three visual tools:

- errdate (formats and presents an error message)
- helpdate (formats and presents a help message)
- valdate (validates the answer to be a date)

The format and description of each visual tool set is shown on the equivalent shell command manual page in Appendix A. For example, the equivalent shell command for the set described above is ckdate. Refer to the manual page ckdate(1) for details on the three visual tools errdate, helpdate, and valdate.

Figure 9-4 lists the visual tool sets and their associated response type.

Figure 9-4: The Visual Tools

Visual Tool Set	Response Type
erryorn, helpyorn, valyorn	yes or no
errint, helpint, valint	integer
errange, helprange, valrange	integer in a range
errstr, helpstr, valstr	string (potentially matching an expression)
errpath, helppath, valpath	pathname
erritem, helpitem	menu item
errgid, helpgid, valgid	existing group
errtime, helptime, valtime	time of day
errdate, helpdate, valdate	date

There are two other visual tools. `dispuid` displays a list of login ids and `dispgid` displays a list of group ids. These two tools can be used with the FMLI `rmenu` keyword to display a list of ids.

The following example shows a field definition written in FMLI using the visual tools:

```
name="Do you want to install the manual page files?"
value=y
choicemsg='helpyorn'
invalidmsg='erryorn -e "~Enter yes to install the manual page files"'
valid='valyorn $F1'
rows=1
columns=1
```

10 Driver Software Packaging

10. DRIVER SOFTWARE PACKAGING

10. DRIVER SOFTWARE PACKAGING

Installable Driver (ID) Implementation

This section describes the Installable Driver (ID) scheme, which allows users to add drivers for peripheral devices to Release 4.0 of UNIX System V/386.

ID provides an automatic method of installing device drivers using the `pkgadd` command delivered in the Base System Package of the UNIX System V/386 Release 4.0 Foundation Set. Users invoke ID when adding new driver(s) to their system. ID involves system reconfiguration, which in the past has required users to know the internals of many system files (`/etc/system`, `/etc/master`, `io.mk`, `space.h`, the `config` command, and so forth). As with many other UNIX system implementations, ID builds a new UNIX system, then has the user reboot the system using the new kernel.

This section provides an overview of what software developers need to do when building an installable device driver package. Driver developers must use the C Programming Language Utilities (CPLU) delivered in the UNIX System V/386 Release 4.0 Software Development Set to compile their driver and build installation scripts for delivery with the device driver software package. The section entitled "Device Driver Development Methodology" provides step-by-step procedures on how to write, compile, debug, and finally package the device driver.

ID provides a packaging strategy applicable to vendor-supplied drivers. Driver writers must develop an add-on Driver Software Package (DSP) similar to those for applications programs. A DSP consists of a driver object module, installation and removal scripts, and device-specific entries for system configuration, initialization and shutdown files, as well as space allocation entries normally associated with `space.h` on earlier UNIX systems.

ID allows replacement of "base" drivers using a special DSP called an Update Driver Software Package (UDSP). Base drivers are defined as those drivers delivered with the UNIX System V/386 Release 4.0 Base System software package.

User Interface

A user may install or remove device drivers using the `pkgadd` and `pkgrm` commands.

 NOTE At this point, we assume a basic knowledge about the layout and implementation of OA&M packages.

User Procedures

The `pkgadd` command installs a DSP from tape or floppy diskette onto the system and initiates automatic procedures to reconfigure the kernel. The `pkgrm` command allows the user to select which package to delete. It then removes the DSP from the system and reconfigures the kernel without the driver.

The `pkginfo` command displays any software packages that the user has installed. DSPs are treated identically to other UNIX System V/386 Release 4.0 software packages. Device drivers that are pre-installed on the system by the Foundation Set tapes or floppy diskettes are not displayed by this command.

User Privileges

The DSP uses the same installation rules as any other add-on software for UNIX System V/386 Release 4.0; therefore, the user needs `root` permissions. A user must be *super-user* to install DSPs.

Interactions with Other UNIX System V Processes

The DSP affects other users or processes no more than installing or removing other software with the exception that the final step is to reboot the system. It is, therefore, not advisable for another user to be logged on using a remote terminal while installing or removing a DSP.

Modifications for ID

Master File

In earlier UNIX systems, the `master` file contained information about all I/O devices that can be configured into a kernel. It also listed tunable parameters and their default values. For UNIX System V/386 Release 4.0, the `master` file has been split into

- `mdevice` – master device file

- `mtune` – master tunable parameter file

The format of `mdevice` and `mtune` are shown in the manual pages in the UNIX System V/386 Release 4.0 *System Files and Devices Reference Manual*.

System File

The `system` file represents a configuration from which a kernel is configured. The `system` file has been split into

- `sdevice` – system device file

- `stune` – system tunable parameter file

- `sassign` – file specifying pseudo-devices `root`, `pipe`, `swap` and `dump`.

The format of `sdevice` and `stune` are shown in the manual pages in the UNIX System V/386 Release 4.0 *System Files and Devices Reference Manual*.

space.c

The amount of storage allocated for each driver data structure is dependent on the number of subdevices configured for a particular device. Because of the need to modularize storage allocation and the fact that space allocation should rightly be done in a " `.c`" file, in UNIX System V/386 Release 4.0, the file `/usr/include/sys/space.h` has become a collection of `space.c` files kept in the `/etc/conf/pack.d` directory. These `space.c` files determine how much storage is required for the main body of the kernel and each of the added drivers. These files are compiled and linked into the kernel during reconfiguration.

ID Directory Structure

The root directory for the ID software is /etc/conf. All files and directories
are writable only by root so that users cannot inadvertently modify anything.
In addition, the /etc/conf directory may not have symbolic links in it. The ID
directory contains the following subdirectories:

- bin – contains all ID commands.

- cf.d – contains configuration-dependent files.

  □ stune, sassign, sdevice, mdevice, mtune – equivalent to the
    master and system files of earlier UNIX systems. The mdevice file
    is built from the Master modules of the installed DSPs. A base
    mdevice file supports corresponding devices in the base system. The
    entries in the Master modules for installed DSPs are added to the
    base mdevice.

  □ mfsys, sfsys – file system type information (see the mfsys(4) and
    sfsys(4) manual pages in the UNIX System V/386 Release 4.0
    System Files and Devices Reference Manual).

  □ init.base – base system part of /etc/inittab.

  □ kernmap – kernel memory mapping information.

  □ Temporary files used by the reconfiguration process:

conf.c	Kernel data structures and function definitions
config.h	Kernel #defines for device and system parameters
direct	Listing of all driver components included in the build
fsconf.c	File system type configuration data
vector.c	Interrupt vector definition
unix	The UNIX operating system kernel; eventually to be linked to /stand/unix.

    These temporary files are created and used by the ID reconfiguration
    software, and are then deleted. If you run the
    /etc/conf/bin/idconfig command manually, it creates these files
    for your review.

- sdevice.d – contains one file for each type of device (that is, controller board or pseudo-device). The file-name is the same as the DSP internal name. Each file contains all of the system configuration entries pertaining to that device. Generally, this file contains a single line entry. (A device might have two entries in the system configuration if there were two devices of that type installed in the system.) These files are copies of the Systems modules of each installed DSP. When concatenated together, these files comprise the file /etc/conf/cf.d/sdevice.

- pack.d – contains one directory for each DSP installed on the system. The directory name is the same as the DSP internal name. The directories in pack.d contain the Driver.o and space.c files for the drivers. This directory can also contain a stubs.c file. stubs.c files are often used as "place holders" for references the kernel needs to resolve for code that has been uninstalled. These files are taken from the Driver.o, Space.c, and Stubs.c files of a DSP. Note the change in capitalization for Stubs.c and Space.c. A DSP must name these files starting with an upper-case letter. The ID tools will install the files into /etc/conf/pack.d using the lower-case forms.

- rc.d – contains startup procedures for each of the installed DSPs. There will be one file per device startup procedure, and the file's contents are to be taken from the Rc module of the DSP. The names of the files are the same as the DSPs internal names. The contents of this directory are linked to /etc/idrc.d whenever a newly configured kernel is first booted.

- sd.d – contains shutdown procedures for each of the installed DSPs. There will be one file per device shutdown procedure, and the file's contents are to be taken from the Shutdown module of the DSP. The names of the files are the same as the DSPs internal names. The contents of this directory are linked to /etc/idsd.d whenever a newly configured kernel is first booted.

- node.d – contains device node definitions (special files in /dev) for each of the installed DSPs. There will be one file per device driver, and the file's contents are taken from the Node module of the DSP. The file-names are the same as the DSP internal names. The contents of this directory are the input to the idmknod command.

■ `init.d` – contains `/etc/inittab` entries for each of the installed DSPs. There will be one file per device driver, and the file's contents are taken from the `Init` module of the DSP. The file names will be the same as the DSP internal names. The contents of this directory is the input to the `idmkinit` command. (It should be noted that this directory may also contain `/etc/inittab` entries other than those associated with DSPs.)

■ `mfsys.d` – contains one FS type master data file for each file system type add-on. These files are taken from the `Mfsys` module of a DSP. When concatenated together, these files comprise the file `/etc/conf/cf.d/mfsys`.

■ `sfsys.d` – contains one FS type system data file for each file system type add-on. These files are taken from the `Sfsys` module of a DSP. When concatenated together, these files comprise the file `/etc/conf/cf.d/sfsys`.

Configuration Process Generated Parameters

The configuration process produces a file config.h that contains device parameters in the form of #defines that specify the number of units, interrupt vectors
used, and other pertinent information. For example, a device driver that controls several subdevices may not know how many subdevices are actually
installed in the system but can determine the number by including config.h
and referencing the proper #define. The parameters generated in config.h
are prefixed with the device handler prefix in all capital letters as shown below:

```
    Per device defines:
    ---------------------------------------------------------------
    #define   PRFX              Set to 1 if device is configured.
    #define   PRFX_CNTLS        Number of entries in System (sdevice) file.
    #define   PRFX_UNITS        Number of subdevices (see below).
    #define   PRFX_CHAN         DMA channel used (-1 if none).
    #define   PRFX_TYPE         Interrupt vector type used.
    #define   PRFX_CMAJORS      Number of multiple Major Numbers supported.
    #define   PRFX_CMAJOR_0     Major Numbers supported.  The first major
                                is PRFX_CMAJOR_0, the second PRFX_CMAJOR_1,
                                and so forth.


    Per controller #defines (PRFX_0 represents the first controller,
    followed by PRFX_1, etc if more than one controller is installed):
    ---------------------------------------------------------------
    #define   PRFX_0            Set to 1 if controller 0 is configured.
    #define   PRFX_0_VECT       Interrupt vector used (0 through 15).
    #define   PRFX_0_SIOA       Starting Input/Output Address.
    #define   PRFX_0_EIOA       Ending Input/Output Address.
    #define   PRFX_0_SCMA       Starting Controller Memory Address.
    #define   PRFX_0_ECMA       Ending Controller Memory Address.
```

It is important to note that since the device driver is delivered as an object
module (Driver.o), the #define cannot be referenced therein. The correct
way to access the value is in the DSPs Space.c file by defining a variable that
is assigned the value of the #define. The driver object module can then simply reference the variable.

Commands for Installing Drivers and Rebuilding the Kernel

The DSP Install script executes idcheck, idinstall, and idbuild. Manual pages for these commands are provided in the UNIX System V/386 Release 4.0 *System Administrator's Reference Manual*. Sample Install and Remove scripts, which use these commands, are provided in the section entitled "A Sample Driver Software Package".

idcheck

The idcheck command is used to obtain selected information about the system configuration. The idcheck command is designed to help driver writers determine if a particular driver package is already installed or to test for interrupt vectors, device addresses, or DMA controllers already in use. It is anticipated that the idcheck command will be used in Install scripts that test for usable IVN, IOA, and CMA values, then will instruct the user to set particular switches or straps on the controller board.

idinstall

The idinstall command is used by the DSPs postinstall and preremove scripts, and its function is to install, remove, or update a DSP.

idbuild

The idbuild command is a shell script that comprises the reconfiguration processes.

- Concatenates the files in /etc/conf/sdevice.d to produce the sdevice file.

- Concatenates the files in /etc/conf/mfsys.d to produce the mfsys file.

- Concatenates the files in /etc/conf/sfsys.d to produce the sfsys file.

Integrated Software Development Guide

- Executes the `idconfig` and `idmkunix` commands.

- Sets a lock file so that on the next system shutdown,
  `/etc/conf/cf.d/unix` is linked to `/stand/unix`. On the next system
  reboot, the same lock file enables the new driver configuration (nodes in
  `/dev`, `/etc/inittab`, and so forth) to be installed.

 NOTE The `idcheck` command does not work properly if `idbuild` has not been
executed after a DSP has been added, deleted, or updated through the use
of `idinstall`. In order to get around this, after executing `idinstall`,
re-synchronize the `sdevice` file or, execute `idbuild`. If not desired,
update the `/etc/conf/cf.d/sdevice` file by doing:

```
cat /etc/confdevice.d/* > /etc/conf/cf.d/sdevice
sync
```

The Driver Software Package (DSP)

This section defines the contents of the Driver Software Package (DSP). The section entitled "A Sample Driver Software Package" contains an example package. Each DSP must have two "names". One is the "external name" that the user sees when the package is installed. The second is an "internal name" that the kernel uses to identify the device. More information is provided about these names below and in the section entitled "Device Driver Development Procedures".

The DSP is to be delivered on installation media as described in the chapter on "Packaging Application Software" in this book. There you will find general descriptions of the files and information on ordering and contents. The driver writer must prepare a DSP consisting of the files (termed modules) described in the following sections.

The package should install the following files as class "volatile" in a `tmp` directory. Its `postinstall` script should `cd` to that directory before invoking the ID commands to add the DSP to the system. An example OA&M prototype is as follows:

```
# packaging files
i pkginfo
i postinstall
i preremove

d none /tmp/foo      755      bin      bin
v none /tmp/foo/Driver.o=/usr/src/pkg/foo/Driver.o ? ? ?
v none /tmp/foo/Master=/usr/src/pkg/foo/Master ? ? ?
v none /tmp/foo/System=/usr/src/pkg/foo/System ? ? ?
v none /tmp/foo/Space.c=/usr/src/pkg/foo/Space.c ? ? ?
v none /tmp/foo/Rc=/usr/src/pkg/foo/Rc ? ? ?
v none /tmp/foo/Shutdown=/usr/src/pkg/foo/Shutdown ? ? ?

# package objects:
!default 555 bin bin
d none    /usr/lib/foo           755      root      sys
f none    /usr/lib/foo/cmd=/usr/src/pkg/foo/cmd
f none    /usr/include/sys/foo.h=/usr/src/pkg/foo/foofblk.h   444   bin   bin
```

Summary of Modules

Table 10-1: Components of Driver Software Package (DSP)

Module	Mandatory/Optional	Definition
preremove	M	Remove DSP
postinstall	M	Install DSP driver files
Driver.o	M	Driver object file
prototype	M	OAM package prototype file
Master	M	Master file entry
System	M	System file entry
Space.c	O	Driver space allocation file
Node	O	Special file entries in /dev
Init	O	/etc/inittab entries
Rc	O	Executed when entering init-level 2
Shutdown	O	Executed when entering init-level 0, 5, and 6
Mfsys	O	File system type master data
Sfsys	O	File system type system data

Driver.o (required)

This is the driver object module that is to be configured into the kernel. This object module must be compiled using the native C Programming Language Utilities (CPLU) delivered in the UNIX System V/386 Release 4.0 Software Development Set. The section entitled "Device Driver Development Methodology" provides procedures for coding, compiling, and debugging the driver object module.

Master (required)

This module contains a one-line description of the device being installed. This module is added to the ID mdevice file. The syntax of this line appears in the mdevice(4) manual page in the UNIX System V/386 Release 4.0 *System Files and Devices Reference Manual*.

Columns 6 and 7 of the Master entry should be set to zero. These are the driver's character and block and character major device numbers. These values are set by ID when the Master entry is added to the kernel configuration. If the device needs to support more than 256 subdevices, multiple major numbers may be specified in either one or both of these fields.

UNIX System V Release 4.0 for the Intel386 and compatible architectures supports multiple major numbers per device. In order to support a large number of subdevices, a new letter "M" (upper-case "m") is used in the third column of the mdevice file.

An "f" in the third field identifies the driver as "new-style" (based on DDI/DKI interfaces described in this book). This applies to STREAMS, block and character drivers. If the driver defines devflag then the Master file must have an "f" in the third field.

In order to specify the specific major numbers, a "range notation" is used that specifies a list of consecutive major numbers to be used. This notation specifies the first and last major numbers separated by a dash (for example, the range 3 – 6, is interpreted as four major numbers between 3 and 6, inclusive). The fifth and sixth columns of the mdevice file (block and character major device numbers, respectively) may contain a range specification of majors. The implementation is backward-compatible with all other mdevice entries that continue to specify a single major number.

Integrated Software Development Guide

Notice the difference in the following example between the specification of single majors versus multiple majors.

Single major:

```
lp    Ioc      iHcSf      lp   0     7        1   2   -1
```

Multiple majors (fictitious device names used):

```
ft    Iocrwi   IHrobcfM   ft   1-4   3-6      1   2   -1
fg    Iocrwi   IHrbcfM    fg   5     20-24    1   2   -1
```

The "ft" entry specifies multiple majors for both block and character numbers; the "fg" entry specifies a single block major and multiple character majors.

For devices that require that both the block and character major ranges be the same, a "u" ("unique") flag may be specified in the third column of Master. Devices that do not specify "u" may be assigned different ranges for block and character majors.

System (required)

When a DSP is installed, this module is added to the files to be included in the kernel the next time the system is rebuilt. During reconfiguration, the system modules for each device are concatenated together to form the ID file sdevice. The syntax of this line appears in the sdevice(4) manual page in the UNIX System V/386 Release 4.0 *System Files and Devices Reference Manual*.

Space.c (optional)

The amount of storage allocated for each driver data structure is dependent on the number of subdevices configured for a particular device. For UNIX System V/386 Release 4.0, each driver can have its own Space.c file containing configuration dependent-data structures. Each driver package brings in its own Space.c file for space allocation.

As an alternative to providing Space.c, the driver writer could preallocate data in the driver, eliminating the need for this file. This is useful when

- the amount of storage required by the driver is static.

- the difference in storage between the minimum and maximum number of subdevices that can be configured for that device is small.

| NOTE | If the driver object file is compiled with special `#ifdefs` turned on, it is important to explicitly turn on these `#ifdefs` in the `space.c` file before including headers so that the compiled `space.c` uses the correct definitions of structures and types. |

Node (optional)

This file is used to generate the device's "special files" in the `/dev` directory on the next reboot after the system has been reconfigured.   Node contains one line for each node that is to be inserted in `/dev`. The columns can be separated by spaces. The syntax of this line is as follows:

Column 1: DSP internal name
Column 2: name of node to be inserted
Column 3: "b" or "c" (block or character device)

> If the device supports multiple majors, a specific major can be specified via the following notation `b:`*offset* or `c:`*offset*, where *offset* is an offset number within the range of majors specified in the `mdevice`(4). This offset starts with "0" to specify the first number in the range. An offset of "1" would specify the second number in the range, and so on.

Column 4: minor device number

Example

```
DSP-internal-name  node0  c   0
DSP-internal-name  node1  c   1
DSP-internal-name  node2  c:0 0   # Selects 1st character major number
DSP-internal-name  node3  c:1 0   # Selects 2nd character major number
```

See the idmknod(1M) manual page in the UNIX System V/386 Release 4.0 *System Administrator's Reference Manual*.

Init (optional)

Some drivers require entries in /etc/inittab to make them operational. An inittab entry is of the following form (see the inittab(4) manual page in the UNIX System V/386 Release 4.0 *System Files and Devices Reference Manual*):

> *id:rstate:action:process*

Each line of the init module must be of the format "*action:process*", or "*-rstate:action:process*". The *id* and *rstate* field are generated by ID (if your entry has an *rstate* field it will be used; otherwise, "2" will be used). The new inittab entries are added to /etc/inittab on the next reboot after the system has been reconfigured. For more information on the init module format, see the idmkinit(1M) manual page in the UNIX System V/386 Release 4.0 *System Administrator's Reference Manual*.

Rc (optional)

This module is an initialization file that is executed when the system is booted. The new Rc file is placed in the directory /etc/idrc.d on the next reboot after the system has been reconfigured and is invoked on every system reboot thereafter upon entering init level 2. (See the init(1M) manual page in the UNIX System V/386 Release 4.0 *System Administrator's Reference Manual*). When creating this module, the file permissions must allow execution by root.

Shutdown (optional)

This file is executed when the system is shut down. The new shutdown file is placed in the directory /etc/idsd.d on the next reboot after the system has been reconfigured and is invoked on every system shutdown thereafter upon entering init state 0, 5 and 6. When creating this module, the file permissions must allow execution by root.

Postinstall (required)

This module performs the following:

- Changes directory to tmp directory where DSP files were installed.

- Uses idcheck to determine conflicts with the installed drivers.

- Invokes the ID command idinstall with the -a option and passes it one argument, the internal DSP name. This moves the contents of the DSP to the proper directories.

- Invokes the ID command idbuild.

- removef any /tmp files installed.

The following is a sample postinstall script:

```
trap '' 1 2 3 5 15
#
#        Intel386 Package Template
#        Driver files installed in /tmp/foo.
#        "foo" will be ID package name for the driver
#
TMP=/tmp/foo.ierr
ERROR1=" Errors have been written to the file $TMP."
rm -f $TMP > /dev/null 2>&1
PRFX=foo

cd /tmp/foo
/etc/conf/bin/idcheck -p ${PRFX} > /dev/null 2>&1
if [ $? != 0 ]
then
        echo "<PACKAGE NAME> has already been installed."
        exit 1
fi

echo "Installing the drivers."
/etc/conf/bin/idinstall -a ${PRFX} 2>> $TMP
if [ $? != 0 ]
then
        echo "\n\tThe installation cannot be completed due to an error
            in the <PACKAGE NAME> driver installation. $ERROR1 "
        exit 1
fi
```

(continued on next page)

```
/etc/conf/bin/idbuild 2>> $TMP
if [ $? != 0 ]
then
        echo "The installation cannot be completed due to an error
            in the driver installation. $ERROR1 "
        /etc/conf/bin/idinstall -d ${PRFX} 2>>/dev/null
        exit 1
fi

installf $PKGINST /usr/options/$PKG.name
echo $NAME > /usr/options/$PKG.name
installf -f $PKGINST

# Needed so the removef works.
removef $PKGINST /tmp/foo/* > /dev/null 2>&1
removef -f $PKGINST

rm -f $TMP
exit 10
```

Preremove (required)

This module does the following:

- Calls the `idinstall` command with the `-d` option and passes it one argument, the internal DSP name. This removes the DSP modules.

- Invokes the ID command `idbuild`.

The following is a sample `preremove` script:

```
trap '' 1 2 3 5 15
#
#        Intel386 generic driver preremove
#        ID package prefix is foo
#
TMP=/tmp/foo.rerr
ERROR1="An error was encountered removing the <PACKAGE NAME> package.
        The file $TMP contains errors reported by the system."
ERROR2="The kernel rebuild failed.  However all software dealing with
         the <PACKAGE NAME> has been removed.  The file $TMP contains
         errors reported by the system."
rm -f $TMP > /dev/null 2>&1

PRFX=foo
/etc/conf/bin/idinstall -d ${PRFX} 2>> $TMP
if [ $? != 0 ]
then
        echo $ERROR1
        exit 1
fi

/etc/conf/bin/idbuild 2>> $TMP
if [ $? != 0 ]
then
        echo $ERROR2
        exit 1
fi

rm -f $TMP
exit 10
```

Base System Drivers

An examination of `/etc/conf/cf.d/mdevice` shows the installed DSPs on UNIX System V Release 4.0 for the Intel386 and compatible architectures. A partial list of the Base System device drivers and software modules is as follows:

Table 10-2: Base System Driver Definitions

Hardware Drivers	Definition
asy	Serial Ports Driver
fd	Floppy Disk
hd	Hard Disk
kd	Keyboard
lp	Line printer (Parallel Port)
rtc	Real-Time Clock

Software Modules	Definition
ipc	Interprocess Communication (IPC)
ld0	TTY Line Disciplines
mem	Memory driver
msg	IPC Messages
prf	Kernel Profiler
sem	IPC Semaphores
shm	IPC Shared Memory
sxt	Shell layers
xt	Layers

The above list does not include several drivers and software modules being packaged as add-ons (such as NFS (Network File System). and RFS (Remote File Sharing). Drivers in the base system are installable drivers that have been delivered in the Base System Package of the UNIX System V/386 Release 4.0 Foundation Set, rather than separate DSPs. They are similar to other DSPs except that there are no `Install` or `Remove` scripts for the base system drivers.

The `pkginfo` and `pkgrm` commands do not show these base system drivers, not only to reduce clutter in those menus, but because it would be unreasonable to remove the base system drivers. Although base drivers cannot be removed, they can be replaced with new drivers by installing an Update Driver Software Package (UDSP).

Update Driver Software Package (UDSP)

This package is specifically designed to replace base system drivers. A UDSP must contain the following files:

- Those modules being replaced. Through special options of the ID commands used to install drivers, the old base driver's modules can be overlaid, removed, or supplemented. Those driver modules that are not changed do not have to be redelivered.

- The `postinstall` module. This module follows the same rules as for other driver packages except that it calls `idinstall` with the −u option.

- The `preremove` module. This module must print the message

      Can not remove base driver

  and return with an exit code of 1.

This scheme allows the user to install an UDSP just as any other ID package. When the user later uses the `pkginfo` command, the updated driver will be listed as "Device_Name Driver Update Package". The `pkgrm` menu displays the same entry, but if the user tries to select the updated driver, the `preremove` script defined above aborts the removal. If a subsequent update to that same driver is ever developed, the requirements for the UDSP are exactly the same as those itemized above for the first update. The second update will simply be loaded on top of the first. The `Name` file and the `Remove` file should remain the same in the second update package. This causes the `pkgrm` and `pkginfo` command results to also remain the same.

Keep in mind that this update scenario is only for use with base drivers. If an add-on driver ever has an update, it is expected that the whole package previously installed will be removed, and the new version then re-installed.

Installation/Removal Summary

The ID commands and the DSPs modules defined above are used together to rebuild and execute a new UNIX operating system kernel. The step-by-step procedure to install, reconfigure, and execute a new kernel is as follows:

1. Execute `pkgadd`.

   `pkgadd` loads files specified by `prototype` and executes the `postinstall` script.

2. `postinstall` script performs the following:

   a. Optionally prompts to determine hardware (IOA or IVN) strappings. This may include calling `idcheck` to test the usability of the IVN or IOA.

   b. Executes `/etc/conf/bin/idinstall` with the `-a` option. This command

      ■ Moves the DSP components to target directories

      ■ Updates the file `/etc/conf/cf.d/mdevice`

   c. Executes `/etc/conf/bin/idbuild`. This command

      ■ Executes `/etc/conf/bin/idconfig`

      ■ Executes `/etc/conf/bin/idmkunix`

   d. Installs any user commands, menus, or files.

3. Upon completing installation, a message to shut down the system is displayed.

4. After the system reboots, the `init` program is the first user-level program executed; `/etc/inittab` executes `/etc/conf/bin/idmkenv`. This command tests to determine if this is the first boot of a new kernel. If so, the command

   a. Links `/etc/conf/rc.d/*` to `/etc/idrc.d`

   b. Links `/etc/conf/sd.d/*` to `/etc/idsd.d`

   c. Executes `/etc/conf/bin/idmkinit`

  d. Executes `/etc/conf/bin/idmknod`

  e. Continues `init` state initializations

  f. The system boot then continues normally.

The process of removing a DSP is very similar to this scenario, with the following exceptions:

- In step 1, invoke `pkgrm`

- In step 2, the `preremove` script deletes commands and files

- The `idinstall` command is called with the `-d` option to delete the DSP.

See the UNIX System V/386 Release 4.0 *System Administrator's Guide* for a detailed description of these procedures.

Tunable System Parameters

The two files `/etc/conf/cf.d/mtune` and `/etc/conf/cf.d/stune` contain kernel tunable parameters, which can profoundly affect system performance. Occasionally an add-on device driver or kernel software module may require you to modify an existing parameter or define a new tunable parameter that is accessible by other add-on drivers.

The UNIX System V/386 Release 4.0 *System Files and Devices Reference Manual* provides manual pages for `mtune`(4) and `stune`(4). As these pages show, the `mtune` file defines a default value along with a minimum and maximum value for each kernel parameter. An add-on package should never modify a predefined system parameter in the `mtune` file.

Modifying An Existing Kernel Parameter

The `stune` file is used to modify a system-tunable parameter from its default value in the `mtune` file. Not every system-tunable parameter is contained in the `stune` file; only those that are to be set to a value other than the system default need be entered there. Although the UNIX System V/386 Release 4.0 Base System defines only a few values in `stune`, other add-on packages may have added additional entries to `stune`. Therefore, if the driver package you are building requires modifying a parameter value, you should use the `idtune` command. See the UNIX System V/386 Release 4.0 *System Administrator's Reference Manual* for the manual page that describes `idtune`(1M). This command takes individual system parameters, verifies that the new value is within the upper and lower bounds specified in `mtune`, searches the `stune` file, and modifies an existing value or adds the parameter to `stune` if not defined.

 NOTE The value selected must always be within the minimum and maximum values in the `mtune` file.

Defining a New Kernel Parameter

If the DSP you are developing is part of a group of kernel software components, there may be a need to define configurable parameters that other packages can reference. If this is the case, the `Install` script can append new tunable parameters to `/etc/conf/cf.d/mtune` by defining lines in the format shown in the `mtune`(4) manual page in the UNIX System V/386 Release 4.0 *System Files and Devices Reference Manual*. The DSP `Remove` script must remove these entries if the user chooses to remove the package. When modifying `mtune`, be careful that you do not modify or delete other values.

Reconfiguring the Kernel to Enable New Parameters

After the `stune` and/or `mtune` files are modified, the system must be reconfigured using the `idbuild` command. If you are modifying the parameter as part of adding your DSP, and your `Install` script already invokes `idbuild`, then, of course, no additional build is required.

Device Driver Development Methodology

We have covered many of the kernel architectural and driver design details you need to know to write a UNIX device driver. Let's now talk about how you actually write the code and compile and package a driver. To accomplish these procedures, you must install the C Programming Language Utilities (CPLU) delivered in the UNIX System V/386 Release 4.0 Software Development Set.

As with any C program, you must compile, link edit, and execute the driver. Since the driver is part of the kernel, it must be link edited together with the kernel and the rest of the device drivers. The following can be used to create a driver object module suitable for the ID:

```
cc -c Driver.c
```

You can call the driver source by any name you want as long as the object module is renamed "Driver.o" for later installation. If your driver is composed of several driver source files, you must compile each as shown above, combine them using "ld -r", and give the name "Driver.o" to the resultant object module.

The ID requires that the driver object file be packaged on an installable tape or floppy diskette, along with the other modules described earlier. While you are initially developing and debugging the driver, it is not necessary to keep writing the tape or floppy diskettes and re-installing everything each time you make a driver modification. The following section presents a methodology for driver development, debugging, and testing without the use of media installation packages. The trace driver provided in the section entitled "A Trace Driver Implementation" is used as a model throughout this section.

Device Driver Development Procedures

Many of the steps that follow require you to modify files and directories owned by `root`; therefore, you must be logged in as `root` or execute as the super-user to develop and debug device drivers.

1. Establish a device "internal name".

   This can be up to eight characters long and must start with a letter, but it can have digits or underscores after the first letter. It is the name that the ID uses to identify the device. For the trace driver, "`trace`" is the name for ID to use. From now on, let's call this `DEV_NAME`.

   The following name definitions based on the internal name are required by the ID implementation in Release 4.0 of UNIX System V/386:

   - Column 1 of the `Master` file. This must be `DEV_NAME`.

   - Column 4 of the `Master` file. This is the driver entry point (function) prefix. It is also called the "handler" field. It can be up to six characters. It is desirable to make this identical to column 1 if `DEV_NAME` is four characters or less. For the trace driver, "`tr`" is this prefix.

   - Column 1 of the `System` file. This must be `DEV_NAME`.

   - "Special file" names listed in the `Node` module. These should be `DEV_NAME0`, `DEV_NAME1`, and so forth, unless other issues, like user perception of the node name, are important. Any numbering for subdevices should match the minor device of that node. The trace driver package uses `trace0`, which causes ID to generate `/dev/trace0`, on the first boot of the new kernel.

   - Function names inside your driver. The function names must use the device prefix defined above. The trace driver uses `tropen`, `trclose`, `trread` and so forth.

   - External variables and internal functions used inside the driver. These should use the prefix defined above or a prefix followed by an underline. The trace driver uses "`tr_`".

2. Manually create a System entry.

   Go to the /etc/conf/sdevice.d directory, and create a file of name DEV_NAME containing the system information. The trace driver uses the following:

   ```
   trace   Y   1   0   0   0   0   0   0   0
   ```

3. Manually create an mdevice entry.

   Because the ID assigns block and/or character major numbers when the package is installed, your Master file is required to have zeros in columns 5 and 6, or 1-x, if multiple majors are required to request "x" major numbers. Although you could manually edit /etc/conf/cf.d/mdevice and assign block and character major numbers, the best approach is to put a file called Master in your local directory (say /tmp) and execute the command:

   ```
   /etc/conf/bin/idinstall -a -m -k DEV_NAME
   ```

   This says add (–a) a Master entry (–m).

    NOTE   Watch out! The Master file in your local directory will be removed by the idinstall command unless you use the –k option.

   The trace driver uses the following:

   ```
   trace   ocri   ioc   tr   0   0   1   1   -1
   ```

   Once idinstall adds the Master entry, examine /etc/conf/cf.d/mdevice and note the block and/or character major number.

4. Create a file in /etc/conf/node.d to tell the ID to create device special files on the next system boot. The file should be named DEV_NAME and conform to the Node module format. For the trace driver, the Node module is as follows:

   ```
   trace   trace0   c   0
   ```

5. Create `/etc/conf/init.d`, `/etc/conf/rc.d`, and `/etc/conf/sd.d` entries if appropriate. This step can probably wait until debugging has proceeded.

6. Create a directory called `/etc/conf/pack.d/DEV_NAME`. Put `Driver.o` and `Space.c` there (if you need them).

7. At this point, it would be a good idea to make a copy of your current UNIX operating system kernel. Execute the following:

   ```
   cp /stand/unix /stand/unix.bak
   ```

8. Manually execute the `/etc/conf/bin/idbuild` shell script. This runs a configuration program and tries to link edit your new driver into the kernel. You will get an initial message followed either by the message

   ```
   UNIX system has been rebuilt
   ```

   message or by error messages from the configuration program or link editor.

   If you get errors, fix them and repeat the above step. If the kernel was built correctly, a new UNIX system image will have been created in the `/etc/conf/cf.d` directory. You can now shut the system down and reboot. Running `/etc/shutdown` causes the system to enter init state 0, 5 or 6 and the new kernel in `/etc/conf/cf.d` is automatically linked to `/stand/unix`. On the next boot, if you specify `/unix` on the `boot:` prompt, the new kernel executes, and upon entering init state 2, the new device nodes, `inittab` entries, and so forth, are installed.

9. When the system comes up, test your driver.

Emergency Recovery (New Kernel Will Not Boot)

The possibility exists that the kernel will fail to boot if your driver contains a serious bug. This can be due to a `panic` call that you put in your driver or some other system problem. If this happens, you should reset your system and boot your original kernel that you hopefully saved as recommended above. To do this, reset your machine, and when you see the message

```
Booting UNIX System ...
```

quickly strike the keyboard space bar to interrupt the default boot. When the boot prompt appears, type "`/unix.bak`" or whatever you named your old kernel. If you did not save a copy of your kernel or some disaster occurred, you cannot gracefully recover, and must reinstall the system using the following emergency procedures to put a bootable `/unix` image back on the hard disk:

1. Insert floppy diskette #1 of the Foundation Set and push the RESET button on the front panel, or power the system down and then back up again. Insert second diskette when prompted.

2. When the following prompt appears:

   ```
   Please press RETURN when ready to install the
   UNIX System
   ```

   press DEL to exit the installation program.

   You are now executing a floppy-bootable UNIX operating system kernel. This is not a standard way to run the system. It should be used for emergency procedures only.

3. Execute the following commands:

   ```
   /etc/fs/bfs/fsck  -y /dev/dsk/0s10      # check the hard disk
   /etc/fs/bfs/mount  /dev/dsk/0s10  /mnt  # mount the hard disk
   cp  /stand/unix  /mnt/unix              # copy a hard disk kernel
   umount /mnt                             # unmount the hard disk
   ```

4. Remove the floppy diskette.

5. Press the RESET Button or power down and then back up again.

The system should now boot normally with a standard foundation kernel. Your new driver and any other drivers you had installed on your system will not be included in `/unix` even though they may appear in the `pkginfo` output.

To fix this, remove your driver and execute `/etc/conf/bin/idbuild`. If that fails, remove and re-install the packages.

This procedure can also be useful if other system files are damaged inadvertently while debugging your driver. There are several reasons your system may fail to boot properly or not let you log in after it has booted. For example, a corrupted password or `inittab` file could prevent console logins.

Because floppy diskette #1 of the Foundation Set software contains a default `/etc/passwd`, `/etc/init`, `/etc/inittab`, and other critical files, you can copy the default file from the floppy diskette to the root file system of the hard disk using the procedures above. Obviously, user logins you have added to `/etc/passwd` or other system changes you have made since installing the original base system will be lost when you overwrite the corrupted file with the floppy diskette default file.

The postinstall Script

The section entitled "A Sample Driver Software Package". contains a sample script you should review. When writing your script, keep the following rules in mind:

1. Use `idcheck` to determine whether your package is already installed and to verify the usability of IVNs/IOAs your driver and controller board use.

2. Call `idinstall` and exit appropriately on errors. Use the `echo` and/or `message` commands to tell the user what failed.

3. Call `idbuild` and check the return code. If non-zero, call `idinstall` to remove your package. If the driver fails kernel reconfiguration, don't leave it partially installed.

The preremove Script

Although there are few reasons a remove operation will fail, the script should still remove the ID components and reconfigure the system first, then remove the user files. Check the return codes from the ID commands and report to the user accordingly. See the section entitled "A Sample Driver Software Package".

How to Document Your Driver Installation

This section is intended to give you some precautionary advice to pass on to your users. If you are developing a DSP that will be installed by users who may not be familiar with the implications of system reconfiguration, some words of caution may be worthwhile:

- Although experience has shown little difficulty in installing and removing a variety of device drivers, there is the possibility that you may have difficulty booting the system. The cause of this would primarily be due to some fault in the added driver. If this occurs, you have to reload the Base System software package, thus losing all user files. It may therefore be advisable to instruct users to back up user files before attempting an installation.

- Since a reconfiguration ends with a system reboot, it is not advisable for other users to be logged on to the system through a remote terminal.

- The user should not press DEL or RESET, power down the system, or in any way try to interrupt an installation. Although interruption protection is built into the ID scheme, total protection of a reboot during an installation can never be completely foolproof.

- Advise your users to run df and determine the free disk space before even trying an installation. Advise them of the number of free blocks needed to install the package.

- Advise the user not to have any background processes running that will be adversely affected by a system reboot, or consume free disk space while a reconfiguration is underway.

  For example, avoid running uucp during an installation.

A Sample Driver Software Package

This section contains sample files needed to install a device driver that is part of an OA&M-style installable software package. The principal files are the postinstall and preremove files. These files contain shell scripts that are used to install and remove the device driver. The prototype file is used to install any commands or header files.

The driver package for the trace driver described in the section entitled "A Trace Driver Implementation" is provided here as an example. Although the driver is a software driver (and hence will not contain hardware-related examples that are needed for hardware driver installation), most of the content of this driver package relates to any device driver.

The postinstall script presented here contains a large amount of diagnostic and recovery information such as checking if the driver is already installed and overwriting the old driver if the user confirms. All errors are redirected to a file in /tmp. It is up to the postinstall script to deal with what errors the user should and shouldn't see on the screen.

Some items to note in the postinstall script:

- make liberal use of the echo and message commands to tell the user what is going on

- make sure you exit with the appropriate return value based on successful or non-successful installation

Figure 10-1: The `postinstall` script for trace driver

```
# Sample OA&M package 'postinstall' script for trace driver.
# Assumes driver object file and related ID files copied into /tmp/trace.
# Will only allow driver to be installed on UNIX SVR4.0 system


FAILURE=1 # fatal error
SUCCESS=10          # success

TMP=/tmp/trace.err
ERROR1=" Errors have been written to the file $TMP."

CONFDIF=${ROOT}/etc/conf
CONFBIN=${CONFDIF}/bin
PACK=${CONFDIF}/pack.d

NOTOOLS="ERROR: The Installable Driver feature has been removed.
         The ${NAME} cannot be installed."

PARTINS="WARNING: A TRACE Driver has been partially installed.  How completely it is
          installed is unknown.  You may continue and overlay it with the ${NAME}."

BASE1="ERROR: The ${NAME} is not compatible with this release of the UNIX System V
        operating system and can not be used with this system."

rm -f $TMP > /dev/null 2>&1 # remove any existing error file

# determine that ID/TP tools are available
if [ -x ${CONFBIN}/idcheck -a -x ${CONFBIN}/idbuild -a -x ${CONFBIN}/idinstall ]
then
        :
else
        message ${NOTOOLS}
        exit $FAILURE
fi

cd /tmp/trace

# verify installation on UNIX System V/386 Release 4
OSVER=`uname -a | cut -d " " -f3`
case ${OSVER} in
        4.*) ;;
        *) message ${BASE1};
           exit $FAILURE;;
esac
```

(continued on next page)

Figure 10-1: The `postinstall` script for trace driver (continued)

```
${CONFBIN}/idcheck -p trace > /dev/null 2>&1
RETTP=$?

################################################################
## If RETTP != 0, then an "trace" driver exists on the system ##
################################################################

WARN=""
if [ $RETTP != 0 ]
then
        message -c ${PARTINS}
        if [ "$?" != "0" ]
        then
                exit ${FAILURE}
        fi
        idinstall -d trace # remove current copy
fi

${CONFBIN}/idinstall -a trace 2>> $TMP
if [ $? != 0 ]
then
        message "The installation cannot be completed due to an error in the
            driver installation.  $ERROR1  Please try the installation again.
            If the error occurs again, contact your Trace Service Representative."
        exit ${FAILURE}
fi

${CONFBIN}/idbuild 2>> $TMP
if [ "$?" -ne "0" ]
then
        message "The installation cannot be completed due to an error in the
            kernel reconfiguration. $ERROR1  Please try the installation again.
            If the error occurs again, contact your Trace Service Representative."
        exit ${FAILURE}
fi

# Needed so the removef works.
removef $PKGINST /tmp/trace/* >/dev/null 2>&1
removef -f $PKGINST >/dev/null 2>&1
rm -f $TMP 1>/dev/null 2>&1
exit ${SUCCESS}
```

Figure 10-2: The `preremove` script for trace driver

```
# Sample OA&M package 'preremove' script for trace driver.
#

FAILURE=1 # fatal error
SUCCESS=10

CONFDIR=/etc/conf
CONFBIN=$CONFDIR/bin

NOTOOLS="ERROR: The Installable Driver feature has been removed.
        The ${NAME} cannot be removed."

TMP=/tmp/trace.err1
ERROR1="An an error was encountered removing the ${NAME}.  The file ${TMP} contains
        errors reported by the system."
ERROR2="The kernel rebuild failed.  However all software dealing with the ${NAME}
        has been removed.  The ${NAME} will still appear in the Show Installed
        Software /Remove Installed Software menus because the kernel still has
        the trace driver in it. Please correct the problem and remove the software
        again.  The file $TMP contains error reported by the system."

rm -f $TMP > /dev/null 2>&1


if [ -x ${CONFBIN}/idcheck -a -x ${CONFBIN}/idbuild -a -x ${CONFBIN}/idinstall ]
then
        :
else
        message ${NOTOOLS}
        exit ${FAILURE}
fi

${CONFBIN}/idcheck -p trace
RES="$?"
if
        [ "${RES}" -ne "100" -a "${RES}" -ne "0" ]
then
        ${CONFBIN}/idinstall -d trace  2>> ${TMP}
        if [ $? != 0 ]
        then
                IDERR=1
        fi
        REBUILD=1
fi
```

(continued on next page)

Figure 10-2: The `preremove` script for trace driver (continued)

```
if [ ${IDERR} != 0 ]
then
        message $ERROR1
        exit ${FAILURE}
fi


RETVAL=0

if
        [ "${REBUILD}" = "1" ]
then
        # rebuild for changes to take effect
        ${CONFBIN}/idbuild 2>> $TMP
        if [ $? != 0 ]
        then
                message $ERROR2
                exit ${FAILURE}
        else
                RETVAL=${SUCCESS}
        fi
fi

rm -f $TMP 1>/dev/null 2>&1

exit ${RETVAL}
```

Figure 10-3: The `pkginfo` file for trace driver

```
# Sample OA&M package 'pkginfo' file for trace driver.
#

PKG="trace"
CLASSES="none"
NAME="386unix Trace Device Driver Package"
RELEASE="4.0"
VERSION="1"
VENDOR="AT&T-SF"
CATEGORY=system
# ARCH is set to i386 because the trace driver is not specific
# to a particular 386 architecture
ARCH="i386"
# The following allows old displaypkg command to show Trace Driver package as installed
PREDEPEND="trace"
```

Figure 10-4: The `prototype` file for trace driver

```
# Sample OA&M package 'prototype' file  for trace driver.

# PACKDIR is where built Driver.o and related ID/TP files are located.
# We use /usr/src/pkg/trace as an example

!PACKDIR=/usr/src/pkg/trace

# the following files should be in the same directory as the prototype file

i pkginfo
i postinstall
i preremove

!PKGINST=trace
!PKGSAV=/var/sadm/pkg/$PKGINST/save

# class "v" files are volatile -- allowed to be removed by package installation

!default 0544 bin bin
d none /tmp/trace           775binbin
v none /tmp/trace/Driver.o=$PACKDIR/Driver.o???
v none /tmp/trace/Master=$PACKDIR/Master???
v none /tmp/trace/System=$PACKDIR/System???
v none /tmp/trace/Node=$PACKDIR/Node???
v none /tmp/trace/Rc=$PACKDIR/Rc???
v none /tmp/trace/Space.c=$PACKDIR/Space.c???


#        directories: default owner=root group=sys mode=0775

!default 0544 root sys
d none    /usr     ?        ??
d none    /usr/bin  ?       ??
d none    /usr/include      ???
d none    /usr/include/sys  ???
# assume "trace" is a command part of the trace driver package
f none    /usr/bin/trace=$PACKDIR/trace


#        header files: default owner=bin group=bin mode=0444
!default 0444 bin bin
f none    /usr/include/sys/trace.h=$PACKDIR/trace.h
```

Figure 10-5: The Master file for trace driver

```
trace ocri   ioc    tr    0    0    1    1    -1
```

Figure 10-6: The System file for trace driver

```
trace Y    1    0    0    0    0    0    0    0
```

Figure 10-7: The Node file for trace driver

```
trace trace0     c    0
```

A Manual Pages

Manual Pages   A-1

A. MANUAL PAGES

Manual Pages

The manual pages included in this appendix are unique to the *Integrated Software Development Guide.* Other manual pages may be applicable as well, but won't be duplicated here; they may be referred to in the appropriate *Reference Manual*.

Table of Contents

1. Commands

4. File Formats

7. Special Files

NAME

ckdate, errdate, helpdate, valdate – prompt for and validate a date

SYNOPSIS

ckdate [–Q] [–W *width*] [–f *format*] [–d *default*] [–h *help*] [–e *error*]
    [–p *prompt*] [–k *pid* [–s *signal*]]

errdate [–W *width*] [–e *error*] [–f *format*]

helpdate [–W *width*] [–h *help*] [–f *format*]

valdate [–f *format*] *input*

DESCRIPTION

ckdate prompts a user and validates the response. It defines, among other
things, a prompt message whose response should be a date, text for help and
error messages, and a default value (which is returned if the user responds with a
RETURN). The user response must match the defined format for a date.

All messages are limited in length to 70 characters and are formatted automatically. Any white space used in the definition (including newline) is stripped.
The –W option cancels the automatic formatting. When a tilde is placed at the
beginning or end of a message definition, the default text is inserted at that point,
allowing both custom text and the default text to be displayed.

If the prompt, help or error message is not defined, the default message (as
defined under NOTES) is displayed.

Three visual tool modules are linked to the ckdate command. They are errdate
(which formats and displays an error message), helpdate (which formats and
displays a help message), and valdate (which validates a response). These
modules should be used in conjunction with FMLI objects. In this instance, the
FMLI object defines the prompt. When *format* is defined in the errdate and
helpdate modules, the messages describe the expected format.

The options and arguments for this command are:

–Q   Do not allow quit as a valid response..

–W   Use *width* as the line length for prompt, help, and error messages.

–f   Verify input using *format*. Possible formats and their definitions are:
        %b = abbreviated month name
        %B = full month name
        %d = day of month (01 – 31)
        %D = date as *%m/%d/%y* (the default format)
        %e = day of month (1 – 31; single digits are preceded by a blank)
        %h = abbreviated month name (for example, jan, feb, mar)
        %m = month number (01 – 12)
        %y = year within century (for example, 91)
        %Y = year as *CCYY* (for example, 1991)

–d   The default value is *default*. The default is not validated and so does not
    have to meet any criteria.

−h   The help message is *help*.

−e   The error message is *error*.

−p   The prompt message is *prompt*.

−k   Send process ID *pid* a signal if the user chooses to abort.

−s   When quit is chosen, send *signal* to the process whose *pid* is specified by the −k option. If no signal is specified, use SIGTERM.

input   Input to be verified against format criteria.

EXIT CODES

0 = Successful execution
1 = EOF on input
2 = Usage error
3 = User termination (quit)
4 = Garbled format argument

NOTES

The default prompt for ckdate is:

    Enter the date [?,q]

The default error message is:

    ERROR − Please enter a date. Format is *format*.

The default help message is:

    Please enter a date. Format is *format*.

When the quit option is chosen (and allowed), q is returned along with the return code 3. The valdate module does not produce any output. It returns zero for success and non-zero for failure.

NAME

ckgid, errgid, helpgid, valgid – prompt for and validate a group ID

SYNOPSIS

ckgid [–Q] [–W *width*] [–m] [–d *default*] [–h *help*] [–e *error*] [–p *prompt*]
[–k *pid* [–s *signal*]]

errgid [–W *width*] [–e *error*]

helpgid [–W *width*] [–m] [–h *help*]

valgid *input*

DESCRIPTION

ckgid prompts a user and validates the response. It defines, among other things, a prompt message whose response should be an existing group ID, text for help and error messages, and a default value (which is returned if the user responds with a RETURN).

All messages are limited in length to 70 characters and are formatted automatically. Any white space used in the definition (including newline) is stripped. The –W option cancels the automatic formatting. When a tilde is placed at the beginning or end of a message definition, the default text is inserted at that point, allowing both custom text and the default text to be displayed.

If the prompt, help or error message is not defined, the default message (as defined under NOTES) is displayed.

Three visual tool modules are linked to the ckgid command. They are errgid (which formats and displays an error message), helpgid (which formats and displays a help message), and valgid (which validates a response). These modules should be used in conjunction with FML objects. In this instance, the FML object defines the prompt.

The options and arguments for this command are:

–Q   Do not allow quit as a valid response.

–W   Use *width* as the line length for prompt, help, and error messages.

–m   Display a list of all groups when help is requested or when the user makes an error.

–d   The default value is *default*. The default is not validated and so does not have to meet any criteria.

–h   The help message is *help*.

–e   The error message is *error*.

–p   The prompt message is *prompt*.

–k   Send process ID *pid* a signal if the user chooses to abort.

–s   When quit is chosen, send *signal* to the process whose *pid* is specified by the –k option. If no signal is specified, use SIGTERM.

input   Input to be verified against /etc/group

EXIT CODES

    0 = Successful execution
    1 = EOF on input
    2 = Usage error
    3 = User termination (quit)

NOTES

The default prompt for ckgid is:

```
Enter the name of an existing group [?,q]
```

The default error message is:

```
ERROR - Please enter the name of an existing group.
```
(if the −m *option of* ckgid *is used, a list of valid groups is displayed here)*

The default help message is:

```
Please enter an existing group name.
```
(if the −m *option of* ckgid *is used, a list of valid groups is displayed here)*

When the quit option is chosen (and allowed), q is returned along with the return code 3. The valgid module does not produce any output. It returns zero for success and non-zero for failure.

NAME

ckint – display a prompt; verify and return an integer value

SYNOPSIS

ckint [-Q] [-W *width*] [-b *base*] [-d *default*] [-h *help*] [-e *error*]
    [-p *prompt*] [-k *pid* [-s *signal*]]

errint [-W *width*] [-b *base*] [-e *error*]

helpint [-W *width*] [-b *base*] [-h *help*]

valint [-b *base*] *input*

DESCRIPTION

ckint prompts a user, then validates the response. It defines, among other things, a prompt message whose response should be an integer, text for help and error messages, and a default value (which is returned if the user responds with a RETURN).

All messages are limited in length to 70 characters and are formatted automatically. Any white space used in the definition (including newline) is stripped. The -W option cancels the automatic formatting. When a tilde is placed at the beginning or end of a message definition, the default text is inserted at that point, allowing both custom text and the default text to be displayed.

If the prompt, help or error message is not defined, the default message (as defined under NOTES) is displayed.

Three visual tool modules are linked to the ckint command. They are errint (which formats and displays an error message), helpint (which formats and displays a help message), and valint (which validates a response). These modules should be used in conjunction with FML objects. In this instance, the FML object defines the prompt. When *base* is defined in the errint and helpint modules, the messages includes the expected base of the input.

The options and arguments for this command are:

-Q   Do not allow quit as a valid response.

-W   Use *width* as the line length for prompt, help, and error messages.

-b   The base for input is *base*. Must be 2 to 36, default is 10.

-d   The default value is *default*. The default is not validated and so does not have to meet any criteria.

-h   The help message is *help*.

-e   The error message is *error*.

-p   The prompt message is *prompt*.

-k   Send process ID *pid* a signal if the user chooses to abort.

-s   When quit is chosen, send *signal* to the process whose *pid* is specified by the -k option. If no signal is specified, use SIGTERM.

input   Input to be verified against *base* criterion.

EXIT CODES
> 0 = Successful execution
> 1 = EOF on input
> 2 = Usage error
> 3 = User termination (quit)

NOTES
> The default base 10 prompt for ckint is:
>
>> Enter an integer [?,q]
>
> The default base 10 error message is:
>
>> ERROR - Please enter an integer.
>
> The default base 10 help message is:
>
>> Please enter an integer.
>
> The messages are changed from "integer" to "base *base* integer" if the base is set to a number other than 10.
>
> When the quit option is chosen (and allowed), q is returned along with the return code 3. The valint module does not produce any output. It returns zero for success and non-zero for failure.

NAME

ckitem – build a menu; prompt for and return a menu item

SYNOPSIS

ckitem [-Q] [-W *width*] [-uno] [-f *file*] [-1 *label*]
    [[-i *invis*] [-i *invis*] . . .] [-m *max*] [-d *default*] [-h *help*] [-e *error*]
    [-p *prompt*] [-k *pid* [-s *signal*]]   [*choice1   choice2* . . .]

erritem [-W *width*] [-e *error*]   [*choice1   choice2* . . .]

helpitem [-W *width*] [-h *help*]   [*choice1   choice2* . . .]

DESCRIPTION

ckitem builds a menu and prompts the user to choose one item from a menu of
items. It then verifies the response. Options for this command define, among
other things, a prompt message whose response is a menu item, text for help and
error messages, and a default value (which is returned if the user responds with a
RETURN).

By default, the menu is formatted so that each item is prepended by a number
and is printed in columns across the terminal. Column length is determined by
the longest choice. Items are alphabetized.

All messages are limited in length to 70 characters and are formatted automatically. Any white space used in the definition (including newline) is stripped.
The -W option cancels the automatic formatting. When a tilde is placed at the
beginning or end of a message definition, the default text is inserted at that point,
allowing both custom text and the default text to be displayed.

If the prompt, help or error message is not defined, the default message (as
defined under NOTES) is displayed.

Two visual tool modules are linked to the ckitem command. They are erritem
(which formats and displays an error message) and helpitem (which formats and
displays a help message). These modules should be used in conjunction with
FML objects. In this instance, the FML object defines the prompt. When *choice* is
defined in these modules, the messages describe the available menu choice (or
choices).

The options and arguments for this command are:

-Q   Do not allow quit as a valid response.

-W   Use *width* as the line length for prompt, help, and error messages.

-u   Display menu items as an unnumbered list.

-n   Do not display menu items in alphabetical order.

-o   Return only one menu token.

-f   *file* contains a list of menu items to be displayed. [The format of this file
    is: *token<tab>description*. Lines beginning with a pound sign ("#") are com-
    ments and are ignored.]

-1   Print *label* above the menu.

-i   *invis* specifies invisible menu choices (choices not to be printed in the menu). For example, "all" used as an invisible choice would mean it is a valid option but does not appear in the menu. Any number of invisible choices may be defined. Invisible choices should be made known to a user either in the prompt or in a help message.

-m   The maximum number of menu choices allowed is *m*.

-d   The default value is *default*. The default is not validated and so does not have to meet any criteria.

-h   The help message is *help*.

-e   The error message is *error*.

-p   The prompt message is *prompt*.

-k   Send process ID *pid* a signal if the user chooses to abort.

-s   When quit is chosen, send *signal* to the process whose *pid* is specified by the -k option. If no signal is specified, use SIGTERM.

choice   Defines menu items. Items should be separated by white space or newline.

EXIT CODES

0 = Successful execution
1 = EOF on input
2 = Usage error
3 = User termination (quit)
4 = No choices from which to choose

NOTES

The user may input the number of the menu item if choices are numbered or as much of the string required for a unique identification of the item. Long menus are paged with 10 items per page.

When menu entries are defined both in a file (by using the -f option) and also on the command line, they are usually combined alphabetically. However, if the -n option is used to suppress alphabetical ordering, then the entries defined in the file are shown first, followed by the options defined on the command line.

The default prompt for ckitem is:

```
Enter selection [?,??,q]:
```

One question mark gives a help message and then redisplays the prompt. Two question marks gives a help message and then redisplays the menu label, the menu and the prompt.

The default error message is:

```
ERROR - Does not match an available menu selection.
Enter one of the following:
- the number of the menu item you wish to select
- the token associated withe the menu item,
- partial string which uniquely identifies the token
   for the menu item
- ?? to reprint the menu
```

The default help message is:

```
Enter one of the following:
- the number of the menu item you wish to select
- the token associated with the menu item,
- partial string which uniquely identifies the token
    for the menu item
- ?? to reprint the menu
```

When the quit option is chosen (and allowed), q is returned along with the return code 3.

NAME

   ckkeywd – prompt for and validate a keyword

SYNOPSIS

   ckkeywd [–Q] [–W *width*] [–d *default*] [–h *help*] [–e *error*] [–p *prompt*]
   [–k *pid* [–s *signal*]] [*keyword* . . .]

DESCRIPTION

   ckkeywd prompts a user and validates the response. It defines, among other
   things, a prompt message whose response should be one of a list of keywords,
   text for help and error messages, and a default value (which is returned if the
   user responds with a RETURN). The answer returned from this command must
   match one of the defined list of keywords.

   All messages are limited in length to 70 characters and are formatted automatically. Any white space used in the definition (including newline) is stripped.
   The –W option cancels the automatic formatting. When a tilde is placed at the
   beginning or end of a message definition, the default text is inserted at that point,
   allowing both custom text and the default text to be displayed.

   If the prompt, help or error message is not defined, the default message (as
   defined under NOTES) is displayed.

   –Q   Do not allow quit as a valid response.

   –W   Use *width* as the line length for prompt, help, and error messages.

   –d   The default value is *default*. The default is not validated and so does
             not have to meet any criteria.

   –h   The help message is *help*.

   –e   The error message is *error*.

   –p   The prompt message is *prompt*.

   –k   Send process ID *pid* a signal if the user chooses to abort.

   –s   When quit is chosen, send *signal* to the process whose *pid* is specified
             by the –k option. If no signal is specified, use SIGTERM.

   keyword   The keyword, or list of keywords, against which the answer is to be
             verified is *keyword*.

EXIT CODES

   0 = Successful execution
   1 = EOF on input
   2 = Usage error
   3 = User termination (quit)
   4 = No keywords from which to choose

NOTES

   The default prompt for ckkeywd is:

        Enter appropriate value [*keyword*[, . . .], ?, q]

The default error message is:

```
ERROR - Please enter one of the following keywords:
```
keyword[, ...]

The default help message is:

```
Please enter one of the following keywords:
```
keyword[, ...]

When the quit option is chosen (and allowed), q is returned along with the return code 3.

NAME

ckpath – display a prompt; verify and return a pathname

SYNOPSIS

ckpath [-Q] [-W *width*] [-a| 1] [*file_options*] [-rtwx] [-d *default*]
     [-h *help*] [-e *error*] [-p *prompt*] [-k *pid* [-s *signal*]]

errpath [-W *width*] [-a| 1] [*file_options*] [-rtwx] [-e *error*]

helppath [-W *width*] [-a| 1] [*file_options*] [-rtwx] [-h *help*]

valpath [-a| 1] [*file_options*] [-rtwx] *input*

DESCRIPTION

ckpath prompts a user and validates the response. It defines, among other things, a prompt message whose response should be a pathname, text for help and error messages, and a default value (which is returned if the user responds with a RETURN).

The pathname must obey the criteria specified by the first group of options. If no criteria are defined, the pathname must be for a normal file that does not yet exist. If neither -a (absolute) or -1 (relative) is given, then either is assumed to be valid.

All messages are limited in length to 70 characters and are formatted automatically. Any white space used in the definition (including newline) is stripped. The -W option cancels the automatic formatting. When a tilde is placed at the beginning or end of a message definition, the default text is inserted at that point, allowing both custom text and the default text to be displayed.

If the prompt, help or error message is not defined, the default message (as defined under NOTES) is displayed.

Three visual tool modules are linked to the ckpath command. They are errpath (which formats and displays an error message), helppath (which formats and displays a help message), and valpath (which validates a response). These modules should be used in conjunction with FACE objects. In this instance, the FACE object defines the prompt.

The options and arguments for this command are:

-Q   Do not allow quit as a valid response.

-W   Use *width* as the line length for prompt, help, and error messages.

-a   Pathname must be an absolute path.

-1   Pathname must be a relative path.

-r   Pathname must be readable.

-t   Pathname must be creatable (touchable). Pathname is created if it does not already exist.

-w   Pathname must be writable.

-x   Pathname must be executable.

-d   The default value is *default*. The default is not validated and so does not have to meet any criteria.

-h   The help message is *help*.

-e   The error message is *error*.

-p   The prompt message is *prompt*.

-k   Send process ID *pid* a signal if the user chooses to abort.

-s   When quit is chosen, send *signal* to the process whose *pid* is specified by the -k option. If no signal is specified, use SIGTERM.

input   Input to be verified against validation options.

file_options are:

-b   Pathname must be a block special file.

-c   Pathname must be a character special file.

-f   Pathname must be a regular file.

-y   Pathname must be a directory.

-n   Pathname must not exist (must be new).

-o   Pathname must exist (must be old).

-z   Pathname must be a file with the size greater than 0 bytes.

The following *file_options* are mutually exclusive: -bcfy, -no, -nz, -bz, -cz.

EXIT CODES

0 = Successful execution
1 = EOF on input
2 = Usage error
3 = User termination (quit)
4 = Mutually exclusive options

NOTES

The text of the default messages for ckpath depends upon the criteria options that have been used. An example default prompt for ckpath (using the -a option) is:

    Enter an absolute pathname [?,q]

An example default error message (using the -a option) is:

    ERROR - Pathname must begin with a slash (/).

An example default help message is:

    A pathname is a filename, optionally preceded by parent
    directories. The pathname you enter:
    — must contain 1 to NAME_MAX characters
    — must not contain a spaces or special characters

NAME_MAX is a system variable is defined in limits.h.

When the quit option is chosen (and allowed), q is returned along with the return code 3. The valpath module does not produce any output. It returns zero for success and non-zero for failure.

NAME

ckrange – prompt for and validate an integer

SYNOPSIS

ckrange [–Q] [–W *width*] [–l *lower*] [–u *upper*] [–b *base*] [–d *default*]
 [–h *help*] [–e *error*] [–p *prompt*] [–k *pid* [–s *signal*]]

errange [–W *width*] [–l *lower*] [–u *upper*] [–e *error*] [–b *base*]

helprange [–W *width*] [–l *lower*] [–u *upper*] [–h *help*] [–b *base*]

valrange [–l *lower*] [–u *upper*] [–b *base*] *input*

DESCRIPTION

ckrange prompts a user and validates the response. It defines, among other things, a prompt message whose response should be an integer in the range specified, text for help and error messages, and a default value (which is returned if the user responds with a RETURN).

This command also defines a range for valid input. If either the lower or upper limit is left undefined, then the range is bounded on only one end.

All messages are limited in length to 70 characters and are formatted automatically. Any white space used in the definition (including newline) is stripped. The –W option cancels the automatic formatting. When a tilde is placed at the beginning or end of a message definition, the default text is inserted at that point, allowing both custom text and the default text to be displayed.

If the prompt, help or error message is not defined, the default message (as defined under NOTES) is displayed.

Three visual tool modules are linked to the ckrange command. They are errange (which formats and displays an error message), helprange (which formats and displays a help message), and valrange (which validates a response). These modules should be used in conjunction with FACE objects. In this instance, the FACE object defines the prompt.

The options and arguments for this command are:

–Q Do not allow quit as a valid response.

–W Use *width* as the line length for prompt, help, and error messages.

–l The lower limit of the range is *lower*. Default is the machine's largest negative integer or long.

–u The upper limit of the range is *upper*. Default is the machine's largest positive integer or long.

–b The base for input is *base*. Must be 2 to 36, default is 10.

–d The default value is *default*. The default is not validated and so does not have to meet any criteria. If *default* is non-numeric, ckrange returns 0 and not the alphabetic string.

–h The help message is *help*.

−e   The error message is *error*.

−p   The prompt message is *prompt*.

−k   Send process ID *pid* a signal if the user chooses to abort.

−s   When quit is chosen, send *signal* to the process whose *pid* is specified by the −k option. If no signal is specified, use SIGTERM.

input   Input to be verified against upper and lower limits and base.

EXIT CODES
0 = Successful execution
1 = EOF on input
2 = Usage error
3 = User termination (quit)

NOTES
The default base 10 prompt for ckrange is:

Enter an integer between *lower* and *upper* [*lower−upper*, q, ?]

The default base 10 error message is:

ERROR − Please enter an integer between *lower* and *upper*.

The default base 10 help message is:

Please enter an integer between *lower* and *upper*.

The messages are changed from "integer" to "base *base* integer" if the base is set to a number other than 10.

When the quit option is chosen (and allowed), q is returned along with the return code 3. The valrange module does not produce any output. It returns zero for success and non-zero for failure.

NAME

ckstr – display a prompt; verify and return a string answer

SYNOPSIS

ckstr [–Q] [–W *width*] [[–r *regexp*] [–r *regexp*] . . .] [–l *length*]
    [–d *default*] [–h *help*] [–e *error*] [–p *prompt*] [–k *pid* [–s *signal*]]

errstr [–W *width*] [–e *error*] [[–r *regexp*] [–r *regexp*] . . .] [–l *length*]

helpstr [–W *width*] [–h *help*] [[–r *regexp*] [–r *regexp*] . . .] [–l *length*]

valstr *input* [[–r *regexp*] [–r *regexp*] . . .] [–l *length*]

DESCRIPTION

ckstr prompts a user and validates the response. It defines, among other things, a prompt message whose response should be a string, text for help and error messages, and a default value (which is returned if the user responds with a RETURN).

The answer returned from this command must match the defined regular expression and be no longer than the length specified. If no regular expression is given, valid input must be a string with a length less than or equal to the length defined with no internal, leading or trailing white space. If no length is defined, the length is not checked. Either a regular expression or a length must be given with the command.

All messages are limited in length to 70 characters and are formatted automatically. Any white space used in the definition (including newline) is stripped. The –W option cancels the automatic formatting. When a tilde is placed at the beginning or end of a message definition, the default text is inserted at that point, allowing both custom text and the default text to be displayed.

If the prompt, help or error message is not defined, the default message (as defined under NOTES) is displayed.

Three visual tool modules are linked to the ckstr command. They are errstr (which formats and displays an error message), helpstr (which formats and displays a help message), and valstr (which validates a response). These modules should be used in conjunction with FACE objects. In this instance, the FACE object defines the prompt.

The options and arguments for this command are:

–Q   Do not allow quit as a valid response.

–W   Use *width* as the line length for prompt, help, and error messages.

–r   Validate the input against regular expression *regexp*. May include white space. If multiple expressions are defined, the answer need match only one of them.

–l   The maximum length of the input is *length*.

–d   The default value is *default*. The default is not validated and so does not have to meet any criteria.

-h   The help message is *help*.

-e   The error message is *error*.

-p   The prompt message is *prompt*.

-k   Send process ID *pid* a signal if the user chooses to abort.

-s   When quit is chosen, send *signal* to the process whose *pid* is specified by
        the -k option. If no signal is specified, use SIGTERM.

input   Input to be verified against format length and/or regular expression cri-
        teria.

EXIT CODES
        0 = Successful execution
        1 = EOF on input
        2 = Usage error
        3 = User termination (quit)

NOTES
        The default prompt for ckstr is:

            Enter an appropriate value [?,q]

        The default error message is dependent upon the type of validation involved.
        The user is told either that the length or the pattern matching failed.

        The default help message is also dependent upon the type of validation involved.
        If a regular expression has been defined, the message is:

            Please enter a string which matches the following pattern:
            regexp

        Other messages define the length requirement and the definition of a string.

        When the quit option is chosen (and allowed), q is returned along with the return
        code 3. The valstr module does not produce any output. It returns zero for
        success and non-zero for failure.

        Unless a "q" for "quit" is disabled by the -Q option, a single "q" to the following

            ckstr -rq

        is treated as a "quit" and not as a pattern match.

NAME

cktime – display a prompt; verify and return a time of day

SYNOPSIS

cktime [–Q] [–W *width*] [–f *format*] [–d *default*] [–h *help*] [–e *error*]
    [–p *prompt*] [–k *pid* [–s *signal*]]

errtime [–W *width*] [–e *error*] [–f *format*]

helptime [–W *width*] [–h *help*] [–f *format*]

valtime [–f *format*] *input*

DESCRIPTION

cktime prompts a user and validates the response. It defines, among other things, a prompt message whose response should be a time, text for help and error messages, and a default value (which is returned if the user responds with a RETURN). The user response must match the defined format for the time of day.

All messages are limited in length to 70 characters and are formatted automatically. Any white space used in the definition (including newline) is stripped. The –W option cancels the automatic formatting. When a tilde is placed at the beginning or end of a message definition, the default text is inserted at that point, allowing both custom text and the default text to be displayed.

If the prompt, help or error message is not defined, the default message (as defined under NOTES) is displayed.

Three visual tool modules are linked to the cktime command. They are errtime (which formats and displays an error message), helptime (which formats and displays a help message), and valtime (which validates a response). These modules should be used in conjunction with FMLI objects. In this instance, the FMLI object defines the prompt. When *format* is defined in the errtime and helptime modules, the messages describe the expected format.

The options and arguments for this command are:

–Q   Do not allow quit as a valid response.

–W   Use *width* as the line length for prompt, help, and error messages.

–f   Verify the input against *format*. Possible formats and their definitions are:

        %H = hour (00 – 23)
        %I = hour (00 – 12)
        %M = minute (00 – 59)
        %p = ante meridian or post meridian
        %r = time as %I:%M:%S %p
        %R = time as %H:%M (the default format)
        %S = seconds (00 – 59)
        %T = time as %H:%M:%S

–d   The default value is *default*. The default is not validated and so does not have to meet any criteria.

-h   The help message is *help*.

-e   The error message is *error*.

-p   The prompt message is *prompt*.

-k *pid*   Send process ID *pid* a signal if the user chooses to abort.

-s *signal*

> When quit is chosen, send *signal* to the process whose *pid* is specified by the -k option. If no signal is specified, use SIGTERM.

input   Input to be verified against format criteria.

EXIT CODES

0 = Successful execution
1 = EOF on input
2 = Usage error
3 = User termination (quit)
4 = Garbled format argument

NOTES

The default prompt for cktime is:

```
Enter a time of day [?,q]
```

The default error message is:

```
ERROR - Please enter the time of day. Format is format.
```

The default help message is:

```
Please enter the time of day. Format is format.
```

When the quit option is chosen (and allowed), q is returned along with the return code 3. The valtime module does not produce any output. It returns zero for success and non-zero for failure.

NAME

    ckuid – prompt for and validate a user ID

SYNOPSIS

    ckuid [–Q] [–W *width*] [–m] [–d *default*] [–h *help*] [–e *error*] [–p *prompt*]
        [–k *pid* [–s *signal*]]

    erruid [–W *width*] [–e *error*]

    helpuid [–W *width*] [–m] [–h *help*]

    valuid *input*

DESCRIPTION

    ckuid prompts a user and validates the response. It defines, among other things,
    a prompt message whose response should be an existing user ID, text for help
    and error messages, and a default value (which is returned if the user responds
    with a RETURN).

    All messages are limited in length to 70 characters and are formatted automati-
    cally. Any white space used in the definition (including newline) is stripped.
    The –W option cancels the automatic formatting. When a tilde is placed at the
    beginning or end of a message definition, the default text is inserted at that point,
    allowing both custom text and the default text to be displayed.

    If the prompt, help or error message is not defined, the default message (as
    defined under NOTES) is displayed.

    Three visual tool modules are linked to the ckuid command. They are erruid
    (which formats and displays an error message), helpuid (which formats and
    displays a help message), and valuid (which validates a response). These
    modules should be used in conjunction with FML objects. In this instance, the
    FML object defines the prompt.

    The options and arguments for this command are:

    –Q   Do not allow quit as a valid response.

    –W   Use *width* as the line length for prompt, help, and error messages.

    –m   Display a list of all logins when help is requested or when the user makes
            an error.

    –d   The default value is *default*. The default is not validated and so does not
            have to meet any criteria.

    –h   The help message is *help*.

    –e   The error message is *error*.

    –p   The prompt message is *prompt*.

    –k   Send process ID *pid* a signal if the user chooses to abort.

    –s   When quit is chosen, send *signal* to the process whose *pid* is specified by
            the –k option. If no signal is specified, use SIGTERM.

    input Input to be verified against /etc/passwd.

EXIT CODES
>0 = Successful execution
>1 = EOF on input
>2 = Usage error
>3 = User termination (quit)

NOTES
>The default prompt for ckuid is:

>>`Enter the login name of an existing user [?,q]`

>The default error message is:

>>`ERROR - Please enter the login name of an existing user.`
>>*(If the* −m *option of* ckuid *is used, a list of valid users is also displayed.)*

>The default help message is:

>>`Please enter the login name of an existing user.`
>>*(If the* −m *option of* ckuid *is used, a list of valid users is also displayed.)*

When the quit option is chosen (and allowed), q is returned along with the return code 3. The valuid module does not produce any output. It returns zero for success and non-zero for failure.

NAME

ckyorn – prompt for and validate yes/no

SYNOPSIS

ckyorn [-Q] [-W *width*] [-d *default*] [-h *help*] [-e *error*] [-p *prompt*]
    [-k *pid* [-s *signal*]]

erryorn [-W *width*] [-e *error*]

helpyorn [-W *width*] [-h *help*]

valyorn *input*

DESCRIPTION

ckyorn prompts a user and validates the response. It defines, among other
things, a prompt message for a yes or no answer, text for help and error messages, and a default value (which is returned if the user responds with a
RETURN).

All messages are limited in length to 70 characters and are formatted automatically. Any white space used in the definition (including newline) is stripped.
The -W option cancels the automatic formatting. For the -h and -e options, placing a tilde at the beginning or end of a message definition causes the default text
to be inserted at that point. This allows both custom text and the default text to
be displayed.

If the prompt, help or error message is not defined, the default message (as
defined under NOTES) is displayed.

Three visual tool modules are linked to the ckyorn command. They are erryorn
(which formats and displays an error message), helpyorn (which formats and
displays a help message), and valyorn (which validates a response). These
modules should be used in conjunction with FACE objects. In this instance, the
FACE object defines the prompt.

The options and arguments for this command are:

-Q   Do not allow quit as a valid response.

-W   Use *width* as the line length for prompt, help, and error messages.

-d   The default value is *default*. The default is not validated and so does not
        have to meet any criteria.

-h   The help message is *help*.

-e   The error message is *error*.

-p   The prompt message is *prompt*.

-k   Send process ID *pid* a signal if the user chooses to abort.

-s   When quit is chosen, send *signal* to the process whose *pid* is specified by
        the -k option. If no signal is specified, use SIGTERM.

input   Input to be verified as y, yes, Y, Yes, YES or n, no, N, No, NO.

EXIT CODES
>   0 = Successful execution
>   1 = EOF on input
>   2 = Usage error
>   3 = User termination (quit)

NOTES
>   The default prompt for ckyorn is:
>
>   >   Yes or No [y,n,?,q]
>
>   The default error message is:
>
>   >   ERROR - Please enter yes or no.
>
>   The default help message is:
>
>   >   Enter y or yes if your answer is yes;
>   >   or no if your answer is no.

When the quit option is chosen (and allowed), q is returned along with the return code 3. The valyorn module does not produce any output. It returns zero for success and non-zero for failure.

NAME

　　　dispgid – displays a list of all valid group names

SYNOPSIS

　　　dispgid

DESCRIPTION

　　　dispgid displays a list of all group names on the system (one group per line).

EXIT CODES

　　　0 = Successful execution
　　　1 = Cannot read the group file

NAME

dispuid – displays a list of all valid user names

SYNOPSIS

dispuid

DESCRIPTION

dispuid displays a list of all user names on the system (one line per name).

EXIT CODES

0 = Successful execution
1 = Cannot read the password file

NAME

mouseadmin - mouse administration

SYNOPSIS

mouseadmin [−nbl] [−d *terminal*] [−a *terminal mouse*]

DESCRIPTION

mouseadmin allows any user with system administrator privileges to add or delete mouse devices. Users without "superuser" privileges will only be allowed to list the current mouse/display assignments. The mouseadmin command issued without arguments will execute in menu mode, providing the user with a listing of current assignments and a selection menu of operations.

OPTIONS

The command line arguments are defined as follows:

−n   build mouse/display pair table without downloading to driver. (This option should only be used within install scripts.)

−b   do not validate for BUS mouse in system configuration. (This option should only be used within install scripts.)

−l   list mouse/display assignments.

−d   delete terminal assignment.

−a   assign mouse device (PS2, BUS, tty00, s0tty0, etc.) to terminal (console, s0vt00, etc.).

When using the −a option, the mouseadmin command format is:

mouseadmin −a *terminal mouse_device*

For example:

```
mouseadmin -a console PS2
mouseadmin -a console BUS
mouseadmin -a s0vt00 tty00
mouseadmin -a s0vt00 tty01
```

FILES

/usr/bin/mouseadmin
/usr/lib/mousemgr

SEE ALSO

mouse(7)
Mouse Driver Administrator's Guide

NAME

newvt – opens virtual terminals.

SYNOPSIS

newvt [-e *prog*] [-n *vt_number*]

DESCRIPTION

Use the newvt command to open a new virtual terminal. The newly opened virtual terminal will inherit your environment.

-e   Specifies a program (*prog*) to execute in the new virtual terminal. Without the -e option, the program pointed to by the $SHELL environment variable is started in the new virtual terminal. If $SHELL is NULL or points to a nonexecutable program, then /bin/sh is invoked.

-n   Specifies a particular virtual terminal (*vt_number*) to open. If the -n option is not specified, then the next available virtual terminal is opened. Close virtual terminals by pressing CTRL-d (control d). Repeat CTRL-d until all open virtual terminals are closed.

DIAGNOSTICS

The newvt command will fail under the following conditions:

If an illegal option is specified.
If the device cannot be opened.
If newvt is invoked from a remote terminal.
If no virtual terminals are available (-n option not specified).
If the requested virtual terminal is not available (-n option specified).
If the requested virtual terminal cannot be opened.
If the specified command cannot be executed (-e option specified).
If the $SHELL program cannot be executed ($SHELL set and -e option not specified).
If /dev/vtmon cannot be opened.

SEE ALSO

vtlmgr(1)
vtgetty(1M) in the *System Administrator's Reference Manual*

NAME

    `pkginfo` – display software package information

SYNOPSIS

    `pkginfo [-q|x|l] [-p|i] [-a` *arch*`] [-v` *version*`]`
        `[-c` *category1*`,[`*category2*`[, . . . ]]] [`*pkginst*`[,`*pkginst*`[, . . . ]]]`

    `pkginfo [-d` *device* `[-q|x|l] [-a` *arch*`] [-v` *version*`]`
        `[-c` *category1*`,[`*category2*`[, . . . ]]] [`*pkginst*`[,`*pkginst*`[, . . . ]]]`

DESCRIPTION

    `pkginfo` displays information about software packages which are installed on the system (with the first synopsis) or which reside on a particular device or directory (with the second synopsis). Only the package name and abbreviation for pre-System V Release 4 packages will be included in the display.

    The options for this command are:

    `-q`   Does not list any information, but can be used from a program to check (that is, query) whether or not a package has been installed.

    `-x`   Designates an extracted listing of package information. It contains the package abbreviation, package name, package architecture (if available) and package version (if available).

    `-l`   Designates long format, which includes all available information about the designated package(s).

    `-p`   Designates that information should be presented only for partially installed packages.

    `-i`   Designates that information should be presented only for fully installed packages.

    `-a`   Specifies the architecture of the package as *arch*.

    `-v`   Specifies the version of the package as *version*. All compatible versions can be requested by preceding the version name with a tilde (~). The list produced by `-v` will include pre-Release 4 packages (with which no version numbers are associated). Multiple white spaces are replaced with a single space during version comparison.

    `-c`   Selects packages to be display based on the category *category*. (Categories are defined in the category field of the `pkginfo` file.) If more than one category is supplied, the package must only match one of the list of categories. The match is not case specific.

    pkginst Designates a package by its instance. An instance can be the package abbreviation or a specific instance (for example, `inst.1` or `inst.beta`). All instances of package can be requested by `inst.*`. When using this format, enclose the command line in single quotes to prevent the shell from interpreting the `*` character.

    `-d`   Defines a device, *device*, on which the software resides. *device* can be a full pathname to a directory or the identifiers for tape, floppy disk, removable disk, and so on. The special token "spool" may be used to indicate the default installation spool directory.

NOTES

Without options, pkginfo lists the primary category, package instance, and name of all completely installed and partially installed packages. One line per package selected is produced.

The −p and −i options are meaningless if used in conjunction with the −d option.

The options −q, −x, and −l are mutually exclusive.

pkginfo cannot tell if a pre-Release 4 package is only partially installed. It is assumed that all pre-Release 4 packages are fully installed.

SEE ALSO

pkgadd(1M), pkgask(1M), pkgchk(1M), pkgrm(1M), pkgtrans(1)

NAME

pkgmk – produce an installable package

SYNOPSIS

pkgmk [−o] [−d *device*] [−r *rootpath*] [−b *basedir*] [−l *limit*] [−a *arch*]
[−v *version*] [−p *pstamp*] [−f *prototype*] [*variable=value* . . .] [*pkginst*]

DESCRIPTION

pkgmk produces an installable package to be used as input to the pkgadd command. The package contents will be in directory structure format.

The command uses the package prototype file as input and creates a pkgmap file. The contents for each entry in the prototype file is copied to the appropriate output location. Information concerning the contents (checksum, file size, modification date) is computed and stored in the pkgmap file, along with attribute information specified in the prototype file.

−o	Overwrites the same instance, package instance will be overwritten if it already exists.
−d *device*	Creates the package on *device*. *device* can be a full pathname to a directory or the identifiers for a floppy disk or removable disk (for example, /dev/diskette). The default device is the installation spool directory.
−r *rootpath*	Ignores destination paths in the prototype file. Instead, uses the indicated *rootpath* with the source pathname appended to locate objects on the source machine.
−b *basedir*	Prepends the indicated *basedir* to locate relocatable objects on the source machine.
−l *limit*	Specifies the maximum size in 512 byte blocks of the output device as *limit*. By default, if the output file is a directory or a mountable device, pkgmk will employ the df command to dynamically calculate the amount of available space on the output device. Useful in conjunction with pkgtrans to create package with datastream format.
−a *arch*	Overrides the architecture information provided in the pkginfo file with *arch*.
−v *version*	Overrides version information provided in the pkginfo file with *version*.
−p *pstamp*	Overrides the production stamp definition in the pkginfo file with *pstamp*.
−f *prototype*	Uses the file *prototype* as input to the command. The default name for this file is either Prototype or prototype.
variable=value	Places the indicated variable in the packaging environment. [See prototype(4) for definitions of packaging variables.]
pkginst	Specifies the package by its instance. pkgmk will automatically create a new instance if the version and/or architecture is different. A user should specify only a package abbreviation; a particular instance should not be specified unless the user is overwriting it.

NOTES

Architecture information is provided on the command line with the −a option or in the prototype file. If no architecture information is supplied at all, the output of uname −m will be used.

Version information is provided on the command line with the −v option or in the prototype file. If no version information is supplied, a default based on the current date will be provided.

Command line definitions for both architecture and version override the prototype definitions.

SEE ALSO

pkgparam(1), pkgproto(1), pkgtrans(1)

NAME

pkgparam – displays package parameter values

SYNOPSIS

pkgparam [−v][−d *device*] *pkginst* [*param*[. . .]]

pkgparam −f *file* [−v] [*param*[. . .]]

DESCRIPTION

pkgparam displays the value associated with the parameter or parameters requested on the command line. The values are located in either the pkginfo file for *pkginst* or from the specific file named with the −f option.

One parameter value is shown per line. Only the value of a parameter is given unless the −v option is used. With this option, the output of the command is in this format:

> *parameter1='value1'*
> *parameter2='value2'*
> *parameter3='value3'*

If no parameters are specified on the command line, values for all parameters associated with the package are shown.

Options and arguments for this command are:

−v   Specifies verbose mode. Displays name of parameter and its value.

−d   Specifies the *device* on which a *pkginst* is stored. It can be a full pathname to a directory or the identifiers for tape, floppy disk or removable disk (for example, /var/tmp, /dev/dsk/f0t, and /dev/dsk/0s2). The default device is the installation spool directory. If no instance name is given, parameter information for all packages residing in *device* is shown.

−f   Requests that the command read *file* for parameter values.

pkginst   Defines a specific package instance for which parameter values should be displayed. The format *pkginst.** can be used to indicate all instances of a package. When using this format, enclose the command line in single quotes to prevent the shell from interpreting the * character.

param   Defines a specific parameter whose value should be displayed.

ERRORS

If parameter information is not available for the indicated package, the command exits with a non-zero status.

NOTES

The −f synopsis allows you to specify the file from which parameter values should be extracted. This file should be in the same format as a pkginfo file. As an example, such a file might be created during package development and used while testing software during this stage.

SEE ALSO

pkgmk(1), pkgparam(3x), pkgproto(1), pgktrans(1)

NAME

pkgproto – generate a prototype file

SYNOPSIS

pkgproto [–i] [–c *class*] [*path1*[=*path2*] . . .]

DESCRIPTION

pkgproto scans the indicated paths and generates a prototype file that may be used as input to the pkgmk command.

–i   Ignores symbolic links and records the paths as ftype=f (a file) versus ftype=s(symbolic link)

–c   Maps the class of all paths to *class*.

path1   Path of directory where objects are located.

path2   Path that should be substituted on output for *path1*.

If no paths are specified on the command line, standard input is assumed to be a list of paths. If the path listed on the command line is a directory, the contents of the directory are searched. However, if input is read from stdin, a directory specified as a path will not be searched.

NOTES

By default, pkgproto creates symbolic link entries for any symbolic link encountered (ftype=s). When you use the –i option, pkgproto creates a file entry for symbolic links (ftype=f). The prototype file would have to be edited to assign such file types as v (volatile), e (editable), or x (exclusive directory). pkgproto detects linked files. If multiple files are linked together, the first path encountered is considered the source of the link.

EXAMPLE

The following two examples show uses of pkgproto and a parial listing of the output produced.

Example 1:

```
$ pkgproto /usr/bin=bin /usr/usr/bin=usrbin /etc=etc
f none bin/sed=/bin/sed 0775 bin bin
f none bin/sh=/bin/sh 0755 bin daemon
f none bin/sort=/bin/sort 0755 bin bin
f none usrbin/sdb=/usr/bin/sdb 0775 bin bin
f none usrbin/shl=/usr/bin/shl 4755 bin bin
d none etc/master.d 0755 root daemon
f none etc/master.d/kernel=/etc/master.d/kernel 0644 root daemon
f none etc/rc=/etc/rc 0744 root daemon
```

Example 2:

```
$ find / -type d -print | pkgproto
d none / 755 root root
d none /usr/bin 755 bin bin
d none /usr 755 root root
d none /usr/bin 775 bin bin
d none /etc 755 root root
d none /tmp 777 root root
```

SEE ALSO
      pkgmk(1), pkgparam(1), pkgtrans(1).

NAME

pkgtrans – translate package format

SYNOPSIS

pkgtrans [-ions] *device1 device2* [*pkginst1* [*pkginst2* [. . .]]]

DESCRIPTION

pkgtrans translates an installable package from one format to another. It translates:

a filesystem format to a datastream

a datastream to a filesystem format

a filesystem format to another filesystem format

The options and arguments for this command are:

-i   Copies only the pkginfo and pkgmap files.

-o   Overwrites the same instance on the destination device, package instance will be overwritten if it already exists.

-n   Creates a new instance if any instance of this package already exists.

-s   Indicates that the package should be written to *device2* as a datastream rather than as a filesystem. The default behavior is to write a filesystem format on devices that support both formats.

device1   Indicates the source device. The package or packages on this device will be translated and placed on *device2*.

device2   Indicates the destination device. Translated packages will be placed on this device.

pkginst   Specifies which package instance or instances on *device1* should be translated. The token all may be used to indicate all packages. *pkginst.* * can be used to indicate all instances of a package. (When using this format, enclose the command line in single quotes to prevent the shell from interpreting the * character.) If no packages are defined, a prompt shows all packages on the device and asks which to translate.

NOTES

Device specifications can be either the special node name (/dev/diskette) or the device alias (diskette1). The device spool indicates the default spool directory. Source and destination devices may not be the same.

By default, pkgtrans will not transfer any instance of a package if any instance of that package already exists on the destination device. Use of the −n option will create a new instance if an instance of this package already exists. Use of the −o option will overwrite the same instance if it already exists. Neither of these options are useful if the destination device is a datastream.

If you're transferring a package in datastream format to floppies and the package spans multiple floppies, use the filesystem format. (The datastream format is not supported across multiple floppies.)

pkgtrans depends on the integrity of the /etc/device.tab file to determine whether a device can support a datastream and/or filesystem formats. Problems in transferring a device in a particular format could mean corruption of /etc/device.tab.

EXAMPLE

The following example translates all packages on the floppy drive /dev/diskette and places the translations on /tmp.

        pkgtrans /dev/diskette /tmp all

The next example translates packages pkg1 and pkg2 on /tmp and places their translations (that is, a datastream) on the 9track1 output device.

        pkgtrans /tmp 9track1 pkg1 pkg2

The next example translates pkg1 and pkg2 on tmp and places them on the diskette in a datastream format.

        pkgtrans -s /tmp /dev/diskette pkg1 pkg2

FILES

    /etc/device.tab

SEE ALSO

    installf(1M), pkgadd(1M), pkgask(1M), pkginfo(1), pkgmk(1), pkgparam(1), pkgproto(1), pkgrm(1M), removef(1M).

NAME

vtlmgr – monitors and opens virtual terminals.

SYNOPSIS

vtlmgr [–k]

DESCRIPTION

When you invoke the vtlmgr command (usually from within your .profile), it places itself in the background and monitors /dev/vtmon for signals from the keyboard/display driver to open new virtual terminals.

Option:

–k   The –k option sends a SIGHUP signal to all open virtual terminals when you log off (by entering CTRL-d from your home virtual terminal). This automatically closes, if possible, existing virtual terminals. For virtual terminals that cannot be automatically closed, you are asked if you want to close them manually.

After running vtlmgr, you open new virtual terminals and then switch between them by entering a hot-key sequence, specifically:

ALT – SYS–REQ *key*

where *key* is either a function key whose number corresponds to the number of the virtual terminal to switch to, for example, pressing F1 switches you to /dev/vt01 (virtual terminal 01), pressing F2 switches you to /dev/vt02 (virtual terminal 02), and so forth, or one of the letters in the following table:

key	Interpretation
h	home virtual terminal (/dev/vt00)
n	next virtual terminal
p	previous virtual terminal
f	force a switch to a virtual terminal

Use the f key only when the current virtual terminal is essentially locked up or stuck in graphics mode. This will cause the virtual terminal to be reset to a sane text state and all processes associated with the virtual terminal will be killed.

When the hot-key sequence is entered, the executable program pointed to by the $SHELL variable is executed in the new virtual terminal. If $SHELL is NULL or pointing to a program which is not executable, /bin/sh is executed. The newly opened virtual terminal inherits the environment in effect when the vtlmgr command is invoked.

You may perform setup on each new virtual terminal as it is created by vtlmgr through the .vtlrc file. This file should be in your home directory. Its contents are a shell script that will be run by /bin/sh before the shell prompt is displayed. In this way it is similar to your .profile file. However, you may not set and export environment variables to the shell for the virtual terminal because a different shell runs the .vtlrc shell script.

The system administrator can control how many virtual terminals are available by setting a parameter in the file /etc/default/workstations. Virtual terminals 0 - 8 are configured by default and the default keyboard map makes up to 13 virtual terminals available (i.e., an additional 4 virtual terminals can readily be defined within the default settings). The default virtual terminals are the home terminal and one corresponding to each function key. An application can make two more available to the end-user (by reprogramming the keyboard map), or can reserve the last two for programmatic use only, making 15 virtual terminals available in all.

Note that processes that are no longer visible may still be continuing. Standard output is directed to the current virtual terminal's screen. For example, you can issue a cat command on one virtual terminal, switch to another virtual terminal to start an application, and then switch to another to do an edit. The cat output will be lost if the virtual terminal scrolls the data off the screen unless you initially redirect the output to a file.

DIAGNOSTICS

The vtlmgr command will fail under the following conditions:

If an illegal option is specified.
If the device cannot be opened.
If the command is invoked from a remote terminal.
If /dev/vtmon cannot be opened.
If $SHELL is set and is not executable.
If $SHELL is not set and /bin/sh cannot be invoked.

SEE ALSO

newvt (1M)
vtgetty(1M), keyboard(7) in the *System Administrator's Reference Manual*

NAME

`delsysadm` – `sysadm` interface menu or task removal tool

SYNOPSIS

`delsysadm` *task* | [*-r*] *menu*

DESCRIPTION

The `delsysadm` command deletes a *task* or *menu* from the `sysadm` interface and modifies the interface directory structure on the target machine.

task | *menu*   The logical name and location of the menu or task within the interface menu hierarchy. Begin with the top menu `main` and proceed to where the menu or the task resides, separating each name with colons. See EXAMPLES.

If the *-r* option is used, this command will recursively remove all sub-menus and tasks for this menu. If the *-r* option is not used, the menu must be empty.

`delsysadm` should only be used to remove items added as "on-line" changes with the `edsysadm` command. Such an addition will have a package instance tag of ONLINE. If the task or menu (and its sub-menus and tasks) have any package instance tags other than ONLINE, you are asked whether to continue with the removal or to exit. Under these circumstances, you probably do not want to continue and you should rely on the package involved to take the necessary actions to delete this type of entry.

The command exits successfully or provides the error code within an error message.

EXAMPLES

To remove the `nformat` task, execute:

`delsysadm main:applications:ndevices:nformat.`

DIAGNOSTICS

0   Successful execution
2   Invalid syntax
3   Menu or task does not exist
4   Menu not empty
5   Unable to update interface menu structure

NOTES

Any menu that was originally a placeholder menu (one that only appears if sub-menus exist under it) will be returned to placeholder status when a deletion leaves it empty.

When the *-r* option is used, `delsysadm` checks for dependencies before removing any subentries. (A dependency exists if the menu being removed contains an entry placed there by an application package). If a dependency is found, the user is shown a list of packages that depend on the menu being deleted and asked whether or not to continue. If the answer is yes, the menu and all of its menus and tasks are removed (even those shown to have dependencies). If the answer is no, the menu is not deleted.

delsysadm should only be used to remove menu or task entries that have been added to the interface with edsysadm.

SEE ALSO

edsysadm(1M), sysadm(1M)

NAME

edsysadm – sysadm interface editing tool

SYNOPSIS

edsysadm

DESCRIPTION

edsysadm is an interactive tool that adds or changes either menu and task definitions in the sysadm interface. It can be used to make changes directly on-line on a specific machine or to create changes that will become part of a software package. The command creates the administration files necessary to achieve the requested changes in the interface and either places them in the appropriate place for on-line changes or saves them to be included in a software package.

edsysadm presents several screens, first prompting for which type of menu item you want to change, menu or task, and then for what type of action to take, add or change. When you select add, a blank menu or task definition (as described below) is provided for you to fill in. When you select change, a series of screens is presented to help identify the definition you wish to change. The final screen presented is the menu or task definition filled in with its current values, which you can then edit.

The menu definition prompts and their descriptions are:

Menu Name
: The name of the new menu (as it should appear in the lefthand column of the screen). This field has a maximum length of 16 alphanumeric characters.

Menu Description
: A description of the new menu (as it should appear in the righthand column of the screen). This field has a maximum length of 58 characters and can consist of any alphanumeric character except at sign (@), carat (ˆ), tilde (˜), back grave (`), grave ('), and double quotes (").

Menu Location
: The location of the menu in the menu hierarchy, expressed as a menu pathname. The pathname should begin with the main menu followed by all other menus that must be traversed (in the order they are traversed) to access this menu. Each menu name must be separated by colons. For example, the menu location for a menu entry being added to the Applications menu is main:applications. Do not include the menu name in this location definition. The complete pathname to this menu entry will be the menu location plus the menu name defined at the first prompt.

: This is a scrollable field, showing a maximum of 50 alphanumeric characters at a time.

Menu Help File Name   Pathname to the item help file for this menu entry. If it resides in the directory from which you invoked edsysadm, you do not need to give a full pathname. If you name an item help file that does not exist, you are placed in an editor (as defined by $EDITOR) to create one. The new file is created in the current directory and named Help.

The task definition prompts and their descriptions are:

Task Name   The name of the new task (as it should appear in the lefthand column of the screen). This field has a maximum length of 16 alphanumeric characters.

Task Description   A description of the new task (as it should appear in the righthand column of the screen). This field has a maximum length of 58 characters and can consist of any alphanumeric character except at sign (@), carat (ˆ), tilde (˜), back grave (`), grave (´), and double quotes (").

Task Location   The location of the task in the menu hierarchy, expressed as a pathname. The pathname should begin with the main menu followed by all other menus that must be traversed (in the order they are traversed) to access this task. Each menu name must be separated by colons. For example, the task location for a task entry being added to the applications menu is main:applications. Do not include the task name in this location definition. The complete pathname to this task entry will be the task location as well as the task name defined at the first prompt.

                         This is a scrollable field, showing a maximum of 50 alphanumeric characters at a time.

Task Help File Name   Pathname to the item help file for this task entry. If it resides in the directory from which you invoked edsysadm, you do not need to give a full pathname. If you name an item help file that does not exist, you are placed in an editor (as defined by $EDITOR) to create one. The new file is created in the current directory and named Help.

Task Action   The FACE form name or executable that will be run when this task is selected. This is a scrollable field, showing a maximum of 58 alphanumeric characters at a time. This pathname can be relative to the current directory as well as absolute.

Task Files   Any FACE objects or other executables that support the task action listed above and might be called from within that action. *Do not include the help file name or the task action in this list.* Pathnames can be relative to the current directory as well as absolute. A dot (.) implies "all files in the current directory" and includes files in subdirectories.

This is a scrollable field, showing a maximum of 50 alphanumeric characters at a time.

Once the menu or task has been defined, screens for installing the menu or task or saving them for packaging are presented. The package creation or on-line installation is verified and you are informed upon completion.

NOTES

For package creation or modification, this command automatically creates a menu information file and a prototype file in the current directory (the directory from which the command is executed). The menu information file is used during package installation to modify menus in the menu structure. A prototype file is an installation file which gives a listing of package contents. The prototype file created by edsysadm lists the files defined under task action and gives them the special installation class of "admin". The contents of this prototype file must be incorporated in the package prototype file.

For on-line installation, edsysadm automatically creates a menu information file and adds or modifies the interface menu structure directly.

The item help file must follow the format shown in the *Application Programmer's Guide* in the "Customizing the Administration Interace" chapter or in the *System Administrator's Guide* in the "Customizing the sysadm Interface" appendix.

SEE ALSO

delsysadm(1M), pkgmk(1), prototype(4), sysadm(1M)

NAME

idbuild – build new UNIX System kernel

SYNOPSIS

/etc/conf/bin/idbuild

DESCRIPTION

This script builds a new UNIX System kernel using the current system configuration in etc/conf/. Kernel reconfigurations are usually done after a device driver is installed, or system tunable parameters are modified. The script uses the shell variable ROOT from the user's environment as its starting path. Except for the special case of kernel development in a non-root source tree, the shell variable ROOT should always be set to null or to "/". idbuild exits with a return code of zero on success and non-zero on failure.

Building a new UNIX System image consists of generating new system configuration files, then link-editing the kernel and device driver object modules in the etc/conf/pack.d object tree. This is done by idbuild by calling the following commands:

etc/conf/bin/idconfig   To build kernel configuration files.

etc/conf/bin/idmkunix   To process the configuration files and link-edit a new UNIX System image.

The system configuration files are built by processing the Master and System files representing device driver and tunable parameter specifications. For the i386 UNIX System the files etc/conf/cf.d/mdevice, and etc/conf/cf.d/mtune represent the Master information. The files etc/conf/cf.d/stune, and the files specified in etc/conf/sdevice.d/* represent the System information. The kernel also has file system type information defined in the files specified by etc/conf/sfsys.d/* and etc/conf/mfsys.d/* .

Once a new UNIX System kernel has been configured, a lock file is set in etc/.new_unix which causes the new kernel to replace /unix on the next system shutdown (i.e., on the next entry to the *init 0* state). Upon the next system boot, the new kernel will be executed.

ERROR MESSAGES

Since idbuild calls other system commands to accomplish system reconfiguration and link editing, it will report all errors encountered by those commands, then clean up intermediate files created in the process. In general, the exit value 1 indicates an error was encountered by idbuild .

The errors encountered fall into the following categories:

Master file error messages.
System file error messages.
Tunable file error messages.
Compiler and Link-editor error messages.

All error messages are designed to be self-explanatory.

SEE ALSO

idinstall(1m), idtune(1m).
mdevice(4), mfsys(4), mtune(4), sdevice(4), sfsys(4), stune(4) in the *Programmer's Reference Manual.*

NAME

idcheck – returns selected information

SYNOPSIS

/etc/conf/bin/idcheck

DESCRIPTION

This command returns selected information about the system configuration. It is
useful in add-on device Driver Software Package (DSP) installation scripts to
determine if a particular device driver has already been installed, or to verify that
a particular interrupt vector, I/O address or other selectable parameter is in fact
available for use. The various forms are:

idcheck –p *device-name* [-i dir] [-r]

idcheck–v *vector* [-i dir] [-r]

idcheck–d *dma-channel* [-i dir] [-r]

idcheck–a –l *lower_address* –u *upper_address* [-i dir] [-r]

idcheck –c –l *lower_address* –u *upper_address* [-i dir] [-r]

This command scans the System and Master modules and returns:

100 if an error occurs.

0 if no conflict exists.

a positive number greater than 0 and less than 100 if a conflict exists.

The command line options are:

–r	Report device name of any conflicting device on stdout.
–p *device-name*	This option checks for the existence of four different components of the DSP. The exit code is the addition of the return codes from the four checks.
	Add 1 to the exit code if the DSP directory under /etc/conf/pack.d exists.
	Add 2 to the exit code if the Master module has been installed.
	Add 4 to the exit code if the System module has been installed.
	Add 8 to the exit code if the Kernel was built with the System module.
	Add 16 to the exit code if a Driver.o is part of the DSP (vs. a stubs.c file).
–v *vector*	Returns 'type' field of device that is using the vector specified (that is, another DSP is already using the vector).
–d *dma-channel*	Returns 1 if the dma channel specified is being used.
–a	This option checks whether the IOA region bounded by "*lower*" and "*upper*" conflict with another DSP ("*lower*" and "*upper*" are specified with the –l and –u options). The exit code is the addition of two different return codes.

	Add 1 to the exit code if the IOA region overlaps with another device.
	Add 2 to the exit code if the IOA region overlaps with another device and that device has the 'O' option specified in the *type* field of the Master module. The 'O' option permits a driver to overlap the IOA region of another driver.
−c	Returns 1 if the CMA region bounded by "*lower*" and "*upper*" conflict with another DSP ("*lower*" and "*upper*" are specified with the −l and −u options).
−l *address*	Lower bound of address range specified in hex. The leading 0x is unnecessary.
−u *address*	Upper bound of address range specified in hex. The leading 0x is unnecessary.
−i *dir*	Specifies the directory in which the ID files sdevice and mdevice reside. The default directory is /etc/conf/cf.d .

ERROR MESSAGES

There are no error messages or checks for valid arguments to options. idcheck interprets these arguments using the rules of scanf(3) and queries the sdevice and mdevice files. For example, if a letter is used in the place of a digit, scanf (3) will translate the letter to 0. idcheck will then use this value in its query.

SEE ALSO

idinstall(1M)

mdevice(4), sdevice(4) in the *Programmer's Reference Manual*

NAME

idconfig – produce a new kernel configuration

SYNOPSIS

/etc/conf/bin/idconfig

DESCRIPTION

The idconfig command takes as its input a collection of files specifying the configuration of the next UNIX System to be built. A collection of output files for use by idmkunix is produced.

The input files expected by idconfig are as follows:

mdevice	– Master device specifications
sdevice	– System device specifications
mtune	– Master parameter specifications
stune	– System parameter specifications
mfsys	– File system type master data
sfsys	– File system type system data
sassign	– Device Assignment File

The output files produced by idconfig are as follows:

conf.c	– Kernel data structures and function definitions
config.h	– Kernel parameter and device definitions
vector.c	– Interrupt vector definitions
direct	– Listing of all driver components included in the build
fsconf.c	– File system type configuration data

The command line options are as follows:

−o *directory* Output files will be created in the directory specified rather than /etc/conf/cf.d.

−i *directory* Input files that normally reside in /etc/conf/cf.d can be found in the directory specified.

−r *directory* The directory specified will be used as the ID "root" directory rather than /etc/conf.

−d *file* Use *file* name rather than sdevice for input.

−t *file* Use *file* name rather than stune for input.

−T *file* Use *file* name rather than mtune for input.

−a *file* Use *file* name rather than sassign for input.

−c *file* Redirect conf.c output to *file* name.

−h *file* Redirect config.h output to *file* name.

−v *file* Redirect vector.c output to *file* name.

−p *file* Redirect direct output to *file* name.

    −D, −m, −s   These options are no longer supported.

    −#   Print debugging information.

This version of UNIX supports multiple major numbers for drivers. idconfig generates additional constants (via defines) in the config.h file so that they can be used by the driver (as they will get referenced in the space.c file to generate appropriate data structures. The information provided by these constants is how many major numbers were assigned to the device and what are their values. The names of the constants are as follows:

    PRFX_CMAJOR_X

    PRFX_BMAJOR_X

where PRFX stands for device prefix. In case of a SCSI device, it would be a SCSI device. The X stands for the list subscript, starting with subscript 0.

In addition, the configuration file conf.c that initializes bdevsw[] and cdevsw[] tables will also add entries for each of the major numbers and, as such, the same driver entry points will be repeated for each one of the entries.

ERROR MESSAGES

An exit value of zero indicates success. If an error i was encountered, idconfig will exit with a non-zero value and report an error message. All error messages are designed to be self-explanatory.

SEE ALSO

dmkunix(1M), idbuild(1M), idinstall(1M), mdevice(4), mtune(4), sdevice(4), stune(4)

NAME

idinstall – add, delete, update, or get device driver configuration data

SYNOPSIS

/etc/conf/bin/idinstall –[adug] [–e] –[msoptnirhcl] *dev_name*

DESCRIPTION

The idinstall command is called by a Driver Software Package (DSP) Install script or Remove script to Add (–a), Delete (–d), Update (–u), or Get (–g) device driver configuration data. idinstall expects to find driver component files in the current directory. When components are installed or updated, they are moved or appended to files in the /etc/conf directory and then deleted from the current directory unless the –k flag is used. The options for the command are as follows:

Action Specifiers:

-a   Add the DSP components

-d   Remove the DSP components

-u   Update the DSP components

-g   Get the DSP components (print to std out, except Master)

Component Specifiers: (*)

-m   Master component

-s   System component

-o   Driver.o component

-p   Space.c component

-t   Stubs.c component

-n   Node (special file) component

-i   Inittab component

-r   Device Initialization (rc) component

-h   Device shutdown (sd) component

-c   Mfsys component: file system type config (Master) data

-l   Sfsys component: file system type local (System) data

(*) If no component is specified, the default is all except for the –g option where a single component must be specified explicitly.

Miscellaneous:

-e   Disable free disk space check

-k   Keep files (do not remove from current directory) on add or update.

In the simplest case of installing a new DSP, the command syntax used by the DSP's Install script should be idinstall –a *dev_name*. In this case the command will require and install a Driver.o, Master and System entry, and optionally install the Space.c, Stubs.c, Node, Init, Rc, Shutdown, Mfsys, and Sfsys components if those modules are present in the current directory.

The Driver.o, Space.c, and Stubs.c files are moved to a directory in /etc/conf/pack.d. The *dev_name* is passed as an argument, which is used as the directory name. The remaining components are stored in the corresponding directories under /etc/conf in a file whose name is *dev_name*. For example, the Node file would be moved to /etc/conf/node.d/dev_name.

The idinstall −m usage provides an interface to the idmaster command which will add, delete, and update mdevice file entries using a Master file from the local directory. An interface is provided here so that driver writers have a consistent interface to install any DSP component.

As stated above, driver writers will generally use only the idinstall −a *dev_name* form of the command. Other options of idinstall are provided to allow an Update DSP (i.e., one that replaces an existing device driver component) to be installed, and to support installation of multiple controller boards of the same type.

If the call to idinstall uses the −u (update) option, it will:

overlay the files of the old DSP with the files of the new DSP.

invoke the idmaster command with the 'update' option if a Master module is part of the new DSP.

idinstall also does a verification that enough free disk space is available to start the reconfiguration process. This is done by calling the idspace command. idinstall will fail if insufficient space exists, and exit with a non-zero return code. The −e option bypasses this check.

This version of UNIX Supports Multiple Major numbers per device. For the case of a DSP package where idinstall is invoked by the installation software in the DSP, the range specification will be used. The range "3.6" will mean four major numbers are being requested. The *ID* Software will then look for the first four available (consecutive) major numbers.

If a driver supports both block and charcter I/O both block and character majors are assigned by idinstall. These major numbers do not have to be the same. For SCSI developers who require them to be the same, a new field 'v' has to be added to the third field of the master file.

idinstall makes a record of the last device installed in a file (/etc/.last_dev_add), and saves all removed files from the last delete operation in a directory (/etc/.last_dev_del). These files are recovered by /etc/conf/bin/idmkenv whenever it is determined that a system reconfiguration was aborted due to a power failure or unexpected system reboot.

ERROR MESSAGES

An exit value of zero indicates success. If an error was encountered, idinstall will exit with a non-zero value, and report an error message. All error messages are designed to be self-explanatory. Typical error message that can be generated by idinstall are as follows:

```
Device package already exists.
Cannot make the driver package directory.
Cannot remove driver package directory.
Local directory does not contain a Driver object (Driver.o) file.
Local directory does not contain a Master file.
Local directory does not contain a System file.
Cannot remove driver entry.
```

SEE ALSO

idspace(1M), idcheck(1M)

mdevice(4), sdevice(4) in the *Programmer's Reference Manual*

NAME

   idmkinit – reads files containing specifications

SYNOPSIS

   /etc/conf/bin/idmkinit

DESCRIPTION

   This command reads the files containing specifications of /etc/inittab entries
   from /etc/conf/init.d and constructs a new inittab file in /etc/conf/cf.d .
   It returns 0 on success and a positive number on error.

   The files in /etc/conf/init.d are copies of the Init modules in device Driver
   Software Packages (DSP). There is at most one Init file per DSP. Each file contains one line for each inittab entry to be installed. There may be multiple lines
   (that is, multiple inittab entries) per file. An inittab entry has the form (the id
   field is often called the *tag*):

   id:rstate:action:process

   The Init module entry must have one of the following forms:

   action:process

   rstate:action:process

   id:rstate:action:process

   When idmkinit encounters an entry of the first type, a valid *id* field will be gen-
   erated, and an *rstate* field of 2 (indicating run on init state 2) will be generated.
   When an entry of the second type is encountered only the *id* field is prepended.
   An entry of the third type is incorporated into the new inittab unchanged.

   Since add-on inittab entries specify init state 2 for their *rstate* field most often,
   an entry of the first type should almost always be used. An entry of the second
   type may be specified if you need to specify other than state 2. DSP's should
   avoid specifying the *id* field as in the third entry, since other add-on applications
   or DSPs may have already used the *id* value you have chosen. The /etc/init
   program will encounter serious errors if one or more inittab entries contain the
   same *id* field.

   idmkinit determines which of the three forms above is being used for the entry
   by requiring each entry to have a valid action keyword. Valid action values are
   as follows:

   off
   respawn
   ondemand
   once
   wait
   boot
   bootwait
   powerfail
   powerwait
   initdefault
   sysinit

The idmkinit command is called automatically upon entering init State 2 on the next system reboot after a kernel reconfiguration to establish the correct /etc/inittab for the running /unix kernel. idmkinit can be called as a user level command to test modification of inittab before a DSP is actually built. It is also useful in installation scripts that do not reconfigure the kernel, but need to create inittab entries. In this case, the inittab generated by idmkinit must be copied to /etc/inittab , and a telinit q command must be run to make the new entry take affect.

The command line options are:

−o *directory*	inittab will be created in the directory specified rather than /etc/conf/cf.d .
−i *directory*	The ID file init.base, which normally resides in /etc/conf/cf.d, can be found in the directory specified.
−e *directory*	The Init modules that are usually in /etc/conf/init.d can be found in the directory specified.
−#	Print debugging information.

ERROR MESSAGES

An exit value of zero indicates success. If an error was encountered, idmkinit will exit with a non-zero value and report an error message. All error messages are designed to be self-explanatory.

SEE ALSO

idbuild(1), idinstall(1M), idmknod(1M), init(1M)

inittab(4) in the *Programmer's Reference Manual*

NAME

idmknod – removes nodes and reads specifications of nodes

SYNOPSIS

idmknod [*options*]

DESCRIPTION

This command performs the following functions:

Removes the nodes for non-required devices (those that do not have an r in field 3 of the the device's mdevice entry) from /dev. Ordinary files will not be removed. If the /dev directory contains subdirectories, those subdirectories will be traversed and nodes found for non-required devices will be removed as well. If empty subdirectories result due to the removal of nodes, the subdirectories are then removed.

Reads the specifications of nodes given in the files contained in /etc/conf/node.d and installs these nodes in /dev. If the node specification defines a path containing subdirectories, the subdirectories will be made automatically.

Returns 0 on success and a positive number on error.

The idmknod command is run automatically upon entering init state 2 on the next system reboot after a kernel reconfiguration to establish the correct representation of device nodes in the /dev directory for the running /unix kernel. idmknod can be called as a user level command to test modification of the /dev directory before a Driver Software Package (DSP) is actually built. It is also useful in installation scripts that do not reconfigure the kernel, but need to create /dev entries.

The files in /etc/conf/node.d are copies of the I. Node modules installed by device DSPs. There is at most one file per DSP. Each file contains one line for each node that is to be installed. The format of each line is:

Name of device entry (field 1) in the mdevice file.

(The mdevice entry will be the line installed by the DSP from its *Master* module.) This field must be from 1 to 8 characters in length. The first character must be a letter. The others may be letters, digits, or underscores.

Name of node to be inserted in /dev.

The first character must be a letter. The others may be letters, digits, or underscores. This field can be a path relative to /dev , and idmknod will create subdirectories as needed.

The character b or c.

A b indicates that the node is a 'block' type device and c indicates 'character' type device.

For devices having multiple major numbers, the following scheme is used to specify which device nodes belong to which major. The third field is expanded to specify a major number offset as follows:

"[b/c]: maj_off", where [b/c] refers to either block or character major and maj_off refers to an offset number within the major number range in the mdevice file. For example, a specification "C:2" refers to a character major offset 2, which for a major range of "15-18" would translate to character major 17.

Minor device number.
   If this field is a non-numeric, it is assumed to be a request for a streams clone device node, and idmknod will set the minor number to the value of the major number of the device specified [see mknod(2) in the *Programmer's Reference Manual* for information on minor device number values].

User id.
   The integer value in this field describes the ownership of the node to be made.

Group id.
   The integer value in this field describes the group ownership of the node to be created.

Permission.
   The value expected must be in octal form, in the manner in which permissions are described to the chmod(1) command (i.e. 0777).

Some example node file entries are as follows:

asy tty00 c 1   makes /dev/tty00 for device asy using minor device 1.

qt rmt/c0s0 c 4 makes /dev/rmt/c0s0 for device qt using minor device 4.

clone net/nau/clone c nau
                    makes /dev/net/nau/clone for device clone. The minor device number is set to the major device number of device nau.

scsi tty1 C:0 5   makes tty1 for device scsi using minor device 1 major_number offset 0.

The command line options are:

−o *directory*   Nodes will be installed in the directory specified rather than /dev.

−i *directory*   The file mdevice which normally resides in /etc/conf/cf.d , can be found in the directory specified.

−e *directory*   The *Node* modules that normally reside in /etc/conf/node.d can be found in the directory specified.

−s   Suppress removing nodes (just add new nodes).

ERROR MESSAGES
An exit value of zero indicates success. If an error was encountered due to a syntax or format error in a *node* entry, an advisory message will be printed to *stdout* and the command will continue. If a serious error is encountered (that is, a required file cannot be found), idmknod will exit with a non-zero value and report an error message. All error messages are designed to be self-explanatory.

SEE ALSO
idinstall(1M), idmkinit(1M)
mdevice(4), mknod(2), sdevice(4) in the *Programmer's Reference Manual*

NAME

idmkunix – build new UNIX System kernel

SYNOPSIS

/etc/conf/bin/idmkunix

DESCRIPTION

The idmkunix command creates a bootable UNIX Operating System kernel in the directory /etc/conf/cf.d . The component kernel "core" files and device driver object files contained in subdirectories of /etc/conf/pack.d are used as input along with device and parameter definition files produced by idconfig. In brief, the required input files are as follows:

/etc/conf/cf.d/conf.c	– Kernel data structures and function definitions
/etc/conf/cf.d/config.h	– Kernel parameter and device definitions
/etc/conf/cf.d/vector.c	– Interrupt vector definitions
/etc/conf/cf.d/direct	– Listing of all driver components included in the build
/etc/conf/cf.d/fsconf.c	– File system type configuration data
/etc/conf/cf.d/vuifile	– Memory management definitions for the kernel
/etc/conf/pack.d/*/Driver.o	– Component kernel object files
/etc/conf/pack.d/*/space.c	– Component kernel space allocation files
/etc/conf/pack.d/*/stubs.c	– Component kernel stubs files

The command line options are as follows:

-o *directory*   The file *unix* be created in the directory specified rather than /etc/conf/cf.d .

-i *directory*   Input files that normally reside in /etc/conf/cf.d can be found in the directory specified.

-r *directory*   The directory specified will be used as the ID "root" directory rather than /etc/conf .

-c, cc, -l, ld   These options are no longer supported.

-#   Print debugging information.

ERROR MESSAGES

An exit value of zero indicates success. If an error was encountered, idmkunix will exit with a non-zero value and report an error message. All error messages are designed to be self-explanatory.

SEE ALSO

idbuild(1M), idconfig(1M), idinstall(1M), mdevice(4), mtune(4), sdevice(4), stune(4)

NAME

idspace – investigates free space

SYNOPSIS

/etc/conf/bin/idspace [−i *inodes*] [−r *blocks*] [−u *blocks*]
[−t *blocks*]

DESCRIPTION

This command investigates free space in /, /usr, and /tmp file systems to deter-mine whether sufficient disk blocks and inodes exist in each of potentially 3 file systems. The default tests that idspace performs are as follows:

Verify that the root file system (/) has 400 blocks more than the size of the current /unix. This verifies that a device driver being added to the current /unix can be built and placed in the root directory. A check is also made to insure that 100 inodes exist in the root directory.

Determine whether a /usr file system exists. If it does exist, a test is made that 400 free blocks and 100 inodes are available in that file system. If the file system does not exist, idspace does not complain since files created in /usr by the reconfiguration process will be created in the root file system and space requirements are covered by the test in (1.) above.

Determine whether a /tmp file system exists. If it does exist, a test is made that 400 free blocks and 100 inodes are available in that file system. If the file system does not exist, idspace does not complain since files created in /tmp by the reconfiguration process will be created in the root file system and space requirements are covered by the test in (1.) above.

The command line options are:

−i *inodes*   This option overrides the default test for 100 inode in all of the idspace checks.

−r *blocks*   This option overrides the default test for /unix size + 400 blocks when checking the root (/) file system. When the −r option is used, the /usr and /tmp file systems are not tested unless explicitly specified.

−u *blocks*   This option overrides the default test for 400 blocks when checking the /usr file system. When the −u option is used, the root (/) and /tmp file systems are not tested unless explicitly specified. If /usr is not a separate file system, an error is reported.

−t *blocks*   This option overrides the default test for 400 blocks when checking the /tmp file system. When the −t option is used, the root (/) and /usr file systems are not tested unless explicitly specified. If /tmp is not a separate file system, an error is reported.

ERROR MESSAGES

An exit value of zero indicates success. If insufficient space exists in a file system or an error was encountered due to a syntax or format error, idspace will report a message. All error messages are designed to be self-explanatory. The specific exit values are as follows:

0   success.

1   command syntax error, or needed file does not exist.

2   file system has insufficient space or inodes.

3   requested file system does not exist (−u and −t options only).

SEE ALSO

idbuild(1M), idinstall(1M)

NAME

idtune – attempts to set value of a tunable parameter

SYNOPSIS

/etc/conf/bin/idtune [-f | -m] *name value*

DESCRIPTION

This script attempts to set the value of a tunable parameter. The tunable parameter to be changed is indicated by *name*. The desired value for the tunable parameter is *value*.

If there is already a value for this parameter (in the stune file), the user will normally be asked to confirm the change with the following message:

Tunable Parameter *name* is currently set to *old_value*.
Is it OK to change it to *value*? (y/n)

If the user answers y, the change will be made. Otherwise, the tunable parameter will not be changed, and the following message will be displayed:

name left at *old_value*.

However, if the -f (force) option is used, the change will always be made and no messages will ever be given.

If the -m (minimum) option is used and there is an existing value which is greater than the desired value, no change will be made and no message will be given.

If system tunable parameters are being modified as part of a device driver or application add-on package, it may not be desirable to prompt the user with the above question. The add-on package Install script may chose to override the existing value using the -f or -m options. However, care must be taken not to invalidate a tunable parameter modified earlier by the user or another add-on package.

In order for the change in parameter to become effective, the UNIX System kernel must be rebuilt and the system rebooted.

DIAGNOSTICS

The exit status will ne non-zero if errors are encountered.

SEE ALSO

idbuild(1).

mtune(4), stune(4) in the *Programmer's Reference Manual*.

NAME

installf – add a file to the software installation database

SYNOPSIS

installf [–c *class*] *pkginst pathname* [*ftype* [[*major minor*]
    [*mode owner group*]]]

installf [–c *class*] *pkginst* –

installf –f [–c *class*] *pkginst*

DESCRIPTION

installf informs the system that a pathname not listed in the pkgmap file is being created or modified. It should be invoked before any file modifications have occurred.

When the second synopsis is used, the pathname descriptions will be read from standard input. These descriptions are the same as would be given in the first synopsis but the information is given in the form of a list. (The descriptions should be in the form: *pathname* [*ftype* [[*major minor*] [*mode owner group*]]].)

After all files have been appropriately created and/or modified, installf should be invoked with the –f synopsis to indicate that installation is final. Links will be created at this time and, if attribute information for a pathname was not specified during the original invocation of installf or was not already stored on the system, the current attribute values for the pathname will be stored. Otherwise, installf verifies that attribute values match those given on the command line, making corrections as necessary. In all cases, the current content information is calculated and stored appropriately.

–c *class*   Class to which installed objects should be associated. Default class is none.

pkginst   Name of package instance with which the pathname should be associated.

pathname   Pathname that is being created or modified.

ftype   A one-character field that indicates the file type. Possible file types include:

f	a standard executable or data file
e	a file to be edited upon installation or removal
v	volatile file (one whose contents are expected to change)
d	directory
x	an exclusive directory
l	linked file
p	named pipe
c	character special device
b	block special device
s	symbolic link

major   The major device number. The field is only specified for block or character special devices.

minor   The minor device number. The field is only specified for block or character special devices.

mode   The octal mode of the file (for example, 0664). A question mark (?) indicates that the mode will be left unchanged, implying that the file already exists on the target machine. This field is not used for linked or symbolically linked files.

owner   The owner of the file (for example, `bin` or `root`). The field is limited to 14 characters in length. A question mark (?) indicates that the owner will be left unchanged, implying that the file already exists on the target machine. This field is not used for linked or symbolically linked files.

group   The group to which the file belongs (for example, `bin` or `sys`). The field is limited to 14 characters in length. A question mark (?) indicates that the group will be left unchanged, implying that the file already exists on the target machine. This field is not used for linked or symbolically linked files.

-f   Indicates that installation is complete. This option is used with the final invocation of `installf` (for all files of a given class).

NOTES

When *ftype* is specified, all applicable fields, as shown below, must be defined:

ftype	Required Fields
p x d f v or e	mode owner group
c or b	major minor mode owner group

The `installf` command will create directories, named pipes and special devices on the original invocation. Links are created when `installf` is invoked with the −f option to indicate installation is complete.

Links should be specified as *path1=path2*. *path1* indicates the destination and *path2* indicates the source file.

For symbolically linked files, *path2* can be a relative pathname, such as ./ or ../. For example, if you enter a line such as

```
        s /foo/bar/etc/mount=../usr/sbin/mount
```

path2 (/foo/bar/etc/mount) will be a symbolic link to ../usr/sbin/mount.

Files installed with `installf` will be placed in the class *none*, unless a class is defined with the command. Subsequently, they will be removed when the associated package is deleted. If this file should not be deleted at the same time as the package, be certain to assign it to a class which is ignored at removal time. If special action is required for the file before removal, a class must be defined with the command and an appropriate class action script delivered with the package.

When classes are used, `installf` must be used as follows:

```
installf -c class1 . . .
installf -f -c class1 . . .
installf -c class2 . . .
installf -f -c class2 . . .
```

EXAMPLE

The following example shows the use of `installf` invoked from an optional preinstall or postinstall script:

```
#create /dev/xt directory
#(needs to be done before drvinstall)
installf $PKGINST /dev/xt d 755 root sys ||
            exit 2
majno=`/usr/sbin/drvinstall -m /etc/master.d/xt
      -d $BASEDIR/data/xt.o -v1.0` ||
            exit 2
i=00
while [ $i -lt $limit ]
do
    for j in 0 1 2 3 4 5 6 7
    do
        echo /dev/xt$i$j c $majno `expr $i * 8 + $j`
            644 root sys |
        echo /dev/xt$i$j=/dev/xt/$i$j
    done
    i=`expr $i + 1`
    [ $i -le 9 ] && i="0$i" #add leading zero
done | installf $PKGINST - || exit 2
# finalized installation, create links
installf -f $PKGINST || exit 2
.ft 1
in 0
```

SEE ALSO

pkgadd(1M), pkgask(1M), pkgchk(1), pkginfo(1), pkgmk(1), pkgparam(1), pkgproto(1), pkgtrans(1), pkgrm(1M), removef(1M)

NAME

pkgadd -. transfer software package to the system

SYNOPSIS

/usr/sbin/pkgadd [−d *device*] [−r *response*] [−n] [−a *admin*] [*pkginst1*]
[*pkginst2*[. . .]]]

/usr/sbin/pkgadd −s *spool* [−d *device*] [*pkginst1* [*pkginst2*[. . .]]]

DESCRIPTION

pkgadd transfers the contents of a software package from the distribution
medium or directory to install it onto the system. Used without the −d option,
pkgadd looks in the default spool directory for the package (/var/spool/pkg).
Used with the −s option, it reads the package to a spool directory instead of installing it.

−d *device*   Installs or copies a package from *device*. *device* can be a full pathname
to a directory or the identifiers for tape, floppy disk or removable disk
(for example, /var/tmp, /dev/rmt/c0s0, /dev/dsk/f0t or
/dev/dsk/f1t). It can also be the device alias (for example, ctape1
for the cartridge tape drive).

−r *response*

Identifies a file or directory, *response*, which contains output from a
previous pkgask session. This file supplies the interaction responses
that would be requested by the package in interactive mode. *response*
must be a full pathname.

−n   Installation occurs in non-interactive mode. The default mode is
interactive.

−a *admin*   Defines an installation administration file, *admin*, to be used in place of
the default administration file. The token none overrides the use of
any *admin* file, and thus forces interaction with the user. Unless a full
path name is given, pkgadd looks in the /var/sadm/install/admin
directory for the file.

pkginst   Specifies the package instance or list of instances to be installed. The
token all may be used to refer to all packages available on the source
medium. The format *pkginst*.* can be used to indicate all instances of
a package. When using this format, enclose the command line in single quotes to prevent the shell from interpreting the * character.

−s *spool*   Reads the package into the directory *spool* instead of installing it.

When executed without options, pkgadd users /var/spool/pkg (the
default spool directory).

NOTES

When transferring a package to a spool directory, the −r, −n, and −a options cannot be used.

The −r option can be used to indicate a directory name as well as a filename.
The directory can contain numerous *response* files, each sharing the name of the
package with which it should be associated. This would be used, for example,
when adding multiple interactive packages with one invocation of pkgadd. Each

package would need a *response* file. If you create response files with the same name as the package (that is, *package1* and *package2*), then name the directory in which these files reside after the −r.

The −n option will cause the installation to halt if any interaction is needed to complete it.

NAME

pkgask – stores answers to a request script

SYNOPSIS

/usr/sbin/pkgask [-d *device*] -r *response* [*pkginst* [*pkginst* [. . .]]]

DESCRIPTION

pkgask allows the administrator to store answers to an interactive package (one
with a request script). Invoking this command generates a *response* file that is
then used as input at installation time. The use of this *response* file prevents any
interaction from occurring during installation since the file already contains all of
the information the package needs.

-d   Runs the request script for a package on *device*. *device* can be a full
        pathname to a directory or the identifiers for tape, floppy disk or
        removable disk (for example, /var/tmp, /dev/dsk/0s2, and
        /dev/dsk/f0t). The default device is the installation spool directory.

-r   Identifies a file or directory, which should be created to contain the
        responses to interaction with the package. The name must be a full
        pathname. The file, or directory of files, can later be used as input to
        the pkgadd command.

pkginst Specifies the package instance or list of instances for which request
        scripts will be created. The token all may be used to refer to all
        packages available on the source medium. The format *pkginst.* * can
        be used to indicate all instances of a package. When using this format,
        enclose the command line in single quotes to prevent the shell from
        interpreting the * character.

NOTES

The -r option can be used to indicate a directory name as well as a filename.
The directory name is used to create numerous *response* files, each sharing the
name of the package with which it should be associated. This would be used, for
example, when you will be adding multiple interactive packages with one invocation of pkgadd. Each package would need a *response* file. To create multiple
response files with the same name as the package instance, name the directory in
which the files should be created and supply multiple instance names with the
pkgask command. When installing the packages, you will be able to identify this
directory to the pkgadd command.

SEE ALSO

installf(1M), pkgadd(1M), pkgchk(1), pkgmk(1), pkginfo(1), pkgparam(1),
pkgproto(1), pkgtrans(1), pkgrm(1M), removef(1M)

NAME

pkgchk − check accuracy of installation

SYNOPSIS

/usr/sbin/pkgchk [−l |−acfqv] [−nx] [−p *path1*[, *path2* . . .] [−i *file*] [*pkginst* . . .]

/usr/sbin/pkgchk −d *device* [−l |v] [−p *path1*[, *path2* . . .] [−i *file*] [*pkginst* . . .]

/usr/sbin/pkgchk −m *pkgmap* [−e *envfile*] [−l |−acfqv] [−nx] [−i *file*]
          [−p *path1*[, *path2* . . .]]

DESCRIPTION

pkgchk checks the accuracy of installed files or, by use of the −l option, displays
information about package files. The command checks the integrity of directory
structures and the files. Discrepancies are reported on stderr along with a
detailed explanation of the problem.

The first synopsis defined above is used to list or check the contents and/or attributes of objects that are currently installed on the system. Package names may be
listed on the command line, or by default the entire contents of a machine will be
checked.

The second synopsis is used to list or check the contents of a package which has
been spooled on the specified device, but not installed. Note that attributes cannot be checked for spooled packages.

The third synopsis is used to list or check the contents and/or attributes of
objects which are described in the indicated *pkgmap*.

The option definitions are:

−l   Lists information on the selected files that make up a package. It is not
        compatible with the a, c, f, g, and v options.

−a   Audits the file attributes only, does not check file contents. Default is to
        check both.

−c   Audits the file contents only, does not check file attributes. Default is to
        check both.

−f   Corrects file attributes if possible. When pkgchk is invoked with this
        option it creates directories, named pipes, links and special devices if
        they do not already exist.

−q   Quiet mode. Does not give messages about missing files.

−v   Verbose mode. Files are listed as processed.

−n   Does not check volatile or editable files. This should be used for most
        post-installation checking.

−x   Searches exclusive directories only, looking for files which exist that are
        not in the installation software database or the indicated *pkgmap* file. If
        used with the −f option, hidden files are removed; no other checking is
        done.

−p	Only checks the accuracy of the pathname or pathnames listed. *pathname* can be one or more pathnames separated by commas (or by white space, if the list is quoted).
−i	Reads a list of pathnames from *file* and compares this list against the installation software database or the indicated *pkgmap* file. Pathnames which are not contained in *inputfile* are not checked.
−d	Specifies the device on which a spooled package resides. *device* can be a directory pathname or the identifiers for tape, floppy disk or removable disk (for example, /var/tmp or /dev/diskette).
−m	Requests that the package be checked against the pkgmap file *pkgmap*.
−e	Requests that the pkginfo file named as *envfile* be used to resolve parameters noted in the specified pkgmap file.
pkginst	Specifies the package instance or instances to be checked. The format *pkginst.*∗ can be used to check all instances of a package. When using this format, enclose the command line in single quotes to prevent the shell from interpreting the ∗ character. The default is to display all information about all installed packages.

NOTES

To remove hidden files only, use the −f and −x options together. To remove hidden files and check attributes and contents of files, use the −f, −x, −c, and −a options together.

SEE ALSO

pkgadd(1M), pkgask(1M), pkginfo(1), pkgrm(1M), pkgtrans(1)

NAME

pkgrm – removes a package from the system

SYNOPSIS

pkgrm [–n] [–a *admin*] [*pkginst1* [*pkginst2*[. . .]]]

pkgrm –s *spool* [*pkginst*]

DESCRIPTION

pkgrm will remove a previously installed or partially installed package from the system. A check is made to determine if any other packages depend on the one being removed. The action taken if a dependency exists is defined in the admin file.

The default state for the command is interactive mode, meaning that prompt messages are given during processing to allow the administrator to confirm the actions being taken. Non-interactive mode can be requested with the –n option.

The –s option can be used to specify the directory from which spooled packages should be removed.

The options and arguments for this command are:

-n   Non-interactive mode. If there is a need for interaction, the command will exit. Use of this option requires that at least one package instance be named upon invocation of the command.

–a *admin*   Defines an installation administration file, *admin*, to be used in place of the default *admin* file.

–s *spool*   Removes the specified package(s) from the directory *spool*.

pkginst   Specifies the package to be removed. The format *pkginst.** can be used to remove all instances of a package. When using this format, enclose the command line in single quotes to prevent the shell from interpreting the * character.

SEE ALSO

installf(1M), pkgadd(1M), pkgask(1M), pkgchk(1), pkginfo(1), pkgmk(1), pkgparam(1), pkgproto(1), pkgtrans(1), removef(1M)

NAME

removef – remove a file from software database

SYNOPSIS

removef pkginst path1 [path2 ...]

removef -f pkginst

DESCRIPTION

removef informs the system that the user, or software, intends to remove a pathname. Output from removef is the list of input pathnames that may be safely
removed (no other packages have a dependency on them).

After all files have been processed, removef should be invoked with the −f
option to indicate that the removal phase is complete.

EXAMPLE

The following shows the use of removef in an optional pre-install script:

```
echo "The following files are no longer part of this package
      and are being removed."
removef $PKGINST /dev/xt[0-9][0-9][0-9] |
while read pathname
do
      echo "$pathname"
      rm -f $pathname
done
removef -f $PKGINST || exit 2
```

SEE ALSO

installf(1M), pkgadd(1M), pkgask(1M), pkgchk(1), pkginfo(1), pkgmk(1),
pkgproto(1), pkgtrans(1), pkgparam(3X)

NAME

compver – compatible versions file

DESCRIPTION

compver is an ASCII file used to specify previous versions of the associated package which are upward compatible. It is created by a package developer.

Each line of the file specifies a previous version of the associated package with which the current version is backward compatible.

Since some packages may require installation of a specific version of another software package, compatibility information is extremely crucial. Consider, for example, a package called "A" which requires version "1.0" of application "B" as a prerequisite for installation. If the customer installing "A" has a newer version of "B" (1.3), the compver file for "B" must indicate that "1.3" is compatible with version "1.0" in order for the customer to install package "A."

NOTES

The comparison of the version string disregards white space and tabs. It is performed on a word-by-word basis. Thus 1.3   Enhanced and 1.3 Enhanced would be considered the same.

EXAMPLE

A sample compver file is shown below.

```
1.3
1.0
```

SEE ALSO

depend(4)

NAME

copyright – copyright information file

DESCRIPTION

copyright is an ASCII file used to provide a copyright notice for a package. The text may be in any format. The full file contents (including comment lines) is displayed on the terminal at the time of package installation.

NAME

depend – software dependencies files

DESCRIPTION

depend is an ASCII file used to specify information concerning software dependencies for a particular package. The file is created by a software developer.

Each entry in the depend file describes a single software package. The instance of
the package is described after the entry line by giving the package architecture
and/or version. The format of each entry and subsequent instance definition is:

> *type pkg name*
> > *(arch)version*
> > *(arch)version*
> > . . .

The fields are:

type
Defines the dependency type. Must be one of the following characters:

> P
> Indicates a prerequisite for installation, for example, the
> referenced package or versions must be installed.
>
> I
> Implies that the existence of the indicated package or ver-
> sion is incompatible.
>
> R
> Indicates a reverse dependency. Instead of defining the
> package's own dependencies, this designates that another
> package depends on this one. This type should be used
> only when an old package does not have a depend file but
> it relies on the newer package nonetheless. Therefore, the
> present package should not be removed if the designated
> old package is still on the system since, if it is removed,
> the old package will no longer work.

pkg
Indicates the package abbreviation.

name
Specifies the full package name.

(arch)version
Specifies a particular instance of the software. A version name
cannot begin with a left parenthesis. The instance specifications,
both *arch* and *version*, are completely optional but each must begin
on a new line that begins with white space. If no version set is
specified, any version of the indicated package will match. A version preceded by a tilde (~) indicates that any compatible version
will be a match. [See compver(4).]

EXAMPLE

Here is a sample depend file:

```
I msvr 3B2 Messaging Server
P ctc Cartridge Tape Utilities
P dfm Directory and File Management Utilities
P ed Editing Utilities
P ipc Inter-Process Communication Utilities
P lp Line Printer Spooling Utilities
```

```
          P shell Shell Programming Utilities
          P sys System Header Files
                    3.0
          P sysadm System Administration Utilities
          P terminf Terminal Information Utilities
          P usrenv User Environment Utilities
          P bnu Basic Networking Utilities
          P x25 X.25 Network Interface
                    1.1
                    1.2
          P windowing Layers Windowing Utilities
                    (3B2)1.0
          R cms 3B2 Call Management System
```

SEE ALSO

compver(4)

NAME

mdevice – file format

SYNOPSIS

mdevice

DESCRIPTION

The mdevice file is included in the directory /etc/conf/cf.d. It includes a one-line description of each device driver and configurable software module in the system to be built [except for file system types, see mfsys(4)]. Each line in mdevice represents the *Master* file component from a Driver Software Package (DSP) either delivered with the base system or installed later via idinstall.

Each line contains several white space-separated fields; they are described below. Each field must be supplied with a value or a '–' (dash). See the individual driver manual pages for information on the values for specific fields.

Device name: This field is the internal name of the device or module, and may be up to 8 characters long. The first character of the name must be an alphabetic character; the others may be letters, digits, or underscores.

Function list: This field is a string of characters that identify driver functions that are present. Using one of the characters below requires the driver to have an entry point (function) of the type indicated. If no functions in the following list are supplied, the field should contain a dash.

o	open routine
c	close routine
r	read routine
w	write routine
i	ioctl routine
s	startup routine
x	exit routine
f	fork routine
e	exec routine
I	init routine
h	halt routine
p	poll routine
E	kenter routine
X	kexit routine

Note that if the device is a 'block' type device (see field 3. below), a *strategy* routine and a *print* routine are required by default.

Characteristics of driver:

This field contains a set of characters that indicate the characteristics of the driver. If none of the characters below apply, the field should contain a dash. The legal characters for this field are:

i	The device driver is installable.
c	The device is a 'character' device.
b	The device is a 'block' device.
[b/c]	For indicating which device nodes belong to which major. See idmknod.
f	The device is DDI/DKI conformant.
t	The device is a tty.
o	This device may have only one *sdevice* entry.
r	This device is required in all configurations of the Kernel. This option is intended for drivers delivered with the base system only. Device nodes (special files in the /dev directory), once made for this device, are never removed. See idmknod.
u	This letter accompanying an 'M' would ensure that the driver will get major numbers starting at the same number for both block and character "multiple majors."
S	This device driver is a STREAMS module.
H	This device driver controls hardware. This option distinguishes drivers that support hardware from those that are entirely software (pseudo-devices).
G	This device does not use an interrupt though an interrupt is specified in the sdevice entry. This is used when you wish to associate a device to a specific device group.
D	This option indicates that the device driver can share its DMA channel.
M	This option indicates that the device requires multiple major numbers.
O	This option indicates that the IOA range of this device may overlap that of another device.

Handler prefix: This field contains the character string prepended to all the externally-known handler routines associated with this driver. The string may be up to 4 characters long.

Block Major number:

This field should be set to zero in a DSP *Master* file. If the device is a 'block' type device, a value will be assigned by idinstall during installation. For devices having multiple major numbers this field is used to specify the "range" of major numbers. (For example, range 3-6 is interpreted as four major numbers between 3-6 inclusive.)

Character Major number:

This field should be set to zero in a DSP *Master* file. If the device is a 'character' type device (or 'STREAMS' type), a value will be assigned by idinstall during installation. For devices having multiple major numbers this field is used to specify the "range" of major numbers. (For example, range 3-6 is interpreted as four major numbers between 3-6 inclusive.)

Minimum units: This field is an integer specifying the minimum number of these devices that can be specified in the sdevice file.

Maximum units: This field specifies the maximum number of these devices that may be specified in the sdevice file. It contains an integer.

DMA channel: This field contains an integer that specifies the DMA channel to be used by this device. If the device does not use DMA, place a '−1' in this field. Note that more than one device can share a DMA channel (previously disallowed).

SPECIFYING STREAMS DEVICES AND MODULES

STREAMS modules and drivers are treated in a slightly different way from other drivers in all UNIX Systems, and their configuration reflects this difference. To specify a STREAMS device driver, its mdevice entry should contain both an 'S' and a 'c' in the *characteristics* field (see 3. above). This indicates that it is a STREAMS driver and that it requires an entry in the UNIX kernel's *cdevsw* table, where STREAMS drivers are normally configured into the system.

A STREAMS module that is not a device driver, such as a line discipline module, requires an 'S' in the *characteristics* field of its mdevice file entry, but should not include a 'c', as a device driver does.

SEE ALSO

mfsys(4), sdevice(4)
idinstall(1M) in the *System Administrator's Reference Manual*

NAME

mfsys – file format

SYNOPSIS

mfsys

DESCRIPTION

The mfsys file contains configuration information for file system types that are to be included in the next system kernel to be built. It is included in the directory /etc/conf/cf.d, and includes a one-line description of each file system type. The mfsys file is coalesced from component files in the directory /etc/conf/mfsys.d. Each line contains the following whitespace-separated fields:

1. *name*: This field contains the internal name for the file system type (for example, S51K, DUFST). This name is no more than 32 characters long, and by convention is composed of upper-case alphanumeric characters.

2. *prefix*: The *prefix* in this field is the string prepended to the *fstypsw* handler functions defined for this file system type (for example, s5, du). The prefix must be no more that 8 characters long.

3. *flags*: The *flags* field contains a hex number of the form "0xNN" to be used in populating the *fsinfo* data structure table entry for this file system type.

4. *notify flags*: The *notify flags* field contains a hex number of the form "0xNN" to be used in population the *fsinfo* data structure table entry for this file system type.

5. *function bitstring*: The *function bitstring* is a string of 28 0's and 1's. Each file system type potentially defines 28 functions to populate the *fstypsw* data structure table entry for itself. All file system types do not supply all the functions in this table, however, and this bitstring is used to indicate which of the functions are present and which are absent. A '1' in this string indicates that a function has been supplied, and a '0' indicates that a function has not been supplied. Successive characters in the string represent successive elements of the *fstypsw* data structure, with the first entry in this data structure represented by the rightmost character in the string.

SEE ALSO

sfsys(4)

idinstall(1m), idbuild(1m) in the *User's/System Administrator's Reference Manual*

NAME

mtune – file format

SYNOPSIS

mtune

DESCRIPTION

The mtune file contains information about all the system tunable parameters. Each tunable parameter is specified by a single line in the file, and each line contains the following whitespace-separated set of fields:

1. *parameter name*: A character string no more than 20 characters long. It is used to construct the preprocessor "#define's" that pass the value to the system when it is built.

2. *default value*: This is the default value of the tunable parameter. If the value is not specified in the stune file, this value will be used when the system is built.

3. *minimum value*: This is the minimum allowable value for the tunable parameter. If the parameter is set in the stune file, the configuration tools will verify that the new value is equal to or greater than this value.

4. *maximum value*: This is the maximum allowable value for the tunable parameter. If the parameter is set in the stune file, the configuration tools will check that the new value is equal to or less than this value.

The file mtune normally resides in /etc/conf/cf.d . However, a user or an add-on package should never directly edit the mtune file to change the setting of a system tunable parameter. Instead the idtune command should be used to modify or append the tunable parameter to the stune file.

In order for the new values to become effective the UNIX System kernel must be rebuilt and the system must then be rebooted.

SEE ALSO

stune(4)

idbuild(1m), idtune(1m) in the *User's/System Administrator's Reference Manual*

NAME

　　　pkginfo – package characteristics file

DESCRIPTION

　　　pkginfo is an ASCII file that describes the characteristics of the package along with information that helps control the flow of installation. It is created by the software package developer.

　　　Each entry in the pkginfo file is a line that establishes the value of a parameter in the following form:

　　　　　　PARAM="value"

　　　There is no required order in which the parameters must be specified within the file. Each parameter is described below. Only fields marked with an asterisk are mandatory.

　　　PKG*　　　　Abbreviation for the package being installed, generally three characters in length (for example, dir or pkg). All characters in the abbreviation must be alphanumeric and the first may not be numeric. The abbreviation is limited to a maximum length of nine characters. install, new, and all are reserved abbreviations.

　　　NAME*　　　Text that specifies the package name (maximum length of 256 ASCII characters).

　　　ARCH*　　　A comma-separated list of alphanumeric tokens that indicate the architecture (for example, 3B2) associated with the package. The pkgmk tool may be used to create or modify this value when actually building the package. The maximum length of a token is 16 characters and it cannot include a comma.

　　　VERSION*　　Text that specifies the current version associated with the software package. The maximum length is 256 ASCII characters and the first character cannot be a left parenthesis. The pkgmk tool may be used to create or modify this value when actually building the package.

　　　CATEGORY*　A comma-separated list of categories under which a package may be displayed. A package must at least belong to the system or application category. Categories are case-insensitive and may contain only alphanumerics. Each category is limited in length to 16 characters.

　　　DESC　　　　Text that describes the package (maximum length of 256 ASCII characters).

　　　VENDOR　　Used to identify the vendor that holds the software copyright (maximum length of 256 ASCII characters).

　　　HOTLINE　　Phone number and/or mailing address where further information may be received or bugs may be reported (maximum length of 256 ASCII characters).

EMAIL
An electronic address where further information is available or bugs may be reported (maximum length of 256 ASCII characters).

VSTOCK
The vendor stock number, if any, that identifies this product (maximum length of 256 ASCII characters).

CLASSES
A space-separated list of classes defined for a package. The order of the list determines the order in which the classes are installed. Classes listed first will be installed first (on a media by media basis). This parameter may be modified by the request script.

ISTATES
A list of allowable run states for package installation (for example, "S s 1").

RSTATES
A list of allowable run states for package removal (for example, "S s 1").

BASEDIR
The pathname to a default directory where "relocatable" files may be installed. If blank, the package is not relocatable and any files that have relative pathnames will not be installed. An administrator can override the default directory.

ULIMIT
If set, this parameter is passed as an argument to the ulimit command, which establishes the maximum size of a file during installation.

ORDER
A list of classes defining the order in which they should be put on the medium. Used by pkgmk in creating the package. Classes not defined in this field are placed on the medium using the standard ordering procedures.

MAXINST
The maximum number of package instances that should be allowed on a machine at the same time. By default, only one instance of a package is allowed. This parameter must be set in order to have multiple instances of a package.

PSTAMP
Production stamp used to mark the pkgmap file on the output volumes. Provides a means for distinguishing between production copies of a version if more than one is in use at a time. If PSTAMP is not defined, the default is used. The default consists of the UNIX system machine name followed by the string "YYMMDDHHMM" (year, month, date, hour, minutes).

INTONLY
Indicates that the package should only be installed interactively when set to any non-NULL value.

PREDEPEND
Used to maintain compatibility with pre-SVR4 package dependency checking. Pre-SVR4 dependency checks were based on whether or not the name file for the required package existed in the /var/options directory. This directory is not maintained for SVR4 packages since the depend file is used for checking dependencies. However, entries can be created in this directory to maintain compatibility. Setting the PREDEPEND parameter to y or yes creates a /usr/option entry for the package.

(Packages that are new for SVR4 do not need to use this parameter.)

EXAMPLES

Here is a sample pkginfo:

```
PKG="oam"
NAME="OAM Installation Utilities"
VERSION="3"
VENDOR="AT&T"
HOTLINE="1-800-ATT-BUGS"
EMAIL="attunix!olsen"
VSTOCK="0122c3f5566"
CATEGORY="system.essential"
ISTATES="S 2"
RSTATES="S 2"
```

NOTES

Developers may define their own installation parameters by adding a definition to this file. A developer-defined parameter must begin with a capital letter, followed by lowercase letters.

NAME

　　pkgmap – package contents description file

DESCRIPTION

　　pkgmap is an ASCII file that provides a complete listing of the package contents. It is automatically generated by pkgmk(1) using the information in the prototype file.

　　Each entry in pkgmap describes a single "deliverable object file." A deliverable object file includes shell scripts, executable objects, data files, directories, and so on. The entry consists of several fields of information, each field separated by a space. The fields are described below and must appear in the order shown.

　　part　　　　An optional field designating the part number in which the object resides. A part is a collection of files, and is the atomic unit by which a package is processed. A developer can choose the criteria for grouping files into a part (for example, based on class). If no value is defined in this field, part 1 is assumed.

　　ftype　　　A one-character field that indicates the file type. Valid values are:

　　　　　　　f　　a standard executable or data file
　　　　　　　e　　a file to be edited upon installation or removal
　　　　　　　v　　volatile file (one whose contents are expected to change)
　　　　　　　d　　directory
　　　　　　　x　　an exclusive directory
　　　　　　　l　　linked file
　　　　　　　p　　named pipe
　　　　　　　c　　character special device
　　　　　　　b　　block special device
　　　　　　　i　　installation script or information file
　　　　　　　s　　symbolic link

　　class　　　The installation class to which the file belongs. This name must contain only alphanumeric characters and be no longer than 12 characters. It is not specified if the ftype is i (information file).

　　pathname　The pathname where the object will reside on the target machine, such as /usr/bin/mail. Relative pathnames (those that do not begin with a slash) indicate that the file is relocatable.

　　　　　　For linked files (ftype is either l or s), pathname must be in the form of *path1=path2*, with *path1* specifying the destination of the link and *path2* specifying the source of the link.

　　　　　　For symbolically linked files, *path2* can be a relative pathname, such as ./ or ../. For example, if you enter a line such as

　　　　　　　　s /foo/bar/etc/mount=../usr/sbin/mount

　　　　　　path2 (/foo/bar/etc/mount) will be a symbolic link to ../usr/sbin/mount.

pathname may contain variables which support relocation of the file. A *$parameter* may be embedded in the pathname structure. $BASEDIR can be used to identify the parent directories of the path hierarchy, making the entire package easily relocatable. Default values for *parameter* and BASEDIR must be supplied in the pkginfo file and may be overridden at installation.

major   The major device number. The field is only specified for block or character special devices.

minor   The minor device number. The field is only specified for block or character special devices.

mode   The octal mode of the file (for example, 0664). A question mark (?) indicates that the mode will be left unchanged, implying that the file already exists on the target machine. This field is not used for linked files, packaging information files or non-installable files.

owner   The owner of the file (for example, bin or root). The field is limited to 14 characters in length. A question mark (?) indicates that the owner will be left unchanged, implying that the file already exists on the target machine. This field is not used for linked files or non-installable files. It is used optionally with a package information file. If used, it indicates with what owner an installation script will be executed.

Can be a variable specification in the form of $[A-Z]. Will be resolved at installation time.

group   The group to which the file belongs (for example, "bin" or "sys"). The field is limited to 14 characters in length. A question mark (?) indicates that the group will be left unchanged, implying that the file already exists on the target machine. This field is not used for linked files or non-installable files. It is used optionally with a package information file. If used, it indicates with what group an installation script will be executed.

Can be a variable assignment in the form of $[A-Z]. Will be resolved at installation time.

size   The actual size of the file in bytes. This field is not specified for named pipes, special devices, directories or linked files.

cksum   The checksum of the file contents. This field is not specified for named pipes, special devices, directories or linked files.

modtime   The time of last modification, as reported by the stat(2) function call. This field is not specified for named pipes, special devices, directories or linked files.

Each pkgmap must have one line that provides information about the number and maximum size (in 512-byte blocks) of parts that make up the package. This line is in the following format:

: number_of_parts maximum_part_size

Lines that begin with "#" are comment lines and are ignored.

When files are saved during installation before they are overwritten, they are normally just copied to a temporary pathname. However, for files whose mode includes execute permission (but which are not editable), the existing version is linked to a temporary pathname and the original file is removed. This allows processes which are executing during installation to be overwritten.

EXAMPLES

The following is an example of a pkgmap file.

```
:2 500
1 i pkginfo 237 1179 541296672
1 b class1 /dev/diskette 17 134 0644 root other
1 c class1 /dev/rdiskette 17 134 0644 root other
1 d none bin 0755 root bin
1 f none bin/INSTALL 0755 root bin 11103 17954 541295535
1 f none bin/REMOVE 0755 root bin 3214 50237 541295541
1 l none bin/UNINSTALL=bin/REMOVE
1 f none bin/cmda 0755 root bin 3580 60325 541295567
1 f none bin/cmdb 0755 root bin 49107 51255 541438368
1 f class1 bin/cmdc 0755 root bin 45599 26048 541295599
1 f class1 bin/cmdd 0755 root bin 4648 8473 541461238
1 f none bin/cmde 0755 root bin 40501 1264 541295622
1 f class2 bin/cmdf 0755 root bin 2345 35889 541295574
1 f none bin/cmdg 0755 root bin 41185 47653 541461242
2 d class2 data 0755 root bin
2 p class1 data/apipe 0755 root other
2 d none log 0755 root bin
2 v none log/logfile 0755 root bin 41815 47563 541461333
2 d none save 0755 root bin
2 d none spool 0755 root bin
2 d none tmp 0755 root bin
```

NOTES

The pkgmap file may contain only one entry per unique pathname.

NAME

prototype – package information file

DESCRIPTION

prototype is an ASCII file used to specify package information. Each entry in the file describes a single deliverable object. An object may be a data file, directory, source file, executable object, and so on. This file is generated by the package developer.

Entries in a prototype file consist of several fields of information separated by white space. Comment lines begin with a "#" and are ignored. The fields are described below and must appear in the order shown.

part   An optional field designating the part number in which the object resides. A part is a collection of files, and is the atomic unit by which a package is processed. A developer can choose criteria for groupig files into a part (for example, based on class). If this field is not used, part 1 is assumed.

ftype   A one-character field which indicates the file type. Valid values are:

      f   a standard executable or data file
      e   a file to be edited upon installation or removal
      v   volatile file (one whose contents are expected to change)
      d   directory
      x   an exclusive directory
      l   linked file
      p   named pipe
      c   character special device
      b   block special device
      i   installation script or information file
      s   symbolic link

class   The installation class to which the file belongs. This name must contain only alphanumeric characters and be no longer than 12 characters. The field is not specified for installation scripts. (admin and all classes beginning with capital letters are reserved class names.)

pathname The pathname where the file will reside on the target machine, for example, /usr/bin/mail or bin/ras_proc. Relative pathnames (those that do not begin with a slash) indicate that the file is relocatable. The form

     path1=path2

may be used for two purposes: to define a link and to define local pathnames.

For linked files, *path1* indicates the destination of the link and *path2* indicates the source file. (This format is mandatory for linked files.)

For symbolically linked files, *path2* can be a relative pathname, such as ./ or ../. For example, if you enter a line such as

     s /foo/bar/etc/mount=../usr/sbin/mount

path2 (/foo/bar/etc/mount) will be a symbolic link to ../usr/sbin/mount.

For local pathnames, *path1* indicates the pathname an object should have on the machine where the entry is to be installed and *path2* indicates either a relative or fixed pathname to a file on the host machine which contains the actual contents.

A pathname may contain a variable specification, which will be resolved at the time of installation. This specification should have the form $[A-Z].

major   The major device number. The field is only specified for block or character special devices.

minor   The minor device number. The field is only specified for block or character special devices.

mode   The octal mode of the file (for example, 0664). A question mark (?) indicates that the mode will be left unchanged, implying that the file already exists on the target machine. This field is not used for linked files or packaging information files.

owner   The owner of the file (for example, bin or root). The field is limited to 14 characters in length. A question mark (?) indicates that the owner will be left unchanged, implying that the file already exists on the target machine. This field is not used for linked files or packaging information files.

Can be a variable specification in the form of $[A-Z]. Will be resolved at installation time.

group   The group to which the file belongs (for example, bin or sys). The field is limited to 14 characters in length. A question mark (?) indicates that the group will be left unchanged, implying that the file already exists on the target machine. This field is not used for linked files or packaging information files.

Can be a variable specification in the form of $[A-Z]. Will be resolved at installation time.

An exclamation point (!) at the beginning of a line indicates that the line contains a command. These commands are used to incorporate files in other directories, to locate objects on a host machine, and to set permanent defaults. The following commands are available:

search   Specifies a list of directories (separated by white space) to search for when looking for file contents on the host machine. The basename of the *path* field is appended to each directory in the ordered list until the file is located.

include   Specifies a pathname which points to another prototype file to include. Note that search requests do not span include files.

default   Specifies a list of attributes (mode, owner, and group) to be used
                 by default if attribute information is not provided for prototype
                 entries which require the information. The defaults do not apply
                 to entries in include prototype files.

param=value   Places the indicated parameter in the current environment.

The above commands may have variable substitutions embedded within them, as
demonstrated in the two example prototype files below.

Before files are overwritten during installation, they are copied to a temporary
pathname. The exception to this rule is files whose mode includes execute permission, unless the file is editable (that is, *ftype* is e). For files which meet this
exception, the existing version is linked to a temporary pathname, and the original file is removed. This allows processes which are executing during installation
to be overwritten.

EXAMPLES

Example 1:

```
!PROJDIR=/usr/proj
!BIN=$PROJDIR/bin
!CFG=$PROJDIR/cfg
!LIB=$PROJDIR/lib
!HDRS=$PROJDIR/hdrs
!search /usr/myname/usr/bin /usr/myname/src /usr/myname/hdrs
i pkginfo=/usr/myname/wrap/pkginfo
i depend=/usr/myname/wrap/depend
i version=/usr/myname/wrap/version
d none /usr/wrap 0755 root bin
d none /usr/wrap/usr/bin 0755 root bin
! search $BIN
f none /usr/wrap/bin/INSTALL 0755 root bin
f none /usr/wrap/bin/REMOVE 0755 root bin
f none /usr/wrap/bin/addpkg 0755 root bin
!default 755 root bin
f none /usr/wrap/bin/audit
f none /usr/wrap/bin/listpkg
f none /usr/wrap/bin/pkgmk
# The logfile starts as a zero length file, since the source
# file has zero length. Later, the size of logfile grows.
v none /usr/wrap/logfile=/usr/wrap/log/zero_length 0644 root bin
# the following specifies a link (dest=src)
l none /usr/wrap/src/addpkg=/usr/wrap/bin/rmpkg
! search $SRC
!default 644 root other
f src /usr/wrap/src/INSTALL.sh
f src /usr/wrap/src/REMOVE.sh
f src /usr/wrap/src/addpkg.c
f src /usr/wrap/src/audit.c
f src /usr/wrap/src/listpkg.c
f src /usr/wrap/src/pkgmk.c
```

```
d none /usr/wrap/data 0755 root bin
d none /usr/wrap/save 0755 root bin
d none /usr/wrap/spool 0755 root bin
d none /usr/wrap/tmp 0755 root bin
d src /usr/wrap/src 0755 root bin
```

Example 2:

```
# this prototype is generated by 'pkgproto' to refer
# to all prototypes in my src directory
!PROJDIR=/usr/dew/projx
!include $PROJDIR/src/cmd/prototype
!include $PROJDIR/src/cmd/audmerg/protofile
!include $PROJDIR/src/lib/proto
```

SEE ALSO

pkginfo(4), pkgmk(1)

NOTES

Normally, if a file is defined in the prototype file but does not exist, that file is created at the time of package installation. However, if the file pathname includes a directory that does not exist, the file will not be created. For example, if the prototype file has the following entry:

```
f none /usr/dev/bin/command
```

and that file does not exist, it will be created if the directory /usr/dev/bin already exists or if the prototype also has an entry defining the directory:

```
d none /usr/dev/bin
```

NAME

sdevice − file format

SYNOPSIS

sdevice

DESCRIPTION

The sdevice file contains local system configuration information for each of the devices specified in the mdevice file. It contains one or more entries for each device specified in mdevice. sdevice is present in the directory /etc/conf/cf.d, and is coalesced from component files in the directory /etc/conf/sdevice.d. Files in /etc/conf/sdevice.d are the *System* file components either delivered with the base system or installed later via idinstall.

Each entry must contain the following whitespace-separated fields:

1. *Device name:* This field contains the internal name of the driver. This must match one of the names in the first field of an mdevice file entry.

2. *Configure:* This field must contain the character 'Y' indicating that the device is to be installed in the Kernel. For testing purposes, an 'N' may be entered indicating that the device will not be installed.

3. *Unit:* This field can be encoded with a device dependent numeric value. It is usually used to represent the number of subdevices on a controller or psuedo-device. Its value must be within the minimum and maximum values specified in fields 7 and 8 of the mdevice entry.

4. *Ipl:* The *ipl* field specifies the system ipl level at which the driver's interrupt handler will run in the new system kernel. Legal values are 0 through 8. If the driver doesn't have an interrupt handling routine, put a 0 in this field.

5. *Type:* This field indicates the type of interrupt scheme required by the device. The permissible values are:

    0   The device does not require an interrupt line.

    1   The device requires an interrupt line. If the driver supports more than one hardware controller, each controller requires a separate interrupt.

    2   The device requires an interrupt line. If the driver supports more than one hardware controller, each controller will share the same interrupt.

    3   The device requires an interrupt line. If the driver supports more than one hardware controller, each controller will share the same interrupt. Multiple device drivers having the same ipl level can share this interrupt.

6. *Vector:* This field contains the interrupt vector number used by the device. If the *Type* field contains a 0 (that is, no interrupt required), this field should be encoded with a 0. Note that more than one device can share an interrupt number.

7.   *SIOA:* The *SIOA* field (Start I/O Address) contains the starting address on the I/O bus through which the device communicates. This field must be within 0x1 and 0xFFFE. (If this field is not used, it should be encoded with the value zero.)

8.   *EIOA:* The field (End I/O Address) contains the end address on the I/O bus through which the device communicates. This field must be greater than the value specified in the seventh field and no greater than 0XFFFF. (If this field is not used, it should be encoded with the value zero.)

9.   *SCMA:* The *SCMA* field (Start Controller Memory Address) is used by controllers that have internal memory. It specifies the starting address of this memory. The start address is 0X10000. (If this field is not used, it should be encoded with the value zero.)

10.   *ECMA:* The *ECMA* (End Controller Memory Address) specifies the end of the internal memory for the device. Its value must be greater than the value of the eighth field. (If this field is not used, it should be encoded with the value zero.)

SEE ALSO

mdevice(4)

idinstall(1m) in the *System Administrator's Reference Manual*

NAME

sfsys – file format

SYNOPSIS

sfsys

DESCRIPTION

The sfsys file contains local system information about each file system type specified in the mfsys file. It is present in the directory /etc/conf/cf.d, and contains a one-line entry for each file system type specified in the mfsys file. The sfsys file is coalesced from component files in the directory /etc/conf/sfsys.d. Each line in this file is a whitespace-separate set of fields that specify:

1. *name*: This field contains the internal name of the file system type (for example, DUFST, S51K). By convention, this name is up to 32 characters long, and is composed of all uppercase alphanumeric characters.

2. *Y/N*: This field contains either an uppercase 'Y' (for "yes") or an uppercase 'N' (for "no") to indicate whether the named file system type is to be configured into the next system kernel to be built.

SEE ALSO

mfsys(4)

idinstall(1m), idbuild(1m) in the *User's/System Administrator's Reference Manual*

NAME

space – disk space requirement file

DESCRIPTION

space is an ASCII file that gives information about disk space requirements for the target environment. It defines space needed beyond that which is used by objects defined in the prototype file—for example, files which will be installed with the installf command. It should define the maximum amount of additional space which a package will require.

The generic format of a line in this file is:

pathname blocks inodes

Definitions for the fields are as follows:

pathname Specifies a directory name which may or may not be the mount point for a filesystem. Names that do not begin with a slash (/) indicate relocatable directories.

blocks Defines the number of disk blocks required for installation of the files and directory entries contained in the pathname (using a 512-byte block size).

inodes Defines the number of inodes required for installation of the files and directory entries contained in the pathname.

EXAMPLE

```
# extra space required by config data which is
# dynamically loaded onto the system
data 500   1
```

SEE ALSO

installf(1M), prototype(4)

NAME
   stune − file format
SYNOPSIS
   stune
DESCRIPTION
   The stune file contains local system settings for tunable parameters. The parameter settings in this file replace the default values specified in the mtune file, if the
   new values are within the legal range for the parameter specified in mtune. The
   file contains one line for each parameter to be reset. Each line contains two
   whitespace-separated fields:

   1.   *external name*: This is the external name of the tunable parameter used in the
        mtune file.

   2.   *value*: This field contains the new value for the tunable parameter.

   The file stune normally resides in /etc/conf/cf.d. However, a user or an
   add-on package should never directly edit the mtune file. Instead the idtune
   command should be used.

   In order for the new values to become effective the UNIX kernel must be rebuilt
   and the system must then be rebooted.

SEE ALSO
   mtune(4)
   idbuild(1m), idtune(1m) in the *User's/System Administrator's Reference Manual*

NAME

display – system console display

DESCRIPTION

The system console (and user's terminal) is composed of two separate pieces: the keyboard [see keyboard (7)] and the display. Because of their complexity, and because there are three possible display interfaces (monochrome, color graphics, and enhanced graphics adapters), they are discussed in separate manual entries.

The display normally consists of 25 lines of 80 columns each; 40-column lines are also supported by the color/graphics adapter, and 43 lines of 80-columns each are supported by the enhanced graphics adapter. Writing characters to the console or one of its virtual screens (/dev/console or /dev/vtxx) has an effect which depends on the characters. All characters written to /dev/console are first processed by the terminal interface [see termio (7)]. For example, mapping new-line characters to carriage return plus new-line, and expanding tabs to spaces, will be done before the following processing:

x	Where x is not one of the following, displays x.
BEL	Generates a bell (audible tone, no modulation).
CR	Places the cursor at column 1 of the current line.
LF, VT	Places the cursor at the same column of the next line (scrolls if the the current line is line 25).
FF	Clears the screen and places the cursor at line 1, column 1.
BS	If the cursor is not at column 1, it is moved to the left one position on the same line. If the cursor is at column 1 but not line 1, it is moved to column 79 of the previous line. Finally, if the cursor is at column 1, line 1, it is not moved.

The display can be controlled by means of ANSI X3.64 *escape sequences*, which are specific sequences of characters, preceded by the ASCII character ESC. The escape sequences, which work on either the monochrome, color graphics, or enhanced graphics adapter, are the following:

ESC c	Clears the screen and places the cursor at line 1, column 1.
ESC Q *n* '*string*'	Defines the function key *n* with *string*. The string delimiter ' may be any character not in *string*. Function keys are numbered 0 through 11 (F1 = 0, F2 = 1, and so on.)
ESC [*n* @	Insert character—inserts *n* blanks at the current cursor position.
ESC [*n* `	Horizontal Position Absolute—moves active position to column given by *n*.
ESC [*n* A	Cursor up—moves the cursor up *n* lines (default: *n*=1).
ESC [*n* a	Horizontal Position Relative—moves active position *n* characters to the right (default: *n*=1).

ESC[*n* B   Cursor down—moves the cursor down *n* lines (default: *n*=1).

ESC[*n* C   Cursor right—moves the cursor right *n* columns (default: *n*=1).

ESC[*n* c   where n is 0 (underline cursor), 1(blockcursor), or 2(no cursor). 0 is the default value for n.

ESC[*n* D   Cursor left—moves the cursor left *n* columns (default: *n*=1).

ESC[*n* d   Vertical Position Absolute—moves active position to line given by *n*.

ESC[*n* E   Cursor next line—moves the cursor to column 1 of the next line, then down *n*−1 lines (default: *n*=1).

ESC[*n* e   Vertical Position Relative—moves the active position down *n* lines (default: *n*=1).

ESC[*n* F   Cursor previous line—moves the cursor to column 1 of the current line, then up *n* lines (default: *n*=1).

ESC[*n* G   Cursor horizontal position—moves the cursor to column *n* of the current line (default: *n*=1).

ESC[*n* ; *m* H
              Position cursor—moves the cursor to column *m* of line *n* (default: *n*=1, *m*=1).

ESC[*n* ; *m* f
              Position cursor—moves the cursor to column *m* of line *n* (default: *n*=1, *m*=1).

ESC[*n* J   Erase window—erases from the current cursor position to the end of the window if *n*=0, from the beginning of the window to the current cursor position if *n*=1, and the entire window if *n*=2 (default: *n*=0).

ESC[*n* K   Erase line—erases from the current cursor position to the end of the line if *n*=0, from the beginning of the line to the current cursor position if *n*=1, and the entire line if *n*=2 (default: *n*=0).

ESC[*n* L   Insert line—inserts *n* lines at the current cursor position (default: *n*=1).

ESC[*n* M   Delete line—deletes *n* lines starting at the current cursor position (default: *n*=1).

ESC[*n* P   Delete character—deletes *n* characters from a line starting at the current cursor position (default: *n*=1).

ESC[*n* S   Scroll up—scrolls the characters in the current window up *n* lines. The bottom *n* lines are cleared to blanks (default: *n*=1).

ESC[*n* T   Scroll down—scrolls the characters in the current window down *n* lines. The top *n* lines are cleared to blanks (default: *n*=1).

ESC[*n* X   Erase character—erases *n* character positions starting at the current cursor position (default: *n*=1).

ESC[*n* Z   Cursor Backward Tabulation—moves active position back *n* tab stops.

ESC[2 h   Locks the keyboard and ignores keyboard input until unlocked. Characters are not saved.

ESC[2 i   Sends the screen to the host. The current screen display is sent to the application.

ESC[2 l   Unlocks the keyboard. Re-enables keyboard input.

ESC[*Ps* ; *Ps*; m

Character attributes—each *Ps* is one of the following characters; multiple characters are separated by semicolons. These parameters apply to successive characters being displayed, in an additive manner (e.g., both bold and underscoring can be selected). Only the parameters through 7 apply to the monochrome adapter; all parameters apply to the color/graphics adapter and the enhanced graphics adapter. (Default: *Ps*=0).

Ps	Meaning		
0	all attributes off (normal display) (white foreground with black background)		
1	bold intensity		
4	underscore on (white foreground with red background on color)		
5	blink on		
6	VGA only: if blink (5) is on, turn blink off and background color to its light equivalent (that is, brown to yellow).		
7	reverse video		
30	black	(gray)	foreground
31	red	(light red)	foreground
32	green	(light green)	foreground
33	brown	(yellow)	foreground
34	blue	(light blue)	foreground
35	magenta	(light magenta)	foreground
36	cyan	(light cyan)	foreground
37	white	(bright white)	foreground
40	black	(gray)	background
41	red	(light red)	background
42	green	(light green)	background
43	brown	(yellow)	background
44	blue	(light blue)	background
45	magenta	(light magenta)	background
46	cyan	(light cyan)	background
47	white	(bright white)	background

Note that for character attributes 30–37, the color selected for foreground will depend on whether the *bold intensity* attribute (1) is currently on. If not, the first color listed will result; otherwise the second color listed will result.

Similarly, for character attributes 40–47, the color selected for background will depend on whether the *blink* attribute (5) is currently on and bright background (6) has been turned on. If *blink* is not turned on or bright background has not been selected, the first listed color will result. Otherwise, the second color listed will result.

ESC[8 m   sets blank (non-display)

ESC[10 m   selects the primary font

ESC[11 m   selects the first alternate font; lets ASCII characters less than 32 be displayed as ROM characters

ESC[12 m   selects a second alternate font; toggles high bit of extended ASCII code before displaying as ROM characters

ESC[38 m   enables underline option; white foreground with white underscore (see WARNINGS)

ESC[39 m   disables underline option; see WARNINGS

The following non-ANSI X3.64 escape sequences are supplied:

ESC[= *c* A   Sets overscan color.

ESC[= *p* ; *d* B

          Sets bell parameters (where *p* is the pitch in Hz and *d* is the duration in milliseconds)

ESC[= *s* ; *e* C

          Sets cursor parameters (where *s* is the starting and *e* is the ending scanlines of the cursor).

ESC[= *x* D   Enables/disables intensity of background color (where *x* is 0 for enable and 1 for disable).

ESC[= *x* E   Sets/clears blink vs. bold background (where *x* is 0 for set and 1 for clear).

ESC[= *c* F   Sets normal foreground color. See GIO_ATTR for the valid values for *c*.

ESC[= *c* G   Sets normal background color. See GIO_ATTR for the valid values for *c*.

ESC[= *n* g   Displays graphic character *n*.

ESC[= *c* H   Sets reverse foreground color. See GIO_ATTR for the valid values for *c*.

ESC[= *c* I   Sets reverse background color. See GIO_ATTR for the valid values for *c*.

ESC[= *c* J   Sets graphic foreground color. See GIO_ATTR for the valid values for *c*.

ESC[= *c* K   Sets graphic background color. See GIO_ATTR for the valid values for *c*.

ESC[*n* z	Makes virtual terminal number *n* active.
ESC 7	Saves cursor position.
ESC 8	Restores cursor position to saved value.
ESC[0 k	Disables the key-click feature (the default).
ESC[1 k	Enables the key-click feature. A tone is produced for each key press.

ioctl Calls

The following ioctl calls may be used to change the display used for the video monitor. If the virtual terminal has not been put in process mode (see the VT_SETMODE ioctl), setting the display mode to a non-text mode will turn off VT switching. VT switches will be re-enabled after the display mode has been reset to a text mode.

Note: All of the following ioctls are performed on either a file descriptor to the virtual terminals or to the special file /dev/video. ioctls to /dev/video are indicated with an asterisk (*). For the ioctls to /dev/video to work, the controlling tty for the process must be the virtual terminal on which the operation is to be performed. If the tty is not a virtual terminal, the return value will be -1 and errno will be set to EINVAL.

SWAPMONO (*)
> This call selects the monochrome adapter as the output device for the system console.

SWAPCGA (*) This call selects the color/graphics adapter as the output device for the system console.

SWAPEGA (*) This call selects the enhanced graphics adapter as the output device for the system console.

SWAPVGA (*) This call selects the video graphics array as the output device for the system console.

The following ioctl call may be used to obtain more information about the display adapter currently attached to the video monitor:

CONS_CURRENT (*)
> This call returns the display adapter type currently attached to the video monitor. The return value can be one of: MONO, CGA, or EGA.

The following ioctl calls may be used to switch display modes on the various video adapters:

SW_B40x25 (*)
> This call selects 40x25 (40 columns by 25 rows) black and white text display mode. It is valid only for CGA and EGA devices.

SW_C40x25 (*)
> This call selects 40x25 (40 columns by 25 rows) color text display mode. It is valid only for CGA and EGA devices.

SW_B80x25 (*)
> This call selects 80x25 (80 columns by 25 rows) black and white text display mode. It is valid only for CGA and EGA devices.

SW_C80x25 (*)
> This call selects 80x25 (80 columns by 25 rows) color text display mode. It is valid only for CGA and EGA devices.

SW_BG320 (*)
> This call selects 320x200 black and white graphics display mode. It is valid only for CGA and EGA devices.

SW_CG320 (*)
> This call selects 320x200 color graphics display mode. It is valid only for CGA and EGA devices.

SW_BG640 (*)
> This call selects 640x200 black and white graphics display mode. It is valid only for CGA and EGA devices.

SW_CG320_D (*)
> This call selects EGA support for 320x200 graphics display mode (EGA mode D). It is valid only for EGA devices.

SW_CG640_E (*)
> This call selects EGA support for 640x200 graphics display mode (EGA mode E). It is valid only for EGA devices.

SW_EGAMONOAPA (*)
> This call selects EGA support for 640x350 graphics display mode (EGA mode F). It is valid only for EGA devices.

SW_ENH_MONOAPA2 (*)
> This call selects EGA support for 640x350 graphics display mode with extended memory (EGA mode F*). It is valid only for EGA devices.

SW_CG640x350 (*)
> This call selects EGA support for 640x350 graphics display mode (EGA mode 10). It is valid only for EGA devices.

SW_ENH_CG640 (*)
> This call selects EGA support for 640x350 graphics display mode with extended memory (EGA mode 10*). It is valid only for EGA devices.

SW_EGAMONO80x25 (*)
> This call selects EGA monochrome text display mode (EGA mode 7), which emulates support provided by the monochrome adapter. It is valid only for EGA devices.

SW_ENHB40x25 (*)
> This call selects enhanced 40x25 black and white text display mode. It is valid only for EGA devices.

SW_ENHC40x25 (*)
>   This call selects enhanced 40x25 color text display mode. It is valid
>   only for EGA devices.

SW_ENHB80x25 (*)
>   This call selects enhanced 80x25 black and white display mode. It is
>   valid only for EGA devices.

SW_ENHC80x25 (*)
>   This call selects enhanced 80x25 color text display mode. It is valid
>   only for EGA devices.

SW_ENHB80x43 (*)
>   This call selects enhanced 80x43 black and white text display mode.
>   It is valid only for EGA devices.

SW_ENHC80x43 (*)
>   This call selects enhanced 80x43 color text display mode. It is valid
>   only for EGA devices.

SW_MCAMODE (*)
>   This call reinitializes the monochrome adapter. It is valid only for
>   monochrome adapters.

SW_ATT640 (*)
>   This call selects 640x400 16 colormode, when an AT&T Super-Vu
>   video controller is attached.

Switching to an invalid display mode for a display device will result in an error.

The following ioctls may be used to obtain information about the current
display modes:

CONS_GET (*)
>   This call returns the current display mode setting for whatever
>   display adapter is being used. Possible return values include:
>
>   M_B40x25 (0), black and white 40 columns. CGA and EGA only.
>
>   M_C40x25 (1), color 40 columns. CGA and EGA only.
>
>   M_B80x25 (2), black and white 80 columns. CGA and EGA only.
>
>   M_C80x25 (3), color 80 columns. CGA and EGA only.
>
>   M_BG320 (4), black and white graphics 320 by 200. CGA and EGA
>   only.
>
>   M_CG320 (5), color graphics 320 by 200. CGA and EGA only.
>
>   M_BG640 (6), black and white graphics 640 by 200 high-resolution.
>   CGA and EGA only.
>
>   M_EGAMONO80x25 (7), EGA-mono 80 by 25. EGA only.
>
>   M_CG320_D (13), EGA mode D.
>
>   M_CG640_E (14), EGA mode E.

M_EFAMONOAPA (15), EGA mode F.

M_CG640x350 (16), EGA mode 10.

M_ENHMONOAPA2 (17), EGA mode F with extended memory.

M_ENH_CG640 (18), EGA mode 10*.

M_ENH_B40x25 (19), EGA enhanced black and white 40 columns.

M_ENH_C40x25 (20), EGA enhanced color 40 columns.

M_ENH_B80x25 (21), EGA enhanced black and white 80 columns.

M_ENH_C80x25 (22), EGA enhanced color 80 columns.

M_ENH_B80x43 (0x70), EGA black and white 80 by 43.

M_ENH_C80x43 (0x71), EGA color 80 by 43.

M_MCA_MODE (0xff), monochrome adapter mode.

MCA_GET (*) This call returns the current display mode setting of the monochrome adapter. See CONS_GET for a list of return values. If the
monochrome adapter is not installed, the call will fail and *errno* will
be set to 22 (EINVAL).

CGA_GET (*) This call returns the current display mode setting of the
color/graphics adapter. See CONS_GET for a list of return values. If
the color graphics adapter is not installed, the call will fail and
errno will be set to 22 (EINVAL).

EGA_GET (*) This call returns the current display mode setting of the enhanced
graphics adapter. See CONS_GET for a list of return values. If the
enhanced graphics adapter is not installed, the call will fail and
errno will be set to 22 (EINVAL).

The following ioctl calls may be used to map the video adapter's memory into
the user's data space.

MAPCONS (*) This call maps the display memory of the adapter currently being
used into the user's data space.

MAPMONO (*) This call maps the monochrome adapter's display memory into the
user's data space.

MAPCGA (*) This call maps the color/graphics adapter's display memory into the
user's data space.

MAPEGA (*) This call maps the enhanced graphics adapter's display memory into
the user's data space.

MAPVGA (*) This call maps the video graphics array's display memory into the
user's data space.

You can use ioctl calls to input a byte from the graphics adapter port or to output a byte to the graphics adapter port. The argument to the ioctl uses the
port_io_arg data structure:

```
struct port_io_arg {
          struct port_io_struc_args[4];
};
```

As shown in the previous example, the *port_io_arg* structure points to an array of four *port_io_struc* data structures. The *port_io_struc* has the following format:

```
struc port_io_struc {
        char    dir;                /*direction flag (in vs. out)*/
        unsigned short port;        /*port address*/
        char    data;               /*byte of data*/
};
```

You can specify one, two, three, or four of the *port_io_struc* structures in the array for one ioctl call. The value of *dir* can be either IN_ON_PORT (to specify a byte being input from the graphics adapter port) or OUT_ON_PORT (to specify a byte being output to the graphics adapter port). *Port* is an integer specifying the port address of the desired graphics adapter port. *Data* is the byte of data being input or output as specified by the call. If you are not using any of the *port_io_struc* structures, load the *port* with 0, and leave the unused structures at the end of the array. Refer to your hardware manuals for port addresses and functions for the various adapters.

The following ioctl calls may be used to input or output bytes on the graphics adapter port:

MCAIO (*)   This call inputs or outputs a byte on the monochrome adapter port as specified.

CGAIO (*)   This call inputs or outputs a byte on the color/graphics adapter port as specified.

EGAIO (*)   This call inputs or outputs a byte on the enhanced graphics adapter port as specified.

VGAIO (*)   This call inputs or outputs a byte on the video graphics array port as specified.

To input a byte on any of the graphics adapter ports, load *dir* with IN_ON_PORT and load *port* with the port address of the graphics adapter. The byte input from the graphics adapter port will be returned in *data*.

To output a byte, load *dir* with OUT_ON_PORT, load *port* with the port address of the graphics adapter, and load *data* with the byte you want to output to the graphics adapter port.

The following ioctls may be used with either the monochrome, color graphics, or enhanced graphics adapters:

GIO_FONT8x8 (*)
        This call gets the current 8x8 font in use.

GIO_FONT8x14 (*)
        This call gets the current 8x14 font in use.

GIO_FONT8x16 (*)
        This call gets the current 8x16 font in use.

KDDISPTYPE (*)
        This call returns display information to the user. The argument expected is the buffer address of a structure of type *kd_disparam* into which display information is returned to the user. The *kd_disparam*

structure is defined as follows:

```
struct kd_disparam {
        long type;      /*display type*/
        char *addr;     /*display memory address*/
        ushort ioaddr[MKDIOADDR];   /*valid I/O addresses*/
}
```

Possible values for the type field include:

KD_MONO (0x01), for the IBM monochrome display adapter.

KD_HERCULES (0x02), for the Hercules monochrome graphics adapter.

KD_CGA (0x03), for the IBM color graphics adapter.

KD_EGA (0x04), for the IBM enhanced graphics adapter.

KIOCSOUND (*)
    Start sound generation. Turn on sound. The "arg" is the frequency desired. A frequency of 0 turns off the sound.

KDGETLED   Get keyboard LED status. The argument is a pointer to a character. The character will be filled with a boolean combination of the following values:

LED_SCR	0x01	(flag bit for scroll lock)
LED_CAP	0x04	(flag bit for caps lock)
LED_NUM	0x02	(flag bit for num lock)

KDSETLED   Set keyboard LED status. The argument is a character whose value is the boolean combination of the values listed under KDGETLED.

KDMKTONE (*)
    Generate a fixed length tone. The argument is a 32 bit value, with the lower 16 bits set to the frequency and the upper 16 bits set to the duration (in milliseconds).

KDGKBTYPE   Get keyboard type. The argument is a pointer to a character type. The character will be returned with one of the following values:

KB_84	0x01	(84 key keyboard)
KB_101	0x02	(101 key keyboard)
KB_OTHER	0x03	

KDADDIO (*)
    Add I/O port address to list of valid video adaptor addresses. Argument is an unsigned short type which should contain a valid port address for the installed video adaptor.

KDDELIO (*)   Delete I/O port address from list of valid video adaptor addresses. Argument is an unsigned short type which should contain a valid port address for the installed video adaptor.

KDENABIO (*)
> Enable in's and out's to video adaptor ports. No argument.

KDDISABIO (*)
> Disable in's and out's to video adaptor ports. No argument.

KDQUEMODE (*)
> Enable/Disable special queue mode. Queue mode is used by
> AT&T's X-Windows software to establish a shared queue for access
> to keyboard and mouse event information. The argument is a
> pointer to a structure "kd_quemode". If a NULL pointer is sent as
> an argument, the queue will be closed and the mode disabled. The
> structure "kd_quemode" is as follows:

```
struct kd_quemode {
        int     qsize; /* desired # of elements in queue */
        int     signo; /* signal number to send when queue
                                  goes non-empty */
        char    *qaddr;/* user virtual address of queue (set by
                                  driver) */
        };
```

KDSBORDER (*)
> Set screen color border in EGA text mode. The argument is of type
> character. Each bit position corresponds to a color selection. From
> bit position 0 to bit position 6, the color selections are respectively;
> blue, green, red, secondary blue, secondary green, and secondary
> red. Setting the bit position to a logic one will select the desired
> color or colors. See WARNINGS below.

KDSETMODE (*)
> Set console in text or graphics mode. The argument is of type
> integer, which should contain one of the following values:
>
> > KD_TEXT   0x00   (sets console to text mode)
> > KD_GRAPHICS 0x01   (sets console in graphics mode)
>
> If the mode is set to KD_GRAPHICS and the Virtual Terminal is not
> in process mode (see the VT_SETMODE ioctl), no virtual terminal
> switches will be possible until the mode is reset to KD_TEXT,
> KD_TEXT0, or KD_TEXT1.
>
> Note, the user is responsible for programming the color/graphics
> adaptor registers for the appropriate graphical state.

KDGETMODE (*)
> Get current mode of console. Returns integer argument containing
> either KD_TEXT or KD_GRAPHICS as defined in the KDSETMODE ioctl
> description.

KDMAPDISP (*)
> Maps display memory into user process address space. Argument is
> a pointer to structure type "kd_memloc". Structure definition is as
> follows:

```
struct kd_memloc {
        char    *vaddr;        /* virtual address to map to */
        char    *physaddr;     /* physical address to map from */
        long    length;        /* size in bytes to map */
        long    ioflg;         /* enable i/o addresses if set */
        }
```

KDUNMAPDISP (*)

Unmap display memory from user process address space. No argument required.

KDVDCTYPE   This call returns VDC controller/display information.

PIO_FONT8x8 (*)

This call uses the user supplied 8x8 font.

PIO_FONT8x14 (*)

This call uses the user supplied 8x14 font.

PIO_FONT8x16 (*)

This call uses the user supplied 8x16 font.

VT_OPENQRY

Find an available virtual terminal. The argument is a pointer to a long. The long will be filled with the number of the first available "VT" that no other process has open or −1 if none are available.

VT_GETMODE (*)

Determine what mode the active virtual terminal is currently in, either VT_AUTO or VT_PROCESS. The argument to the ioctl is the address of the following type of structure:

```
struct vt_mode {
        char    mode;  /* VT mode */
        char    waitv; /* if set, hang on writes when not active */
        short   relsig;/* signal to use for release request */
        short   acqsig;/* signal to use for display acquired */
        short   frsig; /* not used set to 0 */
        }

#define VT_AUTO 0x00    /* automatic VT switching */
#define VT_PROCESS    0x01   /* process controls switching */
```

The "vt_mode" structure will be filled in with the current value for each field.

VT_GETSTATE (*)

The VT_GETSTATE ioctl returns global virtual terminal state information. It returns the active virtual terminal in the v_active field, and the number of active virtual terminals and a bit mask of the global state in the vt_state field, where bit x is the state of vt x (1 indicates that the virtual terminal is open).

VT_SETMODE (*)
> Set the virtual terminal mode. The argument is a pointer to a "vt_mode" structure, as defined above.

VT_SENDSIG (*)
> The VT_SENDSIG ioctl specifies a signal (in vt_signal) to be sent to a bit mask of virtual terminals (in vt_state).

The data structure used by the VT_GETSTATE and VT_SENDSIG ioctls is:

```
struct vt_stat {
        ushort v_active;        /* active vt*/
        ushort v_signal;        /* signal to send (VT_SENDSIG) */
        ushort v_state;         /* vt bit mask (VT_SENDSIG and
                                   VT_GETSTATE) */
};
```

and is defined in /usr/include/sys/vt.h.

VT_RELDISP (*)
> Used to tell the virtual terminal manager that the display has or has not been released by the process. A non-zero argument indicates that the display has been released; a zero argument indicates refusal to release the display.

VT_ACTIVATE (*)
> Makes the virtual terminal number specified in the argument the active "VT". The "VT" manager will cause a switch to occur in the same manner as if a hotkey sequence had been typed at the keyboard. If the specified "VT" is not open or does not exist, the call will fail and errno will be set to ENXIO.

KIOCINFO   This call tells the user what the device is.

GIO_SCRNMAP (*)
> This call gets the screen mapping table from the kernel.

GIO_ATTR   This call returns the current screen attribute. The bits are interpreted as follows:

Bit 0 determines underlining for black and white monitors (1=underlining on).

Bits 0-2, for color monitors only, select the foreground color. The following list indicates what colors are selected by the given value:

> The value 0 selects black.
> The value 1 selects red.
> The value 2 selects green.
> The value 3 selects brown.
> The value 4 selects blue.
> The value 5 selects magenta.
> The value 6 selects cyan.
> The value 7 selects white.

Bit 3 is the intensity bit (1=blink on).

Bits 4-6, for color monitors only, select the background color. For a list of colors and their values, see the list under foreground colors.

Bit 7 is the blink bit (1=blink on).

GIO_COLOR (*)

This call returns a non-zero value if the current display is a color display, otherwise, it returns a zero.

PIO_SCRNMAP

This call puts the screen mapping table in the kernel.

The screen mapping table maps extended ASCII (8-bit) characters to ROM characters. It is an array [256] of char (typedef *scrnmap_t*) and is indexed by extended ASCII values. The value of the elements of the array are the ROM character to display.

For example, the following will change the ASCII character '#' to be displayed as an English pound sign.

```
#include <sys/console.h>
change_pound() {
scrnmap_t scrntab;
      /*get screen mapping table of standard output*/
if (ioctl(0,GIO_SCRNMAP, scrntab)==-1)
      {
      perror("screenmap read");
      exit(-1);
      }
/*156 is the ROM value of English pound sign and 30
  is the ASCII value of '#'.  */
scrntab[30] = 156;
if (ioctl(0, PIO_SCRNMAP, scrntab) == -1)
      {
      perror("screenmap write");
      exit(-1);
      }
}
```

FILES

```
/dev/console
/dev/vt00-n
/dev/video
/usr/include/sys/kd.h
```

SEE ALSO

stty(1), console(7), keyboard(7), termio(7)
ioctl(2) in the *Programmer's Reference Manual*

NOTES

Although it is possible to write character sequences which set arbitrary bits on the screen in any of the three graphics modes, this mode of operation is not currently supported.

Enable/disable of the underscore option using "ESC[38m" and "ESC[39m" are operative only when the AT&T Rite-Vu color/graphics video adaptor is installed, or else the underscore option is unsupported as the default for all other color/graphics adaptors. Monochrome adaptors support underscore option as the default. After "ESC[38m" has enabled underline and until "ESC[39m" has disabled underline all characters with blue attributes will appear as cyan.

It is currently not possible to access the 6845 start address registers. Thus, it is impossible to determine the beginning of the color monitor's screen memory.

The alternate/background color bit (bit 4) of the color select register does not appear to affect background colors in alphanumeric modes.

KDSBORDER ioctl calls will not work with AT&T's Super-Vu enhanced color/graphics video adaptor. It will however, work with the IBM EGA card and other EGA compatible video adaptors.

The low-resolution graphics mode appears to be 80 across by 100 down.

NAME

keyboard – system console keyboard

DESCRIPTION

The system console is composed of two separate pieces: the keyboard and the display [see display (7)].

The keyboard is used to type data, and send certain control signals to the computer. UNIX software performs terminal emulation on the console screen and keyboard, and, in doing so, makes use of several particular keys and key combinations. These keys and key combinations have special names that are unique to the UNIX system, and may or may not correspond to the keytop labels on your keyboard.

When you press a key, one of the following happens:

- An ASCII value is entered

- The meaning of another key, or keys, is changed.

- A string is sent to the computer.

- A function is initiated.

When a key is pressed (a keystroke), the keyboard sends a scancode to the computer. This scancode is interpreted by the keyboard driver. The actual code sequence delivered to the terminal input routine [see termio (7)] is defined by a set of internal tables in the driver. These tables can be modified by software (see the discussion of ioctl calls below). In addition, the driver can be instructed not to do translations, delivering the keyboard up/down scan codes directly.

Changing Meanings

The action performed by a key can be changed by using certain keys in combination. For example, the SHIFT key changes the ASCII values of the alphanumeric keys. Holding down the CTRL key while pressing another key sends a control code (such as CTRL-D, CTRL-S, and CTRL-Q). Holding down the ALT key also modifies a key's value. The SHIFT, CTRL, and ALT keys can be used in combination.

Switching Screens

To change screens (virtual terminals), first run the vtlmgr command [see vtlmgr(1M)]. Switch the current screen by typing ALT-SYSREQ (also labelled ALT-PRINTSCRN on some systems) followed by a key which identifies the desired screen. Any active screen may be selected by following ALT-SYSREQ with *Fn*, where *Fn* is one of the function keys. F1 refers to the first virtual terminal screen, F2 refers to the second virtual terminal screen, and so on. ALT-SYSREQ 'h' refers to the main console display (/dev/console). The next active screen can be selected with ALT-SYSREQ 'n,' and the previous screen can be selected with ALT-SYSREQ 'p.'

The default screen switch enable sequence (ALT-SYSREQ) is configurable. The SYSREQ table entry can be modified by software (see discussion of ioctl calls below).

Special Keys

The following table shows which keys on a typical console correspond to UNIX system keys. In this table, a hyphen (-) between keys means you must hold down the first key while pressing the second. The mapping between characters which generate signals and the signal actually generated is set with stty(1), and may be changed [see stty(1)].

Name	Keytop	Action
INTR	DEL	Stops current action and returns to the shell. This key is also called the RUB OUT or INTERRUPT key.
BACKSPACE	←	Deletes the first character to the left of the cursor. Note that the "cursor left" key also has a left arrow (←) on its keytop, but you cannot backspace using that key.
CTRL–D	CTRL–D	Signals the end of input from the keyboard; also exits current shell.
CTRL–H	CTRL–H	Deletes the first character to the left of the cursor. Also called the ERASE key.
CTRL–Q	CTRL–Q	Restarts printing after it has been stopped with CTRL–S.
CTRL–S	CTRL–S	Suspends printing on the screen (does not stop the program).
CTRL–U	CTRL–U	Deletes all characters on the current line. Also called the KILL key.
CTRL–\	CTRL–\	Quits current command and creates a core file, if allowed. (Recommended for debugging only.)
ESCAPE	ESC	Special code for some programs. For example, changes from insert mode to command mode in the vi(1) text editor.
RETURN	(down-left arrow or ENTER)	Terminates a command line and initiates an action from the shell.
F*n*	F*n*	Function key *n*. F1–F12 are unshifted, F13–F24 are shifted F1–F12, F25–F36 are CTRL–F1 through F12, and F37–F48 are CTRL–SHIFT–F1 through F12. The next F*n* keys (F49–F60) are on the number pad (unshifted): F49 - '7' F55 - '6' F50 - '8' F56 - '+' F51 - '9' F57 - '1' F52 - '-' F58 - '2' F53 - '4' F59 - '3' F54 - '5' F60 - '0'

Keyboard Map

The keyboard mapping structure is defined in /usr/include/sys/kd.h. Each key can have ten states. The first eight states are:

- BASE   - CTRL-SHIFT
- SHIFT   - ALT-SHIFT
- CTRL   - ALT-CTRL
- ALT   - ALT-CTRL-SHIFT

The two remaining states are indicated by two special bytes. The first byte is a "special state" byte whose bits indicate whether the key is "special" in one or more of the first eight states. The second byte is one of four codes represented by the characters C, N, B, or O which indicate how the lock keys affect the particular key.

The following table describes the default keyboard mapping. All values, except for special keywords (which are described later), are ASCII character values.

Heading	Description
SCAN CODE	This column contains the scan code generated by the keyboard hardware when a key is pressed. There are no table entries for the scan code generated by releasing a key.
BASE	This column contains the normal value of a key press.
SHIFT	This column contains the value of a key press when the SHIFT is also being held down.
LOCK	This column indicates which lock keys affect that particular key:

- C indicates CAPSLOCK
- N indicates NUMLOCK
- B indicates both
- O indicates locking is off

The remaining columns are the values of key presses when combinations of the CTRL, ALT and SHIFT keys are also held down.

The SRQTAB column entry is included in this table to provide a simple index of the default virtual terminal key selectors to the scan code to which it is assigned. The actual SRQTAB table is a stand-alone table which can be read or written via the KDGKBENT and KDSKBENT ioctl calls.

SCAN CODE	BASE	SHIFT	CTRL	CTRL SHIFT	ALT	ALT SHIFT	ALT CTRL	ALT CTRL SHIFT	LOCK	SRQTAB
1	esc	esc	esc	esc	esc	esc	esc	esc	O	nop
2	'1'	'!'	'1'	'1'	escn	escn	nop	nop	O	nop
3	'2'	'@'	'2'	nul	escn	escn	nop	nop	O	nop
4	'3'	'#'	'3'	'3'	escn	escn	nop	nop	O	nop
5	'4'	'$'	'4'	'4'	escn	escn	nop	nop	O	nop
6	'5'	'%'	'5'	'5'	escn	escn	nop	nop	O	nop
7	'6'	'^'	'6'	rs	escn	escn	nop	nop	O	nop
8	'7'	'&'	'7'	'7'	escn	escn	nop	nop	O	nop
9	'8'	'*'	'8'	'8'	escn	escn	nop	nop	O	nop
10	'9'	'('	'9'	'9'	escn	escn	nop	nop	O	nop
11	'0'	')'	'0'	'0'	escn	escn	nop	nop	O	nop
12	'-'	'_'	'-'	ns	escn	escn	nop	nop	O	nop
13	'='	'+'	'='	'='	escn	escn	nop	nop	O	nop
14	bs	bs	bs	bs	bs	bs	bs	bs	O	nop
15	ht	btab	ht	btab	ht	btab	ht	btab	O	nop
16	'q'	'Q'	dc1	dc1	escn	escn	nop	nop	C	nop
17	'w'	'W'	etb	etb	escn	escn	nop	nop	C	nop
18	'e'	'E'	enq	enq	escn	escn	nop	nop	C	nop
19	'r'	'R'	dc2	dc2	escn	escn	nop	nop	C	nop
20	't'	'T'	dc4	dc4	escn	escn	nop	nop	C	nop
21	'y'	'Y'	em	em	escn	escn	nop	nop	C	nop
22	'u'	'U'	nak	nak	escn	escn	nop	nop	C	nop
23	'i'	'I'	ht	ht	escn	escn	nop	nop	C	nop
24	'o'	'O'	si	si	escn	escn	nop	nop	C	nop
25	'p'	'P'	dle	dle	escn	escn	nop	nop	C	K_PREV
26	'['	'{'	esc	nop	escn	escn	nop	nop	O	nop
27	']'	'}'	gs	nop	escn	escn	nop	nop	O	nop
28	cr	cr	cr	cr	cr	cr	cr	cr	O	nop
29	lctrl	lctrl	lctrl	lctrl	lctrl	lctrl	lctrl	lctrl	O	nop
30	'a'	'A'	soh	soh	escn	escn	nop	nop	C	nop
31	's'	'S'	dc3	dc3	escn	escn	nop	nop	C	nop
32	'd'	'D'	eot	eot	escn	escn	nop	nop	C	nop
33	'f'	'F'	ack	ack	escn	escn	nop	nop	C	K_FRCNEXT
34	'g'	'G'	bel	bel	escn	escn	nop	nop	C	nop
35	'h'	'H'	bs	bs	escn	escn	nop	nop	C	K_VTF
36	'j'	'J'	nl	nl	escn	escn	nop	nop	C	nop
37	'k'	'K'	vt	vt	escn	escn	nop	nop	C	nop
38	'l'	'L'	np	np	escn	escn	nop	nop	C	nop
39	';'	':'	';'	':'	escn	escn	nop	nop	O	nop
40	'''	'"'	'''	'"'	escn	escn	nop	nop	O	nop
41	'`'	'~'	'`'	'~'	escn	escn	nop	nop	O	nop
42	lshift	lshift	lshift	lshift	lshift	lshift	lshift	lshift	O	nop
43	'\\'	'|'	fs	'|'	escn	escn	nop	nop	O	nop

SCAN CODE	BASE	SHIFT	CTRL	CTRL SHIFT	ALT	ALT SHIFT	ALT CTRL	ALT CTRL SHIFT	LOCK	SRQTAB
44	'z'	'Z'	sub	sub	escn	escn	nop	nop	C	nop
45	'x'	'X'	can	can	escn	escn	nop	nop	C	nop
46	'c'	'C'	etx	etx	escn	escn	nop	nop	C	nop
47	'v'	'V'	syn	syn	escn	escn	nop	nop	C	nop
48	'b'	'B'	stx	stx	escn	escn	nop	nop	C	nop
49	'n'	'N'	so	so	escn	escn	nop	nop	C	K_NEXT
50	'm'	'M'	cr	cr	escn	escn	nop	nop	C	nop
51	','	'<'	','	'<'	escn	escn	nop	nop	O	nop
52	'.'	'>'	'.'	'>'	escn	escn	nop	nop	O	nop
53	'/'	'?'	'/'	ns	escn	escn	nop	nop	O	nop
54	rshift	rshift	rshift	rshift	rshift	rshift	rshift	rshift	O	nop
55	'*'	'*'	'*'	'*'	escn	escn	nop	nop	O	nop
56	lalt	lalt	lalt	lalt	lalt	lalt	lalt	lalt	O	nop
57	' '	' '	nul	nul	escn	escn	nop	nop	O	nop
58	clock	clock	clock	clock	clock	clock	clock	clock	O	nop
59	fkey1	fkey13	fkey25	fkey37	fkey1	fkey13	fkey25	fkey37	O	K_VTF+1
60	fkey2	fkey14	fkey26	fkey38	fkey2	fkey14	fkey26	fkey38	O	K_VTF+2
61	fkey3	fkey15	fkey27	fkey39	fkey3	fkey15	fkey27	fkey39	O	K_VTF+3
62	fkey4	fkey16	fkey28	fkey40	fkey4	fkey16	fkey28	fkey40	O	K_VTF+4
63	fkey5	fkey17	fkey29	fkey41	fkey5	fkey17	fkey29	fkey41	O	K_VTF+5
64	fkey6	fkey18	fkey30	fkey42	fkey6	fkey18	fkey30	fkey42	O	K_VTF+6
65	fkey7	fkey19	fkey31	fkey43	fkey7	fkey19	fkey31	fkey43	O	K_VTF+7
66	fkey8	fkey20	fkey32	fkey44	fkey8	fkey20	fkey32	fkey44	O	K_VTF+8
67	fkey9	fkey21	fkey33	fkey45	fkey9	fkey21	fkey33	fkey45	O	K_VTF+9
68	fkey10	fkey22	fkey34	fkey46	fkey10	fkey22	fkey34	fkey46	O	K_VTF+10
69	nlock	nlock	nlock	nlock	nlock	nlock	nlock	nlock	O	
70	slock	slock	brk	brk	slock	slock	brk	brk	O	
71	fkey49	'7'	fkey49	'7'	fkey49	escn	nop	nop	N	
72	fkey50	'8'	fkey50	'8'	fkey50	escn	nop	nop	N	
73	fkey51	'9'	fkey51	'9'	fkey51	escn	nop	nop	N	
74	fkey52	'-'	fkey52	'-'	fkey52	escn	nop	nop	N	
75	fkey53	'4'	fkey53	'4'	fkey53	escn	nop	nop	N	
76	fkey54	'5'	fkey54	'5'	fkey54	escn	nop	nop	N	
77	fkey55	'6'	fkey55	'6'	fkey55	escn	nop	nop	N	
78	fkey56	'+'	fkey56	'+'	fkey56	escn	nop	nop	N	
79	fkey57	'1'	fkey57	'1'	fkey57	escn	nop	nop	N	
80	fkey58	'2'	fkey58	'2'	fkey58	escn	nop	nop	N	
81	fkey59	'3'	fkey59	'3'	fkey59	escn	nop	nop	N	
82	fkey60	'0'	fkey60	'0'	fkey60	escn	nop	nop	N	
83	del	'.'	del	'.'	del	escn	rboot	nop	N	
84	fkey60	fkey26	fkey60	nop	sysreq	sysreq	sysreq	sysreq	O	
85	fkey58	fkey58	fkey58	fkey58	fkey58	fkey58	fkey58	fkey58	O	
86	fkey53	fkey53	fkey53	fkey53	fkey53	fkey53	fkey53	fkey53	O	

SCAN CODE	BASE	SHIFT	CTRL	CTRL SHIFT	ALT	ALT SHIFT	ALT CTRL	ALT CTRL SHIFT	LOCK	SRQTAB
87	fkey11	fkey23	fkey35	fkey47	fkey11	fkey23	fkey35	fkey47	O	K_VTF+11
88	fkey12	fkey24	fkey36	fkey48	fkey12	fkey24	fkey36	fkey48	O	K_VTF+12
89	nop	nop	nop	nop	nop	nop	nop	nop	O	K_NOP
90	nop	nop	nop	nop	nop	nop	nop	nop	O	K_NOP
91	nop	nop	nop	nop	nop	nop	nop	nop	O	K_NOP
92	nop	nop	nop	nop	nop	nop	nop	nop	O	K_NOP
93	nop	nop	nop	nop	nop	nop	nop	nop	O	K_NOP
94	nop	nop	nop	nop	nop	nop	nop	nop	O	K_NOP
95	nop	nop	nop	nop	nop	nop	nop	nop	O	K_NOP
96	nop	nop	nop	nop	nop	nop	nop	nop	O	K_NOP
97	nop	nop	nop	nop	nop	nop	nop	nop	O	K_NOP
98	nop	nop	nop	nop	nop	nop	nop	nop	O	K_NOP
99	nop	nop	nop	nop	nop	nop	nop	nop	O	K_NOP
100	nop	nop	nop	nop	nop	nop	nop	nop	O	K_NOP
101	nop	nop	nop	nop	nop	nop	nop	nop	O	K_NOP
102	nop	nop	nop	nop	nop	nop	nop	nop	O	K_NOP
103	nop	nop	nop	nop	nop	nop	nop	nop	O	K_NOP
104	nop	nop	nop	nop	nop	nop	nop	nop	O	K_NOP
105	nop	nop	nop	nop	nop	nop	nop	nop	O	K_NOP
106	nop	nop	nop	nop	nop	nop	nop	nop	O	K_NOP
107	fkey53	fkey53	fkey53	fkey53	fkey53	fkey53	fkey53	fkey53	O	
108	nop	nop	nop	nop	nop	nop	nop	nop	O	K_NOP
109	nop	nop	nop	nop	nop	nop	nop	nop	O	K_NOP
110	nop	nop	nop	nop	nop	nop	nop	nop	O	K_NOP
111	fkey51	fkey51	nop	nop	nop	nop	nop	nop	O	K_NOP
112	nop	nop	nop	nop	nop	nop	nop	nop	O	K_NOP
113	nop	nop	nop	nop	nop	nop	nop	nop	O	K_NOP
114	ralt	ralt	ralt	ralt	ralt	ralt	ralt	ralt	O	K_NOP
115	rctrl	rctrl	rctrl	rctrl	rctrl	rctrl	rctrl	rctrl	O	K_NOP
116	cr	cr	cr	cr	cr	cr	cr	cr	O	K_NOP
117	'/'	'/'	nop	nop	escn	escn	nop	nop	O	K_NOP
118	nop	nop	nop	nop	nop	nop	nop	nop	O	K_NOP
119	brk	brk	brk	brk	brk	brk	brk	brk	O	K_NOP
120	fkey50	fkey50	nop	nop	nop	nop	nop	nop	O	K_NOP
121	del	del	del	del	del	del	del	del	O	K_NOP
122	fkey57	fkey57	nop	nop	nop	nop	nop	nop	O	K_NOP
123	fkey60	fkey60	nop	nop	nop	nop	nop	nop	O	K_NOP
124	nop	nop	nop	nop	nop	nop	nop	nop	O	K_NOP
125	fkey55	fkey55	nop	nop	nop	nop	nop	nop	O	K_NOP
126	fkey59	fkey59	nop	nop	nop	nop	nop	nop	O	K_NOP
127	fkey49	fkey49	nop	nop	nop	nop	nop	nop	O	K_NOP

The following table lists the value of each of the special keywords used in the preceding tables. The keywords are only used in the preceding tables for readability. In the actual keyboard map, a special keyword is represented by its value with the corresponding "special state" bit being set.

Name	Value	Meaning
nop	0	No operation - no action from keypress
lshift	2	Left-hand shift
rshift	3	Right-hand shift
clock	4	Caps lock
nlock	5	Numeric lock
slock	6	Scroll lock
alt	7	Alt key
btab	8	Back tab key - generates fixed sequence (ESC[Z)
ctrl	9	Control key
lalt	10	Left-hand alt key
ralt	11	right-hand alt key
lctrl	12	Left-hand control key
rctrl	13	Right-hand control key
agr	14	ALT-GR key (European keyboards only)
fkey1	27	Function key #1
.	.	.
.		.
.		.
fkey96	122	Function key #96
sysreq	123	System request
brk	124	Break key
escn	125	Generate an ESC N x sequence, where x is the un-alt'ed value of the scan code
esco	126	Generate an ESC O x sequence, where x is the un-alt'ed value of the scan code
escl	127	Generate an ESC L x sequence, where x is the un-alt'ed value of the scan code
rboot	128	Reboot system
debug	129	Invoke kernel debugger
NEXT	130	Switch to next virtual terminal on queue
PREV	131	Switch to previous virtual terminal on queue
FNEXT	132	Forced switch to next virtual terminal on queue
FPREV	133	Forced switch to previous virtual terminal on queue
VTF	134	Virtual Terminal First (VT00)
.	.	.
.		.
.	.	.
VTL	148	Virtual Terminal Last (VT14)

Name	Value	Meaning
MGRF	149	Virtual Terminal Manager First. Allows assigning special significance to key sequence for actions by virtual terminal layer manager. Used in SRQTAB table.
.	.	
.	.	
.	.	
MGRL	179	Virtual Terminal Manager Last. Used in SRQTAB table.

The following table lists names and decimal values for ASCII characters in the preceding table. Names are used in place of numeric constants to make it easier to read the scan code table. Only the decimal values are placed in the ioctl buffer. These values are taken from ascii(5).

Name	Value	Name	Value
nul	0	dc1	17
soh	1	dc2	18
stx	2	dc3	19
etx	3	dc4	20
eot	4	nak	21
enq	5	syn	22
ack	6	etb	23
bel	7	can	24
bs	8	em	25
ht	9	sub	26
nl	10	esc	27
vt	11	fs	28
np	12	gs	29
cr	13	rs	30
so	14	ns	31
si	15	del	127
dle	16		

String Key Mapping

The string mapping table is an array of 512 bytes (typedef strmap_t) containing null-terminated strings that redefine the function keys. The first null-terminated string is assigned to the first function key, the second string is assigned to the second function key, and so on.

There is no limit to the length of any particular string as long as the whole table does not exceed 512 bytes, including nulls. To make a string a null, add extra null characters. The following table contains default function key values.

Default Function Key Values				
Function Key #	Function	Shift Function	Ctrl Function	Ctrl Shift Function
1	ESC OP	ESC Op	ESC OP	ESC Op
2	ESC OQ	ESC Oq	ESC OQ	ESC Oq
3	ESC OR	ESC Or	ESC OR	ESC Or
4	ESC OS	ESC Os	ESC OS	ESC Os
5	ESC OT	ESC Ot	ESC OT	ESC Ot
6	ESC OU	ESC Ou	ESC OU	ESC Ou
7	ESC OV	ESC Ov	ESC OV	ESC Ov
8	ESC OW	ESC Ow	ESC OW	ESC Ow
9	ESC OX	ESC Ox	ESC OX	ESC Ox
10	ESC OY	ESC Oy	ESC OY	ESC Oy
11	ESC OZ	ESC Oz	ESC OZ	ESC Oz
12	ESC OA	ESC Oa	ESC OA	ESC Oa

Ioctl Calls:

KDGKBMODE

> This call gets the current keyboard mode. It returns one of the following values, as defined in /usr/include/sys/kd.h:

```
#defineK_RAW          0x00      /* Send row scan codes */
#defineK_XLATE        0x01      /* Translate to ASCII */
```

KDSKBMODE

> This call sets the keyboard mode. The argument to the call is either K_RAW or K_XLATE. By using raw mode, the program can see the raw up/down scan codes from the keyboard. In translate mode, the translation tables are used to generate the appropriate character code.

KDGKBTYTE

> This call gets the keyboard type. It returns one of the following values, as defined in /usr/include/sys/kd.h:

```
#defineKB_84          0x00      /*84 key keyboard*/
#defineKB_101         0x01      /*101 key keyboard*/
#defineKB_OTHER       0x03      /*Other type keyboard*/
```

KDGKBENT

> This call reads one of the entries in the translation tables. The argument to the call is the address of one of the following structures, defined in /usr/include/sys/kd.h, with the first two fields filled in:

```
struct kbentry {
        unchar kb_table;        /* Table to use */
        unchar kb_index;        /* Entry in table */
        ushort kb_value;        /* Value to get/set */
};
```

Valid values for the *kb_table* field are:

```
#defineK_NORMTAB       0x00    /* Base */
#defineK_SHIFTTAB      0x01    /* Shifted */
#defineK_ALTTAB        0x02    /* Alt */
#defineK_ALTSHIFTTAB   0x03    /* Shifted alt */
#defineK_SRQTAB        0x04    /* Select sysreq
                                  table */
```

The `ioctl` will get the indicated entry from the indicated table and return it in the third field.

The K_SRQTAB value for the kb_table field allows access to the scancode indexed table which allows assignment of a given virtual terminal selector (K_VTF–K_VTL) or the virtual terminal layer manager (K_MGRF–K_MGRL) "specialkey" assignments.

The virtual terminal selector (K_VTF) is normally associated with /dev/tty00, on which the user login shell is commonly found. The following terminal selectors also are used to select virtual terminals:

K_VTF+1 for the 1st virtual terminal (/dev/vt01)
K_VTF+2 for the 2nd virtual terminal (/dev/vt02)
.
.
.
K_VTF+12 for the 12th virtual terminal (/dev/vt12)

KDSKBENT
This call sets an entry in one of the translation tables. It uses the same structure as the KDGKBENT ioctl, but with the third field filled in with the value that should be placed in the translation table. This can be used to partially or completely remap the keyboard.

The kd driver provides support for virtual terminals. The console minor device, /dev/vtmon, provides virtual terminal key requests from the kd driver to the process that has /dev/vtmon open. Two ioctls are provided for virtual terminal support:

VT_GETSTATE
The VT_GETSTATE ioctl returns global virtual terminal state information. It returns the active virtual terminal in the v_active field, and the number of active virtual terminals and a bit mask of the global state in the vt_state field, where bit x is the state of vt x (1 indicates that the virtual terminal is open).

VT_SENDSIG
The VT_SENDSIG ioctl specifies a signal (in vt_signal) to be sent to a bit mask of virtual terminals (in vt_state).

The data structure used by the VT_GETSTATE and VT_SENDSIG ioctls is:

```
struct vt_stat {
    ushort v_active;    /* active vt */
    ushort v_signal;    /* signal to send (VT_SENDSIG) */
    ushort v_state;     /* vt bit mask (VT_SENDSIG and VT_GETSTATE) */
};
```

and is defined in /usr/include/sys/vt.h .

VT_OPENQRY
> The VT_OPENQRY ioctl is used to get the next available virtual terminal. This value is set in the last argument of the ioctl (2) call.

GIO_KEYMAP
> This call gets the entire keyboard mapping table from the kernel. The structure of the argument is given in /usr/include/sys/kd.h.

PIO_KEYMAP
> This call sets the entire keyboard mapping table. The structure of the argument is given in /usr/include/sys/kd.h.

GIO_STRMAP
> This call gets the string key mapping table from the kernel. The structure of the argument is given in /usr/include/sys/kd.h.

PIO_STRMAP
> This call sets the string key mapping table. The structure of the argument is given in /usr/include/sys/kd.h.

TIOCKBOF
> Extended character codes are disabled. This is the default mode.

TIOCKBON
> Allows extended characters to be transmitted to the user program. The extended characters are transmitted as a null byte followed by a second byte containing the character's extended code. When a true null byte is sent, it is transmitted as two consecutive null bytes.

When the keyboard is fully enabled, an 8-bit character code can be obtained by holding down the ALT key and entering the 3-digit decimal value of the character from the numeric keypad. The character is transmitted when the ALT key is released.

Some keyboard characters have special meaning. Under default operations, pressing the DELETE key generates an interrupt signal which is sent to all processes designated with the associated control terminal. When the keyboard is fully enabled, holding down the ALT key and pressing the 8 key on the home keyboard (not on the numeric keypad) returns a null byte followed by 0x7F. This will produce the same effect as the DELETE key (0x7F) unless you have executed the stty(1) command with the −isig option.

KBENABLED
> If the keyboard is fully enabled (TIOCKBON), a non-zero value will be returned. If the keyboard is not fully enabled (TIOCKBOF), a value of zero will be returned.

GETFKEY

> Obtains the current definition of a function key. The argument to the call is the address of one of the following structures defined in /usr/include/sys/kd.h:
>
> ```
> struct fkeyarg {
>     unsigned int   keynum;
>     char   keydef [MAXFK];        /*Comes from ioctl.h via comcrt.h*/
>     char   flen;
> };
> ```
>
> The function key number must be passed in *keynum* (see *arg* structure above). The string currently assigned to the key will be returned in *keydef* and the length of the string will be returned in *flen* when the ioctl is performed.

SETFKEY

> Assigns a given string to a function key. It uses the same structure as the GETFKEY ioctl. The function key number must be passed in *keynum*, the string must be passed in *keydef*, and the length of the string (number of characters) must be passed in *flen*.

FILES

/dev/console
/dev/vt00-n
/usr/include/sys/kd.h

SEE ALSO

stty(1), console(7), display(7), termio(7)
ioctl(2), ascii(5) in the *Programmer's Reference Manual*
vtlmgr(1M) in the *User's Reference Manual*

NAME

mouse - mouse device driver supporting bus, serial, and PS/2 compatible mouse devices.

DESCRIPTION

The Mouse Driver Package, Version 3.0, device driver supports three types of mouse devices:

Logitech bus mouse, which attaches to a plug-in card and is designed to be used in an eight-bit card slot.

Logitech serial type mouse, which plugs directly into a serial port connector.

PS/2 compatible mouse, which connects to a PS/2 auxiliary port.

The driver will support multiple mouse applications running in virtual terminal screens, both under the UNIX System and MS-DOS via SimulTask.

Support for a mouse administration is also provided. See mouseadmin(1).

The following ioctl's are supported:

MOUSEIOCMON   Used exclusively by /usr/lib/mousemgr to receive open/close commands from /dev/mouse driver.

MOUSEISOPEN   Used exclusively by mouseadmin. Returns 16-byte character array indicating which mouse devices are currently open; 1 is open, 0 is not open. The array is in the linear order established by /usr/bin/mouseadmin in building the display/device map pairs.

MOUSEIOCCONFIG

Used exclusively by mouseadmin to configure display/mouse pairs. The mse_cfg data structure is used to pass display/device mapping and map pair count information to the driver:

```
struct mse_cfg {
        struct mousemap *mapping;
        unsigned int    count;
}
struct mousemap {
        dev_t    disp_dev;
        dev_t    mse_dev;
}
```

MOUSEIOCREAD   Read mouse position/status data. The following data structure is used to return mouse position information to a user application:

```
struct mouseinfo {
        unsigned char status;
        char          xmotion:
        char          ymotion;
}
```

MOUSEIOCREAD will set errno to EFAULT for failure to return a valid mouseinfo structure. The status byte contains the button state information according to the following format:

```
0 Mv Lc Mc Rc L M R
```

where:

Mv: is 1 if the mouse has moved since last MOUSEIOCREAD

Lc: is 1 if Left button has changed state since last MOUSEIOCREAD

Mc: is 1 if Middle button has changed state since last MOUSEIOCREAD

Rc: is 1 if Right button has changed state since last MOUSEIOCREAD

L: current state of Left button (1 == depressed)

M: current state of Middle button

R: current state of Right button

The Mv bit is required because the total x and y delta since the last MOUSEIOCREAD ioctl could be 0 yet the mouse may have been moved. The Lc, Mc, and Rc bits are required for a similar reason; if a button had been pushed and released since the last MOUSEIOCREAD ioctl, the current state bit would be unchanged but the application would want to know the button had been pushed.

The xmotion and ymotion fields are signed quantities relative to the previous position in the range -128 to 127. Deltas that would overflow a signed char have been truncated.

MOUSE320   Used to send commands and receive responses from the PS/2 compatible mouse devices. Failed MOUSE320 commands will return ENXIO as the errno value. The following data structure is used to pass commands/status/position information between the driver and a user application:

```
struct cmd_320 {
        int     cmd;
        int     arg1;
        int     arg2;
        int     arg3;
}
```

Legal commands for the PS/2 compatible devices are as follows:

MSERESET   reset mouse

MSERESEND   resend last data

MSESETDEF	set default status
MSEOFF	disable mouse
MSEON	enable mouse
MSESPROMPT	set prompt mode
MSEECHON	set echo mode
MSEECHOFF	reset echo mode
MSESTREAM	set stream mode
MSESETRES	set resolution (counts per millimeter) legal arg1 values are as follows:

> 00 = 1 count/mm.
> 01 = 2 count/mm.
> 02 = 4 count/mm.
> 03 = 8 count/mm.

MSESCALE2	set 2:1 scaling
MSESCALE1	set 1:1 scaling.
MSECHGMOD	set sampling rate (reports per second) legal arg1 values are as follows:

> 0A = 10 reports/sec.
> 14 = 20 reports/sec.
> 28 = 40 reports/sec.
> 3C = 60 reports/sec.
> 50 = 80 reports/sec.
> 64 = 100 reports/sec.
> C8 = 200 reports/sec.

MSEGETDEV	read device type returns a zero (0) for the PS/2 compatible mouse.
MSEREPORT	read mouse report returns three-byte mouse/button position where bytes two and three are 9-bit 2's complement relative motions with the 9th bit (sign bit) coming from byte 1.

> Byte 1
>   b0 - left button   (1 == depressed)
>   b1 - right button
>   b2 - middle button
>   b3 - always 1
>   b4 - X data sign   (1 == negative)
>   b5 - Y data sign
>   b6 - X data overflow
>   b7 - Y data overflow
>
> Byte 2
>   X axis position data

Byte 3
Y axis position data

MSESTATREQ   status request returns three-byte report with the
following format:

Byte 1
b0 - right button   (1 == depressed)
b1 - middle button
b2 - left button
b3 - always 0
b4 - scaling 1:1 = 0, 2:1 = 1
b5 - disabled(0)/enabled(1)
b6 - stream(0)/prompt(1) mode
b7 - always 0

Byte 2
b0 - 6 current resolution
b7 - always 0

Byte 3
b0 - 7 current sampling rate

NOTE

The Mouse 3.0 device driver is intended for use with UNIX System V Release 4.0
or later releases. The version 3.0 mouse also supports queue mode for accessing
mouse input, both motion and button events; see display(7) for more information
on KDQUEMODE.

FILES

/dev/mouse
/usr/lib/mousemgr
/usr/include/sys/mouse.h

SEE ALSO

mouseadmin(1)
Mouse Driver Administrator's Guide

Permuted Index

PERMUTED INDEX

PERMUTED INDEX

I | Index

Index

E

F

fclose(3S) 1: 21
fcntl(2) 2: 13, 15, 20–22
field item help message
  description 9: 14
  example 9: 15
  format 9: 15
file and device input/output 2: 1–9,
  xviii–xix
file and record locking 2: 10–25,
  xviii–xix
file mode (see permissions, files)
FILE structure 1: 20–21
file system, structure 5: 4–6, 38–39
files
  dfile 7: 6
  driver.o 10: 12
  /etc 5: 51–57
  init 10: 15
  lock xviii–xix
  locking (see locking)
  master 10: 3, 12
  mdevice 7: 6, 10: 3, 12
  memory-mapped (see mapped
    files)
  mtune 10: 3
  naming rules 5: 6
  node 10: 14
  ownership 5: 27, 34
  permissions 5: 16–24
  postinstall 10: 16
  preremove 10: 18
  protection 5: 16–24
  rc 10: 15
  regular 5: 4
  renamed in Release 4.0 5: 41–45
  sassign 10: 3

sdevice 7: 6, 31, 10: 3, 13
security 5: 16–24
shutdown 10: 15
space.c 10: 3, 13
special 5: 4
stune 10: 3
system 10: 3
system 10: 13
/usr 5: 60–61
/var 5: 65–67
FMLI xiii–xiv
fopen(3S) 1: 20–21
fork(2) 3: 5–8
fsync(2) 2: 28
full path-name (see path-name)
function calls
  data input and output 7: 20
  syntax 7: 20–21
function naming conventions 7: 23
function prototypes 1: 6
functions
  biodone 7: 17, 45
  biowait 7: 17, 45
  delay 7: 49
  drv_usectohz 7: 46–47
  dtimeout 7: 48
  inb 7: 20
  inl 7: 20
  inw 7: 20
  itimeout 7: 47
  LOCK() 7: 33
  LOCK_ALLOC() 7: 33
  outb 7: 20
  outl 7: 20
  outw 7: 20
  panic 7: 52
  read 7: 21
  repinsb 7: 21

Integrated Software Development Guide

Integrated Software Development Guide

Integrated Software Development Guide